SIR WILLIAM JONES

SELECTED POETICAL AND PROSE WORKS

Sir William Jones, attributed to James Northcote RA (1746–1831).
Reproduced by permission of the National Museum of Wales.

SIR WILLIAM JONES

Selected Poetical and Prose Works

Edited by

MICHAEL J. FRANKLIN

CARDIFF
UNIVERSITY OF WALES PRESS
1995

British Library Cataloguing in Publication Data

A catalogue record for this book is available from the British Library.

ISBN 0-7083-1294-2

Published with the financial support of the Arts Council of England

Recommended by the University of Wales Association for the Study of Welsh Writing in English

Jacket design by Design Principle

Typeset at the University of Wales Press
Printed in Great Britain by Bookcraft Ltd., Midsomer Norton

For

Geraint, Ieuan, and Caroline

Contents

CONTENTS

Preface

The aim of this edition of Jones's selected works is to provide a text which attempts to follow his latest intentions both in substance and in accidentals. It would seem clear that he took immense care in the preparation of works for the press, his concern extending beyond meticulous proof-reading to specific typographical detail. In a letter to Nichols of 14 July 1781 (*Letters*, II.485) he sends explicit instructions for the printing of *The Moallakát*: 'The Bishop of London's *Isaiah* must be the *model*; for my Work, like his Lordship's, will consist of a Dedication, preliminary Discourse, the text and notes; and I would observe the same proportion in the size of the letters'.

William Jones managed to correct and revise proofs of complex legal works even amidst the 'whirlwind of business and dissipation' of the Oxford and Welsh circuits, but his poems were often circulated in a much more haphazard fashion. He placed little value upon his extempore compositions, often encouraging the recipients to consign them to the fire as 'the properest place', and those poems which he regarded more highly were sometimes in danger of faring little better. In sending his translation of Isæus to Walter Pollard, a friend and fellow-lawyer, he includes an Ode, adding in conclusion: 'I entreat you to send back my Carmen ad Libertatem, as I have no other copy in the world', (*Letters*, I.262–3). In Bengal he regretted his failure to purchase one of Boulton's patented copying machines, and lamenting the blunders of Armenian clerks, determined to 'print ten or twenty copies of every thing I compose, which are to be considered as manuscripts', (*Letters*, II.777). These 'manuscripts', some of which are extant among the Althorp Papers, currently being catalogued at the British Library, provide copy-text for several of the Hymns to Hindu deities. Elsewhere the absence of manuscripts constrains an editor to chose first or corrected second editions as closest to the text as Jones wanted it to be read. Where the first publication of a text occurs posthumously in the collected works of 1799 (London: G. G. and J. Robinson; and R. H. Evans; 6 vols. quarto) and 1807 (London: John Stockdale and John Walker; 13 vols. octavo), Jones was very fortunate in an editor who was painstaking, scholarly, and uniquely sympathetic – his widow, Lady Anna Maria, a published poet herself.

Annotation, particularly in respect to the compositions produced in Calcutta, represents something of a problem and it was one which Jones himself acknowledged. Feeling that in 'The Enchanted Fruit; or, The Hindu Wife' he had cluttered the page with footnotes, he decided for the Hymns to provide explanatory introductory 'Arguments'. My experience has been, however, that students, and even colleagues, reading Jones for the first time have often been baffled by the substantial body of erudite (and to a westerner) obscure references in his text. If my annotation seems somewhat heavy it is for the convenience of a modern reader not necessarily familiar with Sanskrit literature or the Hindu pantheon; better a cluttered page than an opaque one.

My edition is primarily concerned with Jones's position in the West, and seeks to enable a university audience of readers of English literature to access the central texts of Jones with a knowledge of their place in eighteenth- and nineteenth-century English and European culture. The texts are arranged in chronological order of composition, and each has a headnote on its particular occasion and general significance to enable the reader to obtain a clear sense of Jones's poetic, intellectual, and political development, his contribution to bourgeois radicalism in Britain and cultural revolution in Bengal.

Capitalization and italicization have been retained as in the original, together with eccentricities of spelling, grammar, and rhetorical punctuation. The long eighteenth-century 's', however, has been modernized throughout. Jones's use of accents for Sanskrit, Persian, and Arabic words has been retained, whereas references in the notes use macrons in accordance with modern diacritical practice. The textual apparatus records all substantive variants.

The illustrations of Hindu deities on pp. 103, 107, 115, 126, 142, 145, 163 and 178 are reproduced from *The Works of Sir William Jones*, ed. Anna Maria Jones, 13 vols. (London, 1807), vol. III.

No one can attempt to consider Jones's work today without acknowledging a real debt to Garland Cannon for his careful editing of the letters, not to mention the biography and his very many academic articles. I am also indebted to Professor Malcolm Kelsall for his perceptive criticism, Professor Jerome J. McGann for his thoughtful encouragement, and Gary McKeone of the Arts Council for his interest in my project. I must also thank Beryl Baldwin and rest of the library staff at University of Wales, Cardiff, the National Library of Wales, St David's University College, Lampeter, and the British Library. Liz Powell of University of Wales Press and typesetter Bryan Turnbull are also to be thanked for their patient efficiency. Without the generous secondment granted by St John the Baptist Comprehensive my research could not have proceeded and I pleased to record my gratitude to the Head and Governors, and to Jennifer George and the rest of the staff of the English Department. My deepest debt is to Caroline.

THE PUBLISHED WORKS OF SIR WILLIAM JONES

Histoire de Nader Shah connu sous le nom de Thahmas Kuli Khan, Empereur de Perse, traduite d'un manuscrit Persan, par ordre de sa majesté le Roi de Danemark, avec des notes chronologiques historiques géographiques et un traité sur la poésie. Londres: P. Elmsly, 1770.

A grammar of the Persian language. London: W. & J. Richardson, 1771.

Dissertation sur la littérature Orientale. Londres: P. Elmsly, 1771.

Lettre à Monsieur A*** du P***, dans laquelle est compris L'examen de sa traduction des livres attribués à Zoroastre. Londres: P. Elmsly, 1771.

Poems, consisting chiefly of translations from the Asiatick languages. Oxford: Clarendon Press, 1772.

The history of the life of Nader Shah, King of Persia. London: J. Richardson for T. Cadell, 1773.

Poeseos Asiaticae commentariorum, Libri sex, cum appendice. Londini: T. Cadell, 1774.

The speeches of Isæus in causes concerning the law of succession to property at Athens. London: J. Nichols for E. & C. Dilly, 1779.

An Address to the University of Oxford (Gough. Oxf.90(2)). Oxford, 1780.

A speech on the nomination of candidates to represent the county of Middlesex. London, 1780.

Ad libertatem. London: J. Nichols, 1780.

An inquiry into the legal mode of suppressing riots with a constitutional plan of future defence. J. Nichols for C. Dilly, 1780.

Corrected second edition of the above, together with *A speech on the nomination of candidates to represent the county of Middlesex* (1780), and *An oration intended to have been spoken in the theatre at Oxford.* 9 July 1773. London: C. Dilly, 1782.

The Muse recalled, an ode, occasioned by the nuptials of Lord Viscount Althorp and Miss Lavinia Bingham, eldest daughter of Charles, Lord Lucan. Strawberry Hill: T. Kirgate, 1781.

An ode in imitation of Alcæus. London, 1782 (printed and distributed gratis by the Society for Constitutional Information).

An essay on the Law of Bailments. London: J. Nichols for C. Dilly, 1781.

A plan for national defence. London, 1782.

A speech to the assembled inhabitants of the Counties of Middlesex and Surry, the Cities of London and Westminster, and the Borough of Southwark. London: C. Dilly, 1782.

The principles of government in a dialogue between a scholar and a peasant. Written by a member of the Society for Constitutional Information. London, 1782 (printed and distributed gratis by the Society).

The Mohamedan law of succession to the property of Intestates. London: J. Nichols for C. Dilly, 1782.

The Moallakát or seven Arabian poems which were suspended on the Temple at Mecca. London: P. Elmsly, 1782.

A letter to a patriot Senator, including the heads of a bill for a constitutional representation of the people. London: J. Nichols for Charles Dilly, 1783.

A discourse on the institution of a society for inquiring into the history, civil and natural, the antiquities, arts, sciences, and literature of Asia, delivered at Calcutta, January 15th. 1784: A charge to the grand jury at Calcutta, December 4th. 1783: and *A hymn to Camdeo.* Translated from the Hindu into Persian, and from Persian into English. London: T. Payne & son, 1784.

Asiatick Researches; or, transactions of the Society, instituted in Bengal, for inquiring into the history and antiquities, the arts, sciences and literature of Asia [Vols. I–IV ed. by Sir William Jones]. Calcutta: Manuel Cantopher, 1788, 1790, 1792, 1794.

The following discourses and papers were addressed to the Asiatick Society:

'A dissertation on the orthography of Asiatick words in Roman letters', *As. Res.* I.1–56.

'On the Gods of Greece, Italy, and India', ibid. 221–75.

'On the literature of the Hindus, from the Sanscrit, communicated by Goverdhan Caul, with a short commentary', ibid. 340–55.

'A conversation with Abraham, an Abyssinian, concerning the city of Gwender and the sources of the Nile', ibid. 383–6.

'On the course of the Nile', ibid. 387–8.

'The second anniversary discourse', ibid. 405–14.

'On the Hindus', ibid. 414–32.

'On the Arabs', *As. Res.* II.1–17.

'On the Tartars' ibid. 19–41.

'On the Persians' ibid. 43–66.

'Remarks on the Island of Hinzuan or Johanna', ibid. 77–107.

'On the chronology of the Hindus', ibid. 111–47.

'On the cure of the Elephantiasis and other disorders of the blood', ibid. 153–8.

'On the Indian game of chess', ibid. 159–65.

'On the second classical book of the Chinese', ibid. 195–204.

'On the antiquity of the Indian zodiack', ibid. 289–306.

'The design of a treatise on the plants of India', ibid. 345–52.

'On the Chinese', ibid. 365–81.

'A supplementary essay on Indian chronology', ibid. 389–403.

'On the Spikenard of the Ancients', ibid. 405–17.

'On the borderers, mountaineers and islanders of Asia', *As. Res.* III.1–16.

'A royal grant of land in Carnatta', ibid. 39–53.

'On the musical modes of the Hindus', ibid. 55–87.

'On the mystical poetry of the Persians and Hindus', ibid. 165–83.

'Gítagóvinda, or the songs of Jayadéva', ibid. 185–207.

'The lunar year of the Hindus', ibid. 257–93.

'On the origin and families of nations', ibid. 479–92.

'On Asiatick history, civil and natural', *As.Res.* IV.1–17.

'On the loris, or slow-paced lemur', ibid. 135–9.

'Additional remarks on the Spikenard of the Ancients', ibid. 109–18.

'Questions and remarks on the astronomy of the Hindus', ibid. 159–63.

'On the philosophy of the Asiaticks', ibid. 165–80.

'Botanical observations on select Indian plants', ibid. 237–312.

There were three pirated London editions of *Asiatick Researches* published by Vernor & Hood: in 1796–1808 (6 vols.); 1798–1811 (10 vols.); 1799–1807 (12 vols.)

Asiatick Researches. Printed verbatim from the Calcutta edition. 20 vols. London: J. Sewell [etc.], 1799–1839.

Asiatick Researches. Another ed. printed verbatim. London: J. Sewell, Vernor & Hood [etc.], 1801–12.

Asiatick Researches. 5 vols. London: Vernor, Hood & Sharpe, 1806–7.

Asiatick Researches. 11 vols. London: Vernor, 1806–12.

Lailà Majnún, a Persian poem of Hátifí. Calcutta: Manuel Cantopher, 1788.

Sacontalá, or the Fatal Ring; an Indian drama by Cálidás. Calcutta: Joseph Cooper, 1789. (Sold for the benefit of insolvent debtors, as were all Jones's subsequent works printed in Calcutta.)

Al Sirajiyyah: or the Mahomedan Law of Inheritance; with a commentary. Calcutta: J. Cooper, 1792.

The seasons: a descriptive poem in the original Sanscrit. Calcutta: Calcutta Gazette, 1792.

Institutes of Hindu Law: or the ordinances of Menu, according to the gloss of Cullúca. Calcutta: printed by Government order, 1794.

A digest of Mohummudan law, according to the tenets of the twelve imams, compiled under the superintendence of Sir William Jones, ed. Capt. John Baillie. Calcutta: The Company's Press, 1805.

Francis Gladwin's *Asiatick Miscellany; consisting of original productions, translations, fugitive pieces, imitations, and extracts from curious publications*. 2 vols. Calcutta: Daniel Stuart, 1785; Calcutta: William Mackay, 1786 published six of Jones's hymn to Hindu deities, and some short translated pieces.

The Works of Sir William Jones, ed. Anna Maria Jones, 6 vols. London: G. G. & J. Robinson, 1799.

Supplementary volumes of the works of Sir William Jones, 2 vols. London, 1801.

The Works of Sir William Jones, ed. Anna Maria Jones, 13 vols. London: John Stockdale & John Walker, 1807.

Memoirs of the life, writings and correspondence of Sir William Jones, by John Shore, Lord Teignmouth. London: J. Hatchard, 1804.

The Poetical Works of Sir William Jones with The Life of the Author, ed. John Bell, 2 vols. London: Cadell and Davies; Longman, *et al.*, 1807.

The Poetical Works of Sir William Jones, ed. Thomas Park, 2 vols. London: J. Sharpe, 1808.

THE PUBLISHED WORKS OF SIR WILLIAM JONES

The Poetical Works of Sir William Jones, 2 vols. London: J. Nichols & Son, 1810.

The works of the English poets from Chaucer to Cowper, ed. Alexander Chalmers, vol.18. London, 1810.

Letters of Sir William Jones, chronologically arranged from Lord Teignmouth's collection. London: J. Davidson, 1821.

Introduction

On the 23 August 1775 William Jones, standing with two lawyer friends on Sir Roger Mostyn's elegantly landscaped lawns, looked out over Conway Bay to 'the isle of Anglesea, the ancient Mona, where my ancestors presided over a free but uncivilized people'.[1] He was enjoying a brief tour between the conclusion of the English judicial circuit and the beginning of the Welsh; the weather was fine, and the fruit garden of his host, the MP for Flintshire, was still producing exquisite peaches and nectarines. As he gazed over the calm waters in the direction of Llanfihangel Tre'r-beirdd, his father's home village of Llanbabo and the very different environs of a simple sheep-farm must have occupied his thoughts.

Jones had never known his father who died before the child was three, but the role-model provided by William Jones sen. was ever present to the young barrister. A mixture of intellect and determination had enabled his father to escape the obscurity of Tyddyn-bach and pursue a career as a celebrated and published mathematician, which culminated in his election to the vice-presidency of the Royal Society, and the friendship of Newton, Halley, Hardwicke, and Johnson.

It was a month before Jones's twenty-ninth birthday and a time to survey more than a mere picturesque prospect. Other vistas presented themselves, as he wrote to a fellow Orientalist: 'What a boundless scene opens to my view! if I had two lives, I should scarcely find time for the due execution of all the public and private projects which I have in mind!'[2] The previous Christmas, for the amusement of his former pupil, Viscount Althorp, he had sketched out what he termed an 'Andrometer' which prescribed a proper career for the humane and accomplished man: thirty years devoted to the acquisition of knowledge, twenty to public and professional vocation, ten years to literary and scientific composition, the final years being dedicated to a glorious retirement and preparation for eternity. Despite his protestations, this was not wholly a joke; classical role-models complemented his paternal one, and much remained to be done: 'I have not quite attained the degree of 28, because my rambles into Arabia and Persia have thrown me backwards two

---

1. *The Letters of Sir William Jones*, ed. Garland Cannon, 2 vols. (Oxford, 1970), I.199; (hereafter cited as *Letters*).
2. *The Works of Sir William Jones*, ed. Anna Maria Jones, 13 vols. (London, 1807), I.167; (hereafter cited as *Works*).

or three years, and mine was the age at which both Demosthenes and Cicero began to take a part in the publick affairs of Athens and Rome.'[3]

So what had this earnest young Welshman accomplished? In his middle twenties he had simply become the greatest Oriental scholar in Europe. The secret of his success lay in diverting the enormous wave of taste for things Oriental into the calmer channels of intellectual rigour, effectively combining sensationalism and scholarship in a manner which Romantics like Robert Southey, Thomas Moore, and Lord Byron were to emulate some forty years later. The tradition of Oriental scholarship at Oxford, centred on Edward Pococke (1604–91) and Thomas Hyde (1636–1703), successive occupants of the Laudian Chair of Arabic, was noble and revered but perhaps rather dusty and dull, and Jones, with his youth, talent, and ardent enthusiasm, was ideally suited to the role of popularizer. 'Asiatic Jones' used the reflected glamour of the Oriental vogue to transform the public conception of the Orientalist. His *Lettre à Monsieur A*** du P**** (1771) even cast him in the prestigious role of national hero, defending Oxford scholarship against disrespectful and dubious French scholarship.[4]

Jones's *Poems, consisting chiefly of translations from the Asiatick languages* (1772), following closely on the heels of five acclaimed Orientalist publications, focused his scholarly aims of extending the resources of English poetry, and of encouraging interest in Asian languages, but the intellectual pill was sugared with delight. 'There is a gayety & splendor in the poems', rhapsodized Mrs Elizabeth Montagu, the 'Queen of the Blue Stockings', 'they breathe Asiatick luxury'.[5]

> Let me on beds of dewy flowers recline,
> And quaff with glowing lips the sparkling wine;
> Grant me to feed on beauty's rifled charms,
> And clasp a willing damsel in my arms;
> Her bosom fairer than a hill of snow,
> And gently bounding like the playful roe,
> Her lips more fragrant than the summer air,
> And sweet as Scythian musk her hyacinthine hair:
>
> 'The Palace of Fortune', ll. 183–90.

These early poems are replete with spicy odours and musky scents, crystal fountains, damsels in diaphanous robes, and all the sensuous paraphernalia of the sumptuous pleasure dome; they present a paradisical pleasance out of Arabia Felix, ready to tempt any Romantic to rejuvenate the genre of the Oriental tale. Of the two accompanying essays, the first applies an Enlightenment relativism to differing

---

3. *Letters*, I.175.
4. Stung to anger by the Frenchman's dismissive treatment of the Orientalists at Oxford, Jones penned this vituperative polemic, denouncing Anquetil-Duperron's *Zend-Avesta, ouvrage de Zoroastre* (Paris, 1771) as a modern forgery. The fact that Jones was completely wrong and that he had thus hindered the progress of Avestan studies was later a matter of bitter regret, but the damage that he did to Anquetil-Duperron's reputation on both sides of the channel indicates Jones's powerful influence in the field of Orientalism.
5. Quoted in *Letters*, I.111.

poetic cultures, considering the influence of climate upon the fertility of the Oriental imagination; while the second, 'On the Arts, Commonly Called Imitative', discounts Aristotelian imitation in favour of theories of the emotional and imaginative origin of poetry, and anticipates the literary criticism of Wordsworth and Coleridge.

All this had earned him, like his father, election to the Royal Society, and, again like his father, the friendship of Johnson, to whose Turk's Head Club Jones was elected in 1773, and where he encountered Edmund Burke, Oliver Goldsmith, Joshua Reynolds, David Garrick, and Edward Gibbon on terms of friendly equality and mutual respect. Celebrated, accomplished, handsome, and high-spirited, he had not neglected to acquire the social graces, and 'Persian Jones' was a great success with the ladies, whether Blue Stockings or bishops' daughters. Renowned for his modesty, he still lusted after nothing more than fame, which he promised he would pursue 'through fire and water, by day and by night'.[6]

Fashionable praise, however, would not make Jones lose his head, although decapitation on the Ciceronian model seemed almost attractive: 'I would willingly lose my head at the age of sixty, if I could pass a life at all analogous to that which Middleton [author of *The Life of Cicero*] describes'.[7] Self-discipline and hard work seemed to come remarkably easily to Jones, and calculating that a legal career would guarantee more lasting laurels and his 'country's highest honours', he calmly announced his decision to abandon Oriental literature at the end of the Preface to his *Grammar of the Persian Language* (1771).

Thus on that August morning, although his appreciation of the dramatic scene would not discredit a Pennant or a Gilpin, the fact that he stands on 'Arvon's shore' does not draw his thoughts towards Gray's evocation of the prophetic Bard; poetry must be dismissed as a temptation, for 'the study of my profession engages my whole attention night and day'.[8]

The colourful narrative of Jones's brief north Welsh tour was designed to entertain the young Viscount Althorp who was about to go up to Cambridge; Jones had been his tutor from 1765 to 1770, and their friendship was to prove life-long. In this too Jones was following a pattern established by his father, a tutor to two future Lords Chancellor, with whom the elder Jones maintained a lasting friendship. But the prospect of a comfortable sinecure held little appeal for the son. He felt in danger of becoming a pedagogic adjunct to the Spencer entourage as he accompanied the family through the intellectual desert of the French Riviera; he was little more than a male governess, a domestic tutor, which, as he wrote to Lady Spencer, constituted, 'a character which I always thought far below one whose natural freedom of mind renders him incapable of bearing the least restraint or inattention'.[9]

---

6. *Works*, I.167.
7. *Letters*, I.103–4.
8. Ibid., I.211.
9. Ibid., I.66. Jones had come close to quarrelling with the family when Lady Spencer's solicitude for her son's health had interfered with Jones's plans for his education; to be an effective private tutor Jones required superintendence of his pupil away from the distractions of the family.

The road to liberty lay via the Middle Temple and the Welsh circuits, but the contretemps perfectly illustrates the ambiguities of his position as 'a philosopher among courtiers', unsure of whether to bow or to harangue the insidious influence of the aristocracy.[10] Thus his late-summer narrative of 1785, like many of his letters from Wales, with its eulogistic description of country seats, is interspersed with references to aristocratic effeteness. At Beaumaris, Lord Bulkeley's cold collation was welcomed, but less so his lunch-time remark that: 'persons of rank were already treated with too little respect'; and Jones ends his letter by advising the young heir to the Earldom of Spencer to avoid decadent young nobles at Cambridge: 'I exhort you *eripere te è turbâ nobilium*, distinguish yourself from the mob of noblemen, and consider birth, fortune, and so forth, as nothing more than steps by which you may climb more rapidly into the temple of virtue, which is far above them all.'[11] Such classical republican advice, modelled on Cicero, exemplifies Jones's earnest wish that his former pupil should share his desire to play an enlightened role in public life; but for the teacher, how might he accomplish the degree of independence necessary to enable him to play that role free from the constraints of patronage or party?

In late August 1783, exactly eight years after he had looked out from a pastoral headland of Wales, with Ynys Môn before him, the Menai Straits and Conway Bay, Sir William Jones stood on board the deck of the frigate *Crocodile*:

> *India* lay before us, and *Persia* on our left, whilst a breeze from *Arabia* blew nearly on our stern. A situation so pleasing in itself, and to me so new, could not fail to awaken a train of reflections in a mind, which had early been accustomed to contemplate with delight the eventful histories and agreeable fictions of this eastern world. It gave me inexpressible pleasure to find myself in the midst of so noble an amphitheatre, almost encircled by the vast regions of *Asia*.[12]

'Oriental Jones' was in the Orient at last, but it was the law rather than Orientalism that had placed him there. A judgeship on the Bengal Supreme Court had also provided him with a knighthood, £6,000 per annum, and, effectively, a wife (as he had determined not to marry Anna Maria Shipley, the daughter of the Bishop of St Asaph, until he had sufficient means). Jones had spent five years in attempting to secure this post, and in the light of what he did achieve in his eleven remaining years, it is chastening to contemplate what he might have effected in India (not least in collaboration with Warren Hastings) had he been appointed immediately following Lemaistre's death in 1778.

At the end of May 1778 Lady Spencer, with whom Jones had worked closely for the Society for Charitable Purposes, was instrumental in arranging a meeting with

---

10. 'I fear I ought to have made my bow before, but I did not know the étiquette, and a philosopher among courtiers who flock together on such occasions, is like a lark or a nightingale in a *ménagerie* of peacocks or Indic pheasants', ibid., I.176.

11. Ibid., I.205.

12. 'A Discourse on the Institution of a Society', *Works*, III.1–2.

the Joint Secretary of the Treasury, who informed him that Lord Bathurst supported his application. In his attempts to achieve independence Jones was not above working the patronage system, but he proved very unlucky; within a few days Bathurst was forced to resign, and his successor as Chancellor, Lord Thurlow, was to block the appointment for so long that Jones came to feel: 'like Homer's "Man in a Dream", *pursuing without approaching*'.[13]

During those five years Jones had accomplished many things which were to render his eventual appointment inevitable. He published an important translation (significantly dedicated to Lord Bathurst) of *The Speeches of Isæus*, (1779), the Athenian orator and master of forensic argument; *An Essay on the Law of Bailments* (1781), regarded as a landmark in legal history; and *The Mahomedan Law of Succession to the Property of Intestates* (1782), which was to help British lawyers exercise justice in Bengal. An adviser to his friend Burke on matters of Indian law, in 1782 he was invited to give expert evidence to a Select Committee on the improvement of the English judicature in India, but it was not until March 1783 that the King, on the recommendations of Lords Ashburton and Shelburne, requested the appointment of Jones.

The delay would have been inexplicable, especially in the light of Jones's unparalleled qualifications, were it not for his independence of mind and his involvement with radical politics, both of which seem inextricably linked. His letters to Althorp during the same period that he was first attempting to secure the Indian judgeship reveal some of the reasons why Jones might have been considered irritating or even threatening to a Tory such as Thurlow. On 2 May 1778 he confesses to a disposition:

> which some men may call, and, I dare say, have called *haughtiness to my superiors*, but which I think only a proper dignity of mind and a zeal for independence. True it is, that, except in compliance with the forms of society, I acknowledge no man as my *superior*, who is not so in virtue or in knowledge, and if this be pride, I am not free from it; but I call it only a sense of that manly ἰσονομία [equality of political rights], which ought to be the basis of every good government, and which is certainly founded on reason.[14]

This reluctance to defer to rank or privilege, which rather shocked Horace Walpole, might be seen as the inevitable result of having been fêted at an early age by London society and Oxford professors. But Jones's reputation for unassuming modesty was almost equal to his reputation as an Orientalist, and the sources of his resistance to aristocratic influence were located in his classical republicanism, bolstered by a profoundly Miltonic austerity. Jones's enduring passion was for social justice and liberal constitutionalism; his attack on authoritarian monarchical government, and pro-American sympathies earning him the admiring friendship of men as dissimilar as Wilkes and Franklin, Bishop Shipley and Major Cartwright,

---

13. *Letters*, II.521.
14. Ibid., I.269.

Lord Shelburne and Henry Laurens.[15] His outspoken support for the American cause, his political association with the Virginia diplomat, Arthur Lee, his authorship of the Latin ode *Ad Libertatem*, his trips to Paris to consult Franklin were unlikely to endear him to Thurlow and North as Jones found, to his cost, when he attempted in 1780 to stand for an Oxford seat in the House of Commons.

Jones came late to the contest, and, without an effective agent or patron, demonstrated a rather naïve faith in exalted but nonpolitical support; his whole campaign, while characteristically strong on integrity, was weak in political nous.[16] Mrs Montagu urged Weller Pepys to support Jones, exclaiming: 'If the Muses were the Electors he would carry the election from every candidate that could offer',[17] but Pepys had no university vote and neither did the Muses. In the real world Jones could count on some solid support from Lord Ashburton and the Whig opposition, but his most vociferous campaigners were radicals like Edmund Cartwright, Richard Price, and John Wilkes, men most likely to antagonize the inherent conservatism of resident Oxford voters. Finally the publication of Jones's *An Inquiry into the Legal Mode of Suppressing Riots* (1780), the product of his first-hand experience of the Gordon Riots, although well received by the critics, was viewed in some influential quarters as 'aimed at curtailing the power of the executive as much as putting down the masses'.[18] In the face of almost inevitable defeat, Jones formally declined the poll on 2 September 1780, deprived of this opportunity to serve his country. Ironically his friend and former pupil, Althorp, was returned for Northampton in the same election.

Disillusioned but not embittered, Jones calmly outlined the reasons for his defeat in a letter to Wilkes, where he acknowledged that his literary reputation had proved 'nothing but moonshine'.[19] He threw himself tirelessly into the support of Wilkes's candidacy at Middlesex, and another journey to Passy to see Franklin. Baulked at home and increasingly depressed at the calamities of North's Ministry, his thoughts turn increasingly towards America:

> I am very ready (as I need not repeat) to traverse immense seas and burning sands, desiring only that the Chancellor will say *Yes* or *No*, and declaring, with perfect coolness, that, if he will not put me out of *suspense*, I will put myself out of it, and will accept a noble offer that has been made to me by the noblest of men, among whom I may not only *plead causes*, but *make laws*, and write them on the banks of my own river under my own oak.[20]

---

15. This former President of the American Congress, was imprisoned in the Tower from 1780 until early 1782, see *A Speech on the Nomination of Candidates*, p.375 below.
16. Garland Cannon's account details his tactical errors, see *The Life and Mind of Oriental Jones* (Cambridge, 1990), pp.114–36; (hereafter cited as *Life*).
17. Quoted in S.N. Mukherjee, *Sir William Jones: A Study in Eighteenth-Century British Attitudes to India* (Cambridge, 1968), p.68.
18. Ibid., p.69.
19. *Letters*, I.435.
20. Ibid., II.528.

Reluctant to compromise his principles for the sake of his career, his politics became, if anything, more radical; he joined Major Cartwright's Society for Constitutional Information, and in his *Speech on the Reformation of Parliament* (1782) he aligned himself with reformers like Wilkes and Richard Price in advocating universal manhood suffrage.

In the face of his frustrations he returned to the demanding delights of Oriental literature, publishing his acclaimed translation of *The Moallakát, or Seven Arabian Poems* in 1782. Engrossing himself in the Arabic manuscripts had helped him exchange, however temporarily, the grim realities of the political situation, for the wild heroism and hedonism of the Bedouin. Such are the chief pleasures of Tarafa:

> First, to rise before the censurers wake, and to drink tawny wine, which sparkles and froths when the clear stream is poured into it.
>
> Next, when a warrior, encircled by foes, implores my aid, to bend towards him my prancing charger, fierce as a wolf among the GADHA-trees, whom the sound of human steps has awakened, and who runs to quench his thirst at the brook.
>
> Thirdly, to shorten a cloudy day, a day astonishingly dark, by toying with a lovely delicate girl under a tent supported by pillars.
>
> 'The Poem of Tarafa', vv. 58–60.

His concern for the constitution, however, persistently recalled his attention to the astonishing darkness of Lord North's ministry, and his own poetry was increasingly recruited to the service of political liberty. His *Ode in Imitation of Alcæus* was published and distributed gratis by the Society for Constitutional Information; his *Ode in Imitation of Callistratus* celebrated the concept of a mixed republic; even an extempore epithalamium celebrating Althorp's marriage, *The Muse Recalled* is transformed into a paean of praise for America.

In the summer of 1782 yet another visit to Paris, and a projected voyage to Virginia, fuelled public speculation that Jones had been appointed 'to assist in the Pacific Negotiations with America'.[21] He would indeed have relished such a role, but the principal reason for the planned trip was more mundane – to assist a friend secure his transatlantic property. While abroad he learned of Rockingham's death, and the appointment of Shelburne as his successor; this certainly gave Jones hope of an end to his waiting. Furthermore, his meeting with Franklin and the Comte de Vergennes did, however, produce what Jones termed a *jeu d'esprit*, *The Principles of government, in a dialogue between a scholar and a peasant*, that was to have historic consequences.

In February 1783 Dean William Shipley, Jones's friend (and future brother-in-law), published in Wrexham an edition of this work in which he had significantly substituted throughout the words 'Gentleman' and 'Farmer', for 'Scholar' and 'Peasant'. The pamphlet was immediately denounced as seditious and subversive

---

21. *Public Advertiser* of 26 June, 1782, quoted in *Life*, p.175. On his first visit to Franklin in 1779 Jones, in a scholarly but somewhat naïve manner, had attempted to play the role of negotiator with his *A Fragment of Polybius*, see *Letters*, I.290–6.

by the High Sheriff of Flintshire, Thomas Fitzmaurice, at almost exactly the same moment that his brother, Lord Shelburne, was recommending its author to the King for the Indian judiciary. While a bill of indictment for seditious libel was being prepared against Dean Shipley, Jones was knighted, and married the defendant's sister. Jones, secure in his knowledge of the law, had no apprehensions about the eventual outcome, and the contemplation of such ironies must have been exceedingly sweet to the new Supreme Court judge as he strode the decks of the *Crocodile*.

Six years later, on 27 February 1789, Jones wrote from 'Aārif-nagar to his friend Charles Wilkins, the Sanskrit scholar and translator of the *Bhagavad-Gītā*, to announce that: 'The ships of this season will carry home seven hundred copies of our first volume of Transactions; and the second will be ready, I hope, next year'.[22] The Asiatic Society of Bengal, which Jones had founded in January 1784, only four months after his arrival in Calcutta, had effectively marked the birth of modern Orientalism, and at last its original research was to be available to eager European scholars. The first volume of *Asiatick Researches*, reflecting the society's objects of enquiry which Jones had described as 'MAN and NATURE: whatever is performed by the one, or produced by the other', contained contributions by civil servants, soldiers, native and European scholars on subjects which ranged from cave inscriptions to Asian astronomy, from the pangolin of Bahar to the fretted Indian lute. A five-month voyage would see this plunder arrive in a Europe absorbed in momentous events, where two of Jones's own contributions, 'The Third Anniversary Discourse' and his essay 'On the Gods of Greece, Italy, and India' were to create something of a cultural revolution.

Can there any good thing come out of Bengal? In 1789 the British public were thrilling to Burke's histrionic invective against Warren Hastings: 'He is not satisfied without sucking the blood of 1400 nobles. He is never corrupt without he is cruel. He never dines without creating a famine.'[23] Bengal was viewed as a nabob factory, churning out contemptible moneyed upstarts who, on their return, attempted to buy up Parliamentary seats and elide class boundaries. A site of European greed and indigenous famine, a culture of monstrous gods, suttee, child marriage, and infanticide, how could Bengal be associated with the concept of renaissance, with its dignified connotations of Western order and classical decorum? Incredibly this association is exactly what Jones and his Asiatic Society achieved; he reanimated a Hindu golden age: '. . . how degenerate and abased so ever the Hindus may now appear, . . . in some early age they were splendid in arts and arms, happy in government; wise in legislation, and eminent in various knowledge . . .'[24] Confidently and persistently relating Hindu civilization to that of

---

22. Ibid., II.827–8.
23. *The History of the Trial of Warren Hastings* (London, 1796), Part 6, p.153. Little attention was given at the trial to Hastings' efforts to combat ethnocentricity and incompetence in company officials, or to his vision of an administration characterized by proficiency in Indian languages and responsiveness to Indian culture. Jones made this his vision, and his personal support for Hastings accompanied an increasing animosity for his former friend, Burke.
24. 'Third Anniversary Discourse', p.360 below.

Europe, he compared Indian philosophy with Pythagoras and Plato, but his syncretist and universalist approach did not blunt his sensitivity to the distinctness and distinctiveness of different cultures. A mere four months after starting to learn Sanskrit he established this well-known cornerstone of the Oriental renaissance:

> The *Sanscrit* language, whatever be its antiquity, is of a wonderful structure; more perfect than the *Greek*, more copious than the *Latin*, and more exquisitely refined than either, yet bearing to both of them a stronger affinity, both in the roots of verbs and in the forms of grammar, than could possibly have been produced by accident; so strong indeed, that no philologer could examine them all three, without believing them to have sprung from some common source, which, perhaps, no longer exists.[25]

The profound impact of Jones's formulation of the Indo-European thesis lies in the fact that it simultaneously founded the modern discipline of comparative-historical linguistics and ensured the prominence of Sanskrit in future linguistic researches. In his dismissal of extravagant conjectural etymology it was his a posteriori or empirical method that was particuarly innovatory, and this was clearly the legacy of his forensic training: 'I have habituated myself to form opinions of men and things from *evidence*, which is the only solid basis of *civil*, as *experiment* is of *natural*, knowledge.'[26] This represents yet another instance of the curious relationship between legal and literary studies in the course of Jones's life. In England he had turned from the literary delights of the Middle East to the legal procedures of the Middle Temple, now here in India his decision to learn Sanskrit to codify native law, leads to linguistic and literary discoveries the huge significance of which dwarfs even that codification which was his life's work.

The fact that Jones had turned to Sanskrit in his attempt to compile a digest of Indian law, an immense task which would occupy him until his death, enables Edward Said to characterize Jones as having: 'an irresistible impulse to codify, to subdue the infinite variety of the Orient'.[27] Jones was continually opening up new and profound vistas to both European and Indian awareness. While it is true that Jones frequently expressed a desire to attain '*a complete knowledge of India*', such knowledge, diffused and communicated by means of *Asiatick Researches*, was equally empowering to the colonized as to the colonists. Said's definition of Orientalism as: 'a Western style for dominating, restructuring and having authority over the Orient'[28] proves totally inadequate to describe the work of the Asiatic Society and its president; Jones's Anniversary Discourses have as little in common

---

25. Ibid., p.361.

26. 'On the Persians', *Works*, III.112.

27. Edward Said, *Orientalism* (London, 1978), p.78. Said, who directs most of his attention towards the Middle East, misunderstands the nature of Orientalism in South Asia largely because he fails to consider the cultural contacts between the Europeans and the Asian intelligentsia explored in Kopf's study (see note 31 below), and exemplified in the relationships between Jones and scholars like Rāmalocana, Rādhākānta Sarman, Govardhana Kaula, and Jagannātha Tarkapañcānana. See Rosane Rocher, 'Weaving knowledge: Sir William Jones and Indian Pandits', paper read at New York University Symposium, 21 April 1994, awaiting publication.

28. Ibid., p.3. Said would have done better to direct his attention towards the Evangelical missionaries and the 'Anglicists', such as James Mill and Lord Macaulay, who attacked both the

with Said's notion of Foucauldian discourse as Jones's Orientalism has in common with Eurocentric imperialism.

Writing to Althorp, Jones attempts to communicate the intimidating uniqueness of his position, and his feelings of privilege in serving as a kind of cultural conduit:

Suppose Greek literature to be known in modern Greece only, and there to be in the hands of priests and philosophers; and suppose them still to be worshippers of Jupiter and Apollo: suppose Greece to have been conquered successively by Goths, Huns, Vandals, Tartars, and lastly by the English; then suppose a court of judicature to be established by the British parliament, at Athens, and an inquisitive Englishman to be one of the judges; suppose him to learn Greek there, which none of his countrymen knew, and to read Homer, Pindar, Plato, which no other Europeans had even heard of. Such am I in this country; substituting Sanscrit for Greek, the *Brahmans*, for the priests of *Jupiter*, and *Vālmic, Vyāsa, Cālīdāsa*, for Homer, Plato, Pindar. Need I say what exquisite pleasure I receive from conversing easily with that class of men, who conversed with Pythagoras, Theles and Solon, but with this advantage over the Grecian travellers, that I have no need of an interpreter.[29]

Here is no colonial heart of darkness: India is a revelation to Jones. Standing between two cultures and two worlds, the heir to one classical tradition and the neophyte of another, he appreciates the arrogance of the imperial mission to rule and civilize. Faced with the evidence of a civilization, the value and maturity of which he can only express in terms of his own classical heritage, he sees the opportunities for transculturation on the basis of equality and mutual respect. He has located loot to be shipped home for the metropolis and its rulers, but the uncovering of this treasure enriches the colony and its subjects.

The ships of the 1789 season were also to carry Jones's translation of *Śakuntalā* to an astonishing reception in Europe. If 'A *Śakuntalā* Era'[30] had been established in the West, the effect in the sub-continent of Kālidāsa's rediscovery was equally far-reaching; in the words of Nirad Chaudhuri: 'Psychologically, the Indian people crossed the line which divides primitive peoples from civilized peoples'.[31] While redirecting European Romanticism towards India, Jones was collating four manuscripts of Kālidāsa's *Ritusaṃhāra* to produce the first publication of a complete text in the original Sanskrit for the enlightenment of Indian intellectuals. Jones was not only making Europe familiar with the drama, but he was also freeing Indian literature, as he had freed Indian law, from exclusive Brahminical control and thus initiating the process of secularization which was to prove vital for India's future.

Hindus and their Orientalist defenders, and imposed Western cultural policy by means of a reductive or dismissive critique of Indian culture.
29. *Letters*, II.755–6.
30. Raymond Schwab, *The Oriental Renaissance: Europe's Discovery of India and the East, 1680–1880*, trans. G. Patterson-Black and V. Reinking (New York, 1984), pp.57–64.
31. Quoted in David Kopf, *British Orientalism and the Bengal Renaissance* (Berkeley and Los Angeles, 1969), p.12.

Appreciating that acculturation and diffusion were two-way processes in the contact-zone of Bengal, Jones managed to reconcile his urge to modernize and reform with his antiquarian interest in India's classical past. In fostering a Hindu cultural renaissance Jones simultaneously transformed British public opinion towards India and the way India saw itself.[32] It suited the motives of the missionaries to see India as a site of monstrous and barbaric 'Otherness'. Even William Carey, a professor of the language at Fort William from 1806, described Sanskrit and its literature as 'a golden casket exquisitely wrought, but in reality filled with pebbles and trash',[33] so strong were his associations with the Baptist Mission at Serampore, whereas the publications of the Asiatic Society revealed in a spirit of secular scholarly enquiry the indisputable evidence of mature civilization at a time when Europe was covering itself in woad. This fresh knowledge of ancient Indian culture created immense excitement, especially in the Germany of the 1790s; Jones's concern to speculate about mankind's monogenesis and the primeval source of his civilization became the centre of scholarly enquiry throughout Europe.

In the years following his arrival in Bengal Jones's increasing familiarity with Hindu mythology also revitalized his creative powers and he composed a series of nine hymns celebrating Hindu deities. From the early 1770s he had maintained that a study of Oriental cultures would invigorate European culture, but these hymns demonstrate that Jones's approach was not simply to ransack Asia for portable literary treasures. His study of 'the Vayds and Purans of the Hindus' had convinced him 'that the doctrines of the Vidanti school are Platonic',[34] and the hymns trace the metaphysical relationship between the beautiful and variegated veil of nature and the Supreme Mind which continuously creates it.

> Wrapt in eternal solitary shade,
>   Th'impenetrable gloom of light intense,
>   Impervious, inaccessible, immense,
>   Ere spirits were infus'd or forms display'd,
>   BREHM his own Mind survey'd,
> As mortal eyes (thus finite we compare
>   With infinite) in smoothest mirrors gaze:
>   Swift, at his look, a shape supremely fair
>   Leap'd into being with a boundless blaze,
>   That fifty suns might daze.
> Primeval MAYA was the Goddess nam'd,
>   Who to her sire, with Love divine inflam'd,
>   A casket gave with rich *Ideas* fill'd,
> From which this gorgeous Universe he fram'd;
>   For, when th'Almighty will'd,
>   Unnumber'd worlds to build,

---

32. Ibid., pp.275–91.
33. See Michael A. Laird, *Missionaries and Education in Bengal 1793–1837* (Oxford, 1972), pp.55–6.
34. In a letter of 24 Sept. 1788 to Lord Monboddo, *Letters*, II.818.

From Unity diversified he sprang,
While gay Creation laugh'd, and procreant Nature rang.
'A Hymn to Náráyena', ll.19–36.

With their emphases on creativity and the nature of perception, Jones's hymns anticipated, and helped to shape, Romantic preoccupations with these themes, both on the continent and in England. As Raymond Schwab has maintained:

> Jones was as famous in England for his original poetry as for his introduction of India. The two aspects of his reputation reinforced one another, and both are present in the hymns he addressed to Hindu divinities celebrating a religion 'Wrapt in eternal solitary shade.' The first German Romantics, Schelling and Novalis among them, were very much taken by these hymns, before they became popular in England.[35]

Their subject matter was both novel and exotic; they represent a detailed introduction to a mythology which was little known in Europe. Furthermore, these poems introduce new aspects of a syncretic view of mythology in which cultural and religious idioms are compared, contrasted and redefined. As a Romantic precursor, and a major influence upon the European Romantics, Jones did more to introduce Oriental elements into Western literature than any other poet. But these hymns, published in Calcutta as well as London, along with Jones's translation of *Gítagóvinda*, his extracts from the Vedas, and essays like 'On the Gods of Greece, Italy, and India', served to refocus attention within the subcontinent upon a more complex, structured and classically pure version of Hinduism.

When Jones was not composing his hymns, or speaking 'the language of the gods' (Sanskrit not Welsh!) with his pandits, or further weakening his eyesight poring over Sanskrit, Persian and Arabic manuscripts, long sittings at the Supreme Court made many demands, and, although he was always most supportive of his colleagues on the bench, Sir Robert Chambers's impunctuality and Justice John Hyde's impetuosity must have proved irritating to say the least.[36]

Vacations would find him at Crishna-nagar, answering a voluminous backlog of correspondence with friends and scholars throughout Europe; during brief but delightful spells of relaxation, surrounded by Anna's flocks and herds, and while a Bengal tiger cub played together with a kid at her feet, he contemplated the Sabine farm of his studious retirement. For Jones was not only shipping home exotic seeds and manuscripts, knowledge and 'books, which Europe never saw before', but India bonds and company bills of credit. By living frugally in a land renowned for dissipated luxury Jones had accumulated almost £30,000, and was asking Sir

---

35. Schwab, *The Oriental Renaissance*, p. 195.
36. See *The Memoirs of William Hickey*, ed. Alfred Spencer, 4 vols. (London, 1923), III.218–35. Hickey, a Supreme Court attorney, refers to 'the glaring blemishes in Sir Robert Chambers as a public magistrate', and relates anecdotes of Hyde's petulance. He also records the details of a case in October 1784, where Jones passionately disagreed with both his fellow judges, pp.247–60.

Joseph Banks to keep an eye on the property market for a suitable Middlesex country estate.[37] India had provided the financial independence to enable him to enter the world of politics on his own terms, and, although the House of Commons did not look so attractive to him now, he would have valued the impartial position of Speaker. Law had offered him the means of escaping dependence on patron or party, but Indian law would allow him no escape.

In early December 1793, her health demanding relief from the rigours of a tropical climate, Anna Maria sailed for England on the *Princess Amelia*; Jones was never to see his wife or England again. His desire to complete his Indian law digest for the good of many millions of native Indians, 'to give stability to their property real and personal, and security to their persons', would not allow him to accompany her. He wished to be remembered not as a judge but as a legislator, a Justinian or Hywel Dda of the East, and his description of the rewards of such work provides a measure of his individuality as an imperial representative of the British Crown in Bengal: '. . . the natives are charmed with the work, and the idea of making their slavery lighter by giving them their own laws, is more flattering to me than the thanks of the company and the approbation of the king.'[38]

Within five months of Anna's departure, Jones was dead. He had succumbed, at the age of forty-seven, to a disease which despatched many Europeans in the sub-continent, inflammation of the liver. His last published work was the *Institutes of Hindu Law; or, the Ordinances of Menu*; his last extant letter was to Samuel Davis, a District Judge at Benares, who possessed an observatory and shared Jones's interest in Indian astronomy. Jones had asked Davis to supply him with some botanical specimens of the Tāmala tree, the holy blossoms of which had been used to bedeck Krishna, and he looked forward to spending the next Sunday with Davis discussing the life and achievements of a brilliant Hindu astronomer, Jai Singh. It is this enormous respect for Indian culture and scholarship which gives the lie to Said's claim that Jones's goal was: 'to domesticate the Orient and thereby turn it into a province of European learning'.[39]

His death was truly a national loss both to the Indian and European communities; learned pandits could not restrain their tears.[40] Jones had significantly changed the psychological use the West was making of the Orient; he had represented India and shown how Indians must represent themselves. This was not simply a matter of recommending government pensions for Bengali pandits, but his life-example of eagerness to learn and readiness to respect. When he voyaged to India in 1783 he came complete with an exalted reputation for Oriental learning, he was universally regarded as an authority on Persian and Arabic culture, and an expert on Indian legislation although he had never ventured out of Europe. In the face of a new and demanding post a certain period of resting on his

---

37. *Letters*, II.895. Jones would have preferred retirement in America or France, but he deferred to his wife's wishes, ibid., p.897.
38. *Letters*, II.885.
39. Said, *Orientalism*, p.78.
40. See Sir John Shore's *Memoir*, *Works*, II.307.

laurels might well have seemed justified, but that was not his way; not content merely to meet the European scholars, he approached the fountain-head of knowledge by consulting the pandits and maulvis. The Flaxman monument to Sir William Jones in University College, Oxford depicts in bas-relief, under a pediment decorated with the Greek lyre, the Hindu *vina*, and the Caducæus, three thoughtful native scholars sitting at his feet, but it was his willingness to reverse these roles which struck the strongest blow against Eurocentricity.[41]

With the insights he gained he constantly modified the exhaustive, interdisciplinary 'Objects of Enquiry' which he had drawn up on the *Crocodile*, abandoning preconceptions and opening his mind to radically new premisses. His publications and his letters underscore his close co-operation with a wide range of Indian scholars, and a Sanskrit pandit, Trivédi Servoru Sarman, who had helped supervise work on the Hindu law digest, composed the following verses in Jones's honour:

1. To you there are many like me; yet to me there is none like you, but yourself; there are numerous groves of night flowers; yet the night flower sees nothing like the moon, but the moon.
2. A hundred chiefs rule the world, but thou art an ocean, and they are mere wells; many luminaries are awake in the sky, but which of them can be compared to the Sun?[42]

But Sarman was wrong in one respect. Jones had established Orientalism as a discipline largely by means of creating a network of communicating experts, infecting many with his own enthusiasm, and the Asiatic Society continued to encourage professional standards of research from amateur scholars. It was, above all, the dynamism and practicality of men like Jones, and his successors, H. T. Colebrooke, H. H. Wilson and James Prinsep, which inspired the new Indian intelligentsia. The contrast between such Orientalists and later representatives of British imperialism is nowhere more forcefully expressed than in the words of Girish Chandra Ghose, a Calcutta journalist, writing in 1862:

'As regards Indian literature . . . history, antiquities, the present race of Anglo-Indians [the British in India] . . . are lamentably ignorant . . . Jones, Colebrooke, Wilson . . . respected our fathers and looked upon us hopefully at least with

---

41. In a recent letter to the *TLS* (19 March 1993, p.15), Edward Said concludes his attack upon the reviewer of his *Culture and Imperialism* by branding the review as 'a shabby performance', and appending a telling final sentence: 'But those are the ways of Orientalism.' Without prejudice to the justice or otherwise of his claims, it is interesting to note that Said's criticism of the reviewer is predicated on the latter's disregard of the relevant Islamic languages and texts, inadequate fieldwork, and arrogant cultural stereotyping. None of these accusations can be brought against Sir William Jones and his were the ways of Orientalism.

42. *Works*, II.307. Coleridge transcribed the first verse, and the changes he made 'suggest the possibility of a poem in embryo', Kathleen Coburn, (ed.) *The Notebooks of S.T. Coleridge*, 3 double vols. (London, 1957–73), II.3130.

melancholy interest, as you would look on the heir of a ruined noble. But to the great unwashed abroad today, we are simply niggers – without a past; perhaps, without a future. They do not choose to know us.[43]

In 1819 in the notes to his *Westöstlicher Diwan*, Goethe described Jones as: 'A far-seeing man, he seeks to connect the unknown to the known'.[44] In making these connections between Asia and the West, Jones was so faithful to the spirit of Indian culture that some contemporary reviewers thought his hymns, despite their neoclassical diction and Pindaric form, to be direct translations of Sanskrit texts, and it is interesting to note that this misconception displayed remarkable longevity; thus in 1969 a critic writes, 'Sir William Jones might have written expressly for Blake his remarks upon the Hymn to Narayena, *which he translated*; for he applies its metaphysical distinctions to the Descartes–Locke–Berkeley theme of primary and secondary sensible qualities' (emphasis mine).[45] There is a certain tension between the substantial claim that is made for the influence of Jones's contribution and the error concerning that contribution which underlines the truth of John Drew's observation: 'In a single decade following [his] landfall he evoked an image of India which then shone as brightly, as it was later to be as eclipsed, as his own literary reputation.'[46]

Fifty years ago R. M. Hewitt stressed Jones's extensive influence on poetry and culture: 'If we were compiling a thesis on the influence of Jones we could collect most of our material from footnotes, ranging from Gibbon (1776) to Tennyson (1827) and including *Vathek* and *The Curse of Kehama*.'[47] It would seem time to rescue Sir William Jones from the footnotes. He was clearly regarded as a major poet in the Romantic period – 1807, for example, saw the publication of his *Complete Works* in thirteen volumes by Stockdale, and his *Poetical Works* in two volumes by Cadell and Davies – but his reputation waned in the Victorian era. From the modern perspective of comparative literature,[48] Jones can be seen as a

---

43. Quoted in Kopf, *The Bengal Renaissance*, p.291.

44. Quoted in Schwab, *Oriental Renaissance*, p.195.

45. Kathleen Raine, *Blake and Tradition*, 2 vols. (London, 1969), I.178. Similarly Jerome McGann in *The New Oxford Book of Romantic Period Verse* (Oxford, 1993) foregrounds Jones's work, underlines its importance for Romanticism, and yet repeatedly describes the hymns as 'celebrated translations from the Sanskrit', see pp. xxi–xxii, 783; furthermore two stanzas are inexplicably transposed in 'A Hymn to Indra', ll.129–43 being relocated at the end of the poem, see pp.35–6. See also Morton D. Paley, '"Wonderful Originals" – Blake and Ancient Sculpture', in Robert N. Essick and Donald Pearce (eds.), *Blake in his Time* (Bloominton and London, 1978), who ascribes editorship of Jones's *Works* to a non-existent daughter, (p.185).

46. John Drew, *India and the Romantic Imagination* (Delhi: Oxford University Press, 1987), p.72. The first attacks upon Jones's reputation issued from James Mill's *History of British India* (1818). Mill, like Said, was anti-Orientalist, but, unlike Said, Mill was also anti-Oriental. See Javed Majeed, *Ungoverned Imaginings: 'The History of British India' and Orientalism* (Oxford, 1992).

47. R.M. Hewitt, 'Harmonious Jones', *Essays and Studies*, 23 (1942), 42–59, (43).

48. 'In considering the foundation of our own discipline, comparative literary studies – if discipline it be – no name is more important than that of Sir William Jones. Indeed, the importance of Jones for the development of Oriental studies, for comparative mythology, philology, and law, as well as for the translation of literary masterpieces from the Arabic, Persian, and Sanskrit, is indisputable', Elinor Shaffer, 'Editor's Note', *Comparative Criticism*, 3 (1981), xv.

crucial integrator, synthesizer, and transmitter of Eastern culture, and one who avoided the gross ethnocentricity of most of his contemporaries. Elinor Shaffer suggests that 'if his work is still too little known, it is perhaps because the extraordinary range of his interests and accomplishments puts him beyond the means of assessment available to specialists in any one field'.[49]

Jones brought to India a mind that was both receptive and empirical; a tolerance born of the Enlightenment, and a speculation which anticipates the Romantics. William Jones succeeded largely because he had the imaginative courage to make connections assumed to be impossible. To appreciate the links between Indian philosophy and the works of Pythagoras and Plato was, perhaps, Jones's greatest contribution to European literature and culture. His investigations of Vedic texts focused attention upon Indian Brahmanism, which was to prove immediately attractive to the metaphysical bias of European Romanticism, while simultaneously helping to define an emergent Hindu identity. His intuitive insights were not the product of any homogenizing essentialist position, but a fine sensitivity to the distinctiveness of individual cultures.

Jones is an important figure in the history of ideas, indeed one of the first to realize that ideas can possess a history, and his combination of a poet's sensibility and a legal scholar's acumen and erudition enabled him to appreciate inter-relationships between discrete disciplines, and draw connections between differing cultures. A man of diverse talents and great humanity, his philosophy might be best encompassed in the words of a later writer of Anglo-Indian literature – 'Only connect'.

---

49. Loc. cit.

POEMS

1

Caïssa, or, The Game at Chess (1763)

[A juvenile piece, composed when Jones was only sixteen, and reflecting his early
enthusiasms both for chess and mock-heroic. Inspired (like the ombre episode in
The Rape of the Lock) by the description of the game in the sixteenth-century
Marcus Hieronymus Vida's 'Ludus Scacchiae', this rhymed technical treatise
relating the story of Caïssa and recounting the origins of chess was frequently
reprinted throughout the nineteenth century, often as an embellishment to chess
manuals. During his final months at Harrow, Jones had studied and practised the
game in François-André Danican's (Philidor) *Analyse du jeu des échecs* (London,
1749), and the 'Great Scholar', as Jones was termed, had been composing
imitations of Ovid for some years. One of the things that cemented the friendship
with Franklin was their mutual fascination with chess; and Jones was to publish an
account of 'The Indian Game of Chess' in *Asiatick Researches* II (1790), 159–65.
When the poem was published as the final verse piece of *Poems, consisting chiefly of
translations from the Asiatick languages* (Oxford: Clarendon Press, 1772), the
Scottish historian and critic, Gilbert Stuart, praised its 'singular art and delicacy,
with a command of language, and a power of harmony which few poets have
displayed' (*Monthly Review*, 46, May 1772, 516). The text followed here is that of
the second edition (1777), with variants noted from the first edition of 1772.]

ADVERTISEMENT

The first idea of the following piece was taken from a Latin poem of Vida, entitled SCACCHIA LUDUS, which was translated into Italian by Marino, and inserted in the fifteenth Canto of his Adonis: the author thought it fair to make an acknowledgement in the notes for the passages which he borrowed from those two poets; but he must also do them the justice to declare, that most of the descriptions, and the whole story of Caïssa, which is written in imitation of Ovid, are his own, and their faults must be imputed by him only. The characters in the poem are no less imaginary than those in the episode; in which the invention of Chess is poetically ascribed to Mars, though it is certain that the game was originally brought from India.

6–7 The quotations from Vida and Marino are omitted. Here and throughout the text authorial footnotes are placed above, and editorial footnotes below, a full-width rule.

CAISSA, OR, THE GAME AT CHESS,
A POEM
Written in the Year 1763

Of armies on the chequer'd field array'd,
And guiltless war in pleasing form display'd;
When two bold kings contend with vain alarms,
In ivory this, and that in ebon arms;
Sing, sportive maids, that haunt the sacred hill   5
Of Pindus, and the fam'd Pierian rill.
Thou, joy of all below, and all above,
Mild Venus, queen of laughter, queen of love;
Leave thy bright island, where on many a rose
And many a pink thy blooming train repose: 10
Assist me, goddess! since a lovely pair
Command my song, like thee divinely fair.

Near yon cool stream, whose living waters play,
And rise translucent in the solar ray;
Beneath the covert of a fragrant bower,   15
Where spring's soft influence purpled every flower;
Two smiling nymphs reclin'd in calm retreat,
And envying blossoms crowded round their seat:
Here Delia was enthron'd, and by her side
The sweet Sirena, both in beauty's pride: 20
Thus shine two roses, fresh with early bloom,
That from their native stalk dispense perfume;
Their leaves unfolding to the dawning day
Gems of the glowing mead, and eyes of May.
A band of youths and damsels sat around,   25
Their flowing locks with braided myrtle bound;
Agatis, in the graceful dance admir'd,
And gentle Thyrsis, by the muse inspir'd;
With Sylvia, fairest of the mirthful train;
And Daphnis, doom'd to love, yet love in vain.   30
Now, whilst a purer blush o'erspreads her cheeks,
With soothing accents thus Sirena speaks:

---

6   Pindus was the mountain sacred to Apollo and the Muses.
30   *Daphnis, doom'd to love, yet love in vain* In a letter to his legal amanuensis, Arthur Pritchard, in June 1781 Jones states: 'I meant myself by Daphnis, and you will see that I was an

'The meads and lawns are ting'd with beamy light,
'And wakeful larks begin their vocal flight;
'Whilst on each bank the dewdrops sweetly smile;   35
'What sport, my Delia, shall the hours beguile?
'Shall heavenly notes, prolong'd with various art,
'Charm the fond ear, and warm the rapturous heart?
'At distance shall we view the sylvan chace?
'Or catch with silken lines the finny race?'   40

    Then Delia thus: 'Or rather, since we meet
'By chance assembled in this cool retreat,
'In artful contest let our warlike train
'Move well-directed o'er the colour'd plain;
'Daphnis, who taught us first, the play shall guide;   45
'Explain its laws, and o'er the field preside:
'No prize we need, our ardour to inflame;
'We fight with pleasure, if we fight for fame.'

    The nymph consents: the maids and youth prepare
To view the combat, and the sport to share;   50
But Daphnis most approv'd the bold design,
Whom love instructed, and the tuneful Nine.
He rose, and on the cedar table plac'd
A polish'd board with differing colours grac'd;
Squares eight times eight in equal order lie;   55
These bright as snow, those dark with sable dye;
Like the broad target by the tortoise born,
Or like the hide by spotted panthers worn.
Then from a chest, with harmless heroes stor'd,
O'er the smooth plain two well-wrought hosts he pour'd;   60
The champions burn'd their rivals to assail,
Twice eight in black, twice eight in milkwhite mail;
In shape and station different, as in name,
Their motions various, nor their power the same.
Say, muse! (for Jove has nought from thee conceal'd)   65
Who form'd the legions on the level field?

    High in the midst the reverend kings appear,
And o'er the rest their pearly scepters rear:

early lover, as the poem was written at sixteen. In truth I have never ceased being in love from that age to more than the double of it, but some of my flames are married, others (more lamented) dead, and others surrounded by invincible obstacles; – but I do not despair of gaining a friend of my bosom, while I am young enough to enjoy such a blessing', (*Letters*, II.477).
  67–72 Writing to Reviczky, early in April 1768, of his concern for the state, a chess analogy

One solemn step, majestically slow,
They gravely move, and shun the dangerous foe;   70
If e'er they call, the watchful subjects spring,
And die with rapture if they save their king;
On him the glory of the day depends,
He once imprison'd, all the conflict ends.

   The queens exulting near their consorts stand;   75
Each bears a deadly falchion in her hand;
Now here, now there, they bound with furious pride,
And thin the trembling ranks from side to side;
Swift as Camilla flying o'er the main,
Or lightly skimming o'er the dewy plain: 80
Fierce as they seem, some bold Plebeian spear
May pierce their shield, or stop their full career.

   The valiant guards, their minds on havock bent,
Fill the next squares, and watch the royal tent;
Though weak their spears, though dwarfish be their height,   85
‡Compact they move, the bulwark of the fight.

   To right and left the martial wings display
Their shining arms, and stand in close array.
Behold, four archers, eager to advance,
Send the light reed, and rush with sidelong glance;   90
Through angles ever they assault the foes,
True to the colour, which at first they chose.
Then four bold knights for courage fam'd and speed,
Each knight exalted on a prancing steed:
Their arching course no vulgar limit knows,   95
Transverse they leap, and aim insidious blows:
Nor friends, nor foes, their rapid force restrain,
By one quick bound two changing squares they gain;
From varying hues renew the fierce attack,
And rush from black to white, from white to black.   100

‡The chief art in the Tacticks of Chess consists in the nice conduct of the royal pawns; in supporting them against every attack; and, if they are taken, in supplying their places with others equally supported: a principle, on which the success of the game in great measure depends, though it seems to be omitted by the very accurate Vida.

---

naturally occurs to Jones: 'When I reflect on our constitution, I seem as it were to contemplate a game at chess, a recreation in which we both delight. For we have a king whose dignity we strenuously defend, but whose power is very limited; the knights, rooks, and other pieces, have some kind of resemblance to the orders of nobility, who are employed in war, and in the management of public affairs; but the principal strength is in the pawns, or people; if these are firmly united they are sure of victory, but if divided and separated, the battle is lost', *Works*, I.105.

Four solemn elephants the sides defend;
Beneath the load of ponderous towers they bend:
In one unalter'd line they tempt the fight;
Now crush the left, and now o'erwhelm the right.
Bright in the front the dauntless soldiers raise   105
Their polish'd spears; their steely helmets blaze:
Prepar'd they stand the daring foe to strike,
Direct their progress, but their wounds oblique.

   Now swell th' embattled troops with hostile rage,
And clang their shields, impatient to engage;   110
When Daphnis thus: A varied plain behold,
Where fairy kings their mimick tents unfold,
As Oberon, and Mab, his wayward queen,
Lead forth their armies on the daisied green.
No mortal hand the wonderous sport contriv'd,   115
By Gods invented, and from Gods deriv'd:
From them the British nymphs receiv'd the game,
And play each morn beneath the crystal Thame;
Hear then the tale, which they to Colin sung,
As idling o'er the lucid wave he hung.   120

   A lovely Dryad rang'd the Thracian wild,
Her air enchanting, and her aspect mild;
To chase the bounding hart was all her joy,
Averse from Hymen, and the Cyprian boy;
O'er hills and valleys was her beauty fam'd,   125
And fair Caïssa was the damsel nam'd.
Mars saw the maid; with deep surprize he gaz'd,
Admir'd her shape, and every gesture prais'd:
His golden bow the child of Venus bent,
And through his breast a piercing arrow sent: 130
The reed was Hope; the feathers, keen Desire;
The point, her eyes; the barbs, ethereal fire.
Soon to the nymph he pour'd his tender strain;
The haughty Dryad scorn'd his amorous pain:
He told his woes, where'er the maid he found,   135
And still he press'd, yet still Caïssa frown'd,
But ev'n her frowns (ah, what might smiles have done!)
Fir'd all his soul, and all his senses won.
He left his car, by raging tigers drawn,
And lonely wander'd o'er the dusky lawn;   140
Then lay desponding near a murmuring stream,
And fair Caïssa was his plaintive theme.

A Naiad heard him from her mossy bed,
And through the crystal rais'd her placid head;
Then mildly spake: 'O thou, whom love inspires,   145
'Thy tears will nourish, not allay thy fires.
'The smiling blossoms drink the pearly dew;
'And ripening fruit the feather'd race pursue;
'The scaly shoals devour the silken weeds;
'Love on our sighs, and on our sorrow feeds.   150
'Then weep no more; but, ere thou canst obtain
'Balm to thy wounds, and solace to thy pain,
'With gentle art thy martial look beguile;
'Be mild, and teach thy rugged brow to smile.
'Canst thou no play, no soothing game devise   155
'To make thee lovely in the damsel's eyes?
'So may thy prayers assuage the scornful dame,
'And ev'n Caïssa own a mutual flame.'
'Kind nymph, said Mars, thy counsel I approve;
'Art, only art, her ruthless breast can move.   160
'But when? or how? Thy dark discourse explain:
'So may thy stream ne'er swell with gushing rain;
'So may thy waves in one pure current flow,
'And flowers eternal on thy border blow!'
  To whom the maid replied with smiling mien: 165
'Above the palace of the Paphian queen
'Love's brother dwells, a boy of graceful port,
'By gods nam'd Euphron, and by mortals, Sport:
'Seek him; to faithful ears unfold thy grief,
'And hope, ere morn return, a sweet relief.   170
'His temple hangs below the azure skies;
'Seest thou yon argent cloud? 'Tis there it lies.'
This said, she sunk beneath the liquid plain,
And sought the mansion of her blue-hair'd train.

  Meantime the god, elate with heart-felt joy,   175
Had reach'd the temple of the sportful boy;
He told Caïssa's charms, his kindled fire,
The Naiad's counsel, and his warm desire.
'Be swift, he added, give my passion aid;
'A god requests.' – He spake, and Sport obey'd.   180

153–8   The Naiad's advice to Mars to use gentler arts in his wooing of the Dryad Caïssa in the devising of a 'soothing game' to intrigue and enthral her represents a subtle and amusing blend of the amatory and the intellectual.

He fram'd a tablet of celestial mold,
Inlay'd with squares of silver and of gold;
Then of two metals form'd the warlike band,
That here compact in show of battle stand;
He taught the rules that guide the pensive game,   185
And call'd it *Cassa* from the Dryad's name:
(Whence Albion's sons, who most its praise confess,
Approv'd the play, and nam'd it thoughtful *Chess*.)
The god delighted thank'd indulgent Sport;
Then grasp'd the board, and left his airy court.   190
With radiant feet he pierc'd the clouds; nor stay'd,
Till in the woods he saw the beauteous maid:
Tir'd with the chase the damsel sat reclin'd,
Her girdle loose, her bosom unconfin'd.
He took the figure of a wanton Faun,   195
And stood before her on the flowery lawn;
Then show'd his tablet: pleas'd the nymph survey'd
The lifeless troops in glittering ranks display'd;
She ask'd the wily sylvan to explain
The various motions of the splendid train;   200
With eager heart she caught the winning lore,
And thought ev'n Mars less hateful than before:
'What spell, said she, deceiv'd my careless mind?
'The god was fair, and I was most unkind.'
She spoke, and saw the changing Faun assume   205
A milder aspect, and a fairer bloom;
His wreathing horns, that from his temples grew,
Flow'd down in curls of bright celestial hue;
The dappled hairs, that veil'd his loveless face,
Blaz'd into beams, and show'd a heavenly grace;   210
The shaggy hide, that mantled o'er his breast,
Was soften'd to a smooth transparent vest,
That through its folds his vigorous bosom show'd,
And nervous limbs, where youthful ardour glow'd:
(Had Venus view'd him in those blooming charms,   215
Not Vulcan's net had forc'd her from his arms.)
With goatlike feet no more he mark'd the ground,
But braided flowers his silken sandals bound.
The Dryad blush'd; and, as he press'd her, smil'd,
Whilst all his cares one tender glance beguil'd.   220

205–18 The gradual metamorphosis of Faun (the shape Mars had assumed) into youthful god
is handled with a competence and confidence remarkable in an author of sixteen.

He ends: *To arms,* the maids and striplings cry,
To arms, the groves, and sounding vales reply.
Sirena led to war the swarthy crew,
And Delia those that bore the lily's hue.
Who first, O muse, began the bold attack;   225
The white refulgent, or the mournful black?
Fair Delia first, as favouring lots ordain,
Moves her pale legions tow'rd the sable train:
From thought to thought her lively fancy flies,
Whilst o'er the board she darts her sparkling eyes.   230

At length the warriour moves with haughty strides;
Who from the plain the snowy king divides:
With equal haste his swarthy rival bounds;
His quiver rattles, and his buckler sounds:
Ah! hapless youths, with fatal warmth you burn;   235
Laws, ever fix'd, forbid you to return.
Then from the wing a short-liv'd spearman flies,
Unsafely bold, and see! he dies, he dies:
The dark-brow'd hero with one vengeful blow
Of life and place deprives his ivory foe.   240
Now rush both armies o'er the burnish'd field,
Hurl the swift dart, and rend the bursting shield.
Here furious knights on fiery coursers prance,
Here archers spring, and lofty towers advance.
But see! the white-rob'd Amazon beholds   245
Where the dark host its opening van unfolds:
Soon as her eye discerns the hostile maid,
By ebon shield, and ebon helm betray'd;
Seven squares she passes with majestick mien,
And stands triumphant o'er the falling queen.   250
Perplex'd, and sorrowing at his consort's fate,
The monarch burn'd with rage, despair, and hate:
Swift from his zone th' avenging blade he drew,
And, mad with ire, the proud virago slew.
Meanwhile sweet-smiling Delia's wary king   255
Retir'd from fight behind his circling wing.

Long time the war in equal balance hung;
Till, unforeseen, an ivory courser sprung,
And, wildly prancing in an evil hour,
Attack'd at once the monarch, and the tower: 260
Sirena blush'd; for, as the rules requir'd,
Her injur'd sovereign to his tent retir'd;

Whilst her lost castle leaves his threatening height,
And adds new glory to th' exulting knight.

    At this, pale fear oppress'd the drooping maid, 265
And on her cheek the rose began to fade:
A crystal tear, that stood prepar'd to fall,
She wip'd in silence, and conceal'd from all;
From all but Daphnis: He remark'd her pain,
And saw the weakness of her ebon train; 270
Then gently spoke: 'Let me your loss supply,
'And either nobly win, or nobly die;
'Me oft has fortune crown'd with fair success,
'And led to triumph in the fields of Chess.'
He said: the willing nymph her place resign'd, 275
And sat at distance on the bank reclin'd.
Thus when Minerva call'd her chief to arms,
And Troy's high turret shook with dire alarms,
The Cyprian goddess wounded left the plain,
And Mars engag'd a mightier force in vain. 280

    Straight Daphnis leads his squadron to the field;
(To Delia's arms 'tis ev'n a joy to yield.)
Each guileful snare, and subtle art he tries,
But finds his art less powerful than her eyes:
Wisdom and strength superiour charms obey; 285
And beauty, beauty, wins the long-fought day.
By this a hoary chief, on slaughter bent,
Approach'd the gloomy king's unguarded tent;
Where, late, his consort spread dismay around,
Now her dark corse lies bleeding on the ground. 290
Hail, happy youth! thy glories not unsung
Shall live eternal on the poet's tongue;
For thou shalt soon receive a splendid change,
And o'er the plain with nobler fury range.
The swarthy leaders saw the storm impend, 295
And strove in vain their sovereign to defend:
Th' invader wav'd his silver lance in air,
And flew like lightning to the fatal square;
His limbs dilated in a moment grew
To stately height, and widen'd to the view; 300
More fierce his look, more lion-like his mien,
Sublime he mov'd, and seem'd a warriour queen.
As when the sage on some unfolding plant
Has caught a wandering fly, or frugal ant,

His hand the microscopick frame applies,   305
And lo! a bright-hair'd monster meets his eyes;
He sees new plumes in slender cases roll'd;
Here stain'd with azure, there bedropp'd with gold;
Thus, on the alter'd chief both armies gaze,
And both the kings are fix'd with deep amaze.   310
The sword, which arm'd the snow-white maid before,
He now assumes, and hurls the spear no more;
Then springs indignant on the dark-rob'd band,
And knights, and archers feel his deadly hand.
Now flies the monarch of the sable shield,   315
His legions vanquish'd, o'er the lonely field:
So when the morn, by rosy coursers drawn,
With pearls and rubies sows the verdant lawn,
Whilst each pale star from heaven's blue vault retires,
Still Venus gleams, and last of all expires.   320
He hears, where'er he moves, the dreadful sound;
Check the deep vales, and *Check* the woods rebound.
No place remains: he sees the certain fate,
And yields his throne to ruin, and Checkmate.

A brighter blush o'erspreads the damsel's cheeks,   325
And mildly thus the conquer'd stripling speaks:
'A double triumph, Delia, hast thou won,
'By Mars protected, and by Venus' son;
'The first with conquest crowns thy matchless art,
'The second points those eyes at Daphnis' heart.'   330
She smil'd; the nymphs and amorous youths arise,
And own, that beauty gain'd the nobler prize.

Low in their chest the mimick troops were lay'd,
*And peaceful slept the sable hero's shade.

---

*A parody of the last line in Pope's translation of the Iliad, 'And peaceful slept the mighty Hector's shade.'

2

The Seven Fountains,
An Eastern Allegory (1767)

[Here Jones mingles elements from *Fatihatu'l-Khulafá* (*The Delight of the Caliphs*) by the fifteenth-century Syrian author, Ibn 'Arabsháh, and the Prince Agib episode from Night 57 of the *Thousand and One Nights* to create an allegory in which a young wanderer is led by a band of damsels to a sumptuous pleasure dome. The youth bathes in each fountain of sensual delight, sinking deeper into the pleasure principle, until he is reminded of mortality by a bearded sage and drinks from the clearer rill of religion. Unlike those whose only access to a *Thousand and One Nights* was via Antoine Galland's *Mille et une nuits* (1704), or the English 'Grub Street' translation of Galland, Jones had read the tales in Arabic from a text 'procured for me by a learned friend at *Aleppo*', while his other Arabic source had been encountered among Pocock's manuscripts at Oxford. Orientalism was for Jones more than a fashionable craze, it was an exacting discipline, and the comparative authenticity of *The Seven Fountains* stands in an interesting relation to Collins's pretended translations in *Persian Eclogues* (1742) (about which Collins himself later admitted that they might just as well have been called *Irish Eclogues*), or Johnson's use of orientalizing phrases to spice *Rasselas* (1759). Jones shares Johnson's desire to clothe morality in the diaphanous garb of Eastern exoticism, simultaneously exposing and veiling the vanity of human wishes. Furthermore by introducing moral allegory into the dramatic tale in verse, he develops the genre of Oriental verse tale, using Eastern sensuality to explore the aesthetic implications of Locke's theories of sense perception and Newton's ideas of colour and light. The text followed here is that of the second edition (1777), collated with the first edition of 1772, and Lady Jones's collected editions of 1799 and 1807.]

THE SEVEN FOUNTAINS,
AN EASTERN ALLEGORY
Written in the Year 1767

Deck'd with fresh garlands, like a rural bride,
And with the crimson streamer's waving pride,
A wanton bark was floating o'er the main,
And seem'd with scorn to view the azure plain:
Smooth were the waves, and scarce a whispering gale   5
Fann'd with his gentle plumes the silken sail.
High on the burnish'd deck, a gilded throne
With orient pearls and beaming diamonds shone;
On which reclin'd a youth of graceful mien,
His sandals purple, and his mantle green;   10
His locks in ringlets o'er his shoulders roll'd,
And on his cheek appear'd the downy gold.
Around him stood a train of smiling boys,
Sporting with idle cheer and mirthful toys;
*Ten comely striplings, girt with spangled wings,   15
Blew piercing flutes, or touch'd the quivering strings;
Ten more, in cadence to the sprightly strain,
Wak'd with their golden oars the slumbering main:
The waters yielded to their guiltless blows,
And the green billows sparkled as they rose.   20

    Long time the barge had danc'd along the deep,
And on its glassy bosom seem'd to sleep;
‡But now a glittering isle arose in view,
Bounded with hillocks of a verdant hue:
Fresh groves, and roseate bowers appear'd above,   25
(Fit haunts, be sure, of pleasure and of love)

*The follies of youth.
‡The world.

1–6   The opening description of the 'wanton bark' introduces the central themes of vainglory and sensuality.

13–20   The graceful young man's companions, who represent the follies of youth, and are depicted 'sporting with idle cheer and mirthful toys', reflect this atmosphere of pleasure and leisure, even those who row ply 'their golden oars' with idle ease.

23–30   It is only on viewing the pleasant isle, which offers hope of amorous encounters, that the oarsmen inject any energy into their rowing. Despite this, all his smiling companions are 'Sunk like a mist beneath the briny dew', and the youth disembarks alone.

And higher still a thousand blazing spires
Seem'd with gilt tops to threat the heav'nly fires.
Now each fair stripling plied his labouring oar,
And straight the pinnace struck the sandy shore.   30
The youth arose, and, leaping on the strand,
Took his lone way along the silver sand;
While the light bark, and all the airy crew,
Sunk like a mist beneath the briny dew.

    With eager steps the young adventurer stray'd   35
Through many a grove, and many a winding glade:
At length he heard the chime of tuneful strings,
That sweetly floated on the Zephyr's wings;
*And soon a band of damsels blithe and fair,
With flowing mantles and dishevel'd hair,   40
Rush'd with quick place along the solemn wood,
Where rapt in wonder and delight he stood:
In loose transparent robes they were array'd,
Which half their beauties hid, and half display'd.

    A lovely nymph approach'd him with a smile,   45
And said, 'O, welcome to this blissful isle!
'For thou art he, whom ancient bards foretold,
'Doom'd in our clime to bring an age of gold:
'Hail, sacred king! and from thy subject's hand,
'Accept the robes and sceptre of the land.'   50

    'Sweet maid, said he, fair learning's heavenly beam
'O'er my young mind ne'er shed her favouring gleam;
'Nor has my arm e'er hurl'd the fatal lance,
'While desperate legions o'er the plain advance:
'How should a simple youth, unfit to bear   55
'The steely mail, that splendid mantle wear!'
'Ah! said the damsel, from this happy shore,
'We banish wisdom, and her idle lore;
'No clarions here the strains of battle sing,
'With notes of mirth our joyful valleys ring.   60
'Peace to the brave! o'er us the beauteous reign,
'And ever-charming pleasures form our train.'

*The follies and vanities of the world.

39–44   The nymph-like approach of the damsels indicates the lightness of vanity, while their 'dishevel'd hair' and 'transparent robes' promise delights unavailable en route.

This said, a diadem, inlay'd with pearls,
She plac'd respectful on his golden curls;
Another o'er his graceful shoulder threw   65
A silken mantle of the rose's hue,
Which, clasp'd with studs of gold, behind him flow'd,
And through the folds his glowing bosom show'd.
Then in a car, by snow-white coursers drawn,
They led him o'er the dew-besprinkled lawn,   70
Through groves of joy and arbours of delight,
With all that could allure his ravish'd sight;
Green hillocks, meads, and rosy grots he view'd,
And verdurous plains with winding streams bedew'd.
On every bank, and under every shade,   75
A thousand youths, a thousand damsels play'd;
Some wantonly were tripping in a ring
On the soft border of a gushing spring;
While some, reclining in the shady vales,
Told to their smiling loves their amorous tales: 80
But when the sportful train beheld from far
The nymphs returning with the stately car,
O'er the smooth plain with hasty steps they came,
And hail'd their youthful king with loud acclaim;
With flowers of every tint the paths they strow'd.   85
And cast their chaplets on the hallow'd road.

At last they reach'd the bosom of a wood,
Where on a hill a radiant palace stood;
A sumptuous dome, by hands immortal made,
Which on its walls and on its gates display'd   90
The gems that in the rocks of Tibet glow,
The pearls that in the shells of Ormus grow.
And now a numerous train advance to meet
The youth, descending from his regal seat;
Whom to a rich and spacious hall they led,   95
With silken carpets delicately spread:

---

68 *And through the folds his glowing bosom show'd* The nature and design of the mantle which
they bestow upon him indicate that as their king he, like them, will be devoted to sensuality.

89 The concept of the immortal pleasure dome, possibly inspired by Françoise Bernier's
description of the 'great and vast dome of white marble' surmounting Shah Jehan's Taj Mahal
(Awnsham Churchill *A Collection of Voyages and Travels,* London, 1744–7, VIII.193.), was to
exert an influence upon many of the Romantics. Frequent references in the notes to *Vathek, An
Arabian Tale* (1786) reveal William Beckford's indebtedness to Sir William Jones, and it is
therefore likely that *Vathek*'s Palaces of the Five Senses owe much to this poem.

There on a throne, with gems unnumber'd grac'd,
Their lovely king six blooming damsels plac'd,*
And, meekly kneeling, to his modest hand
They gave the glittering sceptre of command;   100
Then on six smaller thrones they sat reclin'd,
And watch'd the rising transports of his mind:
When thus the youth a blushing nymph address'd,
And, as he spoke, her hand with rapture press'd:

'Say, gentle damsel, may I ask unblam'd,   105
'How this gay isle, and splendid seats are nam'd?
'And you, fair queens of beauty and of grace,
'Are you of earthly or celestial race?
'To me the world's bright treasures were unknown,
'Where late I wandered, pensive and alone;   110
'And, slowly winding on my native shore,
'Saw the vast ocean roll, but saw no more;
'Till from the waves with many a charming song,
'A barge arose, and gayly mov'd along;
'The jolly rowers reach'd the yielding sands,   115
'Allur'd my steps, and wav'd their shining hands;
'I went, saluted by the vocal train,
'And the swift pinnace cleav'd the waves again;
'When on this island struck the gilded prow,
'I landed full of joy: the rest you know.   120
'Short is the story of my tender years:
'Now speak, sweet nymph, and charm my listening ears.'

'These are the groves, for ever deck'd with flowers,
'The maid replied, and these the fragrant bowers,
'Where Love and Pleasure hold their airy court,   125
'The seat of bliss, of sprightliness, and sport;
'And we, dear youth, are nymphs of heavenly line;
'Our souls immortal, as our forms divine:
'For Maia, fill'd with Zephyr's warm embrace,
'In caves and forests cover'd her disgrace;   130

---

*The pleasures of the senses.

127–34 The 'nymphs of heavenly line' stem from the beautiful youth Mirth, the offspring of
the union between Maia – a name which Jones used two years later for the heroine of *The Palace of
Fortune*, and which possesses both Oriental (*Maya*, the Hindu goddess of illusion, or alternatively,
an Arabic name for the beloved) and Occidental (the mother of Mercury, and most luminous of the
seven sisters forming the Pleiades) connotations – and Zephyr; in other words their father
represents a mingling of attractive illusion and insubstantial lightness.

'At last she rested on this peaceful shore,
'Where in yon grot a lovely boy she bore,
'Whom fresh and wild and frolick from his birth
'She nurs'd in myrtle bowers, and call'd him Mirth.
'He on a summer's morning chanc'd to rove   135
'Through the green labyrinth of some shady grove,
'Where, by a dimpled rivulet's verdant side,
'A rising bank with woodbine edg'd he spied:
'There, veil'd with flowerets of a thousand hues,
'A nymph lay bath'd in slumber's balmy dews;   140
'(This maid by some, for some our race defame,
'Was Folly call'd, but Pleasure was her name:)
'Her mantle, like the sky in April, blue,
'Hung on a blossom'd branch that near her grew;
'For, long disporting in the silver stream,   145
'She shunn'd the blazing day-star's sultry beam,
'And ere she could conceal her naked charms,
'Sleep caught her trembling in his downy arms:
'Borne on the wings of Love, he flew, and press'd
'Her breathing bosom to his eager breast.   150
'At his wild theft the rosy morning blush'd,
'The rivulet smil'd, and all the woods were hush'd.
'Of these fair parents on this blissful coast
'(Parents like Mirth and Pleasure who can boast?)
'I, with five sisters, on one happy morn,   155
'All fair alike, behold us now, were born.
'When they to brighter regions took their way,
'By Love invited to the realms of day,
'To us they gave this large, this gay domain,
'And said, departing, Here let Beauty reign.   160
'Then reign, fair prince, in thee all beauties shine,
'And ah! we know thee of no mortal line.'

    She said; the king with rapid ardour glow'd,
And the swift poison through his bosom flow'd:
But while she spoke he cast his eyes around   165
To view the dazzling roof, and spangled ground;
Then, turning with amaze from side to side,
Seven golden doors, that richly shone he spied,
And said, 'Fair nymph, (but let me not be bold),
'What mean those doors that blaze with burnish'd gold?'   170

147–56   Mirth ravished the sleeping nymph Pleasure, while she lay exhausted and naked after bathing, and Pleasure subsequently gave birth to these sensual sextuplets.

'To six gay bowers, the maid replied, they lead,
'Where Spring eternal crowns the glowing mead;
'Six fountains there, that glitter as they play,
'Rise to the sun with many a colour'd ray.'
'But the seventh door, said he, what beauties grace?'   175
'O, 'tis a cave, a dark and joyless place,
'A scene of nameless deeds, and magick spells,
'Where day ne'er shines, and pleasure never dwells:
'Think not of that. But come, my royal friend,
'And see what joys thy favour'd steps attend.'   180
She spoke, and pointed to the nearest door:
Swift he descends; the damsel flies before;
She turns the lock; it opens at command;
The maid and stripling enter hand in hand.

The wondering youth beheld an opening glade,   185
Where in the midst a crystal fountain play'd;*
The silver sands, that on its bottom grew,
Were strown with pearls and gems of varied hue;
The diamond sparkled like the star of day,
And the soft topaz shed a golden ray;   190
Clear amethysts combin'd their purple gleam
With the mild emerald's sight-refreshing beam;
The sapphire smil'd like yon blue plain above,
And rubies spread the blushing tint of love.
'These are the waters of eternal light,   195
'The damsel said, the stream of heavenly sight;
'See, in this cup (she spoke, and stoop'd to fill
'A vase of jasper with the sacred rill),
'See, how the living waters bound and shine,
'Which this well-polish'd gem can scarce confine!'   200
From her soft hand the lucid urn he took,
And quaff'd the nectar with a tender look:
Straight from his eyes a cloud of darkness flew,
And all the scene was open'd to his view;
Not all the groves, where ancient bards have told,   205
Of vegetable gems, and blooming gold;

*Sight

205–6   *where ancient bards have told/Of vegetable gems, and blooming gold* Cf. 'blooming Ambrosial Fruit/Of vegetable Gold', *Paradise Lost* IV.219–20. On Miltonic echoes in Jones see Ann Gossman, '"Harmonious Jones" and Milton's Invocations', *Notes and Queries*, 199 (1954), 527–29.

Not all the bowers which oft in flowery lays
And solemn tales Arabian poets praise;
Though streams of honey flow'd through every mead,
Though balm and amber dropp'd from every reed;   210
Held half the sweets that Nature's ample hand
Had pour'd luxuriant o'er this wondrous land.
All flowerets here their mingled rays diffuse,
The rainbow's tints to these were vulgar hues;
All birds that in the stream their pinion dip,   215
Or from the brink the liquid crystal sip,
Or show their beauties to the sunny skies,
Here wav'd their plumes that shone with varying dyes;
But chiefly he, that o'er the verdant plain
Spreads the gay eyes which grace his spangled train;   220
And he, who, proudly sailing, loves to show
His mantling wings and neck of downy snow;
Nor absent he, who learns the human sound,
With wavy gold and moving emeralds crowned,
Whose head and breast with polish'd sapphires glow,   225
And on whose wing the gems of Indus grow.
The monarch view'd their beauties o'er and o'er,
He was all eye, and look'd from every pore.
But now the damsel calls him from his trance;
And o'er the lawn delighted they advance: 230
They pass the hall adorn'd with royal state,
And enter now with joy the second gate.*

   A soothing sound he heard, (but tasted first
The gushing stream that from the valley burst),
And in the shade beheld a youthful quire   235
That touch'd with flying hands the trembling lyre:
Melodious notes, drawn out with magick art,
Caught with sweet extasy his ravish'd heart;
An hundred nymphs their charming descants play'd,
And melting voices died along the glade;   240
The tuneful stream that murmur'd as it rose,
The birds that on the trees bewail'd their woes,
The boughs, made vocal by the whispering gale,
Join'd their soft strain, and warbled through the vale.
The concert ends: and now the stripling hears   245
A tender voice that strikes his wondering ears;

*Hearing

21

A beauteous bird, in our rude climes unknown,
That on a leafy arbour sits alone,
Strains his sweet throat, and waves his purple wings,
And thus in human accents softly sings: 250

  'Rise, lovely pair, a sweeter bower invites
'Your eager steps, a bower of new delights;
'Ah! crop the flowers of pleasure while they blow,
'Ere winter hides them in a veil of snow.
'Youth, like a thin anemone, displays   255
'His silken leaf, and in a morn decays.
'See, gentle youth, a lily-bosom'd bride!
'See, nymph, a blooming stripling by thy side!
'Then haste, and bathe your souls in soft delights,
'A sweeter bow'r your wandering steps invites.'   260
He ceas'd; the slender branch, from which he flew
Bent its fair head and sprinkled pearly dew.
The damsel smil'd; the blushing youth was pleas'd,
And by her willing hand his charmer seiz'd:
The lovely nymph, who sigh'd for sweeter joy,   265
To the third gate* conducts the amorous boy;
She turns the key; her cheeks like roses bloom,
And on the lock her fingers drop perfume.

  His ravish'd sense a scene of pleasure meets,
A maze of joy, a paradise of sweets;   270
But first his lips had touch'd th' alluring stream,
That through the grove display'd a silver gleam.
Through jasmine bowers, and violet-scented vales,
On silken pinions flew the wanton gales,
Arabian odours on the plants they left,   275
And whisper'd to the woods their spicy theft;
Beneath the shrubs, that spread a trembling shade,
The musky roes, and fragrant civets, play'd.
As when at eve an Eastern merchant roves
From Hadramut to Aden's spikenard groves,   280

*Smell

267–8 *She turns the key; her cheeks like roses bloom,/And on the lock her fingers drop perfume*
When the Augustan diction becomes a trifle oppressive, and 'the paradise of sweets' seems in danger of becoming too cloying, Jones can produce a couplet which locates the sensual firmly in the actual.

279–80 *As when at eve an Eastern merchant roves/From Hadramut to Aden's spikenard groves*
Hadrumat was famed for the production of musk, see 'On the Poetry of the Eastern Nations', p.321 below. For a similar emphasis upon the fragrant air of *Arabia Odorifera*, see *Paradise Lost*, IV.153–65.

Where some rich caravan not long before
Has pass'd, with cassia fraught, and balmy store,
Charm'd with the scent that hills and vales diffuse,
His grateful journey gayly he pursues;
Thus pleas'd, the monarch fed his eager soul,   285
And from each breeze a cloud of fragrance stole:
Soon the fourth door† he pass'd with eager haste,
And the fourth stream was nectar to his taste.

   Before his eyes, on agate columns rear'd,
On high a purple canopy appeared;   290
And under it in stately form was plac'd
A table with a thousand vases grac'd;
Laden with all the dainties that are found
In air, in seas, or on the fruitful ground.
Here the fair youth reclin'd with decent pride,   295
His wanton nymph was seated by his side:
All that could please the taste the happy pair
Cull'd from the loaded board with curious care;
O'er their enchanted heads a mantling vine
His curling tendrils wove with amorous twine;   300
From the green stalks the glowing clusters hung
Like rubies on a thread of emeralds strung;
With these were other fruits of every hue,
The pale, the red, the golden, and the blue.
An hundred smiling pages stood around,   305
Their shining brows with wreaths of myrtle bound:
They, in transparent cups of agate, bore
Of sweetly-sparkling wines a precious store;
The stripling sipp'd and revel'd, till the sun
Down heaven's blue vault his daily course had run;   310
Then rose, and, follow'd by the gentle maid,
*Op'd the fifth door: a stream before them play'd.

   The king, impatient for the cooling draught,
In a full cup the mystic nectar quaff'd;

†Taste
*Touch

292–309   The description of the fourth fountain (the pleasures of taste) is, however, pallid and insipid, almost totally lacking in any sensuous detail. This is both disappointing and surprising as even a cursory reading of his letters reveals Jones's keen enjoyment of prandial delights, see, for example, p.52 below.

Then with a smile (he knew no higher bliss)   315
From her sweet lip he stole a balmy kiss:
On the smooth bank of violets they reclin'd;
And, whilst a chaplet for his brow she twin'd,
With his soft cheek her softer cheek he press'd,
His pliant arms were folded round her breast.   320
She smil'd, soft lightning darted from her eyes,
And from his fragrant seat she bade him rise;
Then, while a brighter blush her face o'erspread,
To the sixth gate* her willing guest she led.

The golden lock she softly turn'd around;   325
The moving hinges gave a pleasing sound:
The boy delighted ran with eager haste,
And to his lips the living fountain plac'd;
The magick water pierc'd his kindled brain,
And a strange venom shot from vein to vein.   330
Whatever charms he saw in other bowers,
Were here combin'd, fruits, musick, odours, flowers;
A couch besides, with softest silk o'erlaid;
And, sweeter still, a lovely yielding maid,
Who now more charming seem'd, and not so coy,   335
And in her arms infolds the blushing boy:
They sport and wanton, till, with sleep oppress'd,
Like two fresh rose-buds on one stalk, they rest.

When morning spread around her purple flame,
To the sweet couch the five fair sisters came;   340
They hail'd the bridegroom with a cheerful voice,
And bade him make with speed a second choice.
Hard task to choose, when all alike were fair!
Now this, now that, engag'd his anxious care:
Then to the first who spoke his hand he lent;   345
The rest retir'd, and whisper'd as they went.

*The sensual pleasures united.

325–38   The episode of the sixth fountain, which offers the epitome of all five senses combined, culminates in a 'silken couch' and a 'yielding maid'. 'It is a maxim among [the Arabians]', wrote Jones, 'that the three most charming objects in nature are, a green meadow, a clear rivulet, and a beautiful woman; and that the view of these objects at the same time affords the greatest delight imaginable', 'On the Poetry of the Eastern Nations', p.324 below.

339–56   The youth spends a delightful sixty-seven days rotating his willing harem of sisters, until the youngest announces that they are obliged to visit their parents for three days. They depart, leaving him the seven keys, and hoping that the six pleasure fountains will provide some solace in their absence.

The prince enamour'd view'd his second bride;
They left the bower, and wander'd side by side,
With her he charm'd his ears, with her his sight;
With her he pass'd the day, with her the night.   350
Thus all by turns the sprightly stranger led,
And all by turns partook his nuptial bed;
Hours, days, and months, in pleasure flow'd away;
All laugh'd, all sweetly sung, and all were gay.

So had he wanton'd threescore days and seven,   355
More blest, he thought, than any son of heaven:
Till on a morn, with sighs and streaming tears,
The train of nymphs before his bed appears;
And thus the youngest of the sisters speaks,
Whilst a sad shower runs trickling down her cheeks: 360

'A custom which we cannot, dare not fail,
'(Such are the laws that in our isle prevail),
'Compels us, prince, to leave thee here alone,
'Till thrice the sun his rising front has shown:
'Our parents, whom, alas! we must obey,   365
'Expect us at a splendid feast to-day;
'What joy to us can all their splendour give?
'With thee, with only thee, we wish to live.
'Yet may we hope, these gardens will afford
'Some pleasing solace to our absent lord?   370
'Six golden keys, that ope yon blissful gates,
'Where joy, eternal joy, thy steps awaits,
'Accept: the seventh (but that you heard before)
'Leads to a cave, where ravening monsters roar,
'A sullen, dire, inhospitable cell,   375
'Where deathful spirits and magicians dwell.
'Farewel, dear youth; how will our bosoms burn
'For the sweet moment of our blest return!'

The king, who wept, yet knew his tears were vain,
Took the seven keys, and kiss'd the parting train.   380
A glittering car, which bounding coursers drew,
They mounted straight, and through the forest flew.

The youth, unknowing how to pass the day,
Review'd the bowers, and heard the fountains play;
By hands unseen whate'er he wish'd was brought;   385
And pleasures rose obedient to his thought.

Yet all the sweets, that ravish'd him before,
Were tedious now, and charm'd his soul no more:
Less lovely still, and still less gay they grew;
He sigh'd, he wish'd, and long'd for something new: 390
Back to the hall he turn'd his weary feet,
And sat repining on his royal seat.
Now on the seventh bright gate he casts his eyes,
And in his bosom rose a bold surmise:
'The nymph, said he, was sure dispos'd to jest,   395
'Who talk'd of dungeons in a place so blest:
'What harm to open, if it be a cell,
'Where deathful spirits and magicians dwell?
'If dark or foul, I need not pass the door;
'If new or strange, my soul desires no more.'   400
He said, and rose; then took the golden keys,
And op'd the door: the hinges mov'd with ease.

Before his eyes appear'd a sullen gloom,
Thick, hideous, wild; a cavern, or a tomb.
Yet as he longer gaz'd, he saw afar   405
A light that sparkled like a shooting star.
He paus'd: at last, by some kind angel led,
He enter'd, and advanc'd with cautious tread.
Still as he walk'd, the light appear'd more clear;
Hope sooth'd him then, and scarcely left a fear.   410
At length an aged sire surpriz'd he saw,
Who fill'd his bosom with a sacred awe:*
A book he held, which, as reclin'd he lay,
He read, assisted by a taper's ray;
His beard, more white than snow on winter's breast,   415
Hung to the zone that bound his sable vest;
A pleasing calmness on his brow was seen,
Mild was his look, majestick was his mien.
Soon as the youth approach'd the reverend sage,
He rais'd his head, and clos'd the serious page;   420
Then spoke: 'O son, what chance has turn'd thy feet
'To this dull solitude, and lone retreat?'
To whom the youth: 'First, holy father, tell,
'What force detains thee in this gloomy cell?

*Religion

---

411 *an aged sire* the medieval type of the devout hermit, fount of wisdom, was enjoying an enduring vogue in contemporary literature as eighteenth-century sensibility moved towards celebration of the numinous.

'This isle, this palace, and those balmy bowers, 425
'Where six sweet fountains fall on living flowers,
'Are mine; a train of damsels chose me king,
'And through my kingdom smiles perpetual spring.
'For some important cause to me unknown,
'This day they left me joyless and alone; 430
'But, ere three morns with roses strow the skies,
'My lovely brides will charm my longing eyes.'

  'Youth, said the sire, on this auspicious day
'Some angel hither led thy erring way:
'Hear a strange tale, and tremble at the snare, 435
'Which for they steps thy pleasing foes prepare.
'Know, in this isle prevails a bloody law;
'List, stripling, list! (the youth stood fix'd with awe:)
'*But seventy days the hapless monarchs reign,
'Then close their lives in exile and in pain; 440
'Doom'd in a deep and frightful cave to rove,
'Where darkness hovers o'er the iron grove.
'Yet know, thy prudence and thy timely care
'May save thee, son, from this destructive snare.
'†Not far from this a lovelier island lies, 445
'Too rich, too splendid, for unhallow'd eyes:
'On that blest shore a sweeter fountain flows
'Than this vain clime, or this gay palace knows,
'Which if thou taste, whate'er was sweet before
'Will bitter seem, and steal thy soul no more. 450
'But, ere these happy waters thou canst reach,
'Thy weary steps must pass yon rugged beach,
'‡Where the dark sea with angry billows raves,
'And, fraught with monsters, curls his howling waves;
'If to my words obedient thou attend, 455
'Behold in me thy pilot and thy friend.
'A bark I keep, supplied with plenteous store,
'That now lies anchor'd on the rocky shore;
'And, when of all thy regal toys bereft,
'In the rude cave an exile thou art left, 460
'Myself will find thee on the gloomy lea,
'And waft thee safely o'er the dangerous sea.'

*The life of man
†Heaven
‡Death

The boy was fill'd with wonder as he spake,
And from a dream of folly seem'd to wake:
All day the sage his tainted thoughts refin'd;   465
His reason brighten'd, and reform'd his mind:
Through the dim cavern hand in hand they walk'd,
And much of truth, and much of heaven, they talk'd.
At night the stripling to the hall return'd;
With other fires his alter'd bosom burn'd.   470
O! to his wiser soul how low, how mean,
Seem'd all he e'er had heard, had felt, had seen!
He view'd the stars, he view'd the crystal skies,
And bless'd the power all-good, all-great, all-wise;
How lowly now appear'd the purple robe,   475
The rubied sceptre, and the ivory globe!
How dim the rays that gild the brittle earth!
How vile the brood of Folly, and of Mirth!

When the third morning, clad in mantle gray,
Brought in her rosy car the seventieth day,   480
A band of slaves, who rush'd with furious sound,
In chains of steel the willing captive bound;
From his young head the diadem they tore,
And cast his pearly bracelets on the floor;
They rent his robe that bore the rose's hue,   485
And o'er his breast a hairy mantle threw;
Then dragg'd him to the damp and dreary cave,
Drench'd by the gloomy sea's resounding wave.
Meanwhile the voices of a numerous croud
Pierc'd the dun air, as thunder breaks a cloud: 490
The nymphs another hapless youth had found,
And then were leading o'er the guilty ground:
They hail'd him king (alas, how short his reign!)
And with fresh chaplets strow'd the fatal plain.

The happy exile, monarch now no more,   495
Was roving slowly o'er the lonely shore,
At last the sire's expected voice he knew,
And tow'rd the sound with hasty rapture flew,
The promis'd pinnace just afloat he found,
And the glad sage his fetter'd hands unbound;   500

---

500   *And the glad sage his fetter'd hands unbound* Religion frees the youth from the physical
bonds as he had unloosed the 'mind-forged manacles' which shackled him to physical pleasures.

But when he saw the foaming billows rave,
And dragons rolling o'er the fiery wave,
He stopp'd: his guardian caught his lingering hand,
And gently led him o'er the rocky strand;
Soon as he touch'd the bark, the ocean smil'd,   505
The dragons vanish'd, and the waves were mild.

   For many an hour with vigorous arms they row'd,
While not a star his friendly sparkle show'd;
At length a glimmering brightness they behold,
Like a thin cloud which morning dyes with gold: 510
To that they steer; and now, rejoic'd, they view
A shore begirt with cliffs of radiant hue.
They land: a train, in shining mantles clad,
Hail their approach, and bid the youth be glad;
They led him o'er the lea with easy pace,   515
And floated as they went with heavenly grace.
A golden fountain soon appear'd in sight,
That o'er the border cast a sunny light.

   The sage, impatient, scoop'd the lucid wave
In a rich vase, which to the youth he gave;   520
He drank: and straight a bright celestial beam
Before his eyes display'd a dazzling gleam;
Myriads of airy shapes around him gaz'd;
Some prais'd his wisdom, some his courage prais'd,
Then o'er his limbs a starry robe they spread,   525
And plac'd a crown of diamonds on his head.

   His aged guide was gone, and in his place
Stood a fair cherub flush'd with rosy grace;
Who, smiling, spake: 'Here ever wilt thou rest,
'Admir'd, belov'd, our brother and our guest;   530
'So all shall end, whom vice can charm no more
'With the gay follies of that perilous shore.
'See yon immortal towers their gates unfold,
'With rubies flaming and no earthly gold!
'There joys, before unknown, thy steps invite,   535
'Bliss without care, and morn without a night.
'But now farewel! my duty calls me hence;
'Some injur'd mortal asks my just defence.

505–26 The sage having stilled the 'howling waves', they arrive on the blessed shore where the youth tastes the immortal waters of the ultimate fountain, greeted by a radiant train who, unlike the sensual sisters, value wisdom and courage.

'To yon pernicious island I repair,
'Swift as a star.' He speaks, and melts in air.   540

   The youth o'er walks of jasper takes his flight,
And bounds and blazes in eternal light.

3

Solima, An Arabian Eclogue (1768)

[This work represents the first poem in Jones's *Poems consisting chiefly of translations from the Asiatick languages* (Oxford: Clarendon Press, 1772). Together with 'A Persian Song of Hafiz', 'A Turkish Ode of Mesihi', and his 'Elegy on Laura', 'Solima' was reprinted in the *Annual Register* of 1772 (vol. 15, pp.196–205). The Preface explains that its composition was influenced by his reading of Arabian poets on the theme of benevolence and hospitality, connecting passages so as to form 'one continued piece, which I suppose to be written in praise of an *Arabian* princess, who had built a *caravansera* with pleasant gardens, for the refreshment of travellers; an act of munificence not uncommon in *Asia*'. It would seem that the poem was partly inspired by Lady Spencer's benevolent works with her Society for Charitable Purposes, and certainly when Jones sent her a copy in December 1774, he remarked: 'the first of them, called Solima, would never have been written, if I had never had the honour of knowing your Ladyship' (*Letters*, I.177). Furthermore the second edition of *Poems* (London: W. Bowyer and J. Nichols, 1777), to which were added some twelve Latin poems entitled *Carminum Liber*, bore this dedication: 'To the Right Honourable *The Countess Spencer*, these Eastern pieces, and, particularly, the poem of *Solima*, are most respectfully inscribed by her lady's most obliged and faithful servant, *The Author.*' This description of an imaginary caravanserai which Princess Solima provided for travellers, contains much heady and sensuous Oriental imagery. The text followed here is that of the second edition (1777), with variants recorded from the first edition of 1772.]

SOLIMA,
AN ARABIAN ECLOGUE
Written in the Year 1768

Ye maids of Aden, hear a loftier tale
Than e'er was sung in meadow, bower, or dale.
The smiles of Abelah, and Maia's eyes,
Where beauty plays, and love in slumber lies;
The fragrant hyacinths of Azza's hair,   5
That wanton with the laughing summer-air;
Love-tinctur'd cheeks, whence roses seek their bloom,
And lips, from which the Zephyr steals perfume,
Invite no more the wild, unpolish'd lay,
But fly like dreams before the morning ray.   10
Then farewel, love! and farewel, youthful fires!
A nobler warmth my kindled breast inspires.
Far bolder notes the listening wood shall fill:
Flow smooth, ye rivulets; and, ye gales, be still.

See yon fair groves that o'er Amana rise,   15
And with their spicy breath embalm the skies;
Where every breeze sheds incense o'er the vales,
And every shrub the scent of musk exhales!
See through yon opening glade a glittering scene,
Lawns ever gay, and meadows ever green!   20
Then ask the groves, and ask the vocal bowers,
Who deck'd their spiry tops with blooming flowers,
Taught the blue stream o'er sandy vales to flow,
And the brown wild with liveliest hues to glow?

---

1   *maids of Aden* 'It is observable that *Aden* in the Eastern dialects, is precisely the same word with *Eden*, which we apply to the garden of paradise: it has two senses, according to a slight difference in its pronunciation; its first meaning is *a settled abode*, its second, *delight, softness*, or *tranquillity*:' 'On the Poetry of the Eastern Nations', p.321 below.
3   *smiles of Abelah, and Maia's eyes* Typical names for the beloved in Arabic poetry. See 'On the Poetry of the Eastern Nations', p.325 below.
5   *The fragrant hyacinths of Azza's hair* Ibid., p.323, but also cf. *Paradise Lost*, IV.301. Henley, in a note to p.80 of *Vathek* (1786), (London, 1900), quotes this line and the following one while discussing the use of this metaphor in Arabian and Greek literature.
15   Cf. *Song of Solomon* 4.8.

*Fair Solima! the hills and dales will sing,   25
Fair Solima! the distant echoes ring.
But not with idle shows of vain delight,
To charm the soul, or to beguile the sight;
At noon on banks of pleasure to repose,
Where bloom intwin'd the lily, pink, and rose;   30
Not in proud piles to heap the nightly feast,
Till morn with pearls has deck'd the glowing east; –
Ah! not for this she taught those bowers to rise,
And bade all Eden spring before our eyes:
Far other thoughts her heavenly mind employ,   35
(Hence, empty pride! and hence, delusive joy!)
To cheer with sweet repast the fainting guest;
To lull the weary on the couch of rest;
To warm the traveller numb'd with winter's cold;
The young to cherish, to support the old;   40
The sad to comfort, and the weak protect;
The poor to shelter, and the lost direct: –
These are her cares, and this her glorious task;
Can heaven a nobler give, or mortals ask?

Come to these groves, and these life-breathing glades,   45
Ye friendless orphans, and ye dowerless maids!
With eager haste your mournful mansions leave,
Ye weak, that tremble, and, ye sick, that grieve;
Here shall soft tents o'er flowery lawns display'd,
At night defend you, and at noon o'ershade: 50
Here rosy health the sweets of life with shower,
And new delights beguile each varied hour.
Mourns there a widow, bath'd in streaming tears?
Stoops there a sire beneath the weight of years?
Weeps there a maid, in pining sadness left,   55
Of tender parents, and of hope, bereft?
To Solima their sorrows they bewail,
To Solima they pour their plaintive tale.

*It was not easy in this part of the translation to avoid a turn similar to that of Pope in the known description of the Man of Ross.

---

25 *Solima* was an ancient name for Jerusalem, cf. 'Ye Nymphs of Solyma!' at the opening of Pope's *Messiah; A Sacred Eclogue.*

Jones's footnote The Man of Ross created a picturesque walk on the banks of the Wye, creating a reservoir which supplied the town with water; his benevolence was also displayed in supplying the poor with food and medicines, and the foundation of an almshouse. See Pope's *Epistle to Bathurst*, ll.249–284, in *Epistles to Several Persons*, ed. F.W. Bateson (London and New Haven, 1961), pp.113–16.

She hears; and, radiant as the star of day,
Through the thick forest gains her easy way: 60
She asks what cares the joyless train oppress,
What sickness wastes them, or what wants distress;
And, as they mourn, she steals a tender sigh,
Whilst all her soul sits melting in her eye:
Then with a smile the healing balm bestows,   65
And sheds a tear of pity o'er their woes,
Which, as it drops, some soft-eyed angel bears
Transform'd to pearl, and in his bosom wears.

When, chill'd with fear, the trembling pilgrim roves
Through pathless deserts, and through tangled groves,   70
Where mantling darkness spreads her dragon wing,
And birds of death their fatal dirges sing,
While vapours pale a dreadful glimmering cast,
And thrilling horrour howls in every blast;
She cheers his gloom with streams of bursting light,   75
By day a sun, a beaming moon by night,
Darts through the quivering shades her heavenly ray,
And spreads with rising flowers his solitary way.

Ye heavens, for this in showers of sweetness shed
Your mildest influence o'er her favour'd head!   80
Long may her name, which distant climes shall praise,
Live in our notes, and blossom in our lays!
And, like an odorous plant, whose blushing flower
Paints every dale, and sweetens every bower,
Borne to the skies in clouds of soft perfume   85
For ever flourish, and for ever bloom!
These grateful songs, ye maids and youths, renew,
While fresh-blown violets drink the pearly dew;
O'er Azib's banks while love-lorn damsels rove,
And gales of fragrance breathe from Hager's grove.   90

So sung the youth, whose sweetly-warbled strains
Fair Mena heard, and Saba's spicy plains.

69–78   In the Preface Jones cites the Arabic source for this passage, together with the following translation: 'the stranger and the pilgrim well know, when the sky is dark and the north-wind rages, when the mothers leave their sucking infants, when no moisture can be seen in the clouds, that thou art bountiful to them as the spring, that thou art their chief support, that thou art a sun to them by day, and a moon in the cloudy night', *Works*, X.200–1.

90   *Hager's grove*   See Genesis 21.

92   *Saba's spicy plains*   The Queen of Sheba or Saba gave Solomon fabulous quantities of precious spices, I Kings 10.

Sooth'd with his lay, the ravish'd air was calm,
The winds scarce whisper'd o'er the waving palm;
The camels bounded o'er the flowery lawn,   95
Like the swift ostrich, or the sportful fawn;
Their silken bands the listening rose-buds rent,
And twin'd their blossoms round his vocal tent:
He sung, till on the bank the moonlight slept,
And closing flowers beneath the night-dew wept;   100
Then ceas'd', and slumber'd in the lap of rest
Till the shrill lark had left his low-built nest.
Now hastes the swain to tune his rapturous tales
In other meadows, and in other vales.

---

95 *The camels bounded o'er the flowery lawn* To a certain extent Jones's neo-classicism tames
the wild desert landscape into bucolic pastoral, cf. 'On the Poetry of the Eastern Nations',
pp.326–7 below.

4

The Palace of Fortune, An Indian Tale (1769)

[Sir William Jones completed work on this poem in his rooms at University College on the morning of 16 February 1769, having 'dined and supped' the previous evening with Johnson, Goldsmith, Chambers, and Percy. (*Letters*, II.24.) Loosely based upon the tale of Roshana in Alexander Dow's *Tales Translated from the Persian of Inatulla of Delhi* (2 vols., London, 1768) – whose tales, according to Dow's Preface, were originally 'taken from the writings of the Brahmins' – it constitutes the only 'Indian' piece in Jones's *Poems, consisting chiefly of translations from the Asiatick languages* (Oxford: Clarendon Press, 1772). The combination of moral allegory and dramatic tale in verse which Jones pioneers here and in *The Seven Fountains* effectively establishes the basis of the genre of the Oriental verse tale which was to prove so popular with the Romantics and their readers. The tale concerns an Indian girl, significantly called Maia, who, bored with the simplicity of her rustic cell, longs for an environment more appreciative of her youth and beauty. At the command of the goddess Fortune, celestial spirits transport Maia in an aerial car drawn by peacocks to a paradisical palace. Here she witnesses a series of visions which ultimately reveal the vanity of human wishes. From this brief summary the extent of Shelley's indebtedness to Jones for the whole framework of *Queen Mab* (1813) will be apparent. Shelley had ordered Jones's *Works* in December 1812; see E. Koeppel, 'Shelley's "Queen Mab" and Sir William Jones's "The Palace of Fortune"', *Englische Studien*, 28 (1900), 43–53. Furthermore John Drew has pointed out that the fact that Shelley was also influenced by Southey's *The Curse of Kehama* 'does not detract from the debt to Jones since Southey here, as elsewhere, is also indebted to Jones' (*India and the Romantic Imagination*, p.233.) The text followed here is that of the second edition (1777), with variants recorded from the first edition of 1772, and Lady Jones's collected editions of 1799 and 1807.]

THE PALACE OF FORTUNE
AN INDIAN TALE
Written in the Year 1769

Mild was the vernal gale, and calm the day,
When Maia near a crystal fountain lay,
Young Maia, fairest of the blue-eyed maids,
That rov'd at noon in Tibet's musky shades;
But, haply, wandering through the fields of air,   5
Some fiend had whisper'd, – Maia, thou art fair!
Hence, swelling pride had fill'd her simple breast,
And rising passions robb'd her mind of rest;
In courts and glittering towers she wish'd to dwell,
And scorn'd her labouring parent's lowly cell.   10
And now, as gazing o'er the glassy stream,
She saw her blooming cheek's reflected beam,
Her tresses brighter than the morning sky,
And the mild radiance of her sparkling eye,
Low sighs and trickling tears by turns she stole,   15
And thus discharg'd the anguish of her soul:
'Why glow those cheeks, if unadmir'd they glow?
'Why flow those tresses, if unprais'd they flow?
'Why dart those eyes their liquid ray serene,
'Unfelt their influence, and their light unseen?   20
'Ye heavens! was that love-breathing bosom made
'To warm dull groves, and cheer the lonely glade?
'Ah, no: those blushes, that enchanting face
'Some tap'stried hall, or gilded bower, might grace;
'Might deck the scenes, where love and pleasure reign,   25
'And fire with amorous flames the youthful train.'

While thus she spoke, a sudden blaze of sight
Shot through the clouds, and struck her dazzled sight.
She rais'd her head, astonish'd, to the skies,
And veil'd with trembling hands her aching eyes;   30

---

2   The choice of name for this Indian heroine was a careful one, as it simultaneously connotes the European 'May' and the Sanskrit *maya* (the power of illusion). See note to ll.127–34 of *The Seven Fountains*. The simple rustic setting is also reminiscent of the forest home of Śakuntalā.

17   *Why glow those cheeks if unadmir'd they glow?*   Cf. the arguments of Milton's Comus to the Lady.

When through the yielding air she saw from far
A goddess gliding in a golden car,
That soon descended on the flowery lawn,
By two fair yokes of starry peacocks drawn:
A thousand nymphs with many a sprightly glance   35
Form'd round the radiant wheels an airy dance,
Celestial shapes! in fluid light array'd;
Like twinkling stars their beamy sandals play'd;
Their lucid mantles glitter'd in the sun,
(Webs half so bright the silkworm never spun)   40
Transparent robes, that bore the rainbow's hue,
And finer than the nets of pearly dew
That morning spreads o'er every opening flower,
When sportive summer decks his bridal bower.

The queen herself, too fair for mortal sight,   45
Sat in the centre of encircling light.
Soon with soft touch she rais'd the trembling maid,
And by her side in silent slumber laid:
Straight the gay birds display'd their spangled train,
And flew refulgent through th' aerial plain;   50
The fairy band their shining pinions spread,
And, as they rose, fresh gales of sweetness shed;
Fann'd with their flowing skirts, the sky was mild;
And heaven's blue fields with brighter radiance smil'd.

Now in a garden deck'd with verdant bowers   55
The glittering car descends on bending flowers:
The goddess still with looks divinely fair
Surveys the sleeping object of her care;
Then o'er her cheek her magick finger lays,
Soft as the gale that o'er a violet plays,   60
And thus in sounds, that favour'd mortals hear,
She gently whispers in her ravish'd ear:

---

34 *By two fair yokes of starry peacocks drawn* This line suggests the way in which Jones enhanced his contribution to the Oriental fable tradition by introducing authentic and exotic detail. In Hindu mythology the peacock is the mount of the adolescent hero, Kumāra. 'Kumāra rides on the peacock, the killer of serpents, for he defeats the most subtle instincts that bind the spirit of man in his body. The serpent, furthermore, represents the cycle of the years, the peacock is thus the killer of Time', Alain Daniélou, *Hindu Polytheism* (New York: Bollingen Foundation, 1964.), p.300. Long before his voyage to India and twenty years before he read and translated Kālidāsa's *Śakuntalā* (in which an aerial car features in Act VII), Jones was including Oriental material which was both colourful and accurate. Similar celestial cars were subsequently to appear in Southey's *The Curse of Kehama*, XXIV.22–6, and Shelley's *Queen Mab*, I.23–5.

'Awake, sweet maid, and view this charming scene
'For ever beauteous, and for ever green;
'Here living rills of purest nectar flow   65
'O'er meads that with unfading flowerets glow;
'Here amorous gales their scented wings display,
'Mov'd by the breath of ever-blooming May;
'Here in the lap of pleasure shalt thou rest,
'Our lov'd companion, and our honour'd guest.'   70

The damsel hears the heavenly notes distil,
Like melting snow, or like a vernal rill.
She lifts her head, and, on her arm reclin'd,
Drinks the sweet accents in her grateful mind:
On all around she turns her roving eyes,   75
And views the splendid scene with glad surprize;
Fresh lawns, and sunny banks, and roseate bowers,
Hills white with flocks, and meadows gemm'd with flowers;
Cool shades, a sure defence from summer's ray,
And silver brooks, where wanton damsels play,   80
Which with soft notes their dimpled crystal roll'd
O'er colour'd shells and sands of native gold;
A rising fountain play'd from every stream,
Smil'd as it rose, and cast a transient gleam,
Then, gently falling in a vocal shower,   85
Bath'd every shrub, and sprinkled every flower,
That on the banks, like many a lovely bride,
View'd in the liquid glass their blushing pride;
Whilst on each branch, with purple blossoms hung,
The sportful birds their joyous descant sung.   90

While Maia thus entranc'd in sweet delight,
With each gay object fed her eager sight,
The goddess mildly caught her willing hand,
And led her trembling o'er the flowery land:
Soon she beheld, where through an opening glade   95
A spacious lake its clear expanse display'd;

95–120 Jones's brightly enamelled depiction of the palace and its perfumed environs
demonstrates the facility with which he captivated the reading public's taste for the Oriental. The
celebrated Elizabeth Montagu, in a letter of 5 Sept. 1772 to James Beattie, rhapsodized: 'There is a
gayety & splendor in these poems which is naturally derived from the happy soil & climate, of the
Poets & they breathe Asiatick luxury, or else Mr Jones is himself a man of most splendid
imagination. The descriptions are so fine, & all the objects so brilliant, *that the sense aches at them*,
& I wish'd that Ossians poems had been laying by me, that I might have turn'd my eyes from ye
dazzling splendor of the Eastern noon day to the moonlight picture of a bleak mountain. Every
object in these pieces is blooming & beautiful; every plant is odouriferous; the passions too are of
the sort which belong to Paradise', quoted in *Letters*, I.111.

In mazy curls the flowing jasper wav'd
O'er its smooth bed with polish'd agate pav'd;
And on a rock of ice, by magick rais'd,
High in the midst a gorgeous palace blaz'd;   100
The sunbeams on the gilded portals glanc'd,
Play'd on the spires, and on the turrets danc'd;
To four bright gates four ivory bridges led,
With pearls illumin'd, and with roses spread:
And now, more radiant than the morning sun,   105
Her easy way the gliding goddess won;
Still by her hand she held the fearful maid,
And, as she pass'd, the fairies homage paid:
They enter'd straight the sumptuous palace-hall,
Where silken tapestry emblaz'd the wall,   110
Refulgent tissue, of an heavenly woof;
And gems unnumber'd sparkled on the roof,
On whose blue arch the flaming diamonds play'd,
As on a sky with living stars inlay'd;
Of precious diadems a regal store,   115
With globes and sceptres, strew'd the porphyry floor;
Rich vests of eastern kings around were spread,
And glittering zones a starry lustre shed:
But Maia most admir'd the pearly strings,
Gay bracelets, golden chains, and sparkling rings.   120

   High in the centre of the palace shone,
Suspended in mid-air, an opal throne:
To this the queen ascends with royal pride,
And sets the favour'd damsel by her side.
Around the throne in mystick order stand   125
The fairy train, and wait her high command;
When thus she speaks: (the maid attentive sips
Each word that flows, like nectar, from her lips.)

   'Favourite of heaven, my much-lov'd Maia, know,
'From me all joys, all earthly blessings, flow: 130
'Me suppliant men imperial Fortune call,
'The mighty empress of yon rolling ball:
(She rais'd her finger, and the wondering maid
At distance hung the dusky globe survey'd,

99–100 *And on a rock of ice by magick rais'd/High in the midst a gorgeous palace blaz'd* Jones
may have read in the *Ayeen Akbery* of the image of ice called Amernaut which magically appears in
the mountains of Kashmir. Cf. Coleridge's 'sunny pleasure-dome with caves of ice!', 'Kubla Khan',
1.36.

Saw the round earth with foaming oceans vein'd,   135
And labouring clouds on mountain tops sustain'd.)
'To me has fate the pleasing task assign'd
'To rule the various thoughts of humankind;
'To catch each rising wish, each ardent prayer,
'And some to grant, and some to waste in air.   140
'Know farther; as I rang'd the crystal sky,
'I saw thee near the murmuring fountain lie;
'Mark'd the rough storm that gather'd in thy breast,
'And knew what care thy joyless soul opprest.
'Straight I resolv'd to bring thee quick relief,   145
'Ease every weight, and soften every grief;
'If in this court contented thou canst live,
'And taste the joys these happy gardens give:
'But fill thy mind with vain desires no more,
'And view without a wish yon shining store: 150
'Soon shall a numerous train before me bend,
'And kneeling votaries my shrine attend;
'Warn'd by their empty vanities beware,
'And scorn the folly of each human prayer.'

She said; and straight a damsel of her train   155
With tender fingers touch'd a golden chain.
Now a soft bell delighted Maia hears,
That sweetly trembles on her listening ears;
Through the calm air the melting numbers float,
And wanton echo lengthens every note.   160
Soon through the dome a mingled hum arose,
Like the swift stream that o'er a valley flows;
Now louder still it grew, and still more loud,
As distant thunder breaks the bursting cloud:
Through the four portals rush'd a various throng,   165
That like a wintry torrent pour'd along:
A croud of every tongue, and every hue,
Toward the bright throne with eager rapture flew.
*A lovely stripling stepp'd before the rest
With hasty pace, and tow'rd the goddess prest;   170
His mien was graceful, and his looks were mild,
And in his eyes celestial sweetness smil'd:
Youth's purple glow, and beauty's rosy beam,
O'er his smooth cheeks diffus'd a lively gleam;

*Pleasure

41

The floating ringlets of his musky hair   175
Wav'd on the bosom of the wanton air:
With modest grace the goddess he addrest,
And thoughtless thus preferr'd his fond request.

'Queen of the world, whose wide-extended sway,
'Gay youth, firm manhood, and cold age obey,   180
'Grant me, while life's fresh blooming roses smile,
'The day with varied pleasures to beguile;
'Let me on beds of dewy flowers recline,
'And quaff with glowing lips the sparkling wine;
'Grant me to feed on beauty's rifled charms,   185
'And clasp a willing damsel in my arms;
'Her bosom fairer than a hill of snow,
'And gently bounding like a playful roe;
'Her lips more fragrant than the summer air,
'And sweet as Scythian musk her hyacinthine hair: 190
'Let new delights each dancing hour employ,
'Sport follow sport, and joy succeed to joy.'

The goddess grants the simple youth's request,
And mildly thus accosts her lovely guest:
'On that smooth mirror, full of magick light,   195
'Awhile, dear Maia, fix thy wandering sight.'
She looks; and in th' enchanted crystal sees
A bower o'er-canopied with tufted trees:
The wanton stripling lies beneath the shade,
And by his side reclines a blooming maid;   200
O'er her fair limbs a silken mantle flows,
Through which her youthful beauty softly glows,
And part conceal'd, and part disclos'd to sight,
Through the thin texture casts a ruddy light,
As the ripe clusters of the mantling vine   205
Beneath the verdant foliage faintly shine,
And, fearing to be view'd by envious day,
Their glowing tints unwillingly display.

The youth, while joy sits sparkling in his eyes,
Pants on her neck, and on her bosom dies;   210

200–8 In this sensuous description of the maiden whose beauty glowed through her
diaphanous mantle, Jones uses an image which combines colour, weight, and tactuality in a
mingling of the Dionysiac and the Bacchic likely to prove appealing to the young voluptuary who
longs to 'quaff with glowing lips the sparkling wine'.

From her smooth cheek nectareous dew he sips,
And all his soul comes breathing to his lips.
But Maia turns her modest eyes away,
And blushes to behold their amorous play.

She looks again, and sees with sad surprize   215
On the clear glass far different scenes arise:
The bower, which late outshone the rosy morn,
O'erhung with weeds she saw, and rough with thorn;
With stings of asps the leafless plants were wreath'd,
And curling adders gales of venom breath'd: 220
Low sat the stripling on the faded ground,
And in a mournful knot his arms were bound;
His eyes, that shot before a sunny beam,
Now scarcely shed a saddening, dying gleam;
Faint as a glimmering taper's wasted light,   225
Or a dull ray that streaks the cloudy night:
His crystal vase was on the pavement roll'd,
And from the bank was fall'n his cup of gold;
From which th' envenom'd dregs of deadly hue,
Flow'd on the ground in streams of baleful dew,   230
And, slowly stealing through the wither'd bower,
Poison'd each plant, and blasted every flower:
Fled were his slaves, and fled his yielding fair,
And each gay phantom was dissolv'd in air;
Whilst in their place was left a ruthless train,   235
Despair, and grief, remorse, and raging pain.

Aside the damsel turns her weeping eyes,
And sad reflections in her bosom rise;
To whom thus mildly speaks the radiant queen:
'Take sage example from this moral scene;   240
'See, how vain pleasures sting the lips they kiss,
'How asps are hid beneath the bowers of bliss!
'Whilst ever fair the flower of temperance blows,
'Unchang'd her leaf, and without thorn her rose;
'Smiling she darts her glittering branch on high,   245
'And spreads her fragrant blossoms to the sky.'

*Next tow'rd the throne she saw a knight advance;
Erect he stood, and shook a quivering lance;

*Glory

217–36 Implicit in the envenoming of the Spenserian Bower of Bliss is a didacticism which was
to prove attractive to the youthful Shelley.

A fiery dragon on his helmet shone,
And on his buckler beam'd a golden sun;   250
O'er his broad bosom blaz'd his jointed mail
With many a gem, and many a shining scale;
He trod the sounding floor with princely mien,
And thus with haughty words address'd the queen:
'Let falling kings beneath my javelin bleed,   255
'And bind my temples with a victor's meed;
'Let every realm that feels the solar ray,
'Shrink at my frown, and own my regal sway:
'Let Ind's rich banks declare my deathless fame,
'And trembling Ganges dread my potent name.'   260

The queen consented to the warriour's pray'r,
And his bright banners floated in the air:
He bade his darts in steely tempests fly,
Flames burst the clouds, and thunder shake the sky;
Death aim'd his lance, earth trembled at his nod,   265
And crimson conquest glow'd wher'er he trod.

And now the damsel, fix'd in deep amaze,
Th' enchanted glass with eager look surveys:
She sees the hero in his dusky tent,
His guards retir'd, his glimmering taper spent;   270
His spear, vain instrument of dying praise,
On the rich floor with idle state he lays;
His gory falchion near his pillow stood,
And stain'd the ground with drops of purple blood;
A busy page his nodding helm unlac'd,   275
And on the couch his scaly hauberk plac'd:
Now on the bed his weary limbs he throws,
Bath'd in the balmy dew of soft repose:
In dreams he rushes o'er the gloomy field,
He sees new armies fly, new heroes yield;   280
Warm with the vigorous conflict he appears,
And ev'n in slumber seems to move the spheres.
But lo! the faithless page, with stealing tread,
Advances to the champion's naked head;
With his sharp dagger wounds his bleeding breast,   285
And steeps his eyelids in eternal rest:
Then cries, (and waves the steel that drops with gore),
'The tyrant dies; oppression is no more.'

---

288 'In Jones's version (of the Bower of Bliss motif), Glory himself is an oppressor, and
Spenser's chivalric militarism has been converted into something like pacifism', David Duff,
Romance and Revolution: Shelley and the Politics of a Genre (Cambridge, 1994), p.84.

*Now came an aged sire with trembling pace;
Sunk were his eyes, and pale his ghastly face;   290
A ragged weed of dusky hue he wore,
And on his back a pondorous coffer bore.
The queen with faltering speech he thus addrest:
'O, fill with gold thy true adorer's chest!'

'Behold, said she, and wav'd her powerful hand,   295
'Where yon rich hills in glittering order stand:
'There load thy coffer with the golden store;
'Then bear it full away, and ask no more.'

With eager steps he took his hasty way,
Where the bright coin in heaps unnumber'd lay;   300
There hung enamour'd o'er the gleaming spoil,
Scoop'd the gay dross, and bent beneath the toil.
But bitter was his anguish, to behold
The coffer widen, and its sides unfold:
And every time he heap'd the darling ore,   305
His greedy chest grew larger than before;
Till, spent with pain, and falling o'er his hoard,
With his sharp steel his maddening breast he gor'd:
On the lov'd heap he cast his closing eye,
Contented on a golden couch to die.   310

A stripling, with the fair adventure pleas'd,
Stepp'd forward, and the massy coffer seiz'd;
But with surprize he saw the stores decay,
And all the long-sought treasures melt away;
In winding streams the liquid metal roll'd,   315
And through the palace ran a flood of gold.

†Next to the shrine advanc'd a reverend sage,
Whose beard was hoary with the frost of age;
His few gray locks a sable fillet bound,
And his dark mantle flow'd along the ground: 320
Grave was his port, yet show'd a bold neglect,
And fill'd the young beholder with respect;
Time's envious hand had plough'd his wrinkled face,
Yet on those wrinkles sat superiour grace;

*Riches
†Knowledge

---

323 *Time's envious hand had plough'd*   It is not difficult to discern echoes of Shakespeare's sonnets in this and succeeding lines.

Still full of fire appear'd his vivid eye, 325
Darted quick beams, and seem'd to pierce the sky.
At length, with gentle voice and look serene,
He wav'd his hand, and thus address'd the queen:

'Twice forty winters tip my beard with snow,
'And age's chilling gusts around me blow: 330
'In early youth, by contemplation led,
'With high pursuits my flatter'd thoughts were fed;
'To nature first my labours were confin'd,
'And all her charms were open'd to my mind,
'Each flower that glisten'd in the morning dew, 335
'And every shrub that in the forest grew:
'From earth to heaven I cast my wondering eyes,
'Saw suns unnumber'd sparkle in the skies,
'Mark'd the just progress of each rolling sphere,
'Describ'd the seasons, and reform'd the year. 340
'At length sublimer studies I began,
'And fix'd my level'd telescope on man;
'Knew all his powers, and all his passions trac'd,
'What virtue rais'd him, and what vice debas'd:
'But when I saw his knowledge so confin'd, 345
'So vain his wishes, and so weak his mind,
'His soul, a bright obscurity at best,
'And rough with tempests his afflicted breast,
'His life, a flower, ere evening sure to fade,
'His highest joys, the shadow of a shade; 350
'To thy fair court I took my weary way,
'Bewail my folly, and heaven's laws obey,
'Confess my feeble mind for prayers unfit
'And to my Maker's will my soul submit:
'Great empress of yon orb that rolls below, 355
'On me the last best gift of heaven bestow.'

He spoke: a sudden cloud his senses stole,
And thickening darkness swam o'er all his soul;
His vital spark her earthly cell forsook;
And into air her fleeting progress took. 360

Now from the throng a deafening sound was heard,
And all at once their various prayers preferr'd;
The goddess, wearied with the noisy croud,
Thrice wav'd her silver wand, and spoke aloud:

'Our ears no more with vain petitions tire,   365
'But take unheard whate'er you first desire.'
She said: each wish'd, and what he wish'd obtain'd;
And wild confusion in the palace reign'd.

But Maia, now grown senseless with delight,
Cast on an emerald ring her roving sight;   370
And, ere she could survey the rest with care,
Wish'd on her hand the precious gem to wear.

Sudden the palace vanish'd from her sight,
And the gay fabrick melted into night;
But, in its place, she view'd with weeping eyes   375
Huge rocks around her, and sharp cliffs arise:
She sat deserted on the naked shore,
Saw the curl'd waves, and heard the tempest roar;
Whilst on her finger shone the fatal ring,
A weak defence from hunger's pointed sting,   380
From sad remorse, from comfortless despair,
And all the painful family of care!
Frantick with grief her rosy cheek she tore,
And rent her locks, her darling charge no more:
But when the night his raven wing had spread,   385
And hung with sable every mountain's head,
Her tender limbs were numb'd with biting cold,
And round her feet the curling billows roll'd;
With trembling arms a rifted crag she grasp'd,
And the rough rock with hard embraces clasp'd.   390

While thus she stood, and made a piercing moan,
By chance her emerald touch'd the rugged stone;
That moment gleam'd from heaven a golden ray,
And taught the gloom to counterfeit the day:

369–72   Despite having witnessed edifying personifications of pleasure, glory, riches, and knowledge, Maia seems to have learned little. When the goddess Fortune, wearied with the endless procession of selfish appellants, announces that all shall be granted their first desire, Maia, 'now grown senseless with delight', wishes a precious emerald upon her finger.

374   *the gay fabrick melted into night*   Cf. *The Tempest* IV.i.150–1.

379   *Whilst on her finger shone the fatal ring*   Covetting the ring has lost her paradise. It is interesting to note that Jones gave to *Sacontalá* the subtitle 'The Fatal Ring' to reflect the sorrow that the king's ring brought to the eponymous heroine.

392–410   The emerald, touching a rock by chance, summons the genius of the ring. He responds to her plea by transporting her from the wild and rugged shoreline to a fragrant sylvan scene. However when it comes to wishing Maia still has much to learn.

A winged youth, for mortal eyes too fair,   395
Shot like a meteor through the dusky air;
His heavenly charms o'ercame her dazzled sight,
And drown'd her senses in a flood of light;
His sunny plumes descending he display'd,
And softly thus address'd the mournful maid: 400

 'Say, thou, who dost yon wondrous ring possess,
'What cares disturb thee, or what wants oppress;
'To faithful ears disclose thy secret grief,
'And hope (so heaven ordains) a quick relief.'

 The maid replied, 'Ah, sacred genius, bear   405
'A hopeless damsel from this land of care;
'Waft me to softer climes and lovelier plains,
'Where nature smiles, and spring eternal reigns.'

 She spoke; and swifter than the glance of thought
To a fair isle his sleeping charge he brought.   410

 Now morning breath'd: the scented air was mild,
Each meadow blossom'd, and each valley smil'd;
On every shrub the pearly dewdrops hung,
On every branch a feather'd warbler sung;
The cheerful spring her flowery chaplets wove,   415
And incense-breathing gales perfum'd the grove.

 The damsel rose; and, lost in glad surprize,
Cast round the gay expanse her opening eyes,
That shone with pleasure like a starry beam,
Or moonlight sparkling on a silver stream.   420
She thought some nymph must haunt that lovely scene,
Some woodland goddess, or some fairy queen;
At least she hop'd in some sequester'd vale
To hear the shepherd tell his amorous tale:
Led by these flattering hopes from glade to glade,   425
From lawn to lawn with hasty steps she stray'd;
But not a nymph by stream or fountain stood,
And not a fairy glided through the wood;
No damsel wanton'd o'er the dewy flowers,
No shepherd sung beneath the rosy bowers: 430
On every side she saw vast mountains rise,
That thrust their daring foreheads in the skies;

The rocks of polish'd alabaster seem'd,
And in the sun their lofty summits gleam'd.
She call'd aloud, but not a voice replied,   435
Save echo babbling from the mountain's side.

By this had night o'ercast the gloomy scene,
And twinkling stars emblaz'd the blue serene:
Yet on she wander'd, till with grief opprest
She fell; and, falling, smote her snowy breast: 440
Now to the heavens her guilty head she rears,
And pours her bursting sorrow into tears;
Then plaintive speaks, 'Ah! fond mistaken maid,
'How was thy mind by gilded hopes betray'd!
'Why didst thou wish for bowers and flowery hills,   445
'For smiling meadows, and for purling rills;
'Since on those hills no youth or damsel roves,
'No shepherd haunts the solitary groves?
'Ye meads that glow with intermingled dyes,
'Ye flowering palms that from yon hillocks rise,   450
'Ye quivering brooks that softly murmur by,
'Ye panting gales that on the branches die;
'Ah! why has Nature through her gay domain
'Display'd your beauties, yet display'd in vain?
'In vain, ye flowers, you boast your vernal bloom,   455
'And waste in barren air your fresh perfume.
'Ah! leave, ye wanton birds, yon lonely spray;
'Unheard you warble, and unseen you play:
'Yet stay till fate has fix'd my early doom,
'And strow with leaves a hapless damsel's tomb.   460
'Some grot or grassy bank shall be my bier,
'My maiden herse unwater'd with a tear.'

Thus while she mourns, o'erwhelm'd in deep despair,
She rends her silken robes, and golden hair:

443–62   Ultimately realizing her mistake, she sees that a depopulated Arcadia is indeed a barren and cold pastoral; she longs for the youths and shepherds that she once scorned. In lines which echo her earlier complaints ('Why glow those cheeks, if unadmir'd they glow?/Why flow those tresses, if unprais'd they flow?', ll. 17–18), she cries: 'Ah! why has nature through her gay domain/Display'd your beauties, yet display'd in vain?' Despite the parallel, there has been progress; she has gained compassion for trees, flowers, and birds, who waste their fragrance if not on the desert air, then at least unobserved. If the 'quivering brooks' had afforded water snakes Maia would have blessed them; the albatross of egotistical vanity has fallen from her.

456   *waste in barren air your fresh perfume*   Cf. Gray's 'Elegy Written in a Country Church-yard', l.56.

Her fatal ring, the cause of all her woes,   465
On a hard rock with maddening rage she throws;
The gem, rebounding from the stone, displays
Its verdant hue, and sheds refreshing rays:
Sudden descends the genius of the ring,
And drops celestial fragrance from his wing;   470
Then speaks, 'Who calls me from the realms of day?
'Ask, and I grant; command, and I obey.'

   She drank his melting words with ravish'd ears,
And stopp'd the gushing current of her tears;
Then kiss'd his skirts, that like a ruby glow'd,   475
And said, 'O bear me to my sire's abode.'

   Straight o'er her eyes a shady veil arose,
And all her soul was lull'd in still repose.

   By this with flowers the rosy-finger'd dawn
Had spread each dewy hill and verdurous lawn;   480
She wak'd, and saw a new-built tomb that stood
In the dark bosom of a solemn wood,
While these sad sounds her trembling ears invade:
'Beneath yon marble sleeps thy father's shade.'
She sigh'd, she wept; she struck her pensive breast, 485
And bade his urn in peaceful slumber rest.

   And now in silence o'er the gloomy land
She saw advance a slowly-winding band;
Their cheeks were veil'd, their robes of mournful hue
Flow'd o'er the lawn, and swept the pearly dew: 490
O'er the fresh turf they sprinkled sweet perfume,
And strow'd with flowers the venerable tomb.
A graceful matron walk'd before the train,
And tun'd in notes of woe the funeral strain:
When from her face her silken veil she drew,   495
The watchful maid her aged mother knew.
O'erpowered with bursting joy she runs to meet
The mourning dame, and falls before her feet.
The matron with surprize her daughter rears,
Hangs on her neck, and mingles tears with tears.   500

---

476 *O bear me to my sire's abode.* Her final and wisest wish, the product of learned experience, is to be reconciled with her patriarchal village society.

Now o'er the tomb their hallow'd rites they pay,
And form with lamps an artificial day:
Erelong the damsel reach'd her native vale,
And told with joyful heart her moral tale;
Resign'd to heaven, and lost to all beside,
She liv'd contented, and contented died.

5

The Damsels of Cardigan

[The Welsh Circuits obviously provided compensations for Jones. It is likely that Jones, inspired by the researches into the court poets of the Welsh princes undertaken by fellow London Welshmen, initiated the society for off-duty barristers known as the 'Druids'; what is undeniable is that he soon became *pencerdd*, or chief bard of the society. 'The Damsels of Cardigan', in eight nine-line verses, and set to the popular contemporary tune 'Rural Felicity', was written for the occasion of a jolly, judicial, *al fresco* luncheon by the banks of the Teifi. It was the first of three songs composed for the Druids' *fêtes champêtres*. As he confided to Althorp in September 1781: 'We dine, you must know on the circuit by the side of a beautiful spring, which, as I discovered in one of my walks I was bound to celebrate' (*Letters*, II.498). Jones's letters testify to the prandial delights of such occasions: 'We passed the day most luxuriously, having sent from London a store of excellent champaign and burgundy, and provided cold turkey pies and cold meat, lobsters, crabs, and so forth for our dinner: we dined in the boat which was moored on the bank, and kept our wines perfectly cool, by putting the bottles into a natural well of the coldest water I have ever tasted' (*Letters*, I.204.) Professor de Sola Pinto described this song as follows: 'These musical lines with their flowing rhythm suggest a link between Prior and Gray on the one hand and Tom Moore on the other, and make the reader regret that more of Jones's work in this vein has not survived.' ('Sir William Jones and English Literature', *Bulletin of the School of Oriental and African Studies*, 11 (1943–6), 686–94, 692). The poem was first printed in the *Gentleman's Magazine*, 52 (Sept. 1782), 446, and this forms the copy-text, with variants noted from Teignmouth's *Life* (*Works*, I.357–8).]

THE DAMSELS OF CARDIGAN

A Song to the Tune of 'Rural Felicity'.
'Curtæ nescio quid semper abest rei.'

Fair Tivy*, how sweet are they waves gently flowing,
   Thy wild oaken woods, and green eglantine bowers!
Thy banks with the musk-rose and amaranth glowing
     When friendship and mirth claim these labourless hours.
       But weak is our vaunt,   5
       While something we want,
More sweet than the pleasure that Prospects can give
      Come, smile, damsels of Cardigan,
Love can alone make it blissful to live.

How sweet is the nectar that glistens and dances,   10
     While quick from its vase the bright sparkler we pour!
And when to our lips the beguiler advances,
     He bids us be pensive and anxious no more.
       But weak is our vaunt,
       While something we want,   15
More sweet than the pleasures that Nectar can give.
      Come, smile, damsels of Cardigan,
Love can alone make it blissful to live.

How sweet is the scent of the jasmine and roses
     That Zephyr around us so lavishly flings,   20
Perhaps for Blaenpant† fresh perfume he composes,

*Tivy, a famous river in Wales.
†Blaenpant, Bronwith, Cilgaran, Dinevor, Slebeck, and Coedmor, particular places or seats.

A Song 'In the Morn as I walk'd thro' the mead', *Rural Felicity*: A Favourite New Song, P.H.[odgson: London, 1775?], see *The Catalogue of Printed Music in the British Library to 1980* (London, 1986), 49.350.
  Epigraph 'Something is always missing from defective fortune', Horace *Odes* III.24.64.
   2 *wild oaken woods and green eglantine* Six years later, having exchanged the hill-country of Cardigan for that of Chittagong, and surrounded by the more exotic scents of champac and nagasar, Jones wrote to Thomas Milles (1753–1830), his old friend of the Welsh circuits: 'At my leisure I will write more, and meditate a General Epistle to Druids of the Tivy; to whom present my affectionate greetings', *Letters*, II.692.
   21 *Blaenpant* Situated in the beautiful valley of the lower Teifi, Blaenpant was the seat of William Owen Brigstocke, a prominent member of the Tivyside Hunt and the local militia, see David Howell, *Patriarchs and Parasites: The Gentry of South West Wales in the Eighteenth Century* (Cardiff, 1986), p.159.

Or tidings from Bronwith auspiciously brings.
    But weak is our vaunt,
    While something we want,
More sweet than the pleasures which Odours can give.   25
    Come, smile, damsels of Cardigan,
Love can alone make it blissful to live.

How sweet was the strain that enliven'd the spirit,
    And cheer'd us with numbers so frolic and free!
The poet is absent; be just to his merit,   30
    Ah! may he in love be more happy than we!
    For weak is our vaunt,
    While something we want,
More sweet than the pleasure that Music can give.
    Come, smile, damsels of Cardigan,   35
Love can alone make it blissful to live.

How sweet is the circle of friends round our table,
    Where stately Cilgaran o'erhangs the brown dale,
Where none are unwilling, and few are unable,
    To sing a wild song, or relate a wild tale!   40
    But weak is our vaunt,
    While something we want,
More sweet than the pleasure which Friendship can give.
    Come, smile, damsels of Cardigan,
Love can alone make it blissful to live.   45

How vainly we pore over dark Gothic pages,
    To cull a rude gibberish from Statham or Brooke!
Leave Year-books and parchments to grey-bearded sages,

---

22 *Bronwith* Bronwydd, also situated on the fertile banks of the Teifi, was owned by Colonel Thomas Lloyd, who experimented with the latest techniques in husbandry, see Howell, *Patriarchs and Parasites*, pp.77–8.

38 *stately Cilgaran* This early thirteenth-century castle crowning the summit of a precipitous rock overlooking the Teifi was later to become part of the picturesque circuit, and the subject of a painting by Richard Wilson.

39–40 *Where none are unwilling . . . a wild tale* These lines are quoted by Scott in a letter to Anna Seward to convey the noisy but good-humoured atmosphere of a Mess Dinner, *The Letters of Sir Walter Scott*, ed. H.J.C. Grierson (London, 1932), I.195.

47 *To cull a rude gibberish from Statham or Brooke* Nicholas Statham (d.1472), a reader at Lincoln's Inn, and author of *Epitome Annalium temp. Henrici Sexti*. The dry legal rulings of Sir Robert Brooke (d. 1558) were similarly recorded in manuscript tomes.

48–9 *Leave Year-books and parchments to grey-bearded sages,/Be nature our law, and fair woman our book* For the amusement of his original audience of circuiteers, Jones mocks their chosen career as dusty and worm-eaten, while anticipating the theme of Wordsworth's 'Expostulation and Reply' and 'The Tables Turned'.

Be nature our law, and fair woman our book.
>> But weak is our vaunt, 50
>> While something we want,
> More sweet than the pleasure which Learning can give.
>> Come, smile, damsels of Cardigan,
> Love can alone make it blissful to live.

Admit that our labours were crown'd in full-measure, 55
>> And gold were the fruit of rhetorical flowers,
> That India supplied us with long-hoarded treasure,
>> That Dinevor, Slebeck or Coedmor were ours;
>>> Yet weak is our vaunt,
>>> While something we want, 60
> More sweet than the pleasure that Riches can give.
>> Come, smile, damsels of Cardigan,
> Love can alone make it blissful to live.

Or say, that preferring fair Thames to fair Tivy,
>> We gain'd with bright ermine robes purple or red, 65

---

57 *That India supplied us with long-hoarded treasure*   The riches of India were shortly to mean something very different to Jones. His appointment in 1783 to the Bengal bench was accompanied by a knighthood, the remarkable salary of £6,000 per annum, and the dream of political independence virtually within reach, but in the event it was the treasure-house of Sanskrit literature which was to captivate him.

58 *Dinevor*   John Dyer, of nearby Aberglasney, had earlier sung the delights of Dynevor in 'Grongar Hill'. Jones, visiting the impressive double-pile gentry house in March 1775, enthused, 'perhaps the finest situation in the whole island. The house appears elegant enough, but the ruin of a castle, which was the summer palace of the old kings of South Wales, has something in it admirably picturesque, the park and the whole prospect is so exquisitely diversified, that I never saw anything equal to it: the river *Towy* (which is more beauteous than its name is melodious) flows through the valley, and the hill, on which the castle stands, is bosomed by the thickest and richest wood I ever beheld', *Letters*, I.189. The lily was gilded by a visit of Capability Brown later that same spring, Dynevor being the only grounds in south-west Wales to benefit from his improvements, see D. Stroud, *Capability Brown* (London, 1975), p.180. It was the seat of George Rice, a prominent Whig, who was MP for Carmarthenshire until his death in 1779. His son, George Talbot Rice was elevated to the peerage as 3rd Baron Dynevor in 1793, see textual notes, p.405.

Slebeck   Slebech was one of the most important estates in south Pembrokeshire, its hall being rebuilt for John Symmons in 1776, see B. Ll. Morris (ed.), *The Slebech Story* (Haverfordwest, 1948).

Coedmor   The mansion of Coedmor was situated about a mile west of Cilgerran surrounded by luxuriant oak woods, a remnant of the ancient forest of Ceredigion Iscoed. It was the seat of Thomas Lloyd, a magistrate who became the Whig High Sheriff of Cardiganshire in 1798. A popular squire but a notorious rake who, carrying the burden of this song to his heart, took pride in the number of his illegitimate offspring, many of whom served him in a domestic capacity, see Herbert M. Vaughan, *The South Wales Squires* (London, 1926), pp.123–25. Cf. Jones's comments on the licentious profligacy of his brother-lawyers, *Letters*, II.498–9.

65 *bright ermine robes purple or red*   'We all seek happiness; now I am so framed that I must act conscientiously, or I cannot be happy: is it not better then to live, as I do, moderately yet independently, like a philosopher yet like a gentleman, than to hanker after silk gowns or red gowns, or all the trumpery of a courtly bar?' *Letters*, I.241.

And peep'd through large perukes, like owlets through ivy,
  Or grant that rich coronets blaz'd on our head;
    Yet weak is our vaunt,
    While something we want,
More sweet than the pleasure that Honours can give.   70
    Come, smile, damsels of Cardigan,
Love can alone make it blissful to live.

---

70 *the pleasure that Honours can give* On 18 September 1780 Jones wrote to Althorp: 'You have, by this time, received my speech, [*A Speech on the Nomination of Candidates*, item 29 below] which would be only a lively prelude to others actually spoken, if I had any lively hope; but really my hope of seeing better things is almost evanescent, a *fluxionary* quantity; and as I am not a man to expect impossibilities or to strive against the stream, I shall do nothing but sing *the damsels of Cardigan*, if the new parliament should go on addressing, chastising, obeying, like the last', *Letters*, I.440.

6

Kneel to the Goddess (1780)

[Never published in Jones's lifetime, these verses were found by Lady Llanover among the papers of Mary Granville, Mrs Delany (1700–88), who had been a friend of Swift, had introduced Frances Burney at court, and was on good terms with the Spencers. The manuscript was apparently incomplete, but the poem of eight ten-line stanzas, with the first line of a ninth stanza, appeared in *The Autobiography and Correspondence of Mary Granville, Mrs. Delany*, (ed. Lady Llanover, 3 vols., London, 1862), 2.539–41. Lady Llanover prefaced the poem thus: 'Among the MS. of this period, the following verses were found, written by the learned Cambrian, Sir W. Jones, after Lord G. Gordon's riots. It was composed in *one hour* for a society called the Druids, to which Sir W. Jones belonged, and who, during the summer circuit at Cardigan, were accustomed to meet and dine in a romantic situation on the banks of the river Teifi.']

What means all this frensy, what mad men are they
  Who broil and are broil'd for a shade in religion?
Since all sage inspirers one doctrine convey
  From Numa's wild nymph to sly Mohamed's pigeon.
    Then Druids arise,   5
    Teach the world to be wise,
And the grape's rosy blood for your sacrifice pour,
    Th'immortals invoke,
    And under this oak
Kneel, kneel to the Goddess whom all men adore.   10

By various high titles this Goddess is nam'd,
  At Ephesus Dian, in Syria Astarte,

---

1 *all this frensy* Throughout early June 1780 Jones was resident at the Temple and had witnessed the Gordon riots: the blue cockades, the cries of 'No Popery!', and the results of 'religious phrenzy . . . succeeded by a desire of general plunder and devastation', *Letters*, I.402.

2 *broil and are broil'd* Throughout the city many Catholic churches had been gutted, with the mob threatening to kill every papist in London. Apprehensive of any increase in the power of the executive, Jones wrote to Lady Spencer: 'The cause of genuine rational Liberty is much injured by the enthusiasm even of many sober men; but the phrenzy which now distracts and alarms us here, is a poniard in the heart of Liberty', *Letters*, I.401.

4 *Numa's wild nymph* Egeria, a nymph associated with Diana, whose divine sanction Numa Pompilius sought to recommend his new regulations to the populace. She became, according to Ovid, the wife of Numa, see *Metamorphoses*, 15.547.

sly Mohamed's pigeon According to a persistent and prejudiced Western tradition from Dante to d'Herbelot, one of Mahomet's impostures was to train a pigeon to pick peas out of his ear so that it might seem that the bird was communicating divine revelation.

5 *Druids arise* The naming of their society was particularly apt, reflecting both the fashionable interest in bardic lore sponsored by the Cymmrodorion and Gwyneddigion societies, and the fact that the Druids were supposed to be the first framers of laws in Britain, see Sir William Dugdale, *Origines Juridiciales* (London, 1666), p.54.

9 *under this oak* The Welsh for 'Druid', as Jones well knew, is 'Derwydd' which means the 'Body of the Oak', or by implication, the 'Man of the Oak'.

10 *Kneel to the Goddess whom all men adore* Seven years later, on the banks of the Ganges rather than the Teifi, after reading one of the sermons of his Welsh nonconformist friend Dr Richard Price, Jones was to write: 'all who believe the *essentials* of religion and act according to the principles of virtue, must be happy . . . After this publication, by good old Price, the *Church of England*, as it is called, would inevitably fall, and the *Religion of the Gospel* be substituted in its place, if it were not for the interest of so many thousands to profess a belief in riddles for the sake of rectories, prebends, and lawn-sleeves . . . if Price's book were accurately and perspicuously translated into Persian, [the Mohammadans] would would certainly not be shocked by the Christian doctrine . . . the Hindus would have less difficulty in admitting the Thirty Nine Articles; because if those articles were written in Sanscrit, they might pass well enough for the composition of a Brahman', *Letters*, II.758.

12 *At Ephesus Dian* The most famous of Diana's temples, one of the seven wonders of the world, where the goddess was represented with a large number of breasts.

Astarte At her magnificent temple in Hierapolis, Astarte, the Syrian Aphrodite, was served by three hundred priests.

In *New* Rome 'tis Mary, Heaven's Regent proclaim'd,
  In *Old* Rome 'twas Venus, the buxom and hearty.
        But crown'd and enthron'd   15
        Her Godhead is own'd
In desert, in valley, on mountain, on shore,
        Then join our gay crew,
        Turk, Roman and Jew,
And kneel to the Goddess, whom all men adore.   20

When sallow Parsees, in vain Anquetil's rant,
  Repeat the strange lessons of false Zoroaster,
Or hymn ruddy Mithra's in rapturous cant
  As their surest preserver from every disaster,
        They worship but one,   25
        Warm and round as the sun,
Which Persia's rich kings on their diadems wore;
        The circle they prize
        Had long left the skies,
And they kneel to the Goddess whom all men adore.   30

When dark visag'd Bramins obsequiously bow
  To the rock whence old Ganges redundantly gushes,
They feign that they bend to the form of a cow,
  And save by this fiction the fair maiden's blushes;
        But from Sanscritan Vedes   35
        The discov'ry proceeds
That her aid, whom we honor, e'en Bramin implores;
        Like us wildly they dance,

21-2 *When sallow Parsees . . . Zoroaster* Nine years earlier Jones had mounted his patriotic intellectual attack upon Anquetil-Duperron, see the Introduction, p.xvi and note. Nine years later in 1789 Jones was to return to the subject of the *Zendávestà* (the *Avesta* is the sacred text of Zoroastrians) in his *Sixth Anniversary Discourse* (*Works*, III.103–36) where he mistakenly described Sanskrit as the source of Avestan, see *Life*, p.299.

23 *ruddy Mithra's* In Iranian texts Mithra is a sun god of light, heat, and fertility. Related to Mitra, the Vedic god of trust and contracts, Mithra displayed more warlike characteristics and was the only Persian deity to be assimilated by the West, appearing in the cult of Mithras, beloved of the Roman legionaries. Jones's use of the epithet 'ruddy' may well refer to the cult's supreme initiation rite, the *taurobolium*, a bath in the blood of a sacrificed ox.

32 *the rock whence old Ganges redundantly gushes* The Vedas describe the purifying Ganges as flowing from the beautiful head of Śiva, cf., for example, Jones's 'A Hymn to Gangá', ll.25-6. However, the reference in l.34 to saving 'the fair maiden's blushes' would seem to indicate that these 'Bramins' are bowing to *Bīja*, or semen, which is worshipped as 'the Ganges flowing from the head of the *linga*', Danielou, *Hindu Polytheism*, p.226.

33 *the form of a cow* Many Hindu goddesses are associated with, or invoked in the form of, a cow, including Priśni, Usas, and Vāc, who are seen as providing sustenance for all.

35 *Sanscritan Vedes* It was Jones's study of the Vedic texts, after he had arrived in India, which confirmed the syncretist approach which is humorously anticipated here, see 'On the Gods of Greece, Italy and India', p.348 below.

Like us lightly advance,
And kneel to the Goddess whom all men adore.   40

You have heard of the mysteries hallow'd in Greece,
    And shewn to th'elect in the groves of Eleusis,
Our learned, about them, have cackled like geese,
    But their learning vain pomp or mere idle abuse is:
        Th'initiate were told,   45
        In verses of gold,
Mad Jove and rough Neptune to worship no more;
        But with love and with truth
        To frolic thro' youth,
And kneel to the Goddess whom all men adore.   50

Say why to sweet Araby pilgrims repair,
    And troop in full caravans yearly to Mecca?
Their mosque is like ours, and no altar is there
    Save that which the Patriarch bless'd in Rebecca;
        The Koran for you,   55
        Ye Mussulmen true,
Has of nymphs with black eyes and black tresses a store:
        Then sink to the ground,
        Tho' turban'd and gown'd,
And kneel to the Goddess whom all men adore.   60

See, Teifi, with joy see our mystical rite
    On steep woody marge after ages renewed;
Here once Taliesin thou heard'st with delight,
    But what was his voice to the voice of our Druid?

---

42 *groves of Eleusis* This town in Attica was the scene of the most celebrated of Greek religious festivals; the ceremony was sacred to Ceres and Proserpine, and involved rites of initiation and purification.

47 *Mad Jove and rough Neptune* The sons of Saturn and Ops, these brothers are alike in their propensity to anger and their shape-shifting seductions. Neptune is often represented as bearded with rough wave-tousled hair.

54 *that which the Patriarch bless'd in Rebecca* See Genesis 24:48.

57 *nymphs with black eyes* 'Mahomet . . . described the pleasures of heaven . . . under the allegory of . . . *black-eyed girls*, as the word *Houri* literally signifies in *Arabick*', 'Essay on the Poetry of Eastern Nations', p.324 below.

62 *after ages renewed* Despite the light-heartedness here, Jones, as a member of the Cymmrodorion, was deeply interested in contemporary attempts to revive ancient customs of bardic congresses and *eisteddfodau*, see *Letters*, II.877.

63 *Here once Taliesin* A sixth-century poet, one of the first of the *Cynfeirdd* (Early Poets) in the heroic age of Britain, who became, in the Middle Ages, the subject of much legendary and magical material. Edward Jones (1752–1824), in a book which was in Sir William Jones's library, records a tradition of the infant Taliesin being exposed in a weir and found by the fishermen of Prince Elphin, see *Musical and Poetical Relicks of the Welsh Bards* (London, 1784), p.5.

Each year will we greet   65
    Thy shady retreat,
And sing to the Naiads our exquisite lore;
    Sweet echo shall laugh
    Whilst brimmers we quaff,
And kneel to the Goddess whom all men adore.   70

Our mystery, Druids, 'tis time to reveal,
    And remove the thin gauze which our discipline covers;
Far hence ye profane, whose cold hearts are of steel,
    But listen devoutly ye passionate lovers.
    Ye zephyrs be dumb,   75
    Cease ye blue flies to hum,
Ye waves kiss the brink of old Teifi no more;
    But each to his fair
    Waft a sigh or a prayer,
And kneel to the Goddess whom all men adore.   80

The young oak is an emblem

[The rest is missing.]

7

*On Seeing Miss * * **
Ride by Him, Without Knowing Her (1780)

[This slight but gently amusing poem is included to illustrate the way in which Jones viewed composition as a recreation from his professional pressures. The summer of 1780 was an extremely fraught period in his life when legal, political and Orientalist concerns vied for his time and attentions; he had hoped to address the electors of Middlesex in August, and both his candidacy and his Arabic and legal researches were drawing him to Oxford. Nevertheless his duties on the Carmarthen circuit had to take priority, and the middle of the month found him deep in west Wales. The unknown equestrienne of Cardigan is celebrated in fifteen quatrains which leaven conventional classical allusion with a significant sprinkling of Eastern images. The poem was first published in the 1807 collected works and this represents the copy-text.]

ON SEEING MISS * * *

RIDE BY HIM, WITHOUT KNOWING HER

Cardigan, Aug. 14, 1780.

So lightly glanc'd she o'er the lawn,
  So lightly through the vale,
That not more swiftly bounds the fawn,
  In Sidon's palmy dale.

Full well her bright-hair'd courser knew,   5
  How sweet a charge he bore,
And proudly shook the tassels blue,
  That on his neck he wore.

Her vest, with liveliest tincture glow'd,
  That Summer-blossoms wear,   10
And wanton down her shoulders flow'd,
  Her hyacinthine hair.

Zephyr in play had loos'd the string,
  And with it laughing flown,
Diffusing from his dewy wing,   15
  A fragrance not his own.

Her shape was like the slender pine,
  With vernal buds array'd,
O heav'n! what rapture would be mine,
  To slumber in its shade.   20

Her cheeks – one rose had *Strephon* seen,
  But dazzled with the sight,
At distance view'd her nymph-like mien,
  And *fainted with delight*.

3–4 *the fawn,/In Sidon's palmy dale*   Jones was working on his translation of the *Mu'allaqāt* at this time, cf. 'The Poem of Tarafa', 6. Here the unknown beauty is seen as both fawn and divine huntress (ll. 25–32).

12 *Her hyacinthine hair*   Cf. 'Essay on the Poetry of Eastern Nations', p.323.

17 *Her shape was like the slender pine*   Cf. the following line from an ode of Hāfiz as translated by Jones: 'O pine, compared with her graceful stature, what honour hast thou in the garden?' 'Essay on the Poetry of Eastern Nations', p.331 below.

21 Strephon   A fond lover from Sidney's *Arcadia*.

He thought *Diana* from the chace,   25
   Was hastening to her bow'r;
For more than mortal seem'd a face,
   Of such resistless pow'r.

Actæon's fatal change he fear'd,
   And trembled at the breeze;   30
High antlers had his fancy rear'd,
   And quiv'ring sunk his knees.

He well might err – that morn confess'd,
   The queen with silver beam,
Shone forth, and *Sylvia* thus address'd,   35
   By Tivy's azure stream:

'Let us this day our robes exchange;
   'Bind on my waxing moon;
'Then through yon woods at pleasure range,
   'And shun the sultry noon.   40

'Whilst I at Cardigan prepare
   'Gay stores of silk and lace,
'Like thine, will seem my flowing hair,
   'Like thine, my heav'nly grace.

'My brother Phœbus lost his heart   45
   'When first he view'd thy charms,
'And would this day, with dang'rous art,
   'Allure thee to his arms.

'But Cynthia, friend to virgins fair,
   'Thy steps will ever guide,   50
'Protect thee from th' enchanting snare,
   'And o'er thy heart preside.

---

29 *Actæon's fatal change he fear'd* While hunting, Actæon saw Diana and her attendants bathing in a woodland pool, the angry goddess transformed him into a stag and he was devoured by his own hounds.

41–2 The domestication of Lucina (Cynthia/Diana), who is prepared to exchange the delights of mount Cynthus for Cardigan with 'its stores of silk and lace', is only to be surpassed by the prospect of humiliating Phoebus Apollo for 'flirting with his sister'.

45–6 *My brother Phœbus . . . thy charms* Implicitly the narratee is compared with the nymph Daphne, who in her attempt to escape the amorous Apollo, was changed not into a pine but a laurel tree.

In vain his wiles he shall essay,
  'And touch his golden lyre;
'Then to the skies shall wing his way,   55
  'With pale, yet raging fire.

'Should he with lies traduce the fair,
  'And boast how oft he kiss'd her,
The gods shall laugh while I declare,
  He flirted with his sister.'   60

8

The Fountain Nymph (1781)

[This 'little *chanson à boire*', as Jones termed it, was also written for the post-prandial celebrations of the Welsh circuiteers. It was published posthumously in the *Monthly Magazine*, May 1804 (vol. 17, pp.347–8), but Jones had sent a copy to Althorp on 28 September 1781. In the letter Jones had included his criticisms of the ode he composed at Althorp's wedding ('The Muse Recalled') which he regarded as 'very *unpoetical*, because it is very *true*, and consequently wants the essence of poetry.' It is in this context that he introduces 'the fountain nymph': 'There is more *fiction* in the little *chanson à boire*, which I enclose, and for which, when you have read it, fire is the fittest element. We dine, you must know on the circuit by the side of a beautiful spring, which, as I discovered [it] in one of my walks, I was bound to celebrate. I therefore wrote the song in a wild grotesque style to the tune of a very lively country-dance, and it was admirably sung by one of our party', *Letters*, II.498. The poem, with its jaunty rhythm and mischievous double and triple rhymes, represents a further example of Jones's facility for extempore composition; on the circuit of 1780 he had delighted the 'Druids' by composing the mock-heroic 'Kneel to the Goddess' in an hour. The text of 'The Fountain Nymph' is printed from the manuscript copy formerly in Earl Spencer's muniment room, and now awaiting cataloguing in the British Library.]

I

Why should old *Tivy*, boys, claim all our duty paid,
And no just homage freely be to charming youth and beauty paid?
See, where the Nymph of the Spring sits inviting us,
With sparkling waters crystalline refreshing and delighting us!
What, tho' his margin proud be rocky steep and willowy,   5
Or what tho' his azure couch be spacious deep and billowy!
She from her sweet paps lilied and roseal
Lies feeding all the laughing birds with dew drops ambrosial.

II

Then with full harmony carol to the fountain-nymph
Far sweeter than a sea-nymph and milder than a mountain-nymph!   10
Long may her stream gush lucid and nectareous!
And long may her gay banks be deck'd with flow'rets multifarious!
Long o'er her arched grot may purple-winged Zephyrus
Come leading on his wanton band of breezes odoriferous!
Yearly to the Naiad shall this roundelay repeated be,   15
And by the chorus jubilant her liquid silver greeted be.

III

Say, can we better, boys, chase our idle time away
Than thus by passing hours in mirth, in melody, and rhime away?
Stretch'd on that green hillock's breast, around its rosy nipple, boys
We merrily will sing and laugh, and merrily will tipple, boys,   20

---

7   *sweet paps lilied and roseal*   In the Corrigenda of *Poems, consisting chiefly of translations from the Asiatick languages* (Oxford: Clarendon Press, 1772) Jones changed 'a rosy-bosom'd bride' in l.257 of 'The Seven Fountains' to 'a lily-bosom'd bride'. The breasts of this Cardiganshire nymph receive the benefit of both floral tributes.

20   *merrily will tipple, boys*   With reference to the drinking habits of his brother-lawyers and Jones's comparatively sober extempore versifying, I came across the following verses written on the end-paper of the National Library of Wales copy of *The Poetical Works of Sir William Jones* (London: Nichols and Son, 1810), bearing the ascription 'Written by Sir Wm Jones on the Oxford Circuit on seeing Bearcroft intoxicated led by Mr. Henry Howarth': 'Immortal Gods! Can this be he,/Who did the fiery Kenyon crush,/Confounded Harding, soften'd Lee,/And made the face of Cooper blush./Conduct him Howarth o'er the lea,/Do thou his tottering footsteps guide,/ Young Hal of Monmouth shalt thou be,/And he be Falstaff by thy side.' [Edward Bearcroft (1720-96), an eminent lawyer, practising on the Brecknock and Oxford circuits, KC, and Chief Justice of Chester from 1788. Henry Howorth (*c*.1746–83), circuiteer and friend of Jones, MP for Abingdon from 1782, see *Letters*, II.535. Lloyd Kenyon (1732–1802), a Flintshire friend who was later to become

Drinking to damsels lovely and delicious;
Oh heav'n, would they but smile on us like Deities propitious!
And if any rebel youth shall miss the cup or mutiny,
Amerc'd shall be the miscreant without appeal or scrutiny.

Lord Chief Justice, but it was his involvement in the prosecution of *The Principles of Government* that led Jones to describe him as 'the hot-headed Welch Chief Justice', see *Letters*, II.638, and below p.393. George Hardinge (1743–1816), eminent judge, poet, and MP, identified as the Jefferies Hardsman of Byron's *Don Juan* XIII:88. Hardinge was a close friend to whom Jones addressed a sonnet, see Teignmouth, *Works*, II.78. John Lee (1733–93), another successful friend of the circuits, appointed Solicitor-General in 1782 and Attorney-General the following year. Sir Grey Cooper (1726–1801), barrister, Rockinghamite, and Secretary of the Treasury, see *Letters*, I.272.]

23–4 *If any rebel youth . . . without appeal or scrutiny* Jones sent this poem in a letter to Viscount Althorp on his return from the Carmarthen circuit in September 1781. Anxious that his former pupil might gain the wrong impression, the serious-minded Jones is quick to reassure him in a passage which sheds light both upon Jones's character, and on the last two lines of the poem: 'Do not imagine, my dear lord, from these light pieces or from any light expression, that I am, or ever was, in principle or practice, a libertine; on the contrary, though I was always deeply sensible of beauty, and naturally loved cheerful company, when my mind was not engaged in any serious pursuit, yet, I believe, no man ever had so supreme a command over his passions as I have; but, let philosophers say what they will, *either a man must not live in society, or he must conform in a certain degree to the society in which he lives*: now it must be allowed, that the manners of my brother-lawyers are most licentiously profligate, (worse, I verily believe than those of the *regular* officers) and, if I had seemed to censure them, I should have been disliked by them, instead of being popular. The fruit, therefore, of one day's excess in wine has been *perpetual temperance* for the rest of my life; for as I convince them that I did not abstain from sullenness or reserve, they now let me drink as little as I please, and very little I please to drink. Even on the day when my song was produced, I confined myself to three or four glasses, with a copious mixture from the fountain', *Letters*, II.498–9.

9

The Muse Recalled; An Ode on the Nuptials of Lord Viscount Althorp and Miss Lavinia Bingham (6 March 1781)

[Written at the insistence of the Duchess of Devonshire and the young ladies present at the important society wedding of his former pupil to the eldest daughter of Charles, Lord Lucan, Jones demonstrated his considerable skills at extempore composition. In a letter to the newly-married Althorp of 18 March, he refers to the circumstances: 'You must make all due allowances for an occasional Ode: nothing was farther from my mind than the idea of writing; for what can words add, either in verse or prose, to friendship like ours? but the young ladies would not hear of an excuse.' (*Letters*, II.461) This epithalamium, written as a Pindaric Ode, is reminiscent of Jones's idol, Milton, in both its octosyllabics and in its addressing of more universal issues. Lord Lucan asked Walpole to print the ode at the Strawberry Hill Press, and 250 copies were printed. (It was reprinted in Paris in 1782, and in the *European Magazine*, (vol. 7, Jan. 1785, pp.62–3.) Walpole approved of the piece: 'There are many beautiful and poetic expressions in it. A wedding to be sure is neither a new or a promising subject, nor will outlast the favours: still I think Mr Jones's ode is uncommonly good for the occasion.' (*The Letters of Horace Walpole*, ed. W. S. Lewis, Oxford and Yale, 1955, xxxv.362.) Despite the fact that the bridegroom, rather than the bride, occupies the real focus of attention, the bride's mother, Lady Lucan, was pleased enough to circulate copies to worthies such as Edward Gibbon and the poet William Hayley, who were delighted with the ode's elegance, see *Memoirs of the Life and Writings of William Hayley, Esq.* (ed. John Johnson, 2 vols., London, 1823), I.470. The copy-text is that of the 1799 edition, with variants noted from the Strawberry Hill imprint.]

THE MUSE RECALLED
AN ODE

Return, celestial Muse,
By whose bright fingers o'er my infant head,
Lull'd with immortal symphony, were spread
Fresh bays and flow'rets of a thousand hues;
  Return! thy golden lyre,   5
Chorded with sunny rays of temper'd fire,
Which in Astræa's fane I fondly hung,
  Bold I reclaim: but ah, sweet maid,
  Bereft of thy propitious aid
My voice is tuneless, and my harp unstrung.   10
In vain I call . . . What charm, what potent spell
Shall kindle into life the long-unwaken'd shell?

Haste! the well-wrought *basket bring,
Which two sister Graces wove,
When the third, whose praise I sing,   15
Blushing sought the bridal grove,
Where the slow-descending sun
Gilt the bow'rs of WIMBLEDON.
In the vase mysterious fling
Pinks and roses gemm'd with dew,   20
Flow'rs of ev'ry varied hue,
Daughters fair of early spring,
Laughing sweet with sapphire eyes,
Or with Iris' mingled dyes:
Then around the basket go,   25
Tripping light with silent pace,

---

*Miss Louisa Bingham, and Miss Frances Molesworth her cousin, decked a basket with ribbands and flowers to hold the nuptial presents.

The Muse Recalled An apt title, for Jones, as he informed Althorp on 16 September 1779, had felt unable to comply with Mrs Poyntz's request for occasional verse: 'I had not written a line of verse these ten years'. The marriage of Althorp's sister, Georgiana, to the Duke of Devonshire five years earlier had tempted Jones to 'renew my acquaintance with the Muse, . . . but poems on such subjects are so common, & praise, however deserved, is so justly liable to the suspicion of flattery, that I left my lyre still hanging on the branches', *Letters*, I.152.

7 *Which in Astræa's fane I fondly hung* The virgin goddess of Justice, represented as holding a pair of scales in one hand, and a sword in the other.

24 *Iris' mingled dyes* Iris was the rainbow messenger of the gods, particularly of Juno, who presided over marriage and childbirth.

While, with solemn voice and slow
Thrice pronouncing, thrice I trace
On the silken texture bright,
Character'd in beamy light,   30
Names of more than mortal pow'r,
Sweetest influence to diffuse;
Names, that from her shadiest bow'r
Draw the soft reluctant muse.

   First, I with living gems enchase   35
The name of Her, whom for this festive day
With zone and mantle elegantly gay
The Graces have adorn'd, herself a Grace,
   MOLESWORTH . . . hark! a swelling note
   Seems on Zephyr's wing to float,   40
Or has vain hope my flatter'd sense beguil'd?
   Next Her, who braided many a flow'r
   To deck her sister's nuptial bow'r,
BINGHAM, with gentle heart and aspect mild:
   The charm prevails . . . I hear, I hear   45
Strains nearer yet, and yet more near.
   Still, ye nymphs and youths, advance,
   Sprinkle still the balmy show'r,
   Mingle still the mazy dance.
Two names of unresisted pow'r,   50
Behold, in radiant characters I write:
O rise! O leave thy secret shrine,
For they, who all thy nymphal train outshine,
DUNCANNON*, heav'nly Muse, and DEVONSHIRE† invite.

   Saw ye not yon myrtle wave?   55
   Heard ye not a warbled strain?
   Yes! the harp, which Clio gave,
   Shall his ancient sound regain.
One dearer name remains. Prepare, prepare!
   She comes . . . how swift th' impatient air   60
   Drinks the rising accent sweet!
   Soon the charm shall be complete.

---

*Lady Henrietta Spencer, second daughter of John earl Spencer, and wife of the lord viscount Duncannon, eldest son of the earl of Besborough.

†Lady Georgiana, eldest daughter of earl Spencer, and wife of William Cavendish, fifth duke of Devonshire.

---

57 *the harp, which Clio gave* The first of the Muses, daughter of Jupiter and Mnemosyne, associated with honour and illustrious reputation.

Return, and wake the silent string;
Return, sweet Muse, for ALTHORP bids me sing.
'Tis she . . . and, as she smiles, the breathing lyre   65
Leaps from his silken bands, and darts ethereal fire.

Bright son of ev'ning, lucid star,
Auspicious rise thy soften'd beam,
Admir'd ere Cynthia's pearly car
O'er heav'n's pure azure spreads her gleam: 70
  Thou saw'st the blooming pair,
  Like thee serenely fair,
By love united and the nuptial vow,
  Thou seest the mirthful train
  Dance to th' unlabour'd strain,   75
Seest bound with myrtle ev'ry youthful brow.
Shine forth, ye silver eyes of night,
And gaze on virtues crown'd with treasures of delight.

And thou, the golden-tressed child of morn,
  Whene'er thy all-inspiring heat   80
Bids bursting rose-buds hill and mead adorn,
See them with ev'ry gift that Jove bestows,
  With ev'ry joy replete,
  Save, when they melt at sight of human woes,

67–104   Cannon suggests that more than three stanzas might have been dedicated to Lavinia Bingham had she 'been less coarse and her father not been North's supporter' (*Life*, p.145). However, the case is more extreme than Cannon states. Of these three stanzas, the first (ll.67–78) is addressed to the evening star that he might shine forth 'on virtues crown'd with treasures of delight'; the second (ll.79–90) implores 'the golden-tressed child of morn' to favour them 'with ev'ry gift that Jove bestows'. This leaves only one stanza dedicated to Lavinia Bingham, and not one word in praise of the bride's beauty, which, despite Walpole's comment ('Mr Jones is not so zealous an idolater at that shrine' [of beauty], *Horace Walpole's Correspondence*, xxxiii.287), seems a remarkable omission in such a poem. The stanza sings the praises of 'LAVINIA's pencil' in its depiction of dignity and grace, and the supreme musical talents of her 'swift fingers', but it is as a creator rather than a creature of beauty that the bride is celebrated. The normally favoured opportunities presented by classical allusion are here neglected, even though such a procedure might have enhanced the heroic stature of his friend. Jones had closed a letter of 1 January congratulating Althorp on the announcement of his engagement: 'Farewell, my dear Æneas, (you know how you acquire this title)'; and on 20 August was to write: 'I shall think those hours the happiest, which I, who am a worse poet, but an honester man than *Virgil*, shall pass with you, who are a better soldier than *Æneas* and as faithful a friend, and with Lady Althorp, who is more amiable as well as more accomplished than the ancient *Lavinia*.' *Letters*, II.455;489.

83   *With ev'ry joy replete*   Although the composition had been virtually extempore, a letter to Althorp of 21 September 1781 reveals the author minutely scrutinizing the printed poem: 'In the sixth stanza the word *replete* occurs in a good sense, though our classical writers, I believe, use it in a bad one as 'replete with *guile* or with *danger*'. (Milton, however, uses the word in both senses, see *Paradise Lost*, 'replete with guile' IX.733, and 'Replete with joy and wonder' XII.468.) After commenting on two Strawberry Hill Press printing errors, he continues: 'The last objection to the Ode, as I have before observed, is fatal; namely that it is very *unpoetical*, because it is very *true*, and in consequence wants the essence of poetry', *Letters*, II.497–8.

Flow smoothly, circling hours,   85
And o'er their heads unblended pleasure pour;
    Nor let your fleeting round
    Their mortal transports bound,
But fill their cup of bliss, eternal pow'rs,
Till time himself shall cease, and suns shall blaze no more.   90

Each morn, reclin'd on many a rose,
LAVINIA's* pencil shall disclose
New forms of dignity and grace,
Th' expressive air, th' impassion'd face,
The curled smile, the bubbling tear,   95
The bloom of hope, the snow of fear,
To some poetick tale fresh beauty give,
And bid the starting tablet rise and live;
Or with swift fingers shall she touch the strings,
And in the magick loom of harmony   100
Notes of such wond'rous texture weave,
As lifts the soul on seraph wings,
    Which, as they soar above the jasper sky,
Below them suns unknown and worlds unnumber'd leave.

While thou, by list'ning crowds approv'd,   105
Lov'd by the Muse and by the poet lov'd,
    ALTHORP, shouldst emulate the fame
Of Roman patriots and th' Athenian name;
Shouldst charm with full persuasive eloquence,
With all thy †mother's grace, and all thy father's sense,   110
    Th' applauding senate; whilst, above they head,
    Exulting Liberty should smile,

*Lady Althorp has an extraordinary talent for drawing historick subjects, and expressing the
passions in the most simple manner.
†Georgiana Poyntz countess Spencer.

95 *curled smile* In expounding Jones's poem to the Countess of Ossory, Walpole writes:
'*Curled smiles*, [sic] . . . is not so beautiful, as the next expression, *the bubbling tear*; but is very
intelligible to anyone who has seen an angel of Correggio, whose mouth is generally curled into a
crescent, and in truth strains grace into almost a grimace', *Horace Walpole's Correspondence*,
xxxiii.287.
105–52 These lines greatly pleased Walpole who remarked that: 'the eighth, ninth, and tenth
stanzas have merit enough to shock Dr Johnson and such sycophant old nurses, and that is enough
for me. How precious is any line of Demosthenes that offended King Philip and the whole court of
Macedon!' *Horace Walpole's Correspondence*, xxxiii.288. Such radical Whig sentiments were
expressed fearlessly despite prejudicing Jones's career.
105–16 It is only with the description of the bridegroom ('Lov'd by the Muse and by the poet
lov'd') that both Jones and his Muse soar skywards; Althorp, emulating the Roman patriot and the
Athenian orator, will gratify 'th'applauding senate', delight 'exulting Liberty', and spread
universal joy.

Then, bidding dragon-born Contention cease,
　　Should knit the dance with meek-ey'd Peace,
　　And by thy voice impell'd should spread　　　　　　115
An universal joy around her cherish'd isle.
But ah! thy publick virtues, youth, are vain
In this voluptuous, this abandon'd age,
　　When Albion's sons with frantick rage,
In crimes alone and recreant baseness bold,　　　　　120
Freedom and Concord, with their weeping train,
Repudiate; slaves of vice, and slaves of gold!
　　They, on starry pinions sailing
　　Through the crystal fields of air,
　　Mourn their efforts unavailing,　　　　　　　　　　125
　　Lost persuasions, fruitless care:
Truth, Justice, Reason, Valour, with them fly
To seek a purer soil, a more congenial sky.

　　Beyond the vast Atlantick deep
A dome by viewless genii shall be rais'd,　　　　　　130
The walls of adamant compact and steep,
The portals with sky-tinctur'd gems emblazed:
There on a lofty throne shall Virtue stand;
To her the youth of Delaware shall kneel;
And, when her smiles rain plenty o'er the land,　　　135
Bow, tyrants, bow beneath th' avenging steel!

117–18 *But ah! thy public virtues, youth! are vain/In this voluptuous, this abandon'd age*　Cf. the congratulatory New Year's day letter to Althorp: '[I] shall be satisfied, if ever it should be said of me, as it was said of Cato, *Urbi pater est urbique maritus*. This quotation has brought gloomy ideas to my mind on the miserable state of our country, which I will not pursue at a time, when you are so happy', (*Letters*, II.454).

129–30 *Beyond the vast Atlantick deep/A dome by viewless genii shall be rais'd*　No mere pleasure dome this, but the new and splendid home for the Muses, the Graces, and all the manly virtues, created by American fighters of tyranny. Jones always admired the American cause and constitution; he favoured re-routing the Grand Tour: 'If young Englishmen had any English spirit, they would finish their education by visiting the United States instead of fluttering about Italy, and strive rather to learn political wisdom from republicans than to pick up a few superficial notions of the fine arts from the poor thralls of bigotry and despotism', (*Letters*, II.821).

136 *Bow, tyrants, bow beneath th'avenging steel!*　Sir Nathaniel William Wraxall (1751–1831), an East India Company judge-advocate and agent for the nawab of Arcot, writes appreciatively of Jones's poetic talents, but it is with regret that he notes: 'He, too, lent his Assistance to the Cause of Rebellion'. After quoting ll.129–36, he adds: 'Here, in a fine Frenzy of Inspiration, he seems to behold as in a Vision, the modern *Washington*, and the Congress met, after successfully throwing off all Subjection to Great Britain. George the Third is pretty clearly designated in the last line, apostrophizing Tyrants', *Historical Memoirs of My Own Time* (3 vols., London: Cadell and Davies, 1818), II.379.

Commerce with fleets shall mock the waves,
And Arts, that flourish not with slaves,
Dancing with ev'ry Grace and ev'ry Muse,
Shall bid the valleys laugh and heav'nly beams diffuse.　140
She ceases; and a strange delight
Still vibrates on my ravish'd ear:
What floods of glory drown my sight!
What scenes I view! What sounds I hear!
This for my friend . . . but, gentle nymphs, no more　145
Dare I with spells divine the Muse recall:
Then, fatal harp, thy transient rapture o'er,
Calm I replace thee on the sacred wall.
Ah, see how lifeless hangs the lyre,
Not lightning now, but glitt'ring wire!　150
Me to the brawling bar and wrangles high
Bright-hair'd Sabrina calls and rosy-bosom'd Wye.

137–8　*Commerce with fleets that mock the waves,/And Arts, that flourish not with slaves*　The juxtaposition of Arts and Commerce here is interesting, as is the idea of American commercial fleets mocking the waves supposedly ruled by Britannia. The reference to slaves combines Jones's utter contempt for the thralls of lust ('slaves of vice, and slaves of gold'), with his outspoken condemnation of the slave trade. See 'A Speech on the Nomination of Candidates', pp.375–6 below.

145–52　The muse having been recalled, Jones himself is recalled to the rigors of the Hereford circuit by 'bright-haired Sabrina' (the nymph of the River Severn) and 'rosy-bosom'd Wye'.

10

An Ode in Imitation of Alcæus (1781)

[The details of the final composition of Jones's most accomplished political poem are contained in a letter to its dedicatee, Viscount Althorp:

Llandovery, 1 April 1781

I send you, my dear lord, a few verses, which contain my system of government, and of morality too. I composed them in my chaise between Abergavenny and Brecon and wrote them down in the mountains of Trecastle. Farewell!

Letters, II.463–4.

Despite the Romantic implication of somewhat spontaneous inspiration, (cf. Jones's 'Essay on the Arts, Commonly Called Imitative', p.337 below), Jones had in fact been working intermittently on this ode since July 1780 (see *Letters*, I.423), and arguably since March 1773 when he had discovered Fragment 29 of Alcæus as quoted by Aristides: 'Not stone and timber, nor the craft of the joiner, make the city; but wheresoever are men who know how to keep themselves safe, there are walls and there a city.' This passage was cited by James Thompson in his Preface to *Areopagitica: A Speech of Mr. John Milton* (London, 1738): 'What makes a city? Not walls and buildings; no – but men, who know themselves to be men, and are sensible that liberty alone exalts them above brutes.'

The poem was privately printed without bibliographical markings and distributed to friends such as Priestley and Franklin. A copy was sent to Dr Samuel Parr, (who had originally provided Jones with the Alcæus fragment), to whom Jones described his poem as '*the last sigh of my departed hope* for a renovation of our free Constitution', *Letters*, II.466. Subsequently it achieved a wider audience being reprinted anonymously by the *Annual Register* of 1781 (vol. 24, p. 183), and the *European Magazine* (vol. 1, February 1782, p. 146). The year 1782 also saw a substantial broadsheet publication (a single leaf in octavo) by the radical Society for Constitutional Information who distributed the poem gratis, adding to its popular accessibility. The dignified and moving rhetoric of the ode struck a timely political chord and 'patriotic Common Councilmen and MPs often dramatically quoted inciting lines', *Life*, p.147. The decorous defiance of these lines is reminiscent of Marvell's *Horatian Ode*. The graceful solidity of the metre, although possibly owing something to Akenside's *Ode to the Honourable Charles Townsend* (1750), has an originality which appealed to later writers such as Felicia Hemans and Emily Brontë. The text followed is the holograph copy which accompanied the letter, (original formerly in Earl Spencer's muniment room, now awaiting cataloguing in the British Library), collated with the 1781 printing, and the 1799 collected edition.]

AN ODE IN IMITATION OF ALCÆUS

Althorp, what forms a state?
Not high-rais'd battlement or labour'd mound,
    Thick wall, and moated gate;
Not cities proud with spires and turrets crown'd;
    Not bays and broad arm'd ports,   5
Where, laughing at the storm, rich navies ride;
    Not starr'd and spangled courts,
Where low-brow'd baseness wafts perfume to Pride;
    No – Men, high-minded men,
With pow'rs as far above dull brutes endued   10
    In forest, brake, or den
As beasts excel cold rocks and brambles rude;
    Men, who their duties know,
But know their rights, and knowing dare maintain,
    Prevent the long-aim'd blow,   15
And crush the tyrant, while they rend the chain;
    These constitute a state,
And sov'reign LAW, that states collected will,

---

7 *Not starr'd and spangled courts* It would be fitting if Jones with his life-long admiration of America should have indirectly inspired its national anthem. It was possibly the words rather than the meaning of this line that lingered in the mind of Francis Scott Key (1779–1843), an American lawyer, who, on seeing the American flag still flying over Fort McHenry after an intensive shelling of Baltimore during the War of 1812, penned the 'The Star-Spangled Banner'.

14 *But know their rights, and knowing dare maintain* In 1795 this line was stamped by the radical bookseller, coin-minter, and member of the London Corresponding Society, Thomas Spence, on a political token. He used tokens to communicate his political message to both literate and illiterate by means of pro-revolutionary iconography. The design of this coin shows three armed soldiers in contemporary uniform, indicating Spence's commitment to 'physical force as a civic duty uniting citizen and soldiery'. Incidentally, Jones was in good radical company as a token dated 1796 bore the sentence 'We also are the people' from Volney's *Ruins of Empire* (ch.XV). The entire poem was quoted in Spence's periodical *Pigs' Meat: or, Lessons for the Swinish Multitude* (vol.I, p.59), the title of which was an ironic radical riposte to Burke's contemptuous description of the people in *Reflections on the Revolution in France* (1791). 'The straightforward egalitarian reading given by Spence to the ode enables it to convey the spirit of Paine and give rebuke to Burke's epithet of "the swinish multitude" since, in Jones's poem, men have "powr's as far above dull brutes" as "beasts excel cold rocks and brambles rude",' David Worrall, *Radical Culture: Discourse, Resistance, and Surveillance 1790–1820* (London, 1992), pp.28–9.

13–20 Cf. Jones's conception of the state as described in a letter to Viscount Althorp of 21 November 1779: 'On another occasion you shall know how widely I differ from *Blackstone*: he defines Law, "a rule prescribed by a superior power." I define it *"The Will of the whole Community as far as it can be collected with convenience"'*, *Letters*, I.333–4.

18 *sov'reign LAW* Jones writes here as a constitutional lawyer; the law, enshrining the collective will of the people is the true sovereign. Cf. 'An Ode in Imitation of Callistratus' (1782): 'Then in

O'er thrones and globes elate
Sits empress, crowning good, repressing ill.   20
    Smit by her sacred frown
The fiend Discretion like a vapour sinks,
    And e'en th' all-dazzling crown
Hides his faint rays and at her bidding shrinks
    Such *was* this heav'n lov'd-isle,   25
Than Lesbos fairer and the Cretan shore!
    No more shall Freedom smile?
Shall *Britons* languish, and be *Men* no more?
    Since all must life resign,
Those sweet rewards, which decorate the brave,   30
    'Tis folly to decline,
And steal inglorious to the silent grave.

Athens all was Peace,/Equal laws and Liberty:/Nurse of Arts, and eye of Greece!/People valiant, firm, and free!' *Works*, X.391–3.

  22 *The fiend Discretion* Cf. the second meaning cited by Johnson in *A Dictionary of the English Language*, 2 vols. (London, 1755): 'Liberty of acting at pleasure; uncontrolled, and unconditional power.' On the radicals' attacks upon discretion in the areas of political patronage, the patron–client nexus in economic relations, and in summary judicial processes, see John Brewer, 'English Radicalism in the Age of George III', in *Three British Revolutions: 1641, 1688, 1776* ed. J. G. A. Pocock (Princeton, 1980), 323–67, pp.347–50.

11

The Enchanted Fruit; or, The Hindu Wife:
An Antediluvian Tale
Written in the Province of Bahar (1784)

[On 12 March 1785 Jones enclosed a copy of 'The Enchanted Fruit' in a letter to Sir John Macpherson, a member of the Supreme Council: 'I send you for your amusement, what has amused me in the composition, a poem on the old philosophy and religion of this country, and you may depend on its orthodoxy.' (*Letters*, II.668–9.) It was published in the first volume of *The Asiatick Miscellany* (Calcutta: Daniel Stuart, 1785, 118–211), which was reprinted in London in 1787.

This elaborate and elegant mock-heroic is based upon the story of princess Draupadī in the *Mahābhārata*. John Parsons in the *Monthly Review* commented: 'let those who have a taste for delicacy, as well as sprightliness and vivacity, gather the fruit for themselves' (76, June 1787, 482). According to Cannon, 'this verse tale set a kind of model that attracted Romantics like Byron and Southey to the form' (*Life*, p. 218). Although it might be claimed that Jones's elaborate footnotes tend to clutter the page, they have been retained to demonstrate the enormous task facing the author in attempting to provide an authentic Indian atmosphere for an audience unfamiliar with most aspects of Hindu culture. They supply detailed references to Hindu mythology, Indian flowers, fruits, and topography. Jones himself thought they might prove distracting, and abandoned the practice with later compositions, preferring to preface an explanatory Argument, but Romantic verse tale authors, desirous of scholarly gravitas, opted for copious notation. The text followed here is that of the first collected edition (1799), collated with *Asiatick Miscellany*.]

THE ENCHANTED FRUIT; OR, THE HINDU WIFE

'O Lovely age,* by *Brahmens* fam'd
'Pure *Setye Yug†* in *Sanscrit* nam'd!
'Delightful ! Not for cups of *gold*,
'Or wives *a thousand centuries* old;
'Or men, degenerate now and small,   5
'Then *one and twenty cubits* tall:
'Not that plump *cows* full udders bore,
'And bowls with *holy curd‡* ran o'er;
'Not that, by Deities defended
'*Fish, Boar, Snake, Lion§*, heav'n-descended, 10
'Learn'd *Pendits*, now grown sticks and clods,
'Redde fast the *Nagry of the Gods* ‖
'And laymen, faithful to *Narayn* ¶
'Believ'd in *Brahmá*'s mystick strain;**
'Not that all Subjects spoke plain truth,   15
'While *Rajas* cherish'd eld and youth,
'No – yet delightful times! because
'*Nature* then reign'd, and *Nature's Laws*;
'When females of the softest kind
'Were unaffected, unconfin'd;   20
'And this grand rule from none was hidden;††
'WHAT PLEASETH, HATH NO LAW FORBIDDEN.'

 Thus, with a lyre in *India* strung,
Aminta's poet would have sung;
And thus too, in a modest way,   25
All virtuous males will sing or say:
But swarthy nymphs of *Hindustan*
Look deeper than short-sighted man,
And thus, in some poetick chime,
Would speak with reason, as with rhyme: 30

---

*A parody on the Ode in *Tasso's Aminta*, beginning, *O bella étá dell' oro!*
†The *Golden Age* of the *Hindus*.
‡Called *Joghrát*, the food of Crishna in his infancy and youth.
§The four first *Avatárs*, or *Incarnations* of the *Divine Spirit*.
‖The *Sanscrit*, or *Sengscrit*, is written in letters so named.
¶*Narayn* or *Náráyan*, the *spirit* of God.
**The *Vayds*, or *Sacred Writings* of *Brahma*, called *Rig, Sám*, and *Yejar*: doubts have been raised concerning the authority of the *fourth*, or *At'herven, Vayd*.
††'Se piace, ei líce.' *Tasso*.

'O lovelier age, by *Brahmens* fam'd,
'Gay *Dwápar Yug* in Sanscrit* nam'd!
'Delightful! though impure with *brass*
'In many a green ill-scented mass;
'Though husbands, but *sev'n* cubits high,   35
'Must in *a thousand summers* die;
'Though, in the lives of dwindled men,
'*Ten* parts were Sin, Religion, *ten*;
'Though *cows* would rarely fill the pail,
'But made th' expected creambowl fail;   40
'Though lazy *Pendits* ill could read
'(No care of ours) their *Yejar Veid*;
'Though *Rajas* look'd a little proud,
'And *Ranies* rather spoke too loud;
'Though *Gods*, display'd to mortal view   45
'In mortal forms, were only *two*;
'(Yet CRISHNA†, sweetest youth, was one,
'*Crishna*, whose cheeks outblaz'd the sun)
'Delightful, ne'ertheless! because
'Not bound by vile unnatural laws,   50
'Which curse this age from *Cáley*‡ nam'd,
'By some base woman-hater fram'd.
'Prepost'rous! that one biped vain
'Should drag ten house-wives in his train,
'And stuff them in a gaudy cage,   55
'Slaves to weak lust or potent rage!
'Not such the *Dwáper Yug*! oh then
'ONE BUXOM DAME MIGHT WED FIVE MEN.'

True History, in solemn terms,
This Philosophick lore confirms;   60

---

*The *Brazen Age*, or that in which Vice and Virtue were in *equal* proportion.
†The *Apollo* of India.
‡The *Earthen* Age, or that of *Caly* or *Impurity*: this verse alludes to *Cáley*, the *Hecate* of the *Indians*.

50–6 The Hindu wife spiritedly rejects the institution of the harem, and the poet uses Indian authority to reverse the sexual politics. Jones detested slavery in any of its manifestations, and described his deep sense of revulsion on witnessing a harem on the island of Hinzuan: 'We saw only two or three miserable creatures with their heads covered, while the favourite, as we supposed, stood behind a coarse curtain, and showed her ankles under it loaded with silver rings; which, if she was capable of reflection, she must have considered as glittering fetters rather than ornaments; but a rational being would have preferred the condition of a wild beast, exposed to perils and hunger in a forest, to the splendid misery of being wife or mistress to Salim', 'Remarks on the Island of Hinzuan or Johanna', *Works*, IV, 269-313, (277–8).

For *India* once, as now cold *Tibet*,*
A groupe unusual might exhibit,
Of sev'ral husbands, free from strife,
Link'd fairly to a single wife!
Thus Botanists, with eyes acute   65
To see prolifick dust minute,
Taught by their learned northern *Brahmen*†
To class by *pistil* and by *stamen*,
Produce from nature's rich dominion
Flow'rs *Polyandrian Monogynian*,   70
Where embryon blossoms, fruits, and leaves
Twenty prepare, and ONE receives.

But, lest my word should nought avail,
Ye Fair, to no unholy tale
Attend.‡ *Five thousand* years§ ago,   75
As annals in *Benares* show,
When *Pándu* chiefs with *Curus* fought,‖
And each the throne imperial sought,
Five brothers of the regal line
Blaz'd high with qualities divine.   80
The first a prince without his peer,
Just, pious, lib'ral *Yudhishteir;*¶
Then *Erjun*, to the base a rod,
An Hero favour'd by a *God;***
Bheima, like mountain-leopard strong,   85
Unrival'd in th' embattled throng,
Bold *Nacul*, fir'd by noble shame
To emulate fraternal fame;
And *Sehdeo*, flush'd with manly grace,
Bright virtue dawning in his face: 90

---

*See the accounts published in the *Philosophical Transactions* from the papers of Mr. *Bogle*.
†*Linnæus*.
‡The story is told by the *Jesuit* BOUCHET, in his Letter to HUET, Bishop of *Avranches*.
§A round number is chosen; but the *Caly Yug*, a little before which *Crishna* disappeared from this world, began *four thousand, eight hundred*, and *eighty four* years ago, that is, according to our Chronologists, *seven hundred* and *forty-seven* before the flood; and by the calculation of *M. Bailly*, but *four hundred* and *fifty-four* after the foundation of the *Indian* empire.
‖This war, which *Crishna* fomented in favour of the *Pandu Prince*, *Yudhishtir*, supplied *Vyás* with the subject of his noble Epick Poem, *Mahábhárat*.
¶This word is commonly pronounced with a strong accent on the last letter, but the preceding vowel is short in *Sengscrit* The prince is called on the Coast *Dherme Ráj*, or Chief Magistrate.
**The *Geita*, containing *Instructions to Erjun*, was composed by *Crishna*, who peculiarly distinguished him.

To these a dame devoid of care,
Blythe *Draupady*, the debonair,
Renown'd for beauty, and for wit,
In wedlock's pleasing chain was knit.*

It fortun'd, at an idle hour,   95
This five-mal'd single-femal'd flow'r
One balmy morn of fruitful May
Through vales and meadows took its way.
A low thatch'd mansion met their eye
In trees umbrageous bosom'd high;   100
Near it (no sight, young maids, for you)
A temple rose to *Mahadew*.†
A thorny hedge and reedy gate
Enclos'd the garden's homely state;
Plain in its neatness: thither wend   105
The princes and their lovely friend.
Light-pinion'd gales, to charm the sense,
Their odorif'rous breath dispense;
From *Béla's*‡ pearl'd, or pointed, bloom,
And *Málty* rich, they steal perfume: 110
There honey-scented *Singarhár*,
And *Júhy*, like a rising star,
Strong *Chempá*, darted by *Cámdew*,
And *Mulsery* of paler hue,
Cayora,§ which the *Ranies* wear   115
In tangles of their silken hair,

Yudhishtir and *Draupady*, called *Drobada* by *M.* Sonnerat, are deified on the Coast; and their feast, of which that writer exhibits an engraving, is named the *Process of Fire*, because she passed *every year from one of her five* husbands to another, after a solemn purification by that element. In the *Bhásh*á language, her name is written, DRÓPTY.

†The *Indian* JUPITER.

‡The varieties of *Bela*, and the *three* flowers next mentioned, are beautiful species of *Jasmin*.

§The *Indian* Spikenard.

---

92   Draupadī, a heroine of the *Mahābhārata*, is often regarded as an incarnation of Śrī-Lakṣmī, with her own cult centred in Tamilnadu. She was granted special dispensation from heaven for her solemn wedding to all the five Pāṇḍava brothers. Draupadī is also the protagonist in a Sanskrit play known to Jones as *The Seizure of the Lock*, see *Sacontalá*, Preface, p.217 below. Drew's speculations (*India and the Romantic Imagination*, pp.64–5) concerning possible Hindu influences on earlier English literature deserve further investigation. On the polyandrous lady herself, see A. Heltebeitel, *The Cult of Draupadī* (Chicago, 1988).

113   *Strong Chempá, darted by Cámdew*' Cf. 'A Hymn to Camdeo', l.55.

114   *Mulsery of paler hue*   The fragrant Bacula which, according to Jones, 'is frequently celebrated in the *Puránas*, and even placed among the flowers of the Hindu paradise', 'Botanical Observations', *Works*, V.110–11.

Round* *Bábul*-flow'rs, and *Gulachein*
Dyed like the shell of Beauty's Queen,
Sweet *Mindy*† press'd for crimson stains,
And sacred *Tulsy*,‡ pride of plains,   120
With *Séwty*, small unblushing rose,
Their odours mix, their tints disclose,
And, as a gemm'd tiara, bright,
Paint the fresh branches with delight.

 One tree above all others tower'd   125
With shrubs and saplings close imbower'd,
For every blooming child of Spring
Paid homage to the verdant King:
Aloft a solitary fruit,
Full sixty cubits from the root,   130
Kiss'd by the breeze, luxuriant hung,
Soft chrysolite with em'ralds strung.
'Try we, said *Erjun* indiscreet,
'If yon proud fruit be sharp or sweet;
'My shaft its parent stalk shall wound: 135
'Receive it, ere it reach the ground.'

 Swift as his word, an arrow flew:
The dropping prize besprent with dew
The brothers, in contention gay,
Catch, and on gather'd herbage lay.   140

 That instant scarlet lightnings flash,
And *Jemna*'s waves her borders lash,
Crishna from *Swerga*'s§ height descends,
Observant of his mortal friends:
Not such, as in his earliest years,   145
Among his wanton cowherd peers,
In *Gocul* or *Brindában*'s‖ glades,
He sported with the dairy-maids;
Or, having pip'd and danc'd enough,
Clos'd the brisk night with *blindman's-buff*;¶   150

---

*The *Mimosa*, or true *Acacia*, that produces the *Arabian* Gum.
†Called *Alhhinná by the Arabs.*
‡Of the kind called *Ocymum.*
§The heaven of *Indra*, or the Empyreum.
‖In the district of *Mat'hura*, not far from *Agra.*
¶This is told in the *Bhágawat.*

(List, antiquaries, and record
This pastime of the *Gopia*'s Lord*)
But radiant with ethereal fire:
Nared alone could bards inspire
In lofty *Slokes*† his mien to trace,   155
And unimaginable grace.
With human voice, in human form,
He mildly spake, and hush'd the storm:
'O mortals, ever prone to ill!
'Too rashly *Erjun* prov'd his skill.   160
'Yon fruit a pious *Muny*‡ owns,
'Assistant of our heav'nly thrones.
'The golden pulp, each month renew'd,
'Supplies him with ambrosial food.
'Should he the daring archer curse,   165
'Not *Mentra*§ deep, nor magick verse,
'Your gorgeous palaces could save
'From flames, your embers, from the wave.‖'

The princes, whom th' immod'rate blaze
Forbids their sightless eyes to raise,   170
With doubled hands his aid implore,
And vow submission to his lore.
'One remedy, and simply one,
'Or take, said he, or be undone:
'Let each his crimes or faults confess,   175
'The greatest name, omit the less;
'Your actions, words, e'en thoughts reveal;
'No part must *Draupady* conceal:
'So shall the fruit, as each applies
'The faithful charm, *ten cubits* rise;   180
'Till, if the dame be frank and true,
'It join the branch, where late it grew.'

---

*GOPY NAT'H, a title of *Crishna*, corresponding with *Nymphagetes*, an epithet of *Neptune*.
†Tetrasticks without rhyme.
‡An inspired Writer: *twenty* are so called.
§Incantation.
‖This will receive illustration from a passage in the *Ramayen*: Even he, who cannot be slain by the ponderous arms of *Indra*, nor by those of *Cály*, nor by the terrible *Checra* (or *Discus*), of *Vishnu*, shall be destroyed, if a *Brahmen* execrate him, *as if he were consumed by fire*.'

---

154 *Nared alone could bards inspire* Nārada was the messenger of the gods, and the inventor of the Indian lute, cf. 'A Hymn to Sereswaty', ll.40–52.

He smil'd, and shed a transient gleam;
Then vanish'd, like a morning dream.

Now, long entranc'd, each waking brother   185
Star'd with amazement on another,
Their consort's cheek forgot its glow,
And pearly tears began to flow;
When *Yudishteir*, high-gifted man,
His plain confession thus began.   190

'Inconstant fortune's wreathed smiles,
'*Duryódhen*'s rage, *Duryódhen*'s wiles,
'Fires rais'd for this devoted head,
'E'en poison for my brethren spread,   195
'My wand'rings through wild scenes of wo,
'And persecuted life, you know.
'Rude wassailers defil'd my halls,
'And riot shook my palace-walls,
'My treasures wasted. This and more
'With resignation calm I bore;   200
'But, when the late-descending god
'Gave all I wish'd with soothing nod,
'When, by his counsel and his aid,
'Our banners danc'd, our clarions bray'd
'(Be this my greatest crime confess'd),   205
'*Revenge* sate ruler in my breast:
'I panted for the tug of arms,
'For skirmish hot, for fierce alarms;
'Then had my shaft *Duryódhen* rent,
'This heart had glow'd with sweet content.'   210

He ceas'd: the living gold upsprung,
And from the bank *ten* cubits hung.

Embolden'd by this fair success,
Next *Erjun* hasten'd to confess:
'When I with *Aswatthámafought*;   215
'My noose the fell assassin caught;

---

189   Yudisthira, leader of the Pāṇḍavas, is the incarnation of Righteousness (*dharma*). As the following stanza makes clear he had gone to the utmost limits to avoid a vengeful war.

192   *Duryódhen's rage* The main story of the *Mahābhārata* concerns the war between the Kauravas, led by Duryodhana, and the Pāṇḍavas (sons of Pāṇḍu), led by Yudhiṣthira. Duryodhana choses to defy Krishna himself.

214   *Erjun* The warrior Arjuna, the son or partial incarnation of Indra, is the bosom-friend of Krishna.

'My spear transfix'd him to the ground:
'His giant limbs firm cordage bound:
'His holy thread extorted awe
'Spar'd by religion and by law;   220
'But, when his murd'rous hands I view'd
'In blameless kindred gore imbued,
'Fury my boiling bosom sway'd,
'And *Rage* unsheath'd my willing blade:
'Then, had not *Crishna*'s arm divine   225
'With gentle touch suspended mine,
'This hand a *Brahmen* had destroy'd,
'And vultures with his blood been cloy'd.'

The fruit, forgiving *Erjun*'s dart,
Ten cubits rose with eager start.   230

Flush'd with some tints of honest shame,
Bheima to his confession came:
' 'Twas at a feast for battles won
'From *Dhriteráshtra*'s guileful son,
'High on the board in vases pil'd   235
'All vegetable nature smil'd:
'Proud *Anaras* * his beauties told,
'His verdant crown and studs of gold,
'To *Dallim*,† whose soft rubies laugh'd
'Bursting with juice, that gods have quaff'd;   240
'Ripe *Kellas* ‡ here in heaps were seen,
'*Kellas*, the golden and the green,
'With *Ambas* § priz'd on distant coasts,
'Whose birth the fertile *Ganga* boasts:
'(Some gleam like silver, some outshine   245
'Wrought ingots from *Besoara*'s mine):
'*Corindas* there, too sharp alone,
'With honey mix'd, impurpled shone;

*Ananas
†Pomegranate
‡Plantains
§Mangos

---

232 Bhīma is one of the elemental forms of Rudra-Śiva, who represents the power of destruction, and performs herculean tasks. He is aptly referred to as 'Wolf-belly' in the *Mahābhārata* 17.2–3.
234 *Dhriteráshtra's guileful son* That is Duryodhana.
235–80 This vast accumulation of fragrantly exotic comestibles represents a formidable mock-epic Hindu feast!

'*Talsans** his liquid crystal spread
'Pluck'd from high *Tara*'s tufted head;   250
'Round *Jamas*† delicate as fair,
'Like rose-water perfum'd the air;
'Bright salvers high-rais'd *Comlas*‡ held
'Like topazes, which *Amrit*§ swell'd;
'While some delicious *Attas*‖ bore,   255
'And *Catels*¶ warm, a sugar'd store;
'Others with *Béla*'s grains were heap'd,
'And mild *Papayas* honey-steep'd;
'Or sweet *Ajéirs* ** the red and pale,
'Sweet to the taste and in the gale.   260
'Here mark'd we purest basons fraught
'With sacred cream and fam'd *Joghrát*;
'Nor saw we not rich bowls contain
'The *Chawla*'s†† light nutritious grain,
'Some virgin-like in native pride,   265
'And some with strong *Haldea*‡‡ dyed,
'Some tasteful to dull palates made
'If *Merich*§§ lend his fervent aid,
'Or *Langa*‖ ‖ shap'd like od'rous nails,
'Whose scent o'er groves of spice prevails,   270
'Or *Adda*,¶¶ breathing gentle heat,
'Or *Joutery*** both warm and sweet.
'*Supiary*††† next (in *Pána*‡‡‡ chewd',
'And *Catha*§§§ with strong pow'rs endued,
'Mix'd with *Elachy*'s‖ ‖ ‖ glowing seeds,   275
'Which some remoter climate breeds),
'Near *Jeifel*¶¶¶ sate, like *Jeifel* fram'd
'Though not for equal fragrance nam'd:
'Last, *Náryal*,**** whom all ranks esteem,
'Pour'd in full cups his dulcet stream: 280
'Long I survey'd the doubtful board
'With each high delicacy stor'd;
'When freely gratified my soul,
'From many a dish, and many a bowl,

*Palmyra-fruit
†Rose-apples
‡Oranges
§The Hindu Nectar
‖Custard-apples
¶Jaik-fruit
**Guayavas
††Rice
‡‡Turmerick
§§Indian Pepper

‖ ‖Cloves
¶¶Ginger
***Mace.
†††Areca-nut
‡‡‡Betel-leaf
§§§What we call Japan-earth
‖ ‖ ‖Cardamums
¶¶¶Nutmeg
****Coconut

'Till health was lavish'd, as my time: 285
'*Intemp'rance* was my fatal crime.'

Uprose the fruit; and now *mid-way*
Suspended shone like blazing day.

Nacal then spoke: (a blush o'erspread
His cheeks, and conscious droop'd his head): 290
'Before *Duryódhen*, ruthless king,
'Taught his fierce darts in air to sing,
'With bright-arm'd ranks, by *Crishna* sent,
'Elate from *Indraprest** I went
'Through *Eastern* realms; and vanquish'd all 295
'From rough *Almóra* to *Nipál*.
'Where ev'ry mansion, new or old,
'Flam'd with Barbarick gems and gold.
'Here shone with pride the regal stores
'On iv'ry roofs, and cedrine floors; 300
'There diadems of price unknown
'Blaz'd with each all-attracting stone;
'Firm diamonds, like fix'd honour true,
'Some pink, and some of yellow hue,
'Some black, yet not the less esteem'd; 305
'The rest like tranquil *Jemna* gleam'd,
'When in her bed the *Gopia* lave
'Betray'd by the pellucid wave.
'Like raging fire the ruby glow'd,
'Or soft, but radiant, water show'd; 310
'Pure amethysts, in richest ore
'Oft found, a purple vesture wore;
'Sapphirs, like yon etherial plain;
'Em'ralds, like *Peipel*† fresh with rain;
'Gay topazes, translucent gold; 315
'Pale chrysolites of softer mould;
'Fam'd beryls, like the surge marine,
'Light-azure mix'd with modest green;
'Refracted ev'ry varying dye,
'Bright as yon bow, that girds the sky. 320
'Here opals, which all hues unite,
'Display'd their many-tinctur'd light,

*DEHLY.
†A sacred tree like an *Aspin*.

---

289 *Nacal* Nakula and Sahadeva are the twin sons of the marvellous Aśvins, who jointly
impregnated the mortal woman Mādrī, the second wife of King Pāṇḍu.

'With turcoises divinely blue
'(Though doubts arise, where first they grew,
'Whether chaste elephantine bone   325
'By min'rals ting'd, or native stone),
'And pearls unblemish'd, such as deck
'*Bhavány*'s * wrist or *Lecshmy*'s † neck.
'Each castle ras'd, each city storm'd,
'Vast loads of pillag'd wealth I form'd,   330
'Not for my coffers; though they bore,
'As you decreed, my lot and more.
'Too pleas'd the brilliant heap I stor'd,
'Too charming seem'd the guarded hoard:
'An odious vice this heart assail'd;   335
'Base *Av'rice* for a time prevail'd.

   Th' enchanted orb *ten* cubits flew,
Strait as the shaft, which *Erjun* drew.

   Sehdio, with youthful ardour bold,
Thus, penitent, his failings told: 340
'From clouds, by folly rais'd, these eyes
'Experience clear'd, and made me wise;
'For, when the crash of battle roar'd,
'When death rain'd blood from spear and sword.
'When, in the tempest of alarms,   345
'Horse roll'd on horse, arms clash'd with arms,
'Such acts I saw by others done,
'Such perils brav'd, such trophies won,
'That, while my patriot bosom glow'd,
'Though some faint skill, some strength I show'd,   350
'And, no dull gazer on the field,
'This hero slew, that forc'd to yield,
'Yet, meek humility, to thee,
'When *Erjun* fought, low sank my knee:
'But, ere the din of war began,   355
'When black'ning cheeks just mark'd the man,
'Myself invincible I deem'd,
'And great, without a rival, seem'd.
'Whene'er I sought the sportful plain,
'No youth of all the martial train   360

*The *Indian* VENUS.
†The *Indian* CERES.

339 *Sehdio* Sahadeva.

'With arm so strong or eye so true
'The *Checra*'s* pointed circle threw;
'None, when the polish'd cane we bent,
'So far the light-wing'd arrow sent;
'None from the broad elastick reed,   365
'Like me, gave *Agnyastra*† speed,
'Or spread its flames with nicer art
'In many an unextinguish'd dart;
'Or, when in imitated fight
'We sported till departing light,   370
'None saw me to the ring advance
'With falchion keen or quiv'ring lance,
'Whose force my rooted seat could shake,
'Or on my steed impression make:
'No charioteer, no racer fleet   375
'O'ertook my wheels or rapid feet.
'Next, when the woody heights we sought,
'With madd'ning elephants I fought:
'In vain their high-priz'd tusks they gnash'd;
'Their trunked heads my *Geda*‡ mash'd.   380
'No buffalo, with phrensy strong,
'Could bear my clatt'ring thunder long:
'No pard or tiger, from the wood
'Reluctant brought, this arm withstood.
'*Pride* in my heart his mansion fix'd,   385
'And with pure drops black poison mix'd.

Swift rose the fruit, exalted now
Ten cubits from his natal bough.

Fair *Draupady* with soft delay,
Then spake: 'Heav'n's mandate I obey;   390
'Though nought, essential to be known.
'Has heav'n to learn, or I to own.
'When scarce a damsel, scarce a child,
'In early bloom your handmaid smil'd,
'*Love of the World* her fancy mov'd,   395
'Vain pageantry her heart approv'd:
'Her form, she thought, and lovely mien,
'All must admire, when all had seen:

*A radiated metalline ring, used as a missile weapon.
†Fire-arms, or rockets, early known in *India*.
‡A mace, or club.

'A thirst of pleasure and of praise
'(With shame I speak) engross'd my days;   400
'Nor were my night-thoughts, I confess,
'Free from solicitude for dress;
'How best to bind my flowing hair
'With art, yet with an artless air
'(My hair, like musk in scent and hue;   405
'Oh! blacker far and sweeter too);
'In what nice braid or glossy curl
'To fix a diamond or a pearl,
'And where to smooth the love-spread toils
'With nard or jasmin's fragrant oils;   410
'How to adjust the golden *Teic*,*
'And most adorn my forehead sleek;
'What *Condals*† should emblaze my ears,
'Like *Seita*'s waves‡ or *Seita*'s tears;§
'How elegantly to dispose   415
'Bright circlets for my well-form'd nose;
'With strings of rubies how to deck,
'Or em'rald rows, my stately neck,
'While some that ebon tow'r embrac'd,
'Some pendent sought my slender waist;   420
'How next my purfled veil to chuse
'From silken stores of varied hues;
'Which would attract the roving view,
'Pink, violet, purple, orange, blue;
'The loveliest mantle to select,   425
'Or unembellish'd or bedeck'd;
'And how my twisted scarf to place
'With most inimitable grace;
'(Too thin its warp, too fine its woof,
'For eyes of males not beauty-proof);   430
'What skirts the mantle best would suit,
'Ornate with stars or tissued fruit,
'The flow'r-embroider'd or the plain
'With silver or with golden vein;

*Properly *Teica*, an ornament of gold, placed above the nose.
†Pendents.
‡Seita Cund, or the *Pool of Seitá*, the wife of Ram, is the name given to the wonderful spring at *Mengeir*, with boiling water of exquisite clearness and purity.
§Her tears, when she was made captive by the giant *Ráwan*.

401–40   This lengthy passage, complete with Jones's notes, is quoted by Southey in the notes to *The Curse of Kehama*, (which, incidentally, contain twenty-one quotations from Jones amidst a plethora of references to *Asiatick Researches*), see *Poetical Works* (London, 1838), VIII.300–1.

'The *Chury** bright, which gayly shows 435
'Fair objects, aptly to compose;
'How each smooth arm and each soft wrist
'By richest *Cosecs*† might be kiss'd;
'While some, my taper ankles round,
'With sunny radiance ting'd the ground. 440
'O waste of many a precious hour!
'O *Vanity*, how vast thy pow'r!'

    Cubits twice four th' ambrosial flew,
Still from its branch disjoin'd by *two*.

    Each husband now, with wild surprise, 445
His compeers and his consort eyes;
When *Yudishteir*: 'Thy female breast
'Some faults, perfidious, hath suppress'd.
'Oh! give the close-lock'd secret room,
'Unfold its bud, expand its bloom; 450
'Lest, sinking with our crumbled halls,
'We see red flames devour their walls.'
Abash'd, yet with a decent pride,
Firm *Draupady* the fact denied;
Till, through an arched alley green, 455
The limit of that sacred scene,
She saw the dreaded *Muny* go
With steps majestically slow;
Then said: (a stifled sigh she stole,
And show'd the conflict of her soul 460
By broken speech and flutt'ring heart)
'One trifle more I must impart:
'A *Brahmen* learn'd, of pure intent
'And look demure, one morn you sent,
'With me, from *Sanscrit* old, to read 465
'Each high *Purán*‡ each holy *Veid*
'His thread, which *Brehmá*'s lineage show'd,
'O'er his left shoulder graceful flow'd;
'Of *Crishna* and his nymphs he redde,
'How with nine maids the dance he led; 470
'How they ador'd, and he repaid
'Their homage in the sylvan shade.

---

*A small mirror worn in a ring.
†Bracelets.
‡A Mythological and Historical Poem.

'While this gay tale my spirits cheer'd,
'So keen the *Pendit*'s eyes appear'd,
'So sweet his voice–a blameless fire   475
'This bosom could not but inspire.
'Bright as a God he seem'd to stand:
'The rev'rend volume left his hand,
'With mine he press'd' – With deep despair
Brothers on brothers wildly stare: 480
From *Erjun* flew a wrathful glance;
Tow'rd them they saw their dread advance;
Then, trembling, breathless, pale with fear,
'Hear, said the matron, calmly hear!
'By *Tulsy*'s leaf the truth I speak –   485
'The *Brahmen* ONLY KISS'D MY CHEEK.'

Strait its full height the wonder rose,
Glad with its native branch to close.

Now to the walk approach'd the Sage
Exulting in his verdant age: 490
His hands, that touch'd his front, express'd
Due rev'rence to each princely guest,
Whom to his rural board he led
In simple delicacy spread,
With curds their palates to regale,   495
And cream-cups from the *Gopia*'s pail.

Could you, ye Fair, like this black wife,
Restore us to primeval life,
And bid that apple, pluck'd for *Eve*
By him, who might all wives deceive,   500
Hang from its parent bough once more
Divine and perfect, as before,
Would you confess your little faults?
(Great ones were never in your thoughts);
Would you the secret wish unfold,   505
Or in your heart's full casket hold?
Would you disclose your inmost mind,
And speak plain truth, to bless mankind?

497–502   Despite the playful tone, it is typical of Jones's comparativist stance to reflect upon the significance of Hindu and Judaic fruit; the Eden narrative is seen to lack this opportunity of restoration, the judgement seems arbitrary and irrevocable.

'What! said the Guardian of our realm,
With waving crest and fiery helm,   510
'What! are the fair, whose heav'nly smiles
'Rain glory through my cherish'd isles,
'Are they less virtuous or less true
'Than *Indian* dames of sooty hue?
'No, by these arms. The cold surmise   515
'And doubt injurious vainly rise.
'Yet dares a bard, who better knows,
'This point distrustfully propose;
'Vain fabler now! though oft before
'His harp has cheer'd my sounding shore.'   520

With brow austere the martial maid
Spoke, and majestick trod the glade:
To that fell cave her course she held,
Where *Scandal*, bane of mortals, dwell'd.
Outstretch'd on filth the pest she found,   525
Black fetid venom streaming round;
A gloomy light just serv'd to show
The darkness of the den below.
Britannia with resistless might
Soon dragg'd him from his darling night: 530
The snakes, that o'er his body curl'd,
And flung his poison through the world,
Confounded with the flash of day,
Hiss'd horribly a hellish lay.
His eyes with flames and blood suffus'd,   535
Long to th' ethereal beam unus'd,
Fierce in their gory sockets roll'd;
And desperation made him bold:
Pleas'd with the thought of human woes,
On scaly dragon feet he rose.   540
Thus, when *Asúrs* with impious rage,
Durst horrid war with *Dévta's* wage,
And darted many a burning mass
E'en on the brow of gemm'd *Cailás*,

509–20   The challenge to British womanhood is proudly answered by Britannia herself, and the
poet is sharply rebuked.
   541   *Asúrs*   These demons or antigods of the *Rig-Veda* are shape-shifters, both frightening and
formidable in battle.
   542   *Dévtas*   Deities.
   544   *the brow of gemm'd Cailás*   Kailāsa, the Pleasure Mountain.

High o'er the rest, on serpents rear'd,   545
The grisly kind of *Deits* appear'd.

The nymph beheld the fiend advance,
And couch'd her far-extending lance:
Dire drops he threw; th' infernal tide
Her helm and silver hauberk dyed: 550
Her moonlike shield before her hung;
The monster struck, the monster stung:
Her spear with many a griding wound
Fast nail'd him to the groaning ground.
The wretch, from juster vengeance free,   555
Immortal born by heav'n's decree,
With chains of adamant secur'd,
Deep in cold gloom she left immur'd.

Now reign at will, victorious Fair,
In *British*, or in *Indian*, air!   560
Still with each envying flow'r adorn
Your tresses radiant as the morn;
Still let each *Asiatick* dye
Rich tints for your gay robes supply;
Still through the dance's labyrinth float,   565
And swell the sweetly lengthen'd note;
Still, on proud steeds or glitt'ring cars,
Rise on the course like beamy stars;
And, when charm'd circles round you close
Of rhyming bards and smiling beaux,   570
Whilst all with eager looks contend
Their wit or worth to recommend,
Still let your mild, yet piercing, eyes,
Impartially adjudge the prize.

---

546 *Deits* Underworld genii (*daityas*). Their king is Bali.

547–58 The evocation of Britannia victorious over an Indian demon, even within the humorous context of this poem, might seem to cast Jones in a glaringly Eurocentric light. Only a miniscule proportion of his metropolitan audience would recognize the ambiguities created by the fact that Śiva himself had already defeated the same demon.

553 *with many a griding wound* Cf. *Paradise Lost*, VI.329.

559–60 *Now reign at will, victorious Fair,/In British, or in Indian, air!* In Jones's revised plan for his long-projected epic *Britain Discovered* the idea of Anglo-Indian conflict is placed on a very different basis. The goddess Gangá urges violent opposition to *Britan* to prevent his foundation of a nation, 'who will possess themselves of her banks, profane her waters, mock the temples of the *Indian* divinities, appropriate the wealth of their adorers, introduce new laws, a new religion, a new government, insult the *Bráhmens*, and disregard the sacred ordinances of *Brihmá*', *Works*, II.445–6.

12

A Hymn to Camdeo (1784)

[This, the first of a series of nine hymns to Hindu deities, is addressed to Camdeo or Kāma the god of love, whose consort is Rati, or sexual desire. Inspired by Jones's reading of Persian translations of the *Bhaviṣya-purāṇa*, the *Bhāgavata Purāṇa* and the *Yogavāsiṣṭha* it celebrates fertility and the processes of creation. Kāma is described in the *Rig-Veda* as the fundamental cohesive bond of the cosmos, the 'first seed of mind' (*Rig-Veda* x.194.4).

Despite a punishing judicial schedule Jones made time to further his studies of the Hindu divinities. In a hurried note from the Courthouse of 15 December 1783 Jones enquired of his friend Richard Johnson if he could supply 'some poetical names of places in India, where *Camdeo* may be supposed to resort, like the *Cyprus* and *Paphos* of the Grecian and Roman deities'. By the 6 January 1784, a proof of 'my Hymn to *Cāmdew*' was sent in another brief note from the Courthouse to the senior Company merchant and Sanskrit scholar, Charles Wilkins, requesting comments and corrections. (*Letters*, II. 624–5)

The hymn was well received by the newly formed Asiatic Society who declared that it was the first correct specimen of Hindu mythology yet to appear. It was first published in *A discourse on the institution of a society*, (London: T. Payne and Son, 1784), together with his First Charge to the Grand Jury. On the title page the hymn was announced as having been 'translated from the Hindú into Persian, and from the Persian into English'. Although labouring under the misapprehension that the work was a direct translation, the London reviewers were as complimentary as the Calcutta audience, and again authenticity was a quality singled out for praise. Charles Burney in the *Monthly Review* declared that the hymn 'will equally delight the admirers of genuine and elegant poetry, and lovers of Eastern allegory', (71, Nov. 1784, 357). It was reprinted in Francis Gladwin's *Asiatic Miscellany* of 1785 in Calcutta, while in London the *Annual Register* also printed it in full (1784–5, pp.137–8). It was not until 1796 that the poem was revealed as an original work, see *Monthly Review* N.S. 21, Oct. 1796, 181. The copy text is that of 1799.]

THE ARGUMENT

The *Hindú* God, to whom the following poem is addressed, appears evidently the same with the *Grecian* EROS and the *Roman* CUPIDO; but the *Indian* description of his person and arms, his family, attendants, and attributes, has new and peculiar beauties.

According to the mythology of *Hindustán*, he was the son of MAYA, or the general *attracting* power, and married to RETTY or *Affection*; and his bosom friend is BESSENT or *Spring*: he is represented as a beautiful youth, sometimes conversing with his mother and consort in the midst of his gardens and temples; sometimes riding by moonlight on a parrot or lory, and attended by dancing girls or nymphs, the foremost of whom bears his colours, which are a *fish* on a red ground. His favourite place of resort is a large tract of country round AGRA, and principally the plains of *Matra*, where KRISHEN also and the nine GOPIA, who are clearly the *Apollo* and *Muses* of the *Greeks*, usually spend the night with musick and dance. His bow of sugar-cane or flowers, with a string of bees, and his *five* arrows, each pointed with an *Indian* blossom of a heating quality, are allegories equally new and beautiful. He has at least twenty-three names, most of which are introduced in the hymn: that of *Cám* or *Cáma* signifies *desire*, a sense which it also bears in ancient and modern *Persian*; and it is possible, that the words *Dipuc* and *Cupid*, which have the same signification, may have the same origin; since we know, that the old *Hetruscans*, from whom great part of the *Roman* language and religion was derived, and whose system had a near affinity with that of the *Persians* and *Indians*, used to write their lines alternately forwards and backwards, as furrows are made by the plough; and, though the two last letters of *Cupido* may be only the grammatical termination, as in *libido* and *capedo*, yet the primary root of *cupio* is contained in the three first letters. The seventh stanza alludes to the bold attempt of this deity to wound the great God *Mahadeo*, for which he was punished by a flame consuming his corporeal nature and reducing him to a mental essence; and hence his chief dominion is over the *minds* of mortals, or such deities as he is permitted to subdue.

HYMN TO CAMDEO

THE HYMN

What potent God from *Agra*'s orient bow'rs
Floats thro' the lucid air, whilst living flow'rs
With sunny twine the vocal arbours wreathe,
And gales enamour'd heav'nly fragrance breathe?
    Hail, pow'r unknown! for at thy beck   5
    Vales and groves their bosoms deck,
    And ev'ry laughing blossom dresses
    With gems of dew his musky tresses.
I feel, I feel thy genial flame divine,
And hallow thee and kiss thy shrine.   10

'Knowst thou not me?' Celestial sounds I hear!
'Knowst thou not me?' Ah, spare a mortal ear!
'Behold' – My swimming eyes entranc'd I raise,
But oh! they shrink before th' excessive blaze.
    Yes, son of *Maya*, yes, I know   15
    Thy bloomy shafts and cany bow,
    Cheeks with youthful glory beaming,
    Locks in braids ethereal streaming,
Thy scaly standard, thy mysterious arms,
And all thy pains and all thy charms.   20

Jones did translate a Sanskrit 'Hymn to CÁMA' from the *Bhaviṣya-purāṇa* which is given here to demonstrate how Jones's hymns lie firmly within an English poetic tradition:
    '1. Hail, God of the flowery bow; hail warrior with a fish on thy banner; hail, powerful divinity, who causeth the firmness of the sage to forsake him, and subduest the guardian deities of eight regions!
    2. O, CANDARPA, thou son of MÁDHAVA! O, MÁRA, thou foe of SAMBHARA! Glory be given to thee, who lovest the goddess RETI; to thee, by whom all worlds are subdued; to thee, who springest from the heart!
    3. Glory be to MADANA, to CÁMA; to Him, who is formed as the God of Gods; to Him, by whom BRAHMÁ, VISHNU, SIVA, INDRA, are filled with emotions of rapture!
    4. May all my mental cares be removed, all my corporeal sufferings terminate! May the object of my soul be attained, and my felicity continue for ever!'
                            'The Lunar Year of the Hindus', *Works*, IV.149.

15   *son of Maya* The spell-binding power of illusion.
16   His five flower-tipped arrows are fired from a sugar-cane bow, the bowstring is made of bees, cf. ll.50–51.
19   *Thy scaly standard, thy mysterious arms* His emblem and vehicle is the *makara*, a shark-like sea-monster or crocodile, cf. *Gítagóvinda* 1.82. Kāma's other mode of conveyance was a parrot or lory, see Jones's Argument; and l. 73.

God of each lovely sight, each lovely sound,
Soul-kindling, world-inflaming, star-ycrown'd,
Eternal *Cáma*! Or doth *Smara* bright,
Or proud *Ananga* give thee more delight?
    Whate'er they seat, whate'er thy name,   25
    Seas, earth, and air, thy reign proclaim;
    Wreathy smiles and roseate pleasures
    Are thy richest, sweetest treasures.
All animals to thee their tribute bring,
And hail thee universal king.   30

Thy consort mild, *Affection* ever true,
Graces thy side, her vest of glowing hue,
And in her train twelve blooming girls advance,
Touch golden strings and knit the mirthful dance.
    Thy dreaded implements they bear,   35
    And wave them in the scented air,
    Each with pearls her neck adorning,
    Brighter than the tears of morning.
Thy crimson ensign, which before them flies,
Decks with new stars the sapphire skies.   40

God of the flow'ry shafts and flow'ry bow,
Delight of all above and all below!
Thy lov'd companion, constant from his birth,
In heav'n clep'd *Bessent*, and gay *Spring* on earth,
    Weaves thy green robe and flaunting bow'rs,   45
    And from thy clouds draws balmy show'rs,
    He with fresh arrows fills thy quiver,
    (Sweet the gift and sweet the giver!)
And bids the many-plumed warbling throng
Burst the pent blossoms with their song.   50

---

22 *world-inflaming* 'One of his many epithets is *Dípaca*, the *Inflamer*', see 'On the Gods of Greece, Italy, and India', *Works*, III.368.

23-4 Camdeo has a variety of epithets which reveal aspects of his nature: *Cáma*, or Kāma, is love; *Smara* is (sweet) memory; *Ananga* is unbodied one.

31 *Thy consort mild, Affection ever true* Jones manages to convey a type of marital fidelity which ill beseems either an Oriental or an Occidental Eros. It is true that, as sexual enjoyment, *Rati* became personified as wife of Kāma, along with *Prīti* who is also synonymous with erotic delight.

44 *In heav'n clep'd Bessent, and gay Spring on earth* Vasanta, or Spring, appears also in the hymns to Sereswaty (126-7), Súrya (131-2), Durgá (II.3.4-7; III.3; XI.1.5-8).

He bends the luscious cane, and twists the string
With bees, how sweet! but ah, how keen their sting!
He with five flow'rets tips thy ruthless darts,
Which thro' five senses pierce enraptur'd hearts:
 Strong *Chumpa*, rich in od'rous gold,   55
 Warm *Amer*, nurs'd in heav'nly mould,
 Dry *Nagkeser* in silver smiling,
 Hot *Kiticum* our sense beguiling,
And last, to kindle fierce the scorching flame,
Loveshaft, which Gods bright *Bela* name.   60

Can men resist thy pow'r, when *Krishen* yields,
Krishen, who still in *Matra*'s holy fields
Tunes harps immortal, and to strains divine
Dances by moonlight with the *Gopia* nine?

51–2   *twists the string/With bees, how sweet! but ah, how keen their sting!*   The conventional Indian sexual image of the bee as lover (the Sanskrit word *bhramara* means both 'bee' and 'paramour') penetrating the virginal flowers and producing both honey and pleasurable pain is frequently enlisted in descriptions of Kāma's (also obviously phallic) arrows. Cf. Jones's translation of Jayadéva: 'The full-blown *Cēsara* gleams like the sceptre of the world's monarch, Love; and the pointed thyrse of the *Cētaca* resembles the darts, by which lovers are wounded. See the bunches of *Pātali*-flowers filled with bees, like the quiver of SMARA full of shafts', (*Gítagóvinda*, ll.31–5)

53–60   Kāma's five arrows are made of five fragrant flowers which inspire lust. Cf. the emphases upon the sensual and emblematic qualities of flowers in *Gítagóvinda*, esp. ll.22–45; 416–20.

55   *Strong Chumpa, rich in od'rous gold*   In his 'Botanical Observations on Select Indian Plants', Sir William Jones writes of 'The strong aromatick scent of the gold-coloured *Champac*', and of the elegant appearance of its blossoms on the black hair of Indian women', *Works*, V.128–9. While Jones was sending seeds and roots of Indian plants to Sir Joseph Banks and the Royal Society, his poems exported 'a nosegay of oriental flowers' (*Letters*, II.786) which was to scent much Romantic Orientalism, see, for example, Shelley's reference to 'Champak odours' in the second stanza of 'The Indian Serenade'.

56   *Warm Amer, nurs'd in heav'nly mould* displays   '*leaflets* mostly five-paired, egg-oblong', *Works* V.125. 'heav'nly mould' presumably refers to the golden egg in which Brahmā was born.

57   Jones writes of the *Nagkeser*, 'the tree is one of the most beautiful on earth, and the delicious odour of its blossoms justly gives these a place in the quiver of CÁMADÉVA. In the poem, called *Naishadha*, there is a wild, but elegant, couplet, where the poet compares the white of the *Nágacésara*, from which the bees were scattering pollen of the numerous gold-coloured anthers, to an alabaster wheel, on which CÁMA was whetting his arrows, while sparks of fire were dispersed in every direction . . . a flower with petals like silver and anthers like gold', *Works*, V.139–40.

58   *Hot Kiticum our sense beguiling*   Possibly the *Cētaca*, or *Pandanus*, of which Jones writes: 'the flowers . . . are celebrated in *Sanscrit*, by poets for their colour or scent, and by physicians for their medical uses', 'On the Fruit of the Mellori', *Works* V.53–4. See also *Gítagóvinda*, ll.42–3, and 'A Hymn to Bhaváni', ll.61–2.

60   *Loveshaft, which Gods bright Bela name*   A beautiful species of Jasmine, see 'The Enchanted Fruit', l.109 and note. See also The Argument to *Two Hymns to Pracriti*, pp.164–7.

61–4   This reconciliation of profane and sacred love in which Krishna sports with the *Gopīs*, or milkmaids, is the central theme of *Gítagóvinda*.

But, when thy daring arm untam'd   65
At *Mahadeo* a loveshaft aim'd,
  Heav'n shook, and, smit with stony wonder,
  Told his deep dread in bursts of thunder,
Whilst on thy beauteous limbs an azure fire
Blaz'd forth, which never must expire.   70

O thou for ages born, yet ever young,
For ages may thy *Bramin*'s lay be sung!
And, when thy lory spreads his em'rald wings,
To waft thee high above the tow'rs of kings,
  Whilst o'er thy throne the moon's pale light   75
  Pours her soft radiance thro' the night,
  And to each floating cloud discovers
  The haunts of blest or joyless lovers,
Thy mildest influence to thy bard impart,
To warm, but not consume, his heart.   80

65ff. Cf. *Śiva Purāṇa* 2.2.2. 30–6: '[Brahmā] said to Kāma, 'Enchant men and women with your five flower arrows and your own beauty, maintaining creation eternally. No one will be able to withstand you – not even Viṣṇu and Śiva and I', (trans. Wendy O'Flaherty, *Asceticism and Eroticism in the Mythology of Śiva* (London, 1975), p.118. In the attempt to rouse *Mahadeo*, or Śiva, from his deeply ascetic meditation, and fill him with sexual desire for Pārvāti, Kāma loosed a love-shaft, but the terrible fire of Śiva's asceticism reduced the love-god to ashes. This episode is recounted in fuller detail in 'A Hymn to Durgá', VIII.1–IX.1.

13

A Hymn to Náráyena (1785)

[Jones's nine hymns on Hindu deities represent his most impressive poetic achievement, and 'A Hymn to Náráyena' is, arguably, the most successful. He had always maintained that a study of Oriental cultures would invigorate European culture, see 'Essay on the Poetry of Eastern Nations' (1772) p.319 below, but this hymn demonstrates that Jones's approach was not simply to ransack Asia for portable literary treasures. This hymn explores the mysterious relationship between the 'Infinite Being' and the transient manifestations of his energized and exhilarating Creation, using the majestic structure of the Pindaric Ode to realize the power of the Omniscient Spirit. It is insufficient merely to view 'A Hymn to Náráyena' as a bridge between the Neoclassicism of Pope's *Essay on Man* and Romantic mystical pantheism of Shelley's 'Hymn to Intellectual Beauty'. Jones's originality here, as in the other hymns, lies in his exploration of the analogies between God's action in the formation of the world and the poet's act of creation. These poems thus, as John Drew has pointed out, 'implicitly deal with their own nature even while they deal explicitly with the nature of existence', (*India and the Romantic Imagination*, pp.73–4).

Jones's prefatory Argument to 'A Hymn to Náráyena' with its valuable insights into the substantial overlap of the artistic and the religious, the philosophic and the literary is in itself a seminal document in the history of Romanticism, in some ways supplementing his earlier *Essay on the Arts, Commonly Called Imitative* (1772), long acknowledged as a fascinating *locus* for pre-Romantic literary criticism. Recently Jerome McGann underlined his conviction that the Argument might be used as an epigraph for a collection of Romantic writing by placing 'A Hymn to Náráyena' as the opening text of his *New Oxford Book of Romantic Period Verse* (Oxford, 1993).

With its emphasis upon the the seminal and amniotic waters of creation, upon creativity and the nature of perception, 'A Hymn to Náráyena' and indeed the whole series of nine hymns anticipated, and helped to shape, Romantic preoccupations with these themes. The hymns represent an influential poetic illustration of Jones's signal intellectual achievement in appreciating and documenting the links between Vedantic doctrines and Platonic thought, providing a weighty corrective to European prejudice which veered between titillated horror at the monstrous images of Hinduism and patronizing admiration for the meek, effeminate, and patient Hindoo.

On 14 April 1785 Jones sent a draft of this hymn to Charles Wilkins with a request for '*more of his names &c.,* that I may insert them in another stanza.' (*Letters*, II, 669–70) These were subsequently used in the construction of the fifth stanza. It was first published in the *Asiatic Miscellany* of 1785 (I, 22–8), being reprinted in both the *Gentleman's Magazine* (57, Feb. 1787, 108–10) and *Dissertations and Miscellaneous Pieces* (II, 1792, 351–6). The *Critical Review* (63, April 1787, 266–9) lauded and generously quoted the poem, and John Parsons, writing for the *Monthly Review*, declared the hymn 'very poetically conceived, and vigorously, as well as elegantly, expressed' (77, May 1787, 417–19). The text followed is that of 1799, collated with the poet's private Calcutta printing (Althorp Papers).]

THE ARGUMENT

A COMPLETE introduction to the following Ode would be no less than a full comment on the VAYDS and PURÁNS of the HINDUS, the remains of *Egyptian* and *Persian* Theology, and the tenets of the *Ionick* and *Italick* Schools; but this is not the place for so vast a disquisition. It will be sufficient here to premise, that the inextricable difficulties attending the *vulgar notion* of   5
material substances, concerning which

'We know this only, that we nothing know,'

induced many of the wisest among the Ancients, and some of the most enlightened among the Moderns, to believe, that the whole Creation was rather an *energy* than a *work*, by which the Infinite Being, who is present at   10
all times in all places, exhibits to the minds of his creatures a set of perceptions, like a wonderful picture or piece of musick, always varied, yet always uniform; so that all bodies and their qualities exist, indeed, to every wise and useful purpose, but exist only as far they are *perceived*; a theory no less pious than sublime, and as different from any principle of Atheism, as   15
the brightest sunshine differs from the blackest midnight. This *illusive operation* of the Deity the *Hindu* philosophers call, MÁYÁ, or *Deception*; and the word occurs in this sense more than once in the commentary on the *Rig Vayd*, by the great VASISHTHA, of which Mr. HALHED has given us an admirable specimen.   20

The first stanza of the Hymn represents the sublimest attributes of the Supreme Being, and the three forms, in which they most clearly appear to us, *Power*, *Wisdom*, and *Goodness*, or, in the language of ORPHEUS and his disciples, *Love*: the *second* comprises the *Indian* and *Egyptian* doctrine of the Divine Essence and Archetypal *Ideas*; for a distinct account of which the   25
reader must be referred to a noble description in the sixth book of PLATO's *Republick*; and the fine explanation of that passage in an elegant discourse by the author of CYRUS, from whose learned work a hint has been borrowed for

---

7 'We know this only, that we nothing know' Cf. Pope's *Essay on Man* IV.260–1.

19 Mr. HALHED Jones's friend Nathaniel Brassey Halhed, whose *A Code of Gentoo Laws* (London, 1776) contained a translation of Vasishtha's commentary. On Halhed, who in the early years of the nineteenth century also wrote some hymns to Hindu deities, see Rosane Rocher, *Orientalism, Poetry, and the Millenium: The Checkered Life of Nathaniel Brassey Halhed 1751–1831* (Delhi, 1983).

28 *the author of* CYRUS John Hoole (1727–1803), poet, playwright (*Cyrus* received its first performance on 3 Dec. 1768), and translator, published no discourse on Plato, but as Hoole was also a member of Johnson's circle, Jones might well have had access to such a work in manuscript.

the conclusion of this piece. The *third* and *fourth* are taken from the Institutes of MENU, and the eighteenth *Puran* of VYÁSÁ, entitled *Srey Bhagawat*, part of which has been translated into *Persian*, not without elegance, but rather too paraphrastically. From BREHME, or the *Great Being*, in the *neuter* gender, is formed BREHMÁ, in the *masculine*; and the second word is appropriated to the *creative power* of the Divinity. 30

The spirit of GOD, call'd NÁRÁYENA, or *moving on the water*, has a multiplicity of other epithets in *Sanscrit*, the principal of which are introduced, expressly or by allusion, in the *fifth* stanza; and two of them contain the names of the *evil beings*, who are feigned to have sprung from the ears of VISHNU; for thus the divine spirit is entitled, when considered as the *preserving power*: the *sixth* ascribes the perception of *secondary* qualities by our *senses* to the immediate influence of MÁYÁ; and the *seventh* imputes to her operation the *primary* qualities of *extension* and *solidity*. 35 40

THE HYMN

Spirit of Spirits, who, through ev'ry part
  Of space expanded and of endless time,
  Beyond the stretch of lab'ring thought sublime,
  Badst uproar into beauteous order start,
    Before Heav'n was, Thou art: 5
Ere spheres beneath us roll'd or spheres above,
  Ere earth in firmamental ether hung,
  Thou satst alone; till, through thy mystick Love,
  Things unexisting to existence sprung,
    And grateful descant sung.   10
What first impell'd thee to exert thy might?
  Goodness unlimited. What glorious light
  Thy pow'r directed? Wisdom without bound.
  What prov'd it first? Oh! guide my fancy right;
    Oh! raise from cumbrous ground   15
    My soul in rapture drown'd,
  That fearless it may soar on wings of fire;
For Thou, who only knowst, Thou only canst inspire.

Wrapt in eternal solitary shade,
  Th' impenetrable gloom of light intense,   20
  Impervious, inaccessible, immense,
  Ere spirits were infus'd or forms display'd,
    BREHM his own Mind survey'd,

1–23 With this essentially Deist conception of the immortal invisible, cf. the Epode, part of a proposed tragedy on the story of Sohrâb, found by Teignmouth among Jones's papers: 'What power, beyond all pow'rs elate,/Sustains this universal frame?/'Tis not nature, 'tis not fate,/'Tis not the dance of atoms blind,/Etherial space, or subtile flame;/No; 'tis one vast eternal mind,/Too sacred for an earthly name./He forms, pervades, directs the whole;/Not like the macrocosm's imag'd soul,/But provident of endless good,/By ways not seen, nor understood,/Which e'en his angels vainly might explore./High, their highest thoughts above,/Truth, wisdom, justice, mercy, love,/Wrought in his heav'nly essence, blaze and soar./Mortals, who his glory seek,/Rapt in contemplation meek,/Him fear, him trust, him venerate, him adore', *Works*, II.512–13.

23 *BREHM his own Mind survey'd* 'the learned *Indians*, as they are instructed by their own books, acknowledge only One Supreme Being, whom they call BRAHME, or THE GREAT ONE in the neuter gender: they believe his Essence to be infinitely removed from the comprehension of any mind but his own; and they suppose him to manifest his power by the operation of his divine spirit, whom they name VISHNU, the *Pervader*, and NÁRÁYAN, or *Moving on the waters*', 'On the Gods of Greece, Italy, and India', p.351.

As mortal eyes (thus finite we compare
  With infinite) in smoothest mirrors gaze: 25
  Swift, at his look, a shape supremely fair
  Leap'd into being with a boundless blaze,
    That fifty suns might daze.
Primeval MAYA was the Goddess nam'd,
  Who to her sire, with Love divine inflam'd,   30
  A casket gave with rich *Ideas* fill'd,
From which this gorgeous Universe he fram'd;
    For, when th' Almighty will'd,
    Unnumber'd worlds to build,
  From Unity diversified he sprang,   35
While gay Creation laugh'd, and procreant Nature rang.

First an all-potent all-pervading sound
  Bade flow the waters – and the waters flow'd,
  Exulting in their measureless abode,
  Diffusive, multitudinous, profound,   40
    Above, beneath, around;
Then o'er the vast expanse primordial wind
  Breath'd gently till a lucid bubble rose,
  Which grew in perfect shape an Egg refin'd:
  Created substance no such lustre shows,   45
    Earth no such beauty knows.
Above the warring waves it danc'd elate,
  Till from its bursting shell with lovely state
  A form cerulean flutter'd o'er the deep,

---

29 On the nature of the goddess Māyā, and her relation to perception see 'On the Gods', p.349 below.

37–8 *First an all-potent all-pervading sound/Bade flow the waters – and the waters flow'd* The primacy of harmonious sound in his depiction of the natural world has been viewed by Javed Majeed (*Ungoverned Imaginings: James Mill's 'The History of British India' and Orientalism* Oxford, 1992, p.39) as reflecting the influence of Mark Akenside's *The Pleasures of Imagination* (1744). In Jones's seminal essay 'On the Musical Modes of the Hindus' (1784), he writes of music 'speaking, as it were, the language of beautiful nature', *Works*, IV. 166–210, (166).

37–54 We can compare Jones's quotation from Menu on this creation myth. 'This world, says he, was all darkness, undiscernible, undistinguishable, altogether as in a profound sleep; till the self-existent invisible GOD, making it manifest with five elements and other glorious forms, perfectly dispelled the gloom. He, desiring to raise up various creatures by an emanation from his own glory, first created the *waters*, and impressed them with a power of motion: by that power was produced a golden Egg, blazing like a thousand suns, in which was born BRAHMÁ, self-existing, the great parent of all rational beings. The waters are called *nárà*, since they are the offspring of NERA (or ÍSWARA); and thence was NÁRÁYANA named, because his first *ayana*, or *moving*, was on them', 'On the Gods of Greece, Italy, and India', p.352 below.

49 *A form cerulean flutter'd o'er the deep* 'Dark blue, approaching to *black*, which is the meaning of the word *Crishna*, is believed to have been his complexion; . . . and hence, in the great reservoir or cistern at *Cátmándu* the capital of *Nepal*, there is placed in a recumbent posture a large well-proportioned image of *blue* marble, representing NÁRÁYAN floating on the waters', 'On the Gods', *Works*, III. 377.

Brightest of beings, greatest of the great: 50
  Who, not as mortals steep,
  Their eyes in dewy sleep,
  But heav'nly-pensive on the Lotos lay,
That blossom'd at his touch and shed a golden ray.

Hail, primal blossom! hail empyreal gem!   55
  KEMEL, or PEDMA, or whate'er high name
  Delight thee, say, what four-form'd Godhead came,
  With graceful stole and beamy diadem,
    Forth from thy verdant stem?
Full-gifted BREHMA! Rapt in solemn thought   60
  He stood, and round his eyes fire-darting threw;
  But, whilst his viewless origin he sought,
  One plain he saw of living waters blue,
    Their spring nor saw nor knew.
Then, in his parent stalk again retir'd,   65
  With restless pain for ages he inquir'd
  What were his pow'rs, by whom, and why conferr'd:
  With doubts perplex'd, with keen impatience fir'd
    He rose, and rising heard
    Th' unknown all-knowing Word,   70
  'BREHMA! no more in vain research persist:
My veil thou canst not move – Go; bid all worlds exist.'

Hail, self-existent, in celestial speech
  NARAYEN, from thy watry cradle, nam'd;
  Or VENAMALY may I sing unblam'd,   75

---

53 *But heav'nly-pensive on the Lotos lay* This Hindu epitome of 'deep self-possession, an intense repose' proved immensely appealing to Coleridge, cf. his letter to John Thelwall of 14 October 1797: 'I should much wish, like the Indian Vishna, to float about along an infinite ocean cradled in the flower of the Lotos', Earl Leslie Griggs, ed., *Collected Letters of Samuel Taylor Coleridge* 6 vols. (Oxford, 1971), I.349–50; see also his *Osorio* V.i.49–56, and *The Night-Scene: A Dramatic Fragment* (1813), ll.50–6.

56 *KEMEL, or PEDMA* Lakshmī is frequently addressed as Kamalā and Padmā, both words meaning 'lotus'. From the moment of her creation in the churning of the ocean, she is associated with the fertility and spiritual purity of the lotus, see 'A Hymn to Lacshmí', 55–72.

74 *NARAYEN, from thy watry cradle nam'd* Nārāyana, the Universal Abode, is one of the twenty-four icons of Vishnu, the all-pervading, centripetal power which holds the universe together. 'When Viṣṇu sleeps, the universe dissolves into its formless state, represented as the causal ocean. The remnants of manifestation are represented as the serpent Remainder (Śeṣa) coiled upon itself and floating upon the abysmal waters. It is on this serpent that the sleeping Viṣṇu rests. Viṣṇu is then called Nārāyana (moving on the waters)', Daniélou, *Hindu Polytheism*, p.151.

75 *VENAMALY* Vana-mālā (Garland-of-the-Forest) The garland of fragrant flowers worn by Vishnu and his incarnations representing the primal energy of creation, see *Viṣṇu Purāṇa* 1.22.72. Jones writes: 'CRISHNA . . . wears a rich garland of sylvan flowers, whence he is named VANAMÁLI', 'On the Gods', *Works*, III.376.

With flow'ry braids, that to thy sandals reach,
   Whose beauties, who can teach?
Or high PEITAMBER clad in yellow robes
   Than sunbeams brighter in meridian glow,
   That weave their heav'n-spun light o'er circling globes?   80
   Unwearied, lotos-eyed, with dreadful bow,
      Dire Evil's constant foe!
Great PEDMANABHA, o'er thy cherish'd world
   The pointed *Checra*, by thy fingers whirl'd,
   Fierce KYTABH shall destroy and MEDHU grim   85
   To black despair and deep destruction hurl'd.
      Such views my senses dim,
      My eyes in darkness swim:
   What eye can bear thy blaze, what utt'rance tell
Thy deed with silver trump or many-wreathed shell?   90

Omniscient Spirit, whose all-ruling pow'r
   Bids from each sense bright emanations beam;
   Glows in the rainbow, sparkles in the stream,
   Smiles in the bud, and glistens in the flow'r
      That crowns each vernal bow'r;   95
Sighs in the gale, and warbles in the throat
   Of ev'ry bird, that hails the bloomy spring,
   Or tells his love in many a liquid note,
   Whilst envious artists touch the rival string,
      Till rocks and forests ring;   100
Breathes in rich fragrance from the sandal grove,
   Or where the precious musk-deer playful rove;
   In dulcet juice from clust'ring fruit distills,
   And burns salubrious in the tasteful clove:
      Soft banks and verd'rous hills   105
      Thy present influence fills;
In air, in floods, in caverns, woods, and plains;
Thy will inspirits all, thy sov'reign MAYA reigns.

---

78   *PEITAMBER clad in yellow robes*   Pītāmbara is the golden yellow veil or robe worn by Vishnu and his incarnations. It is woven of three threads representing the letters of the sacred syllable AUM.

83   *PEDMANABHA*   Another image of Vishnu, Padma-nābha means *He whose Navel is the World's Lotus.*

84   *the pointed Checra, by thy fingers whirl'd*   The *cakra* is Vishnu's discus-like weapon.

85   *Fierce KYTABH shall destroy and MEDHU grim*   Kaitabha and Madhu, two genii who stole the Vedas, were killed by Hayaśirsa, a horse-headed incarnation of Vishnu at the bottom of the ocean, see Daniélou, *Hindu Polytheism*, p.185.

92   Always faithful to the Hindu *purānas*, Jones represents the principal forms of Nature as female emanations of the active power of the intrinsically passive spirit of God.

Blue crystal vault, and elemental fires,
   That in th' ethereal fluid blaze and breathe;   110
   Thou, tossing main, whose snaky branches wreathe
   This pensile orb with intertwisted gyres;
      Mountains, whose radiant spires
Presumptuous rear their summits to the skies,
   And blend their em'rald hue with sapphire light;   115
   Smooth meads and lawns, that glow with varying dyes
   Of dew-bespangled leaves and blossoms bright,
      Hence! vanish from my sight:
Delusive Pictures! unsubstantial shows!
   My soul absorb'd One only Being knows,   120
   Of all perceptions One abundant source,
   Whence ev'ry object ev'ry moment flows:
      Suns hence derive their force,
      Hence planets learn their course;
   But suns and fading words I view no more: 125
GOD only I perceive; GOD only I adore.

109–26   R. M. Hewitt (*Essays and Studies*, 28, 1942, 42–59) briefly considered the influence of this verse and the whole poem upon Shelley's metaphysics. For a much more complete consideration of the impact of this hymn upon Shelley, Coleridge, and Lady Morgan, see Drew, *India and the Romantic Imagination* (Oxford, 1987), pp. 234, 261–3, 268; 193; 243, 258, 282 respectively.

14

A Hymn to Sereswaty (1785)

[This poem, celebrating the Minerva Musica of India in thirteen 13-line Pindaric stanzas, was composed in the summer of 1785. In a note to Richard Johnson of 4 August Jones promised 'In a day or two I will send you and Ld Macartney a Hymn to *Sereswaty* the Goddess of Musick and Speech. It is my intention to compose, at my leisure, *eighteen* such Hymns, the number of the Puráns of Vyása;' (NLW MS 12857C). Published in the first volume of Gladwin's *Asiatick Miscellany* (Calcutta, 1785), it was most favourably reviewed by the *Monthly Review* 76 (June 1787), 481–2. The Sarasvatī of the Vedic hymns is a formidable river goddess, bringer of strength and fertility, whereas her later nature as a goddess of invention, imagination, eloquence, and music is here celebrated by Jones the poet and scholar. The first European to study the intricate modal complexities of Indian music, Jones had been revising his pioneering treatise 'On the Musical Modes of the Hindus' since 1784, collating classical Sanskrit sources such as the *Sangīta-darpana* and the *Rāgavibodha*. Jones was fascinated by the synaesthetic implications of each *rāga* possessing extra-musical association of colour, emotion, season, deity and so on, and his hymn attempts to reproduce faithfully the graphic representation of the modes which he had examined in the ancient paintings of the *Rāgmālās*. The copy text is that of 1799.]

THE ARGUMENT

The *Hindu* Goddesses are uniformly represented as the subordinate *powers* of their respective lords: thus Lachsmy, the consort of Vishnu the *Preserver*, is the Goddess of *abundance* and *prosperity*; Bhavány, the wife of Mahádév, is the genial power of *fecundity*; and Sereswaty, whose husband was the *Creator* Brehmá, possesses the powers of Imagination and Invention, which may justly be termed *creative*. She is, therefore, adored as the patroness of the fine arts, especially of Musick and Rhetorick, as the inventress of the Sanscrit Language, of the *Dévanágry* Letters, and of the sciences, which writing perpetuates; so that her attributes correspond with those of Minerva Musica, in *Greece* and *Italy*, who invented the flute, and presided over literature. In this character she is addressed in the following ode, and particularly as the *Goddess of Harmony*; since the *Indians* usually paint her with a musical instrument in her hand: the seven notes, an artful combination of which constitutes *Musick* and variously affects the passions, are feigned to be her earliest production; and the greatest part of the Hymn exhibits a correct delineation of the Rágmálá, or *Necklace of Musical Modes*, which may be considered as the most pleasing invention of the ancient *Hindus*, and the most beautiful union of Painting with poetical Mythology and the genuine theory of Musick.

The different position of the *two* semitones in the scale of *seven* notes gives birth to seven *primary* modes; and, as the whole series consists of *twelve* semitones, every one of which may be made a *modal* note or *tonick*, there are in nature, (though not universally in practice) *seventy-seven* other modes, which may be called *derivative*: all the *eighty-four* are distributed by the Persians, under the notion of *locality*, into three classes consisting of *twelve* rooms, *twenty-four* angles, and *forty-eight* recesses; but the Hindu arrangement is elegantly formed on the variations of the *Indian* year, and the association of ideas; a powerful auxiliary to the ordinary effect of modulation. The Modes, in this system, are deified; and, as there are *six* seasons in *India*, namely, two Springs, Summer, Autumn, and two Winters, an original Rág, or *God of the Mode*, is conceived to preside over a particular season; each principal mode is attended by *five* Rágnys, or *Nymphs of Harmony*; each has *eight* Sons, or *Genii* of the same divine Art; and each Rág, with his family, is appropriated to a distinct season, in which alone his melody can be sung or played at prescribed hours of the day and night: the mode of Deipec, or Cupid the *Inflamer*, is supposed to be lost; and a tradition is current in *Hindustan*, that a musician, who attempted to restore it, was consumed by fire from heaven. The natural distribution of modes would have been *seven, thirty-three*, and *forty-four*, according to the number of the *minor* and *major* secondary tones; but this order was varied for the sake of the charming fiction above-mentioned. Náred, who is described in the *third* stanza, was one of the first created beings, corresponding with the Mercury of the

Italians, inventor of the Vene, a fretted instrument supported by two large *gourds*, and confessedly the finest used in *Asia*

A full discussion of so copious a subject would require a separate dissertation; but here it will be sufficient to say, that almost every allusion and every epithet in the Poem, as well as the names, are selected from approved treatises, either originally *Persian* or translated from the *Sanscrit*, which contain as lively a display of genius, as human imagination ever exhibited.

The last couplet alludes to the celebrated place of pilgrimage, at the confluence of the *Gangá* and *Yamná*, which the *Sereswaty*, another sacred river, is supposed to join under ground.

THE HYMN

Sweet grace of BREHMA's bed!
Thou, when thy glorious lord
Bade airy nothing breathe and bless his pow'r,
    Satst with illumin'd head,
    And, in sublime accord,   5
Sev'n sprightly notes, to hail th' auspicious hour,
    Ledst from their secret bow'r:
    They drank the air; they came
    With many a sparkling glance,
    And knit the mazy dance,   10
Like yon bright orbs, that gird the solar flame,
    Now parted, now combin'd,
Clear as thy speech and various as thy mind.

    Young Passions at the sound
    In shadowy forms arose,   15
O'er hearts, yet uncreated, sure to reign;
    Joy, that o'erleaps all bound,
    Grief, that in silence grows,
Hope, that with honey blends the cup of pain,
    Pale Fear, and stern Disdain,   20
    Grim Wrath's avenging band,
    Love, nurs'd in dimple smooth,
    That ev'ry pang can soothe;
But, when soft Pity her meek trembling hand
    Stretch'd, like a new-born girl,   25
Each sigh was musick, and each tear a pearl.

---

1 *Sweet grace of BREHMA's bed!* Sarasvatī is the active power, or *śakti*, of the creator, Brahmā. 'Brahmā, desiring to create the world, goes into meditation, whereupon his body divides into two, half male and half female. Enraptured by his female half, who is Sarasvatī, Brahmā desires her, mates with her, and creates the demigod Manu, who subsequently creates the world', David Kinsley, *Hindu Goddesses: Visions of the Divine Feminine in the Hindu Religious Tradition* (Berkeley and London, 1986), p.57.

6 *Sev'n sprightly notes* The practicality and syncretism of Jones's approach is apparent in the following: 'I requested a *German* Professor of musick to accompany with his violin a *Hindu* lutanist, who sung *by note* some popular airs on the loves of CRISHNA and RÁHDÀ; he assured me, that the scales were the same', 'On the Musical Modes of the Hindus', *Works*, IV.189.

Thee her great parent owns
All-ruling Eloquence,
That, like full GANGA, pours her stream divine
    Alarming states and thrones: 30
    To fix the flying sense
Of words, thy daughters, by the varied line
    (Stupendous art!) was Thine;
    Thine, with pointed reed
    To give primeval Truth   35
    Th' unfading bloom of youth,
And paint on deathless leaves high Virtue's meed:
    Fair Science, heav'n-born child,
And playful Fancy on thy bosom smil'd.

    Who bids the fretted *Vene*   40
    Start from his deep repose,
And wakes to melody the quiv'ring frame?
    What youth with godlike mien
    O'er his bright shoulder throws
The verdant gourd, that swells with struggling flame?   45
    NÁRED, immortal name!
    He, like his potent Sire,
    Creative spreads around
    The mighty world of sound,
And calls from speaking wood ethereal fire;   50
    While to th' accordant strings
Of boundless heav'ns and heav'nly deeds he sings.

---

29 *her stream divine* Sarasvatī means 'Flowing-One', and is the name of a sacred river, celebrated in the *Rig-Veda*; she represents the sacrality inherent in rivers or any living water. According to Kinsley: 'The Sarasvatī (and later the Gangā) represents an ever-flowing stream of celestial grace which purifies and fertilizes the earth', *Hindu Goddesses*, p.57. Jones, aware of the goddess's associations in later Vedic literature with speech, poetry, and music, characterizes this stream as one of heavenly eloquence. On the significance of the mythology of Kashmir and the Tantric rites of Sarasvatī for a reading of 'Kubla Khan', and the possible influence of Jones's hymn upon Coleridge, see Drew, *India and the Romantic Imagination*, pp.211–21.

31–2 *To fix the flying sense/Of words* '(Sarasvatī) becomes identified with the dimension of reality that is best described as coherent intelligibility', Kinsley, *Hindu Goddesses*, p.55.

35–6 *To give primeval Truth/Th' unfading bloom of youth* In 'The Lunar Year of the Hindus' Jones translates the following meditation from the *Sáradá Tilaca*: 'May the goddess of speech enable us to attain all possible felicity; she, who wears on her locks a young moon, who shines with exquisite lustre, whose body bends with the weight of her full breasts, who sits reclined on a white lotos, and from the crimson lotos of her hands pours radiance on the instruments of writing, and on the books produced by her favour!' *Works*, IV.143–4.

46 Nārada, son of Brahmā and Sarasvatī, and friend of Krishna, embodies the power of persuasion, and is represented as the inventor of 'the fretted Vene' (*vīnā*) or lute. In both 'On the Musical Modes of the Hindus', *Works*, IV.185, and 'On the Gods Of Greece, Italy, and India', *Works*, III.382, Jones notes 'Náred's' resemblance to Hermes/Mercury.

But look! the jocund hours
A lovelier scene display,
Young HINDOL sportive in his golden swing   55
High-canopied with flow'rs;
While *Rágny's* ever gay
Toss the light cordage, and in cadence sing
The sweet return of Spring:
Here dark *Viráwer* stands;   60
There *Rámcary* divine
And fawn-eyed *Lelit* shine;
But stern *Daysásha* leads her warring bands,
And slow in ebon clouds
Petmenjary her fading beauty shrouds.   65

Ah! where has DEIPEC veil'd
His flame-encircled head?
Where flow his lays too sweet for mortal ears?
O loss how long bewail'd!
Is yellow *Cámód* fled?   70

53–156   The six primary modes or *Rāgas* (Passions) are arranged according to the six Indian seasons. Each of these is 'a Genius, or Demigod, wedded to five *Ráginis* or Nymphs, and father of *eight* little Genii, called his *Putras*, or Sons', 'Musical Modes', p.193. With a characteristic comparativist stance Jones continues: 'the fancy of SHAKESPEARE and the pencil of ALBANO might have been finely employed in giving speech and form to this assemblage of new aërial beings, who people the fairy-land of *Indian* imagination'. Jones's evocation of these musical allegories was to influence the conception of Luxima in Lady Morgan's *The Missionary*, and Shelley's portrayal of the Spirits of the Hours in Act IV of *Prometheus Unbound*.

55   *HINDOL sportive in his golden swing*   The first of the six masculine modes featured in this hymn is a Spring *rāga*. Hindola (the name means 'swing') is often portrayed, 'rocked, as the sages say, by women with ample hips', see Alain Daniélou, *The Rāga-s of Northern Indian Music* (London, 1968), p.346. This stanza, like each of the following six (with the exception of stanza 7), also describes the respective *ragínīs* wedded to each demigod mode. Jones supplies tables denoting the scales of these *rāgas* in 'Musical Modes', *Works*, IV.198–203.

60   *dark Viráwer*   Velāvalī, or Bilāval, who has the dark lustre of the blue lotus, see Daniélou, *Rāga-s*, p.190.

61   *Rámcary divine*   Rāmakrī, or Rāmakalī. 'A shining woman in the posture of heroes, thus should Rāmākriyā be seen. Dark like the jambu fruit she holds a bow and an arrow', *Rāga-sāgara* 3.18, quoted in Daniélou, *Rāga-s*, p.128.

62   *fawn-eyed Lelit*   Lalitā, associated with sensual playfulness and the beauty of dawn, see Daniélou, *Rāga-s*, p.101.

63   *stern Daysásha*   Deshī. 'Tall and amorous, with lovely limbs, her skin prickling in the rapture of the heroic mood . . . Deshī shines, beloved of Hindola', *Chatvārimshach'hata-rāga-nirūpanam*, p.20, quoted in Daniélou, *Rāga-s*, p.155.

65   *Petmanjary her fading beauty shrouds*   'Grown lean and tarnished sundered from her lover, Pathamanjarī decks with flowers her withered beauty', *Sangīta-darpana* 2.62, quoted in Daniélou, *Rāga-s*, p.158.

66   *DEIPEC* (Dīpaka) the Indian Cupid, also known as Kāma or Camdeo, is the second *rāga*, associated with 'languor during the dry heats', 'Musical Modes', *Works*, IV.192. According to Daniélou, Dīpaka is the Fire *rāga* to be played at sunset, see *Rāga-s*, p.253.

70   *Is yellow Cámód fled*   'In the forest, dressed in yellow and with lovely hair, Kāmodī looks about on every side with terror. Thinking of her lover, even the cuckoo's happy cry fills her with

And blythe *Cárnáty* vaunting o'er her peers?
   Where stream *Caydára's* tears
   Intent on scenes above,
   A beauteous anchorite?
No more shall *Daysa* bright   75
With gentle numbers call her tardy love?
   Has *Netta*, martial maid,
Lock'd in sad slumbers her sky-temper'd blade?

   Once, when the vernal noon
   Blaz'd with resistless glare,   80
The Sun's eye sparkled, and a God was born:
   He smil'd; but vanish'd soon –
   Then groan'd the northern air;
The clouds, in thunder mutt'ring sullen scorn,
   Delug'd the thirsty corn.   85
   But, earth-born artist, hold!
   If e'er thy soaring lyre
   To *Deipec's* notes aspire,
Thy strings, thy bow'r, thy breast with rapture bold,
   Red lightning shall consume;   90
Nor can thy sweetest song avert the doom.

   See sky-form'd MAYGH descend
   In fertilising rain,
Whilst in his hand a falchion gleams unsheath'd!
   Soft nymphs his car attend,   95
   And raise the golden grain,
Their tresses dank with dusky spikenard wreath'd:
   (A sweeter gale ne'er breath'd)
   Tenca with laughing eyes,
   And *Gujry's* bloomy cheek,   100

---

desperation', *Sangīta-darpana* 2, 68, quoted in Daniélou, *Rāga-s*, p.272.

71 *blythe Cárnáty* Chhāyānata, often represented as a male deity, is associated with joyful feelings, see Daniélou, *Rāga-s*, p.274.

72 *Caydára's tears* Kedārā is portrayed as a tender devotee of Śiva, Lord of Sleep. 'Wearing the veil that Yogins use in meditation, her mind immersed in contemplation of the Lord of Sleep upholder of the Ganges, Kedārikā is the rāginī of Dīpaka, the rāga of fire', *Shiva-tattva-ratnākara* 6.8.93, quoted in Daniélou, *Rāga-s*, p.277.

77 *Netta, martial maid* Nata is commonly depicted as a male deity, riding triumphantly through the field of battle, see Daniélou, *Rāga-s*, p.234.

92 *See sky-form'd MAYGH descend/In fertilising rain* Megha, the third *rāga*, invokes musical strains associated with 'refreshment by the first rains, which cause in this climate a second spring', 'Musical Modes', *Works*, IV.192.

100 *Gujry's bloomy cheek* Gurjarī. 'Praised be Ghurjarī whose cheeks are like the young Lodhra tree', *Rāga-sāgara* 3.23, quoted in Daniélou, *Rāga-s*, p.136.

Melár with dimple sleek,
On whose fair front two musky crescents rise:
  While *Dayscár* his rich neck
And mild *Bhopály* with fresh jasmin deck.

Is that the King of Dread   105
  With ashy musing face,
From whose moon-silver'd locks fam'd GANGA springs?
  'Tis BHAIRAN, whose gay bed
  Five blushing damsels grace,
And rouse old Autumn with immortal strings,   110
  Till ev'ry forest rings;
  Bengály lotos-crown'd,
  Vairáty like the morn,
  Sindvy with looks of scorn,
And *Bhairavy*, her brow with *Champa's* bound;   115
  But *Medhumádha's* eyes
Speak love, and from her breast pomegranates rise.

Sing loud, ye lucid spheres;
  Ye gales, more briskly play,
And wake with harmony the drooping meads: 120
  The cooler season cheers
  Each bird, that panting lay,
And SIRY bland his dancing bevy leads
  Hymning celestial deeds:

---

101 *Melár* The word Mallār denotes the mid-year rainy season.
103 *Dayscár* Desha expresses passion, desire, and the abundant Monsoon rains.
104 *mild Bhopály* According to Daniélou, Bhūpālī conveys harmony and contentment, see *Rāga-s*, pp.280–1.
105–8 BHAIRAN Bhairava (the Terrible) is an aspect of Śiva, 'From whose moon-silver'd locks' the Ganges flows, cf. 'A Hymn to Gangā', ll.25–6. The music of this fourth *rāga* evokes harvest merriment.
112 *Bengály* Bāngālī is described as a beautiful devotee of Śiva, see Daniélou, *Rāga-s*, p.122.
114 *Sindvy with looks of scorn* Saindhavī, or Sindhurā. 'United with Shiva . . . brandishing a trident in the fearful anger of the hero mood, Saindhavī, the rāginī of Bhairava', *Shiva-tattva-ratnākara* 6.8.85, quoted in Daniélou, *Rāga-s*, p.298.
115 *Bhairavy, her brow with Champa's bound* Bhairavī is the golden consort of Bhairava. On the flower Champa, see 'A Hymn to Camdeo', 55n.
116 *Medhumádha's eyes* 'Madhyamādi, lotus-eyed, her golden skin smeared with saffron, laughingly embraced by her husband, kisses and is kissed by him, the sages tell, after her heart's desire', *Shiva-tattva-ratnākara* 6.8.57, quoted in Daniélou, *Rāga-s*, p.209.
123 SIRY Srírāga, the associations of the fifth *rāga* are with cooling breezes and flowery shade. In order that his European audience 'will think the *Sanscrit* language equal to *Italian* in softness and elegance', Jones quotes a description of this *rāga* from the *Náráyan*, translating it as follows: 'The demigod SRĪRĀGA, famed over all this earth, sweetly sports with his nymphs, gathering fresh blossoms in the bosom of yon grove; and his divine lineaments are distinguished through his graceful vesture', 'Musical Modes', *Works*, IV.194.

Marvá with robes like fire,   125
Vasant whose hair perfumes
With musk its rich-eyed plumes,
Ásávery, whom list'ning asps admire,
Dhenásry, flow'r of glades,
And *Málsry*, whom the branching *Amra* shades.   130

MALCAUS apart reclines
Bedeck'd with heav'n-strung pearls,
Blue-mantled, wanton, drunk with youthful pride;
Nor with vain love repines,
While softly-smiling girls   135
Melt on his cheek or frolick by his side,
And wintry winds deride;
Shambháwty leads along
Cocabh with kerchief rent,
And *Gaúry* wine-besprent,   140
Warm *Guncary*, and *Toda* sweet in song,
Whom antelopes surround
With smooth tall necks, and quaff the streaming sound.

---

125 *Marvá with robes like fire* Māravā. 'Her golden limbs are robed in red . . . Māravā, with Ni and Ga (musical notes) like fire', *Rāga-mālā of Pundarika Vitthala*, quoted in Daniélou, *Rāga-s*, p.244.

126–7 *Vasant whose hair perfumes/ With musk its rich-eyed plumes* 'With ear-rings of mango flower and a high diadem spread wide like the fan of a peacock . . . is Vasantī, the darling of Spring', *Rāga-kalpa-druma* p. 20, quoted in Daniélou, *Rāga-s*, p.349. Jones speculates that the mode of Vasanti might well have been 'adapted by JAYADÉVA himself to the most beautiful of his odes', illustrating his thesis with a quatrain from the *Gītagōvinda*, see 'Musical Modes', *Works* IV.208–10.

128 *Ásávery, whom list'ning asps admire* 'Āshāvarī drags forth the serpent from the sandal-trees and wears it as a zone', *Shiva-tattva-ratnākara* 6.8.113, quoted in Daniélou, *Rāga-s*, p.164.

129 *Dhenásry, flow'r of glades* Dhanāshrī, whose beautiful body is often compared with sacred grass. 'Charming is Dhanāshrī, her body sombre like the durvā grass. Her cheeks are pale with the torment of separation. The tear drops falling on her breast, she is writing to her beloved', *Sangīta-darpana* 2.74, quoted in Daniélou, *Rāga-s*, p.220.

130 *Málsry* Mālavashrī, who is often depicted sitting at the foot of a mango-tree or *Amra*, Daniélou, *Rāga-s*, p.223.

131 MALCAUS *apart reclines/Bedeck'd with heav'n-strung pearls* In Jones's seasonal interpretation this final *rāga* is no frosty Hiems, and the wanton frolic ignores the wintry winds' derision. The Sanskrit texts, however, generally present Mālakosha garlanded with skulls, while his mace runs with blood, see Daniélou, *Rāga-s*, p.324.

139 *Cocabh* Kakubha expresses the joyous mood of love, see Daniélou, *Rāga-s*, p.196.

140 *Gaúry wine-besprent* Gaurī is the goddess of liquor.

141 *Warm Guncary* Gunakirī, or Gunakalī, is sometimes adorned with golden pigment, see Daniélou, *Rāga-s*, p.131.

141–2 *Toda sweet in song,/Whom antelopes surround* 'The woodland deer are spellbound at the sight of Todī splendid, holding a lute', *Sangīta-darpana* 2.53, quoted in Daniélou, *Rāga-s*, p.145.

Nor deem these nuptial joys
    With lovely fruit unblest: 145
No; from each God an equal race proceeds,
    From each eight blooming boys;
    Who, their high birth confess'd,
With infant lips gave breath to living reeds
    In alleys, groves, and meads: 150
    Mark how they bound and glance!
    Some climb the vocal trees,
    Some catch the sighing breeze,
Some, like new stars, with twinkling sandals dance;
    Some the young *Shamma* snare,   155
Some warble wild, and some the burden bear.

    These are thy wond'rous arts;
    Queen of the flowing speech,
Thence SERESWATY nam'd and VÁNY bright!
    Oh, joy of mortal hearts,   160
    Thy mystick wisdom teach;
Expand thy leaves, and, with ethereal light,
    Spangle the veil of night.
    If LEPIT please thee more,
    Or BRÁHMY, awful name,   165
    Dread BRÁHMY's aid we claim,
And thirst, VÁCDÉVY, for thy balmy lore
    Drawn from that rubied cave,
Where meek-ey'd pilgrims hail the triple wave.

---

147   *eight blooming boys* The *putras* (sons) of the primary *rāgas* and secondary *rāginīs*, see note to ll.53-156 above. Indian music, like that of the West, is based on the octave.

152   *the vocal trees* Cf. 'Smooth-sliding *Mincius*, crown'd with vocal reeds', *Lycidas* l.86.

155   *young Shamma snare* Possibly the *haṁsa*, or Bar-headed goose, accorded a semi-divine status as a symbol of grace, purity, knowledge, and spiritual aspiration. The *haṁsa* is the *vāhana* or vehicle of Brahmā and of his consort Sarasvatī, Haṁsādhirūḍhā (mounted on a goose) being one of her epithets.

159–69   This stanza includes some of the names of Sarasvatī: 'VÁNY' and 'VÁCDÉVY' refer to divinely-inspired eloquence and 'BRÁHMY' to the Power-of-the-Immense-Being.

169   *the triple wave* The pilgrimage site of Trivenī at the confluence of three sacred rivers, see Jones's Argument, *Letters*, II.922–3, and 'A Hymn to Gangá', ll.77–8.

15

A Hymn to Gangá (1785)

[Composed late in 1785, and published in the first volume of Gladwin's *Asiatick Miscellany* (Calcutta, 1785), the thirteen 13-line stanzas of this hymn sing of the goddess's birth, wanderings, and marriage to Brahmaputra. The Ganges is the essential element of ritual purification. As Jones makes clear, in his modification of stanza form he was anxious to express 'the long and solemn march of the great *Asiatick* rivers'. In this he was particularly successful, effectively conveying dramatic changes of flow and course by means of subtle yet powerful modulations of rhythm and pace. As Jones was motivated by a desire to legitimize British rule in India, in the hymns he frequently poses as a Hindu poet. This hymn, as the Argument explains, 'is feigned to have been the work of a Brahmen, in an early age of Hindu antiquity, who, by a prophetical spirit, discerns the toleration and equity of the BRITISH government, and concludes with a prayer *for its peaceful duration under good laws well administered.*' Here the objectives of the poet, Orientalist, lawyer, and patriot can be seen to coalesce. The text followed is that of 1799, with variants noted from the Calcutta printing (Althorp Papers).]

THE ARGUMENT

This poem would be rather obscure without geographical notes; but a short introductory explanation will supply the place of them, and give less interruption to the reader.

We are obliged to a late illustrious *Chinese* monarch named Can-hí, who directed an accurate survey to be made of *Pótyid* or (as it is called by the *Arabs*) *Tebbut*, for our knowledge, that a chain of mountains nearly parallel with *Imaus*, and called *Cantésè* by the Tartars, forms a line of separation between the sources of two vast rivers; which, as we have abundant reason to believe, run at first in opposite directions, and, having finished a winding circuit of two thousand miles, meet a little below *Dhácà*, so as to inclose the richest and most beautiful peninsula on earth, in which the British nation, after a prosperous course of brilliant actions in peace and war, have now the principal sway. These rivers are *deified* in India; that, which rises on the *western* edge of the mountain, being considered as the daughter of Mahádéva or Siva, and the other as the son of Brahmá: their loves, wanderings, and nuptials are the chief subject of the following Ode, which is feigned to have been the work of a Bráhmen, in an early age of Hindu antiquity, who, by a prophetical spirit, discerns the toleration and equity of the British government, and concludes with a prayer *for its peaceful duration under good laws well administered.*

After a general description of the *Ganges*, an account is given of her fabulous birth, like that of *Pallas*, from the forehead of *Siva*, the *Jupiter Tonans* and *Genitor* of the *Latins*; and the creation of her lover by an act of *Brahmà's* will is the subject of another stanza, in which his course is delineated through the country of *Pótyid*, by the name of *Sanpò*, or *Supreme Bliss*, where he passes near the fortress of *Rimbù*, the island of *Palté* or *Yambrò* (known to be the seat of a high priestess almost equally venerated with the Goddess *Bhawáni*) and *Trashilhumbo* (as a *Pótya* or *Tebbutian* would pronounce it), or the sacred mansion of the *Lama* next in dignity to that of *Pótala*, who resides in a city, to the south of the *Sanpò*, which the *Italian* travellers write *Sgigatzhè*, but which, according to the letters, ought rather to be written in a manner, that would appear still more barbarous in our orthography. The *Brahmaputra* is not mentioned again till the *twelfth* stanza, where his progress is traced, by very probable conjecture, through *Rangamáti*, the ancient *Rangamriticà* or *Rangamar*, celebrated for the finest spikenard, and *Sríhàt* or *Siret*, the *Serratæ* of *Elian*, whence the fragrant essence extracted from the *Malobathrum*, called *Sádah* by the *Persians*, and *Téjapátra* by the *Indians*, was carried by the *Persian* gulf to *Syria*, and from that coast into *Greece* and *Italy*. It is not, however, positively certain, that the *Brahmaputra* rises as it is here described: two great geographers are decidedly of opposite opinions on this very point; nor is it impossible that the *Indian* river may be one arm of the *Sanpò*, and the *Nau-cyan*, another; diverging from the mountains of *Ashám*, after they have been enriched by many rivers from the rocks of *China*,

The *fourth* and *fifth* stanzas represent the Goddess obstructed in her passage to the west by the hills of *Emodi*, so called from a *Sanscrit* word signifying *snow*, from which also are derived both *Imaus* and *Himálaya* or *Himola*. The *sixth* describes her, after her entrance into *Hindústan* through the straits of *Cúpala*, flowing near *Sambal*, the *Sambalaca* of *Ptolemy*, famed for a beautiful plant of the like name, and thence to the once opulent city and royal place of residence, *Cányacuvja*, erroneously named *Calinipaxa* by the *Greeks*, and *Canauj*, not very accurately, by the modern *Asiaticks*: here she is joined by the *Calinadi*, and pursues her course to *Prayága*, whence the people of *Bahár* were named *Prasii*, and where the *Yamunà*, having received the *Sereswati* below *Indraprest'ha* or *Dehlì*, and watered the poetical ground of *Mat'hurà* and *Agarà*, mingles her noble stream with the *Gangà* close to the modern fort of *Ilahábàd*. This place is considered as the confluence of *three* sacred rivers, and known by the name of *Tivéni*, or the *three plaited locks*; from which a number of pilgrims, who there begin the ceremonies to be completed at *Gayà*, are continually bringing vases of water, which they preserve with superstitious veneration, and are greeted by all the *Hindus*, who meet them on their return.

Six of the principal rivers, which bring their tribute to the *Ganges*, are next enumerated, and are succinctly described from real properties: thus the *Gandac*, which the *Greeks* knew by a similar name, abounds, according to *Giorgi*, with *crocodiles* of enormous magnitude; and the *Mahanadi* runs by the plain of *Gaura*, once a populous district with a magnificent capital, from which the *Bengalese* were probably called *Gangaridæ*, but now the seat of desolation, and the haunt of wild beasts. From *Prayága* she hastens to *Càsì*, or as the *Muslimans* name it, *Benáres*; and here occasion is taken to condemn the cruel and intolerant spirit of the crafty tyrant Aurangzíb, whom the *Hindus* of *Cashmìr* call *Aurangásùr*, or the *Demon*, not the *Ornament*, of the *Throne*. She next bathes the skirts of *Pátaliputra*, changed into *Patna*, which, both in situation and name, agrees better on the whole with the ancient *Palibothra*, than either *Prayága*, or *Cányacuvja*; if *Megasthenes* and the ambassadors of *Seleucus* visited the last-named city, and called it *Palibothra*, they were palpably mistaken. After this are introduced the beautiful hill of *Muctigiri*, or *Mengìr*, and the wonderful pool of *Sítá*, which takes its name from the wife of *Ráma*, whose conquest of *Sinhaldwíp*, or *Sílàn*, and victory over the giant *Ráwan*, are celebrated by the immortal *Válmíci*, and by other epick poets of *India*.

The pleasant hills of *Cáligràm* and *Gangá-presàd* are then introduced, and give occasion to deplore and extol the late excellent Augustus Clevland, Esq. who nearly completed by lenity the glorious work, which severity could not have accomplished, of civilizing a ferocious race of *Indians*, whose mountains were formerly, perhaps, a rocky island, or washed at least by that sea, from which the fertile champaign of *Bengal* has been gained in a course of ages. The western arm of the *Ganges* is called *Bhágirathì*, from a poetical fable of a demigod or holy man, named *Bhágírat'ha*, whose devotion had obtained from *Siva* the privilege of leading after him a great part of the heavenly water, and who drew it accordingly in two branches; which embrace the fine island, now denominated from *Kásimbázàr*, and famed for the defeat of the monster *Sirájuddaulah*, and, having met near the venerable *Hindu* seminary of *Nawadwìp* or *Nedíyá*, flow in a copious stream by the several *European* settlements, and reach the Bay at an island which assumes the name of *Ságar*, either from the *Sea* or from an ancient Raja of distinguished piety. The *Sundarabans* or *Beautiful Woods*, an appellation to which they are justly entitled, are incidentally mentioned, as lying between the *Bhágirat'hì* and the *Great River*, or *Eastern* arm, which, by its junction with the *Brahmáputra*, forms many considerable islands; one of which, as well as a town near the conflux, derives its name from *Lacshmì*, the Goddess of Abundance.

It will soon be perceived, that the *form* of the stanza, which is partly borrowed from GRAY, and to which he was probably partial, as he uses it *six* times in *nine*, is enlarged in the following Hymn by a line of *fourteen* syllables, expressing the long and solemn march of the great *Asiatick* rivers.

THE HYMN

How sweetly GANGÁ smiles, and glides
Luxuriant o'er her broad autumnal bed!
Her waves perpetual verdure spread,
Whilst health and plenty deck her golden sides:
As when an eagle, child of light,   5
On *Cambala*'s unmeasur'd height,
By *Pótala*, the pontiff's throne rever'd,
O'er her eyry proudly rear'd
Sits brooding, and her plumage vast expands,
Thus GANGÁ o'er her cherish'd lands,   10
To *Brahmà*'s grateful race endear'd,
Throws wide her fost'ring arms, and on her banks divine
Sees temples, groves, and glitt'ring tow'rs, that in her crystal shine.

Above the stretch of mortal ken,
On bless'd *Cailása*'s top, where ev'ry stem   15
Glow'd with a vegetable gem,
MAHÉSA stood, the dread and joy of men;
While *Párvatì*, to gain a boon,
Fix'd on his locks a beamy moon,
And hid his frontal eye, in jocund play,   20
With reluctant sweet delay:
All nature straight was lock'd in dim eclipse
Till *Bráhmans* pure, with hallow'd lips
And warbled pray'rs restor'd the day;
When GANGÁ from his brow by heav'nly fingers press'd   25
Sprang radiant, and descending grac'd the caverns of the west.

---

12 *her fost'ring arms* Faithful to Hindu tradition, Jones emphasizes the maternal aspect of Gangā, comforting and nourishing all she encounters.

14–26 Southey quotes this stanza, and acknowledges his indebtedness to Jones's poem, in the notes to *The Curse of Kehama, Poetical Works* (London, 1838), VIII.264.

15 *Cailása* Kailāsa, the Pleasure Mountain.

17 *MAHÉSA* Maheśvara, the Lord of Knowledge is one of Śiva's titles.

18 *Párvatì* The consort of Śiva, cf. 'A Hymn to Durgá', I.3.6ff.

20 *And hid his frontal eye* Śiva's three eyes represent the three sources of light, the sun, the moon, and fire. 'The frontal eye, the eye of fire, is the eye of higher perception', Svāmi Karapātri, 'Śrī Śiva tattva', *Siddhānta*, II (1941–2), 116, quoted by Daniélou, *Hindu Polytheism*, p.214. On the incident when she playfully covers his eyes and thus plunges the world into darkness, see the *Mahābhārata* 13.140.

25 *When GANGÁ from his brow by heav'nly fingers press'd* Cf. 'A Hymn to Sereswaty', ll.105–7, cf. *The Curse of Kehama*, X.2.

26 *descending grac'd the caverns of the west* 'It is because the Ganga descended in her

The sun's car blaz'd, and laugh'd the morn;
What time near proud *Cantésa*'s eastern bow'rs,
(While *Dévatà's* rain'd living flow'rs)
A river-god, so *Brahmà* will'd, was born,   30
And roll'd mature his vivid stream
Impetuous with celestial gleam:
The charms of GANGÁ, through all worlds proclaim'd,
Soon his youthful breast inflam'd,
But destiny the bridal hour delay'd;   35
Then, distant from the west'ring maid,
He flow'd, now blissful *Sanpò* nam'd.
By *Paltè* crown'd with hills, bold *Rimbu*'s tow'ring state,
And where sage *Trashilhumbo* hails her *Lama*'s form renate.

But she, whose mind, at *Siva*'s nod,   40
The picture of that sov'reign youth had seen,
With graceful port and warlike mien,
In arms and vesture like his parent God,
Smit with the bright idea rush'd,
And from her sacred mansion gush'd,   45
Yet ah! with erring step – The western hills
Pride, not pious ardour, fills:
In fierce confed'racy the giant bands
Advance with venom-darting hands,
Fed by their own malignant rills;   50
Nor could her placid grace their savage fury quell:
The madding rifts and should'ring crags her foamy flood repell.

'Confusion wild and anxious wo
'Haunt your waste brow, she said, unholy rocks,
'Far from these nectar-dropping locks!   55
'But thou, lov'd Father, teach my waves to flow.'
Loud thunder her high birth confess'd;
Then from th' inhospitable west
She turn'd, and, gliding o'er a lovelier plain,
Cheer'd the pearled East again: 60
Through groves of nard she roll'd, o'er spicy reeds,
Through golden vales and em'rald meads;

---

avatarana (incarnation) that she is a place of ascent as a *tīrtha* (sacred crossing-place)', Diana Eck, 'Gangā: The Goddess in Hindu Sacred Geography', in John Stratton Hawley and Donna Wulff, eds., *The Divine Consort: Rādhā and the Goddesses of India* (Berkeley, 1982), p.176.

46 The Himalayan range is pictured as jealously intervening between the youthful lovers; the Ganges and Brahmaputra are kept apart.

53–60 The mountains suffer her curse of aridity, and she invokes Śiva who is instrumental in diverting her course eastwards.

Till, pleas'd with INDRA's fair domain,
She won through yielding marl her heav'n-directed way:
With lengthen'd notes her eddies curl'd, and pour'd a blaze of day.   65

　　Smoothly by *Sambal*'s flaunting bow'rs,
Smoothly she flows, where *Calinadi* brings
To *Cányacuvja*, seat of kings,
On prostrate waves her tributary flow'rs;
While *Yamunà*, whose waters clear   70
Fam'd *Indraprestha*'s vallies cheer,
With *Sereswati* knit in mystick chain,
Gurgles o'er the vocal plain
Of *Mathurà*, by sweet *Brindávan*'s grove,
Where *Gópa*'s love-lorn daughters rove,   75
And hurls her azure stream amain,
Till blest *Prayága*'s point beholds three mingling tides,
Where pilgrims on the far-sought bank drink nectar, as it glides.

　　From *Himola*'s perennial snow,
And southern *Palamau*'s less daring steep,   80
Sonorous rivers, bright though deep,
O'er thirsty deserts youth and freshness throw.
'A goddess comes,' cried *Gumti* chaste,
And roll'd her flood with zealous haste:
Her follow'd *Sona* with pellucid wave   85
Dancing from her diamond cave,
Broad *Gogra*, rushing swift from northern hills,
Red *Gandac*, drawn by crocodiles,
(Herds, drink not there, nor, herdsmen, lave!)
Cosa, whose bounteous hand *Népálian* odour flings,   90
And *Mahanadi* laughing wild at cities, thrones, and kings.

70　*Yamunà*　The Jumna river.

74–5　*Of Mathurà, by sweet Brindávan's grove,/Where Gópa's love-lorn daughters rove*
Mathurā is the sacred city of Krishna, who sported with the *gopīs* (milkmaids) in the fragrant groves of Vrndāvana. See *Gítagóvinda*, pp.300–2 below.

77–8　*blest Prayága's point* ('Place of sacrifice') This sacred pilgrimage site (later Allāhābād), situated at the confluence of the Gangā and Yamunā rivers with the mythical subterranean Sarasvatī, is also called Trivenī or 'triple braid', cf. 'A Hymn to Sereswaty', l.169 and n.

Thy temples, CÁSÍ, next she sought,
And verd'rous plains by tepid breezes fann'd,
Where health extends her pinions bland,
Thy groves, where pious *Válmic* sat and thought,   95
Where *Vyása* pour'd the strain sublime,
That laughs at all-consuming time,
And *Bráhmans* rapt the lofty *Véda* sing.
Cease, oh! cease – a ruffian king,
The demon of his empire, not the grace,   100
His ruthless bandits bids deface
The shrines, whence gifts ethereal spring:
So shall his frantick sons with discord rend his throne,
And his fair-smiling realms be sway'd by nations yet unknown.

Less hallow'd scenes her course prolong;   105
But *Cáma*, restless pow'r, forbids delay:
To Love all virtues homage pay,
E'en stern religion yields. How full, how strong
Her trembling panting surges run,
Where *Pátali*'s immortal son   100
To domes and turrets gives his awful name
Fragrant in the gales of fame !
Nor stop, where RÁMA, bright from dire alarms,
Sinks in chaste *Sítà*'s constant arms,
While bards his wars and truth proclaim: 115
There from a fiery cave the bubbling crystal flows,
And *Muctigir*, delightful hill, with mirth and beauty glows.

Oh! rising bow'rs, great *Cáli*'s boast,
And thou, from *Gangà* nam'd, enchanting mount,
What voice your wailings can recount   120
Borne by shrill echoes o'er each howling coast,

---

92   *CÁSÍ*   Kāsī, resplendent city of Śiva, now called Vārānasī (Benares), is sited at another triple confluence, this time on a wholly symbolic plane, for here the three Ganges (the celestial Ganges or Milky Way, the 'Underworld Ganges', and the earthly river) were believed to cross one another.
95   *Válmic*   The sage Vālmīki, creator of epic poetry and author of the *Rāmāyana*.
96   *Vyása*   Vyāsa was the founder of the Vedānta philosophy, who was favoured with the vision of *Suméru* which forms the subject of Jones's 'A Hymn to Indra'.
99   *a ruffian king*   Aurangzīb, see Jones's Argument.
106   *Cáma*   The god of love and subject of Jones's first hymn.
110–12   *Pátali*   Pātaliputra, formerly the splendid capital of northern India which extended for miles along the banks of the Ganges, and derived its name from the 'exquisitely fragrant' *pátali* or trumpetflower, see 'Botanical Observations', *Works*, V.131–4.
113   *Ráma*   Rāma is the incarnation of the solar aspect of Vishnu. Lacshmī became his consort as Sītā, or Nature, see *Padma Purāna* 6.270.29–31.
118   *Cáli*   It is the fearful aspect of Kālī, consort of Śiva the Destroyer, which is stressed here.

When He, who bade your forests bloom,
Shall seal his eyes iron gloom?
Exalted youth! The godless mountaineer,
Roaming round his thickets drear,   125
Whom rigour fir'd, nor legions could appall,
I see before they mildness fall,
Thy wisdom love, thy justice fear:
A race, whom rapine nurs'd, whom gory murder stains,
Thy fair example wins to peace, to gentle virtue trains.   130

But mark, where old *Bhágírath* leads
(This boon his pray'rs of *Mahádèv* obtain:
Grace more distinguish'd who could gain?)
Her calmer current o'er his western meads,
Which trips the fertile plains along,   135
Where vengeance waits th' oppressor's wrong;
Then girds, fair *Nawadwip*, thy shaded cells,
Where the *Pendit* musing dwells;
Thence by th' abode of arts and commerce glides,
Till *Ságar* breasts the bitter tides;   140
While She, whom struggling passion swells,
Beyond the labyrinth green, where pards by moonlight prowl,
With rapture seeks her destin'd lord, and pours her mighty soul.

Meanwhile o'er *Pótyid*'s musky dales,
Gay *Rangamar*, where sweetest spikenard blooms,   145
And *Siret*, fam'd for strong perfumes,
That, flung from shining tresses, lull the gales,
Wild *Brahmaputra* winding flows,
And murmurs hoarse his am'rous woes;
Then, charming GANGÁ seen, the heav'nly boy   150
Rushes with tumultuous joy:

124–30 Augustus Cleveland (1755–84), to whom Jones here pays homage, was the collector and magistrate of Bhagalpur. He bravely dedicated himelf to curbing the martial traits of the mountain tribes, preventing their feuds with the plains tribes. On his early death, monuments were erected to his memory by both the natives and Warren Hastings. He was the cousin of Jones's friend and biographer, Sir John Shore.

131 *old Bhágírath* Bhagiratha performed centuries of heroic penance to absolve the impious sins of the Sagara dynasty. Eventually *Mahádèv* (Śiva) was persuaded to allow the heavenly Ganges to descend to earth, breaking her fall with his mighty head. The purifying waters, guided by Bhagīratha, moistened the ashes of King Sagara's sixty thousand sons, cleansing and releasing their souls. *Bhāgavata-purāṇa* 9.8–9.

145 *sweetest spikenard blooms* Cf. 1.61 above. Jones had undertaken careful botanical research to establish the identity of this plant. See 'On the Spikenard of the Ancients', and 'Additional Remarks on the Spikenard of the Ancients', *Works*, V.13–31,32–46.

(Can aught but Love to men or Gods be sweet?)
When she, the long-lost youth to greet,
Darts, not as earth-born lovers toy,
But blending her fierce waves, and teeming verdant isles;   155
While buxom *Lacshmí* crowns their bed, and sounding ocean smiles.

    What name, sweet bride, will best allure
Thy sacred ear, and give thee honour due?
Vishnupedì? Mild *Bhíshmasù*?
Smooth *Suranimnagà*? *Trisrótà* pure?   160
By that I call? Its pow'r confess;
With growing gifts thy suppliants bless,
Who with full sails in many a light-oar'd boat
On thy jasper bosom float;
Nor frown, dread Goddess, on a peerless race   165
With lib'ral heart and martial grace,
Wafted from colder isles remote:
As they preserve our laws, and bid our terror cease,
So be their darling laws preserv'd in wealth, in joy, in peace!

---

165 *Nor frown, dread Goddess, on a peerless race* The poet, via the Brahman narrator, attempts to enlist the approval of the potent organic symbol of the Ganges in a validation of British rule.

168–9 Cf. the revised plan of 1787 for Jones's projected epic, *Britain Discovered*, in which the goddess Gangā is initially vehemently opposed to the founding of Britain on the the grounds that the Britons 'will possess themselves of her banks, mock the temples of the *Indian* divinities, appropriate the wealth of their adorers, introduce new laws, a new religion, a new government, insult the *Brahméns*, and disregard the sacred ordinances of *Brihmá*'. Gangā is presumably mollified by the prophecy of Britanus's druidic attendant spirit which 'recommends the government of *Indians* by their own laws', *Works*, II.444–54.

16

A Hymn to Indra (1785)

[On the 11 May 1785 Jones sent Charles Wilkins the first stanza of his poem to Indra, requesting the god's 'most poetical names, his parentage, attributes, and attendants', (*Letters*, II.671). It is clear that Jones's continuing series of hymns provided a focus for his deepening knowledge of Hindu mythology, and for his fruitful collaboration with fellow Orientalists. He frequently spent seven hours on the bench and two in chambers, but as he explained to Warren Hastings and Samuel Davis: 'I really find poetry a relief to my mind after its severer employment in the discharge of my public duty', (*Letters*, II.705).

Indra, the courageous ruler of the cloud-region, receives by far the largest share of the devout attentions of the Vedic singer of the 'Orphick Hymns' in the *Rig-Veda*, some of which Jones had read in Persian translations. The completed hymn was published in 1786, together with 'The Hymn to Súrya', in Gladwin's second volume of *Asiatick Miscellany* (Calcutta, 1786). The text is that of 1799, with variants noted from the Calcutta printing (Althorp Papers).]

THE ARGUMENT

So many allusions to *Hindu* Mythology occur in the following Ode, that it would be scarce intelligible without an explanatory introduction, which, on every account and on all occasions, appears preferable to notes in the margin.

A distinct idea of the God, whom the poem celebrates, may be collected from a passage in the ninth section of the *Gítà*, where the sudden change of measure has an effect similar to that of the finest modulation:

> *tè punyamásádya suréndra lócam*
> *asnanti divyán dividévabhógán,*
> *tè tam bhuctwà swergalócam visálam*
> *eshinè punyè mertyalócam visant*

'These, having through virtue reached the mansion of the king of *Sura's*, feast on the exquisite heavenly food of the Gods: they, who have enjoyed this lofty region of SWERGA, *but* whose virtue is exhausted, revisit the habitation of mortals.'

INDRA, therefore, or the *King* of Immortals, corresponds with one of the ancient *Jupiters* (for several of that name were worshipped in *Europe*), and particularly with *Jupiter* the *Conductor*, whose attributes are so nobly described by the *Platonick* Philosophers: one of his numerous titles is *Dyupeti*, or, in the nominative case before certain letters, *Dyupetir*; which means the *Lord of Heaven*, and seems a more probable origin of the *Hetruscan* word than *Juvans Pater*; as *Diespiter* was, probably, not the *Father*, but the *Lord*, of *Day*. He may be considered as the JOVE of ENNIUS in his memorable line:

> 'Aspice hoc sublime candens, quem invocant omnes *Jovem*,'

where the poet clearly means the firmament, of which INDRA is the personification. He is the God of thunder and the five elements, with inferior Genii under his command; and is conceived to govern the Eastern quarter of the world, but to preside, like the *Genius* or *Agathodœmon* of the Ancients, over the celestial bands, which are stationed on the summit of MÉRU, or the North-pole, where he solaces the Gods with nectar and heavenly musick: hence, perhaps, the *Hindus*, who give evidence, and the magistrates, who hear it, are directed to stand fronting the East or the North.

This imaginary mount is here feigned to have been seen in a vision at *Váránasì*,

---

Aspice hoc sublime candens, quem invocant omnes Jovem ('Behold this sublime light, whom all invoke as Jove') Quintus Ennius (239–170 BC), *Thyestes* V.345.

very improperly called *Banáris*, which takes its name from two rivulets, that embrace the city; and the bard, who was favoured with the sight, is supposed to have been VYÁSA, surnamed *Dwaipáyana*, or *Dwelling in an Island*; who, if he really composed the *Gítà*, makes very flattering mention of himself in the tenth chapter. The plant *Latà*, which he describes weaving a net round the mountain *Mandara*, is transported by a poetical liberty to *Suméru*, which the great author of the *Mahabhárat* has richly painted in four beautiful couplets: it is the generick name for a *creeper*, though represented here as a species, of which many elegant varieties are found in *Asia*.

The Genii named *Cinnara's* are the male dancers in *Swerga*, or the Heaven of INDRA; and the *Apsarà's* are his dancing-girls, answering to the *fairies* of the PERSIANS, and to the damsels called in the KORAN *hhùru'lûyùn*, or *with antelopes' eyes*. For the story of *Chitrarat'ha*, the chief musician of the *Indian* paradise, whose *painted car* was burned by ARJUN, and for that of *Chaturdesaretna*, or *fourteen gems*, as they are called, which were produced by churning the ocean, the reader must be referred to Mr. WILKINS's learned annotations on his accurate version of the *Bhagavadgítà*. The fable of the pomegranate-flower is borrowed from the popular mythology of *Népàl* and *Tibet*.

In this poem the same form of stanza is repeated with *variations*, on a principle entirely new in modern lyrick poetry, which on some future occasion may be fully explained.

THE HYMN

But ah! what glories yon blue vault emblaze?
What living meteors from the zenith stream?
Or hath a rapt'rous dream
Perplex'd the isle-born bard in fiction's maze?
He wakes; he hears; he views no fancied rays.   5
'Tis INDRA mounted on the sun's bright beam;
And round him revels his empyreal train:
How rich their tints! how sweet their strain!

   Like shooting stars around his regal seat
A veil of many-colour'd light they weave,   10
That eyes unholy would of sense bereave:
Their sparkling hands and lightly-tripping feet
Tir'd gales and panting clouds behind them leave.
With love of song and sacred beauty smit
Thy mystick dance they knit;   15
Pursuing, circling, whirling, twining, leading,
Now chasing, now receding;
Till the gay pageant from the sky descends
On charm'd *Suméru*, who with homage bends.

1–8 The original first stanza sent to Wilkins consisted of ten lines and reads as follows:
               But ah! what glories from the zenith break?
                  What lucid forms yon jasper vault emblaze?
               Like living suns their airy course they take:
                  Fall back, ye nations, and enraptured gaze!
               Mazy dances briskly knitting,
                  Now they meet, and now retire,
               Round their Prince, in splendor sitting,
                  Weaving veils of heav'nly fire:
               High on a milk-white Elephant he rides,
                  Whose agate hoof the buxom air divides.   (*Letters*, II.671)
Ultimately Jones decided to introduce the king of heaven 'mounted on the sun's bright beam',
relegating Indra's elephant to stanza ten.
    4   *the isle-born bard* As Jones explains in his Argument, the outer frame of this 'dream poem'
is the glorious vision of *Suméru* granted to Vyāsa, the island-born founder of the Vedānta
philosophy. It is Jones's task, as another isle-born bard, to communicate both the vision and the
philosophy to an Occidental audience.
    7–19 Indra's 'empyreal train' of *ráginis* embody the divine graces of music, poetry, and dance.
Cf. 'A Hymn to Sereswaty', ll.55ff.
    10 *A veil of many-colour'd light they weave* Cf. the eighth line of the rejected first stanza
('Weaving veils of heav'nly fire:'), and with Shelley's 'weave the mystic measure/ Of music, and
dance, and shapes of light,' (*Prometheus Unbound* IV. 77–8).
    19ff. *Suméru* The golden mountain, the pleasure ground of the gods constructed of mystic
semen. See *Mahābhārata* 1. 1098; 14. 214.

    Hail, mountain of delight,   20
Palace of glory, bless'd by glory's king!
With prosp'ring shade embow'r me, whilst I sing
Thy wonders yet unreach'd by mortal flight.

    Sky-piercing mountain! In thy bow'rs of love
No tears are seen, save where medicinal stalks   25
Weep drops balsamick o'er the silver'd walks;
No plaints are heard, save where the restless dove
Of coy repulse and mild reluctance talks;
Mantled in woven gold, with gems enchas'd,
With em'rald hillocks grac'd,   30
From whose fresh laps in young fantastick mazes
Soft crystal bounds and blazes
Bathing the lithe convolvulus, that winds
Obsequious, and each flaunting arbour binds.

    When sapient BRAHMÁ this new world approv'd,   35
On woody wings eight primal mountains mov'd;
But INDRA mark'd *Suméru* for his own,
And motionless was ev'ry stone.

    Dazzling the moon he rears his golden head:
Nor bards inspir'd, nor heav'n's all-perfect speech   40
Less may unhallow'd rhyme his beauties teach,
Or paint the pavement which th' immortals tread;
Nor thought of man his awful height can reach:
Who sees it, maddens; who approaches, dies;
For, with flame-darting eyes,   45
Around it roll a thousand sleepless dragons;
While from their diamond flagons
The feasting Gods exhaustless nectar sip,
Which glows and sparkles on each fragrant lip.

    This feast, in mem'ry of the churned wave   50
Great INDRA gave, when *Amrit* first was won
From impious demons, who to *Máyà*'s eyes
Resign'd the prize, and rued the fight begun.

---

51   *when Amrit first was won*   *Amṛta*, the seed-of-life and nectar of the gods. The reference here is to the myth of the churning of the ocean of milk and the prevention of the demons from partaking of the immortal elixir. See *Bhāgavata Purāṇa* 8.7.
52   *Máyà*   This divinity represents the power of illusion, the source of the cosmos and of perception.

Now, while each ardent *Cinnara* persuades
The soft-ey'd *Apsarà* to break the dance,   55
And leads her loth, yet with love-beaming glance,
To banks of marjoram and *Champac* shades,
Celestial *Genii* tow'rd their king advance
(So call'd by men, in heav'n *Gandharva's* nam'd)
For matchless musick fam'd.   60
Soon, where the bands in lucid rows assemble,
Flutes breathe, and citherns tremble;
Till CHITRARATHA sings – His painted car,
Yet unconsum'd, gleams like an orient star.

Hush'd was ev'ry breezy pinion,   65
Ev'ry stream his fall suspended:
Silence reign'd; whose sole dominion
Soon was rais'd, but soon was ended.

He sings, how 'whilom from the troubled main
'The sov'reign elephant *Airávan* sprang;   70
'The breathing shell, that peals of conquest rang;
'The parent cow, whom none implores in vain;
'The milkwhite steed, the bow with deaf'ning clang;
'The Goddesses of beauty, wealth, and wine;
'Flow'rs, that unfading shine,   75

54　*each ardent Cinnara persuades*　Jones's explanation in the Argument that the '*Cinnara's* are the male dancers in *Swerga*' seems to indicate that he has conflated *cārana* (The Wanderers), dancers and singers of panegyric and *kinnara* (The Heavenly-Humans), centaur-like musicians, and *kinnars*, celestial singing girls. See Daniélou, *Hindu Polytheism*, pp.145, 306–7.

55　*soft-ey'd Apsarà*　The *apsarases* (Essences) are heavenly courtesans.

59　*Gandharva's*　These are celestial singers and musicians, who feed on the fragrance of herbs, and are said to possess limitless sexual potency. See B. Rāmacandra Śarmā, 'Some Aspects of the Vedic Gandharva and Apsarases', *Poona Orientalist*, 13 (1948), 65.

64　Chitraratha, whose name means Owner-of-the-Wonder-Chariot, is King of the *gandharvas*, and chief musician of *Suméru* (n.19ff.). His song provides a subtly modulated inner frame for the poem. In the words of S. Viswanathan, 'The instantaneous impact which the singing has on Indra is depicted carefully, so that the poem becomes at once a celebration of the powers of music and an instance of the exploitation of lyrical music in verse', 'The Hymns of Sir William Jones', 493.

69–79　In this stanza Chitraratha celebrates what was produced by the churning of the ocean of milk, see *Bhāgavata Purāṇa* 8.8; *Mahābhārata* 1.18.48–53.

70　The four-tusked, milk-white '*Airávan*', the prototype of the earth-supporting elephants, emerged from the churning and was appropriated by Indra. Airāvana is said to have been the reincarnation of an ancient serpent-king, and when Indra is seated on his royal mount he sends life-giving rain, see *Mahābhārata* 6.95.

71　*breathing shell*　The conch Pāncajanya, symbol of the origin of existence.

72　*The parent cow, whom none implores in vain*　The wish-cow Surabhi (Fragrant Earth) which grants all requests.

73　Indra's white steed is named Uccaihsravas or Loud-neigh. The bow Śārnga is associated with the origin of sensory perception.

74　*The Goddesses of beauty, wealth, and wine*　Lakshmī represents the first two blessings, Vāruṇī, the third.

'Náráyan's gem, the moonlight's tender languish;
'Blue venom, source of anguish;
'The solemn leech, slow-moving o'er the strand,
'A vase of long-sought *Amrit* in his hand.

'To soften human ills dread Siva drank   80
'The pois'nous flood, that stain'd his azure neck;
'The rest thy mansions deck
High *Swerga*, stor'd in many a blazing rank.

'Thou, God of thunder, satst on *Méru* thron'd,
'Cloud-riding, mountain-piercing, thousand-ey'd,   85
'With young Pulómajá, thy blooming bride,
'Whilst air and skies thy boundless empire own'd;
'Hail, Dyupetir, dismay to Bala's pride!
'Or speaks Purander best thy martial fame,
'Or Sacra, mystick name?   90
'With various praise in odes and hallow'd story
'Sweet bards shall hymn thy glory.
'Thou, Vásava, from this unmeasur'd height
'Shedst pearl, shedst odours o'er the sons of light!'

The Genius rested; for his pow'rful art   95
Had swell'd the monarch's heart with ardour vain,
That threaten'd rash disdain, and seem'd to low'r
On Gods of loftier pow'r and ampler reign.

---

76 *Náráyan's gem* The brilliant jewel called Kaustubha (Treasure-of-the-Ocean) represents consciousness.

77 *Blue venom* This is the poison (*háláhala*) which Siva drank.

80 In later mythology Indra is regarded as an aspect of Siva. Siva alone could drink the deadly poison and thus free the world from its effect, see Daniélou, *Hindu Polytheism*, p.276.

86 *Pulómajá* Indrāní, the daughter of Puloman, chosen on account of her sensuousness. Indra ravished her and slew her father to escape his curse. She is also known as Sacī (Divine-Grace), see *Rig-Veda* 10.159. Cf. ll.115ff. below.

88ff. Jones provides a roll-call of Indra's resonant names as supplied by Charles Wilkins: *Dyupetir* Deva-pati (Lord-of-the-Gods) who defeated Bala, king of the demons; *Purander* Puramdara (Destroyer-of-Cities); *Sacra* Sakra (Divine Courage); *Vásava* (Lord-of-the-Spheres).

He smil'd; and, warbling in a softer mode,
Sang, 'the red light'ning, hail, and whelming rain   100
'O'er *Gócul* green and *Vraja*'s nymph-lov'd plain
'By INDRA hurl'd, whose altars ne'er had glow'd,
'Since infant CRISHNA rul'd the rustick train
'Now thrill'd with terrour – Them the heav'nly child
'Call'd, and with looks ambrosial smil'd,   105
'Then with one finger rear'd the vast *Govérdhen*,
'Beneath whose rocky burden
'On pastures dry the maids and herdsmen trod:
'The Lord of thunder felt a mightier God!'

What furies potent modulation soothes!   110
E'en the dilated heart of INDRA shrinks:
His ruffled brow he smoothes,
His lance half-rais'd with listless languor sinks.

A sweeter strain the sage musician chose:
He told, how 'SACHI, soft as morning light,   115
'Blythe SACHI, from her Lord INDRÁNÍ hight,
'When through clear skies their car ethereal rose,
'Fix'd on a garden trim her wand'ring sight,
'Where gay pomegranates, fresh with early dew,
'Vaunted their blossoms new: 120
"Oh! pluck, she said, yon gems, which nature dresses
"To grace my darker tresses."
'In form a shepherd's boy, a God in soul,
'He hasten'd, and the bloomy treasure stole.

'The reckless peasant, who those glowing flow'rs,   125
'Hopeful of rubied fruit, had foster'd long,
'Seiz'd and with cordage strong
'Shackled the God, who gave him show'rs.

99–113 Having celebrated the majesty of the Thunderer, the celestial minstrel Chitraratha modulates both tone and rhythm and, *warbling in a softer mode*, recounts less auspicious events. He sings of how Krishna persuaded the pastoral people of Vraja to abandon their traditional worship of Indra. Krishna, ignoring Indra's wrath, the lightning and the ensuing deluge, lifted up the mountain Govardhana with one finger and held it for seven days as a shelter until Indra acknowledged *a mightier God*. Cf. *Bhāgavata Purāṇa* 10.24–25.

115 SACHI An alternative title for the beautiful Indrani, which suggests the concept of *śákti*, or creative female power.

'Straight from sev'n winds immortal Genii flew,
'Green *Varuna*, whom foamy waves obey,   130
'Bright *Vahni* flaming like the lamp of day,
'*Cuvéra* sought by all, enjoyed by few,
'*Marut*, who bids the winged breezes play,
'Stern *Yama*, ruthless judge, and *Isa* cold
'With *Nairrit* mildly bold: 135
'They with the ruddy flash, that points his thunder,
'Rend his vain bands asunder.
'Th' exulting God resumes his thousand eyes,
'Four arms divine, and robes of changing dyes.'

Soft memory retrac'd the youthful scene: 140
The thund'rer yielded to resistless charms,
Then smil'd enamour'd on his blushing queen,
And melted in her arms.

Such was the vision, which, on *Varan*'s breast
Or *Asì* pure with offer'd blossoms fill'd,   145
Dwaipáyan slumb'ring saw; (thus Náred will'd)
For waking eye such glory never bless'd,
Nor waking ear such musick ever thrill'd.
It vanish'd with light sleep: he, rising, prais'd
The guarded mount high-raised,   150
And pray'd the thund'ring pow'r, that sheafy treasures,
Mild show'rs and vernal pleasures,
The lab'ring youth in mead and vale might cheer,
And cherish'd herdsmen bless th' abundant year.

---

130 *Varuna* is Lord of the waters, ruler of the sea, see *Mahābhārata* 2.9.
131 *Vahni* (the Conveyor) is one of the names of Agni (Fire), who also mediates between men and gods.
132 *Cuvéra* or Kubera is the god of wealth, who guards the earth's treasure of gems.
133 *Marut, who bids the winged breezes play* Marutvan (Lord-of-the-Winds) is another name for Indra, who is the chief of the Maruts, the genii of the storm.
134 *Yama* is the sovereign of the infernal regions and judge of the dead.
135 *Nairrit* Jones might intend the goddess Nirṛti who represents misery, disease and destruction, or possibly, Nirṛta, the god of ghosts and night-travellers.
138 *his thousand eyes* The marks of Indra's lasciviousness. The sage Gautama, in revenge for the seduction of his wife, imprinted a thousand pudenda-shaped marks upon the god, which were later transformed into eyes.
144–5 *on Varan's breast/Or Asì pure* The holy city of Vārānasī (Benares), see Jones's Argument, and 'A Hymn to Gangá', l.92.
146 DWAIPÁYAN The surname of Vyāsa, the Compiler, who divided the Veda into its several branches, and was gifted with this vision of Meru, the axial northern mountain home of the gods.

Thee, darter of the swift blue bolt, he sang;   155
Sprinkler of genial dews and fruitful rains
O'er hills and thirsty plains!
'When through the waves of war thy charger sprang,
'Each rock rebellow'd and each forest rang,
'Till vanquish'd *Asurs* felt avenging pains.   160
'Send o'er their seats the snake, that never dies,
'But waft the virtuous to thy skies!'

155–62   It is fitting that Jones should in conclusion stress Indra's ever-renewed battle with the malicious demons of darkness and drought, for the recovery of the heavenly light and the rain-spending cows of the sky, as these themes predominate in several hymns of the *Rig-Veda*.

160   *Asurs*   Cruel and destructive anti-gods.

17

Hymn to Súrya (1786)

[This, Jones's sixth hymn, was written in September 1786 in twelve 17-line stanzas, and was first published in the second volume of Francis Gladwin's *Asiatick Miscellany* (William Mackay: Calcutta, 1786). His principal sources were Charles Wilkins's translation of the *Bhagavad-Gītā* and an episode from the *Mahābhārata*, and his Argument makes clear his proselytizing zeal for the riches of Indian literature. Whereas in 'A Hymn to Gangá' Jones posed as a Hindu poet, here he introduces himself as one of the first Europeans to learn the 'celestial tongue' of Sanskrit in order to draw 'orient knowledge from its fountains pure,/Through caves obstructed long, and paths too long obscure.' His reference in the Argument to 'Súrya, the Phoebus of *European* heathens', displays his obvious fascination with comparative mythology, but a coolly dispassionate and somewhat disarming re-exportation of all the cultural freight burdening the term 'heathens'.

S. Viswanathan ('The Hymns of Sir William Jones', *The Aryan Path* 90 [1969], 487–93, 543–50 [547]) has shown that 'Shelley's 'Hymn to Intellectual Beauty' carries as many echoes of 'A Hymn to Súrya' as (it does) of 'A Hymn to Náráyena', but it is perhaps Jones's evocations of an abstract and pervasive power informing all creation which links him most closely with the Romantics. Above all it was his explorations of the Vedic philosophy that sees the whole created world as brought into being and continuously sustained by mind which were to prove most influential for poets such as Blake and Coleridge. The text followed is that of 1799.]

THE ARGUMENT

A PLAUSIBLE opinion has been entertained by learned men, that the principal source of idolatry among the ancients was their enthusiastick admiration of the Sun; and that, when the primitive religion of mankind was lost amid the distractions of establishing regal government, or neglected amid the allurements of vice, they ascribed to the great visible luminary, or to the wonderful fluid, of which it is the general reservoir, those powers of pervading all space and animating all nature, which their wiser ancestors had attributed to one eternal MIND, by whom the substance of fire had been created as an inanimate and secondary cause of natural phenomena. The Mythology of the East confirms this opinion; and it is probable, that the *triple Divinity* of the *Hindus* was originally no more than a personification of the Sun, whom they call *Treyitenu*, or *Three-bodied*, in his triple capacity of producing forms by his genial *heat*, preserving them by his *light*, or destroying them by the concentrated force of his *igneous* matter: this, with the wilder conceit of a *female power* united with the Godhead, and ruling nature by his authority, will account for nearly the whole system of *Egyptian*, *Indian*, and *Grecian* polytheism, distinguished from the sublime Theology of the Philosophers, whose understandings were too strong to admit the popular belief, but whose influence was too weak to reform it.

SÚRYA, the PHŒBUS of *European* heathens, has near fifty names or epithets in the *Sanscrit* language; most of which, or at least the meanings of them, are introduced in the following Ode; and every image, that seemed capable of poetical ornament, has been selected from books of the highest authority among the *Hindus*: the title *Arca* is very singular; and it is remarkable, that the *Tibetians* represent the Sun's car in the form of a *boat*.

It will be necessary to explain a few other particulars of the *Hindu* Mythology, to which allusions are made in the poem. SOMA, or the Moon, is a *male* Deity in the *Indian* system, as *Mona* was, I believe, among the *Saxons*, and *Lunus* among some of the nations, who settled in *Italy*: his titles also, with one or two of the ancient fables, to which they refer, are exhibited in the second stanza. Most of the *Lunar mansions* are believed to be the daughters of *Casyapa*, the first production of *Brahmà*'s head, and from their names are derived those of the twelve months, who are here feigned to have married as many constellations: this primeval *Bráhman* and *Vinatà* are also supposed to have been the parents of *Arun*, the charioteer of the Sun, and of the bird *Garuda*, the eagle of the great *Indian* JOVE, one of whose epithets is *Mádhava*.

After this explanation the Hymn will have few or no difficulties, especially if the reader has perused and studied the *Bhagavadgítà*, with which our literature has been lately enriched, and the fine episode from the *Mahábhárat*, on the production of the *Amrita*, which seems to be almost wholly astronomical, but abounds with poetical beauties. Let the following description of the demon *Ráhu*, decapitated by *Náráyan*, be compared with similar passages in *Hesiod* and *Milton*:

> *tach ch'hailasringapratiman dánavasya sirò mahat*
> *chacrach'hinnam c'hamutpatya nenádíti bhayancaram,*
> *tat cabandham pepátásya visp'hurad dharanítalè*
> *sapervatavanadwípán daityasyácampayanmahím.*

THE HYMN

Fountain of living light,
That o'er all nature streams,
Of this vast microcosm both nerve and soul;
Whose swift and subtil beams,
Eluding mortal sight,   5
Pervade, attract, sustain th' effulgent whole,
Unite, impel, dilate, calcine,
Give to gold its weight and blaze,
Dart from the diamond many-tinted rays,
Condense, protrude, transform, concoct, refine   10
The sparkling daughters of the mine;
Lord of the lotos, father, friend, and king,
O Sun, thy pow'rs I sing:
Thy substance *Indra* with his heav'nly bands
Nor sings nor understands;   15
Nor e'en the *Védas* three to man explain
Thy mystick orb triform, though *Brahmà* tun'd the strain.

   Thou, nectar-beaming Moon,
Regent of dewy night,
From yon black roe, that in thy bosom sleeps,   20
Fawn-spotted *Sasin* hight;
Wilt thou desert so soon
Thy night-flow'rs pale, whom liquid odour steeps,
And *Oshadhi*'s transcendent beam
Burning in the darkest glade?   25
Will no lov'd name thy gentle mind persuade
Yet one short hour to shed thy cooling stream?
But ah! we court a passing dream:
Our pray'r nor *Indu* nor *Himánsu* hears;
He fades; he disappears –   30

---

16   *the Védas three*   The *Rig-Veda* (*c*.1000 BC) consists of 1,028 hymns and prayers; the *Sama Veda*, which is basically a rearrangement of *Rig-Veda* materials for singing; the *Yajur Veda* contains explanations and ritual formulae.

20–1   *From yon black roe, that in thy bosom sleeps,/Fawn-spotted Sasin hight*   According to Daniélou, Śaśin means 'Marked-with-a-Hare', and the epithet Mṛgānka denotes 'Marked-like-a-Deer', *Hindu Polytheism*, p.100.

24   *Oshadhi*   On account of its magical association with plant growth the Moon is known as Osadhipati (Lord of Herbs), see *Śatapatha Brāhmaṇa* II.2.4.

29   *Indu*   This title of the Moon, meaning the Drop (of Soma), recalls the association in the later hymns of the *Rig-Veda* between the Moon and the Divine Offering/ambrosia/hallucinogenic plant/deity/semen which constitutes Soma.

E'en *Casyapa*'s gay daughters twinkling die,
And silence lulls the sky,
Till *Chátacs* twitter from the moving brake,
And sandal-breathing gales on beds of ether wake.

Burst into song, ye spheres;   35
A greater light proclaim,
And hymn, concentrick orbs, with sev'nfold chime
The God with many a name;
Nor let unhallow'd ears
Drink life and rapture from your charm sublime: 40
'Our bosoms, *Aryama*, inspire,
'Gem of heav'n, and flow'r of day,
'*Vivaswat*, lancer of the golden ray,
'*Divácara*, pure source of holy fire,
'Victorious *Ráma*'s fervid sire,   45
'Dread child of *Aditi*, *Martunda* bless'd,
'Or *Súra* be address'd,
'*Ravi*, or *Mihira*, or *Bhánu* bold,
'Or *Arca*, title old,
'Or *Heridaswa* drawn by green-hair'd steeds,   50
'Or *Carmasachi* keen, attesting secret deeds.

'What fiend, what monster fierce
'E'er durst thy throne invade?
'Malignant *Ráhu*. Him thy wakeful sight,
'That could the deepest shade   55

---

31 *Casyapa* Kaśyapa is the god of Vision.
33 *Chátacs* The *cātaka* or crested cuckoo, which is reputed to drink only from rainclouds, cf. *Sacontalá*, III.289–91.
35–8 '*Astronomy* was the fifth of the *Védángas* as it was delivered by SÚRYA, and other divine persons:' 'On the Literature of the Hindus', *Works*, IV.95.
41–51 In these lines Jones lists many of the names of Súrya, including '*Vivaswat*' (resplendent); '*Divácara*' (maker of the day); 'child of *Aditi*' (son of the Primordial Vastness [Aditi]); '*Martunda*' (born from a lifeless egg); '*Ravi*' (the Divider); '*Mihira*' Mitra, god of friendship [influenced by the Persian Mithra, god of light]; '*Bhánu*' (shining); '*Arca*' (radiant one); '*Carmasacshi*' Karma-sāksin (the Witness-of-Deeds). *Aryama* (l.41) is not one of Súrya's names; Aryaman (Chivalry) is one of the Ādityas (Sovereign Principles, which govern the universe and human life), responsible for the maintenance of aristocratic society. The fact that Aryaman is frequently invoked to make clear Súrya's path (*Śatapatha Brāhmana* V.3.1.) might account for Jones's confusion here.
54 *Ráhu* Rāhu is the demon spirit who causes eclipses by attempting to devour the sun and moon. 'While the gods were sharing the nectar, a *dānava* (spirit) named Rāhu, disguised as a god, was drinking his share; the Sun and the Moon discovered him when the nectar had only reached his throat, and they informed the other gods. Vishnu instantly cut off with his discus the *dānava*'s head, which was thrown into the sky and began to utter piteous cries, while the headless trunk fell upon the ground and, rolling thereon, made the earth tremble, with her mountains, forests, and islands. From that time a quarrel had existed between Rāhu's head and the sun and the moon, and to this day it always attempts to swallow the sun and the moon.' (*Bhāgavata Purāna* 10.8.9.)

'Of snaky *Narac* pierce,
'Mark'd quaffing nectar; when by magick sleight
'A *Sura*'s lovely form he wore,
'Rob'd in light, with lotos crown'd,
'What time th' immortals peerless treasures found   60
'On the churn'd Ocean's gem-bespangled shore,
'And *Mandar*'s load the tortoise bore:
'Thy voice reveal'd the daring sacrilege;
'Then, by the deathful edge
'Of bright *Sudersan* cleft, his dragon head   65
'Dismay and horror spread
'Kicking the skies, and struggling to impair
'The radiance of thy robes, and stain thy golden hair.

'With smiles of stern disdain
'Thou, sov'reign victor, seest   70
'His impious rage: soon from the mad assault
'Thy coursers fly releas'd;
'Then toss each verdant mane,
'And gallop o'er the smooth aerial vault;
'Whilst in charm'd *Gócul*'s od'rous vale   75
'Blue-ey'd *Yamunà* descends
'Exulting, and her tripping tide suspends,
'The triumph of her mighty sire to hail:
'So must they fall, who Gods assail!
'For now the demon rues his rash emprise,   80
'Yet, bellowing blasphemies
'With pois'nous throat, for horrid vengeance thirsts,
'And oft with tempest bursts,
'As oft repell'd he groans in fiery chains,
'And o'er the realms of day unvanquish'd *Súrya* reigns.'   85

Ye clouds, in wavy wreathes
Your dusky van unfold;
O'er dimpled sands, ye surges, gently flow,
With sapphires edg'd and gold!

---

56   *snaky Narac*   A Hindu netherworld.
62   *And Mandar's load the tortoise bore*   Mandara (the Slow-Mountain) was the churning rod supported by Vishnu in the shape of a tortoise. See notes to 'A Hymn to Indra', 1.50, 'A Hymn to Lacshmí', 1.1.
64–5   *the deathful edge/Of bright Sudersan cleft*   Sudarśana (Fair to see) is the name of Vishnu's sharpened discus or *cakra*, cf. 'A Hymn to Náráyena', 1.84. In some Vedic hymns the *cakra* denotes a cosmic wheel and a symbol of Súrya, the sun, (see *Rig-Veda* I.115); it is depicted on India's national flag.
76   *Blue-ey'd Yamunà*   The river Jumna is the daughter of Súrya and Samjnā (Knowledge).

Loose-tressed morning breathes, 90
And spreads her blushes with expansive glow;
But chiefly where heav'n's op'ning eye
Sparkles at her saffron gate,
How rich, how regal in his orient state!
Erelong he shall emblaze th' unbounded sky: 95
The fiends of darkness yelling fly;
While birds of liveliest note and lightest wing
The rising daystar sing,
Who skirts th' horizon with a blazing line
Of topazes divine; 100
E'en, in their prelude, brighter and more bright,
Flames the red east, and pours insufferable light.*

First o'er blue hills appear,
With many an agate hoof
And pasterns fring'd with pearl, sev'n coursers green; 105
Nor boasts yon arched woof,
That girds the show'ry sphere,
Such heav'n-spun threads of colour'd light serene,
As tinge the reins, which *Arun* guides,
Glowing with immortal grace, 110
Young *Arun*, loveliest of *Vinatian* race,
Though younger He, whom *Mádhava* bestrides,
When high on eagle-plumes he rides:
But oh! what pencil of a living star
Could paint that gorgeous car, 115
In which, as in an ark supremely bright,
The lord of boundless light

*See GRAY's Letters, p. 382, 4to. and the note.

---

102   *and pours insufferable light*   The letter to which Jones refers in his footnote is to Mr Nicholls (19 November 1764). Gray, describing a walk at daybreak, writes: 'all at once a little line of insufferable brightness that (before I can write these five words) was grown to half an orb, and now to a whole one, too glorious to be distinctly seen'. Gray's editor, William Mason, compares a passage from Dr Jeremy Taylor's *Holy Dying* (London, 1651), p.17, the sun 'sends away the spirits of darkness; he gives light to the cock and calls up the lark to mattins; and by and by gilds the fringes of a cloud, and peeps over the eastern hills thrusting out his golden horns . . .', see *The Poems of Mr. Gray, To Which are Prefixed Memoirs of his Life and Writings*, second edition, (London, 1775), p.382.
103–5   Seven bright green mares draw the chariot of Súrya.
111   *Young Arun, loveliest of Vinatian race*   Aruna (the red one) one of the sons of Kaśyapa (Vision) and Vinatā (She-before-whom-Knowledge-Bows), acts as the charioteer of Súrya.
112   *Though younger He, whom Mádhava bestrides/When high on eagle plumes he rides*   Garuda (Wings of Speech), who is half golden bird, half man, is the younger brother of Aruna, and the aerial mount of Mádhava (Vishnu). Garuda represents the hermetic utterances of the Vedas, see Daniélou, *Hindu Polytheism*, pp.160–2.

Ascending calm o'er th' empyrean sails,
And with ten thousand beams his awful beauty veils.

Behind the glowing wheels   120
Six jocund seasons dance,
A radiant month in each quick-shifting hand;
Alternate they advance,
While buxom nature feels
The grateful changes of the frolick band: 125
Each month a constellation fair
Knit in youthful wedlock holds,
And o'er each bed a varied sun unfolds,
Lest one vast blaze our visual force impair,
A canopy of woven air.   130
Vasanta blythe with many a laughing flow'r
Decks his *Candarpa*'s bow'r;
The drooping pastures thirsty *Grìshma* dries,
Till *Vershà* bids them rise;
Then *Sarat* with full sheaves the champaign fills,   135
Which *Sisira* bedews, and stern *Hémanta* chills.

Mark, how the all-kindling orb
Meridian glory gains!
Round *Méru*'s breathing zone he winds oblique
O'er pure cerulean plains: 140
His jealous flames absorb
All meaner lights, and unresisted strike
The world with rapt'rous joy and dread.
Ocean, smit with melting pain,
Shrinks, and the fiercest monster of the main   145
Mantles in caves profound his tusky head
With sea-weeds dank and coral spread:
Less can mild earth and her green daughters bear
The noon's wide-wasting glare;

131 *Vasanta blythe with many a laughing flow'r* The season of Spring.
132 *Candarpa* The Inflamer-of-the-Creator, one of the many names of Kāma, cf. 'A Hymn to Durgá', II.3.8.
133 *thirsty Grìshma* The time of heat. On the Hindu seasons see Jones's essay 'On the Musical Modes of the Hindus', *Works*, IV.191–2.
134 *Till Vershà bids them rise* *Vershà* is the rainy season.
135 *Then Sarat with full sheaves the champaign fills* This corresponds to part of our autumn.
136 *Which Sisira bedews and stern Hémanta chills* Months derived from words which signify 'dew' and 'frost' respectively.
139 *Méru* The Olympus of India, the axial northern mountain, sometimes known as Suméru, see 'A Hymn to Indra', l.20n.

To rocks the panther creeps; to woody night   150
The vulture steals his flight;
E'en cold cameleons pant in thickets dun,
And o'er the burning grit th' unwinged locusts run!

But when thy foaming steeds
Descend with rapid pace   155
Thy fervent axle hast'ning to allay,
What majesty, what grace
Dart o'er the western meads
From thy relenting eye their blended ray!
Soon may th' undazzled sense behold   160
Rich as *Vishnu*'s diadem,
Or *Amrit* sparkling in an azure gem,
Thy horizontal globe of molten gold,
Which pearl'd and rubied clouds infold.
It sinks; and myriads of diffusive dyes   165
Stream o'er the tissued skies,
Till *Sóma* smiles, attracted by the song
Of many a plumed throng
In groves, meads, vales; and, whilst he glides above,
Each bush and dancing bough quaffs harmony and love.   170

Then roves thy poet free,
Who with no borrow'd art
Dares hymn thy pow'r, and durst provoke thy blaze,
But felt thy thrilling dart;
And now, on lowly knee,   175
From him, who gave the wound, the balsam prays.
Herbs, that assuage the fever's pain,
Scatter from thy rolling car,
Cull'd by sage *Aswin* and divine *Cumàr*;
And, if they ask, 'What mortal pours the strain?'   180
Say (for thou seest earth, air, and main)
Say: 'From the bosom of yon silver isle,
'Where skies more softly smile,

---

167   *Sóma*   The god of the Moon, see note to l.29 above.

173–4   *Dares hymn thy pow'r, and durst provoke thy blaze,/But felt thy thrilling dart*   Cf. Jones's letter of St David's Day 1785 to Charles Wilkins: 'The powerful *Surye*, whom I worship only that he may do me no harm, confines me to my house, as long as he appears in the heavens', *Letters*, II.665.

179   *sage Aswin*   The Aśvins are actually beautiful twins, givers of health, youth and fecundity. They are the physicians to the gods, skilled in all the secrets of medicinal herbs.

   divine Cumàr   Kumāra, or Skanda, an adolescent hero conceived of the seed of Śiva to defeat the powers of evil.

'He came; and, lisping our celestial tongue,
'Though not from *Brahmà* sprung,   185
'Draws orient knowledge from its fountains pure,
'Through caves obstructed long, and paths too long obscure.'

   Yes; though the *Sanscrit* song
Be strown with fancy's wreathes,
And emblems rich, beyond low thoughts refin'd,   190
Yet heav'nly truth it breathes
With attestation strong,
That, loftier than thy sphere, th' Eternal Mind,
Unmov'd, unrival'd, undefil'd,
Reigns with providence benign: 195
He still'd the rude abyss, and bade it shine
(Whilst Sapience with approving aspect mild
Saw the stupendous work, and smil'd);
Next thee, his flaming minister, bade rise
O'er young and wondering skies.   200
Since thou, great orb, with all-enlight'ning ray
Rulest the golden day,
How far more glorious He, who said serene,
BE, and *thou wast* – Himself unform'd, unchang'd, unseen!

193–204   Jones's profound Deism is apparent here, and it seems to matter little whether this prime 'unmov'd' mover be conceived in Vedic or Mosaic terms, cf. 'On the Gods of Greece, Italy, and India', pp.352–3 below.

18

A Hymn to Lacshmí (1788)

[First published in the fourth volume of Gladwin's periodical (now re-titled *The New Asiatic Miscellany* [Calcutta: Joseph Cooper, 1789] pp.1–12), this was Jones's seventh hymn, comprising fourteen 18-line stanzas. The hymn was composed 'in ten or twelve hours' in September 1788 (*Letters* II.817), and a manuscript portion is extant in the National Archives of India, New Delhi (Home Public Dept. Records, Consultation 2 October, No. 16 – 1788). Inspired by his reading of his friend Charles Wilkins's *Bhagavad-Gita* (London, 1785), it celebrates Lakshmī, the 'Ceres of Hindustan' as Jones termed her. The goddess of fortune, prosperity, and fertility, she is widely worshipped as the consort of Vishnu, whose all-pervading, preserving power she actively embodies. The copy-text is that of 1799, with variants noted from Jones's Calcutta printing (Althorp Papers).]

THE ARGUMENT

MOST of the allusions to *Indian* Geography and Mythology, which occur in the following Ode to the Goddess of Abundance, have been explained on former occasions; and the rest are sufficiently clear. LACSHMÍ, or SRÍ, the CERES of *India*, is the *preserving power* of nature, or, in the language of allegory, the consort of VISHNU or HERI, a personification of the divine goodness; and her origin is variously deduced in the several *Puráná's*, as we might expect from a system wholly figurative and emblematical. Some represent her as the daughter of BHRIGU, a son of BRAHMÁ; but, in the *Márcandéya Puràn*, the *Indian* ISIS, or *Nature*, is said to have assumed three transcendent forms, according to her three *guna's* or *qualities*, and, in each of them, to have produced a pair of divinities, BRAHMÁ and LACSHMÍ, MAHÉSA and SERESWATÍ, VISHNU and CÁLÍ; after whose intermarriage, BRAHMÁ and SERESWATÍ formed the mundane Egg, which MAHÉSA and CÁLÍ divided into halves; and VISHNU together with LASCHMÍ preserved it from destruction: a third story supposes her to have sprung from the *Sea of milk*, when it was churned on the second incarnation of HERI, who is often painted reclining on the serpent ANANTA, the emblem of eternity; and this fable, whatever may be the meaning of it, has been chosen as the most poetical. The other names of SRÍ, or *Prosperity*, are HERIPRIYÁ, PEDMÁLAYÁ, or PEDMÁ, and CAMALÁ; the first implying the wife of VISHNU, and the rest derived from the names of the Lotos. As to the tale of SUDÁMAN, whose wealth is proverbial among the *Hindus*, it is related at considerable length in the *Bhágavat*, or great *Puràn* on the Achievements of CRISHNA: the *Bráhmen*, who read it with me, was frequently stopped by his tears. We may be inclined perhaps to think, that the wild fables of idolaters are not worth knowing, and that we may be satisfied with mispending our time in learning the Pagan Theology of old *Greece* and *Rome*; but we must consider, that the allegories contained in the Hymn to LACSHMÍ constitute at this moment the prevailing religion of a most extensive and celebrated Empire, and are devoutly believed by many millions, whose industry adds to the revenue of *Britain*, and whose manners, which are interwoven with their religious opinions, nearly affect all *Europeans*, who reside among them.

THE HYMN

Daughter of Ocean and primeval Night,
Who, fed with moonbeams dropping silver dew,
And cradled in a wild wave dancing light,
Saw'st with a smile new shores and creatures new,
Thee, Goddess, I salute; thy gifts I sing,   5
      And, not with idle wing,
Soar from this fragrant bow'r through tepid skies,
Ere yet the steeds of noon's effulgent king
Shake their green manes and blaze with rubied eyes:
Hence, floating o'er the smooth expanse of day,   10
      Thy bounties I survey,
See through man's oval realm thy charms display'd,
See clouds, air, earth, performing thy behest,
Plains by soft show'rs, thy tripping handmaids, dress'd,
And fruitful woods, in gold and gems array'd,   15
      Spangling the mingled shade;
While autumn boon his yellow ensign rears,
And stores the world's true wealth in rip'ning ears.

But most that central tract thy smile adorns,
Which old *Himála* clips with fost'ring arms,   20
As with a waxing moon's half-circling horns,
And shields from bandits fell, or worse alarms
Of *Tatar* horse from *Yunan* late subdued,
      Or *Bactrian* bowmen rude;
Snow-crown'd *Himála*, whence, with wavy wings   25
Far spread, as falcons o'er their nestlings brood,
Fam'd *Brahmaputra* joy and verdure brings,
And *Sindhu*'s five-arm'd flood from *Cashghar* hastes,
      To cheer the rocky wastes,

---

1 *Daughter of Ocean* The sea of milk is an undifferentiated mass of infinite fertility and potentiality. Vishnu in his avatar of a tortoise creates in the depths of the ocean the stable foundation on which rises the axis of the world, Mount Mandara. Tortoise and mountain become a divine churning stick and the elements of creation begin to appear; first the moon, then Lakshmī, and ultimately the nectar of immortality.

8–9 See 'A Hymn to Súrya', ll.102–18.

19–36 With this celebration of the rivers of northern India cf. 'A Hymn to Gangá'.

27–36 According to the myth, the sacred rivers invite Lakshmī to bathe in their immortal waters, and the sacred elephants pour the holy waters of the Ganges from golden vessels over her body. 'With a golden complexion, bathed in the stream of ambrosia flowing from golden vessels held by the trunks of four white elephants, she looks like the abode of snow, the Himálaya. Her hands grant boons, allay fear, and hold two lotoses', *Kamalā Tantrum* 518.

Through western this and that through orient plains;　　　30
While bluish *Yamunà* between them streams,
And *Gangà* pure with sunny radiance gleams,
Till *Vánì*, whom a russet ochre stains,
　　　Their destin'd confluence gains:
Then flows in mazy knot the triple pow'r　　　35
O'er laughing *Magadh* and the vales of *Gour*.

Not long inswath'd the sacred infant lay
(Celestial forms full soon their prime attain):
Her eyes, oft darted o'er the liquid way,
With golden light emblaz'd the darkling main;　　　40
And those firm breasts, whence all our comforts well,
　　　Rose with enchanting swell;
Her loose hair with the bounding billows play'd,
And caught in charming toils each pearly shell,
That idling through the surgy forest stray'd;　　　45
When ocean suffer'd a portentous change,
　　　Toss'd with convulsion strange;
For lofty *Mandar* from his base was torn,
With streams, rocks, woods, by God and Demons whirl'd,
While round his craggy sides the mad spray curl'd,　　　50
Huge mountain, by the passive Tortoise borne:
　　　Then sole, but not forlorn,
Shipp'd in a flow'r, that balmy sweets exhal'd,
O'er waves of dulcet cream PEDMÁLÁ sail'd.

So name the Goddess from her Lotos blue,　　　55
Or CAMALÁ, if more auspicious deem'd:
With many-petal'd wings the blossom flew,
And from the mount a flutt'ring sea-bird seem'd,
Till on the shore it stopp'd, the heav'n-lov'd shore,
　　　Bright with unvalued store　　　60

33　*Vánì*　Vānī (Speech) is another title for Sarasvatī, the sacred river which was supposed to flow underground to join the confluence of the Ganges and the Jumna at the sacred pilgrimage site of Trivéni, see Jones's Argument to 'A Hymn to Gangà', and 'A Hymn to Sereswaty', l.169 and n.

37–72　With this description of the churning of the ocean of milk, whence Lakshmī arose, cf. 'A Hymn to Indra', ll.69–83, and *Rāmāyaṇa* I.45.40–3.

41　*And those firm breasts, whence all our comforts well*　'. . . in very ancient temples near *Gayá*, we see images of LACSHMÍ, with full breasts and a *cord* twisted under her arm like a *horn of plenty*, which look very much like the old *Grecian* and *Roman* figures of CERES', 'On the Gods', *Works*, III.347.

54–6　PÉDMÁLA . . . CAMALÁ　Lakshmī is frequently entitled Padmā and Kamalā, 'lotos'. The lotos represents the fertile power of organic life, the beautiful creative processes of the world. It also symbolizes purity and spiritual perfection, its aspiring blossoms transcend the primordial mud in which it is rooted.

Of gems marine by mirthful INDRA won;
But she, (what brighter gem had shone before?)
No bride for old MÁRÍCHA's frolick son,
On azure HERI fix'd her prosp'ring eyes:
    Love bade the bridegroom rise;   65
Straight o'er the deep, then dimpling smooth, he rush'd;
And tow'rd th' unmeasur'd snake, stupendous bed,
The world's great mother, not reluctant, led:
All nature glow'd, whene'er she smil'd or blush'd;
    The king of serpents hush'd   70
His thousand heads, where diamond mirrors blaz'd,
That multiplied her image, as he gaz'd.

Thus multiplied, thus wedded, they pervade,
In varying myriads of ethereal forms,
This pendent Egg by dovelike MÁYÁ laid,   75
And quell MAHÉSA's ire, when most it storms;
Ride on keen lightning and disarm its flash,
    Or bid loud surges lash
Th' impassive rock, and leave the rolling barque
With oars unshatter'd milder seas to dash;   80
And oft, as man's unnumber'd woes they mark,
They spring to birth in some high-favour'd line,
    Half human, half divine,
And tread life's maze transfigur'd, unimpair'd:

---

63   *old MÁRÍCHA's frolic son*   The son of Marīci (Light), Kaśyapa (Vision), whose name, according to the *Mārkaṇḍeya Purāṇa* means 'wine-drinker'.

64   *azure HERI*   Hari ('the Remover') is Vishnu, who takes away sorrow and ignorance. 'Vishnu is always presented as black or dark blue. Darkness is the colour of ether, the formless, pervasive substance of the spatial universe, and thus a symbol of the Pervader', Daniélou, *Hindu Polytheism*, p.159.

65–72   These lines provide an effective blend of dignity and sensuality as befits a union of such cosmic significance, performed upon the 'stupendous bed' of the serpent Ananta whose thousand mirrored heads infinitely reduplicate this act of primeval potency. The vibrant description of the coiled Ananta, (otherwise known as Seshanaga, or Śeṣa, cf. 'A Hymn to Náráyena', 1.74), who represents eternity or absence of time, while sustaining and reflecting all created things may well have influenced both Southey and Shelley. In the opinion of John Drew: 'It is in this hymn, if anywhere, that Shelley would have become familiar with Seshanaga as well as with the goddess who, I have argued, was the prototype, by way of Miss Owenson's Luxima, for his own Asia', *India and the Romantic Imagination*, pp.266–70.

73–84   The pervasive manifestation of 'varying myriads of ethereal forms' is based upon an archetypal triad of male, female, and serpent, which Shelley was also to use in *Prometheus Unbound*. See S. R. Swaminathan, 'Keats and Shelley: Comparative Studies in Two Types of Poetic Imagery', unpublished D.Phil. thesis, Oxford, 1957, pp.634–54.

75   *This pendent Egg*   See 'A Hymn to Náráyena', ll.37–54 and n.

76   *MAHÉSA*   Maheśvara, the Lord of Knowledge is one of Śiva's titles.

As when, through blest *Vrindávan*'s od'rous grove,   85
They deign'd with hinds and village girls to rove,
And mirth or toil in field or dairy shar'd,
      As lowly rusticks far'd;
Blythe RÁDHÁ she, with speaking eyes, was nam'd,
He CRISHNA, lov'd in youth, in manhood fam'd.   90

Though long in *Mathurá* with milkmaids bred,
Each bush attuning with his past'ral flute,
ANANDA's holy steers the Herdsman fed,
His nobler mind aspir'd to nobler fruit:
The fiercest monsters of each brake or wood   95
      His youthful arm withstood,
And from the rank mire of the stagnant lake
Drew the crush'd serpent with ensanguin'd hood;
Then, worse than rav'ning beast or fenny snake,
A ruthless king his pond'rous mace laid low,   100
      And heav'n approv'd the blow:
No more in bow'r or wattled cabin pent,
By rills he scorn'd and flow'ry banks to dwell;
His pipe lay tuneless, and his wreathy shell
With martial clangor hills and forests rent;   105
      On crimson wars intent
He sway'd high *Dwáracá*, that fronts the mouth
Of gulfy *Sindhu* from the burning south.

A Bráhmen young, who, when the heav'nly boy
In *Vraja* green and scented *Gócul* play'd,   110
Partook each transient care, each flitting joy,
And hand in hand through dale or thicket stray'd,

85–90   Vishnu/Krishna becomes incarnate as the cowherd Govinda and Lakshmī as the cowherdess Rādhā. See *Gítagóvinda*, and cf. 'A Hymn to Gangá', ll.74–5.

91   *Mathurá*   The sacred birthplace of Krishna, the abode of wisdom.

93   ANANDA's *holy steers the Herdsman fed*   'CRISHNA was fostered by an honest herdsman surnamed ANANDA, or *Happy*', 'On the Gods', *Works*, III.374.

96–8   As a boy he slew the dreadful serpent *Cáliya*, not to mention a number of giants and monsters. See 'On the Gods', *Works*, III.377.

100   *A ruthless king his pond'rous mace laid low*   The reference is to his wicked uncle, King Kamsa, or CANSA, as Jones has it, ibid.

104   *His pipe lay tuneless, and his wreathy shell*   Krishna's flute delights the gazelle-eyed women. See *Gítagóvinda*, ll.71–2. The sacred shell was the left-handed buccinum. See 'On the Gods', *Works*, III.376.

107   *He sway'd high Dwáraca*   the mighty city built by the heavenly architect Viśkarman, and the capital of Krishna's kingdom.

109ff.   *A Bráhmen young*   Sudáman, or Śrídáman, was a companion of Krishna's youth in the village of Vraja. The visit of Sudáman to the palace of Dvárakā, with its emphasis upon loving devotion rewarded, is a parable of divine love. See *Bhāgavata Purāṇa* X.80.6–X.81.41.

By fortune sever'd from the blissful seat,
    Had sought a lone retreat;
Where in a costless hut sad hours he pass'd,   115
Its mean thatch pervious to the daystar's heat,
And fenceless from night's dew or pinching blast:
Firm virtue he possess'd and vig'rous health,
    But they were all his wealth.
SUDÁMAN was he nam'd; and many a year   120
(If glowing song can life and honour give)
From sun to sun his honour'd name shall live:
Oft strove his consort wise their gloom to cheer,
    And hide the stealing tear;
But all her thrift could scarce each eve afford   125
The needful sprinkling of their scanty board.

    Now Fame, who rides on sunbeams, and conveys
To woods and antres deep her spreading gleam,
Illumin'd earth and heav'n with CRISHNA's praise:
Each forest echoed loud the joyous theme,   130
But keener joy SUDÁMAN's bosom thrill'd,
    And tears ecstatick rill'd:
'My friend, he cried, is monarch of the skies!'
Then counsell'd she, who nought unseemly will'd:
'Oh! haste; oh! seek the God with lotos eyes;   135
'The pow'r, that stoops to soften human pain,
    'None e'er implor'd in vain.'
To *Dwáracá*'s rich tow'rs the pilgrim sped,
Though bashful penury his hope depress'd;
A tatter'd cincture was his only vest,   140
And o'er his weaker shoulder loosely spread
    Floated the mystick thread:
Secure from scorn the crowded paths he trode
Through yielding ranks, and hail'd the Shepherd God.

    'Friend of my childhood, lov'd in riper age,   145
'A dearer guest these mansions never grac'd:
'O meek in social hours, in council sage!'
So spake the Warriour, and his neck embrac'd;
And e'en the Goddess left her golden seat
    Her lord's compeer to greet: 150

149–50 *And e'en the Goddess left her golden seat/Her lord's compeer to greet* Lakshmī becomes Rukminī when Vishnu appears as Krishna. Jones indicates divine condescension here on the part of queen Rukminī, but the *Purāṇa* pictures her fanning Sudāman while Krishna washes the Brahman's feet.

He charm'd, but prostrate on the hallow'd floor,
Their purfled vestment kiss'd and radiant feet;
Then from a small fresh leaf, a borrow'd store
(Such off'rings e'en to mortal kings are due)
      Of modest rice he drew.   155
Some proffer'd grains the soft-ey'd Hero ate,
And more had eaten, but, with placid mien,
Bright RUCMINÍ (thus name th' all-bounteous Queen)
Exclaim'd: 'Ah, hold! enough for mortal state!'
      Then grave on themes elate   160
Discoursing, or on past adventures gay,
They clos'd with converse mild the rapt'rous day.

  At smile of dawn dismiss'd, ungifted, home
The hermit plodded, till sublimely rais'd
On granite columns many a sumptuous dome   165
He view'd, and many a spire, that richly blaz'd,
And seem'd, impurpled by the blush of morn,
      The lowlier plains to scorn
Imperious: they, with conscious worth serene,
Laugh'd at vain pride, and bade new gems adorn   170
Each rising shrub, that clad them. Lovely scene
And more than human! His astonish'd sight
      Drank deep the strange delight:
He saw brisk fountains dance, crisp riv'lets wind
O'er borders trim, and round inwoven bow'rs,   175
Where sportive creepers, threading ruby flow'rs
On em'rald stalks, each vernal arch intwin'd,
      Luxuriant though confin'd;

---

156 *Some proffer'd grains the soft-eyed Hero ate* This seems a very different god from the young revolutionary who sported with milkmaids and humiliated Indra. Now married and mature, he shows a protective and respectful attitude towards Brahmans.

163–9 *At smile of dawn dismiss'd, ungifted, home/The hermit plodded* The opening, with its rather prosaic diction and short vowels, creates a monochrome and pedestrian atmosphere which is transformed by the expansive sumptuousness of the rest of the stanza as surely as the thatched hut is metamorphosed into a golden palace. Dawn's simple smile had lighted Sudāman's departure, but the domes and spires of his palace *richly blaz'd, impurpled by the blush of morn* as they imperiously scorn the surrounding plain.

169–80 *they, with conscious worth serene,/Laugh'd at vain pride, and bade new gems adorn/Each rising shrub that clad them* The *lowlier plains* represent Nature, and to some extent Sudāman himself, as such palatial splendour might seem incompatible with Brahman spirituality. Certainly the beauty he drinks deep is the beauty of nature, and of nature controlled. The borders are trim, the *crisp riv'lets* flow past *inwoven bowers*; Lakshmī's abundance is regulated by the gardener's art. For a moment the mention of *sportive creepers* recalls the riotous profusion of sensual plants by the Jumna where Krishna dallied with the *gopīs*. This vegetation, however, is entwined in ordered rustic arches, and like the mind of a Brahman, *luxuriant though confin'd.*

And heard sweet-breathing gales in whispers tell
From what young bloom they sipp'd their spicy smell.   180

   Soon from the palace-gate in broad array
A maiden legion, touching tuneful string,
Descending strow'd with flow'rs the brighten'd way,
And straight, their jocund van in equal wings
Unfolding, in their vacant centre show'd   185
     Their chief, whose vesture glow'd
With carbuncles and smiling pearls atween;
And o'er her head a veil translucent flow'd,
Which, dropping light, disclos'd a beauteous queen,
Who, breathing love, and swift with timid grace,   190
     Sprang to her lord's embrace
With ardent greeting and sweet blandishment;
His were the marble tow'rs, th' officious train,
The gems unequal'd and the large domain:
When bursting joy its rapid stream had spent,   195
     The stores, which heav'n had lent,
He spread unsparing, unattach'd employ'd,
With meekness view'd, with temp'rate bliss enjoy'd.

   Such were thy gifts, PEDMÁLÁ, such thy pow'r!
For, when thy smile irradiates yon blue fields,   200
Observant INDRA sheds the genial show'r,
And pregnant earth her springing tribute yields
Of spiry blades, that clothe the champaign dank,
     Or skirt the verd'rous bank,
That in th' o'erflowing rill allays his thirst: 205
Then, rising gay in many a waving rank,
The stalks redundant into laughter burst;
The rivers broad, like busy should'ring bands,
     Clap their applauding hands;
The marish dances and the forest sings;   210
The vaunting trees their bloomy banners rear;
And shouting hills proclaim th' abundant year,
That food to herds, to herdsmen plenty brings,
     And wealth to guardian kings.
Shall man unthankful riot on thy stores?   215
Ah, no! he bends, he blesses, he adores.

---

201 *Observant INDRA sheds the genial show'r* The choice of the epithet 'observant' indicates that Jones was conversant with other traditions which associate Lakshmī with Indra, to make a pairing, common in many world religions, of earth mother and rain/sky god.

But, when his vices rank thy frown excite,
Excessive show'rs the plains and valleys drench,
Or warping insects heath and coppice blight,
Or drought unceasing, which no streams can quench, 220
The germin shrivels or contracts the shoot,
    Or burns the wasted root:
Then fade the groves with gather'd crust imbrown'd,
The hills lie gasping, and the woods are mute,
Low sink the riv'lets from the yawning ground; 225
Till Famine gaunt her screaming pack lets slip,
    And shakes her scorpion whip;
Dire forms of death spread havock, as she flies,
Pain at her skirts and Mis'ry by her side,
And jabb'ring spectres o'er her traces glide; 230
The mother clasps her babe, with livid eyes,
    Then, faintly shrieking, dies:
He drops expiring, or but lives to feel
The vultures bick'ring for their horrid meal.

From ills, that, painted, harrow up the breast, 235
(What agonies, if real, must they give!)
Preserve thy vot'ries: be their labours blest!
Oh! bid the patient *Hindu* rise and live.
His erring mind, that wizard lore beguiles
    Clouded by priestly wiles, 240
To senseless nature bows for nature's GOD.
Now, stretch'd o'er ocean's vast from happier isles,
He sees the wand of empire, not the rod:
Ah, may those beams, that western skies illume,
    Disperse th' unholy gloom! 245

217–34 The hymns express Jones's delight in the fecundity of the created world, but while he was engaged in the composition of this ode to the 'Ceres of Hindustan' the results of a devastating drought were only too apparent. As he wrote to Althorp: 'The Goddess of Abundance, indeed, has not been kind this year; for we are just escaped from a famine: thousands have perished in the late dearth, and thousands are now fed every day in Calcutta, where rice is distributed by English gentlemen, most of whom have subscribed 500 rupees to purchase it: I subscribed 1000, & will double my subscription, if the dearth be not removed by the approaching harvest', *Letters*, II.813.
238–45 Jones's appeal to Lakshmī to enlighten the erring Hindu, whose mind has been *Clouded by priestly wiles*, sits ill with the subsequent exhortation that the Hindu should look westward: *may those beams, that western skies illume,/Disperse th'unholy gloom!* These lines, together with the final couplet, provide a somewhat unconvincing conclusion for a hymn to an Indian divine. Such a Serampore mood is not characteristic of a man whose Enlightenment objectivity was both dispassionate and tolerant as is evidenced in the final sentence of Jones's Argument to this poem.

Meanwhile may laws, by myriads long rever'd,
Their strife appease, their gentler claims decide;
So shall their victors, mild with virtuous pride,
To many a cherish'd grateful race endear'd,
      With temper'd love be fear'd: 250
Though mists profane obscure their narrow ken,
They err, yet feel; though pagans, they are men.

19 & 20
Two Hymns to Pracriti

THE ARGUMENT

IN all our conversations with learned *Hindus* we find them enthusiastick admirers of Poetry, which they consider as a divine art, that had been practised for numberless ages in heaven, before it was revealed on earth by VÁLMÍC, whose great Heroick Poem is fortunately preserved: the *Bráhmans* of course prefer that poetry, which they believe to have been *actually inspired*; while the *Vaidyas*, who are in general perfect grammarians and good poets, but are not suffered to read any of the *sacred* writings except the *Ayurvéda*, or *Body of Medical Tracts*, speak with rapture of their innumerable *popular* poems, *Epick*, *Lyrick*, and *Dramatick*, which were composed by men not literally inspired, but called, metaphorically, the sons of SERESWATI, or MINERVA; among whom the *Pandits* of all sects, nations, and degrees are unanimous in giving the prize of glory to CÁLÍDÁSA, who flourished in the court of VICRAMÁDITYA, fifty-seven years before Christ. He wrote several *Dramas*, one of which, entitled SACONTALÁ, is in my possession; and the subject of it appears to be as interesting as the composition is beautiful: besides these he published the *Méghadúta*, or cloud-messenger, and the *Nalódaya*, or rise of NALA, both elegant love-tales; the *Raghuvansa*, an Heroick Poem; and the *Cumára Sambhava*, or birth of CUMÁRA, which supplied me with materials for the first of the following Odes. I have not indeed yet read it; since it could not be correctly copied for me during the short interval, in which it is in my power to amuse myself with literature; but I have heard the story told both in *Sanscrit* and *Persian*, by many *Pandits*, who had no communication with each other; and their outline of it coincided so perfectly, that I am convinced of its correctness: that outline is here filled up, and exhibited in a lyrick form, partly in the *Indian*, partly in the *Grecian*, taste; and great will be my pleasure, when I can again find time for such amusements, in reading the whole poem of CÁLÍDÁSA, and in comparing my descriptions with the original composition. To anticipate the story in a preface would be to destroy the interest, that may be taken in the poem; a disadvantage attending all prefatory arguments, of which those prefixed to the several books of TASSO, and to the Dramas of METASTASIO, are obvious instances; but, that any interest may be taken in the two hymns addressed to PRACRITI, under different names, it is necessary to render them intelligible by a previous explanation of the mythological allusions, which could not but occur in them.

Iswara, or Ísa, and Ísáni or Ísí, are unquestionably the Osiris and Isis of Egypt; for, though neither a resemblance of names, nor a similarity of character, would separately prove the identity of *Indian* and *Egyptian* Deities, yet, when they both concur, with the addition of numberless corroborating circumstances, they form a proof little short of demonstration. The *female* divinity, in the mythological systems of the East, represents the active *power* of the *male*; and that Ísí means *active nature*, appears evidently from the word *śácta*, which is derived from *śacti*, or *power*, and applied to those *Hindus*, who direct their adoration principally to that goddess: this feminine character of Pracriti, or *created nature*, is so familiar in most languages, and even in our own, that the gravest *English* writers, on the most serious subjects of religion and philosophy, speak of *her* operations, as if *she* where actually an animated being; but such personifications are easily misconceived by the multitude, and have a strong tendency to polytheism. The principal operations of nature are, not the absolute annihilation and new creation of what we call *material substances*, but the temporary extinction and reproduction, or, rather in one word, the *transmutation*, of *forms*; whence the epithet *Polymorphos* is aptly given to nature by *European* philosophers: hence Íswara, Siva, Hara (for those are his names and near a thousand more), united with Ísí, represent the *secondary causes*, whatever they may be, of natural phenomena, and principally those of temporary *destruction* and *regeneration*; but the *Indian* Isis appears in a variety of characters, especially in those of Párvatí, Cálí, Durgá, and Bhávání, which bear a strong resemblance to the Juno of Homer, to Hecate, to the armed Pallas, and to the *Lucretian* Venus.

The name Párvatí took its rise from a wild poetical fiction. Himálaya, or the *Mansion of Snow*, is the title given by the *Hindus* to that vast chain of mountains, which limits *India* to the north, and embraces it with its eastern and western arms, both extending to the ocean; the former of those arms is called *Chandraséc'hara*, or the *Moon's Rock*; and the second, which reaches as far west as the mouths of the *Indus*, was named by the ancients *Montes Parveti*. These hills are held sacred by the *Indians*, who suppose them to be the terrestrial haunt of the God Íswara. The mountain *Himálaya*, being personified, is represented as a powerful monarch, whose wife was Méná: their daughter is named Párvatí, or *Mountain-born*, and Durgá, or *of difficult access*; but the *Hindus* believe her to have been married to Siva in a pre-existent state, when she bore the name of Satí. The daughter of Himálaya had two sons; Ganésa, or the *Lord of Spirits*, adored as the wisest of Deities, and always invoked at the beginning of every literary work, and Cumára, Scanda, or Cárticéya, commander of the celestial armies.

The pleasing fiction of Cáma, the *Indian* Cupid, and his friend Vasanta, or the Spring, has been the subject of another poem; and here it must be remembered, that the God of Love is named also Smara, Candarpa, and Ananga. One of his arrows is called *Mellicà, the Nyctanthes* of our Botanists, who very unadvisedly reject the vernacular names of most *Asiatick* plants: it is beautifully introduced by Cálidása into this lively couplet:

Mellicámuculè bháti gunjanmattamadhuvratah,
Prayánè panchaóánasya sanc'hamápúrayanniva.

'The intoxicated bee shines and murmurs in the fresh-blown *Mellicà*, like him who gives breath to a white conch in the procession of the God with five arrows.'

A critick, to whom CÁLÍDÁSA repeated this verse, observed, that the comparison was not exact: since the bee sits on the blossom itself, and does not murmur at the end of the tube, like him who blows a conch: 'I was aware of that, said the poet, and, therefore, described the bee as *intoxicated*: a drunken musician would blow the shell at the wrong end:' There was more than wit in this answer: it was a just rebuke to a dull critick; for poetry delights in *general* images, and is so far from being a perfect imitation, that a scrupulous exactness of descriptions and similes, by leaving nothing for the imagination to supply, never fails to diminish or destroy the pleasure of every reader, who has an imagination to be gratified.

It may here be observed, that *Nymphœa*, not *Lotos*, is the *generick* name in *Europe* of the flower consecrated to Isis: the *Persians* know by the name of *Nílúfer* that species of it, which the Botanists ridiculously call *Nelumbo*, and which is remarkable for its curious *pericarpium*, where each of the seeds contains in miniature the leaves of a perfect vegetable. The *lotos* of HOMER was probably the *sugar-cane*, and that of LINNÆUS is a papilionaceous plant; but he gives the same name to another species of the *Nymphœa*; and the word is so constantly applied among us in *India* to the *Nílúfer*, that any other would be hardly intelligible: the *blue* lotos grows in *Cashmír* and in *Persia*, but not in *Bengal*, where we see only the *red* and the *white*; and hence occasion is taken to feign, that the lotos of *Hindustan* was dyed crimson by the blood of SIVA.

CUVÉRA, mentioned in the fourteenth stanza, is the God of Wealth, supposed to reside in a magnificent city, called *Alacà*; and VRIHASPATI, or the Genius of the planet *Jupiter*, is the preceptor of the gods in *Swerga* or the firmament: he is usually represented as their orator, when any message is carried from them to one of the three superior Deities.

The lamentations of RETÍ, the wife of CAMA, fill a whole book in the *Sanscrit* poem, as I am informed by my teacher, a learned *Vaidya*; who is restrained only from reading the book, which contains a description of the nuptials; for the ceremonies of a marriage where BRAHMÁ himself officiated as the father of the bridegroom, are too holy to be known by any but *Bráhmans*.

The achievements of DURGÁ in her martial character as the patroness of *Virtue*, and her battle with a demon in the shape of a buffalo, are the subject of many episodes in the *Puránas* and *Cávyas*, or *sacred* and *popular* poems; but a full account of them would have destroyed the unity of the Ode, and they are barely alluded to in the last stanza.

It seemed proper to change the measure, when the goddess was to be addressed as BHAVÁNI, or the *power of fecundity*; but such a change, though very common in *Sanscrit*, has its inconveniences in *European* poetry: a distinct Hymn is therefore appropriated to her in that capacity; for the explanation of which we need only premise, that LACSHMÍ is the Goddess of *Abundance*; that the *Cêtaca* is a fragrant and beautiful plant of the *Diœcian* kind, known to Botanists by the name of *Pandanus*; and that the *Dúrgótsava*, or great festival of BHAVÁNI at the close of the rains, ends in throwing the image of the goddess into the *Ganges* or other sacred water.

I am not conscious of having left unexplained any difficult allusion in the two poems; and have only to add (lest *European* criticks should consider a few of the images as inapplicable to *Indian* manners), that the ideas of *snow* and *ice* are familiar to the *Hindus*; that the mountains of *Himálaya* may be clearly discerned from a part of *Bengal*; that the *Grecian* HÆMUS is the *Sanscrit* word *haimas*, meaning *snowy*; and that funeral *urns* may be seen perpetually on the banks of the river.

The two Hymns are neither translations from any other poems, nor imitations of any; and have nothing of PINDAR in them except the measures, which are nearly the same, syllable for syllable, with those of the first and second *Nemean* Odes: more musical stanzas might perhaps have been formed; but, in every art, variety and novelty are considerable sources of pleasure. The style and manner of PINDAR have been greatly mistaken; and, that a distinct idea of them may be conceived by such, as have not access to that inimitable poet in his own language, I cannot refrain from subjoining the first *Nemean* Ode, not only in the same measure as nearly as possible, but almost word for word, with the original; those epithets and phrases only being necessarily added, which are printed in *Italick* letters.

---

first Nemean Ode Omitted. For Jones's translation of Pindar's Ode see *Works*, XIII.337–41.

19 *The Hymn to Durgá* (1788)

[Composed in 1788, and published posthumously, this was his penultimate and longest hymn, inspired by oral recitations of the *Kumārasambhava* of Kālidāsa. In this largely faithful recension, Jones presents Durgā not as the terrifying goddess of destruction (Kālī), but as the destroyer of the world of illusion. Aware that many Europeans were anxious to locate Hinduism in a monstrous mire of thuggery and blood sacrifice, Durgā is portrayed as the presiding deity of devout intellect. In February 1790 he wrote to Jonathan Duncan: 'With all my admiration of the truly learned Brahmens, I abhor the sordid priestcraft of Durgá's ministers, but such fraud no more affects the sound religion of the Hindus, than the lady of Loretto and the Romish impositions affect our own rational faith', *Letters* II.856. Not entirely free from prejudice of his own, it is, nevertheless, this desire to adopt a relativist stance in his pursuit of the sound and the rational that is the benchmark of Jones's Orientalism. As Stuart Curran has written: 'What is most remarkable about his "Hymn to Durgá", composed in nine three-part sections, is the way it testifies to a combined awareness of religious connotations of the triad (both Christian and Indian) and of the symmetry appropriate to the Pindaric ode', (*Poetic Form and British Romanticism*, Oxford, 1986, p.58.) Furthermore Jones simultaneously distances and dramatizes the austere hierophant and the dedicated neophyte against a sublime backdrop of Himalayan grandeur to create an impression of Vedic dignity for his metropolitan audience. The copy-text is that of 1799, with variants noted from Jones's Calcutta printing (Althorp Papers).]

THE HYMN TO DURGÁ

I. 1.

From thee begins the solemn air,
Ador'd GANÉSA; next, thy sire we praise
(Him, from whose red clust'ring hair
A new-born crescent sheds propitious rays,
Fair as GANGÁ's curling foam),
Dread ISWARA; who lov'd o'er awful mountains,
Rapt in prescience deep, to roam,
But chiefly those, whence holy rivers gush,
Bright from their secret fountains,
And o'er the realms of BRAHMÁ rush.

I. 2.

Rock above rock they ride sublime
And lose their summits in blue fields of day,
Fashion'd first, when rolling time,
Vast infant, in his golden cradle lay,
Bidding endless ages run
And wreathe their giant heads in snows eternal
Gilt by each revolving sun;
Though neither morning beam, nor noontide glare,
In wintry sign or vernal,
Their adamantine strength impair;

I. 3.

Nor e'en the fiercest summer heat
Could thrill the palace, where their Monarch reign'd
On his frost-impearled seat,
(Such height had unremitted virtue gain'd!)

Jones's original stanza numbering has been retained as it reflects the series of tri-partite units –
strophe, antistrophe, and epode – fundamental to the Pindaric structure of the poem.
   I.1.2   *GANÉSA* the second son of Śiva and Pārvatī, is the god of wisdom. His name is
frequently invoked at the beginning of literary works as a muse figure to ensure success.
   I.1.6   *Dread ISWARA* Īsvara (the causal-divinity) is a name for Śiva as Lord of all the elements;
the red locks, surmounted by a crescent moon, belong to the traditional iconography, as do the
entwined serpents of II.2.9–10, see T. A. Gopinatha Rao, *Elements of Hindu Iconography* (Madras,
1914–16), II.225–7.

HIMÁLAYA, to whom a lovely child,
Sweet PARVATÍ, sage MÉNA bore,
Who now, in earliest bloom, saw heav'n adore
Her charms; earth languish, till she smil'd.

II. 1.

But she to love no tribute paid;
Great IŚWARA her pious cares engag'd:
Him, who Gods and fiends dismay'd,
She sooth'd with off'rings meek, when most he rag'd.
On a morn, when, edg'd with light,
The lake-born flow'rs their sapphire cups expanded
Laughing at the scatter'd night,
A vale remote and silent pool she sought,
Smooth-footed, lotos-handed,
And braids of sacred blossoms wrought;

II. 2.

Not for her neck, which, unadorn'd,
Bade envying antelopes their beauties hide:
Art she knew not, or she scorn'd;
Nor had her language e'en a name for pride.
To the God, who, fix'd in thought,
Sat in a crystal cave new worlds designing,
Softly sweet her gift she brought,
And spread the garland o'er his shoulders broad,
Where serpents huge lay twining,
Whose hiss the round creation aw'd.

I.3.6 *Sweet PARVATÍ* When she assumes the role of Śiva's wife, Durgā is identified with Pārvatī. Born from Ether (Himalaya) and Intellect (Mena), Pārvatī is a most gentle goddess, modest, devout, and devoted to the ascetic Śiva (IŚWARA).

II.I.1 *she to love no tribute paid* Although this hymn does not foreground Durgā as the infamous battle queen and demon slayer (see the final stanza), it does portray her fierce independence and absolute dedication to the 'untam'd' Śiva. Jones stresses the Pārvatī-like aspects of her character, but still manages to allow her to represent something of a challenge to the submissive stereotype of Hindu woman which emerges from the law-code of Menu, see *Works*, VII.245–73. Kinsley (*Hindu Goddesses*, p.115) contrasts the South Indian tradition which emphasizes Durgā's dangerous qualities with the North Indian tradition of the goddess as gentle young wife; Jones, writing in Bengal, predictably favours the latter.

II.1.2 *Great IŚWARA her pious cares engag'd* Inevitably Pārvatī as the meditating *yoginī* becomes the paradigm for devotees of Śiva/IŚWARA.

II.2.5–6 *the God, who, fix'd in thought,/Sat in a crystal cave new worlds designing* Śiva represents concentrated enlightenment and spiritual energy, a 'phallus of light' which must be held and stabilized by the vulva which is Pārvatī, see Daniélou, *Hindu Polytheism*, pp.265–6.

II. 3.

He view'd, half-smiling, half-severe,
The prostrate maid – That moment through the rocks
He, who decks the purple year,
VASANTA, vain of odorif'rous locks,
With CÁMA, hors'd on infant breezes flew:
(Who knows not CÁMA, nature's king?)
VASANTA barb'd the shaft and fix'd the string;
The living bow CANDARPA drew.

III. 1.

Dire sacrilege! The chosen reed,
That SMARA pointed with transcendent art,
Glanc'd with unimagin'd speed,
And ting'd its blooming barb in SIVA's heart:
Glorious flow'r, in heav'n proclaim'd
Rich *Mellicà*, with balmy breath delicious,
And on earth *Nyctanthes* nam'd!
Some drops divine, that o'er the lotos blue
Trickled in rills auspicious,
Still mark it with a crimson hue.

III. 2.

Soon clos'd the wound its hallow'd lips;
But nature felt the pain: heav'n's blazing eye
Sank absorb'd in sad eclipse,
And meteors rare betray'd the trembling sky;
When a flame, to which compar'd
The keenest lightnings were but idle flashes,
From that orb all-piercing glar'd,

II.3.4 *VASANTA* Vasanta is Spring, the frequent companion of Kāma (CÁMA), or Camdeo, the Indian Cupid.

II.3.8 *CANDARPA* At this dramatic point Kāma is given this name, which means Inflamer-of-the-Creator.

III.1.2 *SMARA* meaning Remembrance, is another of Kāma's many names.

III.I.5–6 *Rich Mellicà, with balmy breath delicious* Jones refers to the rich musky odour of Mallica, see 'Botanical Observations on Select Indian Plants', *Works*, V.73–4. See also the Argument above.

III.2.7–8 Hara, or Hari (the Remover) is the title of Śiva in his aspect of death and destruction. He reduces Kāma to ashes with the fire that flashes from his third eye, cf. 'A Hymn to Camdeo', ll.66–70.

Which in the front of wrathful HARA rolls,
And soon to silver ashes
Reduc'd th' inflamer of our souls.

III. 3.

VASANT, for thee a milder doom,
Accomplice rash, a thund'ring voice decreed:
'With'ring live in joyless gloom,
'While ten gay signs the dancing seasons lead.
'Thy flow'rs, perennial once, now annual made,
'The Fish and Ram shall still adorn;
'But, when the Bull has rear'd his golden horn,
'Shall, like yon idling rainbow, fade.'

IV. 1.

The thunder ceas'd; the day return'd;
But SIVA from terrestrial haunts had fled:
Smit with rapt'rous love he burn'd,
And sigh'd on gemm'd *Cailása*'s viewless head.
Lonely down the mountain steep,
With flutt'ring heart, soft PARVATI descended;
Nor in drops of nectar'd sleep
Drank solace through the night, but lay alarm'd,
Lest her mean gifts offended
The God her pow'rful beauty charm'd.

IV. 2.

All arts her sorr'wing damsels tried,
Her brow, where wrinkled anguish low'r'd, to smoothe,
And, her troubled soul to soothe,
Sagacious MÉNÁ mild reproof applied;
But nor art nor counsel sage,
Nor e'en her sacred parent's tender chiding,
Could her only pain assuage:
The mountain drear she sought, in mantling shade

IV.1.4 Kailāsa is the Pleasure Mountain, the favoured dwelling place when the erotic – which in Śiva alternates with the ascetic – is in the ascendant.

IV.2.8 *the mountain drear she sought* 'Durgā's liminal nature is also evident in her favorite habitats . . . Nearly all of Durgā's myths associate her with mountains, usually the Himalayas or the Vindhyas', Kinsley, *Hindu Goddesses*, p.99.

Her tears and transports hiding,
And oft to her adorer pray'd.

IV. 3.

There on a crag, whose icy rift
Hurl'd night and horror o'er the pool profound,
That with madding eddy swift
Revengeful bark'd his rugged base around,
The beauteous hermit sat; but soon perceiv'd
A *Bráhmen* old before her stand,
His rude staff quiv'ring in his wither'd hand,
Who, falt'ring, ask'd for whom she griev'd.

V. 1.

'What graceful youth with accents mild,
'Eyes like twin stars, and lips like early morn,
'Has thy pensive heart beguil'd?'
'No mortal youth,' she said with modest scorn,
'E'er beguil'd my guiltless heart:
'Him have I lost, who to these mountains hoary
'Bloom celestial could impart.
'Thee I salute, thee ven'rate, thee deplore,
'Dread SIVA, source of glory,
'Which on these rocks must gleam no more!'

V. 2.

'Rare object of a damsel's love,'
The wizard bold replied, 'who, rude and wild,
'Leaves eternal bliss above,
'And roves o'er wastes where nature never smil'd,
'Mounted on his milkwhite bull!
'Seek INDRA with aërial bow victorious,
'Who from vases ever full

IV.3   Cf. the use Gray makes of dramatic and sublime scenery in his influential Pindaric ode,
'The Bard', 'On a rock, whose haughty brow/Frowns o'er old Conway's foaming flood', (I.2.1–2).

IV.3.6   *A Brahmen old*   Cf. *Kumārasambhava* 5.30–4, and the *Śiva-purāṇa*, Rudra-samhita
3.25.45–51; 3.27.10–38, where the god in disguise attempts to dissuade her from her desire to marry
Śiva.

V.2.6   Indra has a reputation for the lasciviousness and the pursuit of pleasure.

'Quaffs love and nectar; seek the festive hall,
'Rich caves, and mansion glorious
'Of young CUVÉRA, lov'd by all;

V. 3.

'But spurn that sullen wayward God,
'That three-ey'd monster, hideous, fierce, untam'd,
'Unattir'd, ill-girt, unshod –'
'Such fell impiety, the nymph exclaim'd,
'Who speaks, must agonize; who hears, must die;
'Nor can this vital frame sustain
'The pois'nous taint, that runs from vein to vein;
'Death may atone the blasphemy.'

VI. 1.

She spoke, and o'er the rifted rocks
Her lovely form with pious phrensy threw;
But beneath her floating locks
And waving robes a thousand breezes flew,
Knitting close their silky plumes,
And in mid-air a downy pillow spreading;
Till, in clouds of rich perfumes
Embalm'd, they bore her to a mystick wood;
Where streams of glory shedding,
The well-feign'd *Bráhmen*, SIVA stood.

VI. 2.

The rest, my song conceal:
Unhallow'd ears the sacrilege might rue.
Gods alone to Gods reveal
In what stupendous notes th' immortals woo.
Straight the sons of light prepar'd
The nuptial feast, heav'n's opal gates unfolding,
Which th' empyreal army shar'd;

V.2.10 *CUVÉRA* Kubera, the Lord of Riches, dwells in a splendid bejewelled palace.

VI.1 In portraying her dramatic response to the 'blasphemy', Jones follows Hindu tradition in associating Pārvatī with Satī, Śiva's first wife, who committed suicide because of an insult to her husband. Pārvatī's devotion and aceticism mirror those of Satī and similarly attract Śiva's attention.

VI.2.4 *In what stupendous notes th'immortals woo* According to the *Śiva-purāṇa*, not only does the earth move for Pārvatī and Śiva during their violent love-making, the frame of the cosmos is shaken to the terror of the gods. (4.1.44–6)

And sage HIMÁLAYA shed blissful tears
With aged eyes beholding
His daughter empress of the spheres.

VI. 3.

Whilst ev'ry lip with nectar glow'd,
The bridegroom blithe his transformation told:
Round the mirthful goblets flow'd,
And laughter free o'er plains of ether roll'd:
'Thee too, like VISHNU, said the blushing queen,
'Soft MÁYÁ, guileful maid, attends;
'But in delight supreme the phantasm ends;
'Love crowns the visionary scene.'

VII. 1.

Then rose VRIHASPATI, who reigns
Beyond red MANGALA's terrifick sphere,
Wand'ring o'er cerulean plains:
His periods eloquent heav'n loves to hear
Soft as dew on waking flow'rs.
He told, how TÁRACA with snaky legions,
Envious of supernal pow'rs,
Had menac'd long old MÉRU's golden head,
And INDRA's beaming regions
With desolation wild had spread:

VII. 2.

How, when the Gods to BRAHMÁ flew
In routed squadrons, and his help implor'd;
'Sons, he said, from vengeance due
'The fiend must wield secure his fiery sword

VI.3.6 *Soft MÁYÁ, guileful maid, attends* Durgā is seen as a personification of *māyā* (the power of illusion) when she deludes the demons Madhu and Kaitabha in order to help Vishnu slay them, see the *Devī-māhātmya*, I.40–74, and 'A Hymn to Náráyena', ll.84–6.

VII.1.1 *VRIHASPATI* or Bṛhaspati is known as the Teacher of the Gods. He controls the movement of the planets, and is devoted to Śiva.

VII.1.2 *red MANGALA* The planet Mars, associated with Kārttikeya, god of war.

VII.1.6 *TÁRACA with snaky legions* It was the ravages of the anti-god Tāraka, and Brahmā's advice that only the seed of Śiva could produce a hero to defeat the powers of evil that lay behind Kāma's attempt to arouse the meditative Śiva to Pārvatī's charms, see *Matsya Purāṇa* 154. 227–55.

'(Thus th' unerring Will ordains),
'Till from the Great Destroyer's pure embraces,
'Knit in love's mysterious chains
'With her, who, daughter to the mountain-king,
'Yon snowy mansion graces,
'CUMÁRA, warrior-child, shall spring;

VII. 3.

'Who, bright in arms of heav'nly proof,
'His crest a blazing star, his diamond mail
'Colour'd in the rainbow's woof,
'The rash invaders fiercely shall assail,
'And, on a stately peacock borne, shall rush
'Against the dragons of the deep;
'Nor shall his thund'ring mace insatiate sleep,
'Till their infernal chief it crush.'

VIII. 1.

'The splendid host with solemn state
'(Still spoke th' ethereal orator unblam'd)
'Reason'd high in long debate;
'Till, through my counsel provident, they claim'd
'Hapless CÁMA's potent aid:
'At INDRA's wish appear'd the soul's inflamer,
'And, in vernal arms array'd,
'Engag'd (ah, thoughtless!) in the bold emprise
'To tame wide nature's tamer,
'And soften Him, who shakes the skies.

VIII. 2.

'See now the God, whom all ador'd,
'An ashy heap, the jest of ev'ry gale!
'Loss by heav'n and earth deplor'd!
'For, love extinguish'd, earth and heav'n must fail.

VII.2.10   The fiery seed of Śiva produced Kūmara, who was to become the secret-chief of the gods' army. *Mahābhārata* 3. 14610

'Mark, how Rĕtĭ bears his urn,
'And tow'rd her widow'd pile with piercing ditty
'Points the flames – ah, see it burn!
'How ill the fun'ral with the feast agrees!
'Come, love's pale sister, pity;
'Come, and the lover's wrath appease.'

VIII. 3.

Tumultuous passions, whilst he spoke,
In heav'nly bosoms mix'd their bursting fire,
Scorning frigid wisdom's yoke,
Disdain, revenge, devotion, hope, desire:
Then grief prevail'd, but pity won the prize.
Not Sĭva could the charm resist:
'Rise, holy love!' he said; and kiss'd
The pearls, that gush'd from Durgá's eyes.

IX. 1.

That instant through the blest abode,
His youthful charms renew'd, Ananga came:
High on em'rald plumes he rode
With Rĕtĭ brighten'd by th' eluded flame;
Nor could young Vasanta mourn
(Officious friend!) his darling lord attending,
Though of annual beauty shorn:
'Love-shafts enow one season shall supply,
'He menac'd unoffending,
'To rule the rulers of the sky.'

IX. 2.

With shouts the boundless mansion rang;
And, in sublime accord, the radiant quire
Strains of bridal rapture sang
With glowing conquest join'd and martial ire:

VIII.2.5–VIII.3.8 Jones presents Kāma's grieving widow Rati (Desire) as appealing to Pārvatī/Durgā to intercede with Śiva.
IX.1.1–4 Śiva allows Kāma to be reborn as Ananga (Bodiless).

'Spring to life, triumphant son,
'Hell's future dread, and heav'n's eternal wonder!
'Helm and flaming habergeon
'For thee, behold, immortal artists weave,
'And edge with keen blue thunder
'The blade, that shall th' oppressor cleave.'

IX. 3.

O DURGÁ, thou hast deign'd to shield
Man's feeble virtue with celestial might,
Gliding from yon jasper field,
And, on a lion borne, hast brav'd the fight;
For, when the demon Vice thy realms defied,
And arm'd with death each arched horn,
Thy golden lance, O goddess mountain-born,
Touch but the pest – He roar'd and died.

IX.3.1–2 *shield/Man's feeble virtue* In the tradition of Vishnu, this cosmic queen is always ready to descend to earth to re-establish order and support her devotees.

IX.3.4–8 According to several accounts the shape-shifting Mahisa was proof against all opponents except a woman, and thus Durgā was created by the gods to defeat the usurping demon. The 'demon Vice' Mahisa assumed many forms during the fight, but ultimately it was as the buffalo, the symbol of death, that he was destroyed by Durgā, see Kinsley, *Hindu Goddesses*, p.96. Transcending her male creators in martial prowess, Durgā represents an unleashing of female power which disrupts patriarchal structures in an invigorating fashion.

20

The Hymn to Bhavání (1788)

[His final hymn, composed in 1788 and published posthumously, celebrates another aspect of *prakṛti* or transcendent Nature, the goddess Bhavānī (Giver-of-Existence). The feminine principle, here personified as the goddess of fecundity, is supreme in the universe as it embodies the active power, or *śakti*, of the passive aspect of the god Śiva. Thus the cult of śakti simultaneously subordinated the male, and transformed delight in female sensuality into sacred worship. The text followed is that of 1799, with variants noted from the Calcutta printing (Althorp Papers).]

THE HYMN TO BHAVÁNÍ

When time was drown'd in sacred sleep,
And raven darkness brooded o'er the deep,
Reposing on primeval pillows
Of tossing billows,
The forms of animated nature lay;   5
Till o'er the wild abyss, where love
Sat like a nestling dove,
From heav'n's dun concave shot a golden ray.

Still brighter and more bright it stream'd,
Then, like a thousand suns, resistless gleam'd;   10
Whilst on the placid waters blooming,
The sky perfuming,
An op'ning Lotos rose, and smiling spread
His azure skirts and vase of gold,
While o'er his foliage roll'd   15
Drops, that impearl BHAVÁNÍ's orient bed.

Mother of Gods, rich nature's queen,
Thy genial fire emblaz'd the bursting scene;

1–2   *When time was drown'd in sacred sleep,/And raven darkness brooded o'er the deep*   In 'On the Gods' Jones quotes Menu (Manu, son of Brahmā) on the creation: 'This world . . . was all darkness, undiscernible, undistinguishable, altogether as in a profound sleep; till the self-existent invisible GOD, making it manifest with five elements and other glorious forms, perfectly dispelled the gloom', p.352 below.

6–7   *where love/Sat like a nestling dove*   Despite the Miltonic ring (cf. *Paradise Lost* I.19–21), Jones conveys two essential aspects of this Hindu creation myth: firstly that the prime movement involved the force of desire – 'Desire came upon that one in the beginning; that was the first seed of mind', *Rig-Veda* 10.129.4; secondly his juxtaposition of raven and dove suggests the Vedic emphasis upon creation as the product of an equilibrium between the opposing principles of light and darkness.

8   *a golden ray*   Hiranyagarbha, the golden egg/seed/womb embryo, see *Rig-Veda* 10.121. Jones's quotation from the *Mánava Sástra* continues: 'He (the self-existent, unnamed god), desiring to raise up various creatures by an emanation from his own glory, first created the *waters*, and impressed them with a power of motion: by that power was produced a golden Egg, blazing like a thousand suns, in which was born BRAHMÁ', 'On the Gods', p.352 below.

13–14   *An op'ning Lotos rose, and smiling spread/His azure skirts and vase of gold*   The opening eight-petalled lotus represents the unfolding of creation. When, after the universal destruction, creation once more arises, it is on a lotos springing from the navel of Vishnu that Brahmā reappears.

17   *Mother of Gods*   Bhavānī /Durgā is here associated with Mahādevī, the mother of all, the creator of Brahmā, Vishnu, and Śiva, the primal life force. Jones was fascinated by the tendency in many branches of Hinduism to locate ultimate reality in a powerful and transcendent female.

For, on th' expanded blossom sitting,
With sun-beams knitting   20
That mystick veil for ever unremov'd,
Thou badst the softly kindling flame
Pervade this peopled frame,
And smiles, with blushes ting'd, the work approv'd.

Goddess, around thy radiant throne   25
The scaly shoals in spangled vesture shone,
Some slowly through green waves advancing,
Some swiftly glancing,
As each thy mild mysterious pow'r impell'd:
E'en orcs and river-dragons felt   30
Their iron bosoms melt
With scorching heat; for love the mightiest quell'd.

But straight ascending vapours rare
O'ercanopied thy seat with lucid air,
While, through young INDRA's new dominions   35
Unnumber'd pinions
Mix'd with thy beams a thousand varying dyes,
Of birds or insects, who pursued
Their flying loves, or woo'd
Them yielding, and with musick fill'd the skies.   40

And now bedeck'd with sparkling isles
Like rising stars, the watry desert smiles;
Smooth plains by waving forests bounded,
With hillocks rounded,
Send forth a shaggy brood, who, frisking light   45
In mingled flocks or faithful pairs,
Impart their tender cares:
All animals to love their kind invite.

Nor they alone: those vivid gems,
That dance and glitter on their leafy stems,   50
Thy voice inspires, thy bounty dresses,

20–1 *With sun-beams knitting/That mystick veil for ever unremov'd* The seeming intrusion of the homely into the cosmic reflects the tranquil kindliness of the Divine Mother; her fire is genial, the smiles which approve the splendour of her creative endeavours are *with blushes ting'd*. Cf. 'A Hymn to Indra', ll.9–10, and Jones's translation of the *Íśávayam*, 'Unveil, O Thou who givest sustenance to the world, that face of the true sun, which is now hidden by a vase of golden light! so that we may see the truth, and know our whole duty!' 'Extracts from the Vedas', *Works*, XIII.376. Cf. also Shelley's sonnet 'Lift not the painted veil'.

Thy rapture blesses,
From yon tall palm, who, like a sunborn king,
His proud tiara spreads elate,
To those, who throng his gate,   55
Where purple chieftains vernal tribute bring.

A gale so sweet o'er GANGÁ breathes,
That in soft smiles her graceful cheek she wreathes.
Mark, where her argent brow she raises,
And blushing gazes   60
On yon fresh *Cétaca*, whose am'rous flow'r
Throws fragrance from his flaunting hair,
While with his blooming fair
He blends perfume, and multiplies the bow'r.

Thus, in one vast eternal gyre,   65
Compact or fluid shapes, instinct with fire,
Lead, as they dance, this gay creation,
Whose mild gradation
Of melting tints illudes the visual ray:
Dense earth in springing herbage lives,   70
Thence life and nurture gives
To sentient forms, that sink again to clay.

Ye maids and youths on fruitful plains,
Where LACHSMÍ revels and BHAVÁNÍ reigns,
Oh, haste! oh, bring your flow'ry treasures,   75
To rapid measures
Tripping at eve these hallow'd banks along:
The pow'r, in yon dim shrines ador'd,
To primal waves restor'd,
With many a smiling race shall bless your song.   80

61–2   *Cétaca, whose am'rous flow'r/Throws fragrance from his flaunting hair*   In 'On the Spikenard of the Ancients' Jones praises the exquisite perfume of this plant: '. . . on the banks of the *Ganges* . . . the *Hindu* women roll up its flowers in their long black hair after bathing in the holy river', *Works,* V.17.

65–9   The universal fecundity unleashed by the goddess culminates in *one vast eternal gyre* of mingling procreation, the elemental dance of *māyā.*

74   *Where LACSHMÍ revels*   Lakshmī is always associated with joyous fertility, cf. 'A Hymn to Lacshmí', ll.199–214.

75–80   The autumnal worship of Bhavānī/Durgā in Bengal, the Durgā Pūjā, emphasizes the interrelationships between human sexuality and crop fertility; wild dancing and passionate love-making culminate in a ceremony wherein the goddess of fecundity is *To primal waves restor'd*, see Pratāpachandara Ghosha, *Durgā Pūjā: With Notes and Illustrations* (Calcutta, 1871).

TRANSLATIONS

21

A Persian Song of Hafiz (1771)

[Much anthologized, this is without doubt one of Jones's finest efforts at versification in sympathy with the spirit of the original. Representing the first verse translation of a Persian poem into English, it was originally published in *A Grammar of the Persian Language* (1771), reappearing the following year in *Poems, consisting chiefly of translations from the Asiatick languages*. On 7 December 1771 in a letter to Charles Reviczky the modest Jones wrote of his translation: 'It is by no means unpopular here in England', (*Letters*, I.107), and it was reprinted in the *Annual Register* of 1772. His printing of the transliterated original displays the fact that Jones had rendered each Persian verse of four short (or two long) mono-rhymed lines into a six-line stanza, rhyming *abcabc*. This was necessary not primarily because contemporary taste preferred 'an elegant prolixity', but for the practical reason that 'the strangeness of the Persian tropes often demands expansion', see A. J. Arberry, 'Orient Pearls at Random Strung', *BSOAS* 11 (1946), 698–712. Jones's use of octosyllabics helped retain the distinctive accent and cadence of the original metre, and he captured the delicacy and charm of Hāfiz with an ease which modern translators continue to admire. The copy-text is the 1777 *Poems*, with variants noted from the 1771 *Grammar*, and the first edition of *Poems* (1772).]

A PERSIAN SONG OF HAFIZ

Sweet maid, if thou would'st charm my sight,
And bid these arms thy neck infold;
That rosy cheek, that lily hand,
Would give thy poet more delight
Than all Bocara's vaunted gold,   5
Than all the gems of Samarcand.

Jones's literal translation, which precedes his metrical one in *A Grammar of the Persian Language*, reads as follows:

If that lovely maid of Shiraz would accept my heart, I would give for the mole on her cheek the cities of Samarcand and Bokhara.

Boy, bring me the wine that remains, for thou wilt not find in paradise the sweet banks of our Rocnabad, or the rosy bowers of our Mosellâ.

Alas! these wanton nymphs, these fair deceivers, whose beauty raises a tumult in our city, rob my heart of rest and patience, like the Turks that are seizing their plunder.

Yet the charms of our darlings have no need of our imperfect love; what occasion has a face naturally lovely for perfumes, paint, and artificial ornaments?

Talk to me of the singers, and of wine, and seek not to disclose the secrets of futurity; for no one, however wise, ever has discovered, or ever will discover them.

I can easily conceive how the inchanting beauties of Joseph affected Zoleikha so deeply, that her love tore the veil of her chastity.

Attend, O my soul! to prudent counsels; for youths of a good disposition love the advice of the aged better than their own souls.

Thou hast spoken ill of me; yet I am not offended; may Heaven forgive thee! thou hast spoken well: but do bitter words become a lip like a ruby, which ought to shed nothing but sweetness?

O Hafiz! when thou composest verses, thou seemest to make a string of pearls: come, sing them sweetly: for Heaven seems to have shed on thy poetry the clearness and beauty of the Pleïads.

Works, V.315–16.

Stanza 1   Walter Leaf's more literal but graceless translation of the first stanza reads as follows: 'An if yon Turk of Shiraz land this heart would take to hold in fee,/Bokhara town and Samarcand to that black mole my dower should be' (*Versions from Hafiz* [London, 1898], p.76). A detailed comparison of six translations is provided by Arberry ('Orient Pearls', 709–12), who concludes: 'they do not add up to anything approaching in excellence Jones's *Persian Song*'. Jones omitted the reference to the beloved's mole, and discreetly changed the sex of the beloved. The rhyme-scheme *abcabc* is novel, and Jones need hardly have apologized for its 'singularity' (see *A Grammar of the Persian Language*, *Works*, V.316). Byron chose to use it in an early lyric, 'Remind Me Not, Remind Me Not', *Complete Poetical Works*, ed. Jerome J. McGann, (Oxford, 1980-92), I.217–18.

5–6   *Than all Bocara's vaunted gold,/Than all the gems of Samarcand*   These lines, instinct with the romance of the exotic, proved hauntingly memorable. Byron casually quotes them in one of his letters to Dallas, *Letters and Journals* 12 vols., ed. Leslie A. Marchand (London, 1973), 2.91. Byron also wrote an amusing parody of Jones's 'Persian Song' entitled 'The Barmaid', *Complete Poetical Works*, I.342–4. According to legend, when the conquering Timur entered Shiraz he summoned Hāfiz before his presence and said: 'Of all my empire, Bokhara and Samarkand are the fairest jewels; how comes it that in thy song thou hast declared that thou would'st exchange them for the black mole on the cheek of thy beloved?' Hāfiz replied: 'It is because of such generosity that I am now as poor as thou seest.'

Boy, let yon liquid ruby flow,
And bid thy pensive heart be glad,
Whate'er the frowning zealots say:
Tell them, their Eden cannot show   10
A stream so clear as Rocnabad,
A bower so sweet as Mosellay.

O! when these fair perfidious maids,
Whose eyes our secret haunts infest,
Their dear destructive charms display;   15
Each glance my tender breast invades,
And robs my wounded soul of rest,
As Tartars seize their destin'd prey.

In vain with love our bosoms glow:
Can all our tears, can all our sighs,   20
New lustre to those charms impart?
Can cheeks, where living roses blow,
Where nature spreads her richest dyes,
Require the borrow'd gloss of art?

Speak not of fate; ah! change the theme,   25
And told of odours, talk of wine,
Talk of the flowers that round us bloom:
'Tis all a cloud, 'tis all a dream;
To love and joy thy thoughts confine,
Nor hope to pierce the sacred gloom.   30

---

7 *let yon liquid ruby flow* Wine remains the consolation of the lover, and Hāfiz frequently explores the theme of the 'intoxicated' lover, whether the cause be beauty, youth, or *sākī*. 'Many zealous admirers of HĀFIZ insist, that by *wine* he invariably means *devotion*; and they have gone so far as to compose a dictionary of words in the *language*, as they call it, of the *Súfis*: in that vocabulary . . . *kisses* and *embraces* [represent] the *raptures of piety*; . . . *the tavern* is a retired oratory, and its *keeper*, a sage instructor; . . . The poet himself gives a colour in many passages to such an interpretation; and without it, we can hardly conceive that his poems, or those of his numerous imitators, would be tolerated in a *Muselman* country', 'On the Mystical Poetry of the Persians and Hindus', *Works*, IV.227.

11 *A stream so clear as Rocnabad* This is the limpid stream in which Caliph Vathek longed to refresh his mind and body. William Beckford's indebtedness to Jones is attested by the frequent acknowledgements in Henley's notes, in which this second stanza is quoted, see *Vathek, An Arabian Tale* (London, 1786).

24 *the borrow'd gloss of art* Jones was perfectly aware of the dangers (not the least of which was ridicule), represented by mystical interpretations where, for example, the mole, powder, and paint on the beloved's face stand for the ink, calligraphy, and lines of the Koran: 'the sublimity of the *mystical allegory*, which, like metaphors and comparisons, should be *general* only, not minutely exact, is diminished, if not destroyed, by an attempt at *particular* and *distinct resemblances*; and that the style itself is open to dangerous misinterpretation, while it supplies real infidels with a pretext for laughing at religion itself', 'Mystical Poetry', *Works*, IV.228.

Beauty has such resistless power,
That even the chaste Egyptian dame
Sigh'd for the blooming Hebrew boy:
For her how fatal was the hour,
When to the banks of Nilus came   35
A youth so lovely and so coy!

But ah! sweet maid, my counsel hear
(Youth should attend when those advise
Whom long experience renders sage):
While musick charms the ravish'd ear;   40
While sparkling cups delight our eyes,
By gay; and scorn the frowns of age.

What cruel answer have I heard!
And yet, by heaven, I love thee still:
Can aught be cruel from thy lip?   45
Yet say, how fell that bitter word
From lips which streams of sweetness fill,
Which nought but drops of honey sip?

Go boldly forth, my simple lay,
Whose accents flow with artless ease,   50
Like orient pearls at random strung:
Thy notes are sweet, the damsels say;
But O! far sweeter, if they please
The nymph for whom these notes are sung.

31–6   The story of the love of Yūsuf for the Oriental type of perfect beauty, Zalīkhā, represents a myth of divine and profane love.

51   *Like orient pearls at random strung*   Arberry ('Orient Pearls', p. 703) takes Jones to task for the insertion of 'at random', which he sees as maligning the skills both of Hāfiz and the oriental jeweller. It would appear that Jones was attempting to emphasize the 'artless ease' of the poet's 'simple lay' in a conclusion which focuses attention on the sweetness of the beloved rather than the celestial structure of the song. When Jones's literal translation is considered, it is clear that in transforming Hāfiz's self-praising 'signature' into a more Occidental envoy, Jones is guilty of a somewhat uncharacteristic distortion.

22

From *The Moallakát, or Seven Arabian Poems Which were suspended on the Temple at Mecca* (1782)

[These poems, according to legend, were transcribed in gold upon Egyptian linen and hung from the Kaaba at Mecca. They are, nonetheless, pre-Moslem, and decidedly hedonistic, mingling as they do the lyrical and the sensual with heroic vaunting. In the *Mu'allaqāt* Hellenistic tradition is fully assimilated to a specifically Bedouin mentality, and these poems represent the supreme art of the herding and hunting nomad. This outburst of poetry in its unexpected confidence and maturity seemed to confirm Jones's contention that the pastoral genre was more alive in the Yemen than in Europe. Despite the difficulty of these poems, Jones was fascinated by their wild beauty, their vigorous and precise imagery, and felt that they should be introduced to a modern European audience. He had sung their praises in three languages – in his 'Traité de la Poésie Orientale' (1770), in his essay 'On the Poetry of the Eastern Nations' (1772), and in the *Poeseos Asiaticae Commentariorum* (1774) – but no scholar had attempted a translation. In the face of his professional commitments, his political involvement, and his legal studies for the *Essay on the Law of Bailments*, he was tirelessly consulting and collating manuscripts throughout 1780 and 1781. However, in a letter to the inventor Edmund Cartwright in November 1780, Jones explained that working on this edition helped to alleviate his depression at the opposition's failure to bring down North's ministry: 'In these rambles into the wilds of Arabia, I soften the anguish which I feel, whenever I reflect on the melancholy times in which we live' (*Letters*, I.444). Jones's work on a projected preliminary discourse and notes was delaying publication so he had the poems printed (by Nichols for Elmsly) on 1 December 1782 and sold unbound; an accompanying advertisement requested the purchaser to bind the volume only when the editorial matter was available. The re-issue of 1783 bore a cancel title and the references to notes and discourse were omitted. Nevertheless, while Edward Gibbon lamented being deprived of such scholarly notation, Jones's edition of the *Moallakát* represents his most important contribution to Oriental studies prior to his departure for India. Coleridge, like Herder, was greatly impressed by the

---

Title: *suspended on the temple at Mecca* This etymology of the term *mu'allaqāt* has generally been rejected by Arabists since the suggestion of Sir Charles Lyall (*Ancient Arabian Poetry*, London, 1885), that the word *a'lāq* should be taken in the sense of 'necklaces', frequently used in the titles of anthologies, to render a translation of 'hanging jewels' more plausible.

Moallakát, and compared its sublimities with 'The Book of Job' (*Table Talk*, pp.72–3). It influenced Samuel Rogers's 'Pleasure of Memory', Landor's *Poems from the Arabic and Persian*, Browning's 'Mulēykeh, a Dramatic Idyl', and Tennyson acknowledged that it gave him the idea of *Locksley Hall*. Cannon believes that Jones's translation was superseded by Blunt's version of 1903 (although he concedes that 'it merits a modern reprinting', *Life*, p.189), but E. S. Shaffer maintains that it 'holds its place to this day as the finest English translation', ('*Kubla Khan' and The Fall of Jerusalem*, Cambridge, 1975, p.331). The text followed is that of 1799.]

ADVERTISEMENT

THE Discourse will comprise observations on the antiquity of the *Arabian* language and letters; on the dialects and characters of *Himyar* and *Koraish*, with accounts of some *Himyarick* poets; on the manners of the *Arabs* in the age immediately preceding that of *Mahomed*; on the temple at *Mecca*, and the *Moâllakát*, or pieces of poetry *suspended* on its walls or gate; lastly, on the lives of the *Seven Poets*, with a critical history of their works, and the various copies or editions of them preserved in *Europe*, *Asia*, and *Africa*.

The Notes will contain authorities and reasons for the translation of controverted passages; will elucidate all the obscure couplets, and exhibit or propose amendments of the text; will direct the reader's attention to particular beauties, or point out remarkable defects; and will throw light on the images, figures, and allusions of the *Arabian* poets, by citations either from writers of their own country, or from such of our *European* travellers as best illustrate the ideas and customs of eastern nations.

But the *Discourse Notes* are ornamental only, not essential to the work; and, by sending it abroad in its present form, the translator may reap no small advantage, if the learned here or on the Continent will favour him in the course of the summer with their strictures and annotations, and will transmit them for that purpose to the publisher. It is hoped, that the war will raise no obstacle to this intercourse with the scholars of *Leyden*, *Paris*, and *Madrid*; for men of letters, as such, ought, in all places and at all times, to carry *flags of truce*.

THE POEM OF AMRIOLKAIS

[This piece, by the distinguished sixth-century poet Amru'-ul-qais, is widely regarded as the finest poem in the Arabic language; it exemplifies the elaborate and often elegiac form of the *qaṣīda* with its long metres in monorhyme. In its complete traditional form it comprises three thematic sections: the *nasīb*, describing the abandoned encampment, scene of longingly remembered amorous encounters; the *raḥīl*, containing description of a desert journey, with elaborate praise of the poet's mount, typically a she-camel; the final unit is most commonly either the *fakhr*, a species of boast concerning the poet's prowess in hunting, drinking, or fighting, or the *madīh*, which enthusiastically celebrates a chieftain or patron. The poet's exalted reputation makes him almost larger than life; introduced to the Byzantine emperor Justinian in Constantinople, named phylarch of Palestine, and, according to legend, charged before the emperor with seducing a princess. For a detailed consideration of the *akhbār* (pseudo-biographical) materials which have surrounded Amru', together with an exploration of the interface between myth and ritual in this poem, see Suzanne Stetkevych, *The Mute Immortals Speak: Pre-Islamic Poetry and the Poetics of Ritual* (Ithaca and London, 1993), pp.241–85.]

THE ARGUMENT

THE poet, after the manner of his countrymen, supposes himself attended on a journey by a company of friends; and, as they pass near a place, where his mistress had lately dwelled, but from which her tribe was then removed, *he desires them to stop awhile*, that he might indulge the painful pleasure of weeping over the deserted remains of her tent. They comply with his request, but exhort him to show more strength of mind, and urge two topicks of consolation; namely, *that he had before been equally unhappy*, and *that he had enjoyed his full share of pleasures*: thus by the recollection of his passed delight his imagination is kindled, and his grief suspended.

He then gives his friends a lively account of his juvenile frolicks, to one of which they had alluded. It seems, he had been in love with a girl named *Onaiza*, and had in vain sought an occasion to declare his passion: one day, when her tribe had struck their tents, and were changing their station, the women, as usual, came behind the rest, with the servants and baggage, in carriages fixed on the backs of camels. *Amriolkais* advanced slowly at a distance, and, when the men were out of sight, had the pleasure of seeing *Onaiza* retire with a party of damsels to a rivulet or pool, called *Daratjuljul*, where they undressed themselves, and were bathing, when the lover appeared, dismounted from his camel, and sat upon their clothes, proclaiming aloud, that *whoever would redeem her dress, must present herself naked before him.*

They adjured, entreated, expostulated; but, when it grew late, they found themselves obliged to submit, and all of them recovered their clothes except *Onaiza*, who renewed her adjurations, and continued a long time in the water: at length she also performed the condition, and dressed herself. Some hours had passed, when the girls complained of cold and hunger: *Amriolkais* therefore instantly *killed the young camel on which he had ridden*, and having called the female attendants together, made a fire and roasted him. The afternoon was spent in gay conversation, not without a cheerful cup, for he was provided with wine in a leathern bottle; but, when it was time to follow the tribe, the prince (for such was his rank) had neither camel nor horse; and *Onaiza*, after much importunity, consented to take him *on her camel before the carriage*, while the other damsels divided among themselves the less agreeable burden of his arms, and the furniture of his beast.

He next relates his courtship of *Fathima*, and his more dangerous amour with a girl of a tribe at war with his own, *whose beauties he very minutely and luxuriantly delineates.* From these love-tales he proceeds to the commendation of his own fortitude, when he was passing a desert in the darkest night; and the mention of the morning, which succeeded, leads him to *a long description of his hunger, and of a chase in the forest*, followed by a feast on the game, which had been pierced by his javelins.

Here his narrative seems to be interrupted by *a storm of lightning and violent rain*: he nobly describes the shower and the torrent, which it produced down all the adjacent mountains, and, his companions retiring to avoid the storm, the drama (for the poem has the form of a dramatick pastoral) ends abruptly.

The metre is of the *first* species, called *long verse*, and consists of the *bacchius*, or *amphibrachys*, followed by the first *epitrite*; or, in the *fourth* and *eighth* places, of the distich, by the *double iambus*, the last syllable being considered as a long one: the regular form, taken from the second chapter of *Commentaries on Asiatick Poetry*, is this;

'Amator | puellarum | miser sæ | pe fallitur
'Ocellis | nigris, labris | odoris, | nigris comis.'

THE POEM OF AMRIOLKAIS

1   'Stay – Let us weep at the remembrance of our beloved, *at the sight of* the station *where her tent was raised*, by the edge of yon bending sands between DAHUL and HAUMEL,

2   'TUDAM and MIKRA; *a station*, the marks of which are not wholly effaced, though the south wind and the north have woven the twisted sand.'

3   *Thus I spoke, when* my companions stopped their coursers by my side, and said, 'Perish not through despair: only be patient.'

4   A profusion of tears, *answered I*, is my sole relief; but what avails it to shed them over the remains of a deserted mansion?

5   'Thy condition, *they replied*, is not more painful than when thou leftest HOWAIRA, before thy present passion, and her neighbour REBABA, *on the hills of* MASEL.'

6   *Yes, I rejoined*, when those two damsels departed, musk was diffused from their robes, as the eastern gale sheds the scent of clove-gillyflowers:

7   Then gushed the tears from my eyes, through excess of regret, and flowed down my neck, till my sword-belt was drenched in the stream.

Note: references are to stanzas, not line numbers.

     Stanzas 1–2   Following the *istīqāf* convention, the poet implores his companions to stop and weep at the deserted camping-place, its traces almost erased by contending winds.

   After the second verse Jones inexplicably omits two verses, they read as follows in a modern translation: 'there, all about its yards, and away in the dry hollows/you may see the dung of antelopes spattered like peppercorns./Upon the morning of separation, the day they loaded to part,/by the tribe's acacias it was like I was splitting a colocynth*", A. J. Arberry, *The Seven Odes: The First Chapter in Arabic Literature* (London, 1957), p.61. (*The acid juice of the pods produces tears like the onion).

   5–41   The *nasīb* or melancholy love-prelude becomes in the hands of Amru' an opportunity to recall an extensive series of erotic encounters.

    6   Oriental fragrance and exotic imagery were essential ingredients for the Western consumer, and Southey copied this verse, together with verses 30, 33, and 35, into his commonplace book (*Southey's Common-Place Book* Fourth Series, ed. J.W. Warter, London, Longmans, 1850, p.256).

8   'Yet hast thou passed many days in sweet converse with the fair; but none so sweet as the day, which thou spentest by *the pool of* DARAT JULJUL.'

9   On that day I killed my camel to give the virgins a feast; and oh! how strange was it, that they should carry his trappings and furniture!

10   The damsels continued till evening helping one another to the roasted flesh, and to the delicate fat like the fringe of white silk finely woven.

11   On that happy day I entered the carriage, the carriage of ONAIZA, who said, 'Wo to thee! thou wilt compel me to travel on foot.'

12   She added (while the vehicle was bent aside with our weight), 'O AMRIOLKAIS, descend, or my beast also will be killed.'

13   I answered: 'Proceed, and loosen his rein; nor withhold from me the fruits of thy love, which again and again may be tasted with rapture.

14   'Many a fair one like thee, though not *like thee* a virgin, have I visited by night; and many a lovely mother have I diverted from the care of her yearling infant adorned with amulets:

15   'When the suckling behind her cried, she turned round to him with half

---

8   For the incident beside the pool of Daratjuljul (which recalls a similar legend of Krishna), see Jones's Argument, p.191.

9–10   Despite the often lyrical tribute to the charms of the camel which is almost *de rigueur* in the *qasida* (see *Tarafa*, 11–38 for example), this poet displays a practical and unsentimental attitude: the camel can also bear furniture, transport ladies, and provide a virgins' feast.

10   *helping one another to the roasted flesh*   This is an error of translation as noted by A. S. Tritton, 'The Student of Arabic', *BSOAS*, 11 (1946), 695–8, who argues it should read 'throwing at one another'. Jones's mistake serves to render the feast a more sedate occasion.

11–14   *On that happy day . . . have I visited by night*   Henley, in a note to p.62 of *Vathek* (London, 1900), quotes this passage to illustrate the precariousness of the howdah for love-making purposes. There are no fewer than fourteen references to the *Moallakát* in Henley's notes, containing twelve quotations, six of which are from *The Poem of Amriolkais*. Beckford's indebtedness to Jones is evident in the fact that only d'Herbelot's encyclopaedic *Bibliothèque Orientale, ou Dictionnaire . . . des Peuples de l'Orient* receives a greater number of acknowledgements in the notes to *Vathek*.

11   ONAIZA   The name of the poet's mistress reminds us of Southey's detailed knowledge of Jones's writings on Arabic and Persian subjects. *The Moallakát* provided *Thalaba* (1804) with more than the name of its heroine; detailed textual notes quoted Jones's translation to illustrate exotic imagery and desert custom. See, for example, *Poetical Works*, IV. 117–18;170.

14–15   The celebration of the seduction of nursing mothers is, perhaps, an unusual erotic motif. Stetkevych describes the episode as 'among the most scandalous in the classical poetic canon', and argues that the lover is presented as essentially anti-social, if not deviant, especially 'in the light of the pre-Islamic belief that sexual intercourse with a nursing mother was harmful to the nursling', *Mute Immortals Speak*, p.265.

her body; but half of it, pressed beneath my embrace, was not turned from me.'

16   Delightful too was the day, when FATHIMA at first rejected me on the summit of yon sand-hill, and took an oath, which she declared inviolable.

17   'O FATHIMA, said I, away with so much coyness; and, if thou hadst resolved to abandon me, yet at last relent.

18   'If, indeed, my disposition and manners are unpleasing to thee, rend at once the mantle of my heart, that it may be detached from thy love.

19   'Art thou so haughty, because my passion for thee destroys me; and because whatever thou commandest, my heart performs?

20   *'Thou weepest* – yet thy tears flow merely to wound my heart with the shafts of thine eyes; my heart, already broken to pieces and agonizing.'

21   *Besides these* – with many a spotless virgin, whose tent had not yet been frequented, have I holden soft dalliance at perfect leisure.

22   *To visit one of them*, I passed the guards of her bower and a hostile tribe, who would have been eager to proclaim my death.

23   It was the hour, when the Pleiads appeared in the firmament, like the folds of a silken sash variously decked with gems.

24   I approached – she stood *expecting me* by the curtain; and, *as if she was preparing* for sleep, had put off all her vesture, but her night-dress.

25   She said – 'By him who created me (and gave me her lovely hand), I am unable to refuse thee; for I perceive, that the blindness of thy passion is not to be removed.'

---

17   Fātima belonged to the Ban Udrha, a 'tribe famed throughout Arabia for the pure and chaste passion of its menfolk; many were the stories of young lovers who would waste away to death rather than betray their chivalrous ideal. That did not prevent our poet-prince from outraging the most hallowed taboo of the desert, and publishing the indelicate words he spoke to the unfortunate victim of his casual fancy', Arberry, *The Seven Odes*, p.35.

22   Evocation of the dangers attendant upon illicit passion was to become a common theme of *fin' amors*, the introduction of which into Europe was arguably by means of the contact zone of Mozarabic Spain. See Peter Dronke *Medieval Latin and the Rise of the European Love-Lyric*, 2 vols. (Oxford, 1965), and Gustave von Grunebaum, *Themes in Medieval Arab Literature* (London, 1981), ch.5 'The Arab Contribution to Troubadour Poetry'.

26   Then I rose with her; and, as we walked, she drew over our footsteps the train of her pictured robe.

27   Soon as we had passed the habitations of her tribe, and come to the bosom of a vale surrounded with hillocks of spiry sand,

28   I gently drew her towards me by her curled locks, and she softly inclined to my embrace: her waist was gracefully slender; but sweetly swelled the part encircled with ornaments of gold.

29   Delicate was her shape; fair her skin; and her body well proportioned: her bosom was as smooth as a mirror,

30   Or like the pure egg of an ostrich of a yellowish tint blended with white, and nourished by a stream of wholesome water not yet disturbed.

31   She turned aside, and displayed her soft cheek: she gave a timid glance with languishing eyes, like those of a roe in *the groves of* WEGERA looking tenderly at her young.

32   Her neck was like that of a milk-white hind, but, when she raised it, exceeded not the justest symmetry; nor was the neck of my beloved so unadorned.

33   Her long coal-black hair decorated her back, thick and diffused like bunches of dates clustering on the palm-tree.

34   Her locks were elegantly turned above her head; and the riband, which bound them, was lost in her tresses, part braided, part dishevelled.

35   She discovered a waist taper as a well-twisted cord; and a leg both as white and as smooth as the stem of a young palm, or a fresh reed, bending over the rivulet.

36   When she sleeps at noon, her bed is besprinkled with musk: she puts on her robe of undress, but leaves the apron *to her handmaids*.

31–5   To an audience familiar with 'The Song of Solomon' the erotic imagery in the description of Fātima would seem familiar, its exotic 'otherness' domesticated in the family Bible. The attitudes implicit in such comparison ultimately led to the Scriptures being read as Oriental literature.

37   She dispenses gifts with small delicate fingers, sweetly glowing at their tips, like the white and crimson worm of DABIA, or dentrifices made of ESEL-wood.

38   The brightness of her face illumines the veil of night, like the evening taper of a recluse hermit.

39   On a girl like her, a girl of a moderate height, between those who wear a frock and those who wear a gown, the most bashful man must look with an enamoured eye.

40   The blind passions of men for common objects of affection are soon dispersed; but from the love of thee my heart cannot be released.

41   O how oft have I rejected the admonitions of a morose adviser, vehement in censuring my passion for thee; nor have I been moved by his reproaches!

42   Often has the night drawn her skirts around me like the billows of the ocean, to make trial of my fortitude in a variety of cares;

43   And I said to her (when she seemed to extend her sides, to drag on her unwieldy length, and to advance slowly with her breast),

44   'Dispel thy gloom, O tedious night, that the morn may rise; although my sorrows are such, that the morning-light will not give me more comfort than thy shades.

45   'O hideous night! a night in which the stars are prevented from rising, as if they were bound to a solid cliff with strong cables!'

---

37   An allusion to the staining of finger-tips and nails with henna to produce a reddish colour in a stanza which emphasizes voluptuous indolence.
the white and crimson worm of DABIA   a variety of sand worm, having a white body and red head.
dentifrices made of ESEL-wood   The Ishil tree, having very soft fibres, provides the best toothsticks.
43   Where traditionally the audience might expect the *raḥīl* (praise of his swift camel) section, the poet describes the interminable tedium of night. Instead of 'lente currite noctis equi', the passage of the night is compared, according to Stetkevych, with 'the slow and ponderous rising of a bulky camel', *Mute Immortals Speak*, p.271.
45   Keenly suffering the pains of separation, sleep evades the poet; the striking image of the stars being bound to the rocky cliff contrasts with the earlier description of the Pleiades compared with the gem-bedecked girdle of his beloved in stanza 23.
After verse 45 Jones omits four stanzas containing a comparison of man and wolf, desolate and outcast in the desert: 'And many a waterskin of the clans have I borne its leathern strap/Upon my shoulder, submissive and much traveled./And many a riverbed, a bare waste like the belly of an ass,

46   Often too I have risen at early dawn, while the birds were yet in their nests, and mounted a hunter with smooth short hair, of a full height, and so fleet as to make captive the beasts of the forest;

47   Ready in turning, quick in pursuing, bold in advancing, firm in backing; and performing the whole with the strength and swiftness of a vast rock, which a torrent has pushed from its lofty base;

48   A bright bay steed, from whose polished back the trappings slide, as drops of rain glide hastily down the slippery marble.

49   Even in his weakest state he seems to boil while he runs; and the sound, which he makes in his rage, is like that of a bubbling cauldron.

50   When other horses, that swim through the air, are languid and kick the dust, he rushes on like a flood, and strikes the hard earth with a firm hoof.

51   He makes the light youth slide from his seat, and violently shakes the skirts of a heavier and more stubborn rider;

52   Rapid as the pierced wood in the hands of a playful child, which he whirls quickly round with a well-fastened cord.

53   He has the loins of an antelope, and the thighs of an ostrich; he trots like a wolf, and gallops like a young fox.

54   Firm are his haunches; and, when his hinder parts are turned towards you, he fills the space between his legs with a long thick tail, which touches not the ground, and inclines not to either side.

55   His back, when he stands in his stall, resembles the smooth stone on which perfumes are mixed for a bride, or the seeds of coloquinteda are bruised.

I crossed,/Where the wolf howled like an outcast profligate with many a mouth to feed./So when he howled I said to him, Our lot is meager sustenance/If you have not gained wealth, [for I have none]./Each of us when he acquires a thing, it soon escapes him,/Whoever tills your tilth and mine, it will leave lean', Stetkevych, *Mute Immortals Speak*, p.254.

    46–61 In this heroic and lyrical description of the beauty and power of his steed the poet blends elements of the traditional *rahīl* and *fakhr* sections in an original formulation. The excitement of the chase and the desirability of the wild cattle – 'the heifers are fair as the virgins in black trailing robes' – culminates with the cook dressing and roasting the game.

    50 As the imagery indicates, the horse is associated with pluvial revitalization and the return of fecundity, see Adnan Haydar, '*The Mu'allaqa of Imru' al-Qays*: Its Structure and Meaning', Part I: *Edebiyât* 2 (1977), 227–61; Part II: *Edebiyât* 3 (1978), 51–82; 2.249.

56   The blood of the swift game, which remains on his neck, is like the crimson juice of *Henna* on grey flowing locks.

57   He bears us speedily to a herd of wild cattle, in which the heifers are fair as the virgins in black trailing robes, who dance round *the idol* DEWAAR:

58   They turn their backs, and appear like the variegated shells of YEMEN on the neck of a youth distinguished in his tribe for a multitude of noble kinsmen.

59   He soon brings us up to the foremost of the beasts, and leaves the rest far behind; nor has the herd time to disperse itself.

60   He runs from wild bulls to wild heifers, and overpowers them in a single heat, without being bathed, or even moistened, with sweat.

61   Then the busy cook dresses the game, roasting part, baking part on hot stones, and quickly boiling the rest in a vessel of iron.

62   In the evening we depart; and, when the beholder's eye ascends to the head of my hunter, and then descends to his feet, it is unable at once to take in all his beauties.

63   His trappings and girths are still upon him: he stands erect before me, not yet loosed for pasture.

64   O friend, seest thou the lightning, whose flashes resemble the quick glance of two hands amid clouds raised above clouds?

65   The fire of it gleams like the lamps of a hermit, when the oil, poured on them, shakes the cord by which they are suspended.

66   I sit gazing at it, while my companions stand between DAARIDGE and ODHAIB; but far distant is the cloud on which my eyes are fixed.

67   Its right side seems to pour its rain on *the hills of* KATAN, and its left on *the mountains of* SITAAR and YADBUL.

   62–3   Jones's translation conveys the poet's delight in his steed, an emblem of potency, of nature tamed and automatically responsive.

   64   His attention is diverted from his Arab hunter by the flash of lightning and the approaching cloud. A storm scene usually plays no part in the closing section of a *qasīda*, although the *nasīb* may sometimes include an *istisqā'*, or prayer for rain. By means of its destructive energy the storm performs a violent but necessary role as a purifying scourge.

68   It continues to discharge its waters over Cotaifa till the rushing torrent lays prostrate the groves of *Canahbel*-trees.

69   It passes over *mount* Kenaan, which it deluges in its course, and forces the wild goats to descend from every cliff.

70   On *mount* Taima it leaves not one trunk of a palm-tree, nor a single edifice, which is not built with well-cemented stone.

71   *Mount* Tebeir stands in the heights of the flood like a venerable chief wrapped in a striped mantle.

72   The summit of Mogaimar, covered with the rubbish which the torrent has rolled down, looks in the morning like the top of a spindle encircled with wool.

73   The cloud unloads its freight on the desert of Ghabeit, like a merchant of Yemen alighting with his bales of rich apparel.

74   The small birds of the valley warble at day-break, as if they had taken their early draught of generous wine mixed with spice.

75   The beasts of the wood, drowned in the floods of night, float, like the roots of wild onions, at the distant edge of the lake.

71–3   The imagery of apparel in these stanzas suggests nature reclothing the stark wastes with new fresh growth.

74–5   After the frightening and dramatic intensity of the desert storm, the bright morning brings birdsong and relief, but the work ends on a stark and melancholic note with the poet reflecting on the swollen carcasses of the drowned animals, victims of the life-giving inundation.

THE POEM OF TARAFA

[Tarafa, or 'Amr ibn ul-'Abd ul-Bakrī, was also a sixth-century Arabian poet, and spent a wild and dissipated youth in Bahrein. These Arab tribes divided their time between warlike raids and gentler pastoral recreations; Tarafa's vaunt is that he excels in both, a refuge to the distressed, and a bountiful host. It was his impudent invective and imprudent courtship of the king's sister which resulted in his early and cruel death at the instigation of the tyrant 'Amr ibn Hind; for a detailed consideration of the *akhbār*, or (pseudo-)biographical, traditions see Arberry, *The Seven Odes*, pp.67–76.]

THE POEM OF TARAFA

THE ARGUMENT

THIS poem was occasioned by a little incident highly characteristic of pastoral manners. TARAFA and his brother MABEB jointly possessed a herd of camels, and had agreed to watch them alternately, each on his particular day, lest, as they were grazing, they should be driven off by a tribe with whom their own clan was at war; but our poet was so immersed in meditation, and so wedded to his muse, that he often neglected his charge, and was sharply reproved by his brother, who asked him sarcastically, *Whether, if he lost the camels, they could be restored by his poetry?* 'You shall be convinced of it,' answered TARAFA; and persisted so long in his negligence, that the whole herd was actually seized by the MODARITES. This was more than he really expected; and he applied to all his friends for assistance in recovering the camels: among others he solicited the help of his cousin MALEC, who, instead of granting it, took the opportunity of rebuking him with acrimony for his remissness in that instance, and for his general prodigality, libertinism, and spirit of contention; telling him, that *he was a disgrace to his family, and had raised innumerable enemies.*

The defence of a poet was likely to be best made in poetical language; and TARAFA produced the following composition in vindication of his character and conduct, which he boldly justifies in every respect, and even claims praise for the very course of life, which had exposed him to censure.

He glories in his passion for women, and begins as usual with lamenting the departure of his beloved KHAULA, or *the tender fawn;* whose beauty he describes in a very lively strain. It were to be wished, that he had said more of his mistress, and less of his camel, of which he interweaves a very long, and not very pleasing, description.

The rest of the poem contains an eloge on his own fortitude, sprightliness, liberality, and valour, mixed with keen expostulations on the unkindness and ingratitude of MALEC, and with all the common topicks in favour of voluptuousness: he even triumphs on having slain and dressed one of his father's camels, and blames the old man for his churlishness and avarice. It is a tradition preserved by *Abu Obeida,* that one of the chiefs, whom the poet compliments in the *eightieth* couplet, made him *a present of a hundred camels,* and enabled him, as he had promised, to convince his brother, *that poetry could repair his loss.*

The metre is the same with that used by AMRIOLKAIS.

THE POEM OF TARAFA

1   'THE mansion of KHAULA is desolate, and the traces of it on the stony hills of TAHMED faintly shine, like the remains of blue figures painted on the back of a hand.'

2   *While I spoke thus to myself*, my companions stopped their coursers by my side, and said, 'Perish not through despair, but act with fortitude.'

3   Ah! *said I*, the vehicles, which bore away my fair one, on the morning when the tribe of MALEC departed, and their camels were traversing the banks of DEDA, resembled large ships

4   Sailing from ADULI; or vessels of *the merchant* IBN YAMIN, which the mariner now turns obliquely, and now steers in a direct course;

5   Ships, which cleave the foaming waves with their prows, as a boy at his play divides with his hand the collected earth.

6   In that tribe was a lovely antelope with black eyes, dark ruddy lips, and a beautiful neck gracefully raised to crop the fresh berries of ERAC, a neck adorned with two strings of pearls and topazes.

7   She strays from her young, and feeds with the herd of roes in the tangled thicket, where she brouzes the edges of the wild fruit, and covers herself with a mantle of leaves:

8   She smiles, and displays her bright teeth rising from their dark-coloured basis, like a privet-plant in full bloom, which pierces a bank of pure sand moistened with dew:

9   To her teeth the sun has imparted his brilliant water; but not to the part where they grow, which is sprinkled with lead-ore, while the ivory remains unspotted.

10   Her face appears to be wrapped in a veil of sunbeams: unblemished is her complexion, and her skin is without a wrinkle.

---

1   The traces of his mistress Khaula's encampment are compared with tattooing on the back of the hand.

2–5   Tarafa adapts the *qasīda* formula, placing a nautical emphasis on the themes of transience and departure.

11 Such cares *as this*, whenever they oppress my soul, I dispel *by taking adventurous journies* on a lean, yet brisk, camel, who runs with a quick pace both morning and evening;

12 Sure-footed, firm and thin as the planks of a bier; whose course I hasten over long-trodden paths, variegated like a striped vest.

13 She rivals the swiftest camels even of the noblest breed, and her hind-feet rapidly follow her fore-feet on the beaten way.

14 In the vernal season, she grazes on yon two hills among others of her race, whose teats are not yet filled with milk, and depastures the lawns, whose finest grass the gentle showers have made luxuriantly green.

15 She turns back at the sound of her rider's voice; and repels the caresses of a thick-haired russet stallion with the lash of her bushy tail,

16 Which appears as if the two wings of a large white eagle were transfixed by an awl to the bone, and hung waving round both her sides:

17 One while it lashes the place of him, who rides hindmost on her; another while, it plays round her teats, which are become wrinkled and flaccid like a leathern bag, their milk no longer distending them.,

18 Her two haunches are plump, and compact as the two smooth valves of a lofty castle-gate.

19 Supple is her back-bone: her ribs are like the strongest bows; and her neck is firmly raised on the well-connected vertebres.

20 The two cavities under her shoulders are spacious as two dens of beasts among the wild lotus-plants; and stiff bows appear to be bent under her sinewy loins.

21 Her two thighs are exceedingly strong, and, when she moves, they diverge like two buckets carried from a well in the hands of a robust drawer of water.

11–39; 42–3   The cares of love are dispelled by adventures on his fleet-foot camel as the *nasīb* gives way to the *rahīl* (desert journey) section. This lyrical 28-verse tribute devoted to the charms of his camel reflects its centrality to Bedouin existence. The description, as one might expect, is anatomically exact; her bone structure is compared with the solidity of Grecian architecture, and *her cheek is smooth and white as paper of* Syria. ' "It were to be wished, that he had said more of his mistress, and less of his camel." So protests the romantic young Welsh heart of William Jones, who in his enchanted view of Arabia Felix fancied to discover the *Mu'allaqāt* to be pastorals, a quality which would recommend them to the genteel drawing-rooms of London society in which he was being received with such flattering esteem', Arberry, *The Seven Odes*, p.78.

22   *Her joints are well knit, and her bones are solid,* like a bridge of Grecian architecture, whose builder had vowed, that he would enclose it with well-cemented bricks.

23   The hair under her chin is of a reddish hue: her back is muscular: she takes long, yet quick, steps with her hind-feet, and moves her fore-feet with agility;

24   She tosses them *from her chest* with the strength and swiftness of cables firmly pulled *by a nervous arm*; and her shoulders are bent like the rafters of a lofty dome:

25   She turns rapidly from the path: exceedingly swift is her pace; long is her head; and her shoulder-bones are strongly united to her sides.

26   The white and hollow marks of the cords, with which her burdens have been tied to her back, resemble pools of water on the smooth brow of a solid rock,

27   Marks, which sometimes unite and sometimes are distinct, like the gores of fine linen, which are sewed under the arms of a well-cut robe.

28   Long is her neck; and, when she raises it with celerity, it resembles the stern of a ship floating aloft on the billowy Tigris.

29   Her skull is firm as an anvil; and the bones, which the sutures unite, are indented, and sharp as a file.

30   Her cheek is smooth and white as paper of Syria; and her lips, as soft as dyed leather of Yemen, exactly and smoothly cut.

31   Her two eyes, like two polished mirrors, have found a hiding-place in the caverns of their orbits, the bones of which are like rocks, in whose cavities the water is collected:

32   Thou beholdest them free from blemish or spot, and resembling in beauty those of a wild cow, the mother of playful young, when the voice of the hunter has filled her with fear.

33   Her ears truly distinguish every sound, to which she listens attentively in her nightly journies, whether it be a gentle whisper or a loud noise;

34   Sharp ears, by which the excellence of her breed is known! ears, like those of a solitary wild-bull in the groves of Haumel.

35   Her heart, easily susceptible of terror, palpitates with a quick motion, yet remains firm *in her chest* as a round solid stone striking a broad floor of marble.

36   If I please, she raises her head to the middle of her trappings, and swims with her fore-legs as swift as a young ostrich.

37   If I please, she moves more slowly; if not, she gallops, through fear of the strong lash formed of twisted thongs.

38   Her upper lip is divided, and the softer part of her nose is bored: when she bends them towards the ground, her pace is greatly accelerated.

39   On a camel like this I continue my course, when the companion of my adventure exclaims: 'Oh! that I could redeem thee, and redeem myself from the impending danger!'

40   While his soul flutters through fear, and, imagining that he has lost the way, he supposes himself on the brink of perdition.

41   When the people say aloud, 'Who is the man *to deliver us from calamity?*' I believe that they call upon me, and I disgrace not their commission by supineness or folly.

42   I shake the lash over my camel, and she quickens her pace, while the sultry vapour rolls in waves over the burning cliffs.

43   She floats proudly along with her flowing tail, as the dancing-girl floats in the banquet of her lord, and spreads the long white skirts of her trailing vest.

44   I inhabit not the lofty hills through fear of enemies or of guests; but, when the tribe or the traveller demand my assistance, I give it eagerly.

45   If you seek me in the circle of the assembled nation, there you find me; and, if you hunt me in the bowers of the vintner, there too you discover your game

46   When you visit me in the morning, I offer you a flowing goblet; and if you make excuses, I bid you drink it with pleasure, and repeat your draught.

47   When all the clan are met to state their pretensions to nobility, you will perceive me raised to the summit of an illustrious house, the refuge of the distressed.

48 My companions in the feast are youths bright as stars, and singing-girls, who advance towards us, clad in striped robes and saffron-coloured mantles:

49 Large is the opening of their vests above their delicate bosoms, through which the inflamed youth touches their uncovered breasts of exquisite softness.

50 When we say to one of them, 'Let us hear *a song*,' she steps before us with easy grace, and begins with gentle notes, in a voice not forced:

51 When she warbles in a higher strain, you would believe her notes to be those of camels lamenting their lost young.

52 Thus I drink old wine without ceasing, and enjoy the delights of life; selling and dissipating my property both newly acquired and inherited;

53 Until the whole clan reject me, and leave me solitary like a diseased camel smeared with pitch:

54 Yet even now I perceive, that the sons of earth (*the most indigent men*) acknowledge my bounty, and the rich inhabitants of yon extended camp *confess my glory*.

55 O thou, who censurest me for engaging in combats and pursuing pleasures, wilt thou, *if I avoid them*, insure my immortality?

56 If thou art unable to repel the stroke of death, allow me, before it comes, to enjoy the good, which I possess.

57 Were it not for three enjoyments, which youth affords, I swear by thy prosperity, that I should not be solicitous how soon my friends visited me on my death-bed:

48–51 Jones effectively conveys the sensuality of Tarafa's description of the singing-girls, and yet he does not avoid a literal translation of the Arabic image comparing the girl's singing with *camels lamenting their lost young*. It would have been easy to change the line, as did Blunt ('a mother's grieving the one son new-slain from her', *The Poetical Works of Wilfrid Scawen Blunt*, 2 vols. [London, 1914], II.87), but Jones believed a genuine understanding of a nation's culture essential to a real appreciation of its poetry.

55 It is this lust for immortality that drives the hero, oriental or occidental, to epic feats of warfare or of love.

57–60 The heady mixture of hedonism and heroism in Tarafa's three enjoyments, culminating in the ultimate pleasure: *Thirdly, to shorten a cloudy day, a day astonishingly dark, by toying with a lovely delicate girl under a tent supported by pillars*, captures the Arabic spirit of the original, perfectly demonstrating Jones's artistry as poet/translator.

58   First; to rise before the censurers awake, and to drink tawny wine, which sparkles and froths when the clear stream is poured into it.

59   Next, when a warriour, encircled by foes, implores my aid, to bend towards him my prancing charger, fierce as a wolf among the GADHA-trees, whom the sound of human steps has awakened, and who runs to quench his thirst at the brook.

60   Thirdly, to shorten a cloudy day, a day astonishingly dark, by toying with a lovely delicate girl under a tent supported by pillars,

61   A girl, whose bracelets and garters seem hung on the stems of OSHAR-trees, or of *ricinus*, not stripped of their soft leaves.

62   Suffer me, whilst I live, to drench my head *with wine*, lest, having drunk too little in my life-time, *I should be thirsty in another state.*

63   A man of my generous spirit drinks his full draught to-day; and to-morrow, when we are dead, it will be known, which of us has not quenched his thirst.

64   I see no difference between the tomb of the anxious miser, gasping over his hoard, and the tomb of the libertine lost in the maze of voluptuousness.

65   You behold the sepulchres of them both raised in two heaps of earth, on which are elevated two broad piles of solid marble among the tombs closely connected.

66   Death, I observe, selects the noblest heroes for her victims, and reserves as her property the choicest possessions of the sordid hoarder.

67   I consider time as a treasure decreasing every night; and that, which every day diminishes, soon perishes for-ever.

68   By thy life, my friend, when death inflicts not her wound, she resembles a camel-driver, who relaxes the cord which remains twisted in his hand.

69   What causes the variance, which I perceive, between me and my cousin MALEC, who, whenever I approach him, retires and flees to a distance?

---

61   *OSHAR-trees, or of ricinus*   the castor-oil plant.
After verse 68 Jones omits a stanza which reads as follows: 'So that if he wishes, on any day, he leads him off by the reins. And he who is *tied* by the rope of death, will have to submit.' See F. E. Johnson, *The Seven Poems, Suspended in the Temple at Mecca* (Bombay, 1893), p.53.
69–79   Jones's Argument provides a prose gloss to this pastoral dispute.

70   He censures me, whilst I know not the ground of his censure; just as Karth, the son of Aabed, reproved me in the assembly of the tribe.

71   He bids me wholly despair of all the good which I seek, as if we had buried it in a gloomy grave;

72   And this for no defamatory words which I have uttered, but only because I sought, without remissness, for the camels of my brother Mabed.

73   I have drawn closer the ties of our relation, and I swear by thy prosperity, that, in all times of extreme distress, my succour is at hand.

74   Whenever I am summoned on momentous enterprises, I am prepared to encounter peril; and, whenever the foe assails thee impetuously, I defend thee with equal vehemence.

75   If any base defamers injure thy good name by their calumnies, I force them, without previous menace, to drain a cup from the pool of death;

76   Yet, without having committed any offence, I am treated like the worst offender, am censured, insulted, upbraided, rejected.

77   Were any other man *but* Malec my cousin, he would have dispelled my cares, or have left me at liberty for a season.

78   By my kinsman strangles me with cruelty, even at the very time when I am giving thanks for past, and requesting new, favours; even when I am seeking from him the redemption of my soul.

79   The unkindness of relations gives keener anguish to every noble breast than the stroke of an Indian cimeter.

80   Permit me then to follow the bent of my nature, and I will be grateful for thy indulgence, although my abode should be fixed at such a distance as the mountains of Darghed.

81   Had it pleased the Author of my being, I might have been illustrious as Kais, the son of Khaled; had it pleased my Creator, I might have been eminent as Amru, the son of Morthed:

---

81 *Kais, the son of Khaled* and *Amru, the son of Morthed* 'Qais-ibn-'Āsim, of the tribe Shaibān, and 'Amru-ibn-Marthad, of the tribe of Bekr-ibn-Vāil, were two Arab chiefs, renowned for their high birth and great wealth.' See Johnson, *The Seven Poems*, p.58.

82 Then should I have abounded in wealth; and the noblest chiefs would have visited me as a chieftain equally noble.

83 I am light, as you know me all, and am nimble; following my own inclinations, and briskly moving as the head of a serpent with flaming eyes.

84 I have sworn, that my side should never cease to line a bright INDIAN blade with two well-polished and well-sharpened edges.

85 A penetrating cimeter! When I advance with it in my defence against a fierce attack, the first stroke makes a second unnecessary: it is not a mere pruning-sickle,

86 But the genuine brother of confidence, not bent by the most impetuous blow; and, when they say to me, 'Gently,' I restrain its rage, and exclaim, 'It is enough.'

87 When the whole clan are bracing on their armour with eager haste, thou mayst find me victorious in the conflict, as soon as my hand can touch the hilt of this cimeter.

88 Many a herd of slumbering camels have I approached with my drawn sabre, when the foremost of them *awakening* have fled through fear of me:

89 But one of them has passed before me, strong-limbed, full-breasted, and well-fed, the highly-valued property of a morose old churl, dry and thin as a fuller's club.

90 He said to me, when the camel's hoof and thigh were dismembered, 'Seest thou not how great an injury thou hast done me?'

91 Then he turned to his attendants, saying, 'What opinion do you form of that young wine-drinker, who assails us impetuously, whose violence is preconcerted?'

92 'Leave him, he added, and let this camel be his perquisite; but, unless you drive off the hindmost of the herd, he will reiterate his mischief.'

93 Then our damsels were busy in dressing the camel's foal, and eagerly served up the luscious bunch.

---

93 Arberry more accurately translates the second part of this verse as 'the tender shredded hump was hastened to regale us', *The Seven Odes*, p.89.

94   O daughter of Mabed, sing my praises, if I am slain, according to my desert, and rend thy vest with sincere affliction!

95   Compare me not with any man, whose courage equals not my courage; whose exploits are not like mine; who has not been engaged in combats, in which I have been distinguished;

96   With a man slow in noble enterprises, but quick in base pursuits; dishonoured in the assembly of the tribe, and a vile outcast.

97   Had I been ignoble among my countrymen, the enmity of the befriended and the friendless might have been injurious to me;

98   But their malevolence is repelled by my firm defiance of them, by my boldness in attack, by my solid integrity, and my exalted birth.

99   By thy life, the hardest enterprises neither fill my day with solicitude, nor lengthen the duration of my night:

100   But many a day have I fixed my station immoveably in the close conflict, and defended a pass, regardless of hostile menaces,

101   On my native field of combat, where even the boldest hero might be apprehensive of destruction; where the muscles of our chargers quake, as soon as they mingle in battle;

102   And many an arrow *for drawing lots* have I seen well-hardened and made yellow by fire, and then have delivered it into the hand of a gamester noted for ill-fortune.

103   *Too much wisdom is folly*; for time will produce events, of which thou canst have no idea; and he, to whom thou gavest no commission, will bring thee unexpected news.

---

98   Despite his proud boast of being the defender of his clan, Tarafa gives the impression of a man peculiarly adept at putting other people's backs up, whether through his neglect as herdsman or his conscientiousness in camel-rustling. Poetry, the secret of his immortality, was also the source of his death; for composing some satiric verses on the king he was buried alive.

103   Southey copied this final verse into his *Commonplace-Book* (p.106); subsequently it served as the motto to the third book of *Thalaba, Works*, IV.81.

The Remaining Five *Mu'allaqāt*

['The Poem of Zohair' (Zuhair ibn Abī Salmā) contrasts with that of Tarafa in containing the practical wisdom of an old and sober man of the world. Lacking some of the fiery impetuosity of the Bedouin, Zuhair gives his thoughts on the horrors of war, and on expedient peace-making, ending with a series of Solomon-like proverbial utterances.

'The Poem of Lebeid' (Labīd ibn Rabī'ah Al 'Amiri) contains some poignant description of his longing for Nawara, and an elevated description of his dromedary, which is compared to a wind-driven cloud, a wild-ass running to a pool, and a wild-cow hastening in search of her calf. Celebration of his prowess in battle, and praise of the virtues of his tribe follow according to the ground-rules of the *qaṣīda*. For Jones's description of this poem, see his *Essay on the Poetry of the Eastern Nations*, pp.326–7 below, where he quotes five stanzas, providing a verse translation which, however, lacks the accuracy of his later prose one, cf. p.327n. below.

'The Poem of Antara' (Antara ibn Shaddad) opens with the question: 'Have the bards who preceded me left any theme unsung? What, therefore, shall be my subject? Love only must supply my lay'. However, while he does describe the beauties of his beloved Abla, his warlike passions soon supplant her as the subject of his lay: 'Broad were the lips of the wound; and the noise of the rushing blood called forth the wolves, prowling in the night, and pinched with hunger' (50).

'The Poem of 'Amru' ('Amr ibn Kulthum) 'is arrogant beyond all imagination, and contains hardly a colour of argument . . . but his production could not fail of becoming extremely popular among his countrymen; and his own family . . . *could scarce ever desist from repeating it . . .*' (The Argument to 'The Poem of Amru' *Works*, X.92). His mistress's charms are not totally neglected: 'Her hips elegantly swelling, which the entrance to the tent is scarce large enough to admit, and her waist, the beauty of which drives me to madness' (17). But the damsels of the tribe entreat the menfolk to protect them, and, as 'Amru is quick to point out: 'nothing can afford our sweet maids so pure a protection as the strokes of our sabres, which make men's arms fly off like the clashing wands of playful boys'.

'The Poem of Hareth' (Harith ibn Hilliza) again displays the haughty spirit of a chieftain boasting of his tribe's preeminence. It is possible that this poem constituted an oration in response to that of Amru in order to settle their bloody tribal feud before the king of Hira who was acting as mediator (*Works*, X.91–2;110–11). Whatever the truth of the matter, Hareth's indignation at unjust accusations soon inflame him to sing of the clash of scimitars on foreheads, and the dreadful fire of vengeance.]

23

Sacontalá by Kālidāsa (1789)

[*Sacontalá, or, the fatal ring; An Indian drama by Cálidás* (Calcutta: Joseph Cooper, 1789) was published for the benefit of insolvent debtors, without even the translator's name. The following year saw a London edition (by Edwards), with another printing in 1792. Despite the doubts expressed in the *Critical Review* (vol. I, Jan. 1791, 18–27) concerning the authenticity of the work, Jones's name was soon associated with the translation, and the critical response was almost universally enthusiastic. Mary Wollstonecraft, writing for the *Analytical Review* (vol.7, 1790, 361–73) suggests the *Sacontalá*'s breadth of appeal:

> This Indian drama, translated by Sir William Jones, if we may credit common fame, will undoubtedly be thought not only by the man of taste, but by the philosopher, a precious *morçeau*; for whilst the latter has an opportunity of tracing human passions clothed in a new modification of manners, the former will immediately be gratified by the perusal of some pathetic scenes, and beautiful poetic similes.

Jones had not merely produced a translation but a text of cultural mediation, and Wollstonecraft testifies to his success in terms which reveal similar universalist Enlightenment preconceptions: 'the poetic delineation of Indian manners and the artless touches of nature . . . come home to the human bosom in every climate'.

The warm reception given by the British critics was, however, tepid by comparison with the continental reception. It is difficult to over-estimate the sensational effect of Jones's publication of Kālidāsa's play upon European cultural awareness. Schwab speaks of 'A *Sakuntalā* Era'; and Goethe proclaimed in 1791, 'Nenn' ich *Sakuntalā* dich, und so ist alles gesagt.' (When I mention *Sakuntalā*, everything is said.) This first link with the authentic India seduced Herder who posited an Indian fatherland for the human race in its infancy. According to Schwab: 'In a mere decade Jones became widely known as the translator of *Sakuntalā*; for Goethe he had become "the incomparable Jones", the famous Sir William Jones, and it was sufficient to quote him without explanations as de Maistre demonstrated when he quoted Jones in his *Soirées*' (*The Oriental Renaissance*, pp. 63–4).

In India also *Sacontalá* had a profound effect. Jones was not only making

Europe familiar with the drama, but he was also freeing it for Indians from the Brahman hegemony. According to S. N. Mukherjee, 'By saving Kālidāsa from the medieval commentators he ushered in what has been called 'an Indian Renaissance', (*Sir William Jones*, p.3); and Nehru (*The Discovery of India*, New York, 1946, p.317), writing in the bicentenary of Jones's birth, acknowledged India's profound debt of gratitude. The copy text is 1799, with variants noted from the first London edition of 1790.]

PREFACE

IN one of the letters which bear the title of EDIFYING, though most of them swarm with ridiculous errours, and all must be consulted with extreme diffidence, I met, some years ago, with the following passage: 'In the north of India there are many books, called Nátac, which, as the Bráhmens assert, contain a large portion of ancient history without any mixture of fable;' and having an eager desire to know the real state of this empire before the conquest of it by the Savages of the North, I was very solicitous, on my arrival in Bengal, to procure access to those books, either by the help of translations, if they had been translated, or by learning the language in which they were originally composed, and which I had yet a stronger 10 inducement to learn from its connection with the administration of justice to the Hindûs; but when I was able to converse with the Bráhmens, they assured me that the Nátacs were not histories, and abounded with fables; that they were extremely popular works, and consisted of conversations in prose and verse, held before ancient Rájás in their publick assemblies, on an infinite variety of subjects, and in various dialects of India: this definition gave me no very distinct idea; but I concluded that they were dialogues on moral or literary topicks; whilst other Europeans, whom I consulted, had understood from the natives that they were discourses on dancing, musick, or poetry. At length a very sensible Bráhmen, named Rádhácánt, who had 20 long been attentive to English manners, removed all my doubts, and gave me no less delight than surprise, by telling me that our nation had compositions of the same sort, which were publickly represented at Calcutta in the cold season, and bore the name, as he had been informed, of plays. Resolving at my leisure to read the best of them, I asked which of their Nátacs was most universally esteemed; and he answered without hesitation, Sacontalá, supporting his opinion, as usual among the Pandits, by a couplet to this effect: 'The ring of Sacontalá, in which the fourth act, and four stanzas of that act, are eminently brilliant, displays all the rich exuberance of Cálidása's genius.' I soon procured a correct copy of it; and, assisted by my teacher 30 Rámalóchan, began with translating it verbally into Latin, which bears so great a resemblance to Sanscrit, that it is more convenient than any modern

---

1   *the title of* EDIFYING   Père Jean-François Pons to Père Halde, *Lettres édifiantes et curieuses* (1740), p.72.

31   Pandit Rámalóchan, who helped Jones complete his original interlinear translation, was a Sanskrit teacher at the University of Nadia, and had been Jones's tutor since 1785. Significantly he was a teacher of the Vaidya caste as Brahmans were still reluctant to unlock the treasures of their sacred language to a foreigner. Jones was in effect freeing the works of Kālidāsa from religious monopoly in the same way as his *Digest of Hindu Law* was intended to free the courts from a Brahmanical stranglehold.

language for a scrupulous interlineary version: I then turned it word for word into English, and afterwards, without adding or suppressing any material sentence, disengaged it from the stiffness of a foreign idiom, and prepared the faithful translation of the Indian drama, which I now present to the publick as a most pleasing and authentick picture of old Hindû manners, and one of the greatest curiosities that the literature of Asia has yet brought to light.

Dramatick poetry must have been immemorially ancient in the Indian empire: the invention of it is commonly ascribed to Bheret, a sage believed to have been inspired, who invented also a system of musick which bears his name; but this opinion of its origin is rendered very doubtful by the universal belief, that the first Sanscrit verse ever heard by mortals was pronounced in a burst of resentment by the great Válmic, who flourished in the silver age of the world, and was author of an Epick Poem on the war of his contemporary, Ráma, king of Ayódhyà; so that no drama in verse could have been represented before his time; and the Indians have a wild story, that the first regular play, on the same subject with the Rámáyan, was composed by Hanumat or Pávan, who commanded an army of Satyrs or Mountaineers in Ráma's expedition against Lancà: they add, that he engraved it on a smooth rock, which, being dissatisfied with his composition, he hurled into the sea; and that, many years after, a learned prince ordered expert divers to take impressions of the poem on wax, by which means the drama was in great measure restored; and my Pandit assures me that he is in possession of it. By whomsoever or in whatever age this species of entertainment was invented, it is very certain, that it was carried to great perfection in its kind, when Vicramáditya, who reigned in the first century before Christ, gave encouragement to poets, philologers, and mathematicians, at a time when the Britons were as unlettered and unpolished as the army of Hanumat: nine men of genius, commonly called the nine gems, attended his court, and were splendidly supported by his bounty; and Cálidás is unanimously allowed to have been the brightest of them. – A modern epigram was lately repeated to me, which does so much honour to the author of Sacontalá, that I cannot forbear exhibiting a literal version of it: 'Poetry was the sportful daughter of Válmic, and, having been educated by Vyása, she chose Cálidás for her bridegroom after the manner of Viderbha: she was the mother of Amara,

40

50

60

---

59 *when Britons were as unlettered and unpolished as the army of Hanumat* Hanumān was the monkey-headed demigod whose army of monkeys helped Rāma to rescue his wife Sītā. In stressing the sophistication of Vikramāditya's court, Jones suggests that Hindu civilization has as noble a pedigree as that of the Greeks. Eighteen years earlier in the Preface to his *Grammar of the Persian Language*, he had maintained that we resemble benighted savages as long as we fail to respond to the beauties of other cultures: 'we all love to excuse, or conceal, our ignorance, and are seldom willing to allow any excellence beyond the limits of our own attainments: like the savages, who thought the sun rose and set for them alone, and could not imagine that the waves, which surrounded their island, left coral and pearls upon any other shore', *Works*, V.166.

Sundar, Sanc'ha, Dhanic; but now, old and decrepit, her beauty faded, and her unadorned feet slipping as she walks, in whose cottage does she disdain to take shelter?'   70

All the other works of our illustrious poet, the Shakespeare of India, that have yet come to my knowledge, are a second play, in five acts, entitled Urvasí; an heroic poem, or rather a series of poems in one book, on the Children of the Sun; another, with perfect unity of action, on the Birth of Cumára, god of war; two or three love tales in verse; and an excellent little work on Sanscrit Metre, precisely in the manner of Terentianus; but he is believed by some to have revised the works of Válmic and Vyása, and to have corrected the perfect editions of them which are now current: this at least is admitted by all, that he stands next in reputation to those venerable bards; and we must regret, that he has left only two dramatick poems, especially as   80 the stories in his Raghuvansa would have supplied him with a number of excellent subjects. – Some of his contemporaries, and other Hindû poets even to our own times, have composed so many tragedies, comedies, farces, and musical pieces, that the Indian theatre would fill as many volumes as that of any nation in ancient or modern Europe: all the Pandits assert that their plays are innumerable; and, on my first inquiries concerning them, I had notice of more than thirty, which they consider as the flower of their Nátacs, among which the Malignant Child, the Rape of Ushá, the Taming of Durvásas, the Seizure of the Lock, Málati and Mádhava, with five or six dramas on the adventures of their incarnate gods, are the most admired after those of   90 Cálidás. They are all in verse, where the dialogue is elevated; and in prose, where it is familiar: the men of rank and learning are represented speaking pure Sanscrit, and the women Prácrit, which is little more than the language of the Bráhmens melted down by a delicate articulation to the softness of Italian; while the low persons of the drama speak the vulgar dialects of the several provinces which they are supposed to inhabit.

The play of Sacontalá must have been very popular when it was first represented; for the Indian empire was then in full vigour, and the national vanity must have been highly flattered by the magnificent introduction of those kings and heroes in whom the Hindûs gloried; the scenery must have   100

71   *the Shakespeare of India*   This reflects the measure of Jones's excitement at his discovery of Kālidāsa, whom he felt certain could by judged by any standards, Occidental or Oriental. Although some reviewers found this description rather extravagant (see, for example *Blackwood's Edinburgh Magazine*, 1820, 418), he was not alone in seeing such a connection; Augustus Wilhelm Schlegel commented that, had not the fidelity of the translation of *Sakuntalā* been attested to by Orientalists (Frederick Schlegel had referred to its 'scrupulous exactness'), it must have appeared that Jones's love of Shakespeare had been too much for him. In private Jones had gone even further; thus, to Thomas Law on 13 May 1788: 'I am deep into the second act of a Sanscrit play, near 2000 years old, and so much like Shakespeare, that I should have thought our great dramatick poet had studied Cālidāsa', *Letters*, II.806. Jones's chronology is incorrect here, although there is still some uncertainty as to whether Kālidāsa flourished in the fifth or sixth century.

95   *the low persons of the drama speak the vulgar dialects*   It is something of a pity that Jones failed to employ any dialectal variety in the dialogue.

been splendid and beautiful; and there is good reason to believe, that the court at Avanti was equal in brilliancy during the reign of Vicramáditya, to that of any monarch in any age or country. – Dushmanta, the hero of the piece, appears in the chronological tables of the Bráhmens among the Children of the Moon, and in the twenty-first generation after the flood; so that, if we can at all rely on the chronology of the Hindûs, he was nearly contemporary with Obed, or Jesse; and Puru, his most celebrated ancestor, was the fifth in descent from Budha, or Mercury, who married, they say, a daughter of the pious king, whom Vishnu preserved in an ark from the universal deluge: his eldest son Bheret was the illustrious progenitor of Curu, 110 from whom Pándu was lineally descended, and in whose family the Indian Apollo became incarnate; whence the poem, next in fame to the Rámáyan, is called Mahábhárat.

As to the machinery of the drama, it is taken from the system of mythology, which prevails to this day, and which it would require a large volume to explain; but we cannot help remarking, that the deities introduced in the Fatal Ring are clearly allegorical personages. Maríchi, the first production of Brahmá, or the Creative Power, signifies light, that subtil fluid which was created before its reservoir, the sun, as water was created before the sea; Casyapa, the offspring of Maríchi, seems to be a personification of 120 infinite space, comprehending innumerable worlds; and his children by Aditi, or his active power (unless Aditi mean the primeval day, and Diti, his other wife, the night), are Indra, or the visible firmament, and the twelve Adityas, or suns, presiding over as many months.

On the characters and conduct of the play I shall offer no criticism; because I am convinced that the tastes of men differ as much as their sentiments and passions, and that, in feeling the beauties of art, as in smelling flowers, tasting fruits, viewing prospects, and hearing melody, every individual must be guided by his own sensations and the incommunicable associations of his own ideas. This only I may add, that if Sacontalá should 130 ever be acted in India, where alone it could be acted with perfect knowledge of Indian dresses, manners, and scenery, the piece might easily be reduced to five acts of a moderate length, by throwing the third act into the second, and the sixth into the fifth; for it must be confessed that the whole of Dushmanta's conversation with his buffoon, and great part of his courtship in the hermitage, might be omitted without any injury to the drama.

---

110 *Bheret* Bharata, the son of Sacontalá and Dushmanta, is the eponym of the Bhāratas, and the divine aspects of his lineage explain the inclusion of the story of Śakuntalā in the *Mahābhārata*, the central matter of which concerns the dynastic succession of the Bhārata clan, see J. A. B. van Buitenen (ed. and trans.) *Mahābhārata* 3 vols. (Chicago, 1973), I.155–71.

128–31 *every individual must be guided by his own sensations and the incommunicable associations of his own ideas* With a nod in the direction of Hartley, Jones maintains his position that taste varies from individual to individual and not from nation to nation; cf. *Letters*, II.716.

It is my anxious wish that others may take the pains to learn Sanscrit, and may be persuaded to translate the works of Cálidás: I shall hardly again employ my leisure in a task so foreign to my professional (which are, in truth, my favourite) studies; and have no intention of translating any other 140 book from any language, except the Law Tract of Menu, and the new Digest of Indian and Arabian laws; but, to show, that the Bráhmens, at least, do not think polite literature incompatible with jurisprudence, I cannot avoid mentioning, that the venerable compiler of the Hindû Digest, who is now in his eighty-sixth year, has the whole play of Sacontalá by heart; as he proved when I last conversed with him, to my entire conviction. Lest, however, I should hereafter seem to have changed a resolution which I mean to keep inviolate, I think it proper to say, that I have already translated four or five other books, and among them the Hitópadésa, which I undertook, merely as an exercise in learning Sanscrit, three years before I knew that Mr. Wilkins, 150 without whose aid I should never have learnt it, had any thought of giving the same work to the publick.

PERSONS OF THE DRAMA

Dushmanta, Emperor of India.
Sacontalá, the Heroine of the Piece.
Anusúyá,
Priyamvadá, } Damsels attendant on her.
Mádhavya, the Emperor's Buffoon.
Gautamí, an old female Hermit.
Sárngarava,
Sáradwata, } two Bráhmens.
Canna, Foster-father of Sacontalá,
Cumbhílaca, a Fisherman.
Misracésí, a Nymph.
Mátali, Charioteer of Indra.
A little Boy.
Casyapa,
Aditi, } Deities, Parents of Indra.

Officers of State and Police, Bráhmens, Damsels, Hermits, Pupils, Chamberlains, Warders of the Palace, Messengers, and Attendants.

---

144 *the venerable compiler of the Hindu Digest* This was his 'favourite Pandit', the venerable Jagganātha Tarkapañcānana, who edited Jones's *Digest of Hindu Laws*, see *Letters*, II.923.

149 *The Hitópadésa* Jones's translation of this collection of the Fables of Vishnusarman, which predated Charles Wilkins's 1787 version, was published posthumously in 1799.

THE PROLOGUE

A Bráhmen *pronounces the benediction.*

WATER was the first work of the Creator; and Fire receives the oblations ordained by law; the Sacrifice is performed with solemnity; the Two Lights of heaven distinguish time; the subtil Ether, which is the vehicle of sound, pervades the universe; the Earth is the natural parent of all increase; and by Air all things breathing are animated: may ÍSA, the God of Nature, apparent in these eight forms, bless and sustain you!

The Manager *enters.*

Man. What occasion is there for a long speech? – [*Looking towards the dressing-room*] –When your decorations, Madam, are completed, be pleased to come forward.

An Actress *enters.*

Actr. I attend, Sir. – What are your commands?   10

Man. This, Madam, is the numerous and polite assembly of the famed Hero, our king Vicramáditya, the patron of every delightful art; and before this audience we must do justice to a new production of Cálidás, a dramatick piece, entitled Sacontalá, or, The Fatal Ring: it is requested, therefore, that all will be attentive.

Actr. Who, Sir could be inattentive to an entertainment so well intended?

Man. [*Smiling*] I will speak, Madam, without reserve. – As far as an enlightened audience receive pleasure from our theatrical talents, and express it, so far, and no farther, I set a value on them; but my own mind is diffident of its powers, how strongly soever exerted.   20

Actr. You judge rightly in measuring your own merit by the degree of pleasure which this assembly may receive; but its value, I trust, will presently appear. – Have you any farther commands?

Man. What better can you do, since you are now on the stage, than exhilarate the souls, and gratify the sense, of our auditory with a song?

Actr. Shall I sing the description of a season? and which of the seasons do you chuse to hear described?

Man. No finer season could be selected than the summer, which is actually begun, and abounds with delights. How sweet is the close of a summer day, which invites our youth to bathe in pure streams, and induces gentle slumber   30

This device of opening the play with a conversation between the stage manager and the chief actress was copied by Goethe for his *Faust*.

under the shades refreshed by sylvan breezes, which have passed over the blooming Pátalis and stolen their fragrance!

Actr. [*Singing.*] 'Mark how the soft blossoms of the Nágacésar are lightly kissed by the bees! Mark how the damsels delicately place behind their ears the flowers of Sirísha!'

Man. A charming strain! the whole company sparkles, as it were, with admiration; and the musical mode to which the words are adapted, has filled their souls with rapture. By what other performance can we ensure a continuance of their favour?

Actr. Oh! by none better than by the Fatal Ring, which you have just announced.   40

Man. How could I forget it! In that moment I was lulled to distraction by the melody of thy voice, which allured my heart, as the king Dushmanta is now allured by the swift antelope.   [*They both go out.*]

---

32 *blooming Pátalis* 'The *Pátali* blossoms early in the spring, before a leaf appears on the tree ... exquisitely fragrant, preferred by the bees to all other flowers, and compared by the poets to the quiver of CÁMADÉVA, or the God of Love', 'Botanical Observations on Select Indian Plants', *Works*, V.131–4.

33 *the soft blossoms of the Nágacésar* One of the fragrant flowers in the quiver of Kāma, see 'A Hymn to Camdeo', l.57 and n.

35 *the flowers of Sirísha* Mimosa odoratissima, see *Letters*, II.895.

SACONTALÁ;

OR,

THE FATAL RING.

ACT I

SCENE – A FOREST.

Dushmanta, *in a car, pursuing an antelope, with a bow and quiver, attended by his* Charioteer.

Char. [*Looking at the antelope, and then at the king.*]

WHEN I cast my eye on that black antelope, and on thee, O king, with thy braced bow, I see before me, as it were, the God Mahésa chasing a hart, with his bow, named pináca, braced in his left hand.

Dushm. The fleet animal has given us a long chase. Oh! there he runs, with his neck bent gracefully, looking back, from time to time, at the car which follows him. Now, through fear of a descending shaft, he contracts his forehand, and extends his flexible haunches; and now, through fatigue, he pauses to nibble the grass in his path with his mouth half opened. See how he springs and bounds with long steps, lightly skimming the ground, and rising high in the air! And now so rapid is his flight, that he is scarce discernible! 10

Char. The ground was uneven, and the horses were checked in their course. He has taken advantage of our delay. It is level now, and we may easily overtake him.

Dushm. Loosen the reins.

Char. As the king commands. – [*He drives the car first at full speed, and then gently.*] – He could not escape. The horses were not even touched by the clouds of dust which they raised; they tossed their manes, erected their ears, and rather glided than galloped over the smooth plain.

Dushm. They soon outran the swift antelope. – Objects which, from their distance, appeared minute, presently became larger: what was really divided, 20 seemed united, as we passed; and what was in truth bent, seemed straight. So swift was the motion of the wheels, that nothing, for many moments, was either distant or near.   [*He fixes an arrow in his bowstring.*]

[*Behind the scenes.*] He must not be slain. This antelope, O king, has an asylum in our forest: he must not be slain.

---

2 *Mahésa* Śiva, whose bow (Pináka) resembles the rainbow.
24 *This antelope, O king, has an asylum in our forest* The fawn anticipates and symbolizes its protectress, the 'girl with antelope's eyes', Sacontalá.

Char. [*Listening and Looking.*] Just as the animal presents a fair mark for your arrow, two hermits are advancing to interrupt your aim.

Dushm. Then stop the car.

Char. The king is obeyed.   [*He draws in the reins.*]

          Enter a Hermit *and his* Pupil.

Herm. [*Raising his hands.*] Slay not, O mighty sovereign, slay not a poor fawn, who has found a place of refuge. No, surely, no; he must not be hurt. An arrow in the delicate body of a deer would be like fire in a bale of cotton. Compared with thy keen shafts, how weak must be the tender hide of a young antelope! Replace quickly, oh! replace the arrow which thou hast aimed. The weapons of you kings and warriors are destined for the relief of the oppressed, not for the destruction of the guiltless.

Dushm. [*Saluting them.*] It is replaced.   [*He places the arrow in his quiver.*]

Herm. [*With joy.*] Worthy is that act of thee, most illustrious of monarchs; worthy, indeed, of a prince descended from Puru. Mayst thou have a son adorned with virtues, a sovereign of the world!

Pup. [*Elevating both his hands.*] Oh! by all means, may thy son be adorned with every virtue, a sovereign of the world!

Dushm. [*Bowing to them.*] My head bears with reverence the order of a Bráhmen.

Herm. Great king, we came hither to collect wood for a solemn sacrifice; and this forest, on the banks of the Malini, affords an asylum to the wild animals protected by Sacontalá, whom our holy preceptor Canna has received as a sacred deposit. If you have no other avocation, enter yon grove, and let the rights of hospitality be duly performed. Having seen with your own eyes the virtuous behaviour of those whose only wealth is their piety, but whose worldly cares are now at an end, you will then exclaim, 'How many good subjects are defended by this arm, which the bowstring has made callous!'

Dushm. Is the master of your family at home?

Herm. Our preceptor is gone to Sómatírt'ha, in hopes of deprecating some calamity, with which destiny threatens the irreproachable Sacontalá; and he has charged her, in his absence, to receive all guests with due honour.

Dushm. Holy man, I will attend her; and she, having observed my devotion, will report it favourably to the venerable sage.

Both. Be it so; and we depart on our own business.

              [*The* Hermit *and his* Pupil *go out.*]

Dushm. Drive on the car. By visiting the abode of holiness, we shall purify our souls.

Char. As the king (may his life be long!) commands.   [*He drives on.*]

Dushm. [*Looking on all sides.*] That we are near the dwelling-place of pious hermits, would clearly have appeared, even if it had not been told.

---

39 *descended from Puru* On Puru, the ancestor of Dushmanta, see *Mahābhārata*, I.171–5.

Char. By what marks?

Dushm. Do you not observe them? See under yon trees the hallowed grains which have been scattered on the ground, while the tender female parrots were feeding their unfledged young in their pendent nests. Mark in other places the shining pieces of polished stone which have bruised the oily fruit of the sacred Ingudì. Look at the young fawns, which, having acquired confidence in man, and accustomed themselves to the sound of his voice, frisk at pleasure, without varying their course. Even the surface of the river is reddened with lines of consecrated bark, which float down its stream. Look again; the roots of yon trees are bathed in the waters of holy pools, which quiver as the breeze plays upon them; and the glowing lustre of yon fresh leaves is obscured, for a time, by smoke that rises from oblations of clarified butter. See too, where the young roes graze, without apprehension from our approach, on the lawn before yonder garden, where the tops of the sacrificial grass, cut for some religious rite, are sprinkled around.

Char. I now observe all those marks of some holy habitation.

Dushm. [*Turning aside.*] This awful sanctuary, my friend, must not be violated. Here, therefore, stop the car; that I may descend.

Char. I hold in the reins. The king may descend at his pleasure.

Dushm. [*Having descended, and looking at his own dress.*] Groves devoted to religion must be entered in humbler habiliments. Take these regal ornaments; – [*the* Charioteer *receives them*] – and, whilst I am observing those who inhabit this retreat, let the horses be watered and dressed.

Char. Be it as you direct!   [*He goes out.*]

Dushm. [*Walking round and looking.*] Now then I enter the sanctuary. – [*He enters the grove.*] – Oh! this place must be holy, my right arm throbs. – [*Pausing and considering*] – What new acquisition does this omen promise in a sequestered grove? But the gates of predestined events are in all places open.

[*Behind the scenes.*] Come hither, my beloved companions; Oh! come hither.

Dushm. [*Listening.*] Hah! I hear female voices to the right of yon arbour. I am resolved to know who are conversing. – [*He walks round and looks.*] – There are some damsels, I see, belonging to the hermit's family who carry water-pots of different sizes proportioned to their strength, and are going to

70

80

90

---

67   *tender female parrots*   The birds protected Sacontalá when she was abandoned as a baby, hence her name from the Sanskrit *śakunta* (birds), cf. VII.186–7 below.

70   *the sacred Ingudì*   The prized oil was used as an unguent to anoint the hair and heal wounds, see II.159; IV.272;, and Jones's 'A Catalogue of Indian Plants', *Works*, V.58.

90   *this place must be holy, my right arm throbs*   A reference to a traditional Indian superstition that a throbbing sensation in any part of the right hand side of the body was an auspicious sign. If felt on the left hand side it was considered an unpropitious sign. For women the sides were reversed, cf. Sacontalá in V.107 below.

water the delicate plants. Oh! how charmingly they look! If the beauty of   100
maids who dwell in woodland retreats cannot easily be found in the recesses
of a palace, the garden flowers must make room for the blossoms of the
forest, which excel them in colour and fragrance. [*He stands gazing at them.*]

Enter Sacontalá, Anusúyá, *and* Priyamvadá.

Anu. O my Sacontalá, it is in thy society that the trees of our father Canna
seem to me delightful; it well becomes thee, who are soft as the fresh-blown
Mallicà, to fill with water the canals which have been dug round these tender
shrubs.

Sac. It is not only in obedience to our father that I thus employ myself,
though that were a sufficient motive, but I really feel the affection of a sister
for these young plants.   [*Watering them.*]   110

Pri. My beloved friend, the shrubs which you have watered flower in the
summer, which is now begun: let us give water to those which have passed
their flowering time; for our virtue will be the greater when it is wholly
disinterested.

Sac. Excellent advice!   [*Watering other plants.*]

Dushm. [*Aside in transport.*] How! is that Canna's daughter, Sacontalá? –
[*With surprise.*] – The venerable sage must have an unfeeling heart, since he
has allotted a mean employment to so lovely a girl, and has dressed her in a
coarse mantle of woven bark. He, who could wish that so beautiful a
creature, who at first sight ravishes my soul, should endure the hardships of   120
his austere devotion, would attempt, I suppose, to cleave the hard wood
Samì with a leaf of the blue lotos. Let me retire behind this tree, that I may
gaze on her charms without diminishing her confidence.   [*He retires.*]

Sac. My friend Priyamvadá has tied this mantle of bark so closely over my
bosom that it gives me pain: Anusúyá, I request you to untie it.

[Anusúyá *unties the mantle.*]

Pri. [*Laughing.*] Well, my sweet friend, enjoy, while you may, that youthful
prime, which gives your bosom so beautiful a swell.

Dushm. [*Aside.*] Admirably spoken, Priyamvadá! No; her charms cannot
be hidden, even though a robe of intertwisted fibres be thrown over her

---

100   Appropriately in a play the opening of which announces water to be *the first work
of the Creator*, and which hymns that element's sacred fertility, Sacontalá and her friends
are discovered watering the delicate plants.

105–6   *soft as the fresh-blown Mallicà*   Jones identifies this as 'Wavy-leaved
NYCTANTHES', mentioning its rich musky odour, see 'Botanical Observations', *Works*,
V.73–4.

121–2   *to cleave the hard wood Samì with a leaf of blue lotos*   The *śami* tree is associated
with weapons in the *Mahābhārata*, and, according to Jones, the wood of this variety of
Mimosa was 'used by the *Bráhmens* to kindle their sacred fire', see 'Botanical
Observations', *Works*, V.155. The binary oppositions reflect Dushmanta's distress that she
should suffer such hardships. (Cf. Miranda's compassion for her 'patient log-man', see *The
Tempest*, III.i.15ff.) Sacontalá's own pain, caused by the constriction of her breasts under a
mantle of coarse woven bark, and her request to Anusúyá to untie her bodice, highlights
her youthful burgeoning and focuses Dushmanta's sensual voyeurism.

shoulders, and conceal a part of her bosom, like a veil of yellow leaves   130
enfolding a radiant flower. The water lily, though dark moss may settle on its
head, is nevertheless beautiful; and the moon with dewy beams is rendered
yet brighter by its black spots. The bark itself acquires elegance from the
features of a girl with antelope's eyes, and rather augments than diminishes
my ardour. Many are the rough stalks which support the water lily; but
many and exquisite are the blossoms which hang on them.

Sac. [*Looking before her.*] Yon Amra tree, my friends, points with the
finger of its leaves, which the gale gently agitates, and seems inclined to
whisper some secret. I will go near it.   [*They all approach the tree.*]

Pri. O my Sacontalá, let us remain some time in this shade.   140

Sac. Why here particularly?

Pri. Because the Amra tree seems wedded to you, who are graceful as the
blooming creeper which twines round it.

Sac. Properly are you named Priyamvadá, or speaking kindly.

Dushm. [*Aside.*] She speaks truly. Yes; her lip glows like the tender leaflet;
her arms resemble two flexible stalks; and youthful beauty shines, like a
blossom, in all her lineaments.

Anu. See, my Sacontalá, how yon fresh Mallicà, which you have surnamed
Vanàdósiní, or Delight of the Grove, has chosen the sweet Amra for her
bridegroom.   150

Sac. [*Approaching, and looking at it with pleasure.*] How charming is the
season, when the nuptials even of plants are thus publickly celebrated!

                    [*She stands admiring it.*]

Pri. [*Smiling.*] Do you know, my Anusúyá, why Sacontalá gazes on the
plants with such rapture?

Anu. No, indeed: I was trying to guess. Pray, tell me.

Pri. 'As the Grove's Delight is united to a suitable tree, thus I too hope for
a bridegroom to my mind.' – That is her private thought at this moment.

Sac. Such are the flights of your own imagination.

                    [*Inverting the water-pot.*]

Anu. Here is a plant, Sacontalá, which you have forgotten, though it has
grown up, like yourself, under the fostering care of our father Canna.   160

Sac. Then I shall forget myself. – O wonderful! – [*approaching the plant.*] –
O Priyamvadá! [*looking at it with joy*] I have delightful tidings for you.

Pri. What tidings, my beloved, for me?

Sac. This Mádhavi-creeper, though it be not the usual time for flowering,
is covered with gay blossoms from its root to its top.

Both. [*Approaching it hastily.*] Is it really so, sweet friend?

Sac. Is it so? look yourselves.

---

137   *Yon Amra*   The mango tree, see 'Botanical Observations', *Works*, V.125.

164   *Mádhavi-creeper*   The Bengal Banisteria, also known as Vásantì, whose flowers,
according to Jones, are 'delicately fragrant; white with a shade of pink'. The plant is
associated with lovers and love-making, cf. *Gítagóvinda*, I.22. 'This was the favourite plant

Pri. [*With eagerness.*] From this omen, Sacontalá, I announce you an excellent husband, who will very soon take you by the hand.

[*Both girls look at* Sacontalá.]

Sac. [*Displeased.*] A strange fancy of yours! 170

Pri. Indeed, my beloved, I speak not jestingly. I heard something from our father Canna. Your nurture of these plants has prospered; and thence it is, that I foretel your approaching nuptials.

Anu. It is thence, my Priyamvadá, that she has watered them with so much alacrity.

Sac. The Mádhavi plant is my sister; can I do otherwise than cherish her?

[*Pouring water on it.*]

Dushm. [*Aside.*] I fear she is of the same religious order with her foster-father. Or has a mistaken apprehension risen in my mind? My warm heart is so attached to her, that she cannot but be a fit match for a man of the military class. The doubts which awhile perplex the good, are soon removed 180 by the prevalence of their strong inclinations. I am enamoured of her, and she cannot, therefore, be the daughter of a Bráhmen, whom I could not marry.

Sac. [*Moving her head.*] Alas! a bee has left the blossom of this Mallicá, and is fluttering round my face. [*She expresses uneasiness.*]

Dushm. [*Aside, with affection.*] How often have I seen our court damsels affectedly turn their heads aside from some roving insect, merely to display their graces! but this rural charmer knits her brows, and gracefully moves her eyes through fear only, without art or affectation. Oh! happy bee, who touchest the corner of that eye beautifully trembling; who, approaching the 190 tip of that ear, murmurest as softly as if thou wert whispering a secret of love; and who sippest nectar, while she waves her graceful hand, from that lip, which contains all the treasures of delight! Whilst I am solicitous to know in what family she was born, thou art enjoying bliss, which to me would be supreme felicity.

Sac. Disengage me, I entreat, from this importunate insect, which quite baffles my efforts.

Pri. What power have we to deliver you? The kind Dushmanta is the sole defender of our consecrated groves.

Dushm. [*Aside.*] This is a good occasion for me to discover myself – 200 [*advancing a little.*] – I must not, I will not, fear. Yet – [*checking himself and*

---

of SACONTALA, which she very justly called the *Delight of the Woods*; for the beauty and fragrance of its flowers give them a title to all the praises which CÁLIDÁS and JAYADÉVA bestow on them: it is a gigantick and luxuriant climber; but, when it meets with nothing to grasp, it assumes the form of a sturdy tree', 'Botanical Observations', *Works*, V.123–4, see also *Letters*, II.895. It is, however, to the *Mallicà* that Sacontalá applies the epithet 'Vanàdósini, or Delight of the Grove', see ll.148–9 and note to ll.105–6 above.

189 *Oh! happy bee* This familiar trope of love poetry both East and West borrows an added erotic charge from the bee's associations with Kāma, cf. V.50–2 below, and 'A Hymn to Camdeo', ll.51–2.

retiring] – my royal character will thus abruptly be known to them. No; I will appear as a simple stranger, and claim the duties of hospitality.

Sac. This impudent bee will not rest. I will remove to another place. – [*Stepping aside and looking round.*] – Away! away! He follows me wherever I go. Deliver me, oh! deliver me from this distress.

Dushm. [*Advancing hastily.*] Ah! While the race of Puru govern the world, and restrain even the most profligate, by good laws well administered, has any man the audacity to molest the lovely daughters of pious hermits?

[*They look at him with emotion.*]

Anu. Sir, no man is here audacious; but this damsel, our beloved friend,   210
was teased by a fluttering bee.   [*Both girls look at* Sacontalá.]

Dushm. [*Approaching her.*] Damsel, may thy devotion prosper!

[Sacontalá *looks on the ground, bashful and silent.*]

Anu. Our guest must be received with due honours.

Pri. Stranger, you are welcome. Go, my Sacontalá; bring from the cottage a basket of fruit and flowers. This river will, in the mean time, supply water for his feet.   [*Looking at the water-pots.*]

Dushm. Holy maid, the gentleness of thy speech does me sufficient honour.

Anu. Sit down awhile on this bank of earth, spread with the leaves of Septaperna: the shade is refreshing, and our lord must want repose after his   220
journey.

Dushm. You too must all be fatigued by your hospitable attentions; rest yourselves, therefore, with me.

Pri. [*Aside to* Sacontalá.] Come, let us all be seated: our guest is contented with our reception of him.   [*They all seat themselves.*]

Sac. [*Aside.*] At the sight of this youth I feel an emotion scarce consistent with a grove devoted to piety.

Dushm. [*Gazing at them alternately.*] How well your friendship agrees, holy damsels, with the charming equality of your ages, and of your beauties!

Pri. [*Aside to* Anusúyá?] Who can this be, my Anusúyá? The union of   230
delicacy with robustness in his form, and of sweetness with divinity in his discourse, indicate a character fit for ample dominion.

Anu. [*Aside to* Priyamvadá.] I too have been admiring him. I must ask him a few questions. – [*Aloud.*] Your sweet speech, Sir, gives me confidence. What imperial family is embellished by our noble guest? What is his native country? Surely it must be afflicted by his absence from it. What, I pray, could induce you to humiliate that exalted form of yours by visiting a forest peopled only by simple anchorites?

Sac. [*Aside.*] Perplex not thyself, O my heart! let the faithful Anusúyá direct with her counsel the thoughts which rise in thee.   240

---

220   *leaves of Septaperna* (Seven-leaved) Jones describes the flowers as 'rather small, greenish white', and the leaves as very soft and a rich dark green, see 'Botanical Observations', *Works*, V.100–102.

Dushm. [*Aside.*] How shall I reveal, or how shall I disguise myself? – [*Musing.*] – Be it so. – [*Aloud to* Anusúyá.] Excellent lady, I am a student of the Véda, dwelling in the city of our king, descended from Puru; and, being occupied in the discharge of religious and moral duties, am come hither to behold the sanctuary of virtue.

Anu. Holy men, employed like you, are our lords and masters.

[Sacontalá *looks modest, yet with affection; while her companions gaze alternately at her and at the king.*]

Anu. [*Aside to* Sacontalá.] Oh! if our venerable father were present –

Sac. What if he were?

Anu. He would entertain our guest with a variety of refreshments.

Sac. [*Pretending displeasure.*] Go to; you had some other idea in your head; I will not listen to you. [*She sits apart.*] 250

Dushm. [*Aside to* Anusúyá *and* Priyamvadá.] In my turn, holy damsels, allow me to ask one question concerning your lovely friend.

Both. The request, Sir, does us honour.

Dushm. The sage Canna, I know, is ever intent upon the great Being; and must have declined all earthly connections. How then can this damsel be, as it is said, his daughter?

Anu. Let our lord hear. There is, in the family of Cusa, a pious prince of extensive power, eminent in devotion and in arms.

Dushm. You speak, no doubt, of Causica, the sage and monarch. 260

Anu. Know, Sir, that he is in truth her father; while Canna bears that reverend name, because he brought her up, since she was left an infant.

Dushm. Left? the word excites my curiosity; and raises in me a desire of knowing her whole story.

Anu. You shall hear it, Sir, in few words. – When that sage king had begun to gather the fruits of his austere devotion, the gods of Swerga became apprehensive of his increasing power, and sent the nymph Ménacà to frustrate, by her allurements, the full effect of his piety.

Dushm. Is a mortal's piety so tremendous to the inferior deities? What was the event? 270

Anu. In the bloom of the vernal season, Causica, beholding the beauty of the celestial nymph, and wafted by the gale of desire –

[*She stops and looks modest.*]

---

260 *Causica, the sage and monarch* Sacontalá's father, also known as 'Viśvámitra, or Universal Friend', was seduced by the *apsaras* (divine courtesan) Ménacà (Menakā) at the command of Indra who was perturbed by Viśvāmitra's powerful austerities; Sacontalá's parentage thus explains her Pārvāti-like mingling of sensuality and piety.

261 *Canna . . . brought her up* According to the epic narrative, the hermit Kanva (Canna) finds Sacontalá abandoned by Menakā on the banks of the river Mālini, and adopts her, see *Mahābhārata*, I.163.

272 *gale of desire* In the *Mahābhārata* version Indra, at Menaká's suggestion, causes the wind to blow her skirt open in order to inflame Viśvāmitra.

Dushm. I now see the whole. Sacontalá then is the daughter of a king, by a nymph of the lower heaven.

Anu. Even so.

Dushm. [*Aside.*] The desire of my heart is gratified. – [*Aloud.*] How, indeed, could her transcendent beauty be the portion of mortal birth? Yon light, that sparkles with tremulous beams, proceeds not from a terrestrial cavern.

[Sacontalá *sits modestly, with her eyes on the ground.*]

Dushm. [*Again aside.*] Happy man that I am! Now has my fancy an ample range. Yet, having heard the pleasantry of her companions on the subject of her nuptials, I am divided with anxious doubt, whether she be not wholly destined for a religious life. 280

Pri. [*Smiling, and looking first at* Sacontalá, *then at the king.*] Our lord seems desirous of asking other questions.

[Sacontalá *rebukes* Priyamvadá *with her hand.*]

Dushm. You know my very heart. I am, indeed, eager to learn the whole of this charmer's life; and must put one question more.

Pri. Why should you muse on it so long? – [*Aside.*] One would think this religious man was forbidden by his vows to court a pretty woman.

Dushm. This I ask. Is the strict rule of a hermit so far to be observed by Canna, that he cannot dispose of his daughter in marriage, but must check the natural impulse of juvenile love? Can she (oh preposterous fate!) be destined to reside for life among her favourite antelopes, the black lustre of whose eyes is far surpassed by hers? 290

Pri. Hitherto, Sir, our friend has lived happy in this consecrated forest, the abode of her spiritual father; but it is now his intention to unite her with a bridegroom equal to herself.

Dushm. [*Aside, with ecstasy.*] Exult, oh my heart, exult. All doubt is removed; and what before thou wouldst have dreaded as a flame, may now be approached as a gem inestimable.

Sac. [*Seeming angry.*] Anusúyá, I will stay here no longer. 300

Anu. Why so, I pray?

Sac. I will go to the holy matron Gautamí, and let her know how impertinently our Priyamvadá has been prattling. [*She rises.*]

Anu. It will not be decent, my love, for an inhabitant of this hallowed wood to retire before a guest has received complete honour.

[Sacontalá, *giving no answer, offers to go*]

Dushm. [*Aside.*] Is she then departing? – [*He rises, as if going to stop her, but checks himself.*] – The actions of a passionate lover are as precipitate as his mind is agitated. Thus I, whose passion impelled me to follow the hermit's daughter, am restrained by a sense of duty.

Pri. [*Going up to* Sacontalá.] My angry friend, you must not retire. 310

Sac. [*Stepping back and frowning.*] What should detain me?

Pri. You owe me the labour, according to our agreement, of watering two more shrubs. Pay me first, to acquit your conscience, and then depart, if you please. [*Holding her.*]

Dushm. The damsel is fatigued, I imagine, by pouring so much water on the cherished plants. Her arms, graced with palms like fresh blossoms, hang carelessly down; her bosom heaves with strong breathing; and now her dishevelled locks, from which the string has dropped, are held by one of her lovely hands. Suffer me, therefore, thus to discharge the debt. – [*Giving his ring to* Priyamvadá. *Both damsels, reading the name* Dushmanta, *inscribed on the ring, look with surprise at each other.*] – It is a toy unworthy of your fixed attention; but I value it as a gift from the king.

Pri. Then you ought not, Sir, to part with it. Her debt is from this moment discharged on your word only. [*She returns the ring.*]

Anu. You are now released, Sacontalá, by this benevolent lord – or favoured, perhaps, by a monarch himself. To what place will you now retire?

Sac. [*Aside.*] Must I not wonder at all this if I preserve my senses?

Pri. Are not you going, Sacontalá?

Sac. Am I your subject? I shall go when it pleases me.

Dushm. [*Aside, looking at* Sacontalá.] Either she is affected towards me, as I am towards her, or I am distracted with joy. She mingles not her discourse with mine; yet, when I speak, she listens attentively. She commands not her actions in my presence; and her eyes are engaged on me alone.

[*Behind the scenes.*] Oh pious hermits, preserve the animals of this hallowed forest! The king Dushmanta is hunting in it. The dust raised by the hoofs of his horses, which pound the pebbles ruddy as early dawn, falls like a swarm of blighting insects on the consecrated boughs which sustain your mantles of woven bark, moist with the water of the stream in which you have bathed.

Dushm. [*Aside.*] Alas! my officers, who are searching for me, have indiscreetly disturbed this holy retreat.

[*Again behind the scenes.*] Beware, ye hermits, of yon elephant, who comes overturning all that oppose him; now he fixes his trunk with violence on a lofty branch that obstructs his way; and now he is entangled in the twining stalks of the Vratati. How are our sacred rites interrupted! How are the protected herds dispersed! The wild elephant alarmed at the new appearance of a car, lays our forest waste.

Dushm. [*Aside.*] How unwillingly am I offending the devout foresters! Yes; I must go to them instantly.

Pri. Noble stranger, we are confounded with dread of the enraged elephant. With your permission, therefore, we retire to the hermit's cottage.

Anu. O Sacontalá, the venerable matron will be much distressed on your account. Come quickly, that we may be all safe together.

Sac. [*Walking slowly.*] I am stopped, alas! by a sudden pain in my side.

Dushm. Be not alarmed, amiable damsels. It shall be my care that no disturbance happen in your sacred groves.

Pri. Excellent stranger, we were wholly unacquainted with your station; and you will forgive us, we hope, for the offence of intermitting awhile the

320

330

340

350

honours due to you: but we humbly request that you will give us once more
the pleasure of seeing you, though you have not now been received with   360
perfect hospitality.

Dushm. You depreciate your own merits. The sight of you, sweet damsels,
has sufficiently honoured me.

Sac. My foot, O Anusúyá, is hurt by this pointed blade of Cusa grass; and
now my loose vest of bark is caught by a branch of the Curuvaca. Help me to
disentangle myself, and support me.   [*She goes out, looking from time
to time at* Dushmanta, *and supported by the damsels.*]

Dushm. [*Sighing.*] They are all departed; and I too, alas! must depart. For
how short a moment have I been blessed with a sight of the incomparable
Sacontalá! I will send my attendants to the city, and take my station at no
great distance from this forest. I cannot, in truth, divert my mind from the   370
sweet occupation of gazing on her. How, indeed, should I otherwise occupy
it? My body moves onward; but my restless heart runs back to her; like a
light flag borne on a staff against the wind, and fluttering in an opposite
direction.   [*He goes out.*]

---

364 *pointed blade of Cusa grass* Jones mentions the multiplicity of Sanskrit references
to the holiness of this grass; he continues: 'Some of the *leaves* taper to a most acute,
evanescent point; whence the *Pandits* often say of a very sharp-minded man, that his
intellects are *acute as the point of a Cuśa* leaf', 'Botanical Observations', *Works*, V.79–80.
365 *Curuvaca Kurubaka*, a fragrant red amaranth said to bloom only when touched,
or gazed upon, by a beautiful maiden.

ACT II

SCENE – *A* PLAIN, *with royal pavilions on the skirt of the forest.*

Mádhavya. [*Sighing and lamenting.*]

STRANGE recreation this! – Ah me! I am wearied to death. – My royal friend
has an unaccountable taste. – What can I think of a king so passionately
fond of chasing unprofitable quadrupeds? – 'Here runs an antelope! there
goes a boar!' – Such is our only conversation. – Even at noon, in excessive
heat, when not a tree in the forest has a shadow under it, we must be
skipping and prancing about, like the beasts whom we follow. – Are we
thirsty? We have nothing to drink but the waters of mountain torrents,
which taste of burned stones and mawkish leaves. – Are we hungry? We must
greedily devour lean venison, and that commonly roasted to a stick. – Have I
a moment's repose at night? – My slumber is disturbed by the din of horses   10
and elephants, or by the sons of slave-girls hollooing out, 'More venison,
more venison!' – Then comes a cry that pierces my ear, 'Away to the forest,
away!' – Nor are these my only grievances: fresh pain is now added to the
smart of my first wounds; for, while we were separated from our king, who
was chasing a foolish deer, he entered, I find, yon lonely place, and there, to
my infinite grief, saw a certain girl, called Sacontalá, the daughter of a
hermit: from that moment not a word of returning to the city! – These
distressing thoughts have kept my eyes open the whole night. – Alas! when
shall we return? – I cannot set eyes on my beloved friend Dushmanta since he
set his heart on taking another wife. – [*Stepping aside and looking*] – Oh!   20
there he is. – How changed! – He carries a bow, indeed, but wears for his
diadem a garland of wood-flowers. – He is advancing: I must begin my
operations. – [*He stands leaning on a staff.*] – Let me thus take a moment's
rest. – [*Aloud.*]

Dushmanta *enters, as described.*

Dushm. [*Aside, sighing.*] My darling is not so easily attainable; yet my
heart assumes confidence from the manner in which she seemed affected:
surely, though our love has not hitherto prospered, yet the inclinations of us
both are fixed on our union. – [*Smiling.*] – Thus do lovers agreeably beguile
themselves, when all the powers of their souls are intent on the objects of
their desire! – But am I beguiled? No; when she cast her eyes even on her   30
companions, they sparkled with tenderness; when she moved her graceful

arms, they dropped, as if languid with love; when her friend remonstrated against her departure, she spoke angrily – All this was, no doubt, on my account. – Oh! how quick-sighted is love in discerning his own advantages!

Mádh. [Bending downward, as before.] Great prince! my hands are unable to move; and it is with my lips only that I can mutter a blessing on you. May the king be victorious!

Dushm. [Looking at him and smiling.] Ah! what has crippled thee, friend Mádhavya?

Mádh. You strike my eye with your own hand, and then ask what makes it weep. 40

Dushm. Speak intelligibly. I know not what you mean.

Mádh. Look at yon Vétas tree bent double in the river. Is it crooked, I pray, by its own act, or by the force of the stream?

Dushm. It is bent, I suppose, by the current.

Mádh. So am I by your Majesty.

Dushm. How so, Mádhavya?

Mádh. Does it become you, I pray, to leave the great affairs of your empire, and so charming a mansion as your palace, for the sake of living here like a forester? Can you hold a council in a wood? I, who am a reverend 50 Bráhmen, have no longer the use of my hands and feet: they are put out of joint by my running all day long after dogs and wild beasts. Favour me, I entreat, with your permission to repose but a single day.

Dushm. [Aside.] Such are this poor fellow's complaints; whilst I, when I think of Canna's daughter, have as little relish for hunting as he. How can I brace this bow, and fix a shaft in the string, to shoot at those beautiful deer who dwell in the same groves with my beloved, and whose eyes derive lustre from hers?

Mádh. [Looking stedfastly at the king.] What scheme is your royal mind contriving? I have been crying, I find, in a wilderness. 60

Dushm. I think of nothing but the gratification of my old friend's wishes.

Mádh. [Joyfully.] Then may the king live long!

[*Rising, but counterfeiting feebleness.*]

Dushm. Stay; and listen to me attentively.

Mádh. Let the king command.

Dushm. When you have taken repose, I shall want your assistance in another business, that will give you no fatigue.

Mádh. Oh! what can that be, unless it be eating rice-pudding?

Dushm. You shall know in due time.

Mádh. I shall be delighted to hear it.

Dushm. Hola! who is there? 70

The Chamberlain *enters.*

Cham. Let my sovereign command me.

Dushm. Raivataca, bid the General attend.

Cham. I obey. – [*He goes out, and returns with the* General.] – Come quickly, Sir, the king stands expecting you.

Gen. [*Aside, looking at* Dushmanta.] How comes it that hunting, which moralists reckon a vice, should be a virtue in the eyes of a king? Thence it is, no doubt, that our emperor, occupied in perpetual toil, and inured to constant heat, is become so lean, that the sunbeams hardly affect him; while he is so tall, that he looks to us little men, like an elephant grazing on a mountain: he seems all soul. – [*Aloud, approaching the king.*] – May our monarch ever be victorious! – This forest, O king, is infested by beasts of prey: we see the traces of their huge feet in every path. – What orders is it your pleasure to give?

Dushm. Bhadraséna, this moralizing Mádhavya has put a stop to our recreation by forbidding the pleasures of the chase.

Gen. [*Aside to* Mádhavya.] Be firm to your word, my friend: whilst I sound the king's real inclinations. – [*Aloud.*] O! Sir, the fool talks idly. Consider the delights of hunting. The body, it is true, becomes emaciated, but it is light and fit for exercise. Mark how the wild beasts of various kind are variously affected by fear and by rage! What pleasure equals that of a proud archer, when his arrow hits the mark as it flies? – Can hunting be justly called a vice? No recreation, surely, can be compared with it.

Mádh. [*Angrily.*] Away, thou false flatterer! The king, indeed, follows his natural bent, and is excusable; but thou, son of a slave girl, hast no excuse. – Away to the wood! – How I wish thou hadst been seized by a tiger or an old bear, who was prowling for a skakàl, like thyself!

Dushm. We are now, Bhadraséna, encamped near a sacred hermitage; and I cannot at present applaud your panegyrick on hunting. This day, therefore, let the wild buffalos roll undisturbed in the shallow water, or toss up the sand with their horns; let the herd of antelopes, assembled under the thick shade, ruminate without fear; let the large boars root up the herbage on the brink of yon pool; and let this my bow take repose with a slackened string.

Gen. As our lord commands.

Dushm. Recall the archers who have advanced before me, and forbid the officers to go very far from this hallowed grove. Let them beware of irritating the pious: holy men are eminent for patient virtues, yet conceal within their bosoms a scorching flame; as carbuncles are naturally cool to the touch; but, if the rays of the sun have been imbibed by them, they burn the hand.

80

90

100

---

99   *let the wild buffalos roll undisturbed in the shallow water* Drew suggests: 'Jones's *Sacontalá*, with its elevation of the animal and the vegetable worlds, leaves a powerful impression on both *Kehama* and *The Missionary* and may well have had more to do than Shelley's comparatively late reading of Plutarch with his decision to lay aside his gun and adopt a vegetarian diet', *India and the Romantic Imagination*, p.260.

107   *a scorching flame* Ascetic austerities (*tapas*) generate a powerful heat (also called *tapas*) such as was feared by Indra in Sacontalá's father, Viśvāmitra.

Mádh. Away now, and triumph on the delights of hunting.   110

Gen. The king's orders are obeyed.   [*He goes out.*]

Dushm. [*To his attendants.*] Put off your hunting apparel; and thou, Raivataca, continue in waiting at a little distance.

Cham. I shall obey.   [*Goes out.*]

Mádh. So! you have cleared the stage: not even a fly is left on it. Sit down, I pray, on this pavement of smooth pebbles, and the shade of this tree shall be your canopy: I will sit by you; for I am impatient to know what will give me no fatigue.

Dushm. Go first, and seat thyself.

Mádh. Come, my royal friend.   [*They both sit under a tree.*]   120

Dushm. Friend Mádhavya, your eyes have not been gratified with an object which best deserves to be seen.

Mádh. Yes, truly; for a king is before them.

Dushm. All men are apt, indeed, to think favourably of themselves; but I meant Sacontalá, the brightest ornament of these woods.

Mádh. [*Aside.*] I must not foment this passion. – [*Aloud.*] What can you gain by seeing her? She is a Bráhmen's daughter, and consequently no match for you!

Dushm. What! Do people gaze at the new moon, with uplifted heads and fixed eyes, from a hope of possessing it? But you must know, that the heart   130
of Dushmanta is not fixed on an object which he must for ever despair of attaining.

Mádh. Tell me how.

Dushm. She is the daughter of a pious prince and warrior, by a celestial nymph; and, her mother having left her on earth, she has been fostered by Canna, even as a fresh blossom of Malati, which droops on its pendent stalk, is raised and expanded by the sun's light.

Mádh. [*Laughing.*] Your desire to possess this rustick girl, when you have women bright as gems in your palace already, is like the fancy of a man, who has lost his relish for dates, and longs for the sour tamarind.   140

Dushm. Did you know her, you would not talk so wildly.

Mádh. Oh! certainly, whatever a king admires must be superlatively charming.

Dushm. [*Smiling.*] What need is there of long description? When I meditate on the power of Brahmà, and on her lineaments, the creation of so transcendent a jewel outshines, in my apprehension, all his other works: she was formed and moulded in the eternal mind, which had raised with its utmost exertion, the ideas of perfect shapes, and thence made an assemblage of all abstract beauties.

Mádh. She must render, then, all other handsome women contemptible.   150

---

136 *fresh blossom of Malati* Great-flowered Jasmine.

147 *formed and moulded in the eternal mind* Sacontalá's divine origins enable Dushmanta to exalt his beloved in an Indian version of Platonism.

Dushm. In my mind she really does. I know not yet what blessed inhabitant of this world will be the possessor of that faultless beauty, which now resembles a blossom whose fragrance has not been diffused; a fresh leaf, which no hand has torn from its stalk; a pure diamond, which no polisher has handled; new honey, whose sweetness is yet untasted; or rather the celestial fruit of collected virtues, to the perfection of which nothing can be added.

Mádh. Make haste, then, or the fruit of all virtues will drop into the hand of some devout rustick, whose hair shines with oil of Ingudì.

Dushm. She is not her own mistress; and her foster-father is at a distance.   160

Mádh. How is she disposed towards you?

Dushm. My friend, the damsels in a hermit's family are naturally reserved: yet she did look at me, wishing to be unperceived; then she smiled, and started a new subject of conversation. Love is by nature averse to a sudden communication, and hitherto neither fully displays, nor wholly conceals, himself in her demeanour towards me.

Mádh. [*Laughing.*] Has she thus taken possession of your heart on so transient a view?

Dushm. When she walked about with her female friends, I saw her yet more distinctly, and my passion was greatly augmented. She said sweetly,   170 but untruly, 'My foot is hurt by the points of the Cusa grass:' then she stopped; but soon, advancing a few paces, turned back her face, pretending a wish to disentangle her vest of woven bark from the branches in which it had not really been caught.

Mádh. You began with chasing an antelope, and have now started new game: thence it is, I presume, that you are grown so fond of a consecrated forest.

Dushm. Now the business for you, which I mentioned, is this: you, who are a Bráhmen, must find some expedient for my second entrance into that asylum of virtue.   180

Mádh. And the advice which I give is this: remember that you are a king.

Dushm. What then?

Mádh. 'Hola! bid the hermits bring my sixth part of their grain.' Say this, and enter the grove without scruple.

Dushm. No, Mádhavya: they pay a different tribute, who, having abandoned all the gems and gold of this world, possess riches far superior. The wealth of princes, collected from the four orders of their subjects, is perishable; but pious men give us a sixth part of the fruits of their piety; fruits which will never perish.

[*Behind the scenes.*] Happy men that we are! we have now attained the   190 object of our desire.

Dushm. Hah! I hear the voices of some religious anchorites.

The Chamberlain *enters.*

Cham. May the king be victorious! – Two young men, sons of a hermit, are waiting at my station, and soliciting an audience.

Dushm. Introduce them without delay.

Cham. As the king commands. – [*He goes out, and re-enters with two* Bráhmens.] – Come on; come this way.

First Bráhm. [*Looking at the king.*] Oh! what confidence is inspired by his brilliant appearance! – Or proceeds it rather from his disposition to virtue and holiness? – Whence comes it, that my fear vanishes? – He now has taken 200 his abode in a wood which supplies us with every enjoyment; and with all his exertions for our safety, his devotion increases from day to day. – The praise of a monarch who has conquered his passions ascends even to heaven: inspired bards are continually singing, 'Behold a virtuous prince!' but with us the royal name stands first: 'Behold, among kings, a sage!'

Second Bráhm. Is this, my friend, the truly virtuous Dushmanta?

First Bráhm. Even he.

Second Bráhm. It is not then wonderful, that he alone, whose arm is lofty and strong as the main bar of his city gate, possesses the whole earth, which forms a dark boundary to the ocean; or that the gods of Swerga, who fiercely 210 contend in battle with evil powers, proclaim victory gained by his braced bow, not by the thunderbolt of INDRA.

Both. [*Approaching him.*] O king, be victorious!

Dushm. [*Rising.*] I humbly salute you both.

Both. Blessings on thee!

Dushm. [*Respectfully.*] May I know the cause of this visit?

First Bráhm. Our sovereign is hailed by the pious inhabitants of these woods; and they implore –

Dushm. What is their command?

First Bráhm. In the absence of our spiritual guide, Canna, some evil 220 demons are disturbing our holy retreat. Deign, therefore, accompanied by thy charioteer, to be master of our asylum, if it be only for a few short days.

Dushm. [*Eagerly.*] I am highly favoured by your invitation.

Mádh. [*Aside.*] Excellent promoters of your design! They draw you by the neck, but not against your will.

Dushm. Raivataca, bid my charioteer bring my car, with my bow and quiver.

Cham. I obey. [*He goes out.*]

First Bráhm. Such condescension well becomes thee, who art an universal guardian. 230

Second Bráhm. Thus do the descendants of Puru perform their engagement to deliver their subjects from fear of danger.

Dushm. Go first, holy men: I will follow instantly.

Both. Be ever victorious! [*They go out.*]

Dushm. Shall you not be delighted, friend Mádhavya, to see my Sacontalá?

Mádh. At first I should have had no objection; but I have a considerable one since the story of the demons.

Dushm. Oh! fear nothing: you will be near me.

Mádh. And you, I hope, will have leisure to protect me from them.

The Chamberlain *re-enters.*

Cham. May our lord be victorious! The imperial car is ready; and all are expecting your triumphant approach. Carabba too, a messenger from the queen-mother, is just arrived from the city.   240

Dushm. Is he really come from the venerable queen?

Cham. There can be no doubt of it.

Dushm. Let him appear before me.

    [*The* Chamberlain *goes out, and returns with the* Messenger.]

Cham. There stands the king – O Carabba, approach him with reverence.

Mess. [*Prostrating himself.*] May the king be ever victorious! – The royal mother sends this message –

Dushm. Declare her command.

Mess. Four days hence the usual fast for the advancement of her son will   250
be kept with solemnity; and the presence of the king (may his life be prolonged!) will then be required.

Dushm. On one hand is a commission from holy Bráhmens; on the other, a command from my revered parent: both duties are sacred, and neither must be neglected.

Mádh. [*Laughing.*] Stay suspended between them both, like king Trisancu between heaven and earth; when the pious men said, 'Rise!' and the gods of Swerga said, 'Fall!'

Dushm. In truth I am greatly perplexed. My mind is principally distracted by the distance of the two places where the two duties are to be performed; as   260
the stream of a river is divided by rocks in the middle of its bed. – [*Musing.*] – Friend Mádhavya, my mother brought you up as her own son, to be my playfellow, and to divert me in my childhood. You may very properly act my part in the queen's devotions. Return then to the city, and give an account of my distress through the commission of these reverend foresters.

Mádh. That I will; – but you could not really suppose that I was afraid of demons!

Dushm. How come you, who are an egregious Bráhmen, to be so bold on a sudden?

Mádh. Oh! I am now a young king.   270

---

256   *Trisancu*   Satyavrata Triśanku was a king of Ayodhā and an ancestor of Rāma who, during a period of exile, befriended the family of Viśvāmitra, Sacontalá's father. In gratitude Viśvāmitra re-installed Triśanku on the throne of Ayodhā, and ultimately sought to elevate him to heaven. The gods, however, exerted an equal downward force so that Triśanku remained suspended in mid-air.

Dushm. Yes, certainly: and I will dispatch my whole train to attend your highness, whilst I put an end to the disturbance in this hermitage.

Mádh. [*Strutting.*] See, I am a prince regnant.

Dushm. [*Aside.*] This buffoon of a Bráhmen has a slippery genius. He will perhaps disclose my present pursuit to the women in the palace. I must try to deceive him. – [*Taking* Mádhavya *by the hand.*] – I shall enter the forest, be assured, only through respect for its pious inhabitants; not from any inclination for the daughter of a hermit. How far am I raised above a girl educated among antelopes; a girl, whose heart must ever be a stranger to love! – The tale was invented for my diversion.   280

Mádh. Yes, to be sure; only for your diversion.

Dushm. Then farewell, my friend; execute my commission faithfully, whilst I proceed – to defend the anchorites.   [*All go out.*]

ACT III

Scene – *The* Hermitage *in a Grove.*

The Hermit's Pupil *bearing consecrated grass.*

Pupil. [*Meditating with wonder.*]

How great is the power of Dushmanta! – The monarch and his charioteer had no sooner entered the grove than we continued our holy rites without interruption. – What words can describe him? – By his barely aiming a shaft, by the mere sound of his bow-string, by the simple murmur of his vibrating bow, he disperses at once our calamities. – Now then I deliver to the priests this bundle of fresh Cusa grass to be scattered round the place of sacrifice – [*Looking behind the scenes.*] – Ah! Priyamvadá, for whom are you carrying that ointment of Usíra root, and those leaves of water lilies? – [*Listening attentively.*] – What say you? – That Sacontalá is extremely disordered by the sun's heat, and that you have procured for her a cooling medicine! Let her,   10
my Priyamvadá, be diligently attended; for she is the darling of our venerable father Canna. – I will administer, by the hand of Gautamí, some healing water consecrated in the ceremony called Vaitána.

[*He goes out.*]

Dushmanta *enters, expressing the distraction of a lover.*

Dushm. I well know the power of her devotion: that she will suffer none to dispose of her but Canna, I too well know. Yet my heart can no more return to its former placid state, than water can reascend the steep, down which it has fallen. – O God of Love, how can thy darts be so keen, since they are pointed with flowers? – Yes, I discover the reason of their keenness. They are tipped with the flames which the wrath of Hara kindled, and which blaze at this moment, like the Bárava fire under the waves: how else couldst thou,   20
who wast consumed even to ashes, be still the inflamer of our souls? By thee and by the moon, though each of you seems worthy of confidence, we lovers are cruelly deceived. They who love as I do, ascribe flowery shafts to thee, and cool beams to the moon, with equal impropriety; for the moon sheds fire on them with her dewy rays, and thou pointest with sharp diamonds those

---

19   *tipped with the flames which the wrath of Hara kindled*   When Kāma's body was destroyed by a glance of Śiva, see 'A Hymn to Camdeo', ll.66–70; 'A Hymn to Durgá', III.2.7–8 and n.
20   *Bárava fire*   The fire of Bhairava (the Terrible), that is of Śiva in his most destructive aspect.

arrows which seem to be barbed with blossoms. Yet this god, who bears a fish on his banners, and who wounds me to the soul, will give me real delight, if he destroy me with the aid of my beloved, whose eyes are large and beautiful as those of a roe. – O powerful divinity, even when I thus adore thy attributes, hast thou no compassion? Thy fire, O Love, is fanned into a blaze by a hundred of my vain thoughts. – Does it become thee to draw thy bow even to thy ear, that the shaft, aimed at my bosom, may inflict a deeper wound? Where now can I recreate my afflicted soul by the permission of those pious men whose uneasiness I have removed by dismissing my train? – [*Sighing.*] – I can have no relief but from a sight of my beloved. – [*Looking up.*] – This intensely hot noon must, no doubt, be passed by Sacontalá with her damsels on the banks of this river over-shadowed with Tamálas. – It must be so: – I will advance thither. – [*Walking round and looking.*] – My sweet friend has, I guess, been lately walking under that row of young trees; for I see the stalks of some flowers, which probably she gathered, still unshrivelled; and some fresh leaves, newly plucked, still dropping milk. – [*Feeling a breeze.*] – Ah! this bank has a delightful air! – Here may the gale embrace me, wafting odours from the water lilies, and cool my breast, inflamed by the bodiless god, with the liquid particles which it catches from the waves of the Málinì, – [*Looking down.*] – Happy lover! Sacontalá must be somewhere in this grove of flowering creepers; for I discern on the yellow sand at the door of yon arbour some recent footsteps, raised a little before, and depressed behind by the weight of her elegant limbs. – I shall have a better view from behind this thick foliage. – [*He conceals himself, looking vigilantly.*] – Now are my eyes fully gratified. The darling of my heart, with her two faithful attendants, reposes on a smooth rock strown with fresh flowers. – These branches will hide me, whilst I hear their charming conversation. [*He stands concealed, and gazes.*]

Sacontalá *and her two Damsels discovered.*

Both. [*Fanning her.*] Say, beloved Sacontalá, does the breeze, raised by our fans of broad lotos leaves, refresh you?

Sac. [*Mournfully.*] Why, alas, do my dear friends take this trouble?

[*Both look sorrowfully at each other.*]

27 *a fish on his banners* The dolphin or shark-like *makara* which is the ensign and mount of the love god Kāma, cf. 'A Hymn to Camdeo', l.19 and n.

38 *Tamálas* With scented leaves and white blossoms, these trees are associated with love-trysts and with Krishna, cf. *Gítagóvinda*, l.1.

47–8 *some recent footsteps, raised a little before, and depressed behind by the weight of her elegant limbs* Garland Cannon and Siddheshwar Pandey discuss the significant linguistic and cultural difficulties of translating Hindu concepts of beauty, concluding that Jones's pioneering rendering compares well with modern attempts: 'he tried to steer a middle course. He wanted to be faithful without giving his Western audience any impression of grossness and vulgarity about Indian culture . . . if the *Śakuntalā* . . . created the wrong impression on the West because of his translation, the very purpose of his stupendous effort would be defeated', 'Sir William Jones Revisited: On his Translation of the *Śakuntalā*', *Journal of the American Oriental Society*, 96 (1976), 528–35, (535).

Dushm. [*Aside.*] Ah! she seems much indisposed. What can have been the fatal cause of so violent a fever? – Is it what my heart suggests? Or – [*Musing.*] – I am perplexed with doubts. – The medicine extracted from the balmy Usíra has been applied, I see, to her bosom: her only bracelet is made   60
of thin filaments from the stalks of a water lily, and even that is loosely bound on her arm. Yet, even thus disordered, she is exquisitely beautiful. – Such are the hearts of the young! Love and the sun equally inflame us; but the scorching heat of summer leads not equally to happiness with the ardour of youthful desires.

Pri. [*Aside to* Anusúyá.] Did you not observe how the heart of Sacontalá was affected by the first sight of our pious monarch? My suspicion is, that her malady has no other cause.

Anu. [*Aside to* Priyamvadá.] The same suspicion had risen in my mind. I will ask her at once. – [*Aloud.*] – My sweet Sacontalá, let me put one question   70
to you. What has really occasioned your indisposition?

Dushm. [*Aside.*] She must now declare it. Ah! though her bracelets of lotos are bright as moon beams, yet they are marked, I see, with black spots from internal ardour.

Sac. [*Half raising herself.*] Oh! say what you suspect to have occasioned it.

Anu. Sacontalá, we must necessarily be ignorant of what is passing in your breast; but I suspect your case to be that which we have often heard related in tales of love. Tell us openly what causes your illness. A physician, without knowing the cause of a disorder, cannot even begin to apply a remedy.

Dushm. [*Aside.*] I flatter myself with the same suspicion.   80

Sac. [*Aside.*] My pain is intolerable; yet I cannot hastily disclose the occasion of it.

Pri. My sweet friend, Anusúyá speaks rationally. Consider the violence of your indisposition. Every day you will be more and more emaciated, though your exquisite beauty has not yet forsaken you.

Dushm. [*Aside.*] Most true. Her forehead is parched; her neck droops; her waist is more slender than before; her shoulders languidly fall; her complection is wan; she resembles a Mádhaví creeper, whose leaves are dried by a sultry gale: yet, even thus transformed, she is lovely, and charms my soul.   90

Sac. [*Sighing.*] What more can I say? Ah! why should I be the occasion of your sorrow?

Pri. For that very reason, my beloved, we are solicitous to know your secret; since, when each of us has a share of your uneasiness, you will bear more easily your own portion of it.

Dushm. [*Aside.*] Thus urged by two friends, who share her pains as well as her pleasures, she cannot fail to disclose the hidden cause of her malady;

59–60   *The medicine extracted from the balmy Usira*   This represents a typical example of Jones's technique of providing a definition of the transliteration which obviated the need for explanatory footnotes.

whilst I, on whom she looked at our first interview with marked affection, am filled with anxious desire to hear her answer.

Sac. From the very instant when the accomplished prince, who has just given repose to our hallowed forest, met my eye – *[She breaks off, and looks modest.* 100

Both. Speak on, beloved Sactontalá.

Sac. From that instant my affection was unalterably fixed on him – and thence I am reduced to my present languor.

Anu. Fortunately your affection is placed on a man worthy of yourself.

Pri. Oh! could a fine river have deserted the sea and flowed into a lake?

Dushm. [*Joyfully.*] That which I was eager to know, her own lips have told. Love was the cause of my distemper, and love has healed it; as a summer's day, grown black with clouds, relieves all animals from the heat which itself had caused. 110

Sac. If it be no disagreeable task, contrive, I entreat you, some means by which I may find favour in the king's eyes.

Dushm. [*Aside.*] That request banishes all my cares, and gives me rapture even in my present uneasy situation.

Pri. [*Aside to* Anusúyá.] A remedy for her, my friend, will scarce be attainable. Exert all the powers of your mind; for her illness admits of no delay.

Anu. [*Aside to* Priyamvadá.] By what expedient can her cure be both accelerated and kept secret?

Pri. [*As before.*] Oh! to keep it secret will be easy; but to attain it soon, almost insuperably difficult. 120

Anu. [*As before.*] How so?

Pri. The young king seemed, I admit, by his tender glances, to be enamoured of her at first sight; and he has been observed, within these few days, to be pale and thin, as if his passion had kept him long awake.

Dushm. [*Aside.*] So it has – This golden bracelet, sullied by the flame which preys on me, and which no dew mitigates, but the tears gushing nightly from these eyes, has fallen again and again on my wrist, and has been replaced on my emaciated arm.

Pri. [*Aloud.*] I have a thought, Anusúyá – Let us write a love letter, which I will conceal in a flower, and, under the pretext of making a respectful offering, deliver it myself into the king's hand. 130

Anu. An excellent contrivance! It pleases me highly; – but what says our beloved Sacontalá?

Sac. I must consider, my friend, the possible consequences of such a step.

Pri. Think also of a verse or two, which may suit your passion, and be consistent with the character of a lovely girl born in an exalted family.

Sac. I will think of them in due time; but my heart flutters with the apprehension of being rejected.

Dushm. [*Aside.*] Here stands the man supremely blessed in thy presence, 140 from whom, O timid girl, thou art apprehensive of a refusal! Here stands the man, from whom, O beautiful maid, thou fearest rejection, though he loves thee distractedly. He who shall possess thee will seek no brighter gem; and thou art the gem which I am eager to possess.

Anu. You depreciate, Sacontalá, your own incomparable merits. What man in his senses would intercept with an umbrella the moonlight of autumn, which alone can allay the fever caused by the heat of the noon?

Sac. [*Smiling.*] I am engaged in thought.   [*She meditates.*]

Dushm. Thus then I fix my eyes on the lovely poetess, without closing them a moment, while she measures the feet of her verse: her forehead is   150
gracefully moved in cadence, and her whole aspect indicates pure affection.

Sac. I have thought of a couplet; but we have no writing implements.

Pri. Let us hear the words; and then I will mark them with my nail on this lotos leaf, soft and green as the breast of a young paroquet: it may easily be cut into the form of a letter. – Repeat the verses.

Sac. 'Thy heart, indeed, I know not: but mine, oh! cruel, love warms by day and by night; and all my faculties are centered on thee.'

Dushm. [*Hastily advancing, and pronouncing a verse in the same measure.*] 'Thee, O slender maid, love only warms; but me he burns; as the day-star only stifles the fragrance of the night-flower, but quenches the very orb of the moon.'   160

Anu. [*Looking at him joyfully.*] Welcome, great king: the fruit of my friend's imagination has ripened without delay.

[Sacontalá *expresses an inclination to rise.*]

Dushm. Give yourself no pain. Those delicate limbs, which repose on a couch of flowers, those arms, whose bracelets of lotos are disarranged by a slight pressure, and that sweet frame, which the hot noon seems to have disordered, must not be fatigued by ceremony.

Sac. [*Aside.*] O my heart, canst thou not rest at length after all thy sufferings?

Anu. Let our sovereign take for his seat a part of the rock on which she reposes.   [Sacontalá *makes a little room.*]   170

Dushm. [*Seating himself.*] Priyamvadá, is not the fever of your charming friend in some degree abated?

Pri. [*Smiling.*] She has just taken a salutary medicine, and will soon be restored to health. But, O mighty prince, as I am favoured by you and by her, my friendship for Sacontalá prompts me to converse with you for a few moments.

Dushm. Excellent damsel, speak openly; and suppress nothing.

Pri. Our lord shall hear.

Dushm. I am attentive.

Pri. By dispelling the alarms of our pious hermits, you have discharged the   180
duty of a great monarch.

Dushm. Oh! talk a little on other subjects.

Pri. Then I must inform you that our beloved companion is enamoured of you, and has been reduced to her present languor by the resistless divinity, love. You only can preserve her inestimable life.

Dushm. Sweet Priyamvadá, our passion is reciprocal; but it is I who am honoured.

Sac. [*Smiling, with a mixture of affection and resentment.*] Why should you detain the virtuous monarch, who must be afflicted by so long an absence from the secret apartments of his palace?   190

Dushm. This heart of mine, oh thou who art of all things the dearest to it, will have no object but thee, whose eyes enchant me with their black splendour, if thou wilt but speak in a milder strain. I, who was nearly slain by love's arrow, am destroyed by thy speech.

Anu. [*Laughing*] Princes are said to have many favourite consorts. You must assure us, therefore, that our beloved friend shall not be exposed to affliction through our conduct.

Dushm. What need is there of many words? Let there be ever so many women in my palace, I will have only two objects of perfect regard; the sea-girt earth, which I govern, and your sweet friend, whom I love.   200

Both. Our anxiety is dissipated.

[Sacontalá *strives in vain to conceal her joy.*]

Pri. [*Aside to* Anusúyá.] See how our friend recovers her spirits by little and little, as the peahen, oppressed by the summer heat, is refreshed by a soft gale and a gentle shower.

Sac. [*To the damsels.*] Forgive, I pray, my offence in having used unmeaning words: they were uttered only for your amusement in return for your tender care of me.

Pri. They were the occasion, indeed, of our serious advice. But it is the king who must forgive: who else is offended?

Sac. The great monarch will, I trust, excuse what has been said either   210
before him or in his absence. – [*Aside to the damsels.*] Intercede with him, I entreat you.

Dushm. [*Smiling.*] I would cheerfully forgive any offence, lovely Sacontalá, if you, who have dominion over my heart, would allow me full room to sit by you, and recover from my fatigue, on this flowery couch pressed by your delicate limbs.

Pri. Allow him room; it will appease him, and make him happy.

Sac. [*Pretending anger, aside to* Priyamvadá.] Be quiet, thou mischief-making girl! Dost thou sport with me in my present weak state?

Anu. [*Looking behind the scenes.*] O! my Priyamvadá, there is our favourite   220
young antelope running wildly and turning his eyes on all sides: he is, no doubt, seeking his mother, who has rambled in the wide forest. I must go and assist his search.

Pri. He is very nimble; and you alone will never be able to confine him in one place. I must accompany you.   [*Both going out.*]

Sac. Alas! I cannot consent to your going far: I shall be left alone.

Both. [*Smiling.*] Alone! with the sovereign of the world by your side!

[*They got out.*]

Sac. How could my companions both leave me?

Dushm. Sweet maid, give yourself no concern. Am not I, who humbly solicit your favour, present in the room of them? – [*Aside.*] – I must declare   230
my passion. – [*Aloud.*] – Why should not I, like them, wave this fan of lotos leaves, to raise cool breezes and dissipate your uneasiness? Why should not I, like them, lay softly in my lap those feet, red as water lilies, and press them, O my charmer, to relieve your pain?

Sac. I should offend against myself, by receiving homage from a person entitled to my respect.   [*She rises, and walks slowly through weakness.*]

Dushm. The noon, my love, is not yet passed; and your sweet limbs are weak. Having left that couch where fresh flowers covered your bosom, you can ill sustain this intense heat with so languid a frame.

[*He gently draws her back.*]

Sac. Leave me, oh leave me. I am not, indeed, my own mistress, or – the   240
two damsels were only appointed to attend me. What can I do at present?

Dushm. [*Aside.*] Fear of displeasing her makes me bashful.

Sac. [*Overhearing him.*] The king cannot give offence. It is my unhappy fate only that I accuse.

Dushm. Why should you accuse so favourable a destiny?

Sac. How rather can I help blaming it, since it has permitted my heart to be affected by amiable qualities, without having left me at my own disposal?

Dushm. [*Aside.*] One would imagine that the charming sex, instead of being, like us, tormented with love, kept love himself within their hearts, to torment him with delay.   [Sacontalá *going out.*]   250

Dushm. [*Aside.*] How! must I then fail of attaining felicity?

[*Following her, and catching the skirt of her mantle.*]

Sac. [*Turning back.*] Son of Puru, preserve thy reason; oh! preserve it. – The hermits are busy on all sides of the grove.

Dushm. My charmer, your fear of them is vain. Canna himself, who is deeply versed in the science of law, will be no obstacle to our union. Many daughters of the holiest men have been married by the ceremony called Gándharva, as it is practised by Indra's band, and even their fathers have approved them. – [*Looking round.*] – What say you? are you still inflexible? Alas! I must then depart.   [*Going from her a few paces, then looking back.*]

Sac. [*Moving also a few steps, and then turning back her face.*] Though I   260
have refused compliance, and have only allowed you to converse with me for a moment, yet, O son of Puru – let not Sacontalá be wholly forgotten.

---

233   *red as water lilies*   Stained with lac, cf. *Gítagóvinda*, I.315.

257   *the ceremony called Gándharva*   'The reciprocal connection of a youth and a damsel, with mutual desire, . . . contracted for the purpose of amorous embraces, and proceeding from sensual inclination', *The Ordinances of Menu, Works*, VII.158.

Dushm. Enchanting girl, should you be removed to the ends of the world, you will be fixed in this heart, as the shade of a lofty tree remains with it even when the day is departed.

Sac. [*Going out, aside.*] Since I have heard his protestations, my feet move, indeed, but without advancing. I will conceal myself behind those flowering Curuvacas, and thence I shall see the result of his passion.

[*She hides herself behind the shrubs.*]

Dushm. [*Aside.*] Can you leave me, beloved Sacontalá; me who am all affection? Could you not have tarried a single moment? Soft is your beautiful 270 frame, and indicates a benevolent soul; yet your heart is obdurate: as the tender Sirísha hangs on a hard stalk.

Sac. [*Aside.*] I really have now lost the power of departing.

Dushm. [*Aside.*] What can I do in this retreat since my darling has left it? – [*Musing and looking round.*] – Ah! my departure is happily delayed. – Here lies her bracelet of flowers, exquisitely perfumed by the root of Usíra which had been spread on her bosom: it has fallen from her delicate wrist, and is become a new chain for my heart. [*Taking up the bracelet with reverence.*]

Sac. [*Aside, looking at her hand.*] Ah me! such was my languor, that the filaments of lotos stalks which bound my arm dropped on the ground 280 unperceived by me.

Dushm. [*Aside, placing it in his bosom.*] Oh! how delightful to the touch! – From this ornament of your lovely arm, O my darling, though it be inanimate and senseless, your unhappy lover has regained confidence – a bliss which you refused to confer.

Sac. [*Aside.*] I can stay here no longer. By this pretext I may return.

[*Going slowly towards him.*]

Dushm. [*With rapture.*] Ah! the empress of my soul again blesses these eyes. After all my misery I was destined to be favoured by indulgent heaven. – The bird Chátac, whose throat was parched with thirst, supplicated for a drop of water, and suddenly a cool stream poured into his bill from the 290 bounty of a fresh cloud.

Sac. Mighty king, when I had gone half way to the cottage, I perceived that my bracelet of thin stalks had fallen from my wrist; and I return because my heart is almost convinced that you must have seen and taken it. Restore it, I humbly entreat, lest you expose both yourself and me to the censure of the hermits.

Dushm. Yes, on one condition I will return it.

Sac. On what condition? Speak –

Dushm. That I may replace it on the wrist to which it belongs.

---

289   *the bird Chátac*   'The folklore behind the allusion is that the Cātaka-bird lives on the drops that rain in a particular season of the year called *Svāti*; it keeps on thirstily looking towards the clouds till it gets the desired drops, but refuses to taste any other kind of water', Cannon and Pandey, 'Sir William Jones Revisited: On his Translation of the *Śakuntalā*', 531.

Sac. [*Aside.*] I have no alternative.   [*Approaching him.*]   300

Dushm. But in order to replace it, we must both be seated on that smooth
rock.   [*Both sit down.*]

Dushm. [*Taking her hand.*] O exquisite softness! This hand has regained its
native strength and beauty, like a young shoot of Cámalatà: or it resembles
rather the god of love himself, when, having been consumed by the fire of
Hara's wrath, he was restored to life by a shower of nectar sprinkled by the
immortals.

Sac. [*Pressing his hand.*] Let the son of my lord make haste to tie on the
bracelet.

Dushm. [*Aside, with rapture.*] Now I am truly blessed. – That phrase, the   310
son of my lord, is applied only to a husband. – [*Aloud.*] – My charmer, the
clasp of this bracelet is not easily loosened: it must be made to fit you better.

Sac. [*Smiling.*] As you please.

Dushm. [*Quitting her hand.*] Look, my darling: this is the new moon which
left the firmament in honour of superior beauty, and, having descended on
your enchanting wrist, has joined both its horns round it in the shape of a
bracelet.

Sac. I really see nothing like a moon: the breeze, I suppose, has shaken
some dust from the lotos flower behind my ears, and that has obscured my
sight.   320

Dushm. [*Smiling.*] If you permit me, I will blow the fragrant dust from
your eye.

Sac. It would be a kindness; but I cannot trust you.

Dushm. Oh! fear not, fear not. A new servant never transgresses the
command of his mistress.

Sac. But a servant over-assiduous deserves no confidence.

Dushm. [*Aside.*] I will not let slip this charming occasion. – [*Attempting to
raise her head* – Sacontalá *faintly repels him, but sits still.*] – O damsel with an
antelope's eyes, be not apprehensive of my indiscretion – [Sacontalá *looks up
for a moment, and then bashfully drops her head* – Dushmanta, *aside, gently*   330
raising her head.] – That lip, the softness of which is imagined, not proved,
seems to pronounce, with a delightful tremour, its permission for me to allay
my thirst.

Sac. The son of my lord seems inclined to break his promise.

---

304   *young shoot of Cámalatà* 'The plant before us is the most beautiful of its order,
both in the colour and form of its leaves and flowers; its elegant blossoms are *celestial rosy*
red, love's proper hue, and have justly procured it the name of *Cámalatà*, or *Love's Creeper*',
'Botanical Observations', *Works*, V.88.

321–2   *I will blow the fragrant dust from your eye*   It was just such dallying with the
innocence of love that inspired Frederick Schlegel to write: 'all is animated with a deep and
lovely tenderness of feeling, an air of sweetness and beauty is diffused over the whole. If the
enjoyment of solitude and musing, the delight which is excited by the beauty of nature,
above all, the world of plants, are here and there enlarged upon, with a gorgeous profusion
of images, this is but the clothing of innocence', *Lectures on the History of Literature,*
Ancient and Modern, 2 vols. (Edinburgh: Blackwood, 1818, I.211–12).

Dushm. Beloved, I was deceived by the proximity of the lotos to that eye which equals it in brightness. [*He blows gently on her eye.*]

Sac. Well: now I see a prince who keeps his word as it becomes his imperial character. Yet I am really ashamed that no desert of mine entitles me to the kind service of my lord's son.

Dushm. What reward can I desire, except that which I consider as the 340 greatest, the fragrance of your delicious lip?

Sac. Will that content you?

Dushm. The bee is contented with the mere odour of the water lily.

Sac. If he were not, he would get no remedy.

Dushm. Yes, this and this – [*Kissing her eagerly.*]

Behind the scenes. Hark! the Chacraváca is calling her mate on the bank of the Málini: the night is beginning to spread her shades.

Sac. [*Listening alarmed.*] O son of my lord, the matron Gautamí approaches to enquire after my health. Hide yourself, I entreat, behind yon trees. 350

Dushm. I yield to necessity. [*He retires.*]

Gautamí *enters with a vase in her hand.*

Gaut. [*Looking anxiously at* Sacontalá.] My child, here is holy water for thee. – What! hast thou no companion here but the invisible gods; thou who art so much indisposed?

Sac. Both Priyamvadá and Anusúyá are just gone down to the river.

Gaut. [*Sprinkling her.*] Is thy fever, my child, a little abated?

[*Feeling her hand.*]

Sac. Venerable matron, there is a change for the better.

Gaut. Then thou art in no danger. Mayst thou live many years! The day is departing: let us both go to the cottage.

Sac. [*Aside, rising slowly.*] O my heart, no sooner hadst thou begun to taste 360 happiness, than the occasion slipped away! [*She advances a few steps, and returns to the arbour.*] – O bower of twining plants, by whom my sorrows have been dispelled, on thee I call; ardently hoping to be once more happy under thy shade. [*She goes out with* Gautamí.]

Dushm. [*Returning to the bower, and sighing.*] How, alas, have my desires been obstructed! – Could I do less than kiss the lips of my charmer, though her modest cheeks were half averted; lips, whose sweetness had enchanted me, even when they pronounced a denial? – Whither now can I go? I will remain a while in this arbour of creepers, which my darling's presence has illuminated. – [*Looking round.*] – Yes; this is her seat on the rock, spread with 370 blossoms, which have been pressed by her delicate limbs. – Here lies her

346 *the Chacraváca* A species of sheldrake which, according to tradition, sorrowfully laments at evening its separation from its mate. Sacontalá's friends provide a coded warning of Gautamí's approach.

exquisite love letter on the leaf of a water lily; here lay her bracelet of tender filaments which had fallen from her sweet wrist. – Though the bower of twining Vétasas be now desolate, since my charmer has left it, yet, while my eyes are fixed on all these delightful memorials of her, I am unable to depart. – [*Musing.*] – Ah! how imperfectly has this affair been conducted by a lover, like me, who, with his darling by his side, has let the occasion slip. – Should Sacontalá visit once more this calm retreat, the opportunity shall not pass again unimproved: the pleasures of youth are by nature transitory. – Thus my foolish heart forms resolutions, while it is distracted by the sudden   380 interruption of its happiness. Why did it ever allow me to quit without effect the presence of my beloved?

Behind the scenes. O king, while we are beginning our evening sacrifice, the figures of blood-thirsty demons, embrowned by clouds collected at the departure of day, glide over the sacred hearth, and spread consternation around.

Dushm. Fear not, holy men. – Your king will protect you.   [*He goes out.*]

ACT IV

S̲cene – *A* L̲awn *before the Cottage.*

The two damsels are discovered gathering flowers.

Anusúyá

O my Priyamvadá, though our sweet friend has been happily married, according to the rites of Gandharvas, to a bridegroom equal in rank and accomplishments, yet my affectionate heart is not wholly free from care; and one doubt gives me particular uneasiness.

Pri. What doubt, my Anusúyá?

Anu. This morning the pious prince was dismissed with gratitude by our hermits, who had then completed their mystick rites: he is now gone to his capital, Hastinápura, where, surrounded by a hundred women in the recesses of his palace, it may be doubted whether he will remember his charming bride.　　　　　　　　　　　　　　　　　　　　　　　　　　　　　10

Pri. In that respect you may be quite easy. Men, so well informed and well educated as he, can never be utterly destitute of honour. – We have another thing to consider. When our father Canna shall return from his pilgrimage, and shall hear what has passed, I cannot tell how he may receive the intelligence.

Anu. If you ask my opinion, he will, I think, approve of the marriage.

Pri. Why do you think so?

Anu. Because he could desire nothing better, than that a husband so accomplished and so exalted should take Sacontalá by the hand. It was, you know, the declared object of his heart, that she might be suitably married;　　20 and, since heaven has done for him what he most wished to do, how can be possibly be dissatisfied?

Pri. You reason well; but – [*Looking at her basket.*] – My friend, we have plucked a sufficient store of flowers to scatter over the place of sacrifice.

Anu. Let us gather more to decorate the temples of the goddesses who have procured for Sacontalá so much good fortune.

　　　　　　　　　　　　　　　　　　　　　[*They both gather more flowers.*]

Behind the scenes. It is I – Hola!

Anu. [*Listening.*] I hear the voice, as it seems, of a guest arrived in the hermitage.

Pri. Let us hasten thither. Sacontalá is now reposing; but though we may,　　30

8　*Hastinápura*　Hastināpura is a city on the Ganges, about sixty miles north-east of Delhi, founded by Hastin, the first Bāhrata King of the Lunar dynasty.

when she wakes, enjoy her presence, yet her mind will all day be absent with her departed lord.

Anu. Be it so; but we have occasion, you know, for all these flowers.

[*They advance.*]

Again behind the scenes. How! dost thou show no attention to a guest? Then hear my imprecations – 'He on whom thou art meditating, on whom alone thy heart is now fixed, while thou neglectest a pure gem of devotion who demands hospitality, shall forget thee, when thou seest him next, as a man restored to sobriety forgets the words which he uttered in a state of intoxication.' [*Both damsels look at each other with affliction.*]

Pri. Wo is me! Dreadful calamity! Our beloved friend has, through mere 40 absence of mind, provoked by her neglect, some holy man who expected reverence.

Anu. [*Looking.*] It must be so; for the cholerick Durvásas is going hastily back.

Pri. Who else has power to consume, like raging fire, whatever offends him? Go, my Anusúyá; fall at his feet, and persuade him, if possible, to return: in the mean time I will prepare water and refreshments for him.

Anu. I go with eagerness. [*She goes out.*]

Pri. [*Advancing hastily, her foot slips.*] Ah! through my eager haste I have 50 let the basket fall; and my religious duties must not be postponed.

[*She gathers fresh flowers.*]

Anusúyá *re-enters.*

Anu. His wrath, my beloved, passes all bounds. – Who living could now appease him by the humblest prostrations or entreaties? yet at last he a little relented.

Pri. That little is a great deal for him. – But inform me how you soothed him in any degree.

Anu. When he positively refused to come back, I threw myself at his feet, and thus addressed him: 'Holy sage, forgive, I entreat, the offence of an amiable girl, who has the highest veneration for you, but was ignorant, through distraction of mind, how exalted a personage was calling to her.'

Pri. What then? What said he? 60

Anu. He answered thus: 'My word must not be recalled; but the spell which it has raised shall be wholly removed when her lord shall see his ring.' Saying this, he disappeared.

Pri. We may now have confidence; for before the monarch departed, he fixed with his own hand on the finger of Sacontalá the ring, on which we saw the name Dushmanta engraved, and which we will instantly recognize. On him therefore alone will depend the remedy for our misfortune.

Anu. Come, let us now proceed to the shrines of the goddesses, and implore their succour. [*Both advance.*]

Pri. [*Looking.*] See, my Anusúyá, where our beloved friend sits, motionless 70 as a picture, supporting her languid head with her left hand. With a mind so intent on one object, she can pay no attention to herself, much less to a stranger.

Anu. Let the horrid imprecation, Priyamvadá, remain a secret between us two: we must spare the feelings of our beloved, who is naturally susceptible of quick emotions.

Pri. Who would pour boiling water on the blossom of a tender Mallicá?

[*Both go out.*]

A Pupil *of* Canna *enters.*

Pup. I am ordered by the venerable Canna, who is returned from the place of his pilgrimage, to observe the time of the night, and am, therefore, come forth to see how much remains of it. [*Walking round, and observing the*   80 *heavens.*] – On one side, the moon, who kindles the flowers of the Oshadhì, has nearly sunk in his western bed; and, on the other, the sun, seated behind his charioteer Arun, is beginning his course: the lustre of them both is conspicuous, when they rise and when they set; and by their example should men be equally firm in prosperous and in adverse fortune. – The moon has now disappeared, and the night flower pleases no more: it leaves only a remembrance of its odour, and languishes like a tender bride whose pain is intolerable in the absence of her beloved. – The ruddy morn impurples the dew drops on the branches of yonder Vadarí; the peacock, shaking off sleep, hastens from the cottages of hermits interwoven with holy grass; and yonder   90 antelope, springing hastily from the place of sacrifice, which is marked with his hoofs, raises himself on high, and stretches his graceful limbs. – How is the moon fallen from the sky with diminished beams! the moon who had set his foot on the head of Suméru, king of mountains, and had climbed, scattering the rear of darkness, even to the central palace of Vishnu! – Thus do the great men of this world ascend with extreme labour to the summit of ambition, but easily and quickly descend from it.

Anusúyá *enters meditating.*

[*Aside.*] Such has been the affection of Sactonalá, though she was bred in austere devotion, averse from sensual enjoyments! – How unkind was the king to leave her!   100

Pup. [*Aside.*] The proper time is come for performing the hóma: I must apprise our preceptor of it.

[*He goes out.*]

---

81   *Oshadhì*   Osadhi is a medicinal herb especially influenced by the generative powers of the moon, cf. 'A Hymn to Súrya', 1.24.

83   *his charioteer, Arun*   Aruna means 'the red one', cf. 'A Hymn to Súrya', ll.109–19.

89   *the branches of yonder Vadarí*   The Badari is the Jujube- or Jojoba-tree, see 'Botanical Observations', *Works*, V.99.

94   *Suméru, king of mountains*   The pleasure ground of the gods, see 'A Hymn to Indra', ll.14–19.

101   *hóma*   Morning sacrifice.

Anu. The shades of night are dispersed; and I am hardly awake; but were I ever so perfectly in my senses, what could I now do? My hands move not readily to the usual occupations of the morning. – Let the blame be cast on love, on love only, by whom our friend has been reduced to her present condition, through a monarch who has broken his word. – Or does the imprecation of Durvásas already prevail? – How else could a virtuous king, who made so solemn an engagement, have suffered so long a time to elapse without sending even a message? – Shall we convey the fatal ring to him? –   110
Or what expedient can be suggested for the relief of this incomparable girl, who mourns without ceasing? – Yet what fault has she committed? – With all my zeal for her happiness, I cannot summon courage enough to inform our father Canna that she is pregnant. – What then, oh! what step can I take to relieve her anxiety?

Priyamvadá *enters.*

Pri. Come, Anusúyá, come quickly. They are making suitable preparations for conducting Sacontalá to her husband's palace.

Anu. [*With surprise.*] What say you, my friend?

Pri. Hear me. I went just now to Sacontalá, meaning only to ask if she had slept well –   120

Anu. What then? oh! what then?

Pri. She was sitting with her head bent on her knee, when our father Canna, entering her apartment, embraced and congratulated her. – 'My sweet child,' said he, 'there has been a happy omen: the young Bráhmen who officiated in our morning sacrifice, though his sight was impeded by clouds of smoke, dropped the clarified butter into the very centre of the adorable flame. – Now, since the pious act of my pupil has prospered, my foster child must not be suffered any longer to languish in sorrow; and this day I am determined to send thee from the cottage of the old hermit who bred thee up, to the palace of the monarch who has taken thee by the hand.'   130

Anu. My friend, who told Canna what passed in his absence?

Pri. When he entered the place where the holy fire was blazing, he heard a voice from heaven pronouncing divine measures. –

Anu. [*Amazed.*] Ah! you astonish me.

Pri. Hear the celestial verse: – 'Know that thy adopted daughter, O pious Bráhmen, has received from Dushmanta a ray of glory destined to rule the world; as the wood Samì becomes pregnant with mysterious fire.'

Anu. [*Embracing* Priyamvadá.] I am delighted, my beloved; I am transported with joy. But – since they mean to deprive us of our friend so soon as to-day, I feel that my delight is at least equalled by my sorrow.   140

108 *the imprecation of Durvásas* This awesome and somewhat irascible Brahman appears elsewhere in the *Mahābhārata*, but the interwoven romance elements of the ring and the curse are wholly Kālidāsa's invention.

137 *the wood Samì* The Brahmans kindled their sacred fire by drilling a *samì* log with a wooden awl to produce sparks, cf. 'Botanical Observations', *Works*, V.155.

Pri. Oh! we must submit patiently to the anguish of parting. Our beloved friend will now be happy; and that should console us.

Anu. Let us now make haste to dress her in bridal array. I have already, for that purpose, filled the shell of a cocoa nut, which you see fixed on an Amra tree, with the fragrant dust of Nágacésaras: take it down, and keep it in a fresh lotos leaf, whilst I collect some Góráchana from the forehead of a sacred cow, some earth from consecrated ground, and some fresh Cusa grass, of which I will make a paste to ensure good fortune.

Pri. By all means.　　　[*She takes down the perfume. –* Anusúyá *goes out.*]

Behind the scenes. O Gautamí, bid the two Misras, Sárngarava and 　150 Sáradwata, make ready to accompany my child Sacontalá.

Pri. [*Listening.*] Lose no time, Anusúyá, lose no time. Our father Canna is giving orders for the intended journey to Hastinápura.

Anusúyá *re-enters with the ingredients of her charm.*

Anu. I am here: let us go, my Priyamvadá　　　[*They both advance.*]

Pri. [*Looking.*] There stands our Sacontalá, after her bath at sunrise, while many holy women, who are congratulating her, carry baskets of hallowed grain. – Let us hasten to greet her.

Enter Sacontalá, Gautamí, *and female Hermits.*

Sac. I prostrate myself before the goddess.

Gaut. My child, thou canst not pronounce too often the word goddess: thus wilt thou procure great felicity for thy lord.　　　　　160

Herm. Mayst thou, O royal bride, be delivered of a hero!

[*The* Hermits *go out.*]

Both damsels. [*Approaching* Sacontalá.] Beloved friend, was your bath pleasant?

Sac. O! my friends, you are welcome: let us sit a while together.

[*They seat themselves.*]

Anu. Now you must be patient, whilst I bind on a charm to secure your happiness.

Sac. That is kind. – Much has been decided this day: and the pleasure of being thus attended by my sweet friends will not soon return.

[*Wiping off her tears.*]

Pri. Beloved, it is unbecoming to weep at a time when you are going to be so happy. – [*Both damsels burst into tears as they dress her.*] – Your elegant　170 person deserves richer apparel: it is now decorated with such rude flowers as we could procure in this forest.

Canna's Pupil *enters with rich clothes.*

Pup. Here is a complete dress. Let the queen wear it auspiciously; and may her life be long!　　　　　[*The women look with astonishment.*]

146　*Góráchana from the forehead of a sacred cow*　A fragrant juice exuded from small ducts in the animal's temples, which is much prized in sacred rituals.

Gaut. My son, Háríta, whence came this apparel?

Pup. From the devotion of our father Canna.

Gaut. What dost thou mean?

Pup. Be attentive. The venerable sage gave this order: 'Bring fresh flowers for Sacontalá from the most beautiful trees;' and suddenly the woodnymphs appeared, raising their hands, which rivalled new leaves in beauty and softness. Some of them wove a lower mantle bright as the moon, the presage of her felicity; another pressed the juice of Lácshà to stain her feet exquisitely red; the rest were busied in forming the gayest ornaments; and they eagerly showered their gifts on us.   180

Pri. [*Looking at* Sacontalá.] Thus it is, that even the bee, whose nest is within the hollow trunk, does homage to the honey of the lotos flower.

Gaut. The nymphs must have been commissioned by the goddess of the king's fortune, to predict the accession of brighter ornaments in his palace.

[Sacontalá *looks modest.*]

Pup. I must hasten to Canna, who is gone to bathe in the Málinì, and let him know the signal kindness of the woodnymphs.   [*He goes out.*]   190

Anu. My sweet friend, I little expected so splendid a dress: – how shall I adjust it properly? – [*Considering.*] – Oh! my skill in painting will supply me with some hints; and I will dispose the drapery according to art.

Sac. I well know your affection for him.

Canna *enters meditating.*

Can. [*Aside.*] This day must Sacontalá depart: that is resolved; yet my soul is smitten with anguish. – My speech is interrupted by a torrent of tears, which my reason suppresses and turns inward: my very sight is dimmed. – Strange that the affliction of a forester, retired from the haunts of men, should be so excessive! – Oh, with what pangs must they who are fathers of families, be afflicted on the departure of a daughter!   200

[*He walks round musing.*]

Pri. Now, my Sacontalá, you are becomingly decorated: put on this lower vest, the gift of sylvan goddesses.   [Sacontalá *rises, and puts on the mantle.*]

Gaut. My child, thy spiritual father, whose eyes overflow with tears of joy, stands desiring to embrace thee. Hasten, therefore, to do him reverence.

[Sacontalá *modestly bows to him.*]

Can. Mayst thou be cherished by thy husband, as Sarmishthà was cherished by Yayáti! Mayst thou bring forth a sovereign of the world, as she brought forth Puru!

Gaut. This, my child, is not a mere benediction; it is a boon actually conferred.

---

182   *Lácshà*   Lac, see *Letters*, II.895.
205–6   *as Sarmishthà was cherished by Yayáti*   King Dushmanta's ancestors who founded the Puru dynasty, see *Mahābhārata*, I.171–92.

Can. My best beloved, come and walk with me round the sacrificial fire. – 210
[*They all advance.*] – May these fires preserve thee! Fires which spring to their
appointed stations on the holy hearth, and consume the consecrated wood,
while the fresh blades of mysterious Cusa lie scattered around them! –
Sacramental fires, which destroy sin with the rising fumes of clarified butter!
– [Sacontalá *walks with solemnity round the hearth.*] – Now set out, my
darling, on thy auspicious journey. – [*Looking round.*] – Where are the
attendants, the two Misras?

Enter Sárngarava *and* Sáradwata.
Both. Holy sage, we are here.
Can. My son, Sárngarava, show thy sister her way.
Sárn. Come, damsel. –   [*They all advance.*]   220
Can. Hear, all ye trees of this hallowed forest; ye trees, in which the sylvan
goddesses have their abode; hear, and proclaim, that Sacontalá is going to
the palace of her wedded lord; she who drank not, though thirsty, before you
were watered; she who cropped not, through affection for you, one of your
fresh leaves, though she would have been pleased with such an ornament for
her locks; she whose chief delight was in the season when your branches are
spangled with flowers!

CHORUS *of invisible* WOODNYMPHS.
May her way be attended with prosperity! May propitious breezes
sprinkle, for her delight, the odoriferous dust of rich blossoms! May pools of
clear water, green with the leaves of the lotos, refresh her as she walks! and   230
may shady branches be her defence from the scorching sunbeams!
                             [*All listen with admiration.*]
Sárn. Was that the voice of the Cócila wishing a happy journey to
Sacontalá? – Or did the nymphs, who are allied to the pious inhabitants of
these woods, repeat the warbling of the musical bird, and make its greeting
their own?
Gaut. Daughter, the sylvan goddesses, who love their kindred hermits,
have wished you prosperity, and are entitled to humble thanks.
                    [Sacontalá *walks round, bowing to the nymphs.*]
Sac. [*Aside to* Priyamvadá.] Delighted as I am, O Priyamvadá, with the
thought of seeing again the son of my lord, yet, on leaving this grove, my
early asylum, I am scarce able to walk.   240
Pri. You lament not alone. – Mark the affliction of the forest itself when
the time of your departure approaches! – The female antelope browses no
more on the collected Cusa grass; and the peahen ceases to dance on the
lawn: the very plants of the grove, whose pale leaves fall on the ground, lose
their strength and their beauty.

232 *Cócila* The Indian cuckoo, associated with the Spring and with love-making as
its song echoes the amorous fifth note of the Indian scale.

Sac. Venerable father, suffer me to address this Mádhaví creeper, whose red blossoms inflame the grove.

Can. My child, I know thy affection for it.

Sac. [*Embracing the plant.*] O most radiant of twining plants, receive my embraces, and return them with thy flexible arms: from this day, though removed to a fatal distance, I shall for ever be thine. – O beloved father, consider this creeper as myself.   250

Can. My darling, thy amiable qualities have gained thee a husband equal to thyself: such an event has been long, for thy sake, the chief object of my heart; and now, since my solicitude for thy marriage is at an end, I will marry thy favourite plant to the bridegroom Amra, who sheds fragrance near her. – Proceed, my child, on thy journey.

Sac. [*Approaching the two damsels.*] Sweet friends, let this Mádhaví creeper be a precious deposit in your hands.

Anu. and Pri. Alas! in whose care shall we be left?   [*They both weep.*]   260

Can. Tears are vain, Anusúyá: our Sacontalá ought rather to be supported by your firmness, than weakened by your weeping.   [*All advance.*]

Sac. Father! when yon female antelope, who now moves slowly from the weight of the young ones with which she is pregnant, shall be delivered of them, send me, I beg, a kind message with tidings of her safety. – Do not forget.

Can. My beloved, I will not forget it.

Sac. [*Advancing, then stopping.*] Ah! what is it that clings to the skirts of my robe, and detains me?   [*She turns round, and looks.*]

Can. It is thy adopted child, the little fawn, whose mouth, when the sharp points of Cusa grass had wounded it, has been so often smeared by thy hand with the healing oil of Ingudì; who has been so often fed by thee with a handful of Syámáka grains, and now will not leave the footsteps of his protectress.   270

Sac. Why dost thou weep, tender fawn, for me, who must leave our common dwelling-place? – As thou wast reared by me when thou hadst lost thy mother, who died soon after thy birth, so will my foster-father attend thee, when we are separated, with anxious care. – Return, poor thing, return – we must part.   [*She bursts into tears.*]

Can. Thy tears, my child, ill suit the occasion: we shall all meet again: be firm: see the direct road before thee, and follow it. – When the big tear lurks beneath thy beautiful eyelashes, let thy resolution check its first efforts to disengage itself. – In thy passage over this earth, where the paths are now high, now low, and the true path seldom distinguished, the traces of thy feet must needs be unequal; but virtue will press thee right onward.   280

Sárn. It is a sacred rule, holy sage, that a benevolent man should accompany a traveller till he meet with abundance of water; and that rule you have carefully observed: we are now near the brink of a large pool. Give us, therefore, your commands, and return.

Can. Let us rest a while under the shade of this Vata tree – [*They all go to*   290
the shade.] – What message can I send with propriety to the noble
Dushmanta?   [*He meditates.*]

Anu. [*Aside to* Sacontalá.] My beloved friend, every heart in our asylum is
fixed on you alone, and all are afflicted by your departure. – Look; the bird
Chacraváca, called by his mate, who is almost hidden by water lilies, gives
her no answer; but having dropped from his bill the fibres of lotos stalks
which he had plucked, gazes on you with inexpressible tenderness.

Can. My son Sárngarava, remember, when thou shalt present Sacontalá to
the king, to address him thus, in my name: 'Considering us hermits as
virtuous, indeed, but rich only in devotion, and considering also thy own   300
exalted birth, retain thy love for this girl, which arose in thy bosom without
any interference of her kindred; and look on her among thy wives with the
same kindness which they experience: more than that cannot be demanded;
since particular affection must depend on the will of heaven.'

Sárn. Your message, venerable man, is deeply rooted in my remembrance.

Can. [*Looking tenderly at* Sacontalá.] Now, my darling, thou too must be
gently admonished. – We, who are humble foresters, are yet acquainted with
the world which we have forsaken.

Sárn. Nothing can be unknown to the wise.

Can. Hear, my daughter, – When thou art settled in the mansion of thy   310
husband, show due reverence to him, and to those whom he reveres: though
he have other wives, be rather an affectionate handmaid to them than a rival.
– Should he displease thee, let not thy resentment lead thee to disobedience.
– In thy conduct to thy domesticks be rigidly just and impartial; and seek not
eagerly thy own gratifications. – By such behaviour young women become
respectable; but perverse wives are the bane of a family. – What thinks
Gautamí of this lesson?

Gaut. It is incomparable: – my child, be sure to remember it.

Can. Come, my beloved girl, give a parting embrace to me and to thy
tender companions.   320

Sac. Must Anusúyá and Priyamvadá return to the hermitage?

Can. They too, my child, must be suitably married; and it would not be
proper for them yet to visit the city; but Gautamí will accompany thee.

Sac. [*Embracing him.*] Removed from the bosom of my father, like a
young sandal tree, rent from the hills of Malaya, how shall I exist in a
strange soil?

Can. Be not so anxious. When thou shalt be mistress of a family, and
consort of a king, thou mayst, indeed, be occasionally perplexed by the
intricate affairs which arise from exuberance of wealth, but wilt then think
lightly of this transient affliction, especially when thou shalt have a son (and   330
a son thou wilt have) bright as the rising day-star. – Know also with

---

290   *Vata tree*   A species of Bengal fig, see 'Botanical Observations', *Works*, V.160.

certainty, that the body must necessarily, at the appointed moment, be separated from the soul: who, then, can be immoderately afflicted, when the weaker bounds of extrinsick relations are loosened, or even broken.

Sac. [*Falling at his feet.*] My father, I thus humbly declare my veneration for you.

Can. Excellent girl, may my effort for thy happiness prove successful.

Sac. [*Approaching her two companions.*] Come, then, my beloved friends, embrace me together.   [*They embrace her.*]

Anu. My friend, if the virtuous monarch should not at once recollect you, only show him the ring on which his own name is engraved.   340

Sac. [*Starting.*] My heart flutters at the bare apprehension which you have raised.

Pri. Fear not, sweet Sacontalá: love always raises ideas of misery, which are seldom or never realised.

Sárn. Holy sage, the sun has risen to a considerable height: let the queen hasten her departure.

Sac. [*Again embracing* Canna.] When, my father, oh! when again shall I behold this asylum of virtue?

Can. Daughter, when thou shalt long have been wedded, like this fruitful   350
earth, to the pious monarch, and shalt have borne him a son, whose car shall be matchless in battle, thy lord shall transfer to him the burden of empire, and thou, with thy Dushmanta, shalt again seek tranquillity, before thy final departure, in this loved and consecrated grove.

Gaut. My child, the proper time for our journey passes away rapidly: suffer thy father to return. – Go, venerable man, go back to thy mansion, from which she is doomed to be so long absent.

Can. Sweet child, this delay interrupts my religious duties.

Sac. You, my father, will perform them long without sorrow; but I, alas! am destined to bear affliction.   360

Can. O! my daughter, compel me not to neglect my daily devotions. – [*Sighing.*] – No, my sorrow will not be diminished. – Can it cease, my beloved, when the plants which rise luxuriantly from the hallowed grains which thy hand has strown before my cottage, are continually in my sight? Go, may thy journey prosper.

[Sacontalá *goes out with* Gautamí *and the two Misras.*]

Both damsels. [*Looking after* Sacontalá *with anguish.*] Alas! alas! our beloved is hidden by the thick trees.

Can. My children, since your friend is at length departed, check your immoderate grief, and follow me.   [*They all turn back.*]

Both. Holy father, the grove will be a perfect vacuity without Sacontalá.   370

Can. Your affection will certainly give it that appearance. – [*He walks round meditating.*] – Ah me! – Yes; at last my weak mind has attained its due firmness after the departure of my Sacontalá – In truth a daughter must sooner or later be the property of another; and, having now sent her to her lord, I find my soul clear and undisturbed, like that of a man who has restored to its owner an inestimable deposit which he long had kept with solicitude.

[*They go out.*]

ACT V

SCENE – *The* PALACE.

An old Chamberlain, *sighing.*

Chamberlain.

ALAS! what a decrepit old age have I attained! – This wand, which I first held for the discharge of my customary duties in the secret apartments of my prince, is now my support, whilst I walk feebly through the multitude of years which I have passed. – I must now mention to the king, as he goes through the palace, an event which concerns himself: it must not be delayed. – [*Advancing slowly.*] – What is it? – Oh! I recollect: the devout pupils of Canna desire an audience. – How strange a thing is human life! – The intellects of an old man seem at one time luminous, and then on a sudden are involved in darkness, like the flame of a lamp at the point of extinction. – [*He walks round and looks.*] – There is Dushmanta: he has been attending to   10
his people, as to his own family; and now with a tranquil heart seeks a solitary chamber; as an elephant the chief of his herd, having grazed the whole morning, and being heated by the meridian sun, repairs to a cool station during the oppressive heats. – Since the king is just risen from his tribunal, and must be fatigued, I am almost afraid to inform him at present that Canna's pupils are arrived: yet how should they who support nations enjoy rest? – The sun yokes his bright steeds for the labour of many hours; the gale breathes by night and by day; the prince of serpents continually sustains the weight of this earth; and equally incessant is the toil of that man, whose revenue arises from a sixth part of his people's income.   20

[*He walks about*]

Enter Dushmanta, Mádhavya, *and Attendants.*

Dushm. [*Looking oppressed with business.*] Every petitioner having attained justice, is departed happy; but kings who perform their duties conscientiously are afflicted without end. – The anxiety of acquiring dominion gives extreme pain; and when it is firmly established, the cares of supporting the nation incessantly harass the sovereign; as a large umbrella, of which a man carries the staff in his own hand, fatigues while it shades him.

Behind the scenes. May the king be victorious!

---

18   *the prince of serpents continually sustains the weight of this earth*   Ananta (Endless), or Śeṣa (Remainder), is sometimes represented with 'his head upholding the earth. He wears as a garland the world with its gods, men, and demons', *Visnu Purāṇa* 2.5.27.

Two Bards *repeat stanzas.*

First Bard. Thou seekest not thy own pleasure: no; it is for the people that thou art harassed from day to day. Such, when thou wast created, was the disposition implanted in thy soul! Thus a branchy tree bears on his head   30
the scorching sunbeams, while his broad shade allays the fever of those who seek shelter under him.

Second Bard. When thou wieldest the rod of justice, thou bringest to order all those who have deviated from the path of virtue: thou biddest contention cease: thou wast formed for the preservation of thy people: thy kindred possess, indeed, considerable wealth; but so boundless is thy affection, that all thy subjects are considered by thee as thy kinsmen.

Dushm. [*Listening.*] That sweet poetry refreshes me after the toil of giving judgements and publick orders.

Mádh. Yes; as a tired bull is refreshed when the people say, 'There goes the   40
lord of cattle.'

Dushm. [*Smiling.*] Oh! art thou here, my friend: let us take our seats together.

[*The king and* Mádhavya *sit down. – Musick behind the scenes.*]

Mádh. Listen, my royal friend. I hear a well-tuned Vínà sounding, as if it were in concert with the lutes of the gods, from yonder apartment. – The queen Hansamatì is preparing, I imagine, to greet you with a new song.

Dushm. Be silent, that I may listen.

Cham. [*Aside.*] The king's mind seems intent on some other business. I must wait his leisure.   [*Retiring on one side.*

SONG. [*Behind the scenes.*]

'Sweet bee, who, desirous of extracting fresh honey, wast wont to kiss the   50
soft border of the new-blown Amra flower, how canst thou now be satisfied with the water lily, and forget the first object of thy love?'

Dushm. The ditty breathes a tender passion.

Mádh. Does the king know its meaning? It is too deep for me.

Dushm. [*Smiling.*] I was once in love with Hansamatì, and am now reproved for continuing so long absent from her. – Friend Mádhavya, inform the queen in my name that I feel the reproof.

Mádh. As the king commands; but – [*Rising slowly.*] – My friend, you are going to seize a sharp lance with another man's hand. I cannot relish your commission to an enraged woman. – A hermit cannot be happy till he has   60
taken leave of all passions whatever.

Dushm. Go, my kind friend: the urbanity of thy discourse will appease her.

Mádh. What an errand!   [*He goes out.*]

Dushm. [*Aside.*] Ah! what makes me so melancholy on hearing a mere song

---

44   *well-tuned Vínà*   The Indian fretted lute.

on absence, when I am not in fact separated from any real object of my affection? – Perhaps the sadness of men, otherwise happy, on seeing beautiful forms and listening to sweet melody, arises from some faint remembrance of past joys and the traces of connections in a former state of existence.

[*He sits pensive and sorrowful.*]

Cham. [*Advancing humbly.*] May our sovereign be victorious! – Two religious men, with some women, are come from their abode in a forest near the Snowy Mountains, and bring a message from Canna. – The king will command. 70

Dushm. [*Surprised.*] What! are pious hermits arrived in the company of women?

Cham. It is even so.

Dushm. Order the priest Sómaratá, in my name, to shew them due reverence in the form appointed by the Véda; and bid him attend me. I shall wait for my holy guests in a place fit for their reception.

Cham. I obey. [*He goes out.*]

Dushm. Warder, point the way to the hearth of the consecrated fire. 80

Ward. This, O king, this is the way. – [*He walks before.*] – Here is the entrance of the hallowed enclosure; and there stands the venerable cow to be milked for the sacrifice, looking bright from the recent sprinkling of mystick water. – Let the king ascend.   [Dushmanta *is raised to the place of sacrifice on the shoulders of his Warders.*]

Dushm. What message can the pious Canna have sent me? – Has the devotion of his pupils been impeded by evil spirits – or by what other calamity? – Or has any harm, alas! befallen the poor herds who graze in the hallowed forest? – Or have the sins of the king tainted the flowers and fruits of the creepers planted by female hermits? – My mind is entangled in a labyrinth of confused apprehensions. 90

Ward. What our sovereign imagines, cannot possibly have happened; since the hermitage has been rendered secure from evil by the mere sound of his bowstring. The pious men, whom the king's benevolence has made happy, are come, I presume, to do him homage.

Enter Sárngarava, Sáradwata *and* Gautamí, *leading* Sacontalá *by the hand; and before them the old* Chamberlain *and the* Priest.

Cham. This way, respectable strangers; come this way.

Sárn. My friend Sáradwata, there sits the king of men, who has felicity at command, yet shows equal respect to all: here no subject, even of the lowest class, is received with contempt. Nevertheless, my soul having ever been free from attachment to worldly things, I consider this hearth, although a crowd now surround it, as the station merely of consecrated fire. 100

Sárad. I was not less confounded than yourself on entering the populous city; but now I look on it, as a man just bathed in pure water, on a man smeared with oil and dust, as the pure on the impure, as the waking on the sleeping, as the free man on the captive, as the independent on the slave.

Priest. Thence it is, that men, like you two, are so elevated above other mortals.

Sac. [*Perceiving a bad omen.*] Venerable mother, I feel my right eye throb! What means this involuntary motion?

Gaut. Heaven avert the omen, my sweet child! May every delight attend thee!   [*They all advance.*]   110

Priest. [*Shewing the king to them.*] There, holy men, is the protector of the people; who has taken his seat, and expects you.

Sárn. This is what we wished; yet we have no private interest in the business. It is ever thus: trees are bent by the abundance of their fruit; clouds are brought low, when they teem with salubrious rain; and the real benefactors of mankind are not elated by riches.

Ward. O king, the holy guests appear before you with placid looks, indicating their affection.

Dushm. [*Gazing at* Sacontalá.] Ah! what damsel is that, whose mantle conceals the far greater part of her beautiful form? – She looks, among the   120 hermits, like a fresh green bud among faded and yellow leaves.

Ward. This at least, O king, is apparent; that she has a form which deserves to be seen more distinctly.

Dushm. Let her still be covered: she seems pregnant; and the wife of another must not be seen even by me.

Sac. [*Aside, with her hand to her bosom.*] O my heart, why dost thou palpitate? – Remember the beginning of thy lord's affection, and be tranquil.

Priest. May the king prosper! The respectable guests have been honoured as the law ordains; and they have now a message to deliver from their spiritual guide: let the king deign to hear it.   130

Dushm. [*With reverence.*] I am attentive.

Both Misras. [*Extending their hands.*] Victory attend thy banners!

Dushm. I respectfully greet you both.

Both. Blessings on our sovereign!

Dushm. Has your devotion been uninterrupted?

Sárn. How should our rites be disturbed, when thou art the preserver of all creatures? How, when the bright sun blazes, should darkness cover the world?

Dushm. [*Aside.*] The name of royalty produces, I suppose, all worldly advantages! – [*Aloud.*] – Does the holy Canna then prosper?   140

Sárn. O king, they who gather the fruits of devotion may command prosperity. He first inquires affectionately whether thy arms are successful, and then addresses thee in these words: –

Dushm. What are his orders?

Sárn. 'The contract of marriage, reciprocally made between thee and this girl, my daughter, I confirm with tender regard; since thou art celebrated as the most honourable of men, and my Sacontalá is Virtue herself in a human

form, no blasphemous complaint will henceforth be made against Brahmá
for suffering discordant matches: he has now united a bride and bridegroom
with qualities equally transcendent. – Since, therefore, she is pregnant by   150
thee, receive her in thy palace, that she may perform, in conjunction with
thee, the duties prescribed by religion.'

Gaut. Great king, thou hast a mild aspect; and I wish to address thee in
few words.

Dushm. [*Smiling.*] Speak, venerable matron.

Gaut. She waited not the return of her spiritual father; nor were thy
kindred consulted by thee. You two only were present, when your nuptials
were solemnized: now, therefore, converse freely together in the absence of
all others.

Sac. [*Aside*] What will my lord say?   160

Dushm. [*Aside, perplexed.*] How strange an adventure!

Sac. [*Aside.*] Ah me! how disdainfully he seems to receive the message!

Sárn. [*Aside.*] What means that phrase which I overhead, 'How strange an
adventure?' – [*Aloud.*] – Monarch, thou knowest the hearts of men. Let a
wife behave ever so discreetly, the world will think ill of her, if she live only
with her paternal kinsmen; and a lawful wife now requests, as her kindred
also humbly entreat, that whether she be loved or not, she may pass her days
in the mansion of her husband.

Dushm. What sayest thou? – Am I the lady's husband?

Sac. [*Aside with anguish.*] O my heart, thy fears have proved just.   170

Sárn. Does it become a magnificent prince to depart from the rules of
religion and honour, merely because he repents of his engagements?

Dushm. With what hope of success could this groundless fable have been
invented?

Sárn. [*Angrily.*] The minds of those whom power intoxicates are
perpetually changing.

Dushm. I am reproved with too great severity.

Gaut. [*To* Sacontalá.] Be not ashamed, my sweet child: let me take off thy
mantle, that the king may recollect thee.   [*She unveils her.*]

Dushm. [*Aside, looking at* Sacontalá.] While I am doubtful whether this   180
unblemished beauty which is displayed before me has not been possessed by
another, I resemble a bee fluttering at the close of night over a blossom filled
with dew; and in this state of mind, I neither can enjoy nor forsake her.

Ward. [*Aside to* Dushmanta.] The king best knows his rights and his
duties: but who would hesitate when a woman, bright as a gem, brings lustre
to the apartments of his palace?

Sárn. What, O king, does thy strange silence import?

Dushm. Holy man, I have been meditating again and again, but have no
recollection of my marriage with this lady. How then can I lay aside all
consideration of my military tribe, and admit into my palace a young woman   190
who is pregnant by another husband?

Sac. [*Aside.*] Ah! wo is me. – Can there by a doubt even of our nuptials? – The tree of my hope, which had risen so luxuriantly, is at once broken down.

Sárn. Beware, lest the godlike sage, who would have bestowed on thee, as a free gift, his inestimable treasure, which thou hadst taken, like a base robber, should now cease to think of thee, who are lawfully married to his daughter, and should confine all his thoughts to her whom thy perfidy disgraces.

Sárad. Rest a while, my Sárngarava; and thou, Sacontalá, take thy turn to   200
speak; since thy lord has declared his forgetfulness.

Sac. [*Aside.*] If his affection has ceased, of what use will it be to recall his remembrance of me? – Yet, if my soul must endure torment, be it so: I will speak to him. – [*Aloud to* Dushmanta.] – O my husband! – [*Pausing.*] – Or (if the just application of that sacred word be still doubted by thee) O son of Puru, is it becoming, that, having been once enamoured of me in the consecrated forest, and having shown the excess of thy passion, thou shouldst this day deny me with bitter expressions?

Dushm. [*Covering his ears.*] Be the crime removed from my soul! – Thou hast been instructed for some base purpose to vilify me, and make me fall   210
from the dignity which I have hitherto supported; as a river which has burst its banks and altered its placid current, overthrows the trees that had risen aloft on them.

Sac. If thou sayst this merely from want of recollection, I will restore thy memory by producing thy own ring, with thy name engraved on it!

Dushm. A capital invention!

Sac. [*Looking at her finger.*] Ah me! I have no ring.

[*She fixes her eyes with anguish on* Gautamí.]

Gaut. The fatal ring must have dropped, my child, from thy hand, when thou tookest up water to pour on thy head in the pool of Sachítírt'ha, near the station of Sacrávatára.   220

Dushm. [*Smiling.*] So skilful are women in finding ready excuses!

Sac. The power of Brahmá must prevail: I will yet mention one circumstance.

Dushm. I must submit to hear the tale.

Sac. One day, in a grove of Vétasas, thou tookest water in thy hand from its natural vase of lotos leaves –

Dushm. What followed?

Sac. At that instant a little fawn, which I had reared as my own child, approached thee; and thou saidst with benevolence: 'Drink thou first, gentle fawn.' He would not drink from the hand of a stranger, but received water   230
eagerly from mine; when thou saidst, with increasing affection: 'Thus every

---

219 *the pool of Sachítírt'ha* 'a sacred pool called *Sāsitírt'ha* [*sic*] or the *Moon's Pilgrimage*', see Jones's letters to Althorp, dated 1–11 Sept. and 22 Oct. 1787, where, in the manner of Scheherazade, he relates the plot of *Sacontalá*, *Letters*, II.766–9; 792 (767).

creature loves its companions; you are both foresters alike, and both alike amiable.'

Dushm. By such interested and honied falsehoods are the souls of voluptuaries ensnared!

Gaut. Forbear, illustrious prince, to speak harshly. She was bred in a sacred grove where she learned no guile.

Dushm. Pious matron, the dexterity of females, even when they are untaught, appears in those of a species different from our own. – What would it be if they were duly instructed! – The female Cócilas, before they fly   240
towards the firmament, leave their eggs to be hatched, and their young fed, by birds who have no relation to them.

Sac. [*With anger.*] Oh! void of honour, thou measurest all the world by thy own bad heart. What prince ever resembled, or ever will resemble, thee, who wearest the garb of religion and virtue, but in truth art a base deceiver; like a deep well whose mouth is covered with smiling plants!

Dushm. [*Aside.*] The rusticity of her education makes her speak thus angrily and inconsistently with female decorum. – She looks indignant; her eye glows; and her speech, formed of harsh terms, faulters as she utters them. Her lip, ruddy as the Bimba fruit, quivers as if it were nipped with frost; and   250
her eyebrows, naturally smooth and equal, are at once irregularly contracted. – Thus having failed in circumventing me by the apparent lustre of simplicity, she has recourse to wrath, and snaps in two the bow of Cáma, which, if she had not belonged to another, might have wounded me. – [*Aloud.*] – The heart of Dushmanta, young woman, is known to all; and thine is betrayed by thy present demeanor.

Sac. [*Ironically.*] You kings are in all cases to be credited implicitly: you perfectly know the respect which is due to virtue and to mankind; while females, however modest, however virtuous, know nothing, and speak nothing truly. – In a happy hour I came hither to seek the object of my   260
affection: in a happy moment I received the hand of a prince descended from Puru; a prince who had won my confidence by the honey of his words, whilst his heart concealed the weapon that was to pierce mine.

[She hides her face and weeps.]

Sárn. This insufferable mutability of the king's temper kindles my wrath. Henceforth let all be circumspect before they form secret connections: a friendship hastily contracted, when both hearts are not perfectly known, must ere long become enmity.

Dushm. Wouldst thou force me then to commit an enormous crime, relying solely on her smooth speeches?

Sárn. [*Scornfully.*] Thou hast heard an answer. – The words of an   270

259–60 *females . . . speak nothing truly* Although she enlists irony, and accuses her husband of base deception, Kālidāsa's Sacontalá reflects a demure reserve; in the earlier narrative she behaves more like an epic heroine, lashing Duhsanta (Dushmanta) at length with her tongue, see *Mahābhārata*, I.166–70.

incomparable girl, who never learned what iniquity was, are here to receive no credit; while they, whose learning consists in accusing others, and inquiring into crimes, are the only persons who speak truth!

Dushm. O man of unimpeached veracity, I certainly am what thou describest; but what would be gained by accusing thy female associate?

Sárn. Eternal misery.

Dushm. No; misery will never be the portion of Puru's descendants.

Sárn. What avails our altercation? – O king, we have obeyed the commands of our preceptor, and now return. Sacontalá is by law thy wife, whether thou desert or acknowledge her; and the dominion of a husband is 280
absolute. – Go before us, Gautamí. [*The two Misras and* Gautamí *returning.*]

Sac. I have been deceived by this perfidious man; but will you, my friends, will you also forsake me?   [*Following them.*]

Gaut. [*Looking back.*] My son, Sacontalá follows us with affectionate supplications. What can she do here with a faithless husband; she who is all tenderness?

Sárn. [*Angrily to* Sacontalá.] O wife, who seest the faults of thy lord, dost thou desire independence?   [Sacontalá *stops, and trembles.*]

Sárad. Let the queen hear. If thou beest what the king proclaims thee, what right hast thou to complain? But if thou knowest the purity of thy own 290
soul, it will become thee to wait as a handmaid in the mansion of thy lord. Stay, then, where thou art: we must return to Canna.

Dushm. Deceive her not, holy men, with vain expectations. The moon opens the night flower; and the sun makes the water lily blossom: each is confined to its own object: and thus a virtuous man abstains from any connection with the wife of another.

Sárn. Yet thou, O king, who fearest to offend religion and virtue, art not afraid to desert thy wedded wife; pretending that the variety of thy publick affairs has made thee forget thy private contract.

Dushm. [*To his Priest.*] I really have no remembrance of any such 300
engagement; and I ask thee, my spiritual counsellor, whether of the two offences be the greater, to forsake my own wife, or to have an intercourse with the wife of another?

Priest. [*After some deliberation.*] We may adopt an expedient between both.

Dushm. Let my venerable guide command.

Priest. The young woman may dwell till her delivery in my house.

Dushm. For what purpose?

Priest. Wise astrologers have assured the king, that he will be the father of an illustrious prince, whose dominion will be bounded by the western and 310
eastern seas: now, if the holy man's daughter shall bring forth a son whose hands and feet bear the marks of extensive sovereignty, I will do homage to her as my queen, and conduct her to the royal apartments; if not, she shall return in due time to her father.

Dushm. Be it as you judge proper.

Priest. [*To* Sacontalá.] This way, my daughter, follow me.

Sac. O earth! mild goddess, give me a place within thy bosom!

She goes out weeping with the Priest; while the two Misras go out by a different way with Gautamí – Dushmanta *stands meditating on the beauty of* Sacontalá; *but the imprecation still clouds his memory.*]

Behind the scenes. Oh! miraculous event!

Dushm. [*Listening.*] What can have happened!

The Priest *re-enters.*

Priest. Hear, O king, the stupendous event. When Canna's pupils had   320
departed, Sacontalá bewailing her adverse fortune, extended her arms and wept; when –

Dushm. What then?

Priest. A body of light, in a female shape, descended near Apsarastírt'ha, where the nymphs of heaven are worshipped; and having caught her hastily in her bosom, disappeared.   [*All express astonishment.*]

Dushm. I suspected from the beginning some work of sorcery. – The business is over; and it is needless to reason more on it. – Let thy mind, Sómaráta, be at rest.

Priest. May the king be victorious.   [*He goes out.*]   330

Dushm. Chamberlain, I have been greatly harassed; and thou, Warder, go before me to a place of repose.

Ward. This way; let the king come this way.

Dushm. [*Advancing, aside.*] I cannot with all my efforts recollect my nuptials with the daughter of the hermit; yet so agitated is my heart, that it almost induces me to believe her story.   [*All go out.*]

---

324 *Apsarastírt'ha, where the nymphs of heaven are worshipped* The *apsarases*, said to be the daughters of Kaśyapa (Vision), are exquisitely beautiful nymphs of air and water, a species of heavenly courtesan. They are particularly fond of tempting ascetics as was demonstrated when Menakā seduced Viśvāmitra and gave birth to Sacontalā.

ACT VI

SCENE – *A* STREET.

Enter a Superintendent of Police with two Officers, leading a man with his hands bound.

First Officer. Striking the prisoner.

TAKE that, Cumbhílaca, if Cumbhílaca be thy name; and tell us now where thou gottest this ring, bright with a large gem, on which the king's name is engraved.

Cumbh. [*Trembling*] Spare me, I entreat your honours to spare me: I am not guilty of so great a crime as you suspect.

First Off. O distinguished Bráhmen, didst thou then receive it from the king as a reward of some important service?

Cumbh. Only hear me: I am a poor fisherman dwelling at Sacrávatára –

Second Off. Did we ask, thou thief, about thy tribe or thy dwelling-place?

Sup. O Súchaca, let the fellow tell his own story. – Now conceal nothing,   10
sirrah.

First Off. Dost thou hear? Do as our master commands.

Cumbh. I am a man who support my family by catching fish in nets, or with hooks, and by various other contrivances.

Sup. [*Laughing.*] A virtuous way of gaining a livelihood!

Cumbh. Blame me not, master. The occupation of our forefathers, how low soever, must not be forsaken; and a man who kills animals for sale may have a tender heart though his act be cruel.

Sup. Go on, go on.

Cumbh. One day having caught a large Róhita fish, I cut it open, and saw   20
this bright ring in its stomach; but when I offered to sell it, I was apprehended by your honours. So far only am I guilty of taking the ring. Will you now continue beating and bruising me to death?

Sup. [*Smelling the ring.*] It is certain, Jáluca, that this gem has been in the body of a fish. The case requires consideration; and I will mention it to some of the king's household.

Both Off. Come on, cutpurse.   [*They advance.*]

Sup. Stand here, Súchaca, at the great gate of the city, and wait for me, while I speak to some of the officers in the palace.

---

20   *Róhita fish* The 'Ro'hitamatsya (which, by the way, is one of the four most delicate fish in this country)', *Letters*, II.767.

Both Off. Go, Rájayucta. May the king favour thee.   30

[*The Superintendent goes out.*]

Second Off. Our master will stay, I fear, a long while.

First Off. Yes; access to kings can only be had at their leisure.

Second Off. The tips of my fingers itch, my friend Jáluca, to kill this cutpurse.

Cumbh. You would put to death an innocent man.

First. Off. [*Looking.*] Here comes our master. – The king has decided quickly. Now, Cumbhílaca, you will either see your companions again, or be the food of skakàls and vultures.

The Superintendent re-enters.

Sup. Let the fisherman immediately –

Cumbh. [*In an agony.*] Oh! I am a dead man.   40

Sup. – be discharged. – Hola! set him at liberty. The king says he knows his innocence; and his story is true.

Second Off. As our master commands. – The fellow is brought back from the mansion of Yama, to which he was hastening.

[*Unbinding the fisherman.*]

Cumbh. [*Bowing.*] My lord, I owe my life to your kindness.

Sup. Rise, friend; and hear with delight that the king gives thee a sum of money equal to the full value of the ring: it is a fortune to a man in thy station.   [*Giving him the money.*]

Cumbh. [*With rapture.*] I am transported with joy.

First Off. This vagabond seems to be taken down from the stake, and set   50
on the back of a state elephant.

Second Off. The king, I suppose, has a great affection for his gem.

Sup. Not for its intrinsick value; but I guessed the cause of his ecstasy when he saw it.

Both Off. What could occasion it?

Sup. I suspect that it called to his memory some person who has a place in his heart; for though his mind be naturally firm, yet, from the moment when he beheld the ring, he was for some minutes excessively agitated.

Second Off. Our master has given the king extreme pleasure.

First Off. Yes; and by the means of this fishcatcher.   60

[*Looking fiercely at him.*]

Cumbh. Be not angry – Half the money shall be divided between you to purchase wine.

First Off. Oh! now thou art our beloved friend. – Good wine is the first object of our affection. – Let us go together to the vintners.

[*They all go out.*]

---

44 *Yama* The Lord of Death.

SCENE – *The* GARDEN *of the* PALACE.

The Nymph Misracési *appears in the air.*

Misr. My first task was duly performed when I went to bathe in the Nymphs' pool; and I now must see with my own eyes how the virtuous king is afflicted. – Sacontalá is dear to this heart, because she is the daughter of my beloved Ménacà, from whom I received both commissions. – [*She looks round.*] – Ah! on a day full of delights the monarch's family seem oppressed with some new sorrow. – By exerting my supernatural power I could know what has passed; but respect must be shown to the desire of Ménacà. I will retire, therefore, among those plants, and observe what is done without being visible.   [*She descends, and takes her station.*]

Enter two Damsels, attendants on the God of Love.

First Dams. [*Looking at an Amra flower.*] – The blossoms of yon Amra, waving on the green stalk, are fresh and light as the breath of this vernal month. I must present the goddess Retí with a basket of them.

Second Dams. Why, my Parabhriticá, dost thou mean to present it alone?

First Dams. O my friend Madhucaricá, when a female Cócilà, which my name implies, sees a blooming Amra, she becomes entranced, and loses her recollection.

Second Dams. [*With transport.*] What! is the season of sweets actually returned?

First Dams. Yes; the season in which we must sing of nothing but wine and love.

Second Dams. Support me, then, while I climb up this tree, and strip it of its fragrant gems, which we will carry as an offering to Cáma.

First Dams. If I assist, I must have a moiety of the reward which the god will bestow.

Second Dams. To be sure, and without any previous bargain. We are only one soul, you know, though Brahmà has given it two bodies. – [*She climbs up, and gathers the flowers.*] – Ah! the buds are hardly opened. – Here is one a little expanded, which diffuses a charming odour – [*Taking a handful of buds.*] – This flower is sacred to the god who bears a fish on his banner. – O sweet blossom, which I now consecrate, thou well deservest to point the sixth arrow of Cámadéva, who now takes his bow to pierce myriads of youthful hearts.

[*She throws down a blossom.*]

---

65   *Misracési*   Miśrakeśi is another of the divine nymphs or *apsarases*.
76   *Retí*   Rati, or Desire, is the wife of Kāma (Cáma, Camdeo, Cámadéva, Smara), cf. 'A Hymn to Camdeo', l.31.

The old Chamberlain *enters.*

Cham. [*Angrily.*] Desist from breaking off those half-opened buds: there will be no jubilee this year; our king has forbidden it.

Both Dams. Oh! pardon us. We really knew not the prohibition.

Cham. You knew it not! – Even the trees which the spring was decking,   100
and the birds who perch on them, sympathize with our monarch. Thence it is, that yon buds, which have long appeared, shed not yet their prolifick dust; and the flower of the Curuvaca, though perfectly formed, remains veiled in a closed chalice; while the voice of the Cócilà, though the cold dews fall no more, is fixed within his throat; and even Smara, the god of desire, replaces the shaft half-drawn from his quiver.

Misr. [*Aside.*] The king, no doubt, is constant and tender-hearted.

First Dams. A few days ago, Mitravasu, the governor of our province, dispatched us to kiss the feet of the king, and we come to decorate his groves and gardens with various emblems: thence it is, that we heard nothing of his   110
interdict.

Cham. Beware then of reiterating your offence.

Second Dams. To obey our lord will certainly be our delight; but if we are permitted to hear the story, tell us, we pray, what has induced our sovereign to forbid the usual festivity.

Misr. [*Aside.*] Kings are generally fond of gay entertainments; and there must be some weighty reason for the prohibition.

Cham. [*Aside.*] The affair is publick: why should I not satisfy them? – [*Aloud.*] – Has not the calamitous desertion of Sacontalá reached your ears?

First Dams. We heard her tale from the governor, as far as the sight of the   120
fatal ring.

Cham. Then I have little to add. – When the king's memory was restored, by the sight of his gem, he instantly exclaimed: 'Yes, the incomparable Sacontalá is my lawful wife; and when I rejected her, I had lost my reason.' – He showed strong marks of extreme affliction and penitence; and from that moment he has abhorred the pleasures of life. No longer does he exert his respectable talents from day to day for the good of his people: he prolongs his nights without closing his eyes, perpetually rolling on the edge of his couch; and when he rises, he pronounces not one sentence aptly; mistaking the names of the women in his apartments, and through distraction, calling   130
each of them Sacontalá: then he sits abashed, with his head long bent on his knees.

Misr. [*Aside.*] This is pleasing to me, very pleasing.

---

102 *prolifick dust* In his correspondence with Sir Joseph Banks, who was much entertained by *Sacontalá*, Jones comments on his attempts to render the translation 'as literal as possible': 'The use of the pollen in flowers is I believe well known to the Brahmens; but I am not sure that I have not added the epithet *prolifick* to distinguish it from common dust, which would have been the exact version of *renu*; but they also call it *rajas*, which means I believe a seminal substance, & they even apply the word to animal seed', *Letters*, II.894.

Cham. By reason of the deep sorrow which now prevails in his heart, the vernal jubilee has been interdicted.

Both Dams. The prohibition is highly proper.

Behind the scenes. Make way! The king is passing.

Cham. [*Listening.*] Here comes the monarch: depart therefore, damsels, to your own province.   [*The two Damsels go out.*]

Dushmanta *enters in penitential weeds, preceded by a Warder, and attended by* Mádhavya.

Cham. [*Looking at the king.*] Ah! how majestick are noble forms in every   140
habiliment! – Our prince, even in the garb of affliction, is a venerable object. – Though he has abandoned pleasure, ornaments, and business; though he is become so thin, that his golden bracelet falls loosened even down to his wrist; though his lips are parched with the heat of his sighs, and his eyes are fixed open by long sorrow and want of sleep, yet am I dazzled by the blaze of virtue which beams in his countenance like a diamond exquisitely polished.

Misr. [*Aside, gazing on* Dushmanta.] With good reason is my beloved Sacontalá, though disgraced and rejected, heavily oppressed with grief through the absence of this youth.

Dushm. [*Advancing slowly in deep meditation.*] When my darling with an   150
antelope's eyes would have reminded me of our love, I was assuredly slumbering; but excess of misery has awakened me.

Misr. [*Aside.*] The charming girl will at last be happy.

Mádh. [*Aside.*] This monarch of ours is caught again in the gale of affection; and I hardly know a remedy for his illness.

Cham. [*Approaching* Dushmanta.] May the king be victorious! – Let him survey yon fine woodland, these cool walks, and this blooming garden; where he may repose with pleasure on banks of delight.

Dushm. [*Not attending to him.*] Warder, inform the chief minister in my name, that having resolved on a long absence from the city, I do not mean to   160
sit for some time in the tribunal; but let him write and dispatch to me all the cases that my arise among my subjects.

Ward. As the king commands.   [*He goes out.*]

Dushm. [*To the* Chamberlain.] And thou, Párvatáyana, neglect not thy stated business.

Cham. By no means.   [*He goes out.*]

Mádh. You have not left a fly in the garden. – Amuse yourself now in this retreat, which seems pleased with the departure of the dewy season.

Dushm. O Mádhavya, when persons accused of great offences prove wholly innocent, see how their accusers are punished! – A phrensy obstructed my   170
remembrance of any former love for the daughter of the sage; and now the heart-born god, who delights in giving pain, has fixed in his bow-string a new shaft pointed with the blossom of an Amra. – The fatal ring having restored my memory, see me deplore with tears of repentance the loss of my best

beloved, whom I rejected without cause; see me overwhelmed with sorrow, even while the return of spring fills the hearts of all others with pleasure.

Mádh. Be still, my friend, whilst I break Love's arrows with my staff.

[*He strikes off some flowers from an Amra tree.*]

Dushm. [*Meditating.*] Yes, I acknowledge the supreme power of Brahmà. – [*To* Mádhavya.] Where now, my friend, shall I sit and recreate my sight with the slender shrubs which bear a faint resemblance to the shape of Sacontalá?   180

Mádh. You will soon see the damsel skilled in painting, whom you informed that you would spend the forenoon in yon bower of Mádhaví creepers; and she will bring the queen's picture which you commanded her to draw.

Dushm. My soul will be delighted even by her picture. – Show the way to the bower.

Mádh. This way, my friend. – [*They both advance,* Misracésì *following them.*] The arbour of twining Mádhavìs, embellished with fragments of stone like bright gems, appears by its pleasantness, though without a voice, to bid thee welcome. – Let us enter it, and be seated.

[*They both sit down in the bower.*]

Misr. [*Aside.*] From behind these branchy shrubs I shall behold the picture   190
of my Sacontalá – I will afterwards hasten to report the sincere affection of her husband.   [*She conceals herself.*]

Dushm. [*Sighing.*] O my approved friend, the whole adventure of the hermitage is now fresh in my memory. – I informed you how deeply I was affected by the first sight of the damsel; but when she was rejected by me you were not present. – Her name was often repeated by me (how, indeed, should it not?) in our conversation. – What! hast thou forgotten, as I had, the whole story?

Misr. [*Aside.*] The sovereigns of the world must not, I find, be left an instant without the objects of their love.   200

Mádh. Oh, no: I have not forgotten it; but at the end of our discourse you assured me that your love tale was invented solely for your diversion; and this, in the simplicity of my heart, I believed. – Some great event seems in all this affair to be predestined in heaven.

Misr. [*Aside.*] Nothing is more true.

Dushm. [*Having meditated.*] O! my friend, suggest some relief for my torment.

Mádh. What new pain torments you? Virtuous men should never be thus afflicted: the most violent wind shakes not mountains.

Dushm. When I reflect on the situation of your friend Sacontalá, who must   210
now be greatly affected by my desertion of her, I am without comfort. – She made an attempt to follow the Bráhmens and the matron: Stay, said the sage's pupil, who was revered as the sage himself: Stay, said he, with a loud voice. Then once more she fixed on me, who had betrayed her, that celestial face, then bedewed with gushing tears; and the bare idea of her pain burns me like an envenomed javelin.

Misr. [*Aside.*] How he afflicts himself! I really sympathize with him.

Mádh. Surely some inhabitant of the heavens must have wafted her to his mansion.

Dushm. No; what male divinity would have taken the pains to carry off a   220
wife so firmly attached to her lord? Ménacà, the nymph of Swerga, gave her birth; and some of her attendant nymphs have, I imagine, concealed her at the desire of her mother.

Misr. [*Aside.*] To reject Sacontalá was, no doubt, the effect of a delirium, not the act of a waking man.

Mádh. If it be thus, you will soon meet her again.

Dushm. Alas! why do you think so?

Mádh. Because no father and mother can long endure to see their daughter deprived of her husband.

Dushm. Was it sleep that impaired my memory? Was it delusion? Was it an   230
error of my judgement? Or was it the destined reward of my bad actions? Whatever it was, I am sensible that, until Sacontalá return to these arms, I shall be plunged in the abyss of affliction.

Mádh. Do not despair: the fatal ring is itself an example that the lost may be found. – Events which were foredoomed by Heaven must not be lamented.

Dushm. [*Looking at his ring.*] The fate of this ring, now fallen from a station which it will not easily regain, I may at least deplore. – O gem, thou art removed from the soft finger, beautiful with ruddy tips, on which a place had been assigned thee; and, minute as thou art, thy bad qualities appear   240
from the similarity of thy punishment to mine.

Misr. [*Aside.*] Had it found a way to any other hand its lot would have been truly deplorable. – O Ménacà, how wouldst thou be delighted with the conversation which gratifies my ears!

Mádh. Let me know, I pray, by what means the ring obtained a place on the finger of Sacontalá.

Dushm. You shall know, my friend. – When I was coming from the holy forest to my capital, my beloved, with tears in her eyes, thus addressed me: 'How long will the son of my lord keep me in his remembrance?'

Mádh. Well; what then?   250

Dushm. Then, fixing this ring on her lovely finger, I thus answered: 'Repeat each day one of the three syllables engraved on this gem; and before thou hast spelled the word Dushmanta, one of my noblest officers shall attend thee, and conduct my darling to her palace.' – Yet I forgot, I deserted her in my phrensy.

Misr. [*Aside.*] A charming interval of three days was fixed between their separation and their meeting, which the will of Brahmà rendered unhappy.

Mádh. But how came the ring to enter, like a hook, into the mouth of a carp?

Dushm. When my beloved was lifting water to her head in the pool of   260

278

Sachitírt'ha, the ring must have dropped unseen.

Mádh. It is very probable.

Misr. [*Aside.*] Oh! it was thence that the king, who fears nothing but injustice, doubted the reality of his marriage; but how, I wonder, could his memory be connected with a ring?

Dushm. I am really angry with this gem.

Mádh. [*Laughing.*] So am I with this staff.

Dushm. Why so, Mádhavya?

Mádh. Because it presumes to be so straight when I am so crooked. – Impertinent stick!   270

Dushm. [*Not attending to him.*] How, O ring, couldst thou leave that hand adorned with soft long fingers, and fall into a pool decked only with water lilies? – The answer is obvious: thou art irrational. – But how could I, who was born with a reasonable soul, desert my only beloved?

Misr. [*Aside.*] He anticipates my remark.

Mádh. [*Aside.*] So; I must wait here during his meditations, and perish with hunger.

Dushm. O my darling, whom I treated with disrespect, and forsook without reason, when will this traitor, whose heart is deeply stung with repentant sorrow, be once more blessed with a sight of thee?   280

A Damsel *enters with a picture.*

Dams. Great king, the picture is finished.   [*Holding it before him.*]

Dushm. [*Gazing on it.*] Yes; that is her face; those are her beautiful eyes; those her lips embellished with smiles, and surpassing the red lustre of the Carcandhu fruit: her mouth seems, though painted, to speak, and her countenance darts beams of affection blended with a variety of melting tints.

Mádh. Truly, my friend, it is a picture sweet as love itself: my eye glides up and down to feast on every particle of it; and it gives me as much delight as if I were actually conversing with the living Sacontalá.

Misr. [*Aside.*] An exquisite piece of painting! – My beloved friend seems to stand before my eyes.   290

Dushm. Yet the picture is infinitely below the original; and my warm fancy, by supplying its imperfections, represents, in some degree, the loveliness of my darling.

Misr. [*Aside.*] His ideas are suitable to his excessive love and severe penitence.

Dushm. [*Sighing.*] Alas! I rejected her when she lately approached me, and now I do homage to her picture; like a traveller who negligently passes by a clear and full rivulet, and soon ardently thirsts for a false appearance of water on the sandy desert.

Mádh. There are so many female figures on this canvas, that I cannot well 300
distinguish the lady Sacontalá

Misr. [*Aside.*] The old man is ignorant of her transcendent beauty; her eyes, which fascinated the soul of his prince, never sparkled, I suppose, on Mádhavya.

Dushm. Which of the figures do you conceive intended for the queen?

Mádh. [*Examining the picture.*] It is she, I imagine, who looks a little fatigued; with the string of her vest rather loose; the slender stalks of her arms falling languidly; a few bright drops on her face, and some flowers dropping from her untied locks. That must be the queen; and the rest, I suppose, are her damsels. 310

Dushm. You judge well; but my affection requires something more in the piece. Besides, through some defect in the colouring, a tear seems trickling down her cheek, which ill suits the state in which I desired to see her painted. – [*To the Damsel.*] – The picture, O Chaturicà, is unfinished. – Go back to the painting room and bring the implements of thy art.

Dams. Kind Mádhavya, hold the picture while I obey the king.

Dushm. No; I will hold it.

[*He takes the picture; and the Damsel goes out.*]

Mádh. What else is to be painted?

Misr. [*Aside.*] He desires, I presume, to add all those circumstances which became the situation of his beloved in the hermitage. 320

Dushm. In this landscape, my friend, I wish to see represented the river Málini, with some amorous Flamingos on its green margin; farther back must appear some hills near the mountain Himálaya, surrounded with herds of Chamaras; and in the foreground, a dark spreading tree, with some mantles of woven bark suspended on its branches to be dried by the sunbeams; while a pair of black antelopes couch in its shade, and the female gently rubs her beautiful forehead on the horn of the male.

Mádh. Add what you please; but, in my judgement, the vacant places should be filled with old hermits, bent, like me, towards the ground.

Dushm. [*Not attending to him.*] Oh! I had forgotten that my beloved herself 330 must have some new ornaments.

Mádh. What, I pray?

Misr. [*Aside.*] Such, no doubt, as become a damsel bred in a forest.

Dushm. The artist had omitted a Sirísha flower with its peduncle fixed behind her soft ear, and its filaments waving over part of her cheek; and between her breasts must be placed a knot of delicate fibres, from the stalks of water lilies, like the rays of an autumnal moon.

Mádh. Why does the queen cover part of her face, as if she was afraid of something, with the tips of her fingers, that glow like the flowers of the Cuvalaya? – Oh! I now perceive an impudent bee, that thief of odours, who 340 seems eager to sip honey from the lotos of her mouth.

Dushm. A bee! drive off the importunate insect.

Mádh. The king has supreme power over all offenders.

Dushm. O male bee, who approachest the lovely inhabitants of a flowery grove, why dost thou expose thyself to the pain of being rejected? – See where thy female sits on a blossom, and, though thirsty, waits for thy return: without thee she will not taste its nectar.

Misr. [Aside.] A wild, but apt, address!

Mádh. The perfidy of male bees is proverbial.

Dushm. [Angrily.] Shouldst thou touch, O bee, the lip of my darling, ruddy   350
as a fresh leaf on which no wind has yet breathed, a lip from which I drank sweetness in the banquet of love, thou shalt, by my order, be imprisoned in the center of a lotos. – Dost thou still disobey me?

Mádh. How can he fail to obey, since you denounce so severe a punishment? *[Aside, laughing.]* – He is stark mad with love and affliction; whilst I, by keeping him company, shall be as made as he without either.

Dushm. After my positive injunction, art thou still unmoved?

Misr. [Aside.] How does excess of passion alter even the wise!

Mádh. Why, my friend, it is only a painted bee.

Misr. [Aside.] Oh! I perceive his mistake: it shows the perfection of the art.   360
But why does he continue musing?

Dushm. What ill-natured remark was that? – Whilst I am enjoying the rapture of beholding her to whom my soul is attached, thou, cruel remembrancer, tellest me that it is only a picture. –   *[Weeping.]*

Misr. [Aside.] Such are the woes of a separated lover! He is on all sides entangled in sorrow.

Dushm. Why do I thus indulge unremitted grief? That intercourse with my darling which dreams would give, is prevented by my continued inability to repose; and my tears will not suffer me to view her distinctly even in this picture.   370

Misr. [Aside.] His misery acquits him entirely of having deserted her in his perfect senses.

The Damsel *re-enters.*

Dams. As I was advancing, O king, with my box of pencils and colours –

Dushm. [Hastily.] What happened?

Dams. It was forcibly seized by the queen Vasumatì, whom her maid Pingalicà had apprised of my errand; and she said: 'I will myself deliver the casket to the son of my lord.'

Mádh. How came you to be released?

Dams. While the queen's maid was disengaging the skirt of her mantle, which had been caught by the branch of a thorny shrub, I stole away.   380

Dushm. Friend Mádhavya, my great attention to Vasumatì has made her arrogant; and she will soon be here: be it your care to conceal the picture.

Mádh. [Aside.] I wish you would conceal it yourself. – *[He takes the picture, and rises.]* – [Aloud.] – If, indeed, you will disentangle me from the net of your secret apartments, to which I am confined, and suffer me to dwell on the wall Méghach'handa which encircles them, I will hide the picture in a place where none shall see it but pigeons.   *[He goes out.]*

Misr. [*Aside.*] How honourably he keeps his former engagements, though his heart be now fixed on another object!

A Warder *enters with a leaf.*

Ward. May the king prosper! 390

Dushm. Warder, hast thou lately seen the queen Vasumati?

Ward. I met her, O king; but when she perceived the leaf in my hand, she retired.

Dushm. The queen distinguishes time: she would not impede my publick business.

Ward. The chief minister sends this message: 'I have carefully stated a case which has arisen in the city, and accurately committed it to writing: let the king deign to consider it.'

Dushm. Give me the leaf. – [*Receiving it, and reading.*] – 'Be it presented at the foot of the king, that a merchant named Dhanavriddhi, who had 400 extensive commerce at sea, was lost in a late shipwreck: he had no child born; and has left a fortune of many millions, which belong, if the king commands, to the royal treasury.' – [*With sorrow.*] – Oh! how great a misfortune it is to die childless! Yet with his affluence he must have had many wives: – let an inquiry be made whether any one of them is pregnant.

Ward. I have heard that his wife, the daughter of an excellent man, named Sácétaca, has already performed the ceremonies usual on pregnancy.

Dushm. The child, though unborn, has a title to his father's property. – Go: bid the minister make my judgement publick.

Ward. I obey. [*Going.*] 410

Dushm. Stay a while. –

Ward. [*Returning.*] I am here.

Dushm. Whether he had or had not left offspring, the estate should not have been forfeited. – Let it be proclaimed, that whatever kinsman any one of my subjects may lose, Dushmanta (excepting always the case of forfeiture for crimes) will supply, in tender affection, the place of that kinsman.

Ward. The proclamation shall be made. – [*He goes out.*]

[Dushmanta *continues meditating.*]

Re-enter Warder.

O king! the royal decree, which proves that your virtues are awake after a long slumber, was heard with bursts of applause.

Dushm. [*Sighing deeply.*] When an illustrious man dies, alas, without an 420 heir, his estate goes to a stranger; and such will be the fate of all the wealth accumulated by the sons of Puru.

Ward. Heaven avert the calamity! [*Goes out.*]

Dushm. Wo is me! I am stripped of all the felicity which I once enjoyed.

Misr. [*Aside.*] How his heart dwells on the idea of his beloved!

Dushm. My lawful wife, whom I basely deserted, remains fixed in my soul: she would have been the glory of my family, and might have produced a son brilliant as the richest fruit of the teeming earth.

Misr. [*Aside.*] She is not forsaken by all; and soon, I trust, will be thine.

Dams. [*Aside.*] What a change has the minister made in the king by sending him that mischievous leaf! Behold, he is deluged with tears.   430

Dushm. Ah me! the departed souls of my ancestors, who claim a share in the funeral cake, which I have no son to offer, are apprehensive of losing their due honour, when Dushmanta shall be no more on earth: – who then, alas, will perform in our family those obsequies which the Véda prescribes? – My forefathers must drink, instead of a pure libation, this flood of tears, the only offering which a man who dies childless can make them.   [*Weeping.*]

Misr. [*Aside.*] Such a veil obscures the king's eyes, that he thinks it total darkness, though a lamp be now shining brightly.

Dams. Afflict not yourself immoderately: our lord is young; and when sons illustrious as himself shall be born of other queens, his ancestors will be redeemed from their offences committed here below.   440

Dushm. [*With agony.*] The race of Puru, which has hitherto been fruitful and unblemished, ends in me; as the river Sereswati disappears in a region unworthy of her divine stream.   [*He faints.*]

Dams. Let the king resume confidence. –   [*She supports him.*]

Misr. [*Aside.*] Shall I restore him? No; he will speedily be roused – I heard the nymph Dévajananì consoling Sacontalá in these words: 'As the gods delight in their portion of sacrifices, thus wilt thou soon be delighted by the love of thy husband.' I go, therefore, to raise her spirits, and please my friend   450
Ménacà with an account of his virtues and his affection.

[*She rises aloft and disappears.*]

Behind the scenes. A Bráhmen must not be slain: save the life of a Bráhmen.

Dushm. [*Reviving and listening.*] Hah! was not that the plaintive voice of Mádhavya?

Dams. He has probably been caught with the picture in his hand by Pingalicà and the other maids.

Dushm. Go, Chaturicà, and reprove the queen in my name for not restraining her servants.

Dams. As the king commands.   [*She goes out.*]   460

Again behind the scenes. I am a Bráhmen, and must not be put to death.

Dushm. It is manifestly some Bráhmen in great danger. – Hola! who is there?

---

444   *the river Sereswati disappears in a region unworthy of her divine stream*   The idea of earthly rivers having their origin in heaven can be traced to the *Rig-Veda*. According to the *Mahābhārata*, the Sarasvatī, or Sarsuti, river was dried up by the curse of a sage named Utathya. Sarasvatī is also the goddess of the liberal arts, see below VII.395–6; 'A Hymn to Sereswaty', ll.169–70; and 'A Hymn to Gangá', ll.77–8.

The old Chamberlain *enters.*

Cham. What is the king's pleasure?

Dushm. Inquire why the faint-hearted Mádhavya cries out so piteously.

Cham. I will know in an instant.   [*He goes out, and returns trembling.*]

Dushm. Is there any alarm, Párvatáyana?

Cham. Alarm enough!

Dushm. What causes thy tremour? – Thus do men tremble through age:
fear shakes the old man's body, as the breeze agitates the leaves of the   470
Pippala.

Cham. Oh! deliver thy friend.

Dushm. Deliver him! from what?

Cham. From distress and danger.

Dushm. Speak more plainly.

Cham. The wall which looks to all quarters of the heavens, and is named,
from the clouds which cover it, Méghach'handa –

Dushm. What of that?

Cham. From the summit of that wall, the pinnacle of which is hardly
attainable even by the blue-necked pigeons, an evil being, invisible to human   480
eyes, has violently carried away the friend of your childhood.

Dushm. [*Starting up hastily.*] What! are even my secret apartments infested
by supernatural agents? – Royalty is ever subjected to molestation. – A king
knows not even the mischiefs which his own negligence daily and hourly
occasions: – how then should be know what path his people are treading;
and how should he correct their manners when his own are uncorrected?

Behind the scenes. Oh, help! Oh, release me.

Dushm. [*Listening and advancing.*] Fear not, my friend, fear nothing. –

Behind the scenes. Not fear, when a monster has caught me by the nape of
my neck, and means to snap my backbone as he would snap a sugar-cane!   490

Dushm. [*Darting his eyes round.*] Hola! my bow –

A Warder *enters with the king's bow and quiver.*

Ward. Here are our great hero's arms.

[Dushmanta *takes his bow and an arrow.*]

Behind the scenes Here I stand; and, thirsting for thy fresh blood, will slay
thee struggling as a tiger slays a calf. – Where now is thy protector,
Dushmanta, who grasps his bow to defend the oppressed?

Dushm. [*Wrathfully.*] The demon names me with defiance. – Stay, thou
basest of monsters. – Here am I, and thou shalt not long exist. – [*Raising his
bow.*] – Show the way, Párvatáyana, to the stairs of the terrace.

Cham. This way, great king! –   [*All go out hastily.*]

470–1   *the leaves of the Pippala*   The sacred fig tree, the abode of Nirrti, goddess of
Misery.

The SCENE *changes to a broad* TERRACE.

Enter Dushmanta.

Dushm. [*Looking round.*] Ah! the place is deserted.   500

Behind the scenes. Save me, oh! save me. – I see thee, my friend, but thou canst not discern me, who, like a mouse in the claws of a cat, have no hope of life.

Dushm. But this arrow shall distinguish thee from thy foe, in spite of the magick which renders thee invisible. – Mádhavya, stand firm; and thou, blood-thirsty fiend, think not of destroying him whom I love and will protect. – See, I thus fix a shaft which shall pierce thee, who deservest death, and shall save a Bráhmen who deserves long life; as the celestial bird sips the milk, and leaves the water which has been mingled with it.

[*He draws the bowstring.*]

Enter Mátali *and* Mádhavya.

Mát. The god Indra has destined evil demons to fall by thy shafts: against   510
them let thy bow be drawn, and cast on thy friends eyes bright with affection.

Dushm. [*Astonished, giving back his arms.*] Oh! Mátali, welcome; I greet the driver of Indra's car.

Mádh. What! this cutthroat was putting me to death, and thou greetest him with a kind welcome!

Mát. [*Smiling.*] O king, live long and conquer! Hear on what errand I am dispatched by the ruler of the firmament.

Dushm. I am humbly attentive.

Mát. There is a race of Dánavas, the children of Cálanémi, whom it is   520
found hard to subdue –

Dushm. This I have heard already from Náred.

Mát. The god with an hundred sacrifices, unable to quell that gigantick race, commissions thee, his approved friend, to assail them in the front of battle; as the sun with seven steeds despairs of overcoming the dark legions of night, and gives way to the moon, who easily scatters them. Mount, therefore, with me, the car of Indra, and, grasping thy bow, advance to assured victory.

Dushm. Such a mark of distinction from the prince of good genii honours

---

508   *the celestial bird sips the milk*   Hamsas, a species of geese, were said to have the magical ability of separating milk from water, cf. *Mahābhārata,* I.169.

514   *the driver of Indra's car*   Mātali is also Indra's friend, his equal in courage and daring.

520   *Dánavas*   Genii, one of whose leaders, Kālanemi, was eventually subdued by Vishnu.

522   *Náred*   Nārada (Giver-of-Advice) is a messenger between men and gods.

523   *the god with a hundred sacrifices*   Śata-kratu (Glorified-in-a-hundred-Sacrifices); 'Divespetir' Divas-pati (Regent-of-Space) These are two of Indra's many names.

me highly; but say why you treated so roughly my poor friend Mádhavya.   530

Mát. Perceiving that, for some reason or another, you were grievously afflicted, I was desirous to rouse your spirits by provoking you to wrath. – The fire blazes when wood is thrown on it; the serpent, when provoked, darts his head against the assailant; and a man capable of acquiring glory, exerts himself when his courage is excited.

Dushm. [*To* Mádhavya.] – My friend, the command of Divespetir must instantly be obeyed: go, therefore, and carry the intelligence to my chief minister; saying to him in my name: 'Let thy wisdom secure my people from danger while this braced bow has a different employment.'

Mádh. I obey; but wish it could have been employed without assistance   540
from my terror.   [*He goes out.*]

Mát. Ascend, great king.

[Dushmanta *ascends, and* Mátali *drives off the car.*]

ACT VII

Dushmanta *with* Mátali *in the car of* Indra, *supposed to be above the clouds.*

Dushmanta.

I AM sensible, O Mátali, that, for having executed the commission which Indra gave me, I deserved not such a profusion of honours.

Mát. Neither of you is satisfied. You who have conferred so great a benefit on the god of thunder, consider it as a trifling act of devotion; whilst he reckons not all his kindness equal to the benefit conferred.

Dushm. There is no comparison between the service and the reward. – He surpassed my warmest expectation, when, before he dismissed me, he made me sit on half of his throne, thus exalting me before all the inhabitants of the Empyreum; and smiling to see his son Jayanta, who stood near him, ambitious of the same honour, perfumed my bosom with essence of heavenly sandal wood, throwing over my neck, a garland of flowers blown in paradise.

Mát. O king, you deserve all imaginable rewards from the sovereign of good genii; whose empyreal seats have twice been disentangled from the thorns of Danu's race; formerly by the claws of the man-lion, and lately by thy unerring shafts.

Dushm. My victory proceeded wholly from the auspices of the god; as on earth, when servants prosper in great enterprises, they owe their success to the magnificence of their lords. – Could Arun dispel the shades of night if the deity with a thousand beams had not placed him before the car of day?

Mát. That case, indeed, is parallel. – [*Driving slowly.*] – See, O king, the full exaltation of thy glory, which now rides on the back of heaven! The delighted genii have been collecting, among the trees of life, those crimson and azure dyes, with which the celestial damsels tinge their beautiful feet; and they now are writing they actions in verses worthy of divine melody.

Dushm. [*Modestly.*] In my transport, O Mátali, after the rout of the giants, this wonderful place had escaped my notice. – In what path of the winds are we now journeying?

Mát. This is the way which leads along the triple river, heaven's brightest ornament, and causes yon luminaries to roll in a circle with diffused beams: it is the course of a gentle breeze which supports the floating forms of the

10

20

30

---

9   *Jayanta*   One of the three sons of Indra and Śacī, appropriately, his name means Victorious.

15   *Danu's race*   Danu is the mother of the *dánavas*.

   the man-lion   Prahlāda, an avatar, or incarnation, of Vishnu, celebrated for valour and piety.

gods; and this path was the second step of Vishnu, when he confounded the proud Vali.

Dushm. My internal soul, which acts by exterior organs, is filled by the sight with a charming complacency. – [*Looking at the wheels.*] – We are now passing, I guess, through the region of clouds.

Mát. Whence do you form that conjecture?

Dushm. The car itself instructs me that we are moving over clouds pregnant with showers; for the circumference of its wheel disperses pellucid water; the horses of Indra sparkle with lightning; and I now see the warbling   40
Chátacas descend from their nests on the summits of mountains.

Mát. It is even so; and in another moment you will be in the country which you govern.

Dushm. [*Looking down.*] Through the rapid, yet imperceptible, descent of the heavenly steeds, I now perceive the allotted station of men. – Astonishing prospect! It is yet so distant from us, that the low lands appear confounded with the high mountain tops; the trees erect their branchy shoulders, but seem leafless; the rivers look like bright lines, but their waters vanish; and, at this instant, the globe of earth seems thrown upwards by some stupendous power.   50

Mát. [*Looking with reverence on the earth.*] How delightful is the abode of mankind! – O king, you saw distinctly.

Dushm. Say, Mátali, what mountain is that which, like an evening cloud, pours exhilarating streams, and forms a golden zone between the western and eastern seas?

Mát. That, O king, is the mountain of Gandharvas, named Hémacúta: the universe contains not a more excellent place for the successful devotion of the pious. There Casyapa, father of the immortals, ruler of men, son of Maríchi, who sprang from the self-existent, resides with his consort Aditi, blessed in holy retirement.   60

Dushm. [*Devoutly.*] This occasion of attaining good fortune must not be neglected: may I approach the divine pair, and do them complete homage?

Mát. By all means. – It is an excellent idea! – We are now descended on earth.

---

32   *the second step of Vishnu, when he confounded the proud Vali*   Bali (Vali), king of the genii, had gained dominion over the universe. The gods appealed to Vishnu, who was born as Vāmana, a priestly dwarf, and managed to persuade Bali to grant him as much land as he might cover in three steps. His first step encompassed the earth, his second the heavens, with his third he pushed Bali down to the infernal regions, see Daniélou, *Hindu Mythology*, pp.169–70.

56   *Gandharvas*   Benevolent celestial harmonies. According to the *Rig-Veda* (10.123.7) Gandarvas generated precious rain.

58–9   *Casyapa . . . son of Maríchi . . . his consort Aditi*   According to the *Vishnu Purāṇa*, Kaśyapa (Vision) was the father of the *gandharvas*. The union of Kaśyapa and Aditi (Primordial-Vastness) also produced Indra. Marīci (Light), the father of Kaśyapa, was born of Brahmā, the 'self-existent'.

Dushm. [*With wonder.*] These chariot wheels yield no sound; no dust arises from them; and the descent of the car gave me no shock.

Mát. Such is the difference, O king, between thy car and that of Indra!

Dushm. Where is the holy retreat of Maríchi?

Mát. [*Pointing.*] A little beyond that grove, where you see a pious Yógì, motionless as a pollard, holding his thick bushy hair, and fixing his eyes on   70
the solar orb. – Mark; his body is half covered with a white ant's edifice made of raised clay; the skin of a snake supplies the place of his sacerdotal thread, and part of it girds his loins; a number of knotty plants encircle and wound his neck; and surrounding birds' nests almost conceal his shoulders.

Dushm. I bow to a man of his austere devotion.

Mát. [*Checking the reins.*] Thus far, and enough. – We now enter the sanctuary of him who rules the world, and the groves which are watered by streams from celestial sources.

Dushm. This asylum is more delightful than paradise itself: I could fancy myself bathing in a pool of nectar.   80

Mát. [*Stopping the car.*] Let the king descend.

Dushm. [*Joyfully descending.*] How canst thou leave the car?

Mát. On such an occasion it will remain fixed: we may both leave it. – This way, victorious hero, this way. – Behold the retreat of the truly pious.

Dushm. I see with equal amazement both the pious and their awful retreat.
– It becomes, indeed, pure spirits to feed on balmy air in a forest blooming with trees of life; to bathe in rills dyed yellow with the golden dust of the lotos, and to fortify their virtue in the mysterious bath; to meditate in caves, the pebbles of which are unblemished gems; and to restrain their passions, even though nymphs of exquisite beauty frolick around them: in this grove   90
alone is attained the summit of true piety, to which other hermits in vain aspire.

Mát. In exalted minds the desire of perfect excellence continually increases. – [*Turning aside.*] – Tell me, Vriddhasácalya, in what business is the divine son of Maríchi now engaged? – What sayest thou? – Is he conversing with the daughter of Dacsha, who practises all the virtues of a dutiful wife, and is consulting him on moral questions? – Then we must await his leisure. – [*To* Dushmanta.] Rest, O king, under the shade of this Asóca tree, whilst I announce thy arrival to the father of Indra.

Dushm. As you judge right. – [Mátali *goes out.* – Dushmanta *feels his right*   100
arm throb.] Why, O my arm, dost thou flatter me with a vain omen? – My former happiness is lost, and misery only remains.

Behind the scenes. Be not so restless: in every situation thou showest thy bad temper.

Dushm. [*Listening.*] Hah! this is no place, surely, for a malignant disposition. – Who can be thus rebuked? – [*Looking with surprise.*] – I see a

---

96   *the daughter of Dacsha*   Aditi was born of Daksa (Ritual Skill) who represents the techniques of effective ritual enabling communion between men and gods.

child, but with no childish countenance or strength, whom two female anchorites are endeavouring to keep in order; while he forcibly pulls towards him, in rough play, a lion's whelp with a torn mane, who seems just dragged from the half-sucked nipple of the lioness!   110

A little Boy *and two female* Attendants *are discovered, as described by the king.*

Boy. Open thy mouth, lion's whelp, that I may count thy teeth.

First Atten. Intractable child! Why dost thou torment the wild animals of this forest, whom we cherish as if they were our own offspring? – Thou seemest even to sport in anger. – Aptly have the hermits named thee Servademana, since thou tamest all creatures.

Dushm. Ah! what means it that my heart inclines to this boy as if he were my own son? – [*Meditating.*] – Alas! I have no son; and the reflection makes me once more soft-hearted.

Second Atten. The lioness will tear thee to pieces if thou release not her whelp.   120

Boy. [*Smiling.*] Oh! I am greatly afraid of her to be sure!

[*He bites his lip, as in defiance of her.*]

Dushm. [*Aside, amazed.*] The child exhibits the rudiments of heroick valour, and looks like fire which blazes from the addition of dry fuels.

First Atten. My beloved child, set at liberty this young prince of wild beasts; and I will give thee a prettier plaything.

Boy. Give it first. – Where is it?   [*Stretching out his hand.*]

Dushm. [*Aside, gazing on the child's palm.*] What! the very palm of his hand bears the marks of empire; and whilst he thus eagerly extends it, shows its lines of exquisite network, and glows like a lotos expanded at early dawn, when the ruddy splendour of its petals hides all other tints in obscurity.   130

Second Atten. Mere words, my Suvrità, will not pacify him. – Go, I pray, to my cottage, where thou wilt find a plaything made for the hermit's child, Sancara: it is a peacock of earthenware painted with rich colours.

First Atten. I will bring it speedily.   [*She goes out.*]

Boy. In the mean time I will play with the young lion.

Second Atten. [*Looking at him with a smile.*] Let him go, I entreat thee.

Dushm. [*Aside.*] I feel the tenderest affection for this unmanageable child. [*Sighing.*] – How sweet must be the delight of virtuous fathers, when they soil their bosoms with dust by lifting up heir playful children, who charm them with inarticulate prattle, and show the white blossoms of their teeth, while   140
they laugh innocently at every trifling occurrence!

Second Atten. [*Raising her finger.*] What! dost thou show no attention to me? – [*Looking round.*] – Are any of the hermits near? – [*Seeing* Dushmanta.]

---

115   *Servedamana*   Sarvadamana means 'all-tamer', cf. *Mahābhārata*, I.165.

– Oh! let me request you, gentle stranger, to release the lion's whelp, who cannot disengage himself from the grasp of this robust child.

Dushm. I will endeavour. – [*Approaching the* Boy *and smiling.*] – O thou, who art the son of a pious anchorite, how canst thou dishonour thy father, whom thy virtues would make happy, by violating the rules of this consecrated forest? It becomes a black serpent only, to infest the boughs of a fragrant sandal tree.   [*The* Boy *releases the lion.*]   150

Second Atten. I thank you, courteous guest; – but he is not the son of an anchorite.

Dushm. His actions, indeed, which are conformable to his robustness, indicate a different birth: but my opinion arose from the sanctity of the place which he inhabits. – [*Taking the* Boy *by the hand.*] – [*Aside.*] – Oh! since it gives me such delight merely to touch the hand of this child, who is the hopeful scion of a family unconnected with mine, what rapture must be felt by the fortunate man from whom he sprang?

Second Atten. [*Gazing on them alternately.*] Oh wonderful!

Dushm. What has raised your wonder?   160

Second Atten. The astonishing resemblance between the child and you, gentle stranger, to whom he bears no relation. – It surprised me also to see, that although he has childish humours, and had no former acquaintance with you, yet your words have restored him to his natural good temper.

Dushm. [*Raising the* Boy *to his bosom.*] Holy matron, if he be not the son of a hermit, what then is the name of his family?

Second Atten. He is descended from Puru.

Dushm. [*Aside.*] Hah! thence, no doubt, springs his disposition, and my affection for him. – [*Setting him down.*] – [*Aloud.*] It is, I know, an established usage among the princes of Puru's race, to dwell at first in rich palaces with   170 stuccoed walls, where they protect and cherish the world, but in the decline of life to seek humbler mansions near the roots of venerable trees, where hermits with subdued passions practise austere devotion. – I wonder, however, that this boy, who moves like a god, could have been born of a mere mortal.

Second Atten. Affable stranger, your wonder will cease when you know that his mother is related to a celestial nymph, and brought him forth in the sacred forest of Casyapa.

Dush. [*Aside.*] I am transported. – This is a fresh ground of hope. – [*Aloud.*] – What virtuous monarch took his excellent mother by the hand?   180

Second Atten. Oh! I must not give celebrity to the name of a king who deserted his lawful wife.

Dushm. [*Aside.*] Ah! she means me. – Let me now ask the name of the sweet child's mother. – [*Meditating.*] – But it is against good manners to inquire concerning the wife of another man.

The First Attendant *re-enters with a toy.*

First Atten. Look Servademana, look at the beauty of this bird, Saconta lávanyam.

Boy. [*Looking eagerly round.*] Sacontalá! Oh, where is my beloved mother?

[*Both* Attendants *laugh.*]

First Atten. He tenderly loves his mother, and was deceived by an equivocal phrase.   190

Second Atten. My child, she meant only the beautiful shape and colours of this peacock.

Dushm. [*Aside.*] Is my Sacontalá then his mother? Or has that dear name been given to some other woman? – This conversation resembles the fallacious appearance of water in a desert, which ends in bitter disappointment to the stag parched with thirst.

Boy. I shall like the peacock if it can run and fly; not else.   [*He takes it.*]

First Atten. [*Looking round in confusion.*] Alas, the child's amulet is not on his wrist!

Dushm. Be not alarmed. It was dropped while he was playing with the lion: 200 I see it, and will put it into your hand.

Both. Oh! beware of touching it.

First Atten. Ah! he has actually taken it up.

[*They both gaze with surprise on each other.*]

Dushm. Here it is; but why would you have restrained me from touching this bright gem?

Second Atten. Great monarch, this divine amulet has a wonderful power, and was given to the child by the son of Maríchi, as soon as the sacred rites had been performed after his birth: whenever it fell on the ground, no human being but the father or mother of this boy could have touched it unhurt.

Dushm. What if a stranger had taken it?   210

First Atten. It would have become a serpent and wounded him.

Dushm. Have you seen that consequence on any similar occasion?

Both. Frequently.

Dushm. [*With transport.*] I may then exult on the completion of my ardent desire.   [*He embraces the child.*]

Second Atten. Come, Suvritá, let us carry the delightful intelligence to Sacontalá, whom the harsh duties of a separated wife have so long oppressed.   [*The* Attendants *go out.*]

Boy. Farewell; I must go to my mother.

Dushm. My darling son, thou wilt make her happy by going to her with   220 me.

Boy. Dushmanta is my father; and you are not Dushmanta.

Dushm. Even thy denial of me gives me delight.

Sacontalá *enters in mourning apparel, with her long hair twisted in a single braid, and flowing down her back.*

Sac. [*Aside.*] Having heard that my child's amulet has proved its divine power, I must either be strangely diffident of my good fortune, or that event which Misracési predicted has actually happened. [*Advancing.*]

Dushm. [*With a mixture of joy and sorrow.*] Ah! do I see the incomparable Sacontalá clad in sordid weeds? – Her face is emaciated by the performance of austere duties; one twisted lock floats over her shoulder; and with a mind perfectly pure, she supports the long absence of her husband, whose   230 unkindness exceeded all bounds.

Sac. [*Seeing him, yet doubting.*] Is that the son of my lord grown pale with penitence and affliction? – If not, who is it, that sullies with his touch the hand of my child, whose amulet should have preserved him from such indignity?

Boy. [*Going hastily to* Sacontalá.] Mother, here is a stranger who calls me son.

Dushm. Oh! my best beloved, I have treated thee cruelly; but my cruelty is succeeded by the warmest affection; and I implore your remembrance and forgiveness.

Sac. [*Aside.*] Be confident, O my heart! – [*Aloud.*] – I shall be most happy   240 when the king's anger has passed away. – [*Aside.*] – This must be the son of my lord.

Dushm. By the kindness of heaven, O loveliest of thy sex, thou standest again before me, whose memory was obscured by the gloom of fascination; as the star Róhiní at the end of an eclipse rejoins her beloved moon.

Sac. May the king be – [*She bursts into tears.*]

Dushm. My darling, though the word victorious be suppressed by thy weeping, yet I must have victory, since I see thee again, though with pale lips and a body unadorned.

Boy. What man is this, mother?   250

Sac. Sweet child, ask the divinity, who presides over the fortunes of us both. [*She weeps.*]

Dushm. O my only beloved, banish from thy mind my cruel desertion of thee. – A violent phrensy overpowered my soul. – Such, when the darkness of illusion prevails, are the actions of the best intentioned; as a blind man, when a friend binds his head with a wreath of flowers, mistakes it for a twining snake, and foolishly rejects it. [*He falls at her feet.*]

Sac. Rise, my husband, oh! rise – My happiness has been long interrupted; but joy now succeeds to affliction, since the son of my lord still loves me. – [*He rises.*] – How was the remembrance of this unfortunate woman restored   260 to the mind of my lord's son?

---

245 *Róhiní* The relationship between the moon (Soma) and his favourite constellation, Rohinī, is a paradigm of fidelity in Sanskrit literature, cf. the *Kāmasūtra*, 5.3.6.: 'His heart was always excessively affectionate toward her, just as the moon's heart always takes its place in the constellation Rohinī.'

Dushm. When the dart of misery shall be wholly extracted from my bosom, I will tell you all; but since the anguish of my soul has in part ceased, let me first wipe off that tear which trickles from thy delicate eye-lash; and thus efface the memory of all the tears which my delirium has made thee shed. [*He stretches out his hand.*]

Sac. [*Wiping off her tears, and seeing the ring on his finger.*] Ah! is that the fatal ring?

Dushm. Yes; by the surprising recovery of it my memory was restored.

Sac. Its influence, indeed, has been great; since it has brought back the lost   270
confidence of my husband.

Dushm. Take it then, as a beautiful plant receives a flower from the returning season of joy.

Sac. I cannot again trust it. – Let it be worn by the son of my lord.

Mátali *enters.*

Mát. By the will of heaven the king has happily met his beloved wife, and seen the countenance of his little son.

Dushm. It was by the company of my friend that my desire attained maturity. – But say, was not this fortunate event previously known to Indra?

Mát. [*Smiling.*] What is unknown to the gods? – But come: the divine Marícha desires to see thee.   280

Dushm. Beloved, take our son by the hand; and let me present you both to the father of immortals.

Sac. I really am ashamed, even in thy presence, to approach the deities.

Dushm. It is highly proper on so happy an occasion. – Come, I entreat thee. [*They all advance.*]

The scene is withdrawn, and Casyapa *is discovered on a throne conversing with* Aditi.

Cas. [*Pointing to the king.*] That, O daughter of Dacsha, is the hero who led the squadrons of thy son to the front of battle, a sovereign of the earth, Dushmanta; by the means of whose bow the thunder-bolt of Indra (all its work being accomplished) is now a mere ornament of his heavenly palace.

Adi. He bears in his form all the marks of exalted majesty.   290

Mát. [*To* Dushmanta.] The parents of the twelve Adityas, O king, are gazing on thee, as on their own offspring, with eyes of affection. – Approach them, illustrious prince.

Dushm. Are those, O Mátali, the divine pair, sprung from Maríchi and Dacsha? – Are those the grand-children of Brahmá, to whom the self-existent gave birth in the beginning; whom inspired mortals pronounce the fountain of glory apparent in the form of twelve suns; they who produced my benefactor, the lord of a hundred sacrifices, and ruler of three worlds?

291 *the twelve Adityas* These are the sovereign principles, personifications of universal divine and human laws.   300

Mát. Even they – [*Prostrating himself with* Dushmanta.] – Great beings, the king Dushmanta, who has executed the commands of your son Vasava,   300 falls humbly before your throne.

Cas. Continue long to rule the world.

Adi. Long be a warrior with a car unshattered in combat.

[Sacontalá and her son prostrate themselves.]

Cas. Daughter, may thy husband be like Indra! May thy son resemble Jayanta! And mayst thou (whom no benediction could better suit) be equal in prosperity to the daughter of Pulóman!

Adi. Preserve, my child, a constant unity with thy lord: and may this boy, for a great length of years, be the ornament and joy of you both! Now be seated near us.   [*They all sit down.*]

Cas. [*Looking at them by turns.*] Sacontalá is the model of excellent wives;   310 her son is dutiful; and thou, O king, hast three rare advantages, true piety, abundant wealth, and active virtue.

Dushm. O divine being, having obtained the former object of my most ardent wishes, I now have reached the summit of earthly happiness through thy favour, and thy benizon will ensure its permanence. – First appears the flower, then the fruit; first clouds are collected, then the shower falls: such is the regular course of causes and effects; and thus, when thy indulgence preceded, felicity generally followed.

Mát. Great indeed, O king, has been the kindness of the primeval Bráhmens.   320

Dushm. Bright son of Maríchi, this thy handmaid was married to me by the ceremony of Gandharvas, and, after a time, was conducted to my palace by some of her family; but my memory having failed through delirium, I rejected her, and thus committed a grievous offence against the venerable Canna, who is of thy divine lineage: afterwards, on seeing this fatal ring, I remembered my love and my nuptials; but the whole transaction yet fills me with wonder. My soul was confounded with strange ignorance that obscured my senses; as if a man were to see an elephant marching before him, yet to doubt what animal it could be, till he discovered by the traces of his large feet that it was an elephant.   330

Cas. Cease, my son, to charge thyself with an offence committed ignorantly, and, therefore, innocently. – Now hear me –

Dushm. I am devoutly attentive.

Cas. When the nymph Ménacà led Sacontalá from the place where thy desertion of her had afflicted her soul, she brought her to the palace of Aditi; and I knew, by the power of meditation on the Supreme Being, that thy forgetfulness of thy pious and lawful consort had proceeded from the

---

300   *Vasava*   Vāsava is one of Indra's titles, meaning 'Lord of the Spheres'.
304   *Daughter, may thy husband be like Indra!*   Kaśyapa, being the father of Menakā, is actually the grandfather of Sacontalá.
306   *the daughter of Pulóman*   Indrānī, wife of Indra, cf. 'A Hymn to Indra', ll.86–7.

imprecation of Durvásas, and that the charm would terminate on the sight of thy ring.

Dushm. [*Aside.*] My name then is cleared from infamy.   340

Sac. Happy am I that the son of my lord, who now recognises me, denied me through ignorance, and not with real aversion. – The terrible imprecation was heard, I suppose, when my mind was intent on a different object, by my two beloved friends, who, with extreme affection, concealed it from me to spare my feelings, but advised me at parting to show the ring if my husband should have forgotten me.

Cas. [*Turning to* Sacontalá.] Thou art apprised, my daughter, of the whole truth, and must no longer resent the behaviour of thy lord. – He rejected thee when his memory was impaired by the force of a charm; and when the gloom was dispelled, his conjugal affection revived; as a mirror whose surface has   350
been sullied, reflects no image; but exhibits perfect resemblances when its polish has been restored.

Dushm. Such, indeed, was my situation.

Cas. My son Dushmanta, hast thou embraced thy child by Sacontalá, on whose birth I myself performed the ceremonies prescribed in the Véda?

Dushm. Holy Maríchi, he is the glory of my house.

Cas. Know too, that his heroick virtue will raise him to a dominion extended from sea to sea: before he has passed the ocean of mortal life, he shall rule, unequalled in combat, this earth with seven peninsulas; and, as he now is called Servademana, because he tames even in childhood the fiercest   360
animals, so, in his riper years, he shall acquire the name of Bhereta, because he shall sustain and nourish the world.

Dushm. A boy educated by the son of Maríchi, must attain the summit of greatness.

Adi. Now let Sacontalá, who is restored to happiness, convey intelligence to Canna of all these events: her mother Ménacà is in my family, and knows all that has passed.

Sac. The goddess proposes what I most ardently wish.

Cas. By the force of true piety the whole scene will be present to the mind of Canna.   370

Dushm. The devout sage must be still excessively indignant at my frantic behaviour.

Cas. [*Meditating.*] Then let him hear from me the delightful news, that his foster-child has been tenderly received by her husband, and that both are happy with the little warrior who sprang from them. – Hola! who is in waiting?

---

361 *Bhereta* 'In the continuing lineage of Bharata there arose great and puissant kings, the likes of Gods, the likes of Brahmā, whose names are famous beyond measure everywhere', *Mahābhārata*, I.171.

A Pupil *enters.*

Pup. Great being, I am here.

Cas. Hasten, Gólava, through the light air, and in my name inform the venerable Canna, that Sacontalá has a charming son by Dushmanta, whose affection for her was restored with his remembrance, on the termination of the spell raised by the angry Durvásas.   380

Pup. As the divinity commands.   *[He goes out.]*

Cas. My son, reascend the car of Indra with thy consort and child, and return happy to thy imperial seat.

Dushm. Be it as Maríchi ordains.

Cas. Henceforth may the god of the atmosphere with copious rain give abundance to thy affectionate subjects; and mayst thou with frequent sacrifices maintain the Thunderer's friendship! By numberless interchanges of good offices between you both, may benefits reciprocally be conferred on the inhabitants of the two worlds!   390

Dushm. Powerful being, I will be studious, as far as I am able, to attain that felicity.

Cas. What other favours can I bestow on thee?

Dushm. Can any favours exceed those already bestowed? – Let every king apply himself to the attainment of happiness for his people; let Sereswatì, the goddess of liberal arts, be adored by all readers of the Véda; and may Siva, with an azure neck and red locks, eternally potent and self-existing, avert from me the pain of another birth in this perishable world, the seat of crimes and of punishment.   *[All go out.]*

24
Gítagóvinda by Jayadéva (1789)

[On 8 December 1791 Jones read 'On the Mystical Poetry of the Persians and Hindus' to the Asiatic Society. It was a significant occasion, despite the fact that only eighteen members were present, as Jones became the first European scholar to establish authoritatively the link between the Vedanta system and that of the Sufis, viewing their mystical theology as completely compatible with orthodox Christian teaching. Introducing Jayadéva's lyric poem at the conclusion of his address, Jones writes:

> Let us return to the *Hindus*, among whom we now find the same emblematical theology, which *Pythagoras* admired and adopted. The loves of CRISHNA and RADHA, or the reciprocal attraction between the divine goodness and the human soul, are told at large in the tenth book of the *Bhágavat*, and are the subject of a little *Pastoral Drama*, entitled *Gítagóvinda*: it was the work of JAYADÉVA, who flourished, it is said before CALIDAS, and was born, as he tells us himself, in CENDULI, which many believe to be in *Calinga*: but, since there is a town of a similar name in *Berdwan*, the natives of it insist that the finest lyric poet of *India* was their countryman, and celebrate in honour of him an annual jubilee, passing a whole night in representing his drama, and in singing his beautiful songs. After having translated the *Gítagóvinda* word for word, I reduced my translation to the form, in which it is now exhibited; omitting only those passages, which are too luxuriant and too bold for an *European* taste, and the prefatory ode on the ten incarnations of VISHNU, with which you have been presented on another occasion: the phrases in *Italicks*, are the *burdens* of the several songs; and you may be assured, that not a single image or idea has been added by the translator'. (*Works*, IV.234–5.)

In 1792 Jones's translation of the *Gítagóvinda* was published in the third volume of *Asiatick Researches*. The poem's blend of mystic and sensual love had an immediate and pronounced effect, especially on the Continent. Goethe wrote: 'What struck me as remarkable are the extremely varied motives by which an extremely simple subject is made endless', (*Correspondence between Goethe and Schiller*, trans. L. D. Schmitz, 2 vols. (London, 1909), II.395.) Raymond Schwab describes the rapturous reception of the work by the German Romantics: 'Jones's *Gitagovinda* had fired Goethe's imagination even before it was retranslated into German by von Dahlberg, and his enthusiasm spread to Jena. For Schelling this poem of mystical love became an important event; he interpreted it as laying open the essential mystery of the human spirit, a mystery which then supposedly passed from India to Egypt, to Eleusis, and finally to an esoteric gospel known to St John and St Paul', (*The Oriental Renaissance*, p.206). Herder, Novalis and Friedrich Schlegel were also under its spell.

Jones saw the twelfth-century Sanskrit *Gítagóvinda* as an example of poetry which 'consists almost wholly of a mystical religious allegory, though it seems on a transient view to contain only the sentiments of a wild and voluptuous libertinism', *Works*, IV.235. Despite this Jones removed some of the most explicit eroticism, fearing to offend a European audience which he earnestly wished to delight. At home it would seem from the reviews that the extent of Jones's bowdlerizing was fairly well-judged, the *Monthly Review* observing that he did not spiritualize it, and that his 'extremely sweet and delicate' style effectively conveyed the Indian imagery. (13, Apr. 1794, 574). The copy-text is the 1799 collected edition, collated with *Asiatick Researches*.]

GÍTAGÓVINDA

OR

THE SONGS OF JAYADÉVA.

'The firmament is obscured by clouds; the woodlands are black with *Tamála*-trees; that youth, who roves in the forest, will be fearful in the gloom of night: go, my daughter; bring the wanderer home to my rustick mansion.' Such was the command of NANDA, the fortunate herdsman; and hence arose the love of RÁDHÁ and MÁDHAVA, who sported on the bank of *Yamunà*, or hastened eagerly to the secret bower.

If thy soul be delighted with the remembrance of HERI, or sensible to the raptures of love, listen to the voice of JAYADÉVA, whose notes are both sweet and brilliant. O THOU, who reclinest on the bosom of CAMALÁ; whose ears flame with gems, and whose locks are embellished with sylvan flowers; thou,   10 from whom the day star derived his effulgence, who slewest the venombreathing CÁLIYA, who beamedst, like a sun, on the tribe of YADU, that flourished like a lotos; thou, who sittest on the plumage of GARURA, who, by subduing demons, gavest exquisite joy to the assembly of immortals; thou,

---

1   *Tamála-trees* With black bark, scented leaves, and white blossoms, these trees are associated with love-trysts and Krishna.

5   *RÁDHÁ* Rādhā (success) is the beautiful daughter of Krishna's foster-father, Nanda. Whereas the tradition of Krishna sporting with the *gopīs* (milkmaids) is an extremely old one, it is only with this work of Jayadéva that Rādhā emerges as a fully developed figure allegorizing the god's union with *prakṛti* (Nature), see Kinsley, *Hindu Goddesses*, pp.82–3.

5   *MÁDHAVA* An epithet of Krishna, meaning 'honey-like' and 'vernal'. Krishna, the embodiment of love and divine joy, the destroyer of sin, is the eighth avatar (incarnation) of Vishnu. He was born at Mathura between Delhi and Agra to Devakī, the sister of the cruel king Kamsa. In response to the prediction of a celestial sage that Kamsa would be killed by his nephew, the king murdered six of Devakī's children. Krishna escaped by being secretly exchanged for the daughter of a simple herdsman, Nanda. Thus he was brought up as a cowherd, delighting in the pastoral accomplishments of flute playing and seduction. Krishna also demonstrated his resourceful bravery in defeating demons and monsters, ultimately killing Kamsa to rule the kingdom, see 'A Hymn to Lacshmi', ll.91–108, and below l.113.

5   *Yamuná* The Jumna river where Krishna teases the bathing milkmaids, and subdues the 'venom-breathing' serpent Kāliya, see ll.11–12.

7   *HERI* Hari ('the remover') is a name for both Vishnu and his earthly incarnation, Krishna.

9   *CAMALÁ* Kamalā means Lotus-Lady, one of the epithets of Lakshmī, consort of Vishnu; *PEDMÁ* (Padmā) in l.18, with the same meaning, is another, cf. 'A Hymn to Lacshmí', ll.54–6 and n.

12   *the tribe of YADU* Krishna is a descendant of Yadu, and often termed Yadunandana (Son of the Yadus), or Yadava (Sprung from Yadu).

13   *GARURA* Garuda (Wings of Speech) is the fabulous bird, half vulture, half man, on which Vishnu rides.

for whom the daughter of JANACA was decked in gay apparel, by whom DÚSHANA was overthrown; thou, whose eye sparkles like the water-lily, who calledst three worlds into existence; thou, by whom the rocks of *Mandar* were easily supported, who sippest nectar from the radiant lips of PEDMÁ, as the fluttering *Chacóra* drinks the moon-beams; *be victorious*, O HERI, *lord of conquest.*

RÁDHÁ sought him long in vain, and her thoughts were confounded by the fever of desire: she roved in the vernal morning among the twining *Vásantis* covered with soft blossoms, when a damsel thus addressed her with youthful hilarity: 'The gale, that has wantoned round the beautiful clove-plants, breathes now from the hills of *Maylaya*; the circling arbours resound with the notes of the *Cócil* and the murmurs of honey-making swarms. Now the hearts of damsels, whose lovers travel at a distance, are pierced with anguish; while the blossoms of *Bacul* are conspicuous among the flowrets covered with bees. The *Tamála*, with leaves dark and odorous, claims a tribute from the musk, which it vanquishes; and the clustering flowers of the *Palása* resemble the nails of CÁMA, with which he rends the hearts of the young. The full-blown *Césara* gleams like the sceptre of the world's monarch, Love; and the pointed thyrse of the *Cétaca* resembles the darts, by which lovers are

---

15 *the daughter of JANACA* Janaka's daughter Sītā (Furrow) was Vishnu's consort in his seventh incarnation, as Rāma. A model of wifely devotion, Sītā is a manifestation of Lakshmī.

16 *DÚSHANA* Dūshana was one of the generals of Rāvana, the demon-king of Ceylon, who captured Rāma's wife, Sītā. Rāma successfully led an expedition to rescue Sītā and destroy the demon.

16–20 The references here are to the creation myth of the churning of the ocean, cf. 'A Hymn to Lacshmí', ll.37–72; 'A Hymn to Indra', ll.69–83.

19 *the fluttering Chacóra drinks the moon-beams* A bird of the partridge family, which, according to tradition, drinks the moonlight.

22 *Vásantis* a species of spring jasmine, see *Sacontalá*, I.164n.

26 *cócil* cuckoo, the bird of spring in the Indian as in the English tradition, cf. *Sacontalá*, IV.232.

28 *bacul* 'a fragrant tree said to blossom only when sprinkled with nectar from a young woman's mouth', see Lee Siegel, *Sacred and Profane Dimensions of Love in Indian Traditions as Exemplified in the Gítagóvinda of Jayadéva* (Delhi: OUP, 1978), p.245.

30–45 Many of these flowers and perfumed blossoms are sacred to Kāma, god of love, cf. the notes to 'A Hymn to Camdeo', ll.50–60, but in the west Herder was one of the first to recognize that for the Hindu a flower can represent a symbol of cosmology: '*Eine schaffende, erhaltende und zerstörende Kraft* war die Grundlage dieses Systems . . . Jede Blume lehrt uns dieses System, (die Indier liebten die Blumen) und was jene lehrten, bestätigen die Blumen des Himmels, Sonnensysteme, Milchstrassen, alle Theile des Universums:' *Denkmale der Vorwelt* XVI.78, quoted in A. Leslie Wilson, *A Mythical Image: The Ideal of India in German Romanticism* (Durham, NC, 1964), p.60.

30–31 *clustering flowers of the Palása resemble the nails of CÁMA* A name for the flame tree, or *kimśuka* (*Butea frondosa*); in Sanskrit poetry the flowers are often compared to a lover's nailmarks scratched on his mistress, see *Kumārasambhava* 3.29. According to Jones this venerable tree 'gave its name to the memorable *plain* called *Plássey*', 'Botanical Observations', *Works*, V.146.

32 *Césara* The *keśara* is a variety of crocus.

33 *Cétaca* The *ketakī* has fragrant white spikey flowers.

wounded. See the bunches of *Pátali*-flowers filled with bees, like the quiver of SMARA full of shafts; while the tender blossom of the *Caruna* smiles to see the whole world laying shame aside. The far-scented *Mádhaví* beautifies the trees, round which it twines; and the fresh *Mallicà* seduces with rich perfume even the hearts of hermits; while the *Amra*-tree with blooming tresses is embraced by the gay creeper *Atimucta*, and the blue streams of *Yamunà* wind round the groves of *Vrindávan. In this charming season, which gives pain to*   40 *separated lovers, young* HERI *sports and dances with a company of damsels.* A breeze, like the breath of love, from the fragrant flowers of the *Cétaca*, kindles every heart, whilst it perfumes the woods with the dust, which it shakes from the *Mallicá* with half-opened buds; and the *Cócila* bursts into song, when he sees the blossoms glistening on the lovely *Rasála.*'

The jealous RÁDHÁ gave no answer; and, soon after, her officious friend, perceiving the foe of MURA in the forest eager for the rapturous embraces of the herdsmen's daughters, with whom he was dancing, thus again addressed his forgotten mistress: 'With a garland of wild flowers descending even to the yellow mantle, that girds his azure limbs, distinguished by smiling cheeks   50 and by ear-rings, that sparkle, as he plays, HERI *exults in the assemblage of amorous damsels.* One of them presses him with her swelling breast, while she warbles with exquisite melody. Another, affected by a glance from his eye, stands meditating on the lotos of his face. A third, on pretence of whispering a secret in his ear, approaches his temples, and kisses them with ardour. One seizes his mantle and draws him towards her, pointing to the bower on the banks of *Yamunà*, where elegant *Vanjulas* interweave their branches. He applauds another, who dances in the sportive circle, whilst her bracelets ring, as she beats time with her palms. Now he caresses one, and kisses another, smiling on a third with complacency; and now he chases her, whose beauty   60 has most allured him. Thus the wanton HERI frolicks, in the season of sweets, among the maids of *Vraja*, who rush to his embraces, as if he were Pleasure itself assuming a human form; and one of them, under a pretext of hymning his divine perfections, whispers in his ear: 'Thy lips, my beloved, are nectar.'

---

34 *Pátali-flowers* 'exquisitely fragrant, preferred by bees to all other flowers, and compared by the poets to the quiver of CÁMADÉVA', 'Botanical Observations', *Works*, V.134.

34–5 *the quiver of* SMARA Smara (Remembrance) is one of Kāma's many titles.

37 *fresh Mallicá seduces with its rich perfume even the hearts of hermits* '*Bráhmens* in the west of *India* distinguish this flower by the word *Castúri*, or *musk*, on account of its very rich odour', 'Botanical Observations', *Works*, V.73–4.

39 *Atimucta* The *Bengal Banisteria*, a fragrant climbing plant, beloved of Sacontalá, see 'Botanical Observations', *Works*, V.124.

47 *the foe of* MURA Mura is a demon associated with another demon named Naraka in the *Mahābhārata* (I.59ff.) Naraka imprisoned the celestial maidens in the city of the *asuras* (demons/anti-gods) called Prāg-jyotisa (City of Ancient Light), where they were guarded by Mura. Vishnu/Krishna rescued the maidens and destroyed the demons.

57 *Vanjulas* groves of reed or cane.

62 *Vraja* The village in which Rādhā and Krishna grow up, surrounded by the idyllic bowers and woods of Vrndāvana.

RÁDHÁ remains in the forest; but resenting the promiscuous passion of HERI, and his neglect of her beauty, which he once thought superior, she retires to a bower of twining plants, the summit of which resounds with the humming of swarms engaged in their sweet labours; and there, falling languid on the ground, she thus addresses her female companion. '*Though he take recreation in my absence, and smile on all around him, yet my soul remembers him,* whose beguiling reed modulates a tune sweetened by the nectar of his quivering lip, while his ear sparkles with gems, and his eye darts amorous glances; Him, whose locks are decked with the plumes of peacocks resplendent with many-coloured moons, and whose mantle gleams like a dark blue cloud illumined with rain-bows; Him, whose graceful smile gives new lustre to his lips, brilliant and soft as a dewy leaf, sweet and ruddy as the blossom of *Bandhujíva*, while they tremble with eagerness to kiss the daughters of the herdsmen; Him, who disperses the gloom with beams from the jewels, which decorate his bosom, his wrists, and his ankles, on whose forehead shines a circlet of sandal-wood, which makes even the moon contemptible, when it sails through irradiated clouds; Him, whose ear-rings are formed of entire gems in the shape of the fish *Macar* on the banners of Love; even the yellow-robed God, whose attendants are the chiefs of deities, of holy men, and of demons; Him, who reclines under a gay *Cadamba*-tree; who formerly delighted me, while he gracefully waved in the dance, and all his soul sparkled in his eye. My weak mind thus enumerates his qualities; and, though offended, strives to banish offence. What else can it do? It cannot part with its affection for CRISHNA, whose love is excited by other damsels, and who sports in the absence of RÁDHÁ. *Bring, O friend*, that vanquisher of the demon CÉSI, *to sport with* me, who am repairing to a secret bower, who look timidly on all sides, who meditate with amorous fancy on his divine transfiguration. Bring him, whose discourse was once composed of the gentlest words, to converse with me, who am bashful on his first approach, and express my thoughts with a smile sweet as honey. Bring him, who formerly slept on my bosom, to recline with me on a green bed of leaves

70

80

90

69–112   Rādhā's lament and appeal to her friend is also a poignant celebration of the majestic and sensual beauty of Krishna; love in separation (*viraha*) is the emotion that dominates the *Gītagōvinda*.

77   *sweet and ruddy as the blossom of Bandhujíva*   This crimson-scarlet flower 'is often mentioned by the best *Indian* poets; but the *Pandits* are strangely divided in opinion concerning the plant, which the ancients knew by that name. RÁDHÁCANT brought me, as the famed *Bandhúca*, some flowers of the *Doubtful* PAPAVER; and his younger brother RAMÁCANT produced on the following day the *Scarlet* IXORA, with a beautiful couplet in which it is named *Bandhúca*: soon after SERVÓRU showed me a book, in which it is said to have the vulgar name *Dóp'hariya*, or *Meridian*', 'Botanical Observations', *Works*, V.80–1.

82   *the fish Macar*   The *makara* is the dolphin/shark-like emblem on the red banner of Kāma, see 1.166 below, and 'A Hymn to Camdeo', 1.19.

84   The *kadamba* has beautiful orange blossoms, the fragrance of which the ancient Indians, according to Jones, compared to the scent of new wine, see 'Botanical Observations on Select Indian Plants', *Works*, V.90. It was from such a tree that Krishna watched the naked milkmaids as they came to claim their stolen clothes.

just gathered, while his lip sheds dew, and my arms enfold him. Bring him, who has attained the perfection of skill in love's art, whose hand used to press these firm and delicate spheres, to play with me, whose voice rivals that of the *Cócil*, and whose tresses are bound with waving blossoms. Bring him, who formerly drew me by the locks to his embrace, to repose with me, whose   100
feet tinkle, as they move, with rings of gold and of gems, whose loosened zone sounds, as it falls; and whose limbs are slender and flexible as the creeping plant. That God, whose cheeks are beautified by the nectar of his smiles, whose pipe drops in his ecstasy, I saw in the grove encircled by the damsels of *Vraja*, who gazed on him askance from the corners of their eyes: I saw him in the grove with happier damsels, yet the sight of him delighted me. Soft is the gale, which breathes over yon clear pool, and expands the cluster-ing blossoms of the voluble *Asóca*; soft, yet grievous to me in the absence of the foe of MADHU. Delightful are the flowers of *Amra*-trees on the mountain-top, while the murmuring bees pursue their voluptuous toil; delightful, yet   110
afflicting to me, O friend, in the absence of the youthful CÉSAVA.'

Meantime the destroyer of CANSA, having brought to his remembrance the amiable RÁDHÁ, forsook the beautiful damsels of *Vraja*: he sought her in all parts of the forest; his old wound from love's arrow bled again; he repented of his levity, and, seated in a bower near the bank of *Yamunà*, the blue daughter of the sun, thus poured forth his lamentation.

'She is departed – she saw me, no doubt, surrounded by the wanton shepherdesses; yet, conscious of my fault, I durst not intercept her flight. *Wo*

105–106 *I saw him in the grove with happier damsels, yet the sight of him delighted me*
Kinsley indicates that the Bengal Vaisnava theologians argue the superiority of Rādhā's illicit love to conjugal love as a devotional metaphor. 'Married love . . . functions according to rights and obligations . . . including sexual gratification. [It] is characterized by *kāma* (sexual lust), while Rādhā's love . . . is characterized by *prema* selfless love for the beloved)', *Hindu Goddesses*, p.89. Such theological thinking is remakably close that of medieval European apologists of *fin' amor* like Andreas Capellanus. See also notes to ll. 112–50, and 170–93 below.

108   *the voluble Asóca* 'The vegetable world scarce exhibits a richer sight than an *Asóca*-tree in full bloom . . . JAYADÉVA gives it the epithet *voluble*: the *Sanscrit* name will, I hope, be retained by botanists, as it perpetually occurs in the old *Indian* poems and in treatises on religious rites'. 'Botanical Observations', *Works*, V.113. Asoca blossoms and leaves are also used in the worship of Kāma, see *Kāmasūtra* 1.4.42. In recognition of Jones's botanical research, this beautiful tree was named by William Roxburgh (1751–1815) the *Jonesia asoca*, see *Asiatick Researches*, 4.355.

109   *the foe of MADHU* Vishnu/Krishna dived to the bottom of the ocean to restore the Vedas stolen by the two *dānava* (genii) Madhu and Kaitabha.

Amra-trees Mango trees.

111   CÉSAVA The Long-Haired One, Vishnu as Krishna.

112   *the destroyer of CANSA* Kamsa is the wicked uncle of Krishna, see note to 1.5 above.

112–50 'the Kṛṣṇa of the *Gítagóvinda*, unlike the *Purānic* Kṛṣṇa, suffers in his separation from Rādhā; he serves her, bows down in obeisance to her, worships her, and by this suffering Kṛṣṇa is more humanized,' *Sacred and Profane*, p.39–40. This, as Siegel makes clear, not only reflects the literary tradition of 'courtly' love, but also the cult of Devī, favoured in Bengal, whose adherents worshipped the power (*sákti*) of the feminine principle, cf. Jones's Argument to 'Two Hymns to Pracriti'.

is me! she feels a sense of injured honour, and is departed in wrath. How will
she conduct herself? How will she express her pain in so long a separation?   120
What is wealth to me? What are numerous attendants? What are the
pleasures of the world? What joy can I receive from a heavenly abode? I seem
to behold her face with eye-brows contracting themselves through her just
resentment: it resembles a fresh lotos, over which two black bees are
fluttering: I seem, so present is she to my imagination, even now to caress her
with eagerness. Why then do I seek her in this forest? Why do I lament
without cause? O slender damsel, anger, I know, has torn thy soft bosom;
but whither thou art retired, I know not. How can I invite thee to return?
Thou art seen by me, indeed, in a vision; thou seemest to move before me.
Ah! why dost thou not rush, as before, to my embrace? Do but forgive me: 130
never again will I commit a similar offence. Grant me but a sight of thee, O
lovely RÁDHICÁ, for my passion torments me. I am not the terrible MAHÉSA: a
garland of water-lilies with subtil threads decks my shoulders; not serpents
with twisted folds: the blue petals of the lotos glitter on my neck; not the
azure gleam of poison; powdered sandal-wood is sprinkled on my limbs; not
pale ashes: O God of Love, mistake me not for MAHÁDÉVA. Wound me not
again; approach me not in anger; I love already but too passionately; yet I
have lost my beloved. Hold not in thy hand that shaft barbed with an *Amra-*
flower! Brace not thy bow, thou conqueror of the world! Is it valour to slay
one who faints? My heart is already pierced by arrows from RÁDHÁ's eyes,   140
black and keen as those of an antelope; yet mine eyes are not gratified with
her presence. Her eyes are full of shafts; her eye-brows are bows; and the tips
of her ears are silken strings: thus armed by ANANGA, the God of Desire, she
marches, herself a goddess, to ensure his triumph over the vanquished
universe. I meditate on her delightful embrace, on the ravishing glances
darted from her eye, on the fragrant lotos of her mouth, on her nectar-

---

132 *O lovely RÁDHICÁ* In his longing for his favourite, Krishna calls her 'Rādhikā', the
White Light. 'From Rādikā, the white light, impregnated by Krishna, the black light, were
born Universal-Intellect (Mahat-tattva), Basic-Nature (Pradhāna), and the Embryo-of-
Splendour (Hiranya-garbha), which is the principle and totality of all subtle bodies. The
love [of Krishna and Rādhā] is an allegory of the union of Supreme-Man (*purusa*) and
Nature (*prakṛti*), from which the universe gradually arose', Svāmī Karapātrī, 'Krsna
tattva', *Siddhānta*, V (1944–5), 113–34.

132–6 Krishna in his mad passion tries to assure the love-god that he is not 'the terrible
MAHÉSA' (Maheśvara, the transcendent divinity, Śiva) who responded to Kāma's love-dart
with celestial wrath, see 'A Hymn to Camdeo', ll.65ff.; 'The Hymn to Durgā', II.3.8–III.2.8.
He asks Kāma not to mistake his love tokens of blue lotus blossoms and powdered sandal-
wood for the blue poison which Śiva drank, and the pale ashes of the ascetic, see 'A Hymn
to Indra', ll.80–1. 'Śiva . . . exemplifies the path of sublimation: through chastity the ascetic
is able to generate *tapas* (the power of asceticism) as a great creative force . . . Krṣna
exemplifies another path – desire quenched by its fulfilment', Siegel, *Sacred and Profane*,
p.78.

136 *O God of Love, mistake me not for MAHÁDÉVA* Krishna insists that he is not
Mahādeva (Transcendent God, another of Śiva's titles), but the honeyed Mádhava, the foe
of the demon Madhu. Jayadéva plays upon the similarity of these names.

dropping speech; on her lips ruddy as the berries of the *Bimba*; yet even my fixed meditation on such an assemblage of charms increases, instead of alleviating, the misery of separation.'

The damsel, commissioned by RÁDHÁ, found the disconsolate God under   150
an arbour of spreading *Vániras* by the side of *Yamunà*; where, presenting herself gracefully before him, she thus described the affliction of his beloved:

'She despises essence of sandal-wood, and even by moon-light sits brooding over her gloomy sorrow; she declares the gale of *Malaya* to be venom, and the sandal-trees, through which it has breathed, to have been the haunt of serpents. *Thus*, O MÁDHAVA, *is she afflicted in thy absence with the pain, which love's dart has occasioned: her soul is fixed on thee.* Fresh arrows of desire are continually assailing her, and she forms a net of lotos-leaves as armour for her heart, which thou alone shouldst fortify. She makes her own bed of the arrows darted by the flowery-shafted God; but, when she hoped   160
for thy embrace, she had formed for thee a couch of soft blossoms. Her face is like a water-lily, veiled in the dew of tears, and her eyes appear like moons eclipsed, which let fall their gathered nectar through pain caused by the tooth of the furious dragon. She draws thy image with musk in the character of the Deity with five shafts, having subdued the *Macar*, or horned shark, and holding an arrow tipped with an *Amra*-flower; thus she draws thy picture, and worships it. At the close of every sentence, "O MÁDHAVA," she exclaims, "at thy feet am I fallen, and in thy absence even the moon, though it be a vase full of nectar, inflames my limbs." Then, by the power of imagination, she figures thee standing before her; thee, who art not easily   170
attained: she sighs, she smiles, she mourns, she weeps, she moves from side to side, she laments and rejoices by turns. Her abode is a forest; the circle of her female companions is a net; her sighs are flames of fire kindled in a thicket; herself (alas! through thy absence) is become a timid roe; and Love is the tiger, who springs on her like YAMA, the Genius of Death. So emaciated is her beautiful body, that even the light garland, which waves over her bosom, she thinks a load. *Such, O bright-haired God, is* RÁDHÁ *when thou art absent.* If powder of sandal-wood finely levigated be moistened and applied to her breasts, she starts, and mistakes it for poison. Her sighs form a breeze long extended, and burn her like the flame, which reduced CANDARPA to ashes. She   180
throws around her eyes, like blue water-lilies with broken stalks, dropping lucid streams. Even her bed of tender leaves appear in her sight like a kindled fire. The palm of her hand supports her aching temple, motionless as the crescent rising at eve. "HERI, HERI," thus in silence she meditates on thy name, as if her wish were gratified, and she were dying through thy absence.

---

164   *the tooth of the furious dragon*   Ráhu's dragon-like head that causes eclipses by attempting to eat the moon, see note to 1.54 of 'A Hymn to Súrya'.

169–92   The symptoms of Rádhá's love-passion as detailed by her friend would be perfectly familiar to a twelfth-century troubadour in Provence; indeed *fin' amor* itself might well have been of Oriental origin, introduced via Mozarabic Spain.

She rends her locks; she pants; she laments inarticulately; she trembles; she pines; she muses; she moves from place to place; she closes her eyes; she falls; she rises again; she faints; in such a fever of love, she may live, O celestial physician, if thou administer the remedy; but, shouldst Thou be unkind, her malady will be desperate. Thus, O divine healer, by the nectar of thy love   190
must RÁDHÁ be restored to health; and, if thou refuse it, thy heart must be harder than the thunderstone. Long has her soul pined, and long has she been heated with sandal-wood, moon-light, and water-lilies, with which others are cooled; yet she patiently and in secret meditates on Thee, who alone canst relieve her. Shouldst thou be inconstant, how can she, wasted as she is to a shadow, support life a single moment? How can she, who lately could not endure thy absence even an instant, forbear sighing now, when she looks with half-closed eyes on the *Rasála* with bloomy branches, which remind her of the vernal season, when she first beheld thee with rapture?'

'Here I have chosen my abode: go quickly to RÁDHÁ; soothe her with my   200
message, and conduct her hither.' So spoke the foe of MADHU to the anxious damsel, who hastened back, and thus addressed her companion: 'Whilst a sweet breeze from the hills of *Malaya* comes wafting on his plumes the young God of Desire; while many a flower points his extended petals to pierce the bosom of separated lovers, *the Deity crowned with sylvan blossoms, laments, O friend, in thy absence.* Even the dewy rays of the moon burn him; and, as the shaft of love is descending, he mourns inarticulately with increasing distraction. When the bees murmur softly, he covers his ears; misery sits fixed in his heart, and every returning night adds anguish to anguish. He quits his radiant palace for the wild forest, where he sinks on a bed of cold   210
clay, and frequently mutters thy name. In yon bower, to which the pilgrims of love are used to repair, he meditates on thy form, repeating in silence some enchanting word, which once dropped from thy lips, and thirsting for the nectar which they alone can supply. Delay not, O loveliest of women; follow the lord of thy heart: behold, he seeks the appointed shade, bright with the ornaments of love, and confident of the promised bliss. *Having bound his locks with forest-flowers, he hastens to yon arbour, where a soft gale breathes over the banks of* Yamunà: there, again pronouncing thy name, he modulates his divine reed. Oh! with what rapture doth he gaze on the golden dust, which the breeze shakes from expanded blossoms; the breeze, which   220
has kissed thy cheek! With a mind, languid as a dropping wing, feeble as a trembling leaf, he doubtfully expects thy approach, and timidly looks on the path which thou must tread. Leave behind thee, O friend, the ring which tinkles on thy delicate ankle, when thou sportest in the dance: hastily cast over thee thy azure mantle, and run to the gloomy bower. The reward of thy speed, O thou who sparklest like lightning, will be to shine on the blue

---

225–228   *The reward of thy speed . . . fluttering in the air*   According to Siegel, 'Rãhdã's friend urges her to make love to Kṛṣṇa in the "inverse" mode (*viparīta-rata* astride her lover)', *Sacred and Profane*, p.167; cf. ll.251; 351–2; 361 below.

bosom of Murári, which resembles a vernal cloud, decked with a string of pearls like a flock of white water-birds fluttering in the air. Disappoint not, O thou lotos-eyed, the vanquisher of Madhu; accomplish his desire; but go quickly: it is night; and the night also will quickly depart. Again and again he 230 sighs; he looks around; he re-enters the arbour; he can scarce articulate thy sweet name; he again smooths his flowery couch; he looks wild; he becomes frantick; thy beloved will perish through desire. The bright-beamed God sinks in the west, and thy pain of separation may also be removed: the blackness of the night is increased, and the passionate imagination of Góvinda has acquired additional gloom. My address to thee has equalled in length and in sweetness the song of the *Cócila*: delay will make thee miserable, O my beautiful friend. Seize the moment of delight in the place of assignation with the son of Dévaci, who descended from heaven to remove the burdens of the universe; he is a blue gem on the forehead of the three 240 worlds, and longs to sip honey, like the bee, from the fragrant lotos of thy cheek.'

But the solicitous maid, perceiving that Rádhá was unable, through debility, to move from her arbour of flowery creepers, returned to Góvinda, who was himself disordered with love, and thus described her situation.

'*She mourns, O sovereign of the world, in her verdant bower*; she looks eagerly on all sides in hope of thy approach; then, gaining strength from the delightful idea of the proposed meeting, she advances a few steps, and falls languid on the ground. When she rises, she weaves bracelets of fresh leaves; she dresses herself like her beloved, and, looking at herself in sport, exclaims, 250 "Behold the vanquisher of Madhu!" Then she repeats again and again the name of Heri, and, catching at a dark blue cloud, strives to embrace it, saying: "It is my beloved who approaches." Thus, while thou art dilatory, she lies expecting thee; she mourns; she weeps; she puts on her gayest ornaments to receive her lord; she compresses her deep sighs within her bosom; and then, meditating on thee, O cruel, she is drowned in a sea of rapturous imaginations. If a leaf but quiver, she supposes thee arrived; she spreads her couch; she forms in her mind a hundred modes of delight: yet, if thou go not to her bower, she must die this night through excessive anguish.'

By this time the moon spread a net of beams over the groves of *Vrindávan*, 260 and looked like a drop of liquid sandal on the face of the sky, which smiled like a beautiful damsel; while its orb with many spots betrayed, as it were, a consciousness of guilt, in having often attended amorous maids to the loss of their family honour. The moon, with a black fawn couched on its disc,

---

227 *Murári* Krishna, the destroyer of Mura, see above 1.47 and n.
236 *Góvinda* Chief of the cowherds.
239 *son of Dévaci* Devakī is Krishna's mother, the wife of King Vasudeva.
251 '*Behold the vanquisher of Madhu!*' This playful assumption of Krishna's role can be viewed simultaneously as longing for identity with the godhead and desire for a superior coital position.

advanced in its nightly course; but MÁDHAVA had not advanced to the bower of RÁDHÁ, who thus bewailed his delay with notes of varied lamentation.

'The appointed moment is come; but HERI, alas! comes not to the grove. Must the season of my unblemished youth pass thus idly away? *Oh! what refuge can I seek, deluded as I am by the guile of my female adviser?* The God with five arrows has wounded my heart; and I am deserted by Him, for whose sake I have sought at night the darkest recess of the forest. Since my best beloved friends have deceived me, it is my wish to die: since my senses are disordered, and my bosom is on fire, why stay I longer in this world? The coolness of this vernal night gives me pain, instead of refreshment: some happier damsel enjoys my beloved; whilst I, alas! am looking at the gems in my bracelets, which are blackened by the flames of my passion. My neck, more delicate than the tenderest blossom, is hurt by the garland, that encircles it: flowers are, indeed, the arrows of Love, and he plays with them cruelly. I make this wood my dwelling: I regard not the roughness of the *Vétas*-trees; but the destroyer of MADHU holds me not in his remembrance! Why comes he not to the bower of bloomy *Vanjulas*, assigned for our meeting? Some ardent rival, no doubt, keeps him locked in her embrace: or have his companions detained him with mirthful recreations? Else why roams he not through the cool shades? Perhaps, the heart-sick lover is unable through weakness to advance even a step!' – So saying, she raised her eyes; and, seeing her damsel return silent and mournful, unaccompanied by MÁDHAVA, she was alarmed even to phrensy; and, as if she actually beheld him in the arms of a rival, she thus described the vision which overpowered her intellect.

'Yes; in habiliments becoming the war of love, and with tresses waving like flowery banners, *a damsel, more alluring than* RÁDHÁ, *enjoys the conqueror of* MADHU. Her form is transfigured by the touch of her divine lover; her garland quivers over her swelling bosom; her face like the moon is graced with clouds of dark hair, and trembles, while she quaffs the nectareous dew of his lip; her bright ear-rings dance over her cheeks, which they irradiate; and the small bells on her girdle tinkle as she moves. Bashful at first, she smiles at length on her embracer, and expresses her joy with inarticulate murmurs; while she floats on the waves of desire, and closes her eyes dazzled with the blaze of approaching CÁMA: and now this heroine in love's warfare falls exhausted and vanquished by the resistless MURÁRI, but alas! in my bosom prevails the flame of jealousy, and yon moon, which dispels the sorrow of others, increases mine. See again, where the *foe of* MURA *sports in yon grove on the bank of the* Yamunà! See, how he kisses the lip of my rival,

270

280

290

300

303–15 *See how he kisses the lip of my rival . . . stains it with the ruddy hue of Yácava.* This passage is one of many which Southey carefully copied into his *Commonplace-Book*, and into his copious notes to the *Curse of Kehama* (*Poetical Works* (London, 1838), VIII.301). Southey and the rest of the Romantic writers of Oriental verse tale used Jones's *Works* as a thesaurus of authentic detail and exotic imagery.

and imprints on her forehead an ornament of pure musk, black as the young antelope on the lunar orb! Now, like the husband of Reti, he fixes white blossoms on her dark locks, where they gleam like flashes of lightning among the curled clouds. On her breasts, like two firmaments, he places a string of gems like a radiant constellation: he binds on her arms, graceful as the stalks of the water-lily, and adorned with hands glowing like the petals of its flower, a bracelet of sapphires, which resemble a cluster of bees. Ah! see,   310
how he ties round her waist a rich girdle illumined with golden bells, which seem to laugh, as they tinkle, at the inferior brightness of the leafy garlands, which lovers hang on their bowers to propitiate the God of Desire. He places her soft foot, as he reclines by her side, on his ardent bosom, and stains it with the ruddy hue of *Yávaca*. Say, my friend, why pass I my nights in this tangled forest without joy, and without hope, while the faithless brother of HALADHERA clasps my rival in his arms? Yet why, my companion, shouldst thou mourn, though my perfidious youth has disappointed me? What offence is it of thine, if he sport with a crowd of damsels happier than I?
Mark, how my soul, attracted by his irresistible charms, bursts from its   320
mortal frame, and rushes to mix with its beloved. *She, whom the God enjoys, crowned with sylvan flowers*, sits carelessly on a bed of leaves with Him, whose wanton eyes resemble blue water-lilies agitated by the breeze. She feels no flame from the gales of *Malaya* with Him, whose words are sweeter than the water of life. She derides the shafts of soul-born CÁMA, with Him, whose lips are like a red lotos in full bloom. She is cooled by the moon's dewy beams, while she reclines with Him, whose hands and feet glow like vernal flowers. No female companion deludes her, while she sports with Him, whose vesture blazes like tried gold. She faints not through excess of passion,
while she caresses that youth, who surpasses in beauty the inhabitants of all   330
worlds. O gale, scented with sandal, who breathest love from the regions of the south, be propitious but for a moment: when thou hast brought my beloved before my eyes, thou mayest freely waft away my soul. Love, with eyes like blue water-lilies, again assails me and triumphs; and, while the

---

305   *the husband of* Reti   Kāma, whose wife is Rati, or Sexual Desire.
315   *the ruddy hue of Yávaca*   Lac, frequently applied by women to their lips, palms and soles.
316–17   *the faithless brother of* HALADHERA   A reference to Krishna's elder brother, Bala-Rāma, whose love of wine was as legendary as Krishna's love of women.
320–1   *Mark, how my soul, . . . rushes to mix with its beloved.*   In more philosophical, or rather, theological mood, she pays tribute to the universality of Krishna's mystico-erotic charms for he embodies the seductiveness of divinity. Jones realized that the passionate sexuality of this mysticism had much in common not only with Judaic tradition represented by the *Song of Songs*, but also with that of the Christian mystics such as St Teresa or St John of the Cross.
323   *whose wanton eyes resemble blue water-lilies agitated by the breeze*   The blue lotus. An image which Thomas Moore borrowed and acknowledged in *Lalla Rookh: An Oriental Romance*, (London, 1863), p.65. The notes to this poem contain twenty-three references to Jones's translations and contributions to *Asiatick Researches*.

perfidy of my beloved rends my heart, my female friend is my foe, the cool breeze scorches me like a flame, and the nectar-dropping moon is my poison. Bring disease and death, O gale of *Malaya!* Seize my spirit, O God with five arrows! I ask not mercy from thee: no more will I dwell in the cottage of my father. Receive me in thy azure waves, O sister of YAMA, that the ardour of my heart may be allayed!'

Pierced by the arrows of love, she passed the night in the agonies of despair, and at early dawn thus rebuked her lover, whom she saw lying prostrate before her and imploring her forgiveness.

'Alas! *alas! Go*, MÁDHAVA, *depart, O* CÉSAVA; *speak not the language of guile; follow her, O lotos-eyed God, follow her, who dispels thy care*. Look at his eye half-opened, red with continued waking through the pleasurable night, yet smiling still with affection for my rival! Thy teeth, O cerulean youth, are azure as thy complexion from the kisses, which thou hast imprinted on the beautiful eyes of thy darling graced with dark blue powder; and thy limbs marked with punctures in love's warfare, exhibit a letter of conquest, written on polished sapphires with liquid gold. That broad bosom, stained by the bright lotos of her foot, displays a vesture of ruddy leaves over the tree of thy heart, which trembles within it. The pressure of her lip on thine wounds me to the soul. Ah! how canst thou assert, that we are one, since our sensations differ thus widely? Thy soul, O dark-limbed God, shows its blackness externally. How couldst thou deceive a girl, who relied on thee; a girl who burned in the fever of love? Thou rovest in woods, and females are thy prey: what wonder? Even thy childish heart was malignant; and thou gavest death to the nurse, who would have given thee milk. Since thy tenderness for me, of which these forests used to talk, has now vanished, and since thy breast, reddened by the feet of my rival, glows as if thy ardent passion for her were bursting from it, the sight of thee, O deceiver, makes me (ah! must I say it?) blush at my own affection.'

Having thus inveighed against her beloved, she sat overwhelmed in grief, and silently meditated on his charms; when her damsel softly addressed her.

'He is gone: the light air has wafted him away. What pleasure now, my beloved, remains in thy mansion? *Continue not, resentful woman, thy indignation against the beautiful* MÁDHAVA. Why shouldst thou render vain those round smooth vases, ample and ripe as the sweet fruit of yon *Tála*-tree? How often and how recently have I said: "forsake not the blooming HERI?" Why sittest thou so mournful? Why weepest thou with distraction,

340

350

360

370

---

339 *sister of* YAMA sister of Death, the River Yamunā (Jumna).

351–2; 361 *That broad bosom, stained by the bright lotus of her foot* This indicates that they have adopted a coital posture in which the woman's feet are placed upon the man's chest. For the significance, both sexual and religious, of sexual positions, see Siegel, *Sacred and Profane*, pp.167–9.

358–59 *thou gavest death to the nurse* The infant Krishna killed the demon Putanā, who had been sent by Kansa to suckle the baby at her poisonous breasts.

369–70 *the sweet fruit of yon Tála-tree* The coconut.

when the damsels are laughing around thee? Thou hast formed a couch of soft lotos-leaves: let thy darling charm thy sight, while he reposes on it. Afflict not thy soul with extreme anguish; but attend to my words, which conceal no guile. Suffer CÉSAVA to approach: let him speak with exquisite sweetness, and dissipate all thy sorrows. If thou art harsh to him, who is amiable; if thou art proudly silent, when he deprecates thy wrath with lowly prostrations; if thou showest aversion to him, who loves thee passionately; if, when he bends before thee, thy face be turned contemptuously away; by the same rule of contrariety, the dust of sandal-wood, which thou hast sprinkled, may become poison; the moon, with cool beams, a scorching sun; the fresh dew, a consuming flame; and the sports of love be changed into agony.' 380

MÁDHAVA was not absent long: he returned to his beloved; whose cheeks were heated by the sultry gale of her sighs. Her anger was diminished, not wholly abated; but she secretly rejoiced at his return, while the shades of night also were approaching, she looked abashed at her damsel, while He, with faultering accents, implored her forgiveness.

'Speak but one mild word, and the rays of thy sparkling teeth will dispel the gloom of my fears. My trembling lips, like thirsty *Chacóras*, long to drink the moon-beams of thy cheek. *O my darling, who art naturally so tender-* 390 *hearted, abandon thy causeless indignation. At this moment the flame of desire consumes my heart: Oh! grant me a draught of honey from the lotos of thy mouth.* Or, if thou beest inexorable, grant me death from the arrows of thy keen eyes; make thy arms my chains; and punish me according to thy pleasure. Thou art my life; thou art my ornament; thou art a pearl in the ocean of my mortal birth: oh! be favourable now, and my heart shall eternally be grateful. Thine eyes, which nature formed like blue water-lilies, are become, through thy resentment, like petals of the crimson lotos: oh! tinge with their effulgence these my dark limbs, that they may glow like the shafts of Love tipped with flowers. Place on my head that foot like a fresh 400 leaf, and shade me from the sun of my passion, whose beams I am unable to bear. Spread a string of gems on those two soft globes; let the golden bells of thy zone tinkle, and proclaim the mild edict of love. Say, O damsel with delicate speech, shall I dye red with the juice of *alactaca* those beautiful feet, which will make the full-blown land-lotos blush with shame? Abandon thy doubts of my heart, now indeed fluttering through fear of thy displeasure, but hereafter to be fixed wholly on thee; a heart, which has no room in it for

393–5   *Or, if thou beest inexorable, grant me death from the arrows of thy keen eyes; make thy arms my chains; and punish me according to thy pleasure.*   A modern verse 410 translation reads: 'If you feel enraged at me, Rādhā,/Inflict arrow-wounds with your sharp nails!/Bind me in your arms! Bite me with your teeth!/Or do whatever excites your pleasure!' (Barbara Stoler Miller, *The Gítagóvinda of Jayadéva: Love Song of the Dark Lord* (Delhi: Motilal Banarsidass, 1984), p.111. Jones obviously considered the sado-masochistic aspects of love-making 'too bold for an *European* taste', and Petrarchanized this passage.
404   *the juice of alactaca*   Lac.
405   *the full-blown land-lotus*   Hibiscus.

another: none else can enter it, but Love, the bodiless God. Let him wing his arrows; let him wound me mortally; decline not, O cruel, the pleasure of seeing me expire. Thy face is bright as the moon, though its beams drop the   410
venom of maddening desire: let thy nectareous lip be the charmer, who alone has power to lull the serpent or supply an antidote for his poison. Thy silence afflicts me: oh! speak with the voice of musick, and let thy sweet accents allay my ardour. Abandon thy wrath, but abandon not a lover, who surpasses in beauty the sons of men, and who kneels before thee, O thou most beautiful among women. Thy lips are a *Bandhujiva*-flower; the lustre of the *Madhuca* beams on thy cheek; thine eye outshines the blue lotos; thy nose is a bud of the *Tila*; the *Cunda*-blossom yields to thy teeth: thus the flowery-shafted God borrows from thee the points of his darts, and subdues the universe. Surely, thou descendest from heaven, O slender damsel, attended by a company of   420
youthful goddesses; and all their beauties are collected in thee.'

He spake; and, seeing her appeased by his homage, flew to his bower, clad in a gay mantle. The night now veiled all visible objects; and the damsel thus exhorted RÁDHÁ, while she decked her with beaming ornaments.

'Follow, *gentle* RÁDHICÁ, *follow the foe of* MADHU: his discourse was elegantly composed of sweet phrases; he prostrated himself at thy feet; and he now hastens to his delightful couch by yon grove of branching *Vanjulas*. Bind round thy ankle rings beaming with gems; and advance with mincing steps, like the pearl-fed *Marála*. Drink with ravished ears the soft accents of HERI; and feast on love, while the warbling *Cócilas* obey the mild ordinance   430
of the flower-darting God. Abandon delay: see, the whole assembly of slender plants, pointing to the bower with fingers of young leaves agitated by the gale, make signals for thy departure. Ask those two round hillocks, which receive pure dew-drops from the garland playing on thy neck, and the buds on whose top start aloft with the thought of thy darling; ask, and they will tell, that thy soul is intent on the warfare of love; advance, fervid warrior, advance with alacrity, while the sound of thy tinkling waist-bells shall represent martial musick. Lead with thee some favoured maid; grasp her hand with thine, whose fingers are long and smooth as love's arrows: march; and, with the noise of thy bracelets, proclaim thy approach to the   440
youth, who will own himself thy slave: "She will come; she will exult on beholding me; she will pour accents of delight; she will enfold me with eager arms; she will melt with affection:" Such are his thoughts at this moment: and, thus thinking, he looks through the long avenue; he trembles; he rejoices; he burns; he moves from place to place; he faints, when he sees thee not coming, and falls in his gloomy bower. The night now dresses in habiliments fit for secrecy, the many damsels, who hasten to their places of assignation: she sets off with blackness their beautiful eyes; fixes dark

---

416   *Madhuca*   A honey-coloured spring flower with smooth velvet petals.
418   *Tila*   The sesame flower. *Cunda-blossom*   Jasmine.
429   *the pearl-fed Marála*   A species of flamingo.

Tamála-leaves behind their ears; decks their locks with the deep azure of water-lilies, and sprinkles musk on their panting bosoms. The nocturnal sky, 450 black as the touchstone, tries now the gold of their affection, and is marked with rich lines from the flashes of their beauty, in which they surpass the brightest *Cashmirians.*'

RÁDHÁ, thus incited, tripped through the forest; but shame overpowered her, when, by the light of innumerable gems, on the arms, the feet, and the neck of her beloved, she saw him at the door of his flowery mansion: then her damsel again addressed her with ardent exultation.

'Enter, sweet RÁDHÁ, the bower of HERI: seek delight, O thou, whose bosom laughs with the foretaste of happiness. Enter, sweet RÁDHÁ, the bower graced with a bed of *Asóca* leaves: seek delight, O thou, whose garland leaps 460 with joy on thy breast. Enter, sweet RÁDHÁ, the bower illumined with gay blossoms; seek delight, O thou, whose limbs far excel them in softness. Enter, O RÁDHÁ, the bower made cool and fragrant by gales from the woods of *Malaya*: seek delight, O thou, whose amorous lays are softer than breezes. Enter, O RÁDHÁ, the bower spread with leaves of twining creepers: seek delight, O thou, whose arms have been long inflexible. Enter, O RÁDHÁ, the bower which resounds with the murmur of honey-making bees: seek delight, O thou, whose embrace yields more exquisite sweetness. Enter, O RÁDHÁ, the bower attuned by the melodious band of *Cócilas*: seek delight, O thou, whose lips, which outshine the grains of the pomegranate, are embellished, 470 when thou speakest, by the brightness of thy teeth. Long has he borne thee in his mind: and now, in an agony of desire, he pants to taste nectar from thy lip. Deign to restore thy slave, who will bend before the lotos of thy foot, and press it to his irradiated bosom; a slave, who acknowledges himself bought by thee for a single glance from thy eye, and a toss of thy disdainful eyebrow.'

She ended; and RÁDHÁ with timid joy, darting her eyes on GÓVINDA, while she musically sounded the rings of her ankles and the bells of her zone, entered the mystic bower of her only beloved. *There she beheld her* MÁDHAVA, *who delighted in her alone; who so long had sighed for her embrace; and whose* 480 *countenance then gleamed with excessive rapture*: his heart was agitated by her sight, as the waves of the deep are affected by the lunar orb. His azure breast glittered with pearls of unblemished lustre, like the full bed of the cerulean *Yamuná*, interspersed with curls of white foam. From his graceful waist, flowed a pale yellow robe, which resembled the golden dust of the water-lily, scattered over its blue petals. His passion was inflamed by the glances of her eyes, which played like a pair of water-birds with azure plumage, that sport near a full-blown lotos on a pool in the season of dew. Bright ear-rings, like two suns, displayed in full expansion the flowers of his cheeks and lips, which glistened with the liquid radiance of smiles. His locks, 490 interwoven with blossoms, were like a cloud variegated with moon-beams, and on his forehead shone a circle of odorous oil, extracted from the sandal

of *Malaya*, like the moon just appearing on the dusky horizon; while his whole body seemed in a flame from the blaze of unnumbered gems. Tears of transport gushed in a stream from the full eyes of Rádhá, and their watery glances beamed on her best beloved. Even shame, which before had taken its abode in their dark pupils, was itself ashamed and departed, when the fawn-eyed Rádhá gazed on the brightened face of Crishna, while she passed by the soft edge of his couch, and the bevy of his attendant nymphs, pretending to strike the gnats from their cheeks in order to conceal their smiles, warily   *500*
retired from his bower.

Góvinda, seeing his beloved cheerful and serene, her lips sparkling with smiles, and her eye speaking desire, thus eagerly addressed her; while she carelessly reclined on the leafy bed strewn with soft blossoms.

'Set the lotos of thy foot on this azure bosom; and let this couch be victorious over all, who rebel against love. *Give short rapture, sweet Rádhá, to Náráyán, thy adorer.* I do thee homage; I press with my blooming palms thy feet, weary with so long a walk. O that I were the golden ring, that plays round thy ankle! Speak but one gentle word; bid nectar drop from the bright moon of thy mouth. Since the pain of absence is removed, let me thus   *510*
remove the thin vest that enviously hides thy charms. Blest should I be, if those raised globes were fixed on my bosom, and the ardour of my passion allayed. O! suffer me to quaff the liquid bliss of those lips; restore with their water of life thy slave, who has long been lifeless, whom the fire of separation has consumed. Long have these ears been afflicted, in thy absence, by the notes of the *Cócila*: relieve them with the sound of thy tinkling waist-bells, which yield musick, almost equal to the melody of thy voice. Why are those eyes half closed? Are they ashamed of seeing a youth, to whom thy careless resentment gave anguish? O! let affliction cease: and let ecstasy drown the remembrance of sorrow.'   *520*

In the morning she rose disarrayed, and her eyes betrayed a night without slumber; when the yellow-robed God, who gazed on her with transport, thus meditated on her charms in his heavenly mind: 'Though her locks be diffused at random, though the lustre of her lips be faded, though her garland and zone be fallen from their enchanting stations, and though she hide their places with her hands, looking toward me with bashful silence, yet even thus disarranged, she fills me with extatic delight.' But Rádhá, preparing to array herself, before the company of nymphs could see her confusion, spake thus with exultation to her obsequious lover.

'Place, O son of Yadu, with fingers cooler than sandal-wood, place a   *530*
circlet of musk on this breast, which resembles a vase of consecrated water, crowned with fresh leaves, and fixed near a vernal bower, to propitiate the God of Love. Place, my darling, the glossy powder, which would make the blackest bee envious, on this eye, whose glances are keener than arrows

---

507   *Náráyán*   The spirit of god, (moving on the waters).

darted by the husband of Reti. Fix, O accomplished youth, the two gems, which form part of love's chain in these ears, whence the antelopes of thine eyes may run downwards and sport at pleasure. Place now a fresh circle of musk, black as the lunar spots, on the moon of my forehead; and mix gay flowers on my tresses with a peacock's feathers, in graceful order, that they may wave like the banners of Cáma. Now replace, O tender hearted, the   540
loose ornaments of my vesture; and refix the golden bells of my girdle on their destined station, which resembles those hills, where the God with five shafts, who destroyed Sambar, keeps his elephant ready for battle.'

While she spake, the heart of Yadava triumphed; and, obeying her sportful behests, he placed musky spots on her bosom and forehead, dyed her temples with radiant hues, embellished her eyes with additional blackness, decked her braided hair and her neck with fresh garlands, and tied on her wrists the loosened bracelets, on her ankles the beamy rings, and round her waist the zone of bells, that sounded with ravishing melody.

Whatever is delightful in the modes of musick, whatever is divine in   550
mediations on Vishnu, whatever is exquisite in the sweet art of love, whatever is graceful in the fine strains of poetry, all that let the happy and wise learn from the songs of Jayadéva, whose soul is united with the foot of Náráyan. May that Heri be your support, who expanded himself into an infinity of bright forms, when, eager to gaze with myriads of eyes on the daughter of the ocean, he displayed his great character of the all-pervading deity, by the multiplied reflections of his divine person in the numberless gems on the many heads of the king of serpents, whom he chose for his couch; that Heri, who removing the lucid veil from the bosom of Pedmá, and fixing his eyes on the delicious buds, that grew on it, diverted her attention by declaring that,   560
when she had chosen him as her bridegroom near the sea of milk, the disappointed husband of Pervati drank in despair the venom, which dyed his neck azure!

540–3 *Now replace . . . ready for battle* Siegel's translation of this difficult verse runs as follows: 'Put ornaments, clothes and the jewelled girdle, O good-hearted-one, upon my passionate hips which are firm and beautiful, which are the cave-dwelling of the elephant who is Love!' He is reliant upon a sixteenth-century commentary by Śankara Miśra, 'who explains that Love (the Killer-of-Śambara) is like an elephant in fierceness and strength; her hips possess that cleft in which the powerful elephant of Love resides', *Sacred and Profane*, p.284.

556 *he displayed his great character of the all-pervading deity* Heri (Hari), or Vishnu, represents the pervasive and cohesive principle of the universe.

557 *multiplied reflections* The king of serpents, Śesa, on whom Vishnu sleeps between creations, has hundreds of jewelled heads, which endlessly reflect the god, cf. 'A Hymn to Lacshmí', ll.65–72.

559 *Pedmá* Padmā is Lakshmī who appears at the time of the churning of the ocean of milk, see 'A Hymn to Náráyena', ll.55–7; 'A Hymn to Lacshmí', ll.53–74.

562 *the disappointed husband of Pervati* Jayadeva playfully casts Śiva (the husband of Pārvatī) in the role of a jealous rival, envious of Vishnu with the fragrant Lotus-lady Lakshmī, and taking poison in despair (whereas Śiva actually drank the poison in a selfless act of protecting creation from its ill effects, cf. 'A Hymn to Indra', ll.80–1).

ESSAYS

25

Essay on the Poetry of the Eastern Nations (1772)

[This essay, significant both in terms of the history of criticism and in terms of modern comparative and Orientalist studies, laments the tired classicism of contemporary European poetry, recommending the study of Oriental literature as a source of image and inspiration. Jones's consideration of the influence of climate upon the fertility of the Oriental imagination, and his description of Persian and Arab cultures as differing cultures of poetry (the former being more sophisticated and urbane, the latter representing a more primitive but nonetheless dynamic culture of untutored bardic genius and noble savagery) reflect an eighteenth-century Enlightenment relativism. In his emphasis upon the primacy of the imagination, however, Jones is a true precursor of the Romantics. His desire to revive the pastoral tradition involved not faint shepherds but full-blooded Bedouin, and in his attempt to inject a certain primitive energy and a basic reality into the genre he anticipates Wordsworth's 'Preface to *Lyrical Ballads*'.

Jones's panegyric on the Arabs marks an attempt to compensate for the relatively low prestige of Arabic culture in Europe. His rose-tinted picture betrays a certain ignorance of actual conditions within a country like the Yemen, but here, and in his translation of the *Mu'allaqāt*, Jones is rewriting pre-Islamic literature in terms easily assimilable to his Occidental audience – thus his emphasis upon the genre of pastoral, which, he asserts, is alive and well, and living in Arabia. In 1762, at the age of sixteen, Jones had composed 'Arcadia, A Pastoral Poem', which contrasted the opposing virtues of polished elegance and unadorned simplicity in the pastoral genre. A decade later Jones is transposing the neo-classical *locus amoenus* from an Arcadian 'Golden-Age' to an Arabian 'present-time'. Some forty years before Byron, acting on the 'oracular' advice of Mme De Staël, was to advise his friend, Thomas Moore, to 'Stick to the East', this essay indicates the ingredients by means of which a succeeding generation of poets were successfully to generate popularity and hard cash from an 'orientalizing' public. The copy text is 1772, with variants noted from 1799.]

On the poetry of the Eastern nations.

I am not a little afraid, lest the reader should form an unfavourable idea of the *Eastern poetry*, from the preceding specimens of it; and lest, if the faults of the translator be imputed to the pieces themselves, I should have injured my cause, instead of supporting it: I will, therefore, endeavour in this essay to efface any impressions, that may have been made to the disadvantage of the *Asiatick* poets; and in the course of my argument I will avoid, as much as I am able, a repetition of the remarks, that were made in a former treatise on the same subject,[1] which I wrote a few years ago in a foreign language, for the use of an amiable Monarch, who admires true genius, in what country soever it is found: though in some places, I fear, I shall be obliged to produce the same observations, and to illustrate them by the same examples.

It is certain (to say no more) that the poets of *Asia* have as much genius as ourselves; and, if it be shown not only that they have more leisure to improve it, but that they enjoy some peculiar advantages over us, the natural conclusion, I think, will be, that their productions must be excellent in their kind: to set this argument in a clear light, I shall describe, as concisely as possible, the manners of the *Arabs*, *Persians*, *Indians*, and *Turks*, the four principal nations, that profess the religion of *Mahomet*.

Arabia, I mean that part of it, which we call the *Happy*,[2] and which the *Asiaticks* know by the name of *Yemen*, seems to be the only country in the world, in which we can properly lay the scene of pastoral poetry; because no nation at this day can vie with the *Arabians* in the delightfulness of their climate, and the simplicity of their manners. There is a valley, indeed, to the north *Indostan*, called *Cashmere*,[3] which, according to an account written by a native of it, is a perfect garden, exceedingly fruitful, and watered by a thousand rivulets: but when its inhabitants were subdued by the stratagem of a *Mogul* prince, they lost their happiness with their liberty, and *Arabia* retained its old title without any rival to dispute it. These are not the fancies of a poet: the beauties of *Yemen* are proved by the concurrent testimony of all travellers, by the descriptions of it in all the writings of *Asia*, and by the nature and situation of the country itself, which lies between the eleventh and fifteenth degrees of northern latitude, under a serene sky, and exposed to the

---

1. *a former treatise on the same subject* This was the 'Traité sur la poësie orientale', which was published together with the *Histoire de Nader Chah*, (London: P. Elmsly, 1770) for the Danish monarch, Christian VII.

2. *Arabia Felix* was a term used to describe the fertile valleys of the Yemen where the air was heavy with the spiced fragrance of clove and balsam.

3. *There is a valley, indeed, to the north of Indostan, called Cashmere* The Oriental motif of the paradise garden and the Indian Caucasus location was to prove attractive to many later writers, Lady Morgan's *The Missionary* and Shelley's 'Zeinab and Kathema' each feature a Kashmir setting. See also note to p.325 below.

most favourable influence of the sun; it is enclosed on one side by vast rocks and deserts, and defended on the other by a tempestuous sea, so that it seems to have been designed by providence for the most secure, as well as the most beautiful, region of the East. I am at a loss to conceive, what induced the illustrious Prince *Cantemir*[1] to contend that *Yemen* is properly a part of *India*; for, not to mention *Ptolemy*, and the other ancients, who considered it as a province of *Arabia*, nor to insist on the language of the country, which is pure *Arabick*, it is described by the *Asiaticks* themselves as a large division of that peninsula, which they call *Jezeiratul Arab*; and there is no more colour for annexing it to *India*, because the sea, which washes one side of it, is looked upon by some writers as belonging to the great *Indian* ocean, than there would be for annexing it to *Persia*, because it is bounded on another side by the *Persian* gulf. Its principal cities are *Sanaa*, usually considered as its metropolis; *Zebîd*, a commercial town, that lies in a large plain near the sea of *Omman*; and *Aden*, surrounded with pleasant gardens and woods, which is situated eleven degrees from the *Equator*, and seventy-six from the *Fortunate Islands*, or *Canaries*, where the geographers of *Asia* fix their first meridian. It is observable that *Aden*, in the Eastern dialects, is precisely the same word with *Eden*, which we apply to the garden of paradise: it has two senses, according to a slight difference in its pronunciation; its first meaning is *a settled abode*, its second, *delight, softness*, or *tranquillity*: the word *Eden* had, probably, one of these senses in the sacred text, though we use it as a proper name. We may also observe in this place that *Yemen* itself takes its name from a word, which signifies *verdure*, and *felicity*; for in those sultry climates, the freshness of the shade, and the coolness of water, are ideas almost inseparable from that of happiness; and this may be a reason why most of the *Oriental* nations agree in a tradition concerning a delightful spot, where the first inhabitants of the earth were placed before their fall. The ancients, who gave the name of *Eudaimon*, or *Happy* to this country, either meaned to translate the word *Yemen*, or, more probably, only alluded to the valuable spice-trees, and balsamick plants, that grow in it, and without speaking poetically, give a real perfume to the air: the writer of an old history of the *Turkish empire* says, '*The air of Egypt sometimes in summer is like any sweet perfume, and almost suffocates the spirits, caused by the wind that brings the odours of the Arabian spices:*' now it is certain that all poetry receives a very considerable ornament from the beauty of natural images; as the roses of *Sharon*, the verdure of *Carmel*, the vines of *Engaddi*, and the dew of *Hermon*, are the sources of many pleasing metaphors and comparisons in the sacred poetry: thus the odours of *Yemen*, the musk of *Hadramut*, and the pearls of *Omman*, supply the *Arabian* poets with a great variety of allusions; and, if the remark of *Hermogenes*[2] be just, that whatever is *delightful to the senses* produces the *Beautiful* when it is

---

1. Demetrius Cantemir (1673–1723), a Moldavian prince and accomplished linguist. Jones greatly admired his *The History of the Turks* which 'renders the compilations of *Knolles* and *Rycaut* entirely useless', *Works*, II.462–7.
2. Hermogenes was a rhetorician of the second century AD.

described, where can we find so much beauty as in the *Eastern* poems, which turn chiefly upon the loveliest objects in nature?

To pursue this topick yet farther: it is an observation of *Demetrius* of *Phalera*,[1] in his elegant treatise upon style, that it is not easy to write on agreeable subjects in a disagreeable manner, and that beautiful *expressions* naturally rise with beautiful images; *for which reason*, says he, *nothing can be more pleasing than Sappho's poetry, which contains the description of gardens, and banquets, flowers and fruits, fountains and meadows, nightingales and turtle-doves, loves and graces*: thus, when she speaks of *a stream softly murmuring among the branches, and the Zephyrs playing through the leaves, with a sound, that brings on a quiet slumber*, her lines flow without labour as smoothly as the rivulet she describes. I may have altered the words of *Demetrius*, as I quote them by memory, but this is the general sense of his remark, which, if it be not rather specious than just, must induce us to think, that the poets of the *East* may vie with those of *Europe* in *the graces of their diction*, as well as in the loveliness of their images: but we must not believe that the *Arabian* poetry can please only by its descriptions of *beauty*; since the gloomy and terrible objects, which produce the *sublime*, when they are aptly described, are no where more common than in the *Desert* and *Stony Arabia's*; and, indeed, we see nothing so frequently painted by the poets of those countries, as wolves and lions, precipices and forests, rocks and wildernesses.[2]

If we allow the natural objects, with which the *Arabs* are perpetually conversant, to be *sublime*, and *beautiful*, our next step must be, to confess that their comparisons, metaphors, and allegories are so likewise; for an allegory is only a string of metaphors, a metaphor is a short simile, and the finest similes are drawn from natural objects. It is true that many of the *Eastern* figures are common to other nations, but some of them receive a propriety from the manners of the *Arabians*, who dwell in the plains and woods, which would be lost, if they came from the inhabitants of cities: thus *the dew of liberality*, and the *odour of reputation*, are metaphors used by most people; but they are wonderfully proper in the mouths of those, who have so much need of being refreshed by *the dews*, and who gratify their sense of smelling with the *sweetest odours* in the world. Again; it is very usual in all countries to make frequent allusions to the brightness of the celestial luminaries, which give their light to all; but the metaphors taken from them have an additional beauty, if we consider them as made by a nation, who pass most of their nights in the open air, or in tents, and consequently see the moon and stars in their

---

1. Demetrius Phalereus, according to Lemprière (*A Classical Dictionary*, Reading, 1788), 'gained such an influence over the Athenians, by his eloquence and the purity of his manners, that he was elected decennial archon'. His appreciation of Sappho is to be found in *De Elocutione*, Sections 132 and 140–67, see W. Rhys Roberts, *Demetrius on Style* (Cambridge, 1902).

2. Jones's concern with the Beautiful and the Sublime, and the passions inextricably linked to them shows a certain indebtedness to his friend Burke's *Philosophical Enquiry into the Origin of our Ideas of the Sublime and Beautiful* (London, 1757). Both are keen to investigate what is essential in human experience, but Jones is chiefly interested in the power of evocation where, in Wordworth's terms, 'the passions of men are incorporated with the beautiful and permanent forms of nature'.

greatest splendour. This way of considering their poetical figures will give many of them a grace, which they would not have in our languages: so, when they compare the *foreheads of their mistresses to the morning, their locks to the night, their faces to the sun, to the moon, or the blossoms of jasmine, their cheeks to roses or ripe fruit, their teeth to pearls, hail-stones, and snow-drops, their eyes to the flowers of the narcissus, their curled hair to black scorpions, and to hyacinths, their lips to rubies or wine, the form of their breasts to pomegranates, and the colour of them to snow, their shape to that of a pine-tree, and their stature to that of a cypress, a palm-tree, or a javelin*, etc. these comparisons, many of which would seem forced in our idioms, have undoubtedly a great delicacy in theirs, and affect their minds in a peculiar manner; yet upon the whole their similes are very just and striking, as that of *the blue eyes of a fine woman, bathed in tears, to violets dropping with dew*,[1] and that of *a warriour, advancing at the head of his army, to an eagle falling through the air, and piercing the clouds with his wings.*

These are not the only advantages, which the natives of *Arabia* enjoy above the inhabitants of most other countries: they preserve to this day the manners and customs of their ancestors, who, by their own account, were settled in the province of *Yemen* above three thousand years ago; they have never been wholly subdued by any nation;[2] and though the admiral of *Selim the First* made a descent on their coast, and exacted a tribute from the people of *Aden*, yet the *Arabians* only keep up a show of allegiance to the sultan, and act, on every important occasion, in open defiance of his power,[3] relying on the swiftness of their horses, and the vast extent of their forests, in which an invading enemy must soon perish: but here I must be understood to speak of those *Arabians*, who, like the old *Nomades*,[4] dwell

---

1. *the blue eyes of a fine woman* compared to *violets dropping with dew* Jones's frequently repeated desire to introduce the lyrical and pastoral imagery of the Orient was vindicated by the number of later poets who ransacked his writings for materials. This simile, appearing in a listing of Arabian imagery, was appropriated by Byron in 'I Saw Thee Weep', one of the *Hebrew Melodies*: 'The big bright tear/Came o'er that eye of blue/And then methought it did appear/A violet dropping dew', *CPW*, III.296. Husain Haddawy in 'Oriental Translations and the Romantic Movement' (a paper read to the Modern Language Association of America, 28 Dec. 1964) compared the image in 'I Saw Thee Weep' with a translation from the Arabic of Ibnul Rumi by Joseph Dacre Carlisle in *Specimens of Arabic Poetry* (Cambridge, 1796, p.75): 'When I beheld thy blue eye shine/Thro' the bright drop that pity drew,/I saw beneath those tears of thine/A blue-eyed violet bath'd in dew.' Obviously Jones had Rumi's poem in mind, but the verbal correspondence would seem to indicate that Byron had been reading Jones rather than Carlisle's translation.

2. *they have never been wholly subdued by any nation* Jones's emphasis upon the proud independence of the nomadic and pastoral tribes anticipates the findings of the German traveller Carsten Niebuhr, whose *Beschreibung von Arabien* was published in Copenhagen later that year (1772). In his *Reisebeschreibung nach Arabien* (Copenhagen, 1774–8), Niebuhr was to write of the Arabs: 'A nation of this character cannot readily sink into servile subjection and arbitrary power', quoted in John Pinkerton, *Collections of Voyages and Travels* (London, 1808), X.85.

3. *the Arabians only keep up a show of allegiance to the sultan, and act, on every important occasion, in open defiance of his power* To the proponents of natural savagery Jones is offering the Arab nomad as a political symbol of resistance to tyrannical power not unrelated to that represented by the Ossianic rebel or the Celtic Highlander. Cf. 'On the Arabs', *Works*, III.49–50;59;68–9.

4. *like the old Nomades* The Rousseauistic emphasis Jones places upon 'their ancient simplicity' in harmony with the innocence of nature encouraged later poets to respond to the essential pastoralism of Arabian nomadic life.

constantly in their tents, and remove from place to place according to the seasons; for the inhabitants of the cities, who traffick with the merchants of Europe in spices, perfumes, and coffee, must have lost a great deal of their ancient simplicity: the others have, certainly, retained it; and, except when their tribes are engaged in war, spend their days in watching their flocks and camels, or in repeating their native songs, which they pour out almost extempore, professing a contempt for the stately pillars, and solemn buildings of the cities, compared with the natural charms of the country, and the coolness of their tents: thus they pass their lives in the highest pleasure, of which they have any conception, in the contemplation of the most delightful objects, and in the enjoyment of perpetual spring; for we may apply to part of *Arabia* that elegant couplet of *Waller* in his poem of the *Summer-island*,

> The gentle spring, that but salutes us here,
> Inhabits there, and courts them all the year.[1]

Yet the heat of the sun, which must be very intense in a climate so near the line, is tempered by the shade of the trees, that overhang the valleys, and by a number of fresh streams, that flow down the mountains: hence it is, that almost all their notions of *felicity* are taken from *freshness*, and *verdure*: it is a maxim among them that the three most charming objects in nature are, *a green meadow, a clear rivulet, and a beautiful woman*, and that the view of these objects at the same time affords the greatest delight imaginable: *Mahomet* was so well acquainted with the maxim of his countrymen, that he described the pleasures of heaven to them, under the allegory of *cool fountains, green bowers, and black-eyed girls*, as the word *Houri* literally signifies in *Arabick*; and in the chapter of the *Morning*, towards the end of his *Alcoran*, he mentions a garden, called *Irem*, which is no less celebrated by the *Asiatick* poets than that of the *Hesperides* by the *Greeks*: it was planted, as the commentators say, by a king, named *Shedad*, and was once seen by an *Arabian*, who wandered very far into the deserts in search of a lost camel: it was, probably, a name invented by the impostor,[2] as a type of a future state of happiness. Now it is certain that the genius of every nation is not a little affected by their climate; for, whether it be that the immoderate heat disposes the *Eastern* people to a life of indolence, which gives them full leisure to cultivate their talents, or whether the sun has a real influence on the imagination, (as one would suppose that the ancients believed, by their making *Apollo* the god of poetry;) whatever be the cause, it has always been remarked, that the *Asiaticks* excel the inhabitants of our colder regions in the liveliness of their fancy, and the richness of their invention.[3]

*Elmao wa'lkhedrato wa'lwijho'lhasano. See the life of *Tamerlane*, published by *Golius*, page 299.

---

1. *The gentle spring, that but salutes us here,/Inhabits there, and courts them all the year*   Edward Waller's 'The Battle of the Summer Islands' (1638), I.40–1, describing the Bermudas.
2. *the impostor*   Despite his enthusiasm for things Arabian, Jones cannot prevent himself from using this traditional Western epithet for Mahomet.
3. Jones here reflects Montesquieu's theories concerning the influence of climate.

To carry this subject one step farther: as the *Arabians* are such admirers of *beauty*, and as they enjoy such ease and leisure, they must naturally be susceptible of *that passion*, which is the true spring and source of agreeable poetry; and we find, indeed, that *love* has a greater share in their poems than any other passion: it seems to be always uppermost in their minds, and there is hardly an elegy, a panegyrick, or even a satire, in their language, which does not begin with the complaints of an unfortunate, or the exultations of a successful lover. It sometimes happens, that the young men of one tribe are in love with the damsels of another; and, as the tents are frequently removed on a sudden, the lovers are often separated in the progress of the courtship: hence almost all the *Arabick* poems open in this manner; the author bewails the sudden departure of his mistress, Hinda, Maia, Zeineb, or Azza,[1] and describes her beauty, comparing her usually to a wanton fawn, that plays among the aromatick shrubs; his friends endeavour to comfort him, but he refuses consolation; he declares his resolution of visiting his beloved, though the way to her tribe lie through a dreadful wilderness, or even through a den of lions; here he commonly gives a description of the horse or camel, upon which he designs to go, and thence passes, by an easy transition, to the principal subject of his poem, whether it be the praise of his own tribe, or a satire on the timidity of his friends, who refuse to attend him in his expedition; though very frequently the piece turns wholly upon love. But it is not sufficient that a nation have a genius for poetry, unless they have the advantage of a rich and beautiful language, that their expressions may be worthy of their sentiments; the *Arabians* have this advantage also in a high degree: their language is expressive, strong, sonorous, and the most copious, perhaps, in the world; for, as almost every tribe had many words appropriated to itself, the poets, for the convenience of their measure, or sometimes for their singular beauty, made use of them all, and, as the poems became popular, these words were by degrees incorporated with the whole language, like a number of little streams, which meet together in one channel, and forming a most plentiful river, flow rapidly into the sea.

If this way of arguing *à priori* be admitted in the present case, (and no single man has a right to infer the merit of the *Eastern* poetry from the poems themselves, because no single man has a privilege of judging for all the rest,) if the foregoing argument have any weight, we must conclude that the *Arabians*, being perpetually conversant with the most beautiful objects, spending a calm, and agreeable life in a fine climate, being extremely addicted to the softer passions, and having the

---

1. With the example of the *Mu'allaqāt* clearly in mind, Jones describes the beginning of a typical Arabian love poem. Shelley borrowed both this opening situation and a heroine's name for his *Esdaile* poem 'Zeinab and Kathema'. Southey, whose footnotes are crowded with references to Jones and *Asiatick Researches*, used the name Zeinab for a mother in his *Thalaba*. Thomas Moore, who similarly makes many acknowledgements to Jones, gives the heroine of 'The Fire Worshippers' in *Lalla Rookh* the name Hinda. A contemporary of Jones, John Scott of Amwell (1730–83), a Quaker friend of Johnson, handsomely acknowledged his debt to 'the learned and ingenious Mr. Jones, in his elegant and judicious Essay on the Poetry of the Eastern Nations', quoting this passage as the inspiration for his 'Zerad; or, The Absent Lover: An Arabian Eclogue', *Poetical Works of John Scott* (London, 1782), p.126.

advantage of a language singularly adapted to poetry, must be naturally excellent poets, provided that their *manners*, and *customs*, be favourable to the cultivation of that art; and that they are highly so, it will not be difficult to prove.

The fondness of the *Arabians* for poetry, and the respect which they show to poets, would be scarce believed, if we were not assured of it by writers of great authority: the principal occasions of rejoicing among them were formerly, and, very probably, are to this day, the birth of a boy, the foaling of a mare, the arrival of a guest, and the rise of a poet in their tribe: when a young *Arabian* has composed a good poem, all the neighbours pay their compliments to his family, and congratulate them upon having a relation capable of recording their actions, and of recommending their virtues to posterity. At the beginning of the seventh century, the *Arabick* language was brought to a high degree of perfection by a sort of poetical academy, that used to assemble at stated times, in a place called *Ocadh* where every poet produced his best composition,[1] and was sure to meet with the applause that it deserved: the most excellent of these poems were transcribed in characters of gold upon *Egyptian* paper, and hung up in the temple, whence they were named *Modhahebat*, or *Golden*, and *Moallakat*,[2] or *Suspended*: the poems of this sort were called *Casseida's* or *eclogues*, *seven of which are preserved in our libraries, and are considered as the finest that were written before the time of *Mahomet*; the fourth of them, composed by *Lebîd*, is purely pastoral,[3] and extremely like the *Alexis of Virgil*, but far more beautiful, because it is more agreeable to nature: the poet begins with praising the charms of the fair *Novâra*, (a word, which in *Arabick* signifies *a timorous fawn*,) but inveighs against her

* These seven poems, clearly transcribed with explanatory notes, are among *Pocock's* manuscripts at *Oxford* No. 164: the names of the seven poets are *Amralkeis*, *Tarafa*, *Zoheir*, *Lebîd*, *Antara*, *Amru*, and *Hareth*. In the same collection, No. 174, there is a manuscript containing above forty other poems, which had the honour of being suspended in the temple at *Mecca*: this volume is an inestimable treasure of ancient *Arabick* literature.[4]

---

1. *every poet produced his best composition* 'To this day the high point of royal or shaykly gatherings in Arabia is the recitation of poetry, sometimes in contest', *The Encyclopaedia of Islam* (Leiden, 1960), under *Mu'allaqāt*. The concept of poetry competitions obviously appealed to Jones at a time when his fellow Cymmrodorion, and other members of the London Welsh community, were establishing local eisteddfodau in Wales.

2. *Moallakat* The traditional explanation of the name *Mu'allaqāt* given here was rejected by Alfred Lyall who translated *a'alāl* as 'necklaces' or 'hanging jewels' in the sense of a beautiful anthology strung together, see *Ancient Arabian Poetry* (London, 1885), p.56. Cf. the remarks of Abu Temam quoted by Jones p.328 below.

3. *purely pastoral* Johann Fück's criticism of Jones's scholarship as intruding classical poetics into Arabic literature (*Die arabischen Studien in Europa bis in den Anfang des 20. Jahrhunderts,* Leipzig, 1955, p.152) has been countered by Jaroslav Stetkevych, who perceives, 'both in William Jones's translations and in his critical formulations a certain underlying truth of genre perception, for the recognition of the "pastoral manner" in pre-Islamic as well as later Arabic poetry is an essentially valid critical discovery', 'Arabic Poetry and Assorted Poetics', in Malcolm Kerr (ed.), *Islamic Studies: A Tradition and its Problems* (California, 1980), pp.103–23, (108).

4. Here, as in his footnote on p.330, he is trying to encourage scholars to work on these accessible manuscripts, but the labours and the rewards were all too frequently left for Jones, who was to produce the first European translations of Persian and Arabic poetry.

unkindness; he then interweaves a description of his young camel, which he compares for its swiftness to a stag, pursued by the hounds; and takes occasion afterwards to mention his own riches, accomplishments, liberality, and valour, his noble birth, and the glory of his tribe: the diction of this poem is easy and simple, yet elegant, the numbers flowing and musical, and the sentiments wonderfully natural; as the learned reader will see by the following passage, which I shall attempt to imitate in verse that the merit of the poet may not be wholly lost in a verbal translation:

'Bel enti la tadrina cam mi'lleilatin,
Thalkin ledhidhin lahwoha wa nedamoha,
Kad bitto sameroha, wa ghayati tajerin
Wafaito idh rofiat, wa azza medamoha,
Besabuhi safiatin wajadhbi carinatin,
Be mowatterin, taâta leho maan ibhamoha,
Bacarto hajataha' ddajaja besohratin,
Leoalla minha heina habba neyamoha.

But ah! thou know'st not in what youthful play
Our nights, beguil'd with pleasure, swam away;
Gay songs, and cheerful tales, deceiv'd the time,
And circling goblets made a tuneful chime;
Sweet was the draught, and sweet the blooming maid,
Who touch'd her lyre beneath the fragrant shade;
We sip'd till morning purpled ev'ry plain;
The damsels slumber'd, but we sip'd again:
The waking birds, that sung on ev'ry tree
Their early notes, were not so blithe as we.[1]

The Mahometan writers tell a story of this poet, which deserves to be mentioned here: it was a custom, it seems, among the old Arabians, for the most eminent versifiers to hang up some chosen couplets on the gate of the temple, as a publick challenge to their brethren, who strove to answer them before the next meeting at Ocadh, at which time the whole assembly used to determine the merit of them all, and gave some mark of distinction to the author of the finest verses. Now Lebid, who, we are told, had been a violent opposer of Mahomet, fixed a poem on the gate, beginning with the following distich, in which he apparently meaned to reflect upon the new religion:

---

1. Cf. Jones's prose translation, some ten years later, of this passage from the mu'allaqa of Labīd: 'Ah! thou knowest not how many serene nights, with sweet sport and mirthful revelry, I pass in gay conversation; and often return to the flag of the wine-merchant, when he spreads it in the air, and sells his wine at a high price: I purchase the old liquor at a dear rate in dark leathern bottles long reposited, or in casks, black with pitch, whose seals I break, and then fill the cheerful goblet. How often do I quaff pure wine in the morning, and draw towards me the fair lutanist, whose delicate fingers skilfully touch the strings! I rise before the cock to take my morning draught, which I sip again and again, when the sleepers of the dawn awake', Works, X.67–8.

Ila cullo sheion ma khala Allaho bathilon,
Wa cullo naîmon la mohaloho zailon.

That is: *Are not all things vain, which come not from God? and will not all honours decay, but those, which He confers?* These lines appeared so sublime, that none of the poets ventured to answer them; till *Mahomet*, who was himself a poet, having composed a new chapter of his *Alcoran*, (the second, I think,) placed the opening of it by the side of *Lebid's* poem, who no sooner read it, than he declared it to be something divine, confessed his own inferiority, tore his verses from the gate, and embraced the religion of his rival; to whom he was afterwards extremely useful in replying to the satires of *Amralkeis*, who was continually attacking the doctrine of *Mahomet*: the *Asiaticks* add, that their lawgiver acknowledged some time after, that no heathen poet had ever produced a nobler distich than that of *Lebid* just quoted.

There are a few other collections of ancient *Arabick* poetry; but the most famous of them is called *Hamassa*,[1] and contains a number of *epigrams*, *odes*, and *elegies*, composed on various occasions: it was compiled by *Abu Temam*, who was an excellent poet himself, and used to say, that *fine sentiments delivered in prose were like gems scattered at random, but that, when they were confined in a poetical measure, they resembled bracelets, and strings of pearls.*[2] When the religion and language of *Mahomet* were spread over the greater part of *Asia*, and the maritime countries of *Africa*, it became a fashion for the poets of *Persia*, *Syria*, *Egypt*, *Mauritania*, and even of *Tartary*, to write in *Arabick*; and the most beautiful verses in that idiom, composed by the brightest genius's of those nations, are to be seen in a large miscellany, entitled *Yateima*;[3] though many of their works are transcribed separately: it will be needless to say much on the poetry of the *Syrians*, *Tartarians*, and *Africans*, since most of the arguments, before-used in favour of the *Arabs*, have equal weight with respect to the other *Mahometans*, who have done little more than imitate their style, and adopt their expressions; for which reason also I shall dwell the shorter time on the genius and manners of the *Persians*, *Turks*, and *Indians*.

The great empire, which we call *Persia*, is known to its natives by the name of *Iran*; since the word *Persia* belongs only to a particular province, the ancient *Persis*, and is very improperly applied by us to the whole kingdom: but, in compliance with the custom of our geographers, I shall give the name of *Persia* to that celebrated country, which lies on one side between the *Caspian* and *Indian* seas, and extends on the other from the mountains of *Candahar*, or *Paropamisus*, to the confluence of

---

1. *Hamassa al-Hamāsah* (prowess) is an anthology collected by abu-Tammām about 836 AD containing 884 poems or extracts on the themes of gallantry, fortitude, and the beauty and love of women. Jones quotes examples of satire from the fifth book in Section VI of 'Traité sur la poësie orientale' (1770). See also 'The History of the Persian Language', *Works*, V.423 and note. Jones owned a manuscript copy of this collection, see *Catalogue of the Library of the late Sir William Jones* (London, 1831), p.14, item 343.
2. *resembled bracelets, and strings of pearls* Cf. *Thalaba*, III.24.
3. *'Yateima* The *Yatimat ad-Dahr*, a famous anthology composed by Abu Mansūr ath-Tha'ālibi (b. 961 AD), a Persian writing in Arabic.

the rivers *Cyrus* and *Araxes*, containing about twenty degrees from south to north, and rather more from east to west.

In so vast a tract of land there must needs be a great variety of climates: the southern provinces are no less unhealthy and sultry, than those of the north are rude and unpleasant; but in the interior parts of the empire the air is mild and temperate, and, from the beginning of May to September, there is scarce a cloud to be seen in the sky: the remarkable calmness of the summer nights, and the wonderful splendour of the moon and stars in that country, often tempt the *Persians* to sleep on the tops of their houses, which are generally flat, where they cannot but observe the figures of the constellations, and the various appearances of the heavens; and this may in some measure account for the perpetual allusions of their poets, and rhetoricians, to the beauty of the heavenly bodies. We are apt to censure the oriental style for being so full of metaphors taken from the sun and moon: this is ascribed by some to the bad taste of the *Asiaticks*; *the works of the Persians*, says *M. de Voltaire*, *are like the titles of their kings, in which the sun and moon are often introduced*: but they do not reflect that every nation has a set of images, and expressions, peculiar to itself, which arise from the difference of its climate, manners, and history.[1] There seems to be another reason for the frequent allusions of the *Persians* to the sun, which may, perhaps, be traced from the old language and popular religion of their country: thus *Mihridâd*, or *Mithridates*, signifies *the gift of the sun*, and answers to the *Theodorus* and *Diodati* of other nations. As to the titles of the *Eastern* monarchs, which seem, indeed, very extravagant to our ears, they are merely formal, and no less void of meaning than those of *European* princes, in which *serenity* and *highness* are often attributed to the most *gloomy*, and *low-minded* of men.

The midland provinces of *Persia* abound in fruits and flowers of almost every kind, and, with proper culture, might be made the garden of *Asia*: they are not watered, indeed, by any considerable river, since the *Tigris* and *Euphrates*, the *Cyrus* and *Araxes*, the *Oxus*, and the five branches of the *Indus*, are at the farthest limits of the kingdom; but the natives, who have a turn for agriculture, supply that defect by artificial canals, which sufficiently temper the dryness of the soil: but in saying they *supply* that defect, I am falling into a common error, and representing the country, not as it *is* at present, but as it *was* a century ago; for a long series of civil wars and massacres have now destroyed the chief beauties of *Persia*, by stripping it of its most industrious inhabitants.

The same difference of climate, that affects the air and soil of this extensive country, gives a variety also to the persons and temper of its natives: in some provinces they have dark complexions, and harsh features; in others they are exquisitely fair, and well-made; in some others, nervous and robust: but the general

---

1. As always Jones is quick to correct prejudiced or patronizing attitudes, even those of Voltaire, in the spirit of Enlightenment relativism. In the introduction to his *Grammar of the Persian Language* (London, 1771), he had attacked those responsible for the neglect of Oriental literature: 'The state of letters seems to be divided into two classes, men of learning who have no taste, and men of taste who have no learning', *Works*, V.168.

character of the nation is that *softness*, and *love of pleasure*, that *indolence*, and *effeminacy*, which have made them an easy prey to all the western and northern swarms, that have from time to time invaded them. Yet they are not wholly void of martial spirit; and, if they are not naturally brave, they are at least extremely docile, and might, with proper discipline, be made excellent soldiers: but the greater part of them, in the short intervals of peace, that they happen to enjoy, constantly sink into a state of inactivity, and pass their lives in a pleasurable, yet studious, retirement;[1] and this may be one reason, why *Persia* has produced more writers of every kind, and chiefly *poets*, than all *Europe* together, since their way of life gives them leisure to pursue those arts, which cannot be cultivated to advantage, without the greatest calmness and serenity of mind: and this, by the way, is one cause, among many others, why the poems in the preceding collection are less finished; since they were composed, not in bowers and shades, by the side of rivulets or fountains, but either amidst the confusion of a metropolis, the hurry of travel, the dissipation of publick places, the avocations of more necessary studies, or the attention to more useful parts of literature. To return: there is a manuscript at Oxford* containing *the lives of an hundred and thirty five of the finest Persian poets*, most of whom left very ample collections of their poems behind them: but the versifiers, and *moderate poets*, if *Horace* will allow any such men to exist, are without number in *Persia.*

   This delicacy of their lives and sentiments has insensibly affected their language, and rendered it the softest, as it is one of the richest, in the world:[2] it is not possible to convince the reader of this truth, by quoting a passage from a *Persian* poet in *European* characters; since the sweetness of sound cannot be determined by the sight, and many words, which are soft and musical in the mouth of a *Persian*, may appear very harsh to our eyes, with a number of consonants and gutturals: it may not, however, be absurd to set down in this place, an Ode of the poet *Hafiz*,[3] which,

---

*In Hyperoo Bodl. 128. There is a prefatory discourse to this curious work, which comprises the lives of ten *Arabian* poets.

---

   1. The cultural stereotype of the sensuous Persian is significantly adjusted here, with the emphasis placed on leisure rather than luxury, anticipating the Romantic championing of idleness and indolence as nurturing creative imagination. In pointing out that '*Persia* has produced more writers of every kind, and chiefly *poets*, than all *Europe* together', Jones was speaking with some authority. His *Grammar*, which had earned him the sobriquet of 'Persian Jones', constituted in effect an introduction to Persian poetry.
   2. The reluctance of European scholars to relinquish the familiar security of the classical tradition, together with their often negative ideas about the value of Oriental languages irritated Jones. 'So in his early literary criticism he had as one objective the refutation of the charge that Persian is difficult or baroque. In disposing of this idea, he was not substituting for it the linguistic one. He merely went to the other extreme by arguing that Persian is sonorous, musical, and easy to learn', Garland Cannon, 'Sir William Jones's Persian Linguistics', *Journal of the American Oriental Society* 78 (1958), 262–73. Such unscientific procedure, anathema to modern linguistics, is annexed to a central tenet (as expressed in the Preface to his *Grammar*) that 'the only office of a grammarian is to open the mine of literature'.
   3. Jones's enthusiasm for the poetry of Hāfiz is reflected in his correspondence (conducted through the scholarly *lingua franca* of Latin) with the Hungarian Orientalist and diplomat, Count Reviczky: 'Our Hāfiz is most assuredly a poet worthy to sup with the gods; every day I take

if it be not sufficient to prove the delicacy of his language, will at least show the liveliness of his poetry:

Ai bad nesîmi yârdari,
Zan nefheï mushcbâr dari:
Zinhar mecun diraz-desti!
Ba turreï o che câr dari?
Ai gul, to cujâ wa ruyi zeibash?
O taza, wa to kharbâr dari.
Nerkes, to cujâ wa cheshmi mestesh?
O serkhosh, wa to khumâr dari.
Ai seru, to ba kaddi bulendesh,
Der bagh che iytebâr dari?
Ai akl, to ba wujûdi ishkesh
Der dest che ikhtiyâr dari?
Rihan, to cujâ wa khatti sebzesh?
O mushc, wa to ghubâr dari.
Ruzi bures bewasli Hafîz,
Gher takati yntizâr dari.

That is, word for word, *O sweet gale, thou bearest the fragrant scent of my beloved; thence it is that thou hast this musky odour. Beware! do not steal: what hast thou to do with her tresses? O rose, what art thou, to be compared with her bright face? She is fresh, and thou art rough with thorns. O narcissus, what art thou in comparison of her languishing eye? Her eye is only sleepy, but thou art sick and faint. O pine, compared with her graceful stature, what honour hast thou in the garden? O wisdom, what wouldst thou choose, if to choose were in thy power, in preference to her love? O sweet basil, what art thou, to be compared with her fresh cheeks? They are perfect musk, but thou art soon withered. Come, my beloved, and charm Hafiz with they presence, if thou canst but stay with him for a single day.* This little song is not unlike a sonnet, ascribed to *Shakespeare*, which deserves to be cited here, as a proof that the Eastern imagery is not so different from the *Europeans* as we are apt to imagine.[1]

The forward violet thus did I chide:
'Sweet thief! whence didst thou steal thy sweet that smells,
'If not from my love's breath? The purple pride,
'Which on thy soft cheek for complexion dwells,
'In my love's veins thou hast too grossly dyed.'
The lily I condemned for thy hand,
And buds of marjoram had stol'n thy hair;
The roses fearfully on thorns did stand,
One blushing shame, another white despair;
A third, nor red, nor white had stol'n of both,

---

pleasure in his work', *Letters*, I.9. He had included French verse translations of ten of Hāfiz's odes in the 'Traité sur la poësie orientale' (1770) and most of the illustrations for his *Persian Grammar* (1771) were also culled from Hāfiz.

1. The comparison of the Hāfiz ode with Shakespeare's sonnet 99 demonstrates Jones's syncretistic approach.

> *And to his robb'ry had annex'd thy breath;*
> *But for his theft, in pride of all his growth,*
> *A vengeful canker eat him up to death.*
> *More flow'rs I noted, yet I none could see,*
> *But sweet or colour it had stol'n from thee.*
> *Shakespeare's* Poems. p.207

The *Persian* style is said to be ridiculously bombast, and this fault is imputed to the slavish spirit of the nation, which is ever apt to magnify the objects that are placed above it: there are bad writers, to be sure, in every country, and as many in *Asia* as elsewhere; but, if we take the pains to learn the *Persian* language, we shall find that those authors, who are generally esteemed in *Persia*, are neither slavish in their sentiments, nor ridiculous in their expressions: of which the following passage in a moral work of *Sadi*, entitled *Bostân*, or, *The Garden*, will be a sufficient proof.[1]

> *Shinidem ke, der wakti nezî rewan,*
> *Be Hormuz chunîn gufti Nushirewan:*
> *Ki khatir nigehdari derwishi bash,*
> *Ne der bendi âsaïshi khishi bash:*
> *Neâsaïd ender diyari to kes,*
> *Chu âsaïshi khishi khahi wa bes.*
> *Neyayid benezdiki dana pesend,*
> *Shubani khufte, wa gurki der kuspend.*
> *Beru; pasi derwishi muhtâji dar,*
> *Ki shah ez raiyet bûd tâji dar.*
> *Raiyet chu bikhest wa soltan dirakht,*
> *Dirakht, ai piser, bashed ez bikhi sakht.*

That is; *I have heard that king Nushirvan, just before his death, spoke thus to his son Hormuz: Be a guardian, my son,[2] to the poor and helpless; and be not confined in the chains of thy own indolence. No one can be at ease in thy dominion, while thou seekest only thy private rest, and sayest, It is enough. A wise man will not approve the shepherd, who sleeps, while the wolf is in the fold. Go, my son, protect thy weak and*

---

1. Jones was later to submit a formal proposal to Oxford that a translation of the *Būstān* by his friend John Uri should be printed by subscription, *Letters*, I.446–9. It was another moral text by Sa'dī, the *Gulistān* (*The Bed of Roses*), that Jones had used to learn Persian with the help of Mirza, a Syrian, whom he had brought to Oxford.

2. *Be a guardian, my son* Jones's prose translation from Sa'dī was itself the basis of a recension by Anna Seward (1742–1809), the 'Swan of Lichfield', entitled 'Sonnet LIV. A Persian King to his Son'. She also used Jones's prose redaction of Mesihi's ode (*Works*, X.271–6) for her 'Eastern Ode'. A third poem, 'Invocation to the Shade of Petrarch, and to the Spirits of the Persian Poets, on their Compositions Being Translated into English, by Sir William Jones', praises Jones 'Who hung with Persian wreathes the Albion Muses's fane' to ensure that 'all the fire of oriental rhyme/Glows in our isles with undiminish'd ray', see *The Poetical Works of Anna Seward: with Extracts from her Literary Correspondence*, 3 vols., ed. Walter Scott (Edinburgh, 1810), I:175; 300–4; 113–14.

indigent people; since through them is a king raised to the diadem. The people are the root, and the king is the tree, that grows from it; and the tree, O my son, derives its strength from the root.

Are these mean sentiments, delivered in pompous language? Are they not rather worthy of our most spirited writers? And do they not convey a fine lesson for a young king? Yet *Sadi's* poems are highly esteemed at *Constantinople*, and at *Ispahan*; though, a century or two ago, they would have been suppressed in *Europe*, for spreading, with too strong a glare, the light of liberty and reason.[1]

As to the great Epick poem of *Ferdusi*, which was composed in the tenth century, it would require a very long treatise, to explain all its beauties with a minute exactness. The whole collection of that poet's works is called *Shahnâma*,[2] and contains the history of *Persia*, from the earliest times to the invasion of the *Arabs*, in a series of very noble poems; the longest and most regular of which is an heroick poem of one great and interesting action; namely, *the delivery of Persia by Cyrus*, from the oppressions of *Afrasiab*, king of the *Transoxan Tartary*, who, being assisted by the emperors of *India* and *China*, together with all the dæmons, giants, and enchanters of *Asia*, had carried his conquests very far, and become exceedingly formidable to the *Persians*. This poem is longer than the *Iliad*; the characters in it are various and striking; the figures bold and animated; and the diction every where sonorous, yet noble; polished, yet full of fire. A great profusion of learning has been thrown away by some cruel, in comparing *Homer* with the heroick poets, who have succeeded him; but it requires very little judgment to see, that no succeeding poet whatever can with any propriety be compared with *Homer*: that great father of the *Grecian* poetry and literature, had a genius too fruitful and comprehensive to let any of the striking parts of nature escape his observation; and the poets, who have followed him, have done little more than transcribe his images, and give a new dress to his thoughts. Whatever elegance and refinements, therefore, may have been introduced into the works of the moderns, the spirit and invention of *Homer* have ever continued without a rival:[3] for which reasons I am far from pretending to assert that the poet of *Persia* is equal to that of *Greece*; but there is

---

1. *they would have been suppressed in Europe* Undercutting Occidental stereotypes of arbitrary despotism and slavish servility, Jones locates 'the light of liberty and reason' in Saʿdī and his royal Persian patrons. In this connexion, John Scott, in his 'On the Ingenious Mr Jones's Elegant Translations and Imitations of Eastern Poetry, and his Resolution to Decline Translating the Persian Poets', writes of Hāfiz and Saʿdī: 'They sing not all of streams and bowers,/Or banquet scenes, or social hours . . . But Freedom's lofty notes sincere,/And Virtue's moral lore severe', *Poetical Works* (London, 1782), pp.332–3.

2. In the 'Traité sur la poësie orientale' Jones had quoted passages from the Sohrab and Rustum story in his attempt to introduce Firdausi's *Shāhnāma* to a European audience; in his *Poeseos Asiaticae Commentariorum* (1774) he was to refer to Firdausi as the Persian Homer, see *Works*, VI.231–2; cf. 'The History of the Persian Language', *Works*, V.426.

3. *the spirit and invention of Homer have ever continued without a rival* Homer can here be viewed as a Eurocentric benchmark, both for Persian Jones and his audience, but Jones's comparativist position was always flexible, and India was a revelation. Thus twelve years later he wrote to Richard Johnson: 'Jūdishteïr, 'Arjen, Corno, and the other warriors of the *M'hab'harat* appear greater in my eyes than Agamemnon, Ajax, and Achilles appeared, when I first read the Iliad', *Letters*, II.652.

certainly a very great resemblance between the works of those extraordinary men: both drew their images from nature herself, without catching them only by reflection, and painting, in the manner of the modern poets, *the likeness of a likeness*; and both possessed, in an eminent degree, *that rich and creative invention, which is the very soul of poetry.*

As the *Persians* borrowed their poetical measures, and the forms of their poems from the *Arabians*, so the *Turks*, when they had carried their arms into *Mesopotamia*, and *Assyria*, took their numbers, and their taste for poetry from the *Persians*;

> *Græcia* capta ferum victorem cepit, et artes
> Intulit agresti *Latio.*

In the same manner as the *Greek* compositions were the models of all the *Roman* writers, so were those of *Persia* imitated by the *Turks*, who considerably polished and enriched their language, naturally barren, by the number of simple and compound words, which they adopted from the *Persian* and *Arabick*. Lady *Wortley Montague* very justly observes that *we want those compound words, which are very frequent, and strong in the Turkish language*; but her interpreters led her into a mistake in explaining one of them, which she translates *stag-eyed*, and thinks *a very lively image of the fire and indifference in the eyes of the royal bride*: now it never entered into the mind of an *Asiatick* to compare his mistress's eyes to those of a *stag*, or to give an image of their *fire and indifference*; the *Turks* mean to express that *fullness*, and, at the same time, that *soft and languishing lustre*, which is peculiar to the eyes of their beautiful women, and which by no means resembles the unpleasing wildness in those of a stag.[1] The original epithet, I suppose, was *Ahû cheshm*, or, *with the eyes of a young fawn*: now I take the *Ahû* to be the same animal with the *Gazâl* of the *Arabians*,[2] and the *Zabi* of the *Hebrews*, to which their poets allude in almost every page. I have seen one of these animals; it is a kind of antelope, exquisitely beautiful, with eyes uncommonly black and large. This is the same sort of roe, to which *Solomon* alludes in this delicate simile: *Thy two breasts are like two young roes, that are twins, which play among the lilies.*

*This epithet seems to answer to the *Greek* ἑλικῶπις, which our grammarians properly interpret *Quæ nigris oculis decora est et venusta*: if it were permitted to make any innovations in a dead language, we might express the *Turkish* adjective by the word δορκῶπις, which would, I dare say, have sounded agreeably to the *Greeks* themselves.

---

1. In this letter of 1 April 1717 Lady Mary Wortley Montagu, admitting, 'I am pretty far gone in Oriental learning', sends Pope some translated verses of the contemporary ruler and poet Ibrahim Pasha: 'I don't doubt that you'll be of my mind, that it is most wonderfully resembling *The Song of Solomon*'. Earlier in the same letter she expresses her admiration for Adrianople, 'a place where truth, for once, furnishes all the ideas of pastoral', 'I no longer look upon Theocritus as a romantic writer', *Complete Letters*, ed. Robert Halsband, 3 vols., (Oxford, 1965–7), I:330–7.

2. *the Gazâl of the Arabians* After the publication of this essay it is difficult to find an Oriental heroine's eye which is not 'wild as the Gazelle's', cf., for example, Byron's *Giaour*, ll.473–4, or his 'To Ianthe', ll.1–3.

A very polite scholar,[1] who has lately translated sixteen Odes of *Hafiz*, with learned illustrations, blames the *Turkish* poets for copying the *Persians* too servilely: but, surely, they are not more blameable than *Horace*, who not only imitated the measures, and expressions of the *Greeks*, but even translated, almost word for word, the brightest passages of *Alcæus*, *Anacreon*, and others; he took less from *Pindar* than from the rest, because the wildness of his numbers, and the obscurity of his allusions, were by no means suitable to the genius of the *Latin* language: and this may, perhaps, explain his ode to *Julius Antonius*, who might have advised him to use more of *Pindar*'s manner in celebrating the victories of *Augustus*. Whatever we may think of this objection, it is certain that the *Turkish* empire has produced a great number of poets;[2] some of whom had no small merit in their way: the ingenious author just-mentioned assured me, that the *Turkish* satires of *Ruhi Bagdadi* were very forcible and striking, and he mentioned the opening of one of them, which seemed not unlike the manner of *Juvenal*.[3] At the beginning of the last century, a work was published at *Constantinople*, containing the finest verses of *five hundred and forty nine Turkish poets*,[4] which proves at least that they are singularly fond of this art, whatever may be our opinion of their success in it.

The descendants of *Tamerlane* carried into *India* the language, and poetry of the *Persians*; and the *Indian* poets to this day compose their verses in imitation of them. The best of their works, that have passed through my hands, are those of *Huzein*, who lived some years ago at *Benáres*, with a great reputation for his parts and learning, and was known to the *English*, who resided there, by the name of *the Philosopher*. His poems are elegant and lively, and one of them, *on the departure of his friends*, would suit our language admirably well, but is too long to be inserted in this essay. The *Indians* are soft, and voluptuous, but artful and insincere, at least to the *Europeans*, whom, to say the truth, they have had no great reason of late years to admire for the opposite virtues: but they are fond of poetry, which they learned from the *Persians*, and may, perhaps, before the close of the century, be as fond of a more formidable art, which they will learn from the *English*.[5]

---

1. *A very polite scholar* Count Reviczky published his Latin translations of sixteen of Hāfiz's *ghazals* in *Specimen Poeseos Persicae* (Vienna, 1771).

2. While writing this essay Jones was also working on 'a Political Treatise' *On the Turks* as he felt he had somewhat neglected Ottoman literature, but only the *Prefatory Discourse* was ever completed, *Works*, II.455–93.

3. *Ruhi Bagdadi* (d.1605) According to H. A. R. Gibb, Rúhí, in his best known poem, 'Terkíb-Bend', 'runs along the whole gamut of moods known to contemporary poetry, beginning in a spirit of lofty and profound mysticism, and passing on through a phase of bitter defiance of all accepted conventionalities, to end in a tone of contented resignation', *A History of Ottoman Poetry*, 12 vols., (London, 1900), III:187.

4. *a work was published at Constantinople, containing the finest verses of five hundred and forty nine Turkish poets* The end of the sixteenth and the beginning of the seventeenth century saw a remarkable flowering of poetic miscellanies and anthologies in Turkey. The compilation to which Jones refers is probably the *Tezkire* of Qináli-záde Hasan Chelebi (1546–1604), which contains extracts from, and notices of, over 600 poets. See Gibb, *A History of Ottoman Poetry*, III:199;203–4.

5. *a more formidable art, which they will learn from the English* The contact zone of the East Indies is viewed not as a potential site of mutual enlightenment, but as an area of one-way influence in which British imperialism is made to seem more barbaric than Persian dominion.

I must once more request, that, in bestowing these praises on the writings of *Asia*, I may not be thought to derogate from the merit of the *Greek* and *Latin* poems, which have justly been admired in every age; yet I cannot but think that our *European* poetry has subsisted too long on the perpetual repetition of the same images, and incessant allusions to the same fables: and it has been my endeavour for several years to inculcate this truth, *That, if the principal writings of the Asiaticks, which are reposited in our publick libraries, were printed with the usual advantage of notes and illustrations, and if the languages of the Eastern nations were studied in our places of education, where every other branch of useful knowledge is taught to perfection, a new and ample field would be opened for speculation; we should have a more extensive insight into the history of the human mind, we should be furnished with a new set of images and similitudes, and a number of excellent compositions would be brought to light, which future scholars might explain, and future poets might imitate.*[1]

---

1. *future scholars might explain, and future poets might imitate* What underlies Jones's hopes that Oriental studies will be placed on a secure academic footing is the consciousness of his decision, reluctantly taken, to abandon Eastern literature in order to devote more time to jurisprudence, see the Preface to *A Grammar of the Persian Language* (1771), *Works*, V:183. John Scott, in a poem which is at once a celebration of Jones's 'Asian Muse' and a lament for the 'loss irreparable', expressed the feeling of the world of letters, see 'On the Ingenious Mr. Jones's Elegant Translations and Imitations of Eastern Poetry, and his Resolution to Decline Translating the Persian Poets', *Poetical Works* (London, 1782), pp.332–3.

26

An Essay on the Arts, Commonly Called Imitative
(1772)

[This, the second essay which appeared in *Poems, consisting chiefly of translations from the Asiatick languages* (1772), constitutes a landmark in the history of literary criticism; it represents a fundamental re-arranging of the aesthetic premises of neo-classicism into the new poetics of Romanticism. Jones's detailed study of classical and Oriental writers had confirmed his belief that the lyric was not a politely languishing minor genre but the purest, and in some respects, the highest expression of poetry. In maintaining that although poetry and music may imitate 'the manners of men, and several objects in nature', their greatest effect is in the expression of passion, Jones upholds the Longinian distinction between the imitative artistic act and nature acting upon the artist. Both M. H. Abrams and René Wellek see Jones's essay as a fascinating *locus* for pre-Romantic literary criticism. Abrams locates in this essay: 'a conjunction of all the tendencies we have been tracing: the ideas drawn from Longinus, the old doctrine of poetic inspiration, recent theories of the emotional and imaginative origin of poetry, and a major emphasis upon the lyric form and on the supposedly primitive and spontaneous poetry of Oriental nations. It was Jones's distinction to be the first writer in England to weave these threads into an explicit and orderly reformulation of the nature and criteria of poetry and of the poetic genres', *The Mirror and the Lamp* (Oxford, 1953, pp. 87–8). The text followed is that of the second edition of *Poems* (1777), with variants noted from the first edition of 1772.]

ESSAY ON *THE ARTS*, COMMONLY CALLED IMITATIVE

It is the fate of those maxims, which have been thrown out by very eminent writers, to be received implicitly by most of their followers, and to be repeated a thousand times, for no other reason, than because they once dropped from the pen of a superior genius: one of these is the assertion of *Aristotle*, that *all poetry consists in imitation*, which has been so frequently echoed from author to author, that it would seem a kind of arrogance to controvert it; for almost all the philosophers and criticks, who have written upon the subject of *poetry*, *musick*, and *painting*, how little soever they may agree in some points, seem of one mind in considering them as arts merely *imitative*: yet it must be clear to any one, who examines what passes in his own mind, that he is affected by the finest *poems*, *pieces of musick*, and *pictures*, upon a principle, which, whatever it be, is entirely distinct from *imitation*. *M. le Batteux* has attempted to prove that all the fine arts have a relation to this common principle of *imitating*:[1] but, whatever be said of *painting*, it is probable, that *poetry* and *musick* had a nobler origin; and, if the first language of man[2] was not both *poetical* and *musical*, it is certain, at least, that in countries, where no kind of *imitation* seems to be much admired, there are *poets* and *musicians* both by nature and by art: as in some *Mahometan* nations; where *sculpture* and *painting* are forbidden by the laws, where *dramatick poetry* of every sort is wholly unknown, yet, where the pleasing arts, *of expressing the passions in verse, and of enforcing that expression by melody*, are cultivated to a degree of enthusiasm. It shall be my endeavour in this paper to prove, that, though *poetry* and *musick* have, certainly, a power of *imitating* the manners of men, and several objects in nature, yet, that their greatest effect is not produced by *imitation*, but by a very different principle; which must be sought for in the deepest recesses of the human mind.

To state the question properly, we must have a clear notion of what we mean by *poetry* and *musick*; but we cannot give a precise definition of them, till we have made a few previous remarks on their origin, their relation to each other, and their difference.

---

1. Charles Batteaux, *Les Beaux Arts réduits à un même principe* (Paris, 1747). Batteaux's redaction of Aristotelian mimetic theory is interrogated by Jones: 'the young William Jones was the first English writer to challenge the time-honoured notion that art ought to "imitate Nature"', V. de Sola Pinto, 'Sir William Jones and English Literature', *BSOAS* 11 (1946), 686–94, (689).

2. *the first language of man* 'Without overinterpreting Jones, his description of a primitive language, innately congruent with emotion, together with his notion that *in the present* such a congruence has been lost, may both be said to provide analogies for one of the most tenacious illusions of modern criticism, that of a "dissociation of sensibility".' David Newton-De Molina, 'Sir William Jones's "Essay on the Arts Commonly Called Imitative" (1772)', *Anglia* 90 (1972), 147–54, (149–50).

It seems probable then that *poetry* was originally no more than a strong and animated expression of the human passions,[1] of *joy* and *grief*, *love* and *hate*, *admiration* and *anger*, sometimes pure and unmixed, sometimes variously modified and combined: for, if we observe the *voice* and *accents* of a person affected by any of the violent passions, we shall perceive something in them very nearly approaching to *cadence* and *measure*; which is remarkably the case in the language of a vehement *Orator*, whose talent is chiefly conversant about *praise* or *censure*; and we may collect from several passages in *Tully*, that the fine speakers of old *Greece* and *Rome* had a sort of rhythm in their sentences, less regular, but not less melodious, than that of the poets.

If this idea be just, one would suppose that the most ancient sort of poetry consisted in *praising the Deity*;[2] for if we conceive a being, created with all his faculties and senses, endued with speech and reason, to open his eyes in a most delightful plain, to view for the first time the serenity of the sky, the splendour of the sun, the verdure of the fields and woods, the glowing colours of the flowers, we can hardly believe it possible, that he should refrain from bursting into an extasy of *joy*, and pouring his praises to the creator of those wonders, and the author of his happiness. This *kind of poetry* is used in all nations; but as it is the sublimest of all, when it is applied to its true object, so it has often been perverted to impious purposes by pagans and idolaters: every one knows that the *dramatick poetry* of the *Europeans* took its rise from the same spring, and was no more at first than a song in praise of *Bacchus*;[3] so that the only species of poetical composition (if we except the Epick) which can in any sense be called *imitative*, was deduced from a natural emotion of the mind, in which *imitation* could not be at all concerned.[4]

The next source of poetry was, probably, *love*, or the mutual inclination, which naturally subsists between the sexes, and is founded upon personal *beauty*: hence

---

1. *poetry was originally no more than a strong and animated expression of the human passions* This, of course, anticipates Wordsworth's famous definition: 'good poetry is the spontaneous overflow of powerful feelings', Preface to the *Lyrical Ballads* (1800).

2. *the most ancient sort of poetry consisted in praising the Deity* 'This theory of the origin of poetry, which one may call the "spontaneous generation" theory, was part of the whole conception of a "natural" evolution of poetry in terms of a biological organism', René Wellek, *The Rise of English Literary History* (New York, 1966), p.72.

3. In maintaining that even the imitative drama sprang from impassioned song in praise of Bacchus, 'Jones inverts the architecture of Aristotle's history of poetry, although incorporating much of the same material, for Aristotle in tracing the origins of poetry from the early hymns and encomia to the dramatic (*Poetics* 4) is tracing a development that to him resulted in more complicated and moving forms of art, whereas Sir William regards the later dramatic forms as top-heavy superstructures reared upon a base of pure poetry, the direct expression of passion', Norman Maclean, 'From Action to Image: Theories of the Lyric in the Eighteenth Century', in *Critics and Criticism*, ed. R. S. Crane, (Chicago, 1952), pp.408–60, (440).

4. Jones's theory that the origins of poetry were derived from 'a natural emotion of the mind, in which *imitation* could not be at all concerned' demonstrates, according to Abrams, 'that inversion of aesthetic values which reached its climax in the theory of John Stuart Mill, some sixty years later. The 'imitative' elements, hitherto held to be a defining attribute of poetry or art, become inferior, if not downright unpoetic; in their place those elements of a poem that express feeling become at once its identifying characteristic and cardinal poetic value', *The Mirror and the Lamp*, p.88.

arose the most agreeable *odes*, and love-songs, which we admire in the works of the ancient lyrick poets, not filled, like our *sonnets* and *madrigals*, with the insipid babble of *darts*, and *Cupids*, but simple, tender, natural; and consisting of such unaffected endearments, and mild complaints,

> *Teneri sdegni, e placide e tranquille
> Repulse, e cari vezzi, e liete paci,[1]

as we may suppose to have passed between the first lovers in a state of innocence, before the refinements of society, and the restraints, which they introduced, had made the passion of *love* so fierce, and impetuous, as it is said to have been in *Dido*, and certainly was in *Sappho*,[2] if we may take her own word for it.†

The *grief* which the first inhabitants of the earth must have felt at the death of their dearest friends, and relations, gave rise to another species of poetry, which originally, perhaps, consisted of short *dirges*, and was afterwards lengthened into *elegies*.

As soon as vice began to prevail in the world, it was natural for the wise and virtuous to express their *detestation* of it in the strongest manner, and to show their *resentment* against the corrupters of mankind: hence *moral poetry* was derived, which, at first, we find, was severe and passionate; but was gradually melted down into cool precepts of morality, or exhortations to virtue: we may reasonably conjecture that *Epick poetry* had the same origin, and that the examples of heroes and kings were introduced, to illustrate some moral truth, by showing the loveliness and advantages of virtue, or the many misfortunes that flow from vice.

Where there is vice, which is *detestable* in itself, there must be *hate*, since *the strongest antipathy in nature*, as *Mr. Pope* asserted in his writings, and proved by his whole life, *subsists between the good and the bad*:[3] now this passion was the source of that poetry, which we call *Satire*, very improperly, and corruptly, since the *Satire* of the *Romans* was no more than a moral piece, which they entitled *Satura* or *Satyra*,‡ intimating, that the poem, like *a dish of fruit and corn offered to Ceres*, contained a variety and plenty of fancies and figures; whereas the true *invectives* of the ancients were called *Iambi*, of which we have several examples in *Catullus*, and in the *Epodes* of *Horace*, who imitated the very measures and manner of *Archilochus*.[4]

These are the principal sources of *poetry*; and of *musick* also, as it shall be my endeavour to show: but it is first necessary to say a few words on *the nature of*

---

*Two lines of *Tasso*.
†See the ode of *Sappho* quoted by *Longinus*, and translated by *Boileau*.
‡Some Latin words were spelled either with an *u* or a *y*, as *Sulla* or *Sylla*.

---

1. *Gerusalemme Liberata* XVI.25.
2. The ode of Sappho referred to is quoted by Longinus in the tenth chapter of his *On the Sublime*, see T. S. Dorsch, *Classical Literary Criticism* (Harmondsworth, 1965), p.114.
3. See *An Essay on Man* II.iii.
4. Archilochus of Paros (*fl. c.*650 BC) was celebrated for his mastery of iambics in which he composed animated and cutting satire.

sound; a very copious subject, which would require a long dissertation to be accurately discussed. Without entering into a discourse on the *vibrations of chords*, or the *undulations of the air*, it will be sufficient for our purpose to observe that there is a great difference between *a common sound*, and *a musical sound*, which consists chiefly in this, that the former is simple and entire in itself like a *point*, while the latter is always accompanied with other sounds, without ceasing to be *one*; like a *circle*, which is an entire figure, though it is generated by a multitude of points flowing, at equal distances, round a common centre. These accessory sounds, which are caused by the aliquots of a sonorous body vibrating at once, are called *Harmonicks*, and the whole system of modern *Harmony* depends upon them; though it were easy to prove that the system is unnatural, and only made tolerable to the ear by habit: for whenever we strike the perfect accord on a harpsichord or an organ, the harmonicks of the third and fifth have also their own harmonicks, which are dissonant from the principal note: these horrid dissonances are, indeed, almost overpowered by the *natural harmonicks* of the principal chord, but that does not prove them agreeable. Since nature has given us a delightful harmony of her own, why should we destroy it by the additions of art? It is like thinking

> – to paint the lily,
> And add a perfume to the violet.[1]

Now let us conceive that some vehement passion is expressed in strong words, exactly measured, and pronounced, *in a common voice*, in just cadence, and with proper accents, such an expression of the passion will be *genuine poetry*; and the famous ode of *Sappho* is allowed to be so in the strictest sense; but if the same ode, with all its natural accents, were expressed in a *musical voice* (that is, in sounds accompanied with their *Harmonicks*), if it were sung in due time and measure, in a simple and pleasing tune, that added force to the words without stifling them, it would then be *pure and original musick*; not merely soothing to the ear, but affecting to the heart; not an *imitation* of nature, but the voice of nature herself. But there is another point in which *musick* must resemble *poetry*, or it will lose a considerable part of its effect: we all must have observed, that a speaker, agitated with passion, or an actor, who is, indeed, strictly an *imitator*, are perpetually changing the tone and pitch of their voice, as the sense of their words varies: it may be worth while to examine how this variation is expressed in *musick*. Every body knows that the musical scale consists of seven notes, above which we find a succession of similar sounds repeated in the same order, and above that, other successions, as far as they can be continued by the human voice, or distinguished by the human ear: now each of these seven sounds has no more meaning, when it is heard separately, than a single letter of the alphabet would have; and it is only by their succession, and their relation to one principal sound, that they take any rank

---

1. A slight misquotation of lines from *King John* which read: 'to paint the lily,/To throw a perfume on the violet'. Jones was evidently quoting from memory, cf. 'On the Poetry of the Eastern Nations', p.322 above.

in the scale; or differ from each other, except as they are *graver*, or more *acute*: but in the regular scale each interval assumes a proper character, and every note stands related to the first or principal one by various proportions. Now *a series of sounds relating to one leading note* is called a *mode*, or a *tone*, and, as there are twelve semitones in the scale, each of which may be made in its turn the leader of a mode, it follows that there are twelve modes; and each of them has a peculiar character, arising from the position of the *modal* note, and from some minute difference in the ratio's, as of 81 to 80, or a comma; for there are some intervals, which cannot easily be rendered on our instruments, yet have a surprizing effect in *modulation*, or in the transitions from one mode to another.

The *modes* of the ancients are said to have had a wonderful effect over the mind; and *Plato*, who permits the *Dorian* in his imaginary republick, on account of its calmness and gravity, excludes the *Lydian*, because of its languid, tender, and effeminate character: not that any series of mere sounds has a power of raising or soothing the passions, but each of these modes was appropriated to a particular kind of poetry, and a particular instrument; and the chief of them, as the *Dorian, Phrygian, Lydian, Ionian, Eolian, Locrian*, belonging originally to the nations, from which they took their names: thus the *Phrygian mode*, which was ardent and impetuous, was usually accompanied with trumpets, and the *Mixolydian*, which, if we believe *Aristoxenus*,[1] was invented by *Sappho*, was probably confined to the pathetick and tragick style: that these modes had a relation to *poetry* as well as to *musick*, appears from a fragment of *Lasus*,[2] in which he says, *I sing of Ceres, and her daughter Melibœa, the consort of Pluto, in the Eolian mode, full of gravity*; and *Pindar* calls one of his *Odes* an *Eolian song*. If the *Greeks* surpassed us in the strength of their modulations, we have an advantage over them in our *minor scale*, which supplies us with twelve new modes, where the two semitones are removed from their natural position between the third and fourth, the seventh and eighth notes, and placed between the second and third, the fifth and sixth; this change of the semitones, by giving a minor third to the *modal* note, softens the general expression of the mode, and adapts it admirably to subjects of *grief* and *affliction*: the minor mode of D is tender, that of C, with three flats, plaintive, and that of F, with four, pathetick and mournful to the highest degree, for which reason it was chosen by the excellent *Pergolesi* in his *Stabat Mater*.[3] Now these twenty-four modes, artfully interwoven, and changed as often as the sentiment changes, may, it is evident, express all the variations in the voice of a speaker, and give an additional beauty to the accents of a poet. Consistently with the foregoing principles, we may define *original and native poetry* to be *the language of the violent passions, expressed in exact measure, with strong accents and significant words*; and *true musick* to be no more than *poetry, delivered in a succession of harmonious sounds, so disposed as to*

---

1. Aristoxenes, a disciple of Aristotle, composed *The Elements of Harmonics* (*c*.320).
2. Lasus (*fl. c*.510 BC) was a Greek lyric poet who developed the potential of the dithyramb. He instructed Pindar in music as well as poetry and wrote the first theoretical treatise on music.
3. On Jones's admiration for Giovanni Battista Pergolesi (1710–36), ('whom the modern Italians are such puppies as to undervalue'), see *Letters*, II.512;736.

please the ear. It is in this view only that we must consider the musick of the ancient *Greeks*, or attempt to account for its amazing effects, which we find related by the gravest historians, and philosophers; it was wholly passionate or descriptive, and so closely united to poetry, that it never obstructed, but always increased its influence; whereas our boasted harmony, with all its fine accords, and numerous parts, paints nothing, expresses nothing, says nothing to the heart, and consequently can only give more or less pleasure to one of our senses; and no reasonable man will seriously prefer a transitory pleasure, which must soon end in satiety, or even in disgust, to a delight of the soul, arising from sympathy, and founded on the natural passions, always lively, always interesting, always transporting. The old divisions of musick into *celestial* and *earthly, divine* and *human, active* and *contemplative, intellective* and *oratorial*, were founded rather upon metaphors, and chimerical analogies, than upon any real distinctions in nature; but the want of making a distinction between *musick of mere sounds*, and the *musick of the passions*, has been the perpetual source of confusion and contradictions both among the ancients and the moderns: nothing can be more opposite in many points than the systems of *Rameau* and *Tartini*,[1] one of whom asserts that melody springs from harmony, and the other deduces harmony from melody; and both are in the right, if the first speaks only of that musick, which took its rise from *the multiplicity of sounds heard at once in the sonorous body*, and the second, of that, which rose from *the accents and inflexions of the human voice, animated by the passions*: to decide, as *Rousseau* says, whether of these two schools ought to have the preference, we need only ask a plain question, Was the voice made for the instruments, or the instruments for the voice?

In defining what true poetry *ought to be*, according to our principles, we have described what it really *was* among the *Hebrews*, the *Greeks* and *Romans*, the *Arabs* and *Persians*. The lamentation of *David*, and his sacred odes, or psalms, the song of *Solomon*, the prophecies of *Isaiah, Jeremiah*, and the other inspired writers, are truly and strictly poetical; but what did *David* or *Solomon* imitate in their divine poems? A man, who is *really* joyful or afflicted, cannot be said to *imitate* joy or affliction. The lyrick verses of *Alcæus*,[2] *Alcman*,[3] and *Ibycus*,[4] the hymns of *Callimachus*,[5] the elegy of *Moschus*[6] on the death of *Bion*, are all beautiful pieces of

---

1. Jean-Philippe Rameau (1683–1764) published his *Traité de l'harmonie réduite à ses principes naturels* in 1722, and the *Nouveau systéme de musique théorique* in 1726. Guiseppe Tartini (1692–1770), a progressive harmonic theorist, composed his *Trattato di musica* in 1754. On the Franco-Italian musical war which forms the background to this dispute, and on Rousseau's spirited interventions in the *Querelle des Bouffons*, see Gerald Abraham, *The Concise Oxford History of Music* (Oxford, 1979), pp.456–8.

2. Alcæus (*fl. c.*600 BC), a celebrated lyric poet and contemporary of Sappho, invented the Alcaic metre, and was regarded as a model by both Horace and Jones, see poem 10 above.

3. Alcman (*fl. c.*670 BC) is credited with being the founder of Doric lyric poetry. He died, according to Lemprière, 'of the lousy disease'.

4. Ibycus (*fl. c.*540 BC) was a lyric poet of Rhegium, famed for his erotic verse.

5. Callimachus (*fl. c.*250 BC) was the foremost Greek elegiac poet, and chief librarian of the Alexandrian library. His extant hymns are both exceptionally learned and devout.

6. Moschus (*fl. c.*150 BC), a Greek bucolic poet, wrote many elegant eclogues in hexameters. He was the pupil of Bion, although the elegy on Bion is probably not his.

poetry; yet *Alcæus* was no *imitator* of love, *Callimachus* was no *imitator* of religious awe and admiration, *Moschus* was no *imitator* of grief at the loss of an amiable friend. *Aristotle* himself wrote a very poetical elegy on the death of a man, whom he had loved; but it would be difficult to say what he imitated in it:

'*O virtue, who proposest many labours to the human race, and art still the alluring object of our life; for thy charms, O beautiful goddess, it was always an envied happiness in Greece even to die, and to suffer the most painful, the most afflicting evils: such are the immortal fruits, which thou raisest in our minds; fruits, more precious than gold, more sweet than the love of parents, and soft repose: for thee Hercules the son of Jove, and the twins of Leda, sustained many labours, and by their illustrious actions sought thy favour; for love of thee, Achilles and Ajax descended to the mansion of Pluto; and, through a zeal for thy charms, the prince of Atarnea also was deprived of the sun's light: therefore shall the muses, daughters of memory, render him immortal for his glorious deeds, whenever they sing the god of hospitality, and the honours due to a lasting friendship.*'[1]

In the preceding collection of poems, there are some *Eastern* fables, some *odes*, a *panegyrick*, and an *elegy*; yet it does not appear to me, that there is the least *imitation* in either of them: *Petrarch* was, certainly, too deeply affected with real *grief*, and the *Persian* poet was too sincere a lover, to *imitate* the passions of others. As to the rest, a fable in verse is no more an *imitation* than a fable in prose; and if every poetical narrative, which describes the manners, and relates the adventures of men, be called *imitative*, every romance, and even every history, must be called so likewise; since many poems are only *romances*, or parts of *history* told in a regular measure.

What has been said of *poetry*, may with equal force be applied to *musick*, which is *poetry*, dressed to advantage; and even to *painting*, many sorts of which are poems to the eye, as all poems, merely descriptive, are pictures to the ear: and this way of considering them will set the refinements of modern artists in their true light; for the *passions*, which were given by nature, never spoke in an unnatural form, and no man, truly affected with *love* or *grief*, ever expressed the one in an *acrostick*, or the other in a *fugue*: these remains, therefore, of the false taste, which prevailed in the dark ages, should be banished from this, which is enlightened with a just one.

It is true, that some kinds of painting are strictly *imitative*, as that which is solely intended to represent the human figure and countenance; but it will be found, that those pictures have always the greatest effect, which represent some *passion*, as the martyrdom of *St. Agnes* by *Domenichino*,[2] and the various representations of the

---

1. This elegy was occasioned by the death of his friend Hermias. This generous ruler of Atarneus and dedicated Platonist gave his adopted daughter in marriage to Aristotle. Hermias was captured by the Persians, tortured and crucified; his last words, 'Tell my friends and companions that I have done nothing unworthy of philosophy', inspired Aristotle's grief and admiration. See H. S. Long, (ed.), *Vitae Philosophorum* 1 (Oxford, 1964), pp. 198–200.
2. Domenichino Zampieri (1581–1641).

crucifixion by the finest masters of *Italy*; and there can be no doubt, but that the famous *sacrifice of Iphigenia* by *Timanthes* was affecting to the highest degree;[1] which proves, not that painting cannot be said to *imitate*, but that its most powerful influence over the mind arises, like that of the other arts, from *sympathy*.

It is asserted also that *descriptive* poetry, and *descriptive* musick, as they are called, are strict *imitations*; but, not to insist that mere *description* is the meanest part of both arts, if indeed it belongs to them at all, it is clear, that words and sounds have no kind of resemblance to visible objects: and what is an imitation, but a resemblance of some other thing? Besides, no unprejudiced hearer will say that he finds the smallest traces of imitation in the numerous *fugues, counterfugues,* and *divisions,* which rather disgrace than adorn the modern musick: even sounds themselves are imperfectly imitated by harmony, and, if we sometimes hear *the murmuring of a brook,* or *the chirping of birds* in a concert, we are generally apprised before-hand of the passages, where we may expect them. Some eminent musicians, indeed, have been absurd enough to think of imitating laughter and other noises, but, if they had succeeded, they could not have made amends for their want of taste in attempting it; for such ridiculous imitations must necessarily destroy the spirit and dignity of the finest poems, which they ought to illustrate by a graceful and natural melody. It seems to me, that, as those parts of *poetry, musick,* and *painting,* which relate to the passions, affect by *sympathy,* so those, which are merely descriptive, act by a kind of *substitution,*[2] that is, by raising in our minds, affections, or sentiments, analogous to those, which arise in us, when the respective objects in nature are presented to our senses. Let us suppose that a poet, a musician, and a painter, are striving to give their friend, or patron, a pleasure similar to that, which he feels at the sight of a beautiful prospect. The first will form an agreeable assemblage of lively images, which he will express in smooth and elegant verses of a sprightly measure; he will describe the most delightful objects, and will add to the graces of his description a certain delicacy of sentiment, and a spirit of cheerfulness. The musician, who undertakes to set the words of the poet, will select some mode, which, on his violin, has the character of mirth and gaiety, as the Eolian, or *E flat,* which he will change as the sentiment is varied: he will express the words in a simple and agreeable melody, which will not disguise, but embellish them, without aiming at any fugue, or figured harmony: he will use the bass, to mark the modulation more strongly, especially in the changes; and he will place the *tenour* generally in unison with the bass, to prevent too great a distance between the parts: in the symphony he will, above all things, avoid a *double melody,* and will

---

1. Timanthes (*fl. c.*350 BC). 'In his celebrated painting of Iphigenia going to be immolated, he represented all the attendants overwhelmed by grief; but his superior genius, by covering the face of Agamemnon, left to the conception of the imagination the deep sorrows of the father', (Lemprière).

2. It is clear that the kernel of Jones's thinking in this part of the essay owes much to his friend Burke's *A Philosophical Enquiry* (1757), esp. Part V, Sections V and VI. For example Burke writes: 'their business (poetry and rhetoric) is to affect rather by sympathy than imitation', and '*descriptive* poetry operates chiefly by *substitution*', ed. Adam Phillips, (Oxford, 1990), p.157.

apply his variations only to some accessory ideas, which the principal part, that is, the voice, could not easily express: he will not make a number of useless repetitions, because the *passions* only repeat the same expressions, and dwell upon the same sentiments, while *description* can only represent a single object by a single sentence. The painter will describe all visible objects more exactly than his rivals, but he will fall short of the other artists in a very material circumstance; namely, that his pencil, which may, indeed, express a simple passion, cannot paint a thought, or draw the shades of sentiment: he will, however, finish his landscape with grace and elegance; his colours will be rich, and glowing; his perspective striking; and his figures will be disposed with an agreeable variety, but not with confusion: above all, he will diffuse over his whole piece such a spirit of liveliness and festivity, that the beholder shall be seized with a kind of rapturous delight, and, for a moment, mistake art for nature.

Thus will each artist gain his end, not by *imitating* the works of nature, but by assuming her power, and causing the same effect upon the imagination, which her charms produce to the senses: this must be the chief object of a poet, a musician, and a painter, who know that *great effects are not produced by minute details, but by the general spirit of the whole piece, and that a gaudy composition may strike the mind for a short time, but that the beauties of simplicity are both more delightful, and more permanent.*

As the *passions* are differently modified in different men, and as even the various objects in nature affect our minds in various degrees, it is obvious, that there must be a great diversity in the pleasure, which we receive from the fine arts, whether that pleasure arises from *sympathy* or *substitution*; and that it were a wild notion in artists to think of pleasing every reader, hearer, or beholder; since every man has a particular set of objects, and a particular inclination, which direct him in the choice of his pleasures, and induce him to consider the productions, both of nature and of art, as more or less elegant, in proportion as they give him a greater or smaller degree of delight: this does not at all contradict the opinion of many able writers, that *there is one uniform standard of taste*;[1] since the *passions*, and, consequently, *sympathy*, are generally the same in all men, till they are weakened by age, infirmity, or other causes.

If the arguments, used in this essay, have any weight, it will appear, that the finest parts of poetry, musick, and painting, are expressive of the *passions*, and operate on our minds by *sympathy*; that the inferior parts of them are *descriptive* of natural *objects*, and affect us chiefly *by substitution*; that the expressions of *love*, *pity*, *desire*, and the *tender* passions, as well as the *descriptions* of objects that delight the senses, produce in the arts what we call the *beautiful*; but that *hate*, *anger*, *fear*, and the *terrible* passions, as well as objects, which are *unpleasing* to the senses, are productive of the *sublime*, when they are aptly expressed, or described.

---

1. *there is one uniform standard of taste* Cf. the second edition (1759) of *A Philosophical Enquiry*, containing the Introduction on Taste where Burke writes: 'So far then as Taste belongs to the imagination, its principle is the same in all men', ed. cit., p.20.

These subjects might be pursued to infinity; but, if they were amply discussed, it would be necessary to write a series of dissertations, instead of an essay.

27

From *On the Gods of Greece, Italy, and India* (1784)

[Pioneering in its attempt to discover universal connections between Oriental and Occidental religions and cultures, this essay was immediately and widely influential in its day. In yet another attempt to change the psychological use the West was making of the Orient, Jones is exploiting a kind of cultural relativism to familiarize Europe with the 'alien' beliefs of the sub-continent. According to Frank E. Manuel, Jones presented the West 'with the mighty challenge of the Hindus as teachers of the Egyptians . . . herald[ing] the Aryan thesis to which the nineteenth-century German scholars devoted themselves', *The Eighteenth Century Confronts the Gods* (Cambridge, Mass.), 1959, p. 114. Initially read to the Society on 24 March 1785, the essay was published, along with ten other substantial papers from Jones's pen in the first volume of *Asiatick Researches* (1788). The copy-text is 1807 with variants noted from *Asiatick Researches*.

Jones begins his discourse by announcing a path-breaking charter for the comparison of mythic traditions: 'when features of resemblance, too strong to have been accidental, are observable in different systems of polytheism, without fancy or prejudice to colour them, we can scarce help believing, that some connection has immemorially subsisted between the several nations, who have adopted them' *Works*, III.319. He proceeds to outline four principal sources of mythology: 'I. Euhemerism, where historical, or natural truth has been perverted into fable by ignorance, imagination, flattery, or stupidity; . . . II. . . . a wild admiration of the heavenly bodies, . . . III. Numberless divinities have been created solely by the magic of poetry; whose essential business it is, to personify the most abstract notions, and to place a nymph or a genius in every grove . . .' The first extract is from *Works*, III.322–4.]

FROM *ON THE GODS OF GREECE, ITALY, AND INDIA*

IV. The metaphors and allegories of moralists and metaphysicians have been also very fertile in Deities; of which a thousand examples might be adduced from PLATO, CICERO, and the inventive commentators on HOMER in their pedigrees of the Gods, and their fabulous lessons of morality: the richest and noblest stream from this abundant fountain is the charming philosophical tale of PSYCHE, or the *Progress of the Soul*; than which, to my taste, a more beautiful, sublime, and well supported allegory was never produced by the wisdom and ingenuity of man. Hence also the Indian MÁYA, or, as the word is explained by some *Hindu* scholars, "the first inclination of the Godhead to diversify himself (such is their phrase) by creating worlds," is feigned to be the mother of universal nature, and of all the inferiour Gods; as a *Cashmirian* informed me, when I asked him, why CÁMA, or *Love*, was represented as her son; but the word MÁYA, or *delusion*, has a more subtile and recondite sense in the *Védánta* philosophy,[1] where it signifies the system of *perceptions*, whether of secondary or of primary qualities, which the Deity was believed by EPICHARMUS,[2] PLATO, and many truly pious men, to raise by his omnipresent spirit in the minds of his creatures, but which had not, in their opinion, any existence independent of mind.

In drawing a parallel between the Gods of the *Indian* and *European* heathens,[3] from whatever source they were derived, I shall remember, that nothing is less favourable to enquiries after truth than a systematical spirit,[4] and shall call to mind the saying of a *Hindu* writer, 'that whoever obstinately adheres to any set of opinions, may bring himself to believe that the freshest sandal wood is a flame of fire:' this will effectually prevent me from insisting, that such a God of *India* was *the* JUPITER of *Greece*; such, *the* APOLLO; such, *the* MERCURY: in fact, since all the causes of polytheism contributed largely to the assemblage of *Grecian* divinities (though

---

1. In September 1788 Jones wrote to Lord Monboddo: 'As my principal object is the jurisprudence, I have not yet examined the philosophy of the Brahmans; but I have seen enough of it to be convinced, that the doctrines of the Vidanti school are Platonic', *Letters*, II.818. 'This identification of the foremost school of Indian philosophy with the philosophy of Pythagoras and Plato informs Jones's whole approach to classical Indian culture and this, together with the sympathetic nature of his response, is perhaps Jones's most important contribution to English letters', Drew, *India and the Romantic Imagination*, p. 49. The strong possibility that Blake discovered Hindu metaphysics through Jones is examined by Kathleen Raine, *Blake and Tradition*, 2 vols. (London, 1969), I.144,177–83;II.324. A detailed examination of Jones's influence upon the longer mythological poems of William Blake has not yet been undertaken.

2. EPICHARMUS A poet and Pythagorean philosopher of fifth and sixth century Sicily.

3. *the Gods of the Indian and European heathens* It is in such apparently innocuous formulations that Jones underlines his syncretism.

4. Jones's own speculative and syncretist spirit is in evidence throughout this discourse, and it is significant that his counsel of caution should be a Hindu writer.

BACON[1] reduces them all to refined allegories, and NEWTON[2] to a poetical disguise of true history), we find many JOVES, many APOLLOS, many MERCURIES, with distinct attributes and capacities; nor shall I presume to suggest more, than that, in one capacity or another, there exists a striking similitude between the chief objects of worship in ancient *Greece* or *Italy* and in the very interesting country, which we now inhabit.

[Jones proceeds to acknowledge a most conventional religious position: 'Either the first eleven chapters of *Genesis*, all due allowances being made for a figurative Eastern style, are true, or the whole fabrick of our national religion is false; a conclusion, which none of us, I trust, would wish to be drawn.' He was well aware, of course, that to adopt any other position would risk incurring in his European readers the very prejudices he wished to allay. Privately, the emphasis was slightly different, the awful injustice of eternal pain appalled him; in a letter to Althorp of 1–11 September 1787 he writes: 'I am no Hindu; but I hold the doctrine of the Hindus concerning a future state to be incomparably more rational, more pious, and more likely to deter men from vice, than the horrid opinions inculcated by Christians on punishments *without end*', *Letters*, II.766. It remains, however, somewhat surprising that this intellectually probing and enlightened Deist should fail to consider the ramifications of his researches. 'He is aware of the revolutionary implications of his work on the antiquity of Hindu civilization and on the parallelism of mythologies, but rejects them . . . His work is a strange mixture of a new and self-professed accuracy, geographic, linguistic, historical, with unfounded traditional views', E. S. Shaffer, *'Kubla Khan' and 'The Fall of Jerusalem'*, p.117.

Jones outlines the similarities between Ganēsa and Janus, Manu or Satyavrata and Saturn, Indra and Jupiter, Nārada and Hermes, Ceres and Lakshmī, including fourteen decorous illustrations of individual Hindu deities. He translates from the *Matsya Purána* the story of the universal deluge, comparing it with its Biblical parallel (III.332–8). He also expounds the ten *Avatárs* (Descents) of the supreme deity, and draws parallels between the four *Yugs* and the classical ages of gold, silver, copper, and iron. It is clear that Jones's description of the still-awaited tenth *avatár*, when Vishnu will descend 'mounted (like the crowned conqueror in the *Apocalyps*) on a white horse, with a cimeter blazing like a comet to mow down all incorrigible and impenitent offenders' inspired Thomas Campbell's vision of divine retribution for the rapacities of the East India Company in 'The Pleasures of Hope' (1799), see *The Pleasures of Hope with other Poems* (Edinburgh, 1813), pp.95–6. On the alleged barbarities of Company policy in Bengal as perceived by writers of sensibility, see Chris Jones, *Radical Sensibility* (London, 1993), p.63. The second extract is from *Works*, III.349–54.]

---

1. Francis Bacon (1561–1626), in *De Sapientia Veterum* (1609) elaborated upon a favourite thesis that the mythology of the Greeks was allegorical, concealing profound philosophic truths.
2. Sir Isaac Newton (1642–1727), in the posthumously published *The Chronology of Ancient Kingdoms Amended* (London, 1728), maintained the euhemeristic position that mythology had a historical basis in hero-worship. Newton, incidentally, was a friend of the mathematician William Jones, sen.

Let us now descend, from these general and introductory remarks, to some particular observations on the resemblance of ZEUS or JUPITER to the triple divinity VISHNU, SIVA, BRAHMÁ; for that is the order, in which they are expressed by the letters A, U, and M, which coalesce and form the mystical word ÓM; a word, which never escapes the lips of a pious *Hindu*, who meditates on it in silence: whether the *Egyptian* ON, which is commonly supposed to mean the Sun, be the *Sanscrit* monosyllable, I leave others to determine. It must always be remembered, 'that the learned *Indians*, as they are instructed by their own books, in truth acknowledge only One Supreme Being, whom they call BRAHME, or THE GREAT ONE in the neuter gender: they believe his Essence to be infinitely removed from the comprehension of any mind but his own; and they suppose him to manifest his power by the operation of his divine spirit, whom they name VISHNU, the *Pervader*, and NÁRÁYAN, or *Moving on the waters*, both in the masculine gender, whence he is often denominated the *First Male*; and by this power they believe, that the whole order of nature is preserved and supported; but the *Védántis*, unable to form a distinct idea of brute matter independent of mind, or to conceive that the work of Supreme Goodness was left a moment to itself, imagine that the Deity is ever present to his work, and constantly supports a series of perceptions, which, in one sense, they call *illusory*, though they cannot but admit the *reality* of all created forms, as far as the happiness of creatures can be affected by them.[1] When they consider the divine power exerted in *creating*, or in giving existence to that which existed not before, they call the deity BRAHMÁ in the masculine gender also; and, when they view him in the light of *Destroyer*, or rather *Changer* of forms, they give him a thousand names, of which SIVA, ÍSA, or ÍSWARA, RUDRA, HARA, SAMBHU, and MAHÁDÉVA or MAHÉSA, are the most common. The first operations of these three *Powers* are variously described in the different *Purána's* by a number of allegories, and from them we may deduce the *Ionian* Philosophy of *primeval water*, the doctrine of the Mundane Egg, and the veneration paid to the *Nymphœa, or Lotos*, which was anciently revered in *Egypt*, as it is at present in *Hindustán, Tibet*, and *Népal*: the *Tibetians* are said to embellish their temples and altars with it, and a native of *Népal* made prostrations before it on entering my study, where the fine plant and beautiful flowers lay for examination. Mr. HOLWEL,[2] in explaining his first plate, supposes BRAHMÁ to be floating on a leaf of *betel* in the midst of the abyss; but it was manifestly intended by a bad painter for a lotos-leaf, or for that of the *Indian* fig-tree; nor is the species of pepper, known in *Bengal* by the name of *Támbúla*, and on the Coast of *Malabar* by that of *betel*, held sacred, as he asserts, by the *Hindus*, or necessarily cultivated under the inspection of *Bráhmans*; though, as the vines are

---

1. Jones had at this time been in India less than two years but he already possessed a sound understanding of the *Advaita Védanta*.
2. John Zephaniah Holwell (1711–98), former governor of Bengal, and one of the first Europeans to study Hindu antiquities and mythology, had pronounced deistic leanings and was one of Voltaire's chief sources of information about India. See A. Aronson, *Europe Looks at India* (Bombay, 1945), p.17, and P. J. Marshall (ed.), *The British Discovery of Hinduism* (Cambridge, 1970), pp.45–106.

tender, all the plantations of them are carefully secured, and ought to be cultivated by a particular tribe of *Súdras*, who are thence called *Támbúli's*.

That *water* was the primitive element and first work of the Creative Power, is the uniform opinion of the *Indian* Philosophers; but, as they give so particular an account of the general deluge and of the Creation, it can never be admitted, that their whole system arose from traditions concerning the flood only, and must appear indubitable, that their doctrine is in part borrowed from the opening of *Birásìt* or *Genesis*, than which a sublimer passage, from the first word to the last, never flowed or will flow from any human pen: '*In the beginning* GOD created the heavens and the earth. – And the earth was void and waste, and darkness was on the face of the deep, and the spirit of GOD *moved upon* the face of the waters; and GOD said: *Let Light be* – and *Light was*.' The sublimity of this passage is considerably diminished by the *Indian* paraphrase of it, with which MENU, the son of BRAHMÁ, begins his address to the sages, who consulted him on the formation of the universe: 'This world, says he, was all darkness, undiscernible, undistinguishable, altogether as in a profound sleep; till the self-existent invisible GOD, making it manifest with five elements and other glorious forms, perfectly dispelled the gloom. He, desiring to raise up various creatures by an emanation from his own glory, first created the *waters*, and impressed them with a power of motion: by that power was produced a golden Egg,[1] blazing like a thousand suns, in which was born BRAHMÁ, self-existing, the great parent of all rational beings. The waters are called *nárà*, since they are the offspring of NERA (or ÍSWARA); and thence was NÁRÁYANA named, because his first *ayana*, or *moving*, was on them.

'THAT WHICH IS, the invisible cause, eternal, self-existing, but unperceived, becoming masculine *from neuter*, is celebrated among all creatures by the name of BRAHMÁ. That God, having dwelled in the Egg, through revolving years, Himself meditating on Himself, divided it into two equal parts; and from those halves formed the heavens and the earth, placing in the midst the subtil ether, the eight points of the world, and the permanent receptacle of waters.'[2]

To this curious description, with which the *Mánava Sástra* begins, I cannot refrain from subjoining the four verses, which are the text of the *Bhágavat*, and are believed to have been pronounced by the Supreme Being to BRAHMÁ: the following version is most scrupulously literal.*

*See the Original, p.294.

---

1. This establishment of a mythic parallel leads Kathleen Raine to ask: 'does "the Mundane Shell" [in Blake's *Jerusalem*] derive in part from the "egg" of Brahmā as well as from the Orphic egg (known to Blake from various early writings of Thomas Taylor), from which Time hatches as the two halves of the shell fall apart to become heaven and earth?' *Blake and Tradition*, I.182.

2. Jones himself translated *Institutes of Hindu Law: or, The Ordinances of Menu* as a primary source for his law digest, and it was printed by order of the Government in Calcutta in 1794. This quotation from Manu differs slightly from the later translation, cf. *Works*, VII.92–3.

3. Footnote This reference is to Charles Wilkins, *The Bhăgvăt-Gēētā* (London, 1785). This work by Jones's friend and mentor represents the first complete translation directly from a major Sanskrit text; it appeared in November 1784 under the auspices of the Asiatic Society of Bengal.

'Even I was even at first, not any other thing; that, which exists, unperceived; supreme: afterwards I AM THAT WHICH IS; and he, who must remain, am I.

'Except the FIRST CAUSE, whatever may appear, and may not appear, in the mind, know that to be the mind's MÁYÁ (or *Delusion*), as light, as darkness.

'As the great elements are in various beings, entering, yet not entering (that is, pervading, not destroying), thus am I in them, yet not in them.

'Even thus far may inquiry be made by him, who seeks to know the principle of mind, in union and separation, which must be EVERYWHERE ALWAYS.'

Wild and obscure as these ancient verses must appear in a naked verbal translation, it will perhaps be thought by many, that the poetry or mythology of *Greece* or *Italy* afford no conceptions more awfully magnificent: yet the brevity and simplicity of the *Mosaick* diction are unequalled.

[Jones continues his investigation of parallel deities, repeatedly comparing Indian and European systems as equally worthy of scholarly research. Not totally to disappoint the expectations of a Western readership, trained over the centuries to associate Indian gods with delightfully repulsive human sacrifice and flattened devotees of Jagganāth, Jones includes the black Goddess Cáli, with her necklace of skulls and taste for bloody ceremonies. He reminds his audience, however, of the no less sanguinary Stygian Diana, or Hecate, in whose temple shipwrecked sailors and innocent victims were cruelly slaughtered.

Jones subscribes to what Martin Bernal (*Black Athena: The Egyptian and Semitic Roots of Ancient Greece*, 3 vols. (London, 1987–90) has termed the 'Ancient Model' of Greek origins, acknowledging the cultural primacy of Egypt and the theory that Greece had been colonized from Egypt at the beginning of the Heroic Age. 'Since *Egypt* appears to have been the grand source of knowledge for the *western*, and *India* for the more *eastern*, parts of the globe, it may seen a material question, whether the *Egyptians* communicated their Mythology and Philosophy to the *Hindus*, or conversely;' (p.386). Egypt and India are thus seen as two Oriental loci of cultural superiority and intellectual predominance while Greek and Roman civilization is perceived as derivative. Again it might be wished that Jones had fully explored the wider implication of what he was asserting here, but his immediate concern (the Hindu diffusion thesis) remains paramount. With forensic scrupulosity and judicial caution he examines the case for a Hindu tradition that Egyptian priests had established a colony on the Ganges. While admitting that the evidence is circumstantial, he is inclined to believe it, but the tradition has now been discredited.

In attacking the missionaries' proselytizing argument 'that the *Hindus* were even now almost *Christians*, because their BRAHMÁ, VISHNU, and MAHÉSA, were no other than the *Christian* Trinity' (p.393), Jones simultaneously distanced himself from such specious theological arguments with their patently ulterior motives, and from fellow Orientalist scholars like Holwell, Dow, and Wilkins whose deist position had been strengthened by those very arguments. Jones saw that using Hinduism as a stick to beat Christianity in the tradition established by Voltaire and the Abbé Raynal was clearly incompatible with the creation of sympathy with things Indian. According to Kenneth Stunkel, however, 'Jones slid into a variety of special pleading unworthy of so fine an intellect and scholar', 'English Orientalism and India, 1784–1830', *Ohio University Review*, 11 (1969), 49–72 (62). Jones argues that, 'The *Indian* Triad, and that of PLATO . . . are infinitely removed from the holiness and sublimity of the doctrine, which pious *Christians* have deduced from texts in the Gospel', and, unwilling to cause offence to Unitarians, he adds: 'though other *Christians*, as pious, openly profess their dissent from them.' All this was grist to the mill of Lord Teignmouth, official biographer of Jones and member of the Clapham Sect, in his pious attempt to prove Jones an evangelist. But while reluctant to generate hostility in his Christian audience, Jones bore no brief for missionaries of any persuasion: 'neither *Muselmans* nor *Hindus* will ever be converted by any mission from the Church of *Rome*, or from any other church'. Ultimately he believed that each sect must be justified by its own faith and good works. If conversion were to be attempted 'the only human mode' would be through translations of Isaiah, together with one of the Gospels to confirm the fulfilment of the prophecies, the emphasis always being placed on reason and patient education, see pp.396–7. The *Gentleman's Magazine* of March 1790 (vol. 60, p.220) wholeheartedly approved: 'How much more rational this mode of propagating true religion than by the sword, or the fanatic rage of destroying every memorial of error, in which many of the noblest works of human taste and art are included! How much it were to be wished that Sir William Jones would himself undertake the desirable work.' The final irony is nicely captured by Elinor Shaffer: 'Jones's faith has a kind of rationalist pathos about it: the Bible as accurate history, and prophecy as prediction was doomed to extinction, in part by his own researches', *'Kubla Khan' and 'The Fall of Jerusalem'*, p.121.]

28

The Third Anniversary Discourse, on the Hindus, delivered to the Asiatic Society, 2 February 1786

[Sir William Jones's historic postulation of the Indo-European thesis, made less than six months after he had begun the study of Sanskrit, established the cornerstone of modern comparative philology. As Hans Aarsleff has written: 'By making it strictly historical, comparative, and structural, Jones caused a revolution in the study of language' (*The Study of Language in England, 1780–1860*, New Jersey, 1967; repr. London, 1983, p. 134). Even more importantly he had established a cultural link between East and West wherein the colonized appeared in a superior light to the colonizer. The discourse, first published in *Asiatick Researches*, 1 (1788), was included, together with erudite notation, in P. J. Marshall (ed.), *The British Discovery of Hinduism in the Eighteenth Century* (Cambridge, 1970), pp.246–61. The copy-text is 1807 with variants noted from *Asiatick Researches*.]

THE THIRD ANNIVERSARY DISCOURSE
DELIVERED 2 FEBRUARY, 1786, BY THE PRESIDENT

In the former discourses, which I had the honour of addressing to you, Gentlemen, on the *institution* and *objects* of our Society, I confined myself purposely to general topicks; giving in the first a distant prospect of the vast career, on which we were entering, and, in the second, exhibiting a more diffuse, but still superficial, sketch of the various discoveries in History, Science, and Art, which we might justly expect from our inquiries into the literature of *Asia*. I now propose to fill up that outline so comprehensively as to omit nothing essential, yet so concisely as to avoid being tedious; and, if the state of my health shall suffer me to continue long enough in this climate, it is my design, with your permission, to prepare for our annual meetings a series of short dissertations, unconnected in their titles and subjects, but all tending to a common point of no small importance in the pursuit of interesting truths.

Of all the works, which have been published in our own age, or, perhaps, in any other, on the History of the Ancient World, and *the first population of this habitable globe*, that of Mr. Jacob Bryant,[1] whom I name with reverence and affection, has the best claim to the praise of deep erudition ingeniously applied, and new theories happily illustrated by an assemblage of numberless converging rays from a most extensive circumference: it falls, nevertheless, as every human work must fall, short of perfection; and the least satisfactory part of it seems to be that, which relates to the derivation of words from *Asiatick* languages. Etymology has, no doubt, some use in historical researches; but it is a medium of proof so very fallacious,[2] that, where it elucidates one fact, it obscures a thousand, and more frequently borders on the ridiculous, than leads to any solid conclusion: it rarely carries with it any *internal* power of conviction from a resemblance of sounds or similarity of letters; yet often, where it is wholly unassisted by those advantages, it may be indisputably proved by *extrinsick* evidence. We know *à posteriori*,[3] that both *fitz* and *hijo*, by the nature of two several dialects, are derived from *filius*; that *uncle* comes from *avus*,

---

1. Jacob Bryant's three volume *A New System, or, an Analysis of Ancient Mythology* (London, 1774–6) had been eagerly read by Jones, despite his reservations about Bryant's synthetic method. 'There is an infinite profusion of learning in his book, but I cannot help thinking his system very uncertain', *Letters*, I.239. Thomas Maurice suggests that Jones had provided John Richardson, a staunch critic of *A New System*, with valuable linguistic ammunition, *Memoirs of the Author of Indian Antiquities* (London, 1819–22), II.41.
2. In linguistic investigation Jones always stressed the dangers of etymological method, preferring to examine grammatical structures in an analytical and empirical fashion.
3. Aarslef writes: 'the decisive turn in language study occurred when the philosophical, a priori method of the eighteenth century was abandoned in favour of the historical, a posteriori method of the nineteenth . . . This method was first introduced, clearly explained, and fully argued by Sir William Jones', *The Study of Language*, p.127.

and *stranger* from *extra*; that *jour* is deducible, through the *Italian*, from *dies*; and *rossignol* from *luscinia*, or the *singer in groves*; that *sciuro*, *écureuil*, and *squirrel* are compounded of two *Greek* words descriptive of the animal; which etymologies, though they could not have been demonstrated *à priori*, might serve to confirm, if any such confirmation were necessary, the proofs of a connection between the members of one great Empire; but, when we derive our *hanger* or *short pendent sword*, from the *Persian*, because ignorant travellers thus mispell the work *khanjar*, which in truth means a different weapon, or *sandal-wood* from the *Greek*, because we suppose, that *sandals* were sometimes made of it, we gain no ground in proving the affinity of nations, and only weaken arguments, which might otherwise be firmly supported. That Cús then, or, as it certainly is written in one ancient dialect, Cút, and in others, probably, Cás, enters into the composition of many proper names, we may very reasonably believe; and that *Algeziras* takes its name from the *Arabick* word for an *island*, cannot be doubted; but, when we are told from *Europe*,[1] that places and provinces in *India* were clearly denominated from those words, we cannot but observe, in the first instance, that the town, in which we now are assembled, is properly written and pronounced *Calicátà*; that both *Cátá and Cút* unquestionably mean *places of strength*; or, in general, any *inclosures*; and that *Gujaràt* is at least as remote from *Jezirah* in sound, as it is in situation.

Another exception (and a third could hardly be discovered by any candid criticism) to the *Analysis of Ancient Mythology*, is, that the *method* of reasoning and arrangement of topicks adopted in that learned work are not quite agreeable to the title, but almost wholly *synthetical*; and, though *synthesis* may be the better mode in pure *science*, where the principles are undeniable, yet it seems less calculated to give complete satisfaction in *historical* disquisitions, where every postulatum will perhaps be refused, and every definition controverted: this may seem a slight objection, but the subject is in itself so interesting, and the full conviction of all reasonable men so desirable, that it may not be lost labour to discuss the same or a similar theory in a method purely analytical, and, after beginning with facts of general notoriety or undisputed evidence, to investigate such truths, as are at first unknown or very imperfectly discerned.

The *five* principal nations, who have in different ages divided among themselves, as a kind of inheritance, the vast continent of *Asia*, with the many islands depending on it, are the *Indians*, the *Chinese*, the *Tartars*, the *Arabs*, and the *Persians*: who they severally were, *whence*, and *when* they came, *where* they now are settled, and *what advantage* a more perfect knowledge of them all may bring to our *European* world, will be shown, I trust, in *five* distinct essays; the last of which will demonstrate the connexion or diversity between them, and solve the great problem, whether they had *any* common origin, and whether that origin was *the same*, which we generally ascribe to them.

---

1. *when we are told from Europe*   Jones rebuts, with some of the impatience of the field-worker, Bryant's etymological deductions concerning places supposedly named after Cush, the son of Ham.

I begin with *India*, not because I find reason to believe it the true centre of population or of knowledge, but, because it is the country, which we now inhabit, and from which we may best survey the regions around us; as, in popular language, we speak of the *rising* sun, and of his *progress through the Zodiack*, although it had long ago been imagined, and is now demonstrated, that he is himself the centre of our planetary system. Let me here premise, that, in all these inquiries concerning the history of *India*, I shall confine my researches downwards to the *Mohammedan* conquests at the beginning of the *eleventh* century, but extend them upwards, as high as possible, to the earliest authentick records of the human species.

India then, on its most enlarged scale, in which the ancients appear to have understood it, comprises an area of near *forty* degrees on each side, including a space almost as large as all *Europe*; being divided on the west from *Persia* by the *Arachosian* mountains, limited on the east by the *Chinese* part of the farther peninsula, confined on the north by the wilds of *Tartary*, and extending to the south as far as the isles of *Java*.[1] This trapezium, therefore, comprehends the stupendous hills of *Potyid*[2] or *Tibet*, the beautiful valley of *Cashmír*, and all the domains of the old *Indoscythians*, the countries of *Népál* and *Butánt*, *Cámrùp* or *Asàm*, together with *Siam*, *Ava*,[3] *Racan*, and the bordering kingdoms, as far as the *China* of the *Hindus* or *Sín* of the *Arabian* Geographers; not to mention the whole western peninsula with the celebrated island of *Sinhala*,[4] or *Lion-like men*, at its southern extremity. By *India*, in short, I mean that whole extent of country, in which the primitive religion and languages of the *Hindus* prevail at this day with more or less of their ancient purity, and in which the *Nágarì* letters are still used with more or less deviation from their original form.

The *Hindus* themselves believe their own country, to which they give the vain epithets of *Medhyama* or *Central*, and *Punyabhúmi*, or the *Land of Virtues*, to have been the portion of BHARAT,[5] one of *nine* brothers, whose father had the dominion of the whole earth; and they represent the mountains of *Himálaya* as lying to the north, and, to the west, those of *Vindhya*, called also *Vindian* by the *Greeks*; beyond which the *Sindhu*[6] runs in several branches to the sea, and meets it nearly opposite to the point of *Dwáracà*, the celebrated seat of their Shepherd God:[7] in the *south-east* they place the great river *Saravatya*; by which they probably mean that of *Ava*, called also *Airávati* in part of its course, and giving perhaps its ancient name to the gulf of *Sabara*. This domain of *Bharat* they consider as the middle of the *Jambudwípa*, which the *Tibetians* also call the Land of *Zambu*; and the appellation

---

1. In redefining India according to the ancients, Jones was not only outlining the scale of his labours, but also establishing the theoretic foundations of a reemergent nationhood.

2. *Potyid* Augustino Antonio Giorgio claimed that 'Potjid' was the name the Tibetans used for their land, *Alphabetum Tibetanum Missionum Apostolicarum* (Rome, 1762), pp.14–15. See below p.363.

3. *Ava* Burma.

4. *island of Sinhala* Sri Lanka.

5. *BHARAT* Bharata, after whom the Indian sub-continent was named Bharatavarsa, was the eldest son of Rsabha (the Bull), or Morality.

6. *the Sindhu* The Indus.

7. *Shepherd God* Krishna.

is extremely remarkable; for *Jambu* is the *Sanscrit* name of a delicate fruit called *Jáman* by the *Muselmans*, and by us *rose-apple*; but the largest and richest sort is named *Amrita*, or *Immortal*; and the Mythologists of *Tibet* apply the same word to a celestial tree bearing *ambrosial fruit*, and adjoining to *four* vast rocks, from which as many sacred rivers derive their several streams.[1]

The inhabitants of this extensive tract are described by Mr. LORD with great exactness, and with a picturesque elegance peculiar to our ancient language: 'A people, says he, presented themselves to mine eyes, clothed in linen garments somewhat low descending, of a gesture and garb, as I may say, maidenly and well nigh effeminate, of a countenance shy and somewhat estranged, yet smiling out a glozed and bashful familiarity.'[2] Mr. ORME,[3] the Historian of *India*, who unites an exquisite taste for every fine art with an accurate knowledge of *Asiatick* manners, observes, in his elegant preliminary Dissertation, that this 'country has been inhabited from the earliest antiquity by a people, who have no resemblance, either in their figure or manners, with any of the nations contiguous to them,' and that, 'although conquerors have established themselves at different times in different parts of *India*, yet the original inhabitants have lost very little of their original character.' The ancients, in fact, give a description of them, which our early travellers confirmed, and our own personal knowledge of them nearly verifies; as you will perceive from a passage in the Geographical Poem of DIONYSIUS,[4] which the Analyst of Ancient Mythology has translated with great spirit:

> 'To th' east a lovely country wide extends,
> INDIA, whose borders the wide ocean bounds;
> On this the sun, new rising from the main,
> Smiles pleas'd, and sheds his early orient beam.
> Th' inhabitants are swart, and in their locks
> Betray the tints of the dark hyacinth.
> Various their functions; some the rock explore,
> And from the mine extract the latent gold;
> Some labour at the woof with cunning skill,
> And manufacture linen; others shape
> And polish iv'ry with the nicest care:
> Many retire to rivers shoal, and plunge

1. *for Jambu – several streams* Southey transcribed this passage, adding the following comment: 'It is odd that Sir W. Jones makes no remark upon this resemblance to the immortalizing milk, or tree of life', *Southey's Common-Place Book,* fourth Series, ed. J. W. Warter (London, 1850), p.254.

2. *maidenly and well nigh effeminate* This extract from Henry Lord's *A Display of Two Forraigne Sects in the East Indies* (London, 1630) provides an early but typical example of the tendency to view the Orient as feminized Other.

3. Robert Orme, a friend with whom Jones corresponded both in England and Bengal, published *A History of the Military Transactions of the British Nation in Indostan from the Year MDCCXLV* (London, 1763; vol. ii in 1778). Jones's letters to Orme gently but persistently attempt to modify the historian's chauvinistic and classical prejudices, and it is, perhaps, surprising that Jones singles out both Lord and Orme for unqualified praise.

4. Dionysius Periegetes, a writer of the Augustan age, composed this geographical treatise in Greek hexameters, see Bryant, *A New System,* III.227–8.

> To seek the beryl flaming in its bed,
> Or glitt'ring diamond. Oft the jasper's found
> Green, but diaphanous; the topaz too
> Of ray serene and pleasing; last of all
> The lovely amethyst, in which combine
> All the mild shades of purple. The rich soil,
> Wash'd by a thousand rivers, from all sides
> Pours on the natives wealth without control.'

Their sources of wealth are still abundant even after so many revolutions and conquests; in their manufactures of cotton they still surpass all the world; and their features have, most probably, remained unaltered since the time of Dionysius; nor can we reasonably doubt, how degenerate and abased so ever the *Hindus* may now appear, that in some early age they were splendid in arts and arms, happy in government, wise in legislation, and eminent in various knowledge:[1] but, since their civil history beyond the middle of the *nineteenth* century from the present time, is involved in a cloud of fables, we seem to possess only *four* general media of satisfying our curiosity concerning it; namely, first, their *Languages* and *Letters*; secondly, their *Philosophy* and *Religion*; thirdly, the actual remains of their old *Sculpture* and *Architecture*; and fourthly, the written memorials of their *Sciences* and *Arts*.

I. It is much to be lamented, that neither the *Greeks*, who attended ALEXANDER into *India*, nor those who were long connected with it under the *Bactrian* Princes, have left us any means of knowing with accuracy, what vernacular languages they found on their arrival in this Empire. The *Mohammedans*, we know, heard the people of proper *Hindustan*, or *India* on a limited scale, speaking a *Bháshá*, or living tongue of a very singular construction, the purest dialect of which was current in the districts round *Agrà*, and chiefly on the poetical ground of *Mat'hurà*; and this is commonly called the idiom of *Vraja*.[2] Five words in six, perhaps, of this language were derived from the *Sanscrit*, in which books of religion and science were composed, and which appears to have been formed by an exquisite grammatical *arrangement*, as the name itself implies, from some unpolished idiom; but the basis of the *Hindustáni*, particularly the inflexions and regimen of verbs, differed as widely from both those tongues, as *Arabick* differs from *Persian*, or *German* from *Greek*. Now the general effect of conquest is to leave the current language of the

---

1. *in some early age they were splendid in arts and arms* . . . Such grandiose statements, endorsed by Jones's reputation for intellectual rigour and probity, succeeded in modifying European perceptions of the Hindus. Many who came to *Asiatick Researches* for exotica or 'orientalia', stayed to witness a new and Eastern renaissance. In John Collegins's encomium ('Literary Characteristics of the Most Distinguished Members of the Asiatic Society', *Asiatic Annual Register* (1802), 708–18) Hastings, Wilkins, and Wellesley are all singled out for praise, but the greatest honours are reserved for Jones, the rediscoverer of India's golden age, the man who made Calcutta the Florence of Asia.

2. *the idiom of Vraga* Vraga or Braja is the area where Krishna spent his youth, and sported with the *Gopīs*, see *Gītagōvinda*, above. According to Marshall: 'One of the earliest forms of Hindi was the dialect spoken around Mathura (Muttra) and known as *Braj-Bhasha*', *The British Discovery of Hinduism*, p.252.

conquered people unchanged, or very little altered, in its groundwork, but to blend with it a considerable number of exotick names both for things and for actions; as it has happened in every country, that I can recollect, where the conquerors have not preserved their own tongue unmixed with that of the natives, like the *Turks* in *Greece*, and the *Saxons* in *Britain*; and this analogy might induce us to believe, that the pure *Hindì*, whether of *Tartarian* or *Chaldean* origin, was primeval in Upper *India*, into which the *Sanscrit* was introduced by conquerors from other kingdoms in some very remote age;[1] for we cannot doubt that the language of the *Véda's* was used in the great extent of country, which has before been delineated, as long as the religion of *Brahmà* has prevailed in it.

The *Sanscrit* language, whatever be its antiquity, is of a wonderful structure; more perfect than the *Greek*, more copious than the *Latin*, and more exquisitely refined than either, yet bearing to both of them a stronger affinity, both in the roots of verbs and in the forms of grammar, than could possibly have been produced by accident;[2] so strong indeed, that no philologer could examine them all three, without believing them to have sprung from some common source, which, perhaps, no longer exists: there is a similar reason, though not quite so forcible, for supposing that both the *Gothick* and the *Celtick*, though blended with a very different idiom, had the same origin with the *Sanscrit*; and the old *Persian* might be added to the same family, if this were the place for discussing any question concerning the antiquities of *Persia*.

The *characters*, in which the languages of *India* were originally written, are called *Nágarí*, from *Nagara*, a city with the word *Déva* sometimes prefixed, because they are believed to have been taught by the Divinity himself, who prescribed the artificial order of them in a voice from heaven. These letters, with no greater variation in their form by the change of straight lines to curves, or conversely, than the *Cusick* alphabet has received in its way to *India*, are still adopted in more than twenty kingdoms and states, from the borders of *Cashgar* and *Khoten*, to *Ráma's* bridge, and from the *Sindhu* to the river of *Siam*; nor can I help believing, although

---

1. As early as 1779 Jones's mind had been working along the lines of a protolanguage as is demonstrated by his answer to a query from the Polish Prince Adam Czartoryski: 'How so many European words crept into the Persian language, I know not with certainty. Procopius, I think, mentions the great intercourse, both in war and peace, between the Persians and the nations in the north of Europe and Asia, whom the ancients knew by the general name of Scythians. Many learned investigators of antiquity are fully persuaded, that a very old and almost primaeval language was in use among these northern nations, from which not only the Celtic dialects, but even the Greek and Latin, are derived', *Letters*, I.285. For a detailed appraisal of Jones's declaration of the affinity of Sanskrit and Greek and Latin, a formulation 'unrivalled in the history of linguistics', see Garland Cannon, 'Jones's "Sprung from Some Common Source": 1786–1986', in Sydney M. Lamb and E. Douglas Mitchell (eds.), *Sprung From Some Common Source: Investigations into the Prehistory of Languages* (California, 1991), pp.23–47.

2. *both in the roots of verbs and in the forms of grammar* Modern linguistic scholars praise Jones's 'methodology of genetic classification', see, for example, J. H. Greenberg, 'Some Problems of Indo-European in Historical Perspective', in *Sprung From Some Common Source*, pp.125–40 (126).

the polished and elegant *Dévanágari*[1] may not be so ancient as the monumental characters in the caverns of *Jarasandha*,[2] that the square *Chaldaick* letters, in which most *Hebrew* books are copied, were originally the same, or derived from the same prototype, both with the *Indian* and *Arabian* characters: that the *Phenician*, from which the *Greek* and *Roman* alphabets were formed by various changes and inversions, had a similar origin, there can be little doubt; and the inscriptions at *Canárah*, of which you now possess a most accurate copy, seem to be compounded of *Nágari* and *Ethiopick* letters, which bear a close relation to each other, both in the mode of writing from the left hand, and in the singular manner of connecting the vowels with the consonants. These remarks may favour an opinion entertained by many, that all the symbols of *sound*, which at first, probably, were only rude outlines of the different organs of speech, had a common origin: the symbols of *ideas*, now used in *China* and *Japan*, and formerly, perhaps, in *Egypt* and *Mexico*, are quite of a distinct nature; but it is very remarkable, that the order of *sounds* in the *Chinese* grammars corresponds nearly with that observed in *Tibet*, and hardly differs from that, which the *Hindus* consider as the invention of their Gods.

II. Of the *Indian* Religion and Philosophy, I shall here say but little; because a full account of each would require a separate volume: it will be sufficient in this dissertation to assume, what might be proved beyond controversy, that we now live among the adorers of those very deities, who were worshiped under different names in old *Greece* and *Italy*,[3] and among the professors of those philosophical tenets, which the *Ionick* and *Attick* writers illustrated with all the beauties of their melodious language. On one hand we see the trident of NEPTUNE, the eagle of JUPITER, the satyrs of BACCHUS, the bow of CUPID, and the chariot of the *Sun*; on another we hear the cymbals of RHEA, the songs of the *Muses*, and the pastoral tales of APOLLO NOMIUS.[4] In more retired scenes, in groves, and in seminaries of learning, we may perceive the *Bráhmans* and the *Sarmanes*, mentioned by CLEMENS,[5] disputing in the forms of *logick*, or discoursing on the vanity of human enjoyments, on the immortality of the soul, her emanation from the eternal mind, her debasement, wanderings, and final union with her source. The *six* philosophical schools, whose principles are explained in the *Dersana Sàstra*, comprise all the metaphysicks of the old *Academy*, the *Stoa*, the *Lyceum*; nor is it possible to read the *Védánta*, or the

---

1. Jones made the Devanagri alphabet the standard for his celebrated system of transliteration, see 'A Dissertation on the Orthography of Asiatick Words in Roman Letters' (1788), *Works*, III.253–318.

2. *the monumental characters in the caverns of Jarasandha* Through the Asiatick Society Jones had inspired a host of amateur scholars to transcribe and record monumental inscriptions encountered in their travels.

3. *we now live among the adorers of those very deities, who were worshiped under different names in old Greece and Italy* Two years earlier, the paper 'On the Gods of Greece, Italy, and India' (1784) had effectively established Jones as the founding father of Indo-European comparative mythology. See above pp.348–54.

4. Apollo, inventor and patron of all the fine arts, received the surname Nomius because he fed the flocks of Admetus for seven years in Thessaly.

5. *CLEMENS* Clemens Alexandrinus, who composed his *Stromata* in the third century AD.

many fine compositions in illustration of it, without believing, that PYTHAGORAS and PLATO derived their sublime theories from the same fountain with the sages of *India*.[1] The *Scythian* and *Hyperborean* doctrines and mythology may also be traced in every part of these eastern regions; nor can we doubt, that WOD or ODEN, whose religion, as the northern historians admit, was introduced into *Scandinavia* by a foreign race, was the same with BUDDH, whose rites were probably imported into *India* nearly at the same time, though received much later by the *Chinese*, who soften his name into Fó.

This may be a proper place to ascertain an important point in the Chronology of the *Hindus*;[2] for the priests of BUDDHA left in *Tibet* and *China* the precise epoch of his appearance, real or imagined, in this Empire; and their information, which had been preserved in writing, was compared by the *Christian* Missionaries and scholars with our own era. COUPLET,[3] DE GUIGNES,[4] GIORGI, and BAILLY,[5] differ a little in their accounts of this epoch, but that of *Couplet* seems the most correct: on taking, however, the medium of the four several dates, we may fix the time of BUDDHA, or the *ninth* great incarnation of VISHNU, in the year one *thousand* and *fourteen* before the birth of CHRIST, or *two thousand seven hundred and ninety-nine* years ago. Now the *Cáshmirians*, who boast of his descent in their kingdom, assert that he appeared on earth about *two* centuries after CRISHNA the *Indian* APOLLO, who took so decided a part in the war of the *Mahábhárat*; and, if an Etymologist were to suppose, that the *Athenians* had embellished their poetical history of PANDION's expulsion and the restoration of ÆGEUS with the *Asiatick* tale of the PÁNDUS and YUDHISHTIR, neither of which words they could have articulated, I should not hastily deride his conjecture: certain it is, that *Pándumandel* is called by the *Greeks* the

---

1. *PYTHAGORAS and PLATO derived their sublime theories from the same fountain with the sages of India* Jones's increasing familiarity with Indian philosophy seemed to confirm Pythagoras's extensive Oriental travel. He wrote to Althorp in August 1787: 'Need I say what exquisite pleasure I receive from conversing easily with that class of men, who conversed with Pythagoras, Thales and Solon, but with this advantage over the Grecian travellers, that I have no need of an interpreter' *Letters*, II.756. Both publically and privately, in the subcontinent and in Europe (where *Asiatick Researches* was repeatedly republished and pirated) Jones was presenting the Hindus not in craven submission to monstrous deities, but adhering to 'the same emblematical theology, which Pythagoras admired and adopted'.

2. In 1788 Jones wrote his 'On the Chronology of the Hindus' (*Works*, IV.1–47) in a brave effort to establish a sequence of Indian events compatible with recorded Western history. His real breakthrough came in 1793 when in his 'Tenth Anniversary Discourse, on Asiatick History, Civil and Natural' he announced his identification of the 'Palibothra' of the Greeks with Paliputra, and 'Sandracottus' with Chandragupta Maurya I, thus providing Indian history with a weighty 'sheet-anchor'. See O. P. Kejariwal, *The Asiatic Society of Bengal and the Discovery of India's Past 1784–1838* (Delhi: OUP, 1988), pp.37–75.

3. Philippe Couplet, a Belgian Jesuit, who wrote *Tabulae Chronologica Monarchiae Sinicae* (Paris, 1686), and *Confucius, Sinarum sive Scientia Sinensis Latine Exposita* (Paris, 1687).

4. A copy of Joseph de Guignes's *Histoire des Huns, des Turcs, des Mongols et des autres Tartares occidentaux* 4 vols. (Paris, 1756) was in Jones's library; but it seems that Jones was unaware of an article by de Guignes effectively identifying both Sandracottus and Palibothra and published in *Histoires et Mémoires de l'Académie des Inscriptions et Belles-Lettres*, xxxviii (1772), 312–36.

5. Jean-Sylvain Bailly's *Traité de l'astronomie indienne et orientale* (Paris, 1787) was the fifth volume of his *Histoire de l'astronomie* and Jones, equally fascinated with Newton's *Principia* and the *Sūrya Siddhānta*, detected many errors, see *Letters*, II.852,857.

country of Pandion. We have, therefore, determined another interesting epoch, by fixing the age of Crishna near the *three thousandth* year from the present time; and, as the three first *Avatàrs*, or descents of Vishnu,[1] relate no less clearly to *an* Universal Deluge, in which eight persons only were saved, than the *fourth* and *fifth* do to the *punishment of impiety* and the *humiliation* of the *proud*, we may for the present assume, that the *second*, or *silver*, age of the *Hindus* was subsequent to the dispersion from *Babel*; so that we have only a dark interval of about a *thousand* years, which were employed in the settlement of nations, the foundation of states or empires, and the cultivation of civil society. The great incarnate Gods of this intermediate age are both named Ráma but with different epithets;[2] one of whom bears a wonderful resemblance to the *Indian* Bacchus, and his wars are the subject of several heroick poems. He is represented as a descendent from Súrya, or the Sun, as the husband of Sítá, and the son of a princess named Caúselyá: it is very remarkable, that the *Peruvians*, whose *Incas* boasted of the same descent, styled their greatest festival *Ramasitoa*;[3] whence we may suppose, that South *America* was peopled by the same race, who imported into the farthest parts of *Asia* the rites and fabulous history of Ráma. These rites and this history are extremely curious; and, although I cannot believe with Newton, that ancient mythology was nothing but historical truth in a poetical dress, nor, with Bacon, that it consisted solely of moral and metaphysical allegories,[4] nor with Bryant, that all the heathen divinities are only different attributes and representations of the Sun or of deceased progenitors, but conceive that the whole system of religious fables rose, like the *Nile*, from several distinct sources, yet I cannot but agree, that one great spring and fountain of all idolatry in the four quarters of the globe was the veneration paid by men to the vast body of fire, which 'looks from his sole dominion like the God of this world;' and another, the immoderate respect shown to the memory of powerful or virtuous ancestors, especially the founders of kingdoms, legislators, and warriors, of whom the *Sun* or the *Moon* were wildly supposed to be the parents.

III. The remains of *architecture* and *sculpture* in *India*, which I mention here as mere monuments of antiquity, not as specimens of ancient art, seem to prove an early connection between this country and *Africa*: the pyramids of *Egypt*, the colossal statues described by Pausanias[5] and others, the sphinx, and the Hermes

---

1. *Avatars, or descents of Vishnu* The *Bhāgavata Purāṇa* (1.3.6–25) lists twenty-two incarnations, the *Ahirbudhnya Samhitā* (5.50-7) thirty-nine, but Jones, following the *Varāha Purāṇa* (15.9-18) and Jayadéva's Hymn to Vishnu (which Jones omitted from his translation of the *Gītagōvinda*, but printed in his essay 'On the Chronology of the Hindus', *Works*, IV.13–14), favours ten. The first three *avatars* are those of the fish (the universal deluge', cf. 'On the Gods', *Works*, III.332–8), the tortoise (the churning of the ocean), and the boar.
2. *both named Rama, but with different epithets* Paraśu-Rama (Rāma-with-the-Axe), and Rāma-candra (the Charming, the Embodiment of Righteousness), see 'On the Gods', *Works*, III.370–3.
3. *Ramasitoa* Marshall pointedly reminds us that, in conflating two separate Inca festivals, *Raymi* and *Situa*, 'Jones appears to be perpetrating the sort of etymological wishful thinking which he so severely castigates in Bryant', *The British Discovery of Hinduism*, p.256.
4. On his divergence from the positions of Newton and Bacon, see 'On the Gods', p.350 above.
5. *the colossal statues described by Pausanias* This celebrated orator of the second century AD

Canis, which last bears a great resemblance to the *Varáh ávatár*, or the incarnation of VISHNU in the form of a *Boar*, indicate the style and mythology of the same indefatigable workmen, who formed the vast excavations of *Cánárah*,[1] the various temples and images of BUDDHA, and the idols, which are continually dug up at *Gayá*, or in its vicinity.[2] The letters on many of those monuments appear, as I have before intimated, partly of *Indian*, and partly of *Abyssinian* or *Ethiopick*, origin; and all these indubitable facts may induce no ill-grounded opinion, that *Ethiopia* and *Hindustán* were peopled or colonized by the same extraordinary race; in confirmation of which, it may be added, that the mountaineers of *Bengal* and *Bahàr* can hardly be distinguished in some of their features, particularly their lips and noses, from the modern *Abyssinians*, whom the *Arabs* call the children of CÚSH: and the ancient *Hindus*, according to STRABO,[3] differed in nothing from the *Africans*, but in the straitness and smoothness of their hair, while that of the others was crisp or woolly; a difference proceeding chiefly, if not entirely, from the respective humidity or dryness of their atmospheres; hence the people who *received the first light of the rising sun*, according to the limited knowledge of the ancients, are said by APULEIUS[4] to be the *Arü* and *Ethiopians*, by which he clearly meant certain nations of *India*; where we frequently see figures of BUDDHA with *curled hair* apparently designed for a representation of it in its natural state.

IV. It is unfortunate, that the *Silpi Sástra*, or *collection of treatises on Arts* and *Manufactures*, which must have contained a treasure of useful information on *dying*, *painting*, and *metallurgy*, has been so long neglected, that few, if any, traces of it are to be found; but the labours of the *Indian* loom and needle have been universally celebrated; and *fine linen* is not improbably supposed to have been called *Sindon*, from the name of the river near which it was wrought in the highest perfection: the people of *Colchis* were also famed for this manufacture, and the *Egyptians* yet more, as we learn from several passages in scripture, and particularly from a beautiful chapter in EZEKIEL[5] containing the most authentick delineation of ancient commerce, of which *Tyre* had been the principal mart.[6] Silk was fabricated immemorially by the *Indians*, though commonly ascribed to the people of *Serica* or

---

wrote a ten-volume history of Greece. On the excavations of cave temples at Kanheri, see R. Gough, *A Comparative View of the Antient Monuments in India, particularly those in the island of Salset* (London, 1785).

1. Architectural and archaeological evidence is enlisted in the service of cultural anthropology, another of Jones's abiding interests.

2. *the idols, which are continually dug up at Gayá* The previous year had seen three important papers on these caves investigated at Jones's suggestion. The inscriptions discovered were sent to Charles Wilkins, the pioneer of Indian epigraphy, providing new evidence of early dynasties.

3. Strabo (b. *c.*63 BC) composed his *Geography* in 17 volumes, book xv deals with Persia and India.

4. Lucius Apuleius (b. *c.* AD 125), Platonic philosopher and rhetorician. Jones refers to his *Florida* (vi), which contains observations and speculations based upon Apuleius's wide travels in the East.

5. Ezekiel xxvii.

6. The emphasis here upon commerce as an indicator of civilization, together with the inherently syncretic approach are key elements in Jones's cultural investigations.

Tancùt, among whom probably the word *Sèr*, which the *Greeks* applied to the *silk-worm*, signified gold; a sense, which it now bears in *Tibet*. That the *Hindus* were in early ages a *commercial* people, we have many reasons to believe; and in the first of their sacred law-tracts, which they suppose to have been revealed by MENU many *millions* of years ago, we find a curious passage on the legal *interest* of money, and the limited rate of it in different cases, with an exception in regard to *adventures* at sea;[1] an exception, which the sense of mankind approves, and which commerce absolutely requires, though it was not before the reign of CHARLES I. that our own jurisprudence fully admitted it in respect of maritime contracts.

We are told by the *Grecian* writers, that the *Indians* were the wisest of nations; and in moral wisdom, they were certainly eminent: their *Níti Sástra*, or *System of Ethicks*, is yet preserved, and the Fables of VISHNUSERMAN,[2] whom we ridiculously call *Pilpay*, are the most beautiful, if not the most ancient, collection of apologues in the world: they were first translated from the *Sanscrit*, in the *sixth* century, by the order of BUZERCHUMIHR, or *Bright as the Sun*, the chief physician and afterwards *Vézír* of the great ANÚSHIREVÁN, and are extant under various names in more than twenty languages; but their original title is *Hitópadésa*, or *Amicable Instruction*; and, as the very existence of ESOP, whom the *Arabs* believe to have been an *Abyssinian*, appears rather doubtful, I am not disinclined to suppose, that the first *moral fables*, which appeared in *Europe*, were of *Indian* or *Ethiopian* origin.

The *Hindus* are said to have boasted of *three* inventions, all of which, indeed, are admirable, the method of instructing by *apologues*, the *decimal scale* adopted now by all civilized nations, and the game of *Chess*,[3] on which they have some curious treatises; but, if their numerous works on Grammar, Logick, Rhetorick, Musick, all which are extant and accessible, were explained in some language generally known, it would be found, that they had yet higher pretensions to the praise of a fertile and inventive genius. Their lighter Poems are lively and elegant; their Epick, magnificent and sublime in the highest degree; their *Purána's* comprise a series of mythological Histories in blank verse from the *Creation* to the supposed incarnation of BUDDHA; and their *Védas*, as far as we can judge from that compendium of them, which is called *Upanishat*, abound with noble speculations in metaphysicks, and fine discourses on the being and attributes of GOD. Their most ancient medical book, entitled *Chereca*, is believed to be the work of SIVA; for each of the divinities in their *Triad* has at least one *sacred* composition ascribed to him; but, as to mere human works on *History* and *Geography*, though they are said to be extant in *Cashmír*, it has not been yet in my power to procure them. What their *astronomical* and *mathematical* writings contain, will not, I trust, remain long a secret: they are easily procured, and their importance cannot be doubted. The

---

1. *an exception in regard to adventures at sea* See Jones's *The Ordinances of Menu*, VII.157 in *Works*, VII.356–7.

2. *the Fables of VISHNUSERMAN* 1786 also saw the completion of Jones's translation of the *Hītopadēsa of Vishnusarman* (*Works*, XIII.1–210).

3. *the game of Chess* From his Harrow days and the early composition of 'Caissa', Jones had retained his love of chess; his discourse 'On the Indian Game of Chess' was published in *Asiatick Researches* II (1791), see *Works*, IV.323–33.

Philosopher, whose works are said to include a system of the universe founded on the principle of *Attraction* and the *Central* position of the sun, is named YAVAN ACHÁRYA,[1] because he had travelled, we are told, into *Ionia*: if this be true, he might have been one of those, who conversed with PYTHAGORAS; this at least is undeniable, that a book on astronomy in *Sanscrit* bears the title of *Yavana Jática*, which may signify the *Ionic Sect*; nor is it improbable, that the names of the planets and *Zodiacal* stars, which the *Arabs* borrowed from the *Greeks*, but which we find in the oldest *Indian* records,[2] were originally devised by the same ingenious and enterprising race, from whom both *Greece* and *India* were peopled; the race, who, as DIONYSIUS describes them,

> – 'first assayed the deep,
> And wafted merchandize to coasts unknown,
> Those, who digested first the starry choir,
> Their motions mark'd, and call'd them by their names.'

Of these cursory observations on the *Hindus*, which it would require volumes to expand and illustrate, this is the result: that they had an immemorial affinity with the old *Persians*, *Ethiopians*, and *Egyptians*, the *Phenicians*, *Greeks*, and *Tuscans*, the *Scythians* or *Goths*, and *Celts*, the *Chinese*, *Japanese*, and *Peruvians*; whence, as no reason appears for believing, that they were a colony from any one of those nations, or any of those nations from them, we may fairly conclude that they all proceeded from some *central* country, to investigate which will be the object of my future Discourses; and I have a sanguine hope, that your collections during the present year will bring to light many useful discoveries; although the departure for *Europe* of a very ingenious member, who first opened the inestimable mine of *Sanscrit* literature,[3] will often deprive us of accurate and solid information concerning the languages and antiquities of *India*.

---

1. *YAVAN ACHÁRYA* means 'Greek teacher'.
2. In his discourse 'On the Antiquity of the Indian Zodiac', read to the Asiatick Society on 5 November 1789, Jones substantiated his claims that the Indian zodiac was not borrowed from the Greeks or Arabs, thereby generating heated controversy in astronomical circles, see *Works*, IV.71–92.
3. Charles Wilkins who, on account of deteriorating health, returned to Britain and settled in Bath.

POLITICAL WRITINGS

29

A Speech on the Nomination of Candidates to Represent the County of Middlesex, ix September, MDCCLXXX

[Privately printed in 1780, this speech was reprinted in the second edition of Jones's *Inquiry into the Legal Mode of Suppressing Riots* (London: C. Dilly, 1782), pp.43–60. The candidates in question were John Wilkes and George Byng, and their nomination being unopposed, Wilkes delivered a long speech to the large meeting at Hackney which was enthusiastically received; formal business succeeded, and Jones judged the occasion inopportune to deliver his planned speech. With its savage attack upon Britain's war with America, upon current colonial and commercial policy, and its indictment of the slave trade, this state of the nation address represents some of Jones's most impassioned radical writing.

Jones attended this meeting only three days after informing Nathan Wetherel, the Master of University College, of his decision not to stand the poll as a Whig candidate for the Oxford University parliamentary seat. It was largely his reputation as a convinced republican which had forced this decision, as Jones himself was well aware: 'Least of all could I have expected to be accused of *wishing* to overturn a constitution, which I prize, because I understand it, and which I would sacrifice my life to *preserve*', *Letters*, I.433–4. Oxford had a long memory, and some of its electors clearly recalled Jones's refusal to compose the expected laudatory oration on the occasion of Lord North's installation as University Chancellor in 1773 (also printed in the second edition of *Inquiry into Riots*, pp.68–75), an irritation refuelled, late in 1779, by Jones's authorship of the Latin ode *Ad Libertatem* (*Works*, X.394–400), which condemned the American war.

It would seem clear that Jones's politics, whether described as advanced Whig or radical, were distorted by his biographer and friend Sir John Shore, Lord Teignmouth, whose association with the aggressive evangelicalism of the Clapham Sect led him to present his subject as free from any taint of godlessness or republicanism. When the *Memoirs* appeared in 1804, they were attacked by Dr William Paley who wrote: 'He was a great Republican when I knew him. The principles which he then avowed so decidedly, he certainly never afterwards disclaimed; and his sentiments on questions of great public importance ought neither to be extenuated nor withheld', (quoted by A. J. Arberry, 'New Light on Sir William Jones', *BSOAS*, 11 [1946], 673–85 [674]). Furthermore, an anonymous contributor to the *Gentleman's Magazine* for 1804 (vol.74, p.1214) maintains that 'the general undisguised opinion' was that, but for the Indian appointment, Jones would have proved 'a second Wilkes', adducing as evidence, 'Sir William's intended "Speech on the Nomination of Candidates to represent the County of Middlesex, in September 1780" [which speech] is to the full as bold as the boldest of Mr Wilkes's.' The text is that of 1782.]

On the 9th of September, 1780, I met the freeholders of Middlesex[1] *assembled for the purpose of nominating two representatives in the new parliament; but, there being no opposition or debate, and only some formal business transacted, I could not with propriety rise to address them on* the general state of the nation. *On my return home, I amused myself with revolving in my mind such topicks as I should probably have urged, if there had been either room or invitation to speak at all; and half an hour's meditation convinced me, that I should have addressed my countrymen, possibly in the following words; but, certainly, to the following purport.*

A SPEECH TO THE FREEHOLDERS OF MIDDLESEX

GENTLEMEN,

Nothing, I assure you, was more distant from my thoughts, on my first entrance into this assembly, than the design of rising to address the county of *Middlesex*, and, through them, the electors of *Britain*, on the multiplied and increasing evils,[2] with which they are at this moment surrounded, and for which they may at this moment, if ever, provide a remedy; but the number and magnitude of those evils, which the sight of so many injured citizens brings fresh to my mind, the nature of the remedy, which has occurred to me, and which the object of the present meeting must instantly suggest, together with my hearty approbation of the principles avowed by the two honourable candidates [*a*], have induced and even impelled me to declare that approbation, and at the same time to present you with a short, though painful enumeration of your calamities, actual or impending, and to enforce, as strongly as I am able, the necessity of employing the only means in your power, by which you may remove, alleviate, or avert them.

[*a*] *John Wilkes* and *George Byng*, Esqrs.[3]

---

1. *the freeholders of Middlesex* In 1768 the freeholders of Middlesex had secured both the election of the outlawed Wilkes to Parliament and their own place in the history of the reform movement, see G. F. E. Rudé, 'The Middlesex Electors of 1768–1769', *English Historical Review*, 75 (1960), 601–17.
   2. *the multiplied and increasing evils* On 27 January 1780 Jones had accompanied Shelburne to a meeting in Wiltshire where he had informed the electors that the nation's grievances could only be redressed by a reformed parliament, see John Norris, *Shelburne and Reform* (London, 1963), pp.126–7.
   3. George Byng (1735–89), who was returned with Wilkes for Middlesex, was an active member of the Westminster Committee of association, and a tireless campaigner for parliamentary reform.

I begin with congratulating you, gentlemen, on the dissolution of an angry, vengeful, implacable parliament,[1] which in six sessions has deprived this country of greater advantages than six centuries will restore to it, and, by all its avenging acts[2] (which I have lately been contemplating with no less attention than anguish), has established a system so compact and well-adapted to every ruinous purpose, that, if any other colonising and commercial nation shall hereafter determine effectually to alienate their colonies and destroy their commerce, they must propose as their model *THE FOURTEENTH PARLIAMENT OF GREAT BRITAIN*: but, unless you resolve, (and when I speak to *you*, I should wish to raise my voice so high, that *all other Englishmen* might hear me), unless you firmly resolve, that the *fifteenth* parliament, which you are now called upon to elect, shall be guided by another star and pursue another course; shall profess, instead of resentment, forbearance; instead of rancour, lenity; instead of revenge, placability; and a conciliating, not a subjugating, spirit; there will be no room for congratulation, none for triumph; but your calamity will then be the last and worst that mortals can suffer, because you will want the only consolation that mortals afflicted in extremity can enjoy, Hope. If six years have dragged you to the brink of perdition, from which you may still be preserved, six more such years will precipitate you into the gulf, from which there will be no redemption: and, that you may perceive the importance of this crisis, which calls aloud for all your virtue and all your resolution, let me request you to view with me from above the horrors of that precipice on which you stand, and on which, if you fall through dizziness or fainting, you will look back in vain.

Turn your eyes for a moment to the *East*,[3] and behold three noble kingdoms in the paradise of *Asia*, together with great dominions on other parts of the *Indian coast*: all these a series of wonderful events, which the hand of time had been weaving for ages, has brought into your sole possession; *yours* I say, because, whether the crown or the company *formally* have the territorial right (a question which I hope the wisdom of the nation will prevent from being discussed), yet in

---

1. *an angry, vengeful, implacable parliament* For Jones the calamities of North's Ministry had strengthened his determination to leave England, whether for India or America: 'be assured, my dear lord, that, if the *system* of government, which has insulted common sense and manliness for the last twenty years, be unchangeable or unchanged, *I will not grow old in England*', *Letters*, II.516–17.

2. *all its avenging acts* As a radical and a lawyer Jones lamented the increased power of the legislature and its proliferation of statutes which introduced judicial procedures involving summary jurisdiction, eroding traditional rights enshrined in common law. Cf. *The Principles of Government*, p.399 below.

3. *Turn your eyes for a moment to the East* Jones wanted the East India Company to succeed both as a viable commercial concern and as a powerful organ of imperial power, and in this he reflected middle-class, and even landed class, opinion within and outside Parliament. His statement that the territories should be 'held *in trust for the benefit of the whole community*' is somewhat weakened by his failure to mention the vital question of patronage, or the issue of returning 'nabobs' purchasing Parliamentary seats. His attempt to steer a middle course between the promoters and the opposers of the East India Judicature Bill (see *Letters*, II.478–9), was complicated by his own long-standing hopes of a lucrative seat on the Bengal bench. He excused himself from assisting Burke in the framing of the bill until he could ascertain the opinions of Thurlow on whom 'my appointment to an Indian judgeship depends so entirely', *Letters*, II.520–1.

either case the territories must necessarily be held *in trust for the benefit of the whole community*. What is the fruit of these dominions? No less than every precious, every useful, commodity; gold and gems, spices and elegant apparel; and these not only producing private wealth to the industrious or fortunate, but filling the coffers of the state with annual treasure, and forming at this instant your chief resource: not to enlarge on the chain of excellent ships, and the nursery of incomparable seamen, by which your navy has been more than once enabled to protect this island from invaders; but you must not forget, that your *Indian* territories border on those of an ambitious and numerous people, with a very warlike spirit and a very hostile disposition [*b*], whose power has been growing for a century, and, if it continue to increase, may possibly endanger even our *settlement* in *Asia*, but must unavoidably require the wisest counsels, the most vigorous exertions, and the most abundant supplies both of gold and arms:[1] there is a power also in this very country, which has long been hovering over the company,[2] but whose violence will, I trust, be averted by a seasonable accommodation. This I may boldly affirm, that, if any sudden revolution in *Asia*, or the continuance of an unaccommodating spirit in *England*, shall overthrow or even shake our *India* company, nothing less than the miraculous discovery of golden mines in this island can supply the expenses of the complicated war, in which we are engaged.

I pass with haste by the coast of *Africa*, whence my mind turns with indignation at the abominable traffick in the human species, from which a part of our countrymen dare to derive their most inauspicious wealth, and which our southern colonies, *while they were ours*, strove in vain to abolish, but will now, I am credibly informed, annihilate *by their own authority*, as soon as times and circumstances shall permit them to emancipate their slaves [*c*]. Sugar, it has been said, would be dear, if it were not worked by *blacks* in the western islands; as if the most laborious, the most dangerous, works were not carried on in every country, but chiefly in *England*, by *free* men: in fact, they are so carried on with infinitely more advantage; for there is an alacrity in a consciousness of freedom, and a gloomy sullen indolence in a consciousness of slavery; but let sugar be as dear as it may; it is better

---

[*b*] This has been too fully proved since the year 1780.

[*c*] This measure has since been greatly advanced, to the immortal honour of Mr. *Laurens*, and other excellent men, who concurred in so glorious a work.[3]

---

1 At this period the Company's priority was to raise increasing amounts of revenue to fund wars against Mysore and the Marathas, see C. A. Bayly, *Indian Society and the Making of the British Empire* (Cambridge, 1988).

2. Jones was opposed to intervention by the national government, sharing his friend Burke's aversion 'from the Ministers of this country taking any part in the direction of India', see P. J. Marshall (ed.), *The Writings and Speeches of Edmund Burke, V: India: Madras and Bengal* (Oxford, 1981), p.191.

3. Henry Laurens (1724–92), former President of the American Congress, was imprisoned in the Tower from 1780 until early 1782. Jones's friendship with Laurens and with the Virginia diplomat, Arthur Lee, his sympathy with the American cause, and his violent opposition to impressment, (which rendered 'the peasantry of Britain no more free than the people of Constantinople or Morocco', *Letters*, II.467), all contributed to Jones's withdrawal from the Oxford election, and considerably delayed his appointment to the Bengal Supreme Court.

to eat none;[1] to eat honey, if sweetness only be palatable; better to eat aloes or coloquinteda than violate a primary law of nature, impressed on every heart not imbruted by avarice, than rob one human creature of those eternal rights, of which no law upon earth can justly deprive him.[2]

I would not here even mention the total decay of your trade to the dominions of the *Turkish* Sultan,[3] since the causes of that irreparable loss are wholly unconnected with our other calamities, and were antecedent to the measures, which have nearly ruined us; but since the advantage, which we have lost, has been transferred to the *French*, and a source of opulence, from which we are excluded, rolls in a plentiful stream on our bitterest enemies, this misfortune also may be added to the afflicting and humiliating catalogue.

A scene far more deplorable presents itself in *the western hemisphere*; with this mixture of consolation, that, if we be firmly united in one wise and virtuous resolution, our certain relief will proceed from that very quarter, whence our calamity sprung, and *America reconciled* will repair the losses, which *America injured* was *forced* to occasion. The war with our colonies, of which the sad detail is too fresh in your memory, began with injustice, was pursued with malignity, and must end, if it be long protracted, in destruction: the *principles* on which it was begun, and by which it has been feebly but insolently vindicated, are no less irrational in themselves than repugnant to the first elements of our constitution; and the bringing of those principles into fashion has been the most envenomed fruit of this miserable contest. It fills me, I declare, with a petrifying astonishment, that the *people of England* are still blind to *the consequences of this war*, and will not see how closely their own liberties are blended and interwoven with those of the *Americans*: were it *possible* to subdue them by force, it would be impossible to keep them in subjection without a constant military establishment; and thus an exhausted dispirited race of slaves, with a desolated country, would be purchased at the expense of our constitutional government; whilst a flattered, caressed, intoxicated army, conquerors without fame, and heroes without laurel, would return to give us law, and make us truckle to a power, which our fore-fathers always suspected, always detested. Such would be the fruits of *victory!* but comfort yourselves, my countrymen, and be assured that you will not be *finally* victorious [d]. All the

[d] A prediction fully accomplished.

1. *it is better to eat none* Jones anticipates the boycotting movement of later in the decade, which was given impetus by the Quaker William Fox's influential pamphlet *An Address to the People of Great Britain on the Propriety of Abstaining from West Indies Sugar and Rum* (London, 1791).

2. The controlled rhetoric underlines the depth of Jones's repugnance for the slave trade. In his second *Charge to the Grand Jury* (10 June 1785) he paints a horrific picture of its evils: 'many of you, I presume, have seen large boats with such children coming down the river for open sale at *Calcutta*; nor can you be ignorant, that most of them were stolen from their parents, or bought, perhaps, for a measure of rice in a time of scarcity', *Works*, VII.16.

3. *the total decay of your trade to the dominions of the Turkish Sultan* In Turkey French commerce had expanded dramatically at the expense of Britain's Levant Company, see James C. Riley, *The Seven Years' War and the Old Regime in France* (Princeton, 1986), pp.105–10.

nations of *Europe* (I speak only what I know) have long envied, and consequently hated, you: they now take a malignant pleasure in laughing at your projects, and deriding what they call the *madness* of your enterprises.

I was last summer at *Paris*,[1] in company every day with sensible and experienced men of different nations; men, who knew *America* perfectly, and as perfectly knew the strength of the *British* navy. 'Your countrymen,' said they, 'must be *mad* in the extreme, to entertain a hope of subduing a people *both commercial and agricultural*: you may certainly obstruct their commerce, and perhaps possess yourselves of every provincial town, *near which your ships can approach*; but your conquest will not be accelerated. The virtuous republicans can subsist, as pleasurably as republicans either ought or wish to subsist, by *agriculture* alone, and your armies will never penetrate, to our positive knowledge, into the *heart* of their provinces,[2] how loudly soever you may boast of success at the *extremities*.' What pain must it give a lover of his country to hear such reproaches from his enemies! but how much must his pain be augmented by a consciousness, that those enemies might perhaps be vanquished by arms, but could not be confuted by reason!

Thus have we lost our flourishing colonies; and lost them irrecoverably, unless we conciliate their minds by renewing their unsuspicious confidence; while the nations of our *European* continent are either openly hostile, or secretly adverse, to us, and our *western islands* seem to lie in the midst of the field, like the prizes in the ancient games, ready to decorate the brows of successive conquerors [e].

As to *IRELAND*, she has for a time been soothed by extorted concessions;[3] but let her ever keep in remembrance, that she owes her late acquisitions to the example and efforts of *her sisters beyond the Atlantick*.

Nor let the generous people of *BRITAIN* disdain to receive advantage from the same once affectionate, and yet kindred, hands. Two strong topicks are now urged in *America* (alas! with how much bitter truth!) against any sort of re-union with this country:[4] first, they insist, that we are degenerate in manners and principles, and that we suffer ourselves to be fed with the moonshine of *forms*, whilst our

---

[e] If the *French* have a PINDAR among them, we have given him too many subjects for *Odes* of triumph.

---

1. *I was last summer at Paris*   On 28 May 1779 Jones had presented Franklin with his 'Fragment of Polybius', an allegorical and idealistic attempt to outline a treaty based on commerce, compromise, and a joint congress, see *Letters*, I.290–6.

2. *into the heart of their provinces*   After two hours' 'delightful conversation' with Henry Laurens, Jones wrote to Althorp in March 1782: 'Did you know that the Americans had flourishing settlements *seven hundred* miles from the coast? Every man among them is a soldier, a *patriot* – Subdue such a people! The king may as easily conquer the moon or wear it on his sleeve', *Letters*, II.516–17.

3. *soothed by extorted concessions*   Grattan had indeed recognized the American precedent, and the Irish Protestant gentry, at the head of a volunteer army, demanded commercial equality.

4. *against any sort of re-union with this country*   Jones was airing Franklin's arguments against re-unification as he had heard them at Paris. The following September he wrote to Franklin: 'All virtue and publick spirit are dead in this country: we have the *shadow* merely of a free constitution, but live in truth under the substance of despotism', *Letters*, II.493–4.

constitutional liberty, without which there can be no union between us and them, is in *substance* extinguished; secondly, they aver, that *many attempts have been made to ensnare them*, which have wholly destroyed their confidence in any set of men, whether ministers or opponents of ministry; so that nothing can remove their distrust but *a national proof of our sincerity* by the lenient acts of a free parliament.

You begin, I am persuaded, to discover the double remedy for all our evils, which I ground on these two objections to a reconciliation; and which, if you suffer this moment to pass, you will never be able to apply. I will hold you no longer in suspense; the remedy is this – 'return a conciliating parliament, and restore the lost balance of your constitution.'[1] I said the *lost* balance, and I said it with boldness; because it is a proposition of the clearest evidence, a truth of the first water, that the due temperature of powers in our mixed system,[2] which MONTESQUIEU,[3] who breathed the spirit of an *Englishman*, and BLACKSTONE,[4] who was the pride of *England*, so lavishly applauded, subsists no more.

The subject, on which I am entering, is vast; but I will restrain myself within proper bounds, and be satisfied with reminding you, that the executive magistrate[5] (of whom it behoves us to speak respectfully, yet freely) has of late acquired two enormous branches, not of just prerogative, but of unconstitutional power; *influence*, by receiving and dispensing at pleasure all the gold, and *force*, by commanding and subjecting to his nod all the steel, of the nation, thus holding in his mighty grasp, as the Thunderer of the ancients is represented on *Olympus*, the two sinews of war; by one of which the coequal parts of the legislature may

---

1. *restore the lost balance of your constitution*　Jones's correspondence, like that of Walpole, Pitt, Burke, Shelburne, and Rockingham, reflects the widespread feeling that the Constitution, under North's Ministry, was in the greatest danger. Writing to Lady Spencer from a London in the aftermath of the Gordon Riots, Jones expresses his fears for 'our form of government, which ought to be so nobly balanced': 'Many of the best-intentioned men, well inclined till now to our mixed constitution, are continually saying, "How much more secure we should have been in France"!' *Letters*, I.409.

2. *the due temperature of powers in our mixed system*　In a letter of 25 April 1782 to Thomas Yeates, Secretary for the Society for Constitutional Information, he writes: 'Care must now be taken, lest, by reducing the Regal power to its just level, we raise the Aristocratical to a dangerous height; since it is from the People alone that we can deduce the obligation of our laws and the authority of our magistrates . . . If the properties of all good government be considered as duly distributed in the different parts of our limited republic, goodness ought to be the distinguished attribute of the Crown, wisdom of the Aristocracy, but power and fortitude of the People', *Letters*, II.534.

3. Montesquieu, Charles de Secondat (1689–1755). Admiring the English constitution as a 'mixed state', he used it as the model for his Theory of the Separation of Powers in *Esprit des Lois*, trans. and ed. Anne M. Cohler *et al.* (Cambridge, 1989), pp.156–66.

4. Jones's great admiration for Sir William Blackstone's *Commentaries* (Oxford, 1765–9) was centred in the latter's championing of Common Law, which is 'eminently favourable to the absolute rights of persons', (*Letters*, II.553), and in his premiss that the spirit of the Constitution required a 'nearly equal and nearly universal representation'. See Jones's speech *On the Reformation of Parliament* (1782), p.391 below.

5. *the executive magistrate*　George III had practically assumed the duty of leader of the government by his constant and meticulous directions to Lord North and other ministers. Debts of over a million pounds on his substantial Civil List, and his unavowed exercise of 'influence' confirmed Jones's opinion that 'this rolling tide of prerogative and influence' theatened the very foundations of the constitution.

continually be sapped, and by the other may at any time be stormed. I have heard undue *prerogative* compared to a *giant*,[1] who bestrides our narrow island, and may at his discretion suspend his massy club over our heads, or reduce us to powder with its weight; whilst *influence* resembles *a fairy*, who plays around us invisibly, or assumes any shape that suits her purpose, and often drops gold or patents in proper places, as a reward or incentive for such as merit the approbation of the little wanton divinity. Attempts to bring back the constitution to its genuine temperament are so far from being seditious or even derogatory from the respect due to the Crown, that they would, if successful, highly augment the splendour of it; unless it be more glorious to rule, like the princes of the continent, over *slaves*, than to be *the chief in a nation of freemen*; an opinion, which no man, who deserves either dignity or freedom, can entertain. As to the first branch, *undue influence*, the well-intended efforts of the petitioning and associated counties[2] have not, unfortunately, been as well directed, but have been obstructed, if not defeated, by a cause very dangerous on similar occasions, though in itself not dishonourable; I mean, by an exuberance of zeal in the promoters of the business, and by a departure from the simplicity of the original plan, which ought all along to have been steadily kept in view. The object of the different associations became too complex, or, as a pleader would term it, *multifarious*;[3] and the petitions, beginning in a single point, on which there could be no diversity of opinion, ended in a variety of points, on which the best and wisest men might and did disagree. A proposition, designed to meet with unanimous concurrence, cannot be too simple; and I may safely assert, that a very judicious motion, which was made in the late parliament by a Senator, whose great popularity is no more than a just reward of his unrivalled talents and unbiassed integrity [f], would never have been carried, if its extreme simplicity had not made it like a stroke of lightning, irresistible. The *time* also,

[f] *John Dunning*, Esq.; now Lord *Ashburton*.[4]

---

1. *undue prerogative compared to a giant* Cf. Jones's labelling of discretion as a fiend in 'An Ode in Imitation of Alcæus', l.22.

2. *the well-intended efforts of the petitioning and associated counties* Despite his reservations concerning their manner of proceeding, Jones, like the other radicals, saw the principle of association as central in any attempt to cleanse the Augean stables of corruption, secure accountability, and restore the balance of the Constitution. Following the lead of the Yorkshire Association, almost forty constituencies had submitted petitions for 'economical reform' by April 1780. In Middlesex the radical Dr John Jebb urged a national association to remodel the constitution and ultimately achieve 'the blessing of an equal, annual, and universal representation of the commons', see Ian R. Christie, *Wilkes, Wyvill and Reform: The Parliamentary Reform Movement 1760–1785* (London, 1962), p.79.

3. *The object of the different associations became too complex* On the failure of the movement to maintain unanimity, see H. Butterfield, *George III, Lord North, and the People* (London, 1949), p.281.

4. John Dunning (first Baron Ashburton), a friend of the circuits, became increasingly close to Jones, who composed an obituary essay upon learning of his death, *Works*, VIII.538–43. Although not a member of the popular reform committees, he played a significant part in the reforming movement of 1779–82 as a lawyer within Parliament, the very role in which Jones might have distinguished himself had things gone differently at the Oxford election. On 6 April 1780 the hitherto docile House of Commons finally accepted Dunning's motion that 'the power of the Crown has increased, is increasing and ought to be diminished'.

when the associations were formed, gave suspicion to many honest men; who were prompted to consider them as an attempt to catch the popular gale *on the approach of a general election*;[1] nor was the suspicion wholly groundless, although I am confident, that numbers of the most exalted virtue and the most independent spirit associated themselves from the noblest motives. The *only* objection against associations, which I was at a loss to answer, was founded on the proximity of that moment, when we might apply a remedy to our accumulated ills by a method strictly legal, without vainly soliciting the authors of our misery to heal the very wounds in our constitution, which they had themselves inflicted.

The second branch of irregular power in the crown, *military force*, appears to have been overlooked by the associated counties, and little considered by the people in general, till the late exertion of it in suppressing the fatal riots in our metropolis;[2] fatal, because in less than a week they operated more forcibly on feeble minds in favour of *pure monarchical authority* than all the speeches and writings of all the courtiers and sycophants could have done in a century; fatal indeed! unless your noble exertions turn the tide of those dangerous opinions, which have been rolling impetuously within the last three months against our glorious constitutional fabrick.

There has indeed been an attempt to check this growing disposition by an unknown person, who seems however to have the welfare of his country at heart; and who has demonstrated, that, if our laws were restored to their genuine vigour, there would be little danger from the vast accession of force, which the crown has gained by the riot act and the *annual* appointment of a standing army [g]; but assure yourselves, that, unless his plan, or some other not dissimilar to it, be generally adopted, *a standing army* paid by the *king*, officered by the *king*, commanded by the *king*, devoted to the *king*, will be made, in form annual, in substance perpetual.

On how great a variety of matter have I touched, and into how wide a field

---

[g] See the *Inquiry into the Legal Mode of Suppressing Riots.*

---

1. *on the approach of a general election* While supporting the reforms urged by the association movement, (see, for example, *On the Reformation of Parliament*, p.386 below), Jones was irritated by the failure of their petitions to confront what he saw as the central issue – the pressing need for an honourable reunion with America, see *Letters*, I.349. Certainly it was opposition to North's handling of the American crisis and to the general incompetence of his ministry, rather than desire for representational reform which influenced electors in September 1780, see Christie, *Wilkes, Wyvill and Reform*, pp.116–17.

2. *suppressing the fatal riots in our metropolis* The Gordon Riots of June 1780 found Jones raising a volunteer company of barristers and students to protect the Inns of Court. Saddened by the loss of life and the destruction, Jones was even more depressed at the thought of the injury to the cause of liberty. He wrote to Lady Spencer: 'A very great magistrate said to me yesterday, "This is the voice of the people!" Good God! No sober man ever used that expression without meaning the voice of the *nation*, or the *whole community*; such as was heard to call so loudly and so nobly at the Revolution', *Letters*, I.404. Alarmed at the thought that the king might now use these riots as a precedent for employing the army against lawful gatherings, Jones drew up *An Inquiry into the Legal Mode of Suppressing Riots* (*Works* VIII.459–98), criticizing the Riot Acts and pointing out that the constitution allows civil power in the shape of a citizen's militia to repress internal revolt.

should I have been led, if my respect for so enlightened an auditory had not restrained me! Intimations to such men, as I am addressing, supply the place of the most copious discussion; and, as I am willing to believe, that my sentiments have been little more than an echo to your own hearts, I have all along considered myself as rather exhorting the people of *Britain* at large, many of whom may be wavering, and many thoughtless, than the firm, the intelligent, the consistent electors of *Middlesex*.

All my countrymen, therefore, in general, through you, my fellow-freeholders, I adjure and supplicate, by whatever they hold estimable in this world, by the endearing relations of friends, families, and country, to follow the example of an individual, who loves and reveres them, in solemnly declaring, what I now solemnly declare, that I would not give my voice, on this occasion, to my best beloved or most respected friend, unless I knew with moral certainty his fixed resolution to restore by the most effectual means in his power *the broken harmony of our limited republick*, and to promote *a conciliatory act for the cessation of hostilities against the Americans*, on terms which nothing but their well-grounded confidence in *national*, not *ministerial*, engagements can induce them to accept.

Since one of our honourable candidates has, I firmly believe, the disposition which I require in my representative, and since he has done the state very signal service,[1] I shall give him my suffrage with the warmest alacrity; and since his intended colleague, whom I have not the honour of knowing, except by the fair fame of his excellent character and sound principles, has engaged himself to support that character, and act conformably to those principles, I beg him with equal cheerfulness to accept my hearty concurrence in his nomination.

Who is this (it will possibly be whispered or exclaimed) that importunes us with his complaints and his exhortations? This only, gentlemen, it will become me to answer. Were I inflamed by resentment against one set of men, or biassed by attachment to another, you might justly suspect the sincerity of my professions; or, if any disappointment in the career of ambition, or abrupt refusal of a favour asked, had ruffled or embittered my temper, you might fairly withdraw your attention and confidence; but, since I am neither agitated by one tumultuous passion, nor constrained by any narrowness of party; since the few favours I ever asked of administration have been either granted with the most obliging facility, or kept, from the justest motives, in suspense; since the first minister himself and many of his confidential friends have attached me personally to them by their manly, noble, unreserved behaviour, and that to a man from whom they could have nothing either to hope or to fear; since others, now in high departments of state, have conferred obligations on me, a grateful sense of which I shall never lose, but with my life; my country cannot with justice distrust my filial affection; nor can those, to whom I am obliged, accuse me of ingratitude, if I confine my regard to

---

1. *he has done the state very signal service* Jones's opinion of John Wilkes had significantly changed since April 1768, when he described him as: 'that villain Wilkes – a man, it is true, of energy and intelligence, but a trouble-maker and a sort of firebrand to light the flames of sedition', *Letters*, I.10.

their *persons*, without extending it blindly to their *actions*, and publickly evince my opinion, that the sacred duty to our country, which transcends all other relations, supersedes at the same time all other ties.

Had it been my good or my bad fortune to have delivered in the great assembly of representatives the sentiments which this bosom contains, a small part of which I have now delivered in a great assembly of electors, I am sensible that my *publick* course of speaking and voting must have clashed in a variety of instances with my *private* obligations; and this conflict of interfering duties constitutes, in my opinion, the nicest part of morality; on which, however, I have completely formed my system, and trust that no views of interest will ever prevent my practice from coinciding with my theory.

Having then imperfectly, I fear, but zealously, I am sure, discharged one duty this morning, to the neglect perhaps of another, but certainly with a total disregard of my own loss or gain, I sit down with an entire conviction, that, if my country-men be virtuously active and deliberately firm at the present crisis, there will be not a dawn only, but a full dayspring, of hope, that BRITAIN may again enjoy the sweets of rational liberty and the charms of peace: if, on the contrary, through drowsiness or oblivion of *English* virtue, you faint before you reach the goal, and suffer this moment to glide away unimproved, I do not see how any power less than that of GOD himself (and, whether this nation have deserved the divine inter-position in their favour, it will become us all to consider) can save our country from slavery and ruin; to the misery of which will be added this painful and agonizing reflection, the last and keenest sting of despair, that you will then have a right to censure no human beings but YOURSELVES.

30

A Speech to the Assembled Inhabitants of the Counties of Middlesex and Surry, the Cities of London and Westminster, and the Borough of Southwark. (On the Reformation of Parliament) xxviii May, MDCCLXXXII

[On the 20 May 1782 Jones wrote to Wilkes to give him notice 'as my friend and representative': 'that, at the next general meeting of the county of Middlesex, I shall make the following motion: "That the committee . . . inquire into the most practicable and constitutional mode of enabling the sheriff and magistrates of this county to defend it by legal force, and to assist government in defending the kingdom, in case of dangerous insurrection or invasion', *Letters*, II.540. Jones, whose preoccupation with 'how the *civil state* is to be armed, not how the *military state* is to be reinforced' originated in his first-hand experience of the Gordon Riots, was evidently intending to recommend the adoption of his *Plan of National Defence* (1782) The proposals concerning re-establishment of the *posse comitatus* published in his first political pamphlet, *An Inquiry into the Legal Mode of Suppressing Riots, with a Constitutional Plan of Future Defence* (1780) had met with much praise, the city of London very nearly implementing his plan, (*Life*, p.132).

In the event however, the meeting of 28 May in the London Tavern produced two resolutions concerning the extension of representation, at which Jones, appreciating the greater priority, abandoned his intended motion to speak on Constitutional law and parliamentary reform. The text of his speech was published by Charles Dilly on the 14 June, and the *Monthly Review* (vol. 67, August 1782, pp.148–9) applauded the 'judicious and spirited oration' for its successful attack on the doctrine of 'virtual representation'. The copy-text is that of 1782.]

ADVERTISEMENT

HAVING been informed, that parts of my Speech on the 28th of May at the London Tavern *were thought obscure, yet important, I have endeavoured to recollect what I then took the liberty to say, and have consented to let the argument go abroad in its rude and unpolished state. What offence this publication may give, either in parts or in the whole, is the last and least of my cares: my first and greatest is, to speak on all occasions what I conceive to be just and true.*

A SPEECH ON THE REFORMATION OF PARLIAMENT

My Lord Mayor,

So far am I from rising to intimate the slightest shade of dissent from this respectable and unanimous assembly, or the minutest disapprobation of the two resolutions proposed, that I despair of finding words sufficiently strong to express my joy and triumph at the perfect harmony, with which the first of them has already passed, and to which the second will, I trust, be thought equally entitled: but, on the last reading of the proposition now before you, it struck me, that, although it was in *substance* unexceptionable, yet it might easily be improved in *form* by the insertion of two or three words referring to the preceding resolution, and thus be rendered more conducive to our great object of generally declaring our concurrent sense, and avoiding any chance of disunion upon specifick points.[1] Every proposition, intended to meet with universal concurrence, ought to have three distinguishing properties; it should be just, simple, comprehensive: without justice, it will be rejected by the wise and good; without simplicity, it will involve complex matter, on which the wisest and the best may naturally differ; and without comprehensiveness, it will never answer any purpose of consequence and extent. The first resolution, 'that petitions ought to be prepared for a more complete representation of the people,' has all of these properties in an eminent degree: it is so just, that, if this meeting had been ten times as large, there would not have been one dissentient voice on that ground; so simple, that it affords no scope or subject for cavil; so comprehensive, that, when the house of commons have the petitions before them, it will give room for every particular plan, which the ingenuity of any member, duly tempered by wisdom, yet actuated by true patriotism, can suggest.

Ought not the *second* proposition, 'that the *sense of the people* should be taken this summer in order to prepare their *several* petitions,' to be somewhat restrained in the generality of the expression? It is just, but rather *too* comprehensive: *the sense of the people* is a phrase of measureless compass, and may include their several opinions, however specifick, however discordant. This is the very evil, which we are anxious to prevent; since we all agree, that no particular mode of reformation should be prescribed to the house, lest they should reject, for no other reason, some good plan, which, if left to the operation of their own minds, they may probably

---

1. *avoiding any chance of disunion on specifick points*   Jones applies his forensic skills to the wording of the second resolution to obviate any potential vagueness or ambiguity. In his intended motion concerning civilian militia he was aware that: 'a lawyer may appear with better grace than a mere soldier', (*Letters*, II.541), and the barrister in Jones is equally as concerned with accuracy as with oratory. As Caroline Robbins maintains: 'His speech at the London Tavern in 1782 reveals clearly the quality of his mind', *The Eighteenth-Century Commonwealthman* (Cambridge, Mass., 1961), p.375.

adopt. Might not the sentence be thus corrected, 'that the sense of the people should be taken *on the preceding resolution?*' But this I offer as a mere suggestion to wiser heads, and will not trouble the assembly by shaping it into a motion: indeed, if both resolutions be taken together, and it be understood, that we mean to recommend petitions on the *general* ground,[1] in order to shun that fatal rock, *diversity of sentiment on particulars*, I desire no more, and am very little solicitous about accuracy of expression; hoping at the same time, although the *five* circles[2] here assembled have no right or pretension to take the lead in the nation, yet that the other counties, districts, and towns in *Great Britain* will approve our idea, and not disdain to follow our example: in that event I smile at the thought of a miscarriage, and am confident, that, with concurrence, perseverance, and moderation, the people of *England* must prevail in a claim so essential to their liberty, and to the permanence of an administration, who profess to govern with their confidence.

Here I should regularly cease; especially, as I now labour under the pressure of the epidemical complaint, which alone can have prevented this meeting from being as numerous as it is respectable: it could not prevent my attendance, for, in health or in sickness, I am devoted to your service; and I shall never forget the words of an old *Roman*, LIGARIUS;[3] who, when the liberties of his country were in imminent danger, and when a real friend to those liberties was condoling with him on his illness at so critical a time, raised himself on his couch, seized the hand of his friend, and said, *If you have any business worthy of yourselves, I am well.*

It was not in truth my design to have spoken at all this evening; but, since I have risen to explain a sudden thought, I will avail myself of your favourable attention, and hazard a few words upon the *general* question itself: on the smallest intimation of your wishes, I will be silent. Numbers will have patience to hear, who have not time to read; besides, that it is always easier to speak than to write; and, as to myself, a very particular and urgent occasion,[4] which calls me for some months

---

1. *to recommend petitions on the general ground*   Despite the Thatched-House Tavern agreement earlier in May that petitions to Parliament be drawn up in general terms, there was dissension between the Revd Christopher Wyvill of the Yorkshire Association, who favoured petitions outlining a programme of specific propositions, and the metropolitan reformers, who argued that the details of reform might be left to the discretion of Parliament, see Christie, *Wilkes, Wyvill and Reform*, pp.145–66.

2. *the five circles*   The *Morning Chronicle* coined the term 'Quintuple Alliance' for this association of county, city, and borough electors, see *Life*, pp.167–8.

3. *LIGARIUS*   Quintus Ligarius, a Roman pro-consul, supporter of Pompey, and friend of Cicero, became one of the conspirators against Cæsar. Cf. 'I am not sick if Brutus have in hand/Any exploit worthy the name of honour', *Julius Cæsar* II.i.316–17, (Shakespeare, following Plutarch, misnames him Caius).

4. *a very particular and urgent occasion, which calls me for some months from England*   Jones's planned trip to Virginia (via Paris and his friend Franklin) was in fact to secure the estate of a friend, John Paradise, but Cannon has shown that John Jay, largely on the basis of this cryptic reference, suspected Jones of being a British agent, and similar speculation was circulating in London. The *Public Advertiser* of 26 June confidently announced: 'The destination of Mr. Jones is not Asia, . . . but *America* . . . When we call to Mind . . . his very confidential Intimacy with the Spencer Family, his peculiar Enthusiasm for Liberty of every Kind and in every Place, and, above all, his Fame not only for Literature, but the Business of Politics, it seems to the highest Degree

from *England*, will deprive me of another opportunity to communicate my sentiments in either form, until the momentous object before us shall be made certainly attainable through the concord, or for ever lost and irrecoverable through the disagreement, of the nation.

The only *specious* argument, that I have anywhere heard, against a change in the parliamentary representation of the people, is, that, 'a *constitution*, which has stood for ages, ought not to be altered.'[1]

This objection appears on a superficial view so plausible, and applies itself so winningly to the hearts of *Englishmen*, who have an honest prejudice for their established system, without having in general very distinct ideas of it, that a detection of the *sophism*, for such I engage to prove it, becomes absolutely necessary for the promotion of your glorious enterprise.

I will risk your impatience; for, though I am aware, that allusions to history and interpretations of old statutes are not very proper in addresses to popular assemblies; yet, when popular assemblies take upon them, as they justly may, to act and resolve upon constitutional points, they are bound to seek or to receive information, lest their actions should be rash and their resolutions ill-founded. A power exerted through passion or caprice, without a deep knowledge of the business in hand, and a fair application of the intellectual faculties, is a *tyrannical* power, whether it be regal, aristocratical, *or popular*; and the prevalence of any such power, by the overbearing strength of king, nobles, *or people*, would form an immediate *tyranny*, and in a moment subvert the constitution.

That constitution, which, I persuade myself, will not be subverted, consists of form and spirit, of body (if I may so express myself), and of soul: but, in a course of years, the form is apt to deviate so widely from the spirit, that it becomes expedient almost every century to restore its genuine purity and loveliness. The objection, which I undertake to remove, is sophistical, either by design or through ignorance; for the proposition is true in one sense of the word *constitution*, and false in the other; and the sense, in which it is true, is inapplicable to the question. It is true, that the *spirit* of the constitution ought not to be changed; it is false, that the *form* ought not to be corrected; and I will now demonstrate, 'that the spirit of our constitution requires a representation of the people, nearly equal and nearly universal.'[2] Such as cannot or will not follow me in the premises, both can and will (or I greatly deceive myself) bear away the conclusion in their memory; and it is of higher importance than they may imagine.

---

probable that Mr Jones is now appointed, and surely with the best possible Reason appointed, to assist in the Pacific Negotiations with America', quoted in *Life*, p.175.

1. *a constitution, which has stood for ages, ought not to be altered* 'Improvement without innovation was the watchword of many politically conservative figures', Paul Langford, *Public Life and the Propertied Englishman 1689–1798* (Oxford, 1991), p.211.

2. *nearly equal and nearly universal* Cf. John Locke, *The Second Treatise of Government* (New York, 1952), paras. 157–8. On Locke's influence upon the reformers see Isaac Kramnick, *Republicanism and Bourgeois Radicalism* (Ithaca and London, 1990), esp. pp.172–94.

There has been a continued war in the constitution of *England* between two jarring principles;[1] the evil principle of the feudal system with his dark auxiliaries, ignorance and false philosophy; and the good principle of increasing commerce,[2] with her liberal allies, true learning and sound reason. The first is the poisoned source of all the abominations, which history too faithfully records: it has blemished and polluted, wherever it has touched, the fair form of our constitution, and for ages even contaminated the spirit. While any dregs of this baneful system[3] remain, you cannot justly boast of general freedom: it was a system of niggardly and partial freedom, enjoyed by great barons only and many acred men, who were perpetually insulting and giving check to the king, while they racked and harrowed the people. Narrow and base as it was, and confined exclusively to landed property, it admitted the *lowest freeholders* to the due enjoyment of that inestimable right, without which it is a banter to call a man *free*; the right of voting in the choice of deputies to assist in making those laws, which may affect not his property only, but his life, and, what is dearer, his liberty; and which are not laws, but tyrannous ordinances, if imposed on him without his suffrage given in person or by deputation. This I conceive to have been the right of every freeholder, even by the feudal polity, from the earliest time; and the statute of HENRY IV. I believe to have been merely declaratory: an act which passed in the *seventh* year of that prince, near four hundred years ago, ordains, that, '*all* they, who are present at the county court, as well suitors *duly summoned* for the same cause, *as others*, shall proceed to the election of their knights for the parliament.' *All suitors*, you see, had the right; and *all freeholders* were *suitors* in the court, however low the value of their freeholds. Observe all along, that one pound in those days was equal to ten at least

---

1. *There has been a continued war in the constitution of England between two jarring principles* This was not merely another rehearsal of the oppositional pattern favoured by the early radicals – the struggle of the English people to free Anglo-Saxon institutions from the dead weight of the Norman yoke. In opposing 'the evil principle of feudalism' and 'the good principle of increasing commerce' Jones demonstrates a faith in commodity exchange and the market with a confidence beyond many of Wilkes's supporters. 'Wilkites . . . did not go so far as to express explicitly the idea that market relations were a viable alternative to the old system', John Brewer, 'English Radicalism in the Age of George III', in *Three British Revolutions: 1641, 1688, 1776*, ed. J. G. A. Pocock (Princeton, 1980), 323–67, p.346. Indeed Jones anticipates the new dichotomy between virtuous commerce and corrupt privilege which was to be drawn by Dissenting middle-class radicals such as Richard Price and Joseph Priestley in the next decade, see Kramnick, *Republicanism and Bourgeois Radicalism*, pp.195–9. The whole passage was published by Capell Lofft in the proceedings of the Society for Constitutional Information, see *London Proc. S.C.I.*, 12 Aug, 1782.

2. *increasing commerce* Jones was well aware that the prime function of government was to protect commerce and foster overseas markets; Adam Smith was a fellow-member of the Turk's Head Club, and had characterized the political economy as a 'natural system of perfect liberty and justice', *An Inquiry into the Nature and Causes of the Wealth of Nations*, 2 vols. (London, 1776), I.66.

3. *this baneful system* Jones's animus against feudalism is largely explained by his fears of aristocratic power, cf. *Principles of Government*, p.400. In this connection it is salutary to note Langford's opinion: 'Sometimes it was precisely the men who complained about the creeping influence of aristocratic power who were themselves responsible for it. William Jones was one such', *Public Life and the Propertied Englishman* , p.558. Certainly Jones was quick to seek electoral support from the Spencers, and to nominate Lord Althorp, his former pupil, for membership of the Literary Club.

in the present time. Here then is a plain declaration, that minuteness of *real* property created no harsh suspicion of a dependent mind; for a harsh suspicion it is, and, by proving too much, proves nothing.

What caused the absurd, yet fatal, distinction between property, personal and real?[1] The feudal principle. What created another odious distinction between *free* and *base* holdings, and thus excluded copyholds of any value? The feudal principle. What introduced an order of men, called *villains*, transferable, like cattle, with the land which they stocked? The feudal principle. What excludes the holders of beneficial leases? The feudal principle. What made personalty, in those times, of little or no estimation? The feudal principle. What raised the silly notion, that the property, not the person, of the subject, was to be represented? The feudal principle. What prevented the large provision in the act of *Henry* IV. by which *all freeholders* were declared electors, from being extended to *all* holders of *property*, however denominated, however inconsiderable? The same infernal principle, which then subdued and stifled the genuine equalising spirit of our constitution. Now, if we find that this demon was himself in process of time subdued, as he certainly was by the extension of commerce under *Elizabeth*, and the enlarged conceptions which extended commerce always produces, by the revival of learning, which dispelled the darkness of *Gothick* ignorance, and by the great transactions of the last century, when the true theory and genuine principles of freedom, were unfolded and illustrated, we shall not hesitate to pronounce, that, by the *spirit* of our constitution, all *Englishmen*, having property of any kind or quantity, are entitled to votes in chusing parliamentary delegates. The *form* soon received a cruel blemish; for, in the *eighth* of Henry VI.[2] the property of suitors qualified to vote, was restrained to '*forty* shillings a year above all charges,' that is, to twenty pounds at least by the present value of money. I agree with those, who consider this act as basely aristocratical, as a wicked invasion of clear popular rights, and therefore in a high degree unconstitutional: it is also a disgraceful confession of legislative weakness; for the evil, pretended to be remedied by it, was, that the county elections were *tumultuary*. What! could not the wisdom of the legislature suggest a mode of preventing tumult, if the laws already subsisting had been insufficient for that purpose, without shaking the obligation of all future laws, by narrowing the circle of those, who, being affected by them, ought by natural equity to assist in framing them? Ridiculous and indefensible!

In the *twelfth* of Charles II. the mighty fabrick of the feudal system was shaken from its basis; but, though its ramparts were overset, its connexions and covered ways destroyed, and its very foundations convulsed, yet the ruins of it have been found replete with mischief, and the mischief operates, even while I speak.

---

1. *the absurd, yet fatal, distinction between property, personal and real* As John Brewer has shown, the emphasis upon moveable property enabled the radicals to extend the movement for reform beyond the traditional rhetoric of country ideology, see *Party Ideology and Popular Politics at the Accession of George III* (Cambridge, 1977), p.255.

2. *in the eighth of Henry VI* This Act of 1430 confined the right to vote for a knight of the shire to 40s. freeholders, resident in the county.

At the Revolution, indeed, the good spirit of the constitution was called forth, and its fair principles expanded: it is only since that auspicious event, that, although we may laugh, when lawyers call their vast assemblage of sense and subtilty *the perfection of human wisdom*, yet we shall deride no man, who asserts the constitution of *England* to be in theory the most perfect of human systems – in theory, not in practice; for, although you are clearly entitled to all the advantages, which the *principles* of the constitution give you, while you claim those advantages by cool and decent petition, yet, either from some unaccountable narrowness in the managers of the Revolution, or from the novelty and difficulty of their situation, they left their noble work so unfinished, and the feudal poison so little exterminated, that, to use the words of your favourite poet, 'they scotched the snake, not killed it.'[1] Who could have imagined, that, in the *eighteenth* of GEORGE II. the statute of *Henry* VI. would have been adopted and almost transcribed? Who could have dreamed, that, in the *thirty-first* of the same king,[2] the last act would have been recited and approved, with a declaration added, that no tenant by copy of court roll should vote at an election for knights of the shire under penalty of fifty pounds? It was the accursed feudal principle, which suggested these laws, when the fairest opportunity presented itself of renovating the constitution. Another gale has now sprung up; and, unless you catch it while it blows, it will be gone for ever.

I have proved, unless I delude myself, 'that the spirit of our constitution requires a representation of the people nearly equal and nearly universal.' Carry this proposition home with you, and keep it as an answer to those, who exclaim 'that the constitution ought not to be changed.' I said *nearly* universal; for I admit, that our constitution, both in form and spirit, requires *some* property in electors,[3] either real or personal, in possession or in action; but I consider a *fair trade* or *profession* as *valuable property*, and an *Englishman*, who can support himself by honest industry, though in a low station, has often a more independent mind than the

---

1. *scotched the snake, not killed it   Macbeth* III.ii.13.

2. *the thirty-first of the same king*   The Act, which received the royal signature on 9 June 1758, effectively reestablished the principles of the Eighth Parliament of Henry VI. Five days before his speech, on 23 May, Jones had written to Major John Cartwright, recommending a copyhold franchise: 'had I been in parliament in the 31st of George II, I should have thought, as a legislator, that copyholders had a natural right, supported by the spirit of our constitution; should have depised the gabble of the feudal lawyers; and should consequently, both have argued and voted against the act by which all tenants, by copy of court-roll, were declared incapable of polling for knights of the shire', *Letters*, II.547. The contrasting tone of the postscript to this letter reveals that Jones was occasionally frustrated by the fact that the Society for Constitutional Information made no attempt to direct popular mobilization: 'P.S. It is my deliberate (though private) opinion, that the people of England will never be a people, in the majestic sense of the word, unless two hundred thousand of the *civil* state be ready, before the first of next November, to take the field, without rashness or disorder, at twenty-four hours' notice'.

3. *our constitution, both in form and spirit, requires some property in electors*   Jones appears to baulk at the idea of universal male suffrage, maintaining that only those with property to be self-supporting should be enfranchised, see C. B. Macpherson, *The Political Theory of Possessive Individualism from Hobbes to Locke* (Oxford, 1963), pp.263–7. As he viewed labour as a source of property, however, he effectively excluded only those 'unable or unwilling to gain any thing by art or labour'.

prodigal owner of a large encumbered estate. When *Prynne*[1] speaks of *every inhabitant and commoner*, to whom he supposes that the right of voting originally belonged, I cannot persuade myself, that he meaned to include such as, having nothing at all, and being unable or unwilling to gain any thing by art or labour, were supported by alms.

If modern authorities be demanded in aid of my opinions, I shall only mention the great judge, Sir *William Blackstone*, and I mention him the more willingly, because he never professed democratical sentiments, and, though we admire him as the systematical arranger of our laws, yet we may fairly doubt the popularity of his political notions: nevertheless, he openly allows in his Commentary, 'that the spirit of our constitution is in favour of a more complete representation of the people.'[2] This too is allowed by the very man, who, in another tract, intimates an opinion, 'that the value of freeholds themselves should be greatly advanced above what is now required by law to give the proprietor a voice in county elections'. I told you, that all reasoning from the statute of *Henry* VI. proved too much, and, consequently, nothing; for, who now would bear the idea of disqualifying those electors of *Surry* and *Middlesex*, whose freeholds were not of the annual value of twenty pounds?

I hear a murmur among you, and perceive other marks of impatience. Indulge me a moment, and I will descend; but let me not be misapprehended. I do not propose to conclude with a specifick motion: it is my deliberate opinion, confirmed by my observations on the event of your associations *to reduce the influence of the Crown*, that your petitions and resolutions must be *very general*. In my own mind I go along with you to the full length of your wishes. If the present system of representation[3] be justly compared to a tree rotten at the heart, I wish to see removed every particle of its rottenness, that a microscopick eye could discern. I deride many of the fashionable doctrines: that of *virtual* representation I hold to be *actual* folly; as childish, as if they were to talk of *negative* representation, and to contend, that it involved any *positive* idea. Substitute the word *delegation* or

---

1. *Prynne* William Prynne (1600–69), Puritan pamphleteer and barrister. His writings had proved very influential with members of the Yorkshire Association, see, for example the tract of the philanthropist Granville Sharp entitled 'Equitable Representation necessary to the Establishment of Law, Peace and good Government; shewn in some Extracts from Mr Prynne's *Brevia Parliamentarii Rediviva*' (1780).

2. *'a more complete representation of the people'* A powerful and influential exponent of the balanced constitution, Blackstone attached importance to strengthening the position of the Commons to maintain Constitutional equilibrium, see Sir William Blackstone, *Commentaries on the Laws of England*, 14th. edn. 4 vols. (London, 1803), I.51, 154, 261. See *A Speech on the Nomination of Candidates*, p.378 note 4 above.

3. *present system of representation* On Jones's advanced ideas see *A Letter to a Patriot Senator, including the Heads of a Bill for a Constitutional Representation of the People* (London: John Nichols for Charles Dilly, 1783), which suggested annual parliaments, measures to counter corruption, and adult male suffrage extended to those with an annual income of at least £25 from property or labour. Anticipating possible lines of attack, Jones writes: 'The whole system, it will be said, is *democratical*, big with danger to publick peace, and evidently tending to revolution, by giving to the people a greater share of power than is consistent with general tranquillity. Idle terrors! vain surmises!' (p.39).

deputation, instead of representation, and you will instantly see the absurdity of the conceit.[1] Does a man, who is *virtually*, not *actually*, represented, delegate or depute any person to make those laws, which may affect his property, his freedom, and his life? None; for he has no suffrage. How then is he represented according to the principles of our constitution? As well might a *Roman* tyrant have urged, that all his vassals were represented in his person: he was augur and high priest; the religious state was, therefore, represented by him: he was tribune of the people; the popular part of the nation were, therefore, represented: he was consul, dictator, master of the horse, every thing he pleased; the civil and military states were, therefore, concentrated in him; the next deduction would have been, that the slaves of his empire were free men. There is no end of absurdities deducible from so idle a play upon words.

That there may be an end of my address to you, which has been too long for the place and occasion, but too short for the subject, I resume my seat with a full conviction, that, if united, and dependent on Yourselves alone, you must succeed; if disunited, or too confident in others, you must fail. Be persuaded also, that the people of *England* can only expect to be the happiest and most glorious, while they are the freest, and can only become the freest, when they shall be the most virtuous, and most enlightened, of nations.

---

1. Virtual representation involved the idea that an MP represented the localities where he resided or held property, or indeed that he represented the country as a whole, and not merely his electors, as Burke had maintained in Bristol (*Speech at the Conclusion of the Poll, 3 Nov. 1774*, Bristol, 1774). This was anathema to Jones, the Wilkesites, and the Bristol voters who wanted members to be answerable to their electoral constituents.

31

The Principles of Government (1782)

[This short pamphlet perfectly illustrates how the modest and scholarly Jones manages to situate himself at the centre of affairs in pre-Revolutionary Europe. In conversation with the French Minister, Vergennes, and his old friend Benjamin Franklin at the latter's house in Paris in July 1782, Jones maintained, despite Vergennes' incredulity and Franklin's doubt, that 'the first principles of government could be made intelligble to plain illiterate readers', (*sic*) *Bibliotheca Parriana, a Catalogue of the Library of the late Samuel Parr* (London, 1827), p.441. But this Socratic dialogue indicates more than the mere winning of an academic debating point, it demonstrates, within the context of the 'Atlantic Revolution', its author's faith in the discipline and independence of a general populace which could be educated into citizenship. *The Principles of Government in a Dialogue between a Scholar and a Peasant*, with its tripartite emphases upon popular education, parliamentary reform, and co-operative association, was welcomed by Major John Cartwright and his Society for Constitutional Information. In April 1782 Jones had been elected to this principal forum of the pre-Jacobin intelligentsia, and the Society promptly published *The Principles of Government* anonymously as a free pamphlet. The *Gentleman's Magazine* supposed it 'to be by no mean hand' (53, April 1783, 332); a later piece in the *Monthly Review* (71, Oct. 1784, 349) praised Jones as an upholder of the great principles of liberty on which constitutional government is founded. It subsequently went into nine editions, one of which was brought out after the Peterloo massacre in 1819 to remind the public of how such horrific occurences could be avoided. It is generally agreed that *The Principles of Government* was, in Mukherjee's words: 'one of the most influential books of the movement for parliamentary reform in the late eighteenth and early nineteenth centuries, and so gave Jones an undeniable position in the history of the reform movement', *Sir William Jones*, p. 53.

But this was not all. In 1783, Jones's friend and future brother-in-law, the Revd William Shipley, Dean of St Asaph, published an edition of *The Principles* in Flintshire. Thomas Fitzmaurice, the sheriff of Flintshire, promptly prosecuted Shipley for seditious libel. Thomas Erskine, a famous defence lawyer, was engaged by the Society for Constitutional Information, and, after a long and intricate trial, Shipley was acquitted and his success celebrated throughout the country with bonfires and fireworks. The trial focused attention upon the problems of trial by jury and directly led towards the enactment of Fox's Libel Act of 1792, which gave the jury the right to decide on the libellous tendency of any publication. Thus Jones's *jeu d'esprit* had a far-reaching effect upon both the movement for parliamentary reform and the legal history of England. On the impact of the pamphlet in Wales, including its incorporation into a lively interlude which represents the first political tract in Welsh, see my *Sir William Jones* (*Writers of Wales* series, Cardiff: University of Wales Press, 1995). The text followed is that of 1799.]

ADVERTISEMENT

A SHORT defence hath been thought necessary, against a violent and groundless attack upon the FLINTSHIRE COMMITTEE, for having testified their approbation of the following Dialogue, which hath been publickly branded with the most injurious epithets; and it is conceived, that the sure way, to vindicate this little Tract from so unjust a character, will be as publickly to produce it. – The friends of the Revolution will instantly see, that it contains no principle, which has not the support of the highest authority, as well as the clearest reason.

If the doctrines which it slightly touches, in a manner suited to the nature of the Dialogue, be 'seditious, treasonable, and diabolical,' Lord *Somers*[1] was an incendiary, *Locke* a traitor, and the *Convention-parliament* a pandæmonium; but, if those names are the glory and boast of *England*, and if that convention secured our liberty and happiness, then the doctrines in question are not only *just* and *rational* but *constitutional* and *salutary*; and the reproachful epithets belong wholly to the system of those, who so grossly misapplied them.

Advertisement: On 24 January 1783 Dean Shipley sent a copy of *The Principles of Government* throughout which he had substituted in his own hand the words 'Gentleman' and 'Farmer', for 'Scholar' and 'Peasant', to the Revd Edward Edwards, his curate at Wrexham, with instructions, 'to get the edition of the enclosed Dialogue printed by Marsh as soon as possible with the following advertisement annexed to it', quoted in Peter Brown, *The Chathamites* (London, 1967), p.376. Samuel Parr ascribes authorship of the advertisement to Bishop Shipley, Dean Shipley's father, and Jones's future father-in-law, (*Bibliotheca Parriana, A Catalogue of the Library of the late Samuel Parr*, London, 1827, p.441.)

1. *Lord Somers* (1651–1716). A close and dedicated supporter of William III, as lord chancellor he superintended the drafting of the Declaration of Rights. Somers was the friend and patron of Addison, Congreve, Steele and Swift.

THE PRINCIPLES OF GOVERNMENT,

IN A DIALOGUE BETWEEN

A GENTLEMAN AND A FARMER.

F. WHY should humble men, like me, sign or set marks to petitions of this nature? It is better for us Farmers to mind our husbandry, and leave what we cannot comprehend to the King and Parliament.

G. You can comprehend more than you imagine; and, as a *free member of a free state*, have higher things to mind than you may conceive.

F. If by *free* you mean *out of prison*, I hope to continue so, as long as I can pay my rent to the 'squire's bailiff; but what is meant by a *free state?*

G. Tell me first what is meant by a club in the village, of which I know you to be a member.

F. It is an assembly of men, who meet after work every Saturday to be   10
merry and happy for a few hours in the week.

G. Have you no other object but mirth?

F. Yes; we have a box, into which we contribute equally from our monthly or weekly savings, and out of which any members of the club are to be relieved in sickness or poverty; for the parish officers are so cruel and insolent, that it were better to starve than apply to them for relief.

G. Did they, or the 'squire, or the parson, or all together, compel you to form this society?

---

4 *you can comprehehend more than you imagine* Ten years later Joseph Priestley informed the Birmingham Dissenters: 'You are told that matters of the state and church are of great mystery, into which you shouldn't delve', *An Appeal to the Public on the Subject of Riots in Birmingham* (Birmingham, 1792), p.14. In this attempt to demystify the state, Jones anticipates the efforts of Priestley, Paine, and Godwin in the 1790s to tear the Burkean veil of baroque mystery and stress the intelligibility of government to the common man; see Kramnick, *Republicanism and Bourgeois Radicalism*, pp.88–90.

8 *Tell me first what is meant* In a letter of 13 April 1784 Jones writes of the dialogue: 'I meant it merely as an imitation of one of Plato's, where a boy wholly ignorant of geometry, is made by a few simple questions to demonstrate a proposition, and I intended to inculcate that the principles of government were so obvious and intelligible, that even a clown might be brought to understand them. As to raising sedition, I as much thought of raising a church', *Letters*, II.642.

   a club in the village Habermas has documented the relevance of the Enlightenment associational tendency in providing a 'training ground for what were to become a future society's norms of behaviour', 'Further Reflections on the Public Sphere', in Craig Calhoun (ed.), *Habermas and the Public Sphere* (Cambridge, Mass., and London, 1992), pp.423–4. However, while Habermas views such societies as 'an exclusively bourgeois affair', it would seem that Jones did not.

13 *we have a box* This pooling of resources in the interests of reciprocal obligation and mutual benevolence freed even humble men from economic, social, and political dependence on patrons or local magnates.

F. Oh! no – we could not be compelled; we formed it by our own choice.

G. You did right – But have you not some head or president of your club?　20

F. The master for each night is chosen by all the company present the week before.

G. Does he make laws to bind you in case of ill temper or misbehaviour?

F. He make laws! He bind us! No; we have all agreed to a set of equal rules, which are signed by every new comer, and were written in a strange hand by young *Spelman*, the lawyer's clerk, whose uncle is a member.

G. What should you do, if any one member were to insist on becoming *perpetual* master, and on altering your rules at his arbitrary will and pleasure?

F. We should expel him.　30

G. What, if he were to bring a sergeant's guard, when the militia are quartered in your neighbourhood, and insist upon your obeying him?

F. We should resist, if we could; if not, the society would be broken up.

G. Suppose that, with his sergeant's guard, he were to take the money out of the box or out of your pockets?

F. Would not that be a robbery?

G. I am seeking information from you. How should you act on such an occasion?

F. We should submit, perhaps, at that time; but should afterwards try to apprehend the robbers.　40

G. What, if you could not apprehend them?

F. We might kill them, I should think; and, if the King would not pardon us, God would.

G. How could you either apprehend them, or, if they resisted, kill them, without a sufficient force in your own hands?

F. Oh! we are all good players at single stick, and each of us has a stout cudgel or quarter-staff in the corner of his room.

G. Suppose that a few of the club were to domineer over the rest, and insist upon making laws for them –

F. We must take the same course; except that it would be easier to restrain　50

19　*we formed it by our own choice*　Jones conceives of the state in very similar terms to Priestley, a fellow member of the Honest Whigs club, 'a simple and useful artefact created by ordinary self-seeking people whose rational common sense prompted them voluntarily to consent to be governed', Kramnick, *Republicanism and Bourgeois Radicalism*, p.88.

24–5　*a set of equal rules*　All members within the club were equal, and officers were elected, often on a rotating basis. 'Such associations were ideal polities, models of a perfect social order', Brewer, 'English Radicalism', p.360.

31–2　*when the militia are quartered in your neighbourhood*　Jones regarded the militia as an army in all but name, favouring the concept of the *posse comitatus*, a more democratic force, as sanctioned by existing law. See his *An Inquiry into the Legal Mode of Suppressing Riots* (1780),and his *Plan of National Defence* (1782), *Works*, VIII.516–24. On the clarity and rectitude of Jones's interpretations of criminal law, see S. G. Vesey-Fitzgerald, 'Sir William Jones the Jurist', *BSOAS* 11 (1946), 807–17.

one man, than a number; but we should be the majority with justice on our side.

G. A word or two on another head. Some of you, I presume, are no great accountants.

F. Few of us understand accounts; but we trust old *Lilly* the schoolmaster, whom we believe to be an honest man; and he keeps the key of our box.

G. If your money should in time amount to a large sun, it might not perhaps be safe, to keep it at his house or in any private house.

F. Where else should we keep it?

G. You might chuse to put it into the funds, or to lend it the 'squire; who   60
has lost so much lately at *Newmarket*, taking his bond or some of his fields as your security for payment with interest.

F. We must in that case confide in young *Spelman*, who will soon set up for himself, and, if a lawyer can be honest, will be an honest lawyer.

G. What power do you give to *Lilly*, or should you give to *Spelman* in the case supposed?

F. No power. We should give them both a due allowance for their trouble, and should expect a faithful account of all they had done for us.

G. Honest men may change their nature. What, if both or either of them were to deceive you.   70

F. We should remove them, put our trust in better men, and try to repair our loss.

G. Did it never occur to you, that every state or nation was only a great *club*?

F. Nothing ever occurred to me on the subject; for I never thought about it.

G. Though you never thought before on the subject, yet you may be able to tell me, why you suppose men to have assembled, and to have formed *nations*, *communities*, or *states*, which all mean the same thing.

F. In order, I should imagine, to be as happy as they can, while they live.   80

G. By *happy* do you mean *merry* only?

F. To be as merry as they can without hurting themselves or their neighbours, but chiefly to secure themselves from danger, and to relieve their wants.

67–8 *No power. . . expect a faithful account* The notion of accountability is premised upon the Lockean concept of government as a contract or trust where high office should yield not individual power but public responsibility.

73 *every state or nation was only a great club?* Brewer has seen the burgeoning of Lockean voluntary association, the private club – tavern, village or tradesmen's clubs, masonic or pseudomasonic organizations, provincial learned societies, associations of electors, and so on – as fundamental to the creation of a 'commercially freer, politically self-reliant body politic', John Brewer, 'Commercialization and Politics', in *The Birth of a Consumer Society: The Commercialization of Eighteenth-Century England*, ed. Neil McKendrick *et al.* (Bloomington, Ind., 1982), p.233.

80 *to be as happy as they can* Among inherent and inalienable rights, the farmer prioritises the pursuit of happiness, reversing the Jeffersonian order.

G. Do you believe, that any King or Emperor compelled them so to associate?

F. How could one man compel a multitude? A King or an Emperor, I presume, is not born with a hundred hands.

G. When a prince of the blood shall in any country be so distinguished by nature, I shall then, and then only, conceive him to be a greater man than   90
you. But might not an army, with a King or General at their head, have compelled them to assemble?

F. Yes; but the army must have been formed by their own choice. One man or a few can never govern many without their consent.

G. Suppose, however, that a multitude of men, assembled in a town or city, were to chuse a King or Governor, might they not give him high power and authority?

F. To be sure; but they would never be so mad, I hope, as to give him a power of making their *laws*.

G. Who else should make them?   100

F. The *whole* nation or people.

G. What, if they disagreed?

F. The opinion of the *greater number*, as in our village-clubs, must be taken and prevail.

G. What could be done, if the society were so large, that all could not meet in the same place?

F. A greater number must chuse a less.

G. Who should be the chusers?

F. All, who are not *upon the parish*, In our club, if a man asks relief of the overseer, he ceases to be one of us, because he must depend on the overseer.   110

G. Could not a few men, one in seven for instance, chuse the assembly of law-makers as well as a larger number?

F. As conveniently, perhaps; but I would not suffer any man to chuse another, who was to make laws, by which my money or my life might be taken from me.

G. Have you a *freehold* in any county of forty shillings a year?

F. I have nothing in the world but my cattle, implements of husbandry, and household goods, together with my farm, for which I pay a fixed rent to the 'squire.

G. Have you a vote in any city or borough?   120

F. I have no vote at all; but am able by my honest labour to support my wife and four children; and, whilst I act honestly, I may defy the laws.

---

109 *All, who are not upon the parish* Cf. *On the Reformation of Parliament*, pp.390–1 above.

116 *Have you a freehold in any county of forty shillings a year?* Jones had developed the Lockean concept that 'everyman has a property in his own person' (see *The Second Treatise of Government*, New York, 1952, ch.5, para. 33), arguing that the qualification for suffrage should be that property which every man held in his own life and labour, see *On the Reformation of Parliament*, loc. cit.

G. Can you be ignorant, that the Parliament, to which members are sent by this county, and by the next market-town, have power to make new laws, by which you and your family may be stripped of your goods, thrown into prison, and even deprived of life?

F. A dreadful power! I never made inquiries, having business of my own, concerning the business of Parliament, but imagined, that the laws had been fixed for many hundred years.

G. The common laws, to which you refer, are equal, just, and humane; but   130
the King and Parliament may alter them, when they please.

F. The King ought, therefore, to be a good man, and the Parliament to consist of men equally good.

G. The King alone can do no harm; but who must judge the goodness of Parliament-men?

F. All those whose property, freedom, and lives may be affected by their laws.

G. Yet six men in seven, who inhabit this kingdom, have, like you, no votes; and the petition, which I desired you to sign, has nothing for its object, but the restoration of you all to the right of chusing those law-makers, by   140
whom your money or your lives may be taken from you. Attend, while I read it distinctly.

F. Give me your pen – I never wrote my name, ill as it may be written, with greater eagerness.

G. I applaud you, and trust, that your example will be followed by millions. Another word before we part. Recollect, your opinion about your club in the village, and tell me what ought to be the consequence, if the King alone were to insist on making laws, or on altering them at his will and pleasure.

F. He too must be expelled.   150

130–1   *The common laws . . . alter them when they please*   The central dilemma for many Englishmen, especially common lawyers, was how 'to reconcile the tradition of Englishmen's inalienable rights (whether civil or natural) and the recognized, unlimited power of a sovereign Parliament', Brewer, 'English Radicalism', p.341. For Jones, grounded in Blackstone, and convinced of the need for equilibrium, the unlimited sovereignty of Parliament represented a violation of the Constitution. To Burke Jones had insisted, 'the Omnipotence of Parliament is a Solecism in Terms', *Letters*, I.258.

138–9   *six men in seven, who inhabit this kingdom, have, like you, no votes*   Cf. Major John Cartwright, founder of the Society for Constitutional Information and friend of Jones: 'What right has $\frac{6}{7}$ of the people who wear laced coats and eat white bread to tell $\frac{6}{7}$ who have plain coats and eat brown bread that they have no right to interfere in the election', *The Legislative Rights of the Commonalty Vindicated; or, Take Your Choice* (London, 1776), p.27.

150   *He too must be expelled*   Jones's belief in the ability of the Constitution to check monarchic power had been shaken by recent events. Nevertheless, he maintained that the 1688 revolution had established the right of the people to expel an oppressive monarch, and this point was taken up by Erskine in his defence: 'If any one sentence from the beginning to the end of it is seditious or libellous, the Bill of Rights (to use the language of the advertisement prefixed to it) was seditious libel; the Revolution was wicked rebellion', J. Gurney, *The Whole Proceedings on the Trial of the King against Shipley* (London, 1784), p.19.

G. Oh! but think of his standing army and of the militia, which now are his in substance, though ours in form.

F. If he were to employ that force against the nation, they would and ought to resist him, or the state would cease to be a state.

G. What, if the great accountants and great lawyers, the *Lillys* and *Spelmans*, of the nation were to abuse their trust, and cruelly injure, instead of faithfully serving, the publick?

F. We must request the King to remove them, and make trial of others, but none should implicitly be trusted.

G. But what, if a few great lords or wealthy men were to keep the king   160
himself in subjection, yet exert his force, lavish his treasure, and misuse his name, so as to domineer over the people, and manage the Parliament.

F. We must fight for the King and ourselves.

G. You talk of fighting, as if you were speaking of some rustick engagement at a wake; but your quarter-staffs would avail you little against bayonets.

F. We might easily provide ourselves with better arms.

G. Not so easily; when the moment of resistance came, you would be deprived of all arms; and those who should furnish you with them, or exhort you to take them up, would be called traitors, and probably put to death.   170

F. We ought always, therefore, to be ready; and keep each of us a strong firelock in the corner of his bed-room.

G. That would be legal as well as rational. Are you, my honest friend, provided with a musket?

F. I will contribute no more to the club, and purchase a firelock with my savings.

G. It is not necessary – I have two, and will make you a present of one with complete accoutrements.

F. I accept it thankfully, and will converse with you at your leisure on other subjects of this kind.   180

---

162   *to domineer over the people, and manage the Parliament*   Jones was also convinced of the dangers of aristocratic hegemony, cf. *Nomination of Candidates*, p.378; and *On the Reformation of Parliament*, p.388 above.

165–6   *quarter-staffs would avail you little against bayonets*   On 6 April 1782 he had written to Althorp: 'I am free to own that, if peace were obtained abroad, I should prefer the horrors of civil war (though I have much to lose) to the enormous prevalence of monarchical or *aristocratical* power; and I wish to God, that every elector of Britain had as bright a bayonet as mine, with as much resolution as I feel myself to possess', *Letters*, II.527.

171–2   *a strong firelock in the corner of his bed-room*   In Jones's *Plan of National Defence* (1782), he had answered Shelburne's ninth proposal ('Proper magazines, or storehouses, to be chosen or erected in each town, for keeping the said arms, &c') in the following manner: 'The said arms, &c to be kept by each man, in *his own house*, for his *legal* protection', *Works*, VIII.522. It would seem that Jones conceived of militiamen along the lines of Lord Charlemont's Irish volunteers, or, perhaps, the minute men of Massachusetts. It was just such an idea of civic manliness that attracted him to the American revolutionaries.

G. In the mean while, spend an hour every morning in the next fortnight in learning to prime and load expeditiously, and to fire and charge with bayonet firmly and regularly. I say every *morning*; because, if you exercise *too late in the evening*, you may fall into some of the legal snares, which have been spread for you by those gentlemen, who would rather secure game for their table, than liberty for the nation.

F. Some of my neighbours, who have served in the militia, will readily teach me; and, perhaps, the whole village may be persuaded to procure arms, and learn their exercise.

G. It cannot be expected, that the villagers should purchase arms, but they   190 might easily be supplied, if the gentry of the nation would spare a little from their vices and luxury.

F. May they turn to some sense of honour and viritue!

G. Farewell, at present; and remember, 'that a free state is only a more numerous and more powerful club, and that he only is a free man, who is member of such a state.'

F. Good morning, Sir! You have made me wiser and better than I was yesterday; and yet, methinks, I had some knowledge in my own mind of this great subject, and have been a politician all my life without perceiving it.

---

184   *legal snares*   For Jones, as for Priestley and many other radicals, the game laws exemplified class privilege, conflicting with the natural rights of men, cf. Joseph Priestley, *First Principles of Government*, 2d. ed. (London, 1771), pp.65, 75, 253–68.

194–5   *a free state is only a more numerous and more powerful club*   With Jones's conception of the state as a friendly society writ large, contrast Lord Braxfield's definition in a judgement of 1793: 'A government in every country should be just like a corporation; and, in this country, it is made up of the landed interest, which alone has the right to be represented; as for the rabble, who have nothing but personal property, what hold has the nation of them? What security for the payment of taxes? They may pack up all their property on their backs, and leave the country in the twinkling of an eye, but landed property cannot be removed', T. B. Howell, ed., *A Complete Collection of State Trials* (London, 1809–26), xxiii.231.

TEXTUAL NOTES

1. *Caïssa, or, The Game at Chess* (page 3)

17   *smiling] beauteous* 1772.
26   *braided myrtle] wreaths of myrtle* 1772.
69   *One solemn step] With solemn steps* 1772.

2. *The Seven Fountains, An Eastern Allegory* (page 14)

23   *But now a glittering isle] And now a pleasant isle* 1772.
41   *Rush'd] Came* 1772.
42   *rapt] wrap'd* 1772. Error corrected in 1772 Corrigenda.
169   *And said] Then said* 1772, altered in 1772 Corrigenda.
177   *nameless deeds] bloody deeds* 1772.
179   *Think not of that] No more of that* 1772.
186   footnote *Sight] Light* 1772. Error corrected in 1772 Corrigenda.
215   *pinion] pinions* 1772.
220   *which] that* 1772.
221   *who] that* 1772.
223   *who] that* 1772.
257   *lily-bosom'd bride] rosy-bosom'd bride* 1772, altered in 1772 Corrigenda.
263   *youth] boy* 1772.
265–6 1772 has *Soon the* **·** *third door he pass'd with eager haste,/And the third stream was nectar to his taste.*
267–8 *She turns the key; her cheeks like roses bloom,/And on the lock her fingers drop perfume]* This couplet is transposed from ll. 285–6 of 1772.
271–2 *But first his lips had touch'd th'alluring stream,/That through the grove display'd a silver gleam]* This couplet altered and transposed from ll.297–8 of the 1772 version, where it reads: *(But first the king had quaff'd the tempting stream,/That through the bow'r display'd a silver gleam:)*.
287–8 The 1772 version reads: *But now the nymph, who sigh'd for sweeter joy,/To the* **·** *fourth gate conducts the blooming boy:* (ll.283–4).
324   footnote *The sensual pleasures united]* absent from first edition.
374   *Leads to a cave, where ravening monsters roar] Leads to a gloomy dungeon, and no more* 1772, altered in 1772 Corrigenda.
379   *The king, who wept, yet knew his tears were vain] The king, who found it useless to complain* 1772, altered in 1772 Corrigenda.
444   *destructive] alarming* 1772.
449   *thou] you* 1772.
450   *thy] your* 1772.
452   *beach]* This is the 1799 reading; *beech* appears in both 1772 and 1777.
457   *keep] have* 1772.
499   *The promis'd] A little* 1772.
510   *which morning dyes] that morning dies* 1772.
539   *pernicious] destructive* 1772.

3. *Solima: an Arabian Eclogue* (page 32)

56   *tender] fondling* 1772.

| 60 | *gains*] *wins* 1772. |
| 85 | *Borne*] *Born* 1772. |

4. *The Palace of Fortune, an Indian Tale* (page 36)

81	*Which*] *That* 1772.
90	*descant*] *ditty* 1772.
118	*lustre*] *radiance* 1772.
210	*on her bosom*] *in her bosom* 1772, altered in 1772 Corrigenda.
235	*ruthless train*] *joyless train* 1772.
247	*tow'rd*] *to* 1772.
357	*spoke*] *spake* 1772.
364	*spoke*] *spake* 1772.
382	*painful family*] *ruthless company* 1772.
401	*thou, who*] *thou that* 1772.
417	*rose*] *wak'd* 1772, altered in 1772 Corrigenda.
436	*babbling*] 1807. Earlier versions have *babling*.
494	*the funeral strain*] *a plaintive strain* 1772, altered in 1772 Corrigenda to *a piercing strain*.

5. *The Damsels of Cardigan* (page 52)

Teignmouth (*Works*, I.356–58) gives no title, but prefaces the poem with the information that it was composed 'for the express purpose of being sung at a kind of fête champêtre'; thereafter subsequent editions provided the title, *Written for a Fête Champêtre in Wales*, see, for example *The Poetical Works of Sir William Jones*, 2 vols., (London: Cadell and Davies, 1807), I.283–5. Teignmouth also omits both the reference to the tune and the Horatian epigraph.

2	*bowers!*] *bow'rs,* Teignmouth.
3	*musk-rose*] *blush rose* Teignmouth.
3	*glowing*] The Teignmouth reading is preferred, *GM* has *flowing*.
5	*But*] *Yet* Teignmouth.
5&6	These refrain lines are combined into a single line in each verse of the Teignmouth version to produce an eight-line stanza.
7	*That*] *which* Teignmouth.
7	*Prospects*] *prospects* Teignmouth.
10–18	This stanza omitted in Teignmouth version.
19	*scent*] *odour* Teignmouth.
20	*flings,*] *flings!* Teignmouth.
21	*Blaenpant*] *Bleanpant* Teignmouth.
21	footnote *The seat of W. Brigstocke, Esq.* Teignmouth.
22	footnote to *Bronwith*] *The seat of Thos. Lloyd, Esq.* Teignmouth.
23	*But*] *Yet* Teignmouth.
25	*Odours*] *odours* Teignmouth.
34	*that Music*] *the muses* Teignmouth.
37	*sweet*] *gay* Teignmouth.
37	*our*] *a* Teignmouth.
38	*Cilgaran*] *Kilgarran* Teignmouth.
38	footnote *A ruin of a castle on the banks of the Tivey.* Teignmouth.
40	*relate*] *repeat* Teignmouth.
43	*Friendship*] *friendship* Teignmouth.
46	*How vainly we pore*] *No longer then pore* Teignmouth.
46	*Gothic*] *gothic* Teignmouth.
47	*Statham*] *Neatham* Teignmouth (Possibly Sir John Needham (d.1480).
49	*Be nature our law*] *Be nature and love* Teignmouth.
49	*book.*] *book;* Teignmouth.
50	*But*] *For* Teignmouth.

52   *which*] *that* Teignmouth.
52   *Learning*] *learning* Teignmouth.
56   *flowers*] *flow'rs* Teignmouth.
58   footnote to *Dinevor*] *Seat of Lord Dinevor's, near Landelo, in Carmarthen.* Teignmouth.
58   footnote to *Slebeck*] *Seat of ____ Philips, Esq. near Haverford West.* Teignmouth.
58   *Coedmor*] *Coidsmore* Teignmouth.
58   footnote *Seat of Thomas Lloyd, Esq. near Cardigan.* Teignmouth.
61   *Riches*] *riches* Teignmouth.
65   *with*] *the* Teignmouth.
65   *purple or red,*] *purple and red;* Teignmouth.
66   *large*] *long* Teignmouth.
66   *through*] *thro'* Teignmouth.
67   *Or grant*] *Or say,* Teignmouth.
67   *rich*] *bright* Teignmouth.
70   *Honours*] *honours* Teignmouth.

9. *The Muse Recalled* (page 69)

99   *shall she touch*] *touch* Strawberry Hill.
114   *knit*] *join* Strawberry Hill.
124   *crystal*] Strawberry Hill has *chrystal*, a printer's error as noted by Jones, see *Letters* II:497–98.
135   *rain*] Strawberry Hill has *reign*, a printer's error as noted by Jones, see *Letters* II:497–98.

10. *An Ode in Imitation of Alcaeus* (page 76)

The *Annual Register* text has the following five-line epigraph from Alcæus:

Οὐ λίθοι, οὐδὲ ξύλα, οὐδὲ
Τέχνη τεκτόνων αἱ πόλεις εἰσίν,
'Αλλ' ὅπου ποτ' ἂν ὦσιν 'ΑΝΔΡΕΣ
Αὑτοὺς σώζειν εἰδότες,
Ἐνταῦθα τείχη καὶ πόλεις,

ALC. quoted by ARISTIDES.

[Cities are not stones or timbers or the craft of builders; but wherever there are men who know how to defend themselves, *there* are walls and cities.] See *Greek Lyric*, with translation by David A. Campbell, 4 vols. (Cambridge, Mass. and London, 1982), I.427.

1   *Althorp, what forms a state?*] Changed upon publication to: *What constitutes a State?*, presumably for the sake of anonymity.
5   *broad arm'd*] *broad-arm'd AnnR* and 1799.
8   *Pride;*] *pride. AnnR* and 1799.
9   *No—Men ... men*] *No:—MEN ... MEN AnnR* and 1799.
13   *duties*] italics in *AnnR* and 1799.
14   *rights*] italics in *AnnR* and 1799.
17   *These*] italics in *AnnR* and 1799.
18   *that state's collected will*] italics in *AnnR* and 1799.
20   *empress*] *Empress AnnR* and 1799.
      ill.] *ill; AnnR* and 1799.
22   *Discretion*] italics in *AnnR* and 1799.
23   *crown*] *Crown* italics in *AnnR* and 1799.
24   *rays*] *rays, AnnR* and 1799.
26   *Lesbos, Cretan*] italics in *AnnR* and 1799.
28   *Men*] *MEN AnnR* and 1799.

11. *The Enchanted Fruit; or, The Hindu Wife: An Antediluvian Tale* (page 80)

6   *cubits*] *AM* has *Cubits*.
10   *Lion*] *AM* has *Lyon*.
77   *chiefs*] *Chiefs AM*.
92   *Draupady*] *AM* in the verse and the footnote has *Dropady*.
        debonair] *debonnair AM*.
94n   *Procession*] *Possession AM*.
        DRÓPTY] *DRAPTY AM*.
99   *low thatched*] *low-thatched AM*.
106   *princes*] *princess AM*.
133   *said Erjun* indiscreet] *AM* encloses in a parenthesis.
153   *ethereal*] *etherial AM*.
184   *morning dream*] *morning-dream AM*.
195   *wo*] *woe AM*.
416   *well-formed*] *well formed AM*.
430   *beauty-proof*] *beauty, proof AM*.
443   *ambrosial*] *ambrosia AM*.
445   *surprise*] *surprize AM*.
466n   *Mythological and Historical*] *mythological and historical AM*.
566   *sweetly lengthen'd*] *sweetly-lengthen'd AM*.

13. *A Hymn to Náráyena* (page 104)

For Hymns 13, and 15–20 Jones's privately printed Calcutta copies are extant among the Althorp papers currently being catalogued at the British Library. ('Armenian clerks make such blunders, that I print ten or twenty copies of every thing I compose, which are to be considered as manuscripts', *Letters*, II.777.) Textual evidence indicates that *Asiatic Miscellany* also used Jones's printed copy.

15. *A Hymn to Gangá* (page 123)

Argument *her*] *his* Althorp, manuscript correction to *her*.
76   *her*] *his* Althorp, manuscript correction to *her*.
113   *stop*] *stops* Althorp, manuscript correction to *stop*.
160   *Trisrótà*] *Tristótà* Althorp, manuscript correction to *Trisrótà*.

16. *A Hymn to Indra* (page 133)

Argument *visant*] *visanti* Althorp.
36   *woody*] *wooddy* Althorp, manuscript correction to *woody*.
46   *flagons*] *flaggons* Althorp.

17. *A Hymn to Súrya* (page 143)

89   *sapphires*] *sapphirs* Althorp.

18. *A Hymn to Lacshmí* (page 153)

109   *Bráhmen*] *BRÁHMEN* Althorp.
228   *havock*] *havoc* Althorp.
229   *Mis'ry*] *mis'ry* Althorp.

19. *The Hymn to Durgá* (page 168)

Argument *critick*] *CRITICK* Althorp.
I.2.8   *morning beam*] *morn* Althorp, adjusted to present reading in printed Corrigenda.
VIII.3.7 *kiss'd*] *kiss'd* In Althorp there is a manuscript insertion of the word *softly* before *kiss'd*.

20. *The Hymn to Bhaváni* (page 179)

16   *orient bed*] *bed* Althorp, adjusted to present reading in printed Corrigenda.
18   *emblaz'd*] *imblaz'd* Althorp.
25   *Goddess, around*] *Around* Althorp, adjusted to present reading in printed Corrigenda.
41   *bedeck'd with*] *with* Althorp, adjusted to present reading in printed Corrigenda.

21. *A Persian Song of Hafiz* (page 185)

In the 1772 and subsequent editions Jones's transliterated version of the original was printed beneath the text, separated by a full-width rule. This is omitted.

5   *Bocara*] *Bokhára* 1771.
7   1771 has the following note: *a melted ruby is a common periphrasis for wine in Persian poetry. See Hafiz, ode 22.*
12   *bower*] *bow'r* 1771 and 1772.
13   *fair perfidious*] *fair, perfidious* 1771.
15   *display;*] *display,* 1771.
19   *glow;*] *glow;* 1771.
22   *cheeks,*] *cheeks* 1771.
23   *dyes*] *dies* 1771 and 1772.
27   *flowers*] *flow'rs* 1771 and 1772.
31   *power*] *pow'r* 1771 and 1772.
32   1771 has the following note: *Zoleikha, Potiphar's wife.*
36   1771 has the following note: *Joseph, called by Persians and Arabians Jusuf.*
37   *hear*] *hear;* 1771; *hear:* 1772.
38   *attend*] *attend,* 1771.
44   *heaven*] *heav'n* 1771.
53   *O!*] *oh,* 1771.
54   *sung.*] *sung!* 1771.

23. *Sacontalá; or, the Fatal Ring* by Kālidāsa (page 213)

Preface, l.37 *publick*] *Publick* 1790.
Preface, l.82 *Hindû*] *Hindu* 1790.
Preface, l.100 *Hindûs*] *Hindus* 1790.
Preface, l.115 *mythology*] *Mythology* 1790.
Preface, l.124 *suns*] *Suns* 1790.
Prologue, first stage direction *benediction*] *Benediction* 1790.
I.18   *galloped*] *gallopped* 1790.
I.19   *outran*] *out ran* 1790.
I.144   *speaking*] *Speaking* 1790.
I.250   *Go to*] 1790 reading preferred; 1799 has *Go too.*
I.268   *frustrate, by her allurements,*] *frustrate by her allurements* 1790.
I.297   *ecstasy*] 1790 reading preferred; 1799 has *ecstacy.*
II.95   *tiger*] *tyger* 1790.
II.96   *skakàl*] *shakal* 1790.
II.134   *warrior*] 1790 reading preferred; 1799 has *warriour.*
II.136   *pendent*] 1790 reading preferred; 1799 has *pendant.*

III.354   *indisposed?*] *indisposed!* 1790.
IV.334   *broken*] *broken?* 1790.
VI.38   *skakàls*] to agree with II.96; 1790 and 1799 have *shakàls*.
VI.64   *vintners*] *vintner's* 1790.
VI.494   *tiger*] to agree with with II.95; 1790 and 1799 have *tyger*.
VII.34   *exterior*] *exteriour* 1790.
VII.303   *warrior*] 1790 reading preferred; 1799 has *warriour*.

24. *Gítagóvinda* by Jayadéva (page 298)

70   *him*] *Him AM*.
80   *sandal-wood*] *sandal wood AM*.
84   *Him*] *him AM*.
104   *ecstasy*] *extasy AM*.
133   *subtil*] *subtile AM*.
189   *thou*] *Thou AM*.
344   *CÉSAVA*] *CÉSAVI AM*.
413   *musick*] *music AM*.
519   *ecstasy*] *extasy AM*.
527   *extatic*] *extatick AM*.
530   *Place*] *Peace AM*.
531   *musk*] *musick AM*.

25. *Essay on the Poetry of the Eastern Nations* (page 319)

The two prefatory paragraphs were omitted in 1799 and later editions.
320, l.19   *Arabia*] *ARABIA* 1799.
320, l.23   *Cashmere*] *Cashmîr* 1799.
321, l.3   *providence*] *Providence* 1799.
321, ll.4–12   *I am at a loss to conceive . . . by the Persian gulf*] dropped to a footnote in 1799 and later editions.
321, l.30–3   *the writer of an old history . . . Arabian spices*] dropped to a footnote in 1799 and later editions.
322, l.31   *world.*] 1799 punctuation preferred. 1772 has *world:*.
323, l.9   *javelin, &c,*] *javelin, &c** 1799 note gives Arabic original.
323, l.12   *dew*] *dew** 1799 note gives Arabic original.
324, l.14   *line*] *Line* 1799.
324, l.32   *ancients*] *Ancients* 1799.
324n   Transliterated line replaced by Arabic in 1799 and later editions.
326, l.2   *manners,*] *manners* 1799.
326, l.2   *customs,*] *customs* 1799.
327, ll.9–16   Transliterated lines replaced by Arabic in 1799 and later editions.
328, ll.1–2   Transliterated lines replaced by Arabic in 1799 and later editions.
328, l.15   *Hamassa*] *Hamása* 1799.
328, l.19   *pearls*] *pearls** 1799 gives the four lines of the original Arabic.
328, l.28   *imitate*] 1772 printed *imitating* Altered in Corrigenda.
328, l.28   *adopt*] 1772 printed *adopting* Altered in Corrigenda.
328, l.30   *Persia*] *PERSIA* 1799.
330, l.7   *studious,*] *studious* 1799.
330, ll.11–16   *and this, by the way . . . To return*] This aside omitted in 1799 and subsequent editions.
330, l.27   *Hafiz*] *Hafez* 1799.
331, l.27   *Hafiz*] *Hafez* 1799.
331, l.28   *sonnet,*] *sonnet* 1799.
331, l.29   *Shakespeare*] 1799 reading preferred. 1772 has *Shakespear*.
332, l.12   *Bostân*] *Bostán* 1799.

332, 1.13–24	Transliterated lines replaced by Persian in 1799 and later editions.
333, 1.8	*glare,*] glare 1799.
333, 1.26	*transcribe*] 1772 printed *transcribing* Altered in Corrigenda.
333, 1.27	*give*] 1772 printed *giving* Altered in Corrigenda.
334, 1.7	*Turks*] *TURKS* 1799.
336, 1.1	*once more request*] request 1799.
336, 1.6	*That*] that 1799.
336, 11.6–14	*That, if the principal ... might imitate*] Concluding section without italics in 1799 and later editions.
336, 1.9	*places of education*] great seminaries of learning 1799.

26. *An Essay on the Arts, Commonly Called Imitative* (page 337)

338, 1.4	*superior*] superiour 1772.
339, 1.12	*Deity*] deity 1772.
339, 1.17	*creator*] creatour 1772.
339, 1.17	*author*] authour 1772.
340, 1.30	*Iambi*] Jambi 1772; error corrected in Corrigenda.
341, 1.14	*note*] note‡ 1772 footnote reads: *Suppose C, E, G, are struck together: then E gives g sharp, b, and G, b, d, which g sharp, b, d, are dissonant from C, the first being its superfluous fifth, and the two last its seventh and second; and, to complete the harmony, as it is called, g sharp and g natural are heard together, than which nothing can be more absurd:*
341, 1.14–17	*these horrid dissonances ... additions of art*] 1772 drops these lines to a footnote.
341, 1.17–19	*It is like thinking ... to the violet.*] 1772 has *It is like painting a face naturally beautiful.*
342, 1.3	*proportions*] proportions* 1772 has the following footnote: *The proportions of the intervals are these: 2ᵈ. maj. 8 to 9. 2ᵈ. min. 15 to 16. 3ᵈ. maj. 4 to 5. 3ᵈ. min. 5 to 6. 4ᵗʰ. 3 to 4. 5ᵗʰ. 2 to 3. 6ᵗʰ.maj. 3 to 5. 6ᵗʰ. min. 5 to 8. 7ᵗʰ. maj. 8 to 15. 7ᵗʰ. min. 5 to 9. These proportions are determined by the length of the strings, but, when they are taken from the vibrations of them, the ratio's are inverted, as 2ᵈ. maj. 9 to 8, 2ᵈ. min. 16 to 15 &c. that is, while one string vibrates nine times, its second major makes eight vibrations, and so forth. It happens that the intervals which have the simplest ratio's are generally the most agreeable; but that simplicity must not be thought to occasion our pleasure, as it is not possible that the ear should determine those proportions.*
342, 1.4	*twelve*] ‡twelve 1772 has the following footnote: *There are no more than six full notes in a scale of eight sounds, or an octave, because the intervals between C D,D E, F G, G A, A B, are equal, and the intervals beytween E F, B C, are also equal, but are almost half as small as the others; and C D E = 2n + E F = $\frac{1}{2}$n + F G A B = 3n + B C = $\frac{1}{2}$n = 6n. But though the interval E F be usually called a semitone; yet it is more properly a Limma, and differs from a semitone by a Comma, or $\frac{81}{80}$; and that it is less than a semitone was asserted by Pythagoras, and thus demonstrated by Euclid of Alexandria, in his treatise On the division of the Monochord: if the diatessaron C F, contain two full tones, and a semitone, then the diapason C c (which comprises two diatessarons, and a whole tone) will be equal to six tones: But the diapason is less than six tones; therefore C F is less than two, and a semitone; for if $\frac{9}{8}$, the ratio of a tone, be six times compounded, it will be a fraction greater than that, which is equal to $\frac{2}{1}$, or the ratio of the diapason; therefore, the diapason is less than six tones. Ptolemy has proved the same truth more at large in the tenthand eleventh chapters of his first book of Harmonicks, where he refutes the assertions of the Aristoxenians, and exposes their errours with great clearness.*
344, 1.12	*Atarnea*] Atarne 1772.
345, 1.1	*crucifixion*] Crucifixion 1772.

27. *On the Gods of Greece, Italy, and India* (page 348)

349, l.22   *sandal wood*] *sandal-wood As Res.*
351, l.22   *deity*] *Deity As Res.*

28. *The Third Anniversary Discourse* (page 355)

365, l.28   *EZEKIEL*] *As Res* reading preferred; 1807 has *EZEKIAL.*
367, l.6   *Ionic*] *Ionick As Res.*
367, l.9   *enterprising*] *enterprizing As Res.*

SELECT BIBLIOGRAPHY

Aarsleff, Hans, *The Study of Language in England, 1780–1860* (New Jersey, 1967; repr. London, 1983).

Abrams, M. H., *The Mirror and the Lamp* (Oxford, 1953).

Ahmad, Aijaz, *In Theory: Classes, Nations, Literatures* (London and New York, 1992).

Arberry, A. J., *Asiatic Jones. The Life and Influence of Sir William Jones* (London, 1946).

—— 'Orient Pearls at Random Strung', *Bulletin of the School of Oriental and African Studies*, 11 (1946), 698–712.

—— *The Seven Odes: The First Chapter in Arabic Literature* (London, 1957)

Aronson, A., *Europe Looks at India* (Bombay, 1945).

Barker, Francis, *et al.* (eds.) *Europe and its Others*, 2 vols. (Colchester, 1985).

Bayly, C. A., *Indian Society and the Making of the British Empire* (Cambridge, 1988).

Bearce, G. D., *British Attitudes towards India* (Oxford, 1961).

Bernal, Martin, *Black Athena: The Egyptian and Semitic Roots of Ancient Greece*, 3 vols. (London, 1987–90)

Bonwick, Colin, *English Radicals and the American Revolution* (Chapel Hill, NC, 1977).

Brown, Peter, *The Chathamites* (London, 1967).

Butler, Marilyn, 'Orientalism', in David B. Pirie (ed.), *Penguin History of Literature, V: The Romantic Period* (Harmondsworth, 1994).

Cannon, Garland, 'Sir William Jones and Edmund Burke', *Modern Philology*, 54 (1957), 165–85.

—— 'Sir William Jones's Persian Linguistics', *Journal of the American Oriental Society* 78 (1958), 262–73.

—— (ed.), *The Letters of William Jones*, 2 vols. (Oxford, 1970).

—— 'Five New Letters by Sir William Jones', *Philological Quarterly*, 51:4 (1972), 951–5.

—— 'Sir William Jones and Anglo-American Relations during the American Revolution', *Modern Philology*, 76 (1978), 29–45.

—— *Sir William Jones: A Bibliography of Primary and Secondary Sources*. Vol. 7. Library and Information Sources in Linguistics. (Amsterdam, 1979).

—— Foundations of Oriental and Comparative Studies: The Correspondence of Sir William Jones', *Comparative Criticism*, 3 (1981), 157–96.

—— 'Sir William Jones's Founding and Directing of the Asiatic Society', *India Office Library and Records Report*, (1984-5), 11–28.

—— 'The Construction of the European Image of the Orient: A Bicentenary Reappraisal of Sir William Jones as Poet and Translator', *Comparative Criticism*, 8 (1986), 167–88.

—— *The Life and Mind of Oriental Jones* (Cambridge, 1990).

—— 'Jones's "Sprung from Some Common Source": 1786–1986', in Sydney M. Lamb and E. Douglas Mitchell (eds.), *Sprung From Some Common Source: Investigations into the Prehistory of Languages* (California, 1991), pp.23–47.

—— and Pandey, Siddheswar, 'Sir William Jones Revisited: On his Translation of the Śakuntalā', *Journal of the American Oriental Society*, 96 (1976), 528–35,

Crane, Verner W., 'The Club of Honest Whigs: Friends of Science and Liberty', *William and Mary Quarterly*, 23 (1966), 210–33.

Derrett, J. Duncan M., *Religion, Law and the State in India* (London, 1968).

Drew, John, *India and the Romantic Imagination* (Delhi: Oxford University Press, 1987).

Edgerton, Franklin, 'Sir William Jones: 1746–1794', *Journal of the American Oriental Society*, 66 (1946), 230–9.

Emeneau, Murray B., 'India and Linguistics', *Journal of the American Oriental Society*, 75 (1955), 145–53.

Evans, R. H., *Catalogue of the Library of the late Sir William Jones*. London: W. Nicol, 1831.

Fan, T. C., 'Sir William Jones's Chinese Studies', *Review of English Studies*, 22 (1946), 304–14.

Figueria, Dorothy, '*Śakuntalā*'s Reception in Nineteenth Century Europe', *South Asian Review*, 8 (1984), 30–37.

Franklin, Michael J., *Sir William Jones*, Writers of Wales series (Cardiff, 1995).

—— 'Accessing India: Orientalism, Anti-"Indianism", and the Rhetoric of Jones and Burke', in T. J. Fulford and Peter J. Kitson (eds.), *Romanticism and Colonialism* (Cambridge University Press, forthcoming).

Gossman, Ann, '"Harmonious Jones" and Milton's Invocations', *Notes and Queries*, 199 (1954), 527–29.

Greenberg, J. H., 'Some Problems of Indo-European in Historical Perspective', in *Sprung From Some Common Source*, pp.125–40, (cited under Cannon above).

Hawley, John Stratton and Wulff, Donna Marie (eds.), *The Divine Consort: Rādhā and the Goddesses of India* (Boston, Mass., 1986).

Hewitt, R. M., 'Harmonious Jones', *Essays and Studies*, 23 (1942), 42–59.

Inden, Ronald, *Imagining India* (Cambridge Mass., and Oxford, 1990).

Iyer, R. (ed.), *The Glass Curtain between Asia and Europe* (London, 1965).

Jones, Sir William, *The Collected Works of Sir William Jones* (Facsimile reprint of the 1807 edition) 13 vols. ed. Garland Cannon, (London, 1993).

Kejariwal, O. P., *The Asiatic Society of Bengal and the Discovery of India's Past 1784–1838* (Delhi: OUP, 1988).

Kinsley, David, *Hindu Goddesses: Visions of the Divine Feminine in the Hindu Religious Tradition* (Berkeley and London, 1986).

Kopf, David, *British Orientalism and the Bengal Renaissance* (Berkeley and Los Angeles, 1969).

Kramnick, Isaac, *Republicanism and Bourgeois Radicalism: Political Ideology in Late Eighteenth-Century Englan and America* (Ithaca and London, 1990).

Leask, Nigel, *British Romantic Writers and the East: Anxieties of Empire* (Cambridge, 1992).

Lehmann, Winfred P, 'The Impact of India on Jones', *South Asian Review*, 8 (1984), 18–21.

—— 'Fick and Kleuker on Jones – Riga 1795', *Historiographia Linguistica*, 13 (1986), 19–26.

—— 'The Impact of Jones in German-Speaking Areas'. Paper read at New York University Symposium, 21 April 1994.

Lloyd, Mary, 'Sir Charles Wilkins, 1749-1836', *India Office Library and Records Report*, (1978), 9–39.

Majeed, Javed, *Ungoverned Imaginings: James Mill's The History of British India and Orientalism* (Oxford, 1992).

Manuel, Frank E., *The Eighteenth Century Confronts the Gods* (Cambridge, Mass., 1959).

Marshall, P. J., *The British Discovery of Hinduism* (Cambridge, 1970).

—— *Bengal: The British Bridgehead. Eastern India 1740–1828* (Cambridge, 1987).

Master, Alfred, 'The Influence of Sir William Jones upon Sanskrit Studies', *Bulletin of the School of Oriental and African Studies*, 11 (1946), 798–806.

Meisami, Julie S., 'Sir William Jones and the Reception of Persian Literature'. *South Asian Review*, 8 (1984), 61–70.

Mitter, Partha, *Much Maligned Monsters: The History of European Reactions to Indian Art* (Oxford, 1977).

Mojumder, Abu Taher, 'Three New Letters by Sir William Jones', *India Office Library and Records Report*, (1981), 24–35.

Moussa-Mahmoud, Fatma, *Sir William Jones and the Romantics* (Cairo, 1962).

Mukherjee, S. N., *Sir William Jones: A Study in Eighteenth-Century British Attitudes to India* (Cambridge, 1968; 2nd edn. London, 1987).

Mukherji, Abhijit, ' European Jones and Asiatic Pundits', *Journal of the Asiatic Society*, 27 (1985), 43–58.

Nehru, Jawaharlal, *The Discovery of India* (New York, 1946).

Newton-de Molina, David, 'Sir William Jones's "Essay on the Arts Commonly Called Imitative" (1772)', *Anglia*, 90 (1972), 147–54.

Norris, John, *Shelburne and Reform* (London, 1963).

Oldham, James C., 'The Survival of Sir William Jones in American Jurisprudence'. Paper read at New York University Symposium, 21 April 1994.

Pachori, Satya S., 'Shelley's "Indian Serenade": Hafiz and Sir William Jones', *Osmania Journal of Indian Studies*, 11 (1974-5), 11–26.

—— ed., *Sir William Jones: A Reader* (Delhi: OUP, 1993).

Pinto, V. De Sola, V., 'Sir William Jones and English Literature', *Bulletin of the School of Oriental and African Studies*, 11 (1946), 686–94.

Polomé, Edgar C., 'Sir William Jones and the Position of Germanic', *Journal of Indo-European Studies*, 16 (1988), 209–32.

Powell, L. F., 'Sir William Jones and The Club', *Bulletin of the School of Oriental and African Studies*, 11 (1946), 818–22.

Raine, Kathleen, *Blake and Tradition*, 2 vols. (London, 1969).

Raychaudhuri, Tapan, *Europe Reconsidered: Perceptions of the West in Nineteenth Century Bengal* (Delhi: OUP, 1988).

Robbins, Caroline, *The Eighteenth-Century Commonwealthman* (Cambridge, Mass., 1961).

Robins, R. H., 'The Evolution of Historical Linguistics', *Journal of the Royal Asiatic Society*, (1986), 5–20.

Rocher, Rosane, 'The Career of Rdhknta Tarkavga, an Eighteenth-Century Pandit in British Employ', *Journal of the American Oriental Society*, 109 (1989), 627–33.

—— 'Nathaniel Brassey Halhed, Sir William Jones, and Comparative Indo-European Linguistics', *Recherches de Linguistique*, 53 (1980), 173–80.

—— *Orientalism, Poetry, and the Millenium: The Checkered Life of Nathaniel Brassey Halhed 1751–1830* (Delhi, 1983).

—— 'Weaving Knowledge: Sir William Jones and Indian Pandits'. Paper read at New York University Symposium, 21 April 1994.

Rowse, A. L., 'Welsh Orientalist: Sir William Jones', *History Today*, 21 (1971), 57–64.

Said, Edward, *Orientalism* (London, 1978).

Schwab, Raymond, *The Oriental Renaissance: Europe's Discovery of India and the East, 1680–1880*, trans. G. Patterson-Black and V. Reinking (New York, 1984).

Shaffer, Elinor, *'Kubla Khan' and The Fall of Jerusalem* (Cambridge, 1975).

—— 'Editor's Note', *Comparative Criticism*, 3 (1981), xv.

Sharafuddin, Mohammed, *Islam and Romantic Orientalism* (London, 1994).

Shaw, Graham, *Printing in Calcutta to 1800* (London, 1981).

—— *The South Asia and Burma Retrospective Bibliography: Stage 1: 1556–1800* (London, 1987).

Siegel, Lee, *Sacred and Profane Dimensions of Love in Indian Traditions as Exemplified in the Gítagóvinda of Jayadéva* (Delhi: OUP, 1978).

Steadman, J. M., 'The Asiatick Society of Bengal', *Eighteenth-Century Studies*, 10 (1977), 464–83.

Stetkevych, Suzanne P., *The Mute Immortals Speak: Pre-Islamic Poetry and the Poetics of Ritual* (Ithaca and London, 1993).

Stewart, J. A., 'Sir William Jones's Revision of the Text of Two Poems of Anacreon', *Bulletin of the School of Oriental and African Studies*, 11 (1946), 669–72.

Stokes, Eric, *The English Utilitarians and India* (Oxford, 1963).

Stunkel, Kenneth, 'English Orientalism and India, 1784–1830', *Ohio University Review*, 11 (1969), 49-72.

Sutherland, L. S. and Mitchell, L. G. (eds.), *The History of the University of Oxford*, vol. V: *The Eighteenth Century* (Oxford, 1986).

Thapar, Romila, 'Imagined Religious Communities? Ancient History and the Modern Search for a Hindu Identity', *Modern Asian Studies*, 23 (1989), 209–31.

Tritton, A. S., 'The Student of Arabic', *Bulletin of the School of Oriental and African Studies*, 11 (1946), 695–8.

Vesey-Fitzgerald, S. G., 'Sir William Jones the Jurist', *Bulletin of the School of Oriental and African Studies*, 11 (1946), 807–17.

Viswanathan, Gauri, *Masks of Conquest: Literary Study and British Rule in India* (New York, 1989).

Viswanathan, S., 'The Hymns of Sir William Jones', *The Aryan Path* 90 (1969), 487–93, 543–50.

Waley, Arthur D., 'Anquetil-Duperron and Sir William Jones', *History Today*, 2 (1952), 23–33.

Wellek, René, *A History of Modern Criticism 1750–1950*, 5 vols. (London, 1955).

Willson, A. Leslie, *A Mythical Image: The Ideal of India in German Romanticism* (Durham, NC, 1964).

Worrall, David, *Radical Culture: Discourse, Resistance, and Surveillance 1790–1820* (London, 1992).

Yohannan, John D., 'The Persian Poetry Fad in England, 1770–1825', *Comparative Literature*, 4 (1952), 137–60.

Young, Robert, *White Mythologies: Writing History and the West* (London, 1990).